CONTENTS

C000091456

Legend for Club Stadium Plans	Legend for Clubs' 10-year League Record	Footnote to Each Club's 10-year Playing Record

Legend for Club Stadium Plans

Covered seating

Covered standing

Uncovered seating

Uncovered standing

Disabled Facilities, wheelchairs access and viewing areas

Main entrances

Main exits

Legend for Clubs' 10-year League Record

Premier Division/S.P.L.

First Division

Second Division

Third Division

Hatched area indicates where the number of teams in the division has been fewer than 12 or 14 (see right).

Footnote to Each Club's 10-year Playing Record

The number of teams playing in each division of The Scottish Football League and The Scottish Premier League has altered on several occasions during the past ten seasons and in order to assist the reader, the following information explains the various formats in operation during the following period:-

SEASON	PREMIER DIVISION	FIRST DIVISION	SECOND DIVISION	THIRD DIVISION
1991/92	12	12	14	N/A
1992/93	12	12	14	N/A
1993/94	12	12	14	N/A
1994/95	10	10	10	10
1995/96	10	10	10	10
1996/97	10	10	10	10
1997/98	10	10	10	10
	S.P.L.	S.F.L. FD	S.F.L. SD	S.F.L. TD
1998/99	10	10	10	10
1999/2000	10	10	10	10
2000/01	12	10	10	10

LOOKING TO THE FUTURE

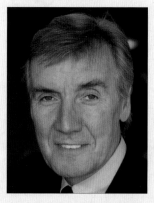

I am once again privileged to have this opportunity in extending to all football fans, a very warm welcome to the 2001/02 edition of The Scottish Football League Review.

As you will by now have noticed, this season's edition has a new title sponsor and I am obviously delighted that Bell's have taken over the sponsorship of this prestigious publication. The Scottish Football League and Bell's have developed an extremely close working relationship during the past few years and their commitment and enthusiasm in sponsoring the three divisions of The Scottish Football League, the Challenge Cup competition as well as many other exciting activities within the Scottish game is greatly appreciated not only by the League Management Committee but also by all member clubs. You will be able to read in greater detail on pages 30 to 33 of the tremendous range of sponsorship activities undertaken by Bell's during the course of a season and I think that it is fair to say that a very positive relationship has been forged between The Scottish Football League, its member clubs and Bell's in recent seasons which has been to the benefit of all parties concerned.

The 2001/02 season witnesses the final year of our three year sponsorship agreement with Bell's and it is no secret that both parties have held discussions with a view to hopefully extending the sponsorship for a further term. However, that topic is for another day and I think that it would be prudent at this point in time to look back on the various events which shaped our national game during the course of the 2000/01 season. It was another eventful season with many issues not being settled until the final couple of weeks of the season.

In the First Division, congratulations must be extended to Livingston in gaining promotion to The Scottish Premier League. It is only five years ago that they won the Third Division title and to move up through two further divisions and now be playing against the top clubs in the country is a remarkable achievement in such a short space of time. Whilst the Lions of Livi took all of the credit, Ayr United must also be commended for keeping the title race alive until the penultimate Saturday of the season and no doubt they will be trying to go one better this term. In the Second Division, my own club, Partick Thistle, dominated proceedings and comprehensively won the Championship with several weeks of the season remaining and I am sure that all Jags' fans will relish the challenges that they will face during the course of this season. The second promotion spot, however, was a much closer affair with Arbroath eventually overcoming gallant efforts from both Berwick Rangers and Stranraer to secure their place in the First Division for the first time since season 1979/80.

The final day drama once again took place in the Third Division with Hamilton Academical and Cowdenbeath contesting the Championship whilst Brechin City still had the opportunity of claiming the second promotion spot. Hollywood could not have scripted it better with the latter two clubs meeting each other at Central Park whilst Hamilton Academical were playing at Montrose. After a tension filled day full of drama and excitement, Accies secured the Championship on goal difference from the Blue Brazil who were also promoted. Although Brechin City narrowly missed out, I am sure that Dick Campbell and his players will be challenging once again this season.

In The CIS Insurance Cup, Celtic's victory in the Final against Kilmarnock not only saw them claim the trophy for the second successive season but also gave them the launchpad to go on and win their first domestic treble since season 1968/69. The Parkhead club went on to win The Scottish Premier League by an impressive 15 point margin and rounded off an incredible season beating Hibernian by three goals to nil in the Tennent's Scottish Cup Final.

The Bell's Challenge Cup Final once again provided an entertaining encounter with Airdrieonians and

Livingston sharing four goals between them before the Diamonds clinched the trophy in emotional circumstances following a dramatic penalty shoot-out.

Towards the end of last season, The Scottish Football League moved its office base from West Regent Street in the city centre of Glasgow to Hampden Park. The Scottish Football League, The Scottish Football Association and The Scottish Premier League therefore are now all located there as well as the other national football bodies which administer the game outwith League football. Hopefully, this will be to the benefit of Scottish football in the long term! Hampden Park is now not just a football venue, but a seven-days-a-week operation. It has a wide range of superb facilities which you can read about on pages 56 and 57 of the Review and will, of course, host the UEFA Champions League Final at the end of this season. As a supporter, you too can enjoy the modern facilities which the stadium has to offer by visiting the new Scottish Football Museum. I can guarantee you that it is an experience not to be missed and lives up to its title as the first national football museum in the world. An article on the Museum is featured elsewhere in this publication...why not come along with friends and family and enjoy a great day out.

I have in previous editions of the Review written about the importance of Scottish football having a fully integrated youth development structure and I am therefore delighted to report that during the course of this season, we will be sitting down with both The Scottish Football Association and The Scottish Premier League as well as the various other affiliated national associations to work towards this objective. Let us all hope that an integrated youth system is in place for the start of the 2002/03 season as it is imperative that our game has a solid foundation to build upon.

Talking about youth development brings me on nicely to a subject that has dominated football matters off the field of play during the past couple of years or so and that has been the threat by the European Commission to abolish the existing transfer system. This would have severe financial implications to the football industry with concerns being expressed by most clubs that it would not be

worth all of the time, effort and most importantly, the considerable expenditure incurred on developing young players. At the time of going to print, there appears to have been a compromise deal reached involving FIFA, UEFA, FIFPRO and the European Commission although all of the implications to the domestic game here in Scotland have still to be considered in greater detail. Hopefully, commonsense will prevail in the end.

Although we have increased the cover price slightly this season to reflect increased printing costs, we have endeavoured to maintain and indeed improve the quality of the Review and I am sure that it will once again be regarded as the most authoritative reference book on Scottish football.

The preparation of the Review involves a tremendous amount of time and effort and I would like to thank the following:-

David C. Thomson (Editor); all of the staff at The Scottish Football League and in particular, Jan Murdoch, Anton Fagan and Brian Jamieson; our member clubs; Alan Elliott and Jim Jeffrey; our contributors; the various sectors of the media for their co-operation and assistance; our sponsors, Bell's, and especially David Longmuir; everyone at PPL Sport and in particular, Bill Cotton, David Kelly, Emma Robinson, Graham Nuttall and Kevin McGoverin.

Finally, I do hope that you, the fan, has an exciting and memorable football season.

HAVE AN ENJOYABLE SEASON.

JAMES OLIVER
President, The Scottish Football League

COVER PHOTOGRAPHS

Craig Ireland (Airdrieonians) with the Bell's Challenge Cup • Danny Lennon (Partick Thistle) with the Bell's Second Division Trophy • Ally Dawson and the Hamilton Academical players with the Bell's Third Division Trophy • David Fernandez and Davide Xausa (Livingston) with the Bell's First Division Trophy.

A word from our Sponsor

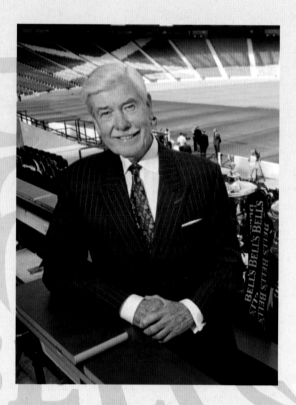

Bell's have always been proud to support Scottish football. We were first sponsors of the League Cup in the late 70's and early 80's, the Bell's League Championship in the mid 90's and are the current sponsors of The Scottish Football League and the Bell's Challenge Cup.

As sponsor of the SFL, I feel it is appropriate for Bell's to support the SFL Review Book. This 'bible' of Scottish football gives fans all the information they need to follow their team, home and away, and as the 'spirit of Scottish football' Bell's want to be with you on your travels.

To show how we value our relationship with all the SFL clubs, at the end of last season we organised a showcase event at our 'home ground', Gleneagles, where the Bell's Player, Young Player and the three divisional Managers of the Year were presented with their awards. Representatives from the 30 SFL clubs were in attendance which gave us the opportunity to thank them all for their help in making our sponsorship a success.

We'd also like to thank you! Bell's is proud of its Scottish roots and heritage and as a fan of your local football team you carry on a tradition where football is at the heart of the community. We are delighted to be involved in such a passionate sport with such loyal fans.

A successful combination - Bell's and Scottish football – it's all in the blend.

Lord Macfarlane of Bearsden KT

The Scottish Football League finished in early May last season wondering if they were about to lose at least one of its member clubs. However, the 2001/02 football season kicked off on a much higher note of optimism with those teams in turmoil, Airdrieonians, Clydebank and Morton, still all in membership.

The very fact that all of these clubs are still in business is just part of a success story often overlooked by many people in the game who only occasionally glance down towards "the lower leagues." To be fair however, there are a number of shrewd managers, coaches and scouts who don't just look, though. The more perceptive of them know when to touch as well and are never backward when it comes to deciding on the players and backroom boys from the Bell's First, Second and Third Divisions who are ready to fly "premier-class" or even higher.

A number of players who began the 2000/01 season plying their trade at the coalface of Scottish football moved on to more glamorous locations during the course of last season and now find themselves playing both with and against the superstars of the game. These players however, can be extremely grateful that Scottish Football League clubs first of all provided good coaching and education and then had the foresight and vision to provide the platform for these young players to develop their undoubted talents by giving them an opportunity to play at a decent level from an early age.

One of the players who stepped into the limelight overnight was Steven Ferguson, who changed the bracing air of East Fife home games at Methil for the glitz, glamour and buzz of London's White Hart Lane with Tottenham Hotspur. Young Steven only made eleven League appearances for the Fifers but during that short period, a number of clubs realised his undoubted potential resulting in the White Hart Lane club snapping him up

David Fernandez

halfway through last season.

Although the skills of David Fernandez are only now being realised by those who by-passed watching First Division games, his impressive performances with Airdrieonians last season were enjoyed not only by Diamonds' fans but all other supporters of that division. Unfortunately, his time at the Excelsior Stadium was cut short as a result of the problems which blighted that club last season and together with other Latino imports to North Lanarkshire, were allowed to leave the club. Two of his team mates last season, Antonio Calderon and Jesus Sanjuan, subsequently moved to SPL club Kilmarnock whilst Fernandez signed for eventual First Division Champions Livingston.

It was a familiar pattern. When Hibernian ran away with the First Division title a couple of years ago, followers of SFL clubs knew Russell Latapy had brought special skills with him from the Caribbean, long before the Old Firm, and ultimately Rangers, made a decisive move for him. The same can be said for Didier Agathe whose pace was a contributory factor in helping Celtic to

the "Treble" last season. However, it was Raith Rovers who initially gave him the opportunity to show off his skills in the SFL First Division.

Back to the indigenous Scotsman and two talented youngsters now playing in the SPL but who started their careers in the lower divisions. Andy Webster graduated through Arbroath's youth development system and secured a move to Heart of Midlothian, whilst former Airdrieonians defender, Austin McCann, also moved to the Gorgie Road club during the course of last season. They are working at Tynecastle under the guidance of Craig Levein, a defender in his day good enough to represent his country at the World Cup Finals but who has never forgotten his roots, starting both his playing and managerial careers with Cowdenbeath and is now in charge of one of the clubs looked on to try and break the Old Firm duopoly when it comes to prize day.

Levein isn't the only young manager who decided that the Bell's SFL First, Second and Third Divisions were good enough for them. John Brownlie, the

Didier Agathe

5

Ray Stewart

means to communities the length and breadth of the country. For example, Livingston attracted more than 64,000 fans for their 18 home games last season, of which nearly 7,500 of them attended the last League encounter against Clyde. Ross County and Inverness Caledonian Thistle attracted between them just short of 100,000 supporters over the season and their own Highland derbies attracted between 5,000 to 6,000 fans per game. Before gaining entry to the SFL, Caledonian and Inverness Thistle were lucky to attract much more than 1,000 fans between them and Caley Thistle now average more than double that at their home games whilst Ross County averaged over 2,700 per game last season.

Hamilton Academical are back up in the Second Division with their bright new home and enjoying figures well in excess of the few hundred who stuck with them during their days as tenants at Firhill. Ally Dawson and his players will be hoping that their new custom built Ballast Stadium will act as the catalyst in their attempts to gain further promotion this season. Whilst clubs in the Third Division do not carry huge supports, it just goes to show that a meaningful encounter can always attract the crowds. The Cowdenbeath versus Brechin City fixture last season was accurately billed as a "winner takes all" contest in deciding the other Third Division promotion place and attracted nearly 3,500 fans to Central Park on the

former Hibernian, Newcastle United and Scotland full-back, guided Arbroath up into the First Division at the end of last season. Then there is Ray Stewart, a classy defender with Dundee United, West Ham United and was capped on ten occasions for Scotland, who is in charge at Stirling Albion and, who it has to be remembered, took Livingston up to the First Division a couple of seasons ago. Neale Cooper, who won every honour with Aberdeen (including a European Cup Winners' Cup medal), as well as playing for Aston Villa and Rangers, has taken all of his football knowledge to make Ross County a success by taking them up two divisions within a short time of the Dingwall club becoming members of the SFL.

Supporters of clubs in The Scottish Football League may turn out in smaller numbers than those who follow the fortunes of clubs playing in the SPL but they manage to retain a special relationship with their favourite team which extends well beyond such matters as big business, corporate identity and share issues.

For a country with a population of only five million inhabitants, the number of fans attending football even at the lower levels of our national game shows the importance that football

Partick Thistle v Queen's Park – the alternative Glasgow derby

The Second Division had one really big crowd-puller last season. Partick Thistle totalled just more than 52,500 fans to Firhill over the season, including just under 5,000 for their last appearance as Champions against Stenhousemuir. The Jags' "alternative Glasgow derbies" with Queen's Park were resurrected and attracted around 4,000 for each of their four meetings. The other promoted club, Arbroath, had more than 2,000 fans at their vital final home game last season against fellow promotion challengers Berwick Rangers.

final day of the season.

Another club which moved to a new stadium during the course of last season was Dumbarton with nearly 2,000 supporters flocking to their first match at the Strathclyde Homes Stadium in the shadow of Dumbarton Rock and they're confident of maintaining higher attendances during the course of this season. Clyde have already been settled in Cumbernauld for a few years and they have further plans to develop their excellent facilities at Broadwood Stadium by building a fourth stand

which will include a gymnasium complex for both the community and the club.

All three divisions of the Bell's Scottish Football League are expected to provide fans with another exciting season. Those people in the know, the bookies, certainly thought so when they set the Championship odds in the summer break. If the games are as meaningful and the tables as tight as last season, they won't be far off target.........remember Bell's even had a helicopter to take the Third Division trophy to either Montrose or Cowdenbeath. As the record books now show, the helicopter took League Secretary, Peter Donald, to Montrose to enable Hamilton Academical to be presented with the trophy on the final day of last season. Although Cowdenbeath went up in second place, such was the tightness of the nine-month marathon finish that if they had lost to Brechin - and it was 1-1 with two minutes to play – the Blue Brazil could

Cowdenbeath v Brechin City – "Winner takes all"

even have missed out on promotion for another year never mind the Championship itself!

The Bell's Challenge Cup, exclusive to the SFL's 30 clubs, has also proved to be a winner. First we had the 4-4 "Mark Cairns" Cup Final when the then Alloa Athletic 'keeper saved a shoot-out penalty then knocked in the winner and this was followed up by last season's showdown between Airdrieonians and Livingston. That gala affair again went into another penalty shoot-out thanks to a 2-2 scoreline after 120 minutes of pulsating action. Then Spaniard Javier Sanchez Broto – another SFL player now playing in the SPL with promoted Livi, - earned the Man of the Match accolade and a winners' medal with some fantastic goalkeeping.

Maybe it all just summed up the roller-coaster ride the SFL can so easily

be as Diamonds' fans were able to switch off the worries over the club's future for a while to celebrate winning a trophy! It may not always provide the glamour and skill on show at the very highest level but the Bell's First, Second and Third Divisions certainly provide fans with entertainment, drama and value-for-money action throughout a long season.

Javier Sanchez Broto

GRAHAM SCOTT
(Evening Times)

Airdrieonians

Excelsior Stadium, Broomfield Park,
Craigneuk Avenue, Airdrie, ML6 8QZ

CHAIRMAN

VICE-CHAIRMAN

DIRECTORS

ACTING SECRETARY
Mrs. Ethel Tappenden

MANAGER
Ian McCall

ASSISTANT MANAGER

FIRST TEAM COACH
Brian Rice

COACHES

RESERVE TEAM COACH

YOUTH TEAM COACHES

COMMERCIAL MANAGER
Morna Watkins (01236) 622000

CLUB DOCTOR
Brian Dunn, M.B.,CLB.,M.R.C.P.(UK)

STADIUM MANAGER
Alistair Cameron

GROUNDSMAN
John McGuire

**FOOTBALL SAFETY OFFICERS'
ASSOCIATION REPRESENTATIVE**
Alistair Cameron (01236) 622000

MATCHDAY PROGRAMME EDITOR
John O'Brien (01236) 441017

TELEPHONES
Ground/Ticket Office/Information
Service (01236) 622000
Fax (01236) 626002

E-MAIL & INTERNET ADDRESS
www.airdrieoniansfc.co.uk
enquiries@airdrieoniansfc.co.uk

CLUB SHOP
The club shop is situated at the stadium.

OFFICIAL SUPPORTERS CLUB
c/o David Johnstone,
16 Deveron Street, Coatbridge
Tel (01236) 423812

TEAM CAPTAIN
Allan McManus

SHIRT SPONSOR

KIT SUPPLIER
IMP Sports

LIST OF PLAYERS 2001-2002

SURNAME	FIRST NAME	MIDDLE NAME	DATE OF BIRTH	PLACE OF BIRTH	DATE OF SIGNING	HEIGHT FT INS	WEIGHT ST LBS	POS. ON PITCH	PREVIOUS CLUB
Armstrong	Paul	George	05/10/78	Dublin	13/07/01	5 11.0	11 4	Def	Brighton & Hove Albion
Beasley	Darren		16/03/81	Rotherham	07/08/01	5 10.5	12 6	Mid	Kilmarnock
Bennett	Neal		29/10/80	Dewsbury	07/08/01	6 1.0	12 12	Gk	Ossip Town
Coyle	Owen	Columba	14/07/66	Paisley	13/07/01	5 11.0	10 6	Fwd	Dunfermline Athletic
Docherty	Stephen		18/02/76	Glasgow	13/07/01	5 10.0	11 0	Mid	Partick Thistle
Dunn	Robert		28/06/79	Glasgow	13/07/01	5 10.0	10 8	Fwd	Partick Thistle
Ferguson	Allan	Thomas	21/03/69	Lanark	22/08/01	5 10.5	12 7	Gk	St. Johnstone
Gardner	Robert	Lee	11/07/70	Ayr	31/07/01	5 8.0	11 0	Mid	Alloa Athletic
James	Kevin	Francis	03/12/75	Edinburgh	03/08/01	6 7.0	13 10	Def	Heart of Midlothian
MacDonald	Stuart		15/05/81	Glasgow	13/07/01	5 11.0	11 5	Def	Morton
Macfarlane	Neil		10/10/77	Dunoon	31/07/01	6 1.0	13 1	Mid	Kilmarnock
McAlpine	Joseph	Charles	12/09/81	Glasgow	19/07/01	5 9.5	11 2	Def	Airdrieonians B.C.
McDonald	Colin		10/04/74	Edinburgh	25/07/01	5 7.0	10 8	Fwd	Falkirk
McKeown	Stephen	James	17/07/81	Rutherglen	19/07/01	5 10.0	12 2	Fwd	Airdrieonians B.C.
McManus	Allan	William	17/11/74	Paisley	13/07/01	6 1.0	12 2	Def	Alloa Athletic
McPherson	Craig		27/03/71	Greenock	13/07/01	5 10.0	11 4	Def	Clyde
Roberts	Mark	Kingsley	29/10/75	Irvine	03/08/01	5 11.0	12 0	Fwd	Falkirk
Smith	Anthony		28/10/73	Bellshill	03/08/01	5 8.0	11 7	Def	Dundee United
Stewart	Alexander		14/10/65	Bellshill	13/07/01	5 8.0	11 4	Def	Partick Thistle
Taylor	Stuart		26/11/74	Glasgow	13/07/01	6 1.0	11 10	Mid	St. Mirren

Milestones

YEAR OF FORMATION: 1878
MOST CAPPED PLAYER: Jimmy Crapnell
NO. OF CAPS: 9
MOST LEAGUE POINTS IN A SEASON: 60 (Division 2 - Season 1973/74) (2 Points for a Win)
        61 (First Division - Season 1994/95) (3 Points for a Win)
MOST LEAGUE GOALS SCORED BY A PLAYER IN A SEASON: Bert Yarnell (Season 1916/17)
NO. OF GOALS SCORED: 39
RECORD ATTENDANCE: 24,000 (-v- Heart of Midlothian – 8.3.1952 at Broomfield Park)
        8,762 (-v- Celtic – 19.8.1998 at Excelsior Stadium)
RECORD VICTORY: 15-1 (-v- Dundee Wanderers – Division 2, 1.12.1894)
RECORD DEFEAT: 1-11 (-v- Hibernian - Division 1, 24.10.1959)

The Diamonds' ten year record

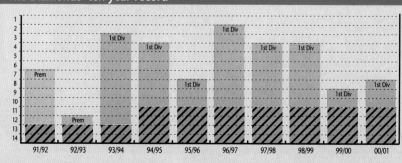

The Diamonds

Date	Venue	Opponents	Att.	Res	Broto J.S.	Alfonso M.	McAlpine J.	Forrest E.	Aguilar M.	Moreau F.	Capin S.	Sanjuan J.	Prest M.	Calderon A.	Fernandez D.	Evans G.	McGuire D.	Boyce S.	Taylor S.	McCann H.A.	Brady D.	Coulter R.	Clark P.	Elliot J.	Elliot B.	Wilson S.	McKeown S.	Armstrong P.	Ireland C.	Phillips T.	Ingram S.	Pilivi T.	Gonzalez R.	McManus T.	Ferguson A.	McPherson C.	Sweeney S.	Bannerman S.	May E.	Dunn M.	Zahana-Oni L.	Davidson S.	Struthers W.	Forge N.	Cameron I.	Wishart F.	Coyle O.	Gardner R.L.	McWilliams D.
Aug 5	A	Inverness Cal. Th.	2,366	0-2	1	2	3	4	5	6	7	8	9	10	11		16	14	17																														
12	H	Raith Rovers	2,854	1-1	1	2	3	4		5	6	7	8^1	10	11		16	9	12																														
19	A	Ayr United	2,705	1-3	1			4		2	6		8	9^1	10	11	14	12	3	7	5	16																											
26	A	Ross County	2,210	1-1	1			4	5^1		6		8	16	10	11	12	2		3	7	15	9																										
Sep 9	H	Alloa Athletic	1,806	2-2	1			4		5	6		8^1	15	10	11^1		2	12	3	9	7	13																										
16	H	Clyde	1,864	1-4	1			4		5	6		8	16^1	10	11		2	12	3	9	7	1	14																									
23	H	Livingston	1,826	1-2	1			4	3	5	6		8	9^1	10	11		15		7	12	16	2																										
30	A	Morton	1,377	5-1	1			4		6^1	16^1	8		10	11^1		12	3	7		15	9^1		2	5^1																									
Oct 7	H	Falkirk	2,879	1-2	1			4		6	15	8	9	10	11			3	7		14		16	2	5^1																									
14	H	Inverness Cal. Th.	1,555	1-2	1			4		6	16	8	9	10	11^1			7	3		14			2	5																									
21	A	Raith Rovers	1,930	1-1				5			7		9	10		15	3	8		4		11^1		2	6	13	16																							
28	H	Ross County	1,431	5-1				5	12	16			15^1	10^1	11^1		2	8^1		3	4		9^1		7	6																								
Nov 4	H	Alloa Athletic	1,220	0-2				5	12		8	9	10	15	2		3	4		11			7	6	1	14																								
11	A	Livingston	3,915	2-2				5	12	7		9	10^1	11	15		2	8^1		3	4		14		6																									
22	H	Clyde	1,513	1-3				5		8	16	15	10	11	9			3^1		4	7			2	6	14																								
25	H	Falkirk	2,867	2-0				5		11^1	7	8	10		12			3		4				2	6	9	16^1																							
Dec 2	H	Morton	1,643	1-1	1			5^1		11	7	8	14	10	12			16		3	4			2	6	9																								
9	A	Ayr United	1,572	0-0	1			5		7		8	9	10	11			2		3	4		12		6		16																							
16	A	Inverness Cal. Th.	1,570	0-4	1			5		7		8	9	10	11		14	2		3	4	6			15																									
26	H	Alloa Athletic	1,427	2-1	1			5		7		8^2	9	10	11		15	2		3	4			6		12	13																								
Jan 2	A	Clyde	1,769	1-1	1	6		5		10^1	7	8	9				15	2		3	4		12			11																								
6	H	Livingston	2,382	1-1	1	6		5		7^1	12	8	9	10			15	2		3	4					16	11																							
13	A	Morton	2,602	3-0	1	6		5		7^1		8	10	11^1	12		14	2		3	4					9^1																								
Feb 3	A	Ayr United	2,060	2-2	1	6	3	5		7^1		8^1	10	11	12			4		2						9																								
10	H	Raith Rovers	1,753	3-0	1	6	3	5		7	16	8	10	11^2	12^1		4	15		2						9																								
Mar 24	A	Falkirk	1,644	1-2	12									2	4^1		6									1	3	5	7	8	9	10	11	14															
27	A	Alloa Athletic	632	0-6					2			6			4			1		7						3	8	10	9			14		5	11															
31	H	Clyde	1,309	1-0	12				15	6					2			1					3	5		7	16										8		4	9^1	10	11							
Apr 3	A	Ross County	1,645	4-3	12				15	6^1					2			1					3	5	7	14^1											8		4	9^2	10	11							
7	A	Falkirk	2,040	1-1					15	6					2			1					3	5	7	12											8		4	9^1	10	11							
10	H	Ross County	1,211	2-2					16	6					2			1					3	5	7^1	15	12										8		4	9^1	10	11							
14	H	Morton	1,331	0-2	14					6					2			1					3	5	7	15	12										8		4	9	10	11							
21	A	Inverness Cal. Th.	805	0-5	3				15	6					2									5	7	12												8		4	9^1	10	11							
28	A	Raith Rovers	2,186	0-5	3				12	6					13									5	7	8	11			15										4	9	10								
May 1	A	Livingston	3,295	0-5	12				3		6				2			1						5	7	11	16	14										8		4	9	10								
5	H	Ayr United	1,228	1-1	12				3		6				2			1						5	11^1	7	14										8		4	9	10								
TOTAL FULL APPEARANCES					23	12	6	25	1	21	7	21	13	24	19		2	13	14	20	20	6	1	7	2	2		26	12	1	2	4	7	1	3	7	10	9	4	5	1	2		1	9	9	9	9	6
TOTAL SUB APPEARANCES					(7)			(3)	(7)	(1)	(5)		(1)	(4)	(11)	(9)	(5)		(1)					(2)	(8)	(1)	(2)	(3)				(1)	(3)	(5)	(1)						(2)	(6)		(3)	(3)			
TOTAL GOALS SCORED								2		6	1	5	4	2	7		1		4	1								2	1					2				2					1	2			6

Small bold figures denote goalscorers. † denotes opponent's own goal.

Excelsior Stadium

CRAIGNEUK AVENUE — CAR PARK — CAR PARK — NORTH STAND — EAST STAND — SOUTH STAND — STAND — CAR PARK — CAR PARK — JACK DALZIEL STAND — PETERSBURN ROAD — CAR PARK — CAR PARK

CUMBERNAULD — A73 — NEWHOUSE

CAPACITY: 10,170 (All Seated)

PITCH DIMENSIONS: 115 yds x 74 yds

FACILITIES FOR DISABLED SUPPORTERS: Disabled facilities are provided in the North, East & South Stands

Team playing kits

How to get there

Excelsior Stadium can be reached by the following routes:

BUSES: Nos 260 or 15 from Airdrie Town Centre.

TRAINS: From Glasgow Queen Street to Airdrie there is a train every 15 minutes. From the Station beyond Airdrie, Drumgelloch, there is a train every 30 minutes, then a 10 minute walk to the stadium.

CARS: From Glasgow or Edinburgh leave the M8 at Newhouse junction (A73) and the stadium is 2½ miles north of Newhouse. From Cumbernauld, the stadium is 6 miles south on the A73.

email: info@sfl.scottishfootball.com • website: www.scottishfootball.com

Arbroath

Gayfield Park,
Arbroath, Angus, DD11 1QB

PRESIDENT
John D. Christison

VICE-PRESIDENT
Charles W. Kinnear

COMMITTEE
R. Alan Ripley (Treasurer),
George Johnson, Michael Caird,
David G. Hodgens, Michael J. Leonard,
Brian W. Lumgair & William J. Thomson

SECRETARY
Charles W. Kinnear

OFFICE ADMINISTRATOR
Sheena Docherty

MANAGER
John Brownlie

ASSISTANT MANAGER
Stephen Kirk

FIRST TEAM COACH/RESERVECOACH
Jake Ferrier

YOUTH CO-ORDINATOR
Gordon Wallace

FITNESS COACH
Jim Stewart

U-18 YOUTH TEAM COACH
Gordon Wallace

U-16 YOUTH TEAM COACH
Jim Smith

CLUB DOCTOR
Dr. Dick Spiers

PHYSIOTHERAPIST
Jim Crosbie

**FOOTBALL SAFETY OFFICERS'
ASSOCIATION REPRESENTATIVE**
William Scorgie (Bus)(01241) 878778

GROUNDSMAN
Charles Lamb

COMMERCIAL MANAGER
George Cant
Bus. (01241) 872000

MATCHDAY PROGRAMME EDITOR
George Cant (Herald Press)
Bus. (01241) 872000

TELEPHONES
Ground/Fax/Ticket Office/Club Shop
(01241) 872157
Telefax (01241) 431125
Sec. Home (01241) 876640
Sec. Bus. (01382) 424336

E-MAIL & INTERNET ADDRESS
www.arbroathfc.co.uk

CLUB SHOP
Gayfield Park, Arbroath, DD11 1QB.
Open on home matchdays.
Premier Sports, West Port, Arbroath,
DD11 1RF. Open Mon. to Sat.

TEAM CAPTAIN
John McAulay

SHIRT SPONSOR
Abbeyfruit

KIT SUPPLIER
ERREA

LIST OF PLAYERS 2001-2002

SURNAME	FIRST NAME	MIDDLE NAME	DATE OF BIRTH	PLACE OF BIRTH	DATE OF SIGNING	HEIGHT FT INS	WEIGHT ST LBS	POS. ON PITCH	PREVIOUS CLUB
Arbuckle	David		12/08/73	Bellshill	21/05/98	5 10.0	11 5	Mid	Queen's Park
Bayne	Graham		22/08/79	Kirkcaldy	07/08/01	6 1.0	12 7	Fwd	Dundee
Brownlie	Paul	Jack	30/08/77	Falkirk	31/07/99	5 9.0	10 8	Fwd	Raith Rovers
Cargill	Andrew		02/09/75	Dundee	30/05/01	5 6.5	10 8	Mid	Dundee
Cunningham	David		08/09/81	Broxburn	25/10/00	5 10.0	11 0	Def	Broxburn Athletic
Cusick	John	James	16/01/75	Kirkcaldy	14/06/00	5 8.0	12 8	Def/Mid	East Fife
Durno	Paul		19/06/84	Arbroath	07/06/00	5 10.0	11 0	Mid	S Form
Fallon	Steven		08/05/79	Paisley	20/07/01	5 8.5	11 6	Def	Dundee United
Florence	Steven		28/10/71	Dundee	20/05/88	5 6.0	11 6	Mid	Arbroath Lads Club
Gallagher	Stephen		29/07/81	Glasgow	27/07/01	6 0.0	12 0	Def	Maryhill
Gardner	James		27/09/67	Dunfermline	20/07/01	5 11.0	12 10	Mid	Stirling Albion
Graham	Ewan	Douglas	11/01/83	Arbroath	07/06/00	5 11.0	11 0	Def	St. Johnstone
Heenan	Kevin	Alexander	07/03/82	Dundee	24/05/01	5 9.0	10 8	Fwd	S Form
Henslee	Greig		13/01/83	Dundee	20/02/01	5 10.0	11 10	Mid	S Form
Hinchcliffe	Craig	Peter	05/05/72	Glasgow	04/08/95	5 11.0	13 0	Gk	Elgin City
Kirk	Stephen	David	03/01/63	Kirkcaldy	14/11/00	5 11.0	13 7	Mid	Hill of Beath Hawthorn
Laverick	Scott		02/03/84	Arbroath	07/06/00	5 8.0	10 0	Mid	S Form
Leahy	Steven		13/11/83	Dundee	17/01/01	5 5.0	10 0	Mid	Brechin City
Mackay	David		02/05/81	Rutherglen	01/08/01	5 5.0	11 0	Def	Dundee
Mallan	Stephen	Patrick	30/08/67	Glasgow	26/07/00	5 11.0	12 4	Fwd	Queen of the South
McAulay	John		28/04/72	Glasgow	04/07/95	5 9.0	11 7	Def	Clyde
McGlashan	John		03/06/67	Dundee	15/08/00	6 1.0	12 0	Mid	Ross County
McInally	David		03/03/81	Glasgow	23/07/01	5 6.0	9 7	Mid	Raith Rovers
McKinnon	Colin	Graham	29/08/69	Glasgow	05/03/01	6 0.0	11 7	Mid	Stenhousemuir
McMillan	Kenneth		26/08/83	Dundee	07/06/00	6 2.0	11 4	Def	S Form
Mercer	James		30/07/74	Glasgow	18/07/98	6 5.0	13 7	Fwd	Queen's Park
Rowe	John	George	23/08/68	Glasgow	14/07/00	6 0.0	12 10	Def	Queen of the South
Spink	Darren		08/01/81	Arbroath	08/09/00	5 11.0	12 0	Def	Broughty Athletic
Steele	Kevin	James	11/10/81	Dundee	02/09/00	5 11.0	10 7	Fwd	Broughty Ferry
Swankie	Gavin		22/11/83	Arbroath	20/02/01	5 8.5	9 0	Mid	S Form
Wight	Craig	MacDonald	24/07/78	Glasgow	09/10/97	6 2.0	12 5	Gk	Hibernian

Milestones

YEAR OF FORMATION: 1878
MOST CAPPED PLAYER: Ned Doig
NO. OF CAPS: 2
MOST LEAGUE POINTS IN A SEASON: 57 (Division 2 – Season 1966/67)(2 Points for a Win)
68 (Third Division – Season 1997/98)(3 Points for a Win)
MOST LEAGUE GOALS SCORED BY A PLAYER IN A SEASON: David Easson (Season 1958/59)
NO. OF GOALS SCORED: 45
RECORD ATTENDANCE: 13,510 (-v- Rangers – Scottish Cup, 23.2.1952)
RECORD VICTORY: 36-0 (-v- Bon Accord – Scottish Cup, 12.9.1885)
RECORD DEFEAT: 1-9 (-v- Celtic – League Cup, 25.8.1993)

The Red Lichties' ten year league record

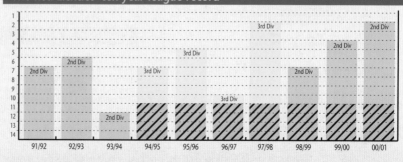

THE RED LICHTIES' CLUB FACTFILE 2000/2001
RESULTS... APPEARANCES... SCORERS... ATTENDANCES...

BELL'S
SCOTTISH FOOTBALL LEAGUE

Date	Venue	Opponents	Att.	Res	Hinchcliffe C.	King T.	Fotheringham K.	Cusick J.	Rowe J.G.	Thomson J.	Arbuckle D.	Bryce T.	McGlashan C.	Mallan S.	Mercer J.	Brownlie P.	Good I.	Tindal K.	Florence S.	McGlashan J.	McAulay J.	Crawford J.	Webster A.	Heenan K.	Henslee G.	Peters S.	Steele K.	Cunningham D.	McInally D.	Wight C.	McDonald C.	McKinnon C.	Maughan R.	Graham E.	Swankie G.	Kirk S.
Aug 5	H	Partick Thistle	1,456	1-1	1	2	3	4	5^1	6	7	8	9	10	11	12	14	16																		
12	A	Berwick Rangers	498	1-2	1	2	3	7	5	4		8	9	10^1	11	14	6	15	12																	
19	H	Clydebank	691	1-0	1	2	11	14	5^1			8	9	12	7	10	4			3	6															
26	A	Stranraer	426	1-2	1	2	6	4	5			8	9	10^1	11	12	16	15	3	7																
Sep 9	H	Forfar Athletic	876	3-4	1				5				9^1	10	11	7^1	3		2	8^1	4	6														
16	H	Stenhousemuir	541	3-0	1	2	11	6	5	4			9^1		7^1	10			3	8^1			12	15	16												
23	A	Queen's Park	721	0-0	1	2	11	6	5				9	10	7				3	8			4	12													
30	H	Queen of the South	667	2-0	1	2	11	6	5	4			9	10^1	7				3	8^1	14		15	16													
Oct 7	H	Stirling Albion	576	0-0	1	2	11	6	5	4			9	10	7		16		3	8	12			15													
14	A	Partick Thistle	2,242	1-1	1		11^1	6	5	4			9	10	15	7			3	8	12		16	2													
21	H	Berwick Rangers	648	0-2	1		11	6	5	4			9	10		7			3	8	14		15	2	15												
28	H	Stranraer	528	1-1	1		11			5			9^1	10	8		14		3		4	6	7	2	15												
Nov 4	A	Forfar Athletic	834	1-0	1		11	12	2	5			9	10^1	8	7			3		4	6		16													
11	H	Queen's Park	573	2-2	1		11	12	2	5			9	10^1	8	7^1	14		3		4	6		16													
18	A	Stenhousemuir	369	1-3	1		11^1		2	5			9		8	7	3				4	6	16		14	10											
25	H	Stirling Albion	550	†3-2	1				2	5			9	10^1	8				11		4	6	16^1	7		15	12	3									
Dec 2	A	Queen of the South	1,087	1-1	1			14		2	5		9^1	10	8				11		4	6	16^1	7		12	3										
16	H	Partick Thistle	1,054	1-1	1			11	12	2^1	5			9	8				10		4	6				7	3										
23	A	Clydebank	131	2-1	1			11^1	14	2	5			9	8				10^1		4	6	16			7	3	13									
Jan 2	H	Forfar Athletic	1,061	1-1	1			11	10	2	5		12^1	9	8						4	6				14	3	1									
13	H	Stenhousemuir	575	5-0	1			11^1	4	2^1				8	9^1				7	10^1	12^1	6	5	14		17		3	1								
20	A	Queen's Park	1,148	1-1	1			11	4	2	5		12	8	9^1				7	10	14	6	3			17		1									
Feb 3	A	Stirling Albion	676	1-1					4	2	5		11	8	9				7	10	12	6	3	14^1		15		1									
17	H	Clydebank	537	4-2					4	2	5			8	9^1				7	10	14	6	3	15		12		1	11^3								
Mar 10	H	Stranraer	670	2-1					15	2			14	8^1	9				3	10	4	6	5	12				1	11	7^1							
17	H	Queen's Park	605	2-0	1				14	2			9^1	8					3	10	12	6	5^1	7		15			11	4							
20	H	Queen of the South	698	†5-2	1				4	2	3		17	9^1	8	11^2				14	6	5	7					13	10^1								
25	A	Stranraer	394	1-0	1				4	2^1	3		14	9	8	11				12	6	5		15				7	10								
31	A	Stenhousemuir	475	1-0	1				4	2^1	3		12	9	8	11				5	6		7			15		10									
Apr 7	H	Stirling Albion	711	1-1	1					2	3		14	9^1	8	11			15	5	6		7			17		10	4								
14	A	Queen of the South	1,141	0-1	1					2	5		11	9	8		3			15	6		7			17		10	4								
17	A	Berwick Rangers	613	0-1	1				11	2	5		9		8		3		12	4	6		15			14		10	7								
21	A	Partick Thistle	3,003	1-0	1					4	2	5		9	8		3		11	12	6		7			15			10^1	17							
24	A	Forfar Athletic	1,065	1-1	1					4	2	5		9^1	8		3		11	12	6		7			15			10								
28	H	Berwick Rangers	2,124	2-0	1				3^1		5		14	9	8^1	17			10	2	6		7			11			4	15							
May 5	A	Clydebank	243	1-3					16		5	2	9		8		3	7					11		10			1			4	6	12^1	15			
TOTAL FULL APPEARANCES					29	8	19	21	33	29	2	4	20	27	34	16	5		23	23	15	25	9	12	1	3	2	2	7	7	4	11	4	1	
TOTAL SUB APPEARANCES					(1)	(8)						(7)	(2)	(1)	(4)	(5)	(3)	(1)		(2)	(14)		(4)	(12)	(2)	(1)	(17)	(4)		(1)	(1)		(2)		(1)	(1)
TOTAL GOALS SCORED							4	1	6				5	10	3	7				5	1		1	1						3	3		1	

Small bold figures denote goalscorers. † denotes opponent's own goal.

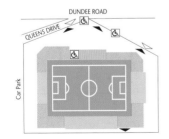

Gayfield Park

DUNDEE ROAD
QUEENS DRIVE
Car Park

CAPACITY: 4,020; Seated 715, Standing 3,305
PITCH DIMENSIONS: 115 yds x 71 yds

FACILITIES FOR DISABLED SUPPORTERS:
Enclosure at west end of Stand with wide steps to take a wheelchair. Toilet facilities are also available.

Team playing kits

How to get there

The following routes may be used to reach Gayfield Park:

BUSES: Arbroath is on the main route from both Glasgow and Edinburgh to Aberdeen. Buses from these three cities, plus Stirling, Dundee and Perth all stop at Arbroath Bus Station at hourly intervals. There is also a local service between Dundee-Arbroath and Montrose and this service is half hourly until 7.00 p.m. Between 7.00 p.m. and 10.45 p.m. the service is hourly. The bus station is 10 minutes walk from the ground.

TRAINS: Arbroath is on the Inter-City 125 route from London to Aberdeen and there are frequent local services between Arbroath, Dundee and Edinburgh. Trains also travel north from Glasgow, Stirling and Perth. The station is a 15 minute walk from the ground.

CARS: There is free parking for 500 cars just next to the ground in Queen's Drive.

The Red Lichties

email: info@sfl.scottishfootball.com • website: www.scottishfootball.com

Somerset Park, Tryfield Place,
Ayr, KA8 9NB

CHAIRMAN
William J. Barr, O.B.E.,
C. Eng., F.I.C.E., F.C.I.O.B., F.I.Mgt

VICE-CHAIRMAN
Donald R. Cameron B.Sc.

DIRECTORS
George H. Smith,
John E. Eyley, B.A., ACMA,
Kenneth W. MacLeod, M.A.S.I. &
Roy G. Kennedy A.R.I.C.S.

COMPANY SECRETARY
John E. Eyley, B.A., ACMA

ADMINISTRATOR
Brian Caldwell

MANAGER
Gordon Dalziel

COACH
Iain Munro

YOUTH COACH
I. Campbell Money

YOUTH COACHES
Eric Morris (U18),
Sammy Conn (U16),
Peter Leonard (U15),
Lawrie Dinwoodie (U14),
David Agnew (U13),

CLUB DOCTOR
Dr. John A.M. Hannah, B.Sc (Hons)
M.B.Ch.B., M.R.C.G.P., D.R.C.O.G.

PHYSIOTHERAPIST
John Kerr, L.V.M.C. Inst. of H.T.

**FOOTBALL SAFETY OFFICERS'
ASSOCIATION REPRESENTATIVES**
Roy Kennedy & Jim Crombie

GROUNDSMAN
David Harkness

LOTTERY MANAGER
Andrew Downie

MATCHDAY PROGRAMME EDITOR
Brian Caldwell (01292) 263435

TELEPHONES
Ground/Ticket Office
(01292) 263435/6
Fax (01292) 281314
Information Line (09068) 121552

E-MAIL & INTERNET ADDRESS
info@aufc.co.uk
www.aufc.co.uk

CLUB SHOP
During weekdays Mon-Fri at the
Centrum Arena, Ayr Road, Prestwick,
(01292 678822) 10.00am - 6.00 p.m.
During all first team home matchdays,
shop is open at the ground, Tryfield
Place, Ayr 10.30 a.m. - 6.00 p.m.

OFFICIAL SUPPORTERS CLUB
c/o Ayr United F.C., Somerset Park,
Ayr, KA8 9NB

TEAM CAPTAIN
John Hughes

SHIRT SPONSOR
First Choice Playing Kit: Aurigin
Second Choice Playing Kit: Barr Steel

KIT SUPPLIER
TFG

LIST OF PLAYERS 2001-2002

SURNAME	FIRST NAME	MIDDLE NAME	DATE OF BIRTH	PLACE OF BIRTH	DATE OF SIGNING	HEIGHT FT INS	WEIGHT ST LBS	POS. ON PITCH	PREVIOUS CLUB
Annand	Edward		24/03/73	Glasgow	01/06/00	5 11.0	11 1	Fwd	Dundee
Black	Aaron		19/12/83	Larne	06/09/00	6 0.0	11 0	Mid	Larne Youth
Bradford	John		15/12/79	Irvine	13/01/98	5 11.0	11 0	Fwd	Dalry Thistle
Bruce	Robert		20/02/82	Dumfries	09/05/00	5 9.0	10 7	Mid	Wigtown & Bladnoch
Burns	Gordon		02/12/78	Glasgow	19/01/00	6 1.0	13 10	Def/Mid	Troon Juniors
Campbell	Mark	Thomas	04/02/78	Irvine	26/02/99	6 0.0	10 12	Def	Stranraer
Chaplain	Scott		09/10/83	Bellshill	27/07/00	5 9.0	10 0	Mid	Rangers
Craig	David	William	11/06/69	Glasgow	16/06/98	6 2.0	13 0	Def	Hamilton Academical
Crilly	Mark		23/05/80	Glasgow	26/09/97	5 10.0	11 0	Mid	Gleniffer Thistle
Dodds	John		16/12/81	Edinburgh	01/10/99	6 3.0	12 11	Gk	Maybole Juniors
Duffy	Cornelius		05/06/67	Glasgow	01/07/99	6 1.0	13 5	Def/Mid	Dundee United
Duncan	Lee		23/01/83	Irvine	22/03/00	5 10.0	11 0	Mid	Maybole Juniors
Dunlop	Michael		05/11/82	Glasgow	24/08/01	6 1.0	11 7	Def	Renfrew
Ferry	Martin	Neil	18/04/83	Glasgow	30/06/01	6 0.0	12 0	Def	Ayr United Youth
Grady	James		14/03/71	Paisley	01/06/00	5 7.0	10 0	Fwd	Dundee
Hamilton	Brian		06/02/84	Glasgow	04/08/00	6 0.0	10 4	Gk	Ayr United B.C.
Hughes	John		09/09/64	Edinburgh	01/07/00	6 0.0	13 7	Def	Hibernian
Kean	Stewart		04/03/83	Irvine	15/01/00	5 9.0	10 0	Fwd	Craigmark Burntonians
Love	Alan	Kenneth	01/04/83	Omagh	06/09/00	5 10.0	10 2	Mid	Dungannon Swifts
Lovering	Paul	James	25/11/75	Glasgow	24/05/00	5 10.0	11 1	Def	Hibernian
Lyle	William		14/04/84	Irvine	27/07/00	5 10.0	10 1	Def	S Form
McColl	Mark	James	26/12/84	Greenock	27/06/01	5 8.0	10 2	Fwd	Morton
McEwan	Craig	George	03/10/77	Glasgow	22/09/00	5 8.5	11 0	Def	Raith Rovers
McGinlay	Patrick	David	30/05/67	Glasgow	01/07/00	5 10.0	11 1	Mid	Hibernian
McLaughlin	Brian		14/05/74	Bellshill	16/08/01	5 4.0	9 10	Mid	Wigan Athletic
McVeigh	Aidan		24/06/83	Portadown	26/05/00	5 11.0	11 7	Fwd	Glenavon
Molloy	Thomas		23/01/83	Greenock	17/08/01	5 11.0	11 7	Def	Morton
Nelson	Craig	Robert	28/05/71	Coatbridge	13/07/98	6 1.0	12 3	Gk	Falkirk
Potter	Craig		18/09/84	Irvine	27/07/00	5 9.0	9 6	Def	S Form
Renwick	Michael		29/02/76	Edinburgh	01/06/00	5 9.0	11 6	Def	Hibernian
Robertson	John	Alexander	28/03/76	Irvine	15/05/01	6 0.0	11 0	Def	Oxford United
Rovde	Marius		26/06/72	Trondheim	31/03/00	6 3.0	13 10	Gk	L.F. Honefoss
Scally	Neil		14/08/78	Paisley	16/02/98	5 11.0	12 0	Mid	Glenafton
Sharp	Lee		22/05/75	Glasgow	12/01/01	5 8.0	11 10	Def/Mid	St. Mirren
Sheerin	Paul	George	28/08/74	Edinburgh	01/06/01	5 10.0	12 4	Mid	Inverness Caledonian Thistle
Smyth	Marc		27/12/82	Edinburgh	09/06/01	6 0.0	11 9	Def	Blackpool
Stevenson	Craig	Andrew	16/02/82	Dumfries	29/08/00	6 0.0	12 0	Def	Morton
Teale	Gary		21/07/78	Glasgow	02/10/98	6 0.0	11 4	Fwd	Clydebank
Wilson	Marvyn		01/12/73	Bellshill	06/07/99	5 7.5	10 0	Mid	Airdrieonians

Milestones

YEAR OF FORMATION: 1910
MOST CAPPED PLAYER: Jim Nisbett
NO. OF CAPS: 3
MOST LEAGUE POINTS IN A SEASON: 61 (Second Division – Season 1987/88)(2 Points for a Win)
77 (Second Division – Season 1996/97)(3 Points for a Win)
MOST LEAGUE GOALS SCORED BY A PLAYER IN A SEASON: Jimmy Smith (Season 1927/28)
NO. OF GOALS SCORED: 66
RECORD ATTENDANCE: 25,225 (-v- Rangers – 13.9.1969)
RECORD VICTORY: 11-1 (-v- Dumbarton – League Cup, 13.8.1952)
RECORD DEFEAT: 0-9 (-v- Rangers, Heart of Midlothian, Third Lanark – Division 1)

The Honest Men's ten year league record

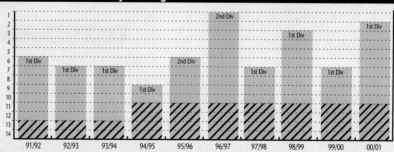

BELL'S
SCOTTISH FOOTBALL LEAGUE

Date	Venue	Opponents	Att.	Res	Rowde M.	Renwick M.	Lovering P.	McGinlay P.	Hughes J.	Duffy C.	Hurst G.	Wilson M.	Armand E.	Grady J.	Teale G.	Reynolds M.	Scally N.	Crilly M.	Bradford J.	Craig D.	Connolly P.	Burns G.	Campbell M.	Benlaredj M.	Nelson C.	McEwan C.	Boyack S.	Robertson H.	Sharp L.	Kean S.
Aug 5	H	Ross County	2,740	1-0	1	2	3	4	5	6	7	8	9[1]	10	11	12	14													
12	A	Alloa Athletic	1,274	1-1	1	2	3	4	5	6	7	8	9[1]	10	12		11		17											
19	H	Airdrieonians	2,705	3-1	1	2	3	11[2]	5	4	9[1]	8		10	12	14	7		17	6											
26	H	Falkirk	3,213	5-2	1	2	3	11[1]	5	4	9[3]	8		10						6	7[1]	17									
Sep 9	A	Livingston	5,271	0-2	1	2	3	11	5	4	9	8							16	6	7	10	14	17						
16	A	Morton	1,308	1-1			3	11		4		8	9[1]		7		16	12		6	10		5		1	2				
23	H	Clyde	2,715	2-1			3	4[1]		5	9	8	12[1]		7	14	11			6	10		16		1	2				
30	H	Inverness Cal. Th.	2,070	3-3			3	4	5		9[2]	8	12[1]		7	11		16		6	10		14		1	2				
Oct 7	H	Raith Rovers	1,858	3-1			3	11		6	9[2]	8	10		12					5	7[1]		4		1	2				
14	A	Ross County	2,567	1-1			3	11[1]		6	9	8	10		12					5			4		1	2	7			
21	H	Alloa Athletic	2,259	3-1			3	11	5	4	9[2]	8	10		12	14		17		6					1	2	7[1]			
28	A	Falkirk	3,783	0-3			3	4	5	2	9		8	10	17		11			6					1		7			
Nov 4	H	Livingston	3,082	1-1			3	4	5		9		12	10	7[1]	17	11			6					1	2	8	11		
11	A	Clyde	1,318	1-0		5	3	4			12	9			7		14			10	6				1	2	8[1]	11		
18	H	Morton	2,256	1-1		5	3	4[1]			12	9			7	17				10	6				1	2	8	11		
25	H	Raith Rovers	2,212	4-2		5	3	4			9[1]		10[1]		7	17				6					1	2	8[1]	11[1]		
Dec 2	H	Inverness Cal. Th.	1,513	3-7		2	3	4	5		9[1]		10[1]		7	17		16		6					1	12	8	11[1]		
9	A	Airdrieonians	1,572	0-0	1	2	14	11	5	4	9	8	10	16	12					6							7	3		
16	H	Ross County	2,007	0-2	1			4	5	6	9	12	14	10	7		11								2		8	3		
Jan 2	A	Morton	2,866	6-0	1	2		4	5	6	9[5]	8		10[1]	7	14	16						12				11	3		
6	H	Clyde	2,481	2-0	1	2	3	4	5[1]	6	9	8		10[1]	7	14												11		
13	H	Inverness Cal. Th.	2,534	1-1		2	3	4[1]	5	6	9	8	17		10	7	14	16										11		
Feb 3	A	Airdrieonians	2,060	2-2			3[1]		5		8	9	10	7[1]	16	11			17	6			4		1	2		14		
17	A	Raith Rovers	1,217	4-1			3	10[3]	4	8	12	9[1]		6		2	11	17	5	4					1			16		
24	A	Falkirk	2,668	2-1				10		5	11	9[1]		7	12				8[1]	6			4		1	2		3		
Mar 3	H	Livingston	2,726	1-1				10		5	11	9	17	7	12				8[1]	6			4		1	2		3		
6	H	Falkirk	2,041	6-0				10		5		9[1]	17	7[1]	11	16			8[1]	6[1]			4[1]		1	2		3[1]		
13	A	Alloa Athletic	539	2-0	12			10		5		9[2]	17	7	11				8	6			4		1	2		3		
17	A	Clyde	1,416	2-2	12	14			5			9[1]	17	7	11				8	6			4		1	2		3		
20	A	Livingston	2,731	1-0				10		5		9[1]	8	7	11	16		17		6			4		1	2		3		
31	H	Morton	2,111	3-0		14		10		5		9[2]	8	7	11	16				6			4		1	2		3[1]		
Apr 7	H	Raith Rovers	2,026	2-0		14		10		5		9[1]	8[1]		11				7	6			4		1	2		3		17
14	A	Inverness Cal. Th.	2,269	0-1		14		10		5		9	8	7	11	17				6			4		1	2		3		
21	A	Ross County	1,942	1-0		14		10[1]		5	12	9	8	7	11	17				6			4		1	2		3		
28	A	Alloa Athletic	2,234	4-1		14		10[2]		5	12	9[1]		7	11	8				6			4		1	2		3[1]		
May 5	A	Airdrieonians	1,228	1-1		14		10	4	5		9		7[1]	11	8				6			12		1	2		3		17
TOTAL FULL APPEARANCES					10	13	21	34	18	29	19	18	26	13	27	4	13	5	10	30	6	1	16		26	24	10	8	15	
TOTAL SUB APPEARANCES						(2)	(8)				(6)	(5)	(5)	(2)	(14)	(10)	(5)	(12)			(2)	(4)	(1)		(1)				(2)	(2)
TOTAL GOALS SCORED							1	13	1		17		18	3	5					3	1	2	1				3	2	3	

Small bold figures denote goalscorers. † denotes opponent's own goal.

The Honest Men

Somerset Park

HOME SUPPORTERS
A77 ►
SOMERSET ROAD
VISITING SUPPORTERS
HOME SUPPORTERS
TRYFIELD PLACE

CAPACITY: 10,185; Seated 1,597, Standing 8,588
PITCH DIMENSIONS: 110 yds x 72 yds
FACILITIES FOR DISABLED SUPPORTERS:
Enclosure and toilet facilities for wheelchairs. Match commentary available for blind persons at all first team matches.

Team playing kits

How to get there

Somerset Park can be reached by the following routes:

TRAINS: There is a half hourly train service from Glasgow to either Ayr or Newton-on-Ayr. The ground is a ten minute walk from both stations.

BUSES: There are several buses from the town centre with a frequency approximately every five minutes. Fans should board buses bound for Dalmilling, Whitletts or any bus passing Ayr Racecourse. The ground is only a ten minute walk from the town centre.

CARS: A77 to Ayr and at Whitletts Roundabout, take third exit (A719) and follow until after Ayr Racecourse. Take first right at traffic lights then left and right into Somerset Road. Car parking facilities are available at Craigie Road, Ayr Racecourse and also at Somerset Road car parks.

email: info@sfl.scottishfootball.com • website: www.scottishfootball.com

Clyde

**Broadwood Stadium,
Cumbernauld, G68 9NE**

CHAIRMAN
William B. Carmichael

CHIEF EXECUTIVE
Ronald D. MacDonald

DIRECTORS
John F. McBeth, F.R.I.C.S.,
Gerard W. Dunn, M.A.,
Harry McCall, B.A., C.Eng., M.I.C.E.,
John D. Taylor, A.C.I.B. &
Ronald D. MacDonald

SECRETARY
John D. Taylor, A.C.I.B.
Bus. (01236) 451511

OFFICE ADMINISTRATION
Mrs. Lynn Calder

MANAGER
Allan Maitland

ASSISTANT MANAGER
Denis McDaid

HEAD COACH
Billy Reid

PLAYER/COACH
Andy Millen

FITNESS COACH
Paul Caton

DIRECTOR OF YOUTH DEVELOPMENT
John Bean

YOUTH TEAM COACHES
Robert Ferguson, Cameron Watt,
& Derek Steel (U16)
Billy Reid, Gerry Ronald,
& Iain Clark (U15)
Colin Mitchell & John Bean (U14)
Jim Strathdee (U13), Gary O'Rourke,
& Steven Harvey (U13)

CLUB DOCTOR
John A. MacLean

FIRST TEAM PHYSIOTHERAPIST
John Watson

CHIEF SCOUT
Stevie Campbell

**DIRECTOR OF STADIUM
OPERATIONS/FOOTBALL SAFETY
OFFICERS' ASSOCIATION
REPRESENTATIVE**
Denis Gowans
(01236) 451511

COMMERCIAL MANAGER
Sharron McCarthy (01236) 451511

GROUNDSMAN/KIT MAN
Douglas Fraser

MEDIA LIAISON OFFICER
Sharron McCarthy (01236) 451511

MATCHDAY PROGRAMME EDITOR
John D. Taylor (01236) 451511

TELEPHONES
Ground (01236) 451511
Fax (01236) 733490

E-MAIL & INTERNET ADDRESS
clydefc@sysnet.co.uk
www.clydefc.co.uk

CLUB SHOP
Situated at Ground
Open on Home Matchdays 1 hour
before and for 1 hour after match.

TEAM CAPTAIN
Andrew McClay

SHIRT SPONSOR

First Choice Playing Kit: Compaq
Second & Third Choice Playing Kit:
Cullen Packaging
KIT SUPPLIER
VIRMA

LIST OF PLAYERS 2001-2002

SURNAME	FIRST NAME	MIDDLE NAME	DATE OF BIRTH	PLACE OF BIRTH	DATE OF SIGNING	HEIGHT FT INS	WEIGHT ST LBS	POS. ON PITCH	PREVIOUS CLUB
Aitken	Christopher	Ian	31/03/81	Glasgow	06/06/00	5 9.0	10 8	Mid	Morton
Bingham	Craig		22/12/79	Irvine	06/07/00	6 0.0	11 4	Mid	Irvine Meadow
Budinauckas	Kevin		16/09/74	Bellshill	17/05/00	5 10.0	11 0	Gk	Partick Thistle
Convery	Steven		27/10/72	Glasgow	31/07/98	5 11.0	11 6	Fwd	Arthurlie
Cook	Barry		06/06/79	Glasgow	21/08/01	6 2.0	13 5	Gk	Pollok Juveniles
Cranmer	Craig	Hamilton	21/02/68	Johnstone	31/07/98	6 2.0	12 12	Def	Pollok
Crawford	Brian		27/07/78	Lanark	13/12/00	5 9.0	11 5	Fwd	Cumbernauld United
Dunn	David	Hugh	01/11/81	Bellshill	19/10/99	5 11.0	12 3	Mid	Motherwell
Grant	Allan		01/07/73	Glasgow	31/07/98	5 10.0	11 0	Fwd	Maryhill
Halliwell	Bryn	Steven	01/10/80	Epsom	12/06/00	6 1.0	12 10	Gk	Wimbledon
Hinds	Leigh	Michael	17/08/78	Beckenham	19/03/01	5 10.0	12 0	Fwd	Wimbledon
Kane	Andrew		07/12/76	Paisley	28/06/00	6 0.0	12 8	Fwd	Rutherglen Glencairn
Keogh	Patrick	Sebastian	07/05/76	Redlands	04/08/98	6 2.0	12 10	Def	Maryhill
McClay	Andrew		26/11/72	Glasgow	31/07/98	5 6.0	9 12	Mid	Maryhill
McCusker	Richard		24/08/70	Glasgow	31/07/98	6 0.0	12 0	Mid	Maryhill
McLaughlin	Mark		02/12/75	Greenock	28/07/99	6 2.0	13 5	Def	Arthurlie
Millen	Andrew	Frank	10/06/65	Glasgow	13/01/01	5 11.0	11 4	Def	Morton
Miller	Kevin		24/09/81	Glasgow	21/08/01	6 2.0	13 0	Mid	Knightswood Juveniles
Mitchell	Jamie		06/01/76	Glasgow	05/03/99	5 7.0	10 0	Mid	Scarborough
Murray	Darren	Thomas	25/01/74	Glasgow	31/07/98	6 1.0	11 10	Def	Maryhill
Okikiolu	Samuel	Kolawole	15/01/82	London	17/08/01	5 11.0	14 0	Def	Wimbledon
Ross	John	James	05/06/76	Falkirk	02/07/99	6 1.0	11 5	Mid	Camelon Juniors
Smith	Bryan	James	21/08/70	Clydebank	31/07/98	5 10.0	11 0	Def	Petershill
Tolland	Michael		02/11/79	Glasgow	14/08/01	5 8.0	10 6	Fwd	Knightswood Juveniles

Milestones

YEAR OF FORMATION: 1878
MOST CAPPED PLAYER: Tommy Ring
NO. OF CAPS: 12
MOST LEAGUE POINTS IN A SEASON: 64 (Division 2 – Season 1956/57) (2 Points for a Win)
          65 (Second Division – Season 1999/2000) (3 Points for a Win)
MOST LEAGUE GOALS SCORED BY A PLAYER IN A SEASON: Bill Boyd (Season 1932/33)
NO. OF GOALS SCORED: 32
RECORD ATTENDANCE: 52,000 (-v- Rangers – 21.11.1908 – at Shawfield Stadium)
          7,382 (-v- Celtic – 14.8.1996 (Coca-Cola Cup) – at Broadwood Stadium)
RECORD VICTORY: 11-1 (-v- Cowdenbeath – Division 2, 6.10.1951)
RECORD DEFEAT: 0-11 (-v- Dumbarton and Rangers, Scottish Cup)

The Bully Wee's ten year league record

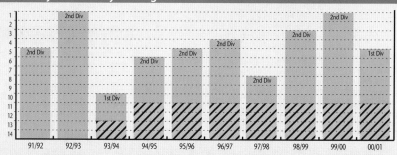

THE BULLY WEE'S CLUB FACTFILE 2000/2001
RESULTS... APPEARANCES... SCORERS... ATTENDANCES...

Date	Venue	Opponents	Att.	Res	Halliwell B.	Murray D.	McLaughlin M.	Smith B.	Cranmer C.	Ross J.	Convery S.	Sellars B.	Proudlock A.	Keogh P.	Grant A.	Greer G.	Henderson N.	Aitken C.	McCusker R.	Kane A.	McPherson C.	Mitchell J.	Bingham C.	Carnie P.	Dunn D.	Hay P.	Hanley D.	Henry J.	Boniface F.	McAuley S.	Crawford B.	McClay A.	Millen A.	Macfarlane N.	Hinds L.
Aug 5	H	Falkirk	2,706	3-1	1	2	3	4	5	6	7	8	9¹	10	11	12	14	15																	
12	A	Ross County	2,645	2-0	1	2	2	4	5	6	7	8	9¹	10¹	11		14		15	16															
19	H	Livingston	1,781	1-1	1	2	3	4	5	6	7	8	9	10	11	12			14	16¹															
26	H	Morton	1,480	0-3	1	2			4	5	6		9	10	11	12	8			16	3	7	15												
Sep 9	A	Inverness Cal. Th.	1,484	2-1	1		3	4	5	6	14²	7		8			2	9		10	11	15	16												
16	H	Airdrieonians	1,864	4-1	1	15	3¹	4	5	6¹	7	16		8			2	9		11¹		10		17¹											
23	A	Ayr United	2,715	1-2	1	15	3	4	5	6	7¹	16		8	11	2		17				10		9											
30	H	Raith Rovers	1,202	0-0	1	2		4	5	6	7	15		8				10	11		3		9	16	14										
Oct 7	A	Alloa Athletic	740	1-3	1	2	3¹		5	6	7	9		8	15			10	11				14	4	13										
14	A	Falkirk	3,003	2-3	2	3			6	7¹				8	5			9¹	12		11	16	10	4	1	15									
21	A	Ross County	987	2-2	2	3¹			6					4¹	5	14		11			7	16	10		1	8	9	15							
28	A	Morton	1,051	1-1	1	2	3		6	17				4	5			11	10	7				15¹	9	8									
Nov 4	H	Inverness Cal. Th.	935	1-1	1	2	3		6	12				4	5	15		11	10¹	7	14				9	8									
11	H	Ayr United	1,318	0-1	1	2	3		6	7				4	5	8		11	10	15	16				9	14									
22	A	Airdrieonians	1,513	3-1	1		3	4	12	6	7			5	2	8¹		11¹		10	15	14				9¹									
25	H	Alloa Athletic	1,012	0-0	1	2		4		6	12			3	15	5		11		10		7	16			9									
Dec 2	A	Raith Rovers	1,810	2-1	1	5	3	4		6	7			8¹	2			11		10	15					9¹									
9	A	Livingston	3,230	0-2	1	5	3	4		6	7			8	16	2		14		11	10	15				9									
16	H	Falkirk	1,629	0-3	1		3	4	5	6	7			8	14	2		10		11		9								15	16				
23	A	Inverness Cal. Th.	1,588	2-2	1		3	4	5		7			8		2		10¹		11		9	12¹	14		6				16					
Jan 2	A	Airdrieonians	1,769	1-1	1		3	4	5	6				10		2		8	14	11	16					9¹									
6	A	Ayr United	2,481	0-2	1	3			4	5	6			10		2		8	15	11	16					9									
13	A	Raith Rovers	1,305	3-1	1	5	3	4						9¹	11	2		15	6			14				7²	10	8							
Feb 3	H	Livingston	2,506	0-3	1	2	3		6	15				4	5	12		11	7				14			9	10	8							
17	H	Morton	1,609	1-1	1	2			4	5	6	7			11			16	10			14		3		9¹	12	8							
24	A	Morton	1,221	1-0	1	2			6						3		14	11	7	15	10		8			9¹				4	5				
Mar 10	A	Alloa Athletic	818	0-0	1	2			6					4	3		14	15	7	16	10		9			11				8	5				
17	H	Ayr United	1,416	2-2	1	2		12	6					3			14	11¹	7		10		8			9				4¹	5				
20	A	Ross County	2,115	0-2	1	2			6					9	3		14	11	7		10		15			8				4	5	16			
27	A	Inverness Cal. Th.	657	0-1	1	2			6					9¹	3		14	11¹	7		10		8			15				4	5				
31	A	Airdrieonians	1,309	0-1	1	2		12	6					10	3		14	5	11	7			9			8				4		16			
Apr 7	H	Alloa Athletic	1,006	1-1	1	2			4	12	6			10	3			11	7	8		12	9								5	16¹			
14	A	Raith Rovers	1,817	1-0	1	2			4	12	6	16			3			11	7		10		15				8	5	9¹						
21	A	Falkirk	2,200	1-1	1	2			4	3	6	16			5		14	11¹	7		10		15				8		9						
28	H	Ross County	1,313	2-0	1	2			4	3	6¹	16³					14	11	7	8	10		15				5		9						
May 5	A	Livingston	6,835	2-0	1	2			4	12	6	11			3		14		7¹	8	10		16				5		9¹						
TOTAL FULL APPEARANCES					34	29	20	23	16	34	18	5	4	28	9	27	3	7	4	25	1	25	10	4	11	2	2	7	8	2	11	3	13	7	4
TOTAL SUB APPEARANCES						(2)		(2)	(4)		(8)	(3)			(4)	(3)	(2)	(11)	(6)	(8)	(2)	(1)	(5)	(11)	(7)	(1)	(1)	(4)		(2)	(7)	(2)		(3)
TOTAL GOALS SCORED							3			2	5		4	5				2		7		2		2				1	2		5		1	3

Small bold figures denote goalscorers. † denotes opponent's own goal.

Broadwood Stadium

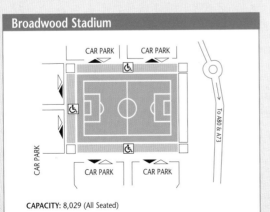

CAPACITY: 8,029 (All Seated)
PITCH DIMENSIONS: 112 yds x 76 yds
FACILITIES FOR DISABLED SUPPORTERS:
Facilities available in Home, Away and New Stands.

Team playing kits

How to get there

The following routes may be used to reach Broadwood Stadium:

BUSES: From Buchanan Street Bus Station in Glasgow, fans should board Bus No. 36A (Glasgow to Westfield).

TRAINS: There are regular trains from Queen Street Station, Glasgow to Croy Station. The Stadium is a 15 minute walk from here.

CARS: From Glasgow City Centre, fans should take the Stepps By-Pass joining the A80 towards Stirling. Take Broadwood turn-off to Stadium.

The Bully Wee

email: info@sfl.scottishfootball.com • website: www.scottishfootball.com

FALKIRK

Brockville Park, Hope Street,
Falkirk, FK1 5AX
CHAIRMAN
Campbell Christie, C.B.E.
VICE-CHAIRMAN
Colin Liddell
DIRECTORS
W. Martin Ritchie O.B.E., Ann M. Joyce,
Colin McLachlan, Graham Crawford,
Douglas Paterson & George Craig
ADVISOR TO THE BOARD
David Brown (Stadium City Ltd)
SECRETARY
Alexander Blackwood
GENERAL MANAGER
Crawford B. Baptie
MANAGER
Alexander Totten
PLAYER/ASSISTANT MANAGER
Kevin McAllister
RESERVE TEAM COACH
Tony Docherty
YOUTH TEAM COACHES
Ian McIntyre (U18),
Bryan Purdie, Andy Dunleavie (U16),
David Docherty (U15),
Ian Fergus & John Darian (U14),
Joe McBride, Peter Deans &
Billy Kirkwood (U13),
CLUB DOCTORS
Dr. R. Gillies Sinclair &
Dr. Ivan Brenkel F.R.C.S.
PHYSIOTHERAPIST
Alexander MacQueen
**COMMUNITY/YOUTH
DEVELOPMENT OFFICERS**
Tony Docherty, Ian McIntyre
& Fraser Cooper
COMMERCIAL MANAGER
Sarah Scott
**FOOTBALL SAFETY OFFICERS'
ASSOCIATION REPRESENTATIVE**
Crawford Baptie (01324) 624121
CHIEF SCOUT
Bill Parker
GROUNDSMAN
James Dawson
MEDIA LIAISON OFFICER
Crawford Baptie (01324) 624121
MATCHDAY PROGRAMME EDITOR
Gordon Dunbar
TELEPHONES
Ground/Commercial/
Ticket Office/Information Service
(01324) 624121 Fax (01324) 612418
E-MAIL & INTERNET ADDRESS
post@falkirkfc.co.uk
www.falkirkfc.co.uk
falkirkfc@lineone.net
CLUB SHOP
47 Glebe Street, Falkirk, FK1 1HX
Tel (01324) 639366
Open Mon. – Sat. 9.30 a.m. – 12 Noon
and 1.00 p.m. – 5.00 p.m.
OFFICIAL SUPPORTERS CLUB
Association of Falkirk F.C. Supporters
Clubs–Chairman: Gordon McFarlane
Tel (01324) 638104
TEAM CAPTAIN
Greig Denham
SHIRT SPONSOR
johnweir.co.uk
KIT SUPPLIER
TFG

LIST OF PLAYERS 2001-2002

SURNAME	FIRST NAME	MIDDLE NAME	DATE OF BIRTH	PLACE OF BIRTH	DATE OF SIGNING	HEIGHT FT INS	WEIGHT ST LBS	POS. ON PITCH	PREVIOUS CLUB
Adams	Neil		22/07/83	Falkirk	07/07/00	5 10.0	11 10	Def	S Form
Archer	Dale	Aaron	12/08/82	London	21/07/01	6 2.0	11 9	Fwd	Crown Manor F.C.
Atai	Michael		15/03/84	Edinburgh	10/07/01	6 1.0	12 2	Gk	Falkirk D Form Under 16
Boyle	Joseph		16/05/83	Glasgow	11/08/99	6 0.5	11 8	Mid	Westfield B.C.
Christie	Kevin		01/04/76	Aberdeen	28/04/99	6 1.0	12 8	Def	Motherwell
Craig	Steven		05/02/81	Blackburn	26/09/00	5 10.0	11 11	Fwd	Broxburn Athletic
Creaney	Philip		12/02/83	Bellshill	09/06/00	5 11.5	11 5	Mid	S Form
Cringean	Stuart	Charles	20/07/83	Glasgow	24/08/01	6 1.5	12 11	Def	Clyde
Denham	Greig	Paterson	05/10/76	Glasgow	09/06/00	6 2.0	13 6	Def	Motherwell
Deuchar	Kenneth	Robert J.	06/07/80	Stirling	26/08/99	6 3.0	13 0	Fwd	Camelon Juniors
Dodds	Ian		05/11/83	Sunderland	10/07/01	6 3.0	12 0	Def	Billericay F.C.
Gray	Alan		14/01/82	Glasgow	03/07/98	6 1.0	13 2	Def	Falkirk B.C.
Henry	John		31/12/71	Vale of Leven	09/09/99	5 10.0	11 0	Mid	Kilmarnock
Hill	Darren		03/12/81	Falkirk	07/07/98	6 1.0	12 3	Gk	Falkirk B.C.
Hogarth	Myles		30/03/75	Falkirk	31/03/99	6 2.5	12 9	Gk	Heart of Midlothian
Kerr	Mark		02/03/82	Bellshill	03/07/98	5 11.5	10 11	Mid	Falkirk B.C.
Lawrie	Andrew		24/11/78	Galashiels	18/06/96	6 0.0	12 6	Def	Falkirk Under 16's
MacSween	Ian		07/06/84	Edinburgh	10/07/01	5 11.0	11 0	Fwd	Falkirk Form D Under 16
Mair	Lee		09/12/80	Aberdeen	19/07/01	6 0.0	12 0	Mid	Dundee
McAllister	Kevin		08/11/62	Falkirk	08/01/97	5 5.0	11 0	Fwd	Hibernian
McHendry	Mark		13/03/83	Glasgow	09/06/00	5 9.5	10 10	Def	S Form
McQuilken	James	Charles	03/10/74	Glasgow	14/07/98	5 9.0	11 2	Def	Hibernian
McStay	Garry		21/11/79	Bellshill	06/11/98	5 10.5	11 11	Mid	Bonnybridge Juniors
Miller	Lee		18/05/83	Lanark	09/06/00	6 2.0	11 7	Mid	S Form
Morris	Ian		28/08/81	Edinburgh	01/07/98	6 0.5	11 11	Fwd	Rangers B.C.
Murray	Joseph		08/01/84	Edinburgh	10/07/01	5 9.0	10 10	Mid	Falkirk Form D Under 16
Pearson	Charles		21/04/82	Falkirk	03/07/98	5 8.0	11 10	Fwd	Falkirk B.C.
Porteous	Fraser		26/01/83	Edinburgh	22/08/00	6 0.0	10 6	Mid	Hibernian
Rennie	Steven		03/08/81	Stirling	19/07/97	6 2.0	10 12	Def	Hutchison Vale Under 15's
Rodgers	Andrew		18/10/83	Falkirk	07/07/00	5 10.5	10 1	Fwd	S Form
Stewart	Dean		14/06/84	Edinburgh	10/07/01	5 8.0	10 12	Mid	Heart of Midlothian Under 16's
Thomson	Mark		19/03/83	Glasgow	26/08/99	6 1.0	11 2	Def	Zeneca
Waddell	Richard		04/02/81	Falkirk	14/11/97	5 9.0	11 7	Fwd	Stenhousemuir
Watson	Stephen		04/04/73	Liverpool	06/07/01	6 1.0	13 10	Mid	Yee Hope F.C. Hong Kong
Wright	Paul	Hamilton	17/08/67	East Kilbride	24/07/01	5 8.0	11 7	Fwd	Kilmarnock

Milestones

YEAR OF FORMATION: 1876
MOST CAPPED PLAYER: Alex H. Parker
NO. OF CAPS: 14
MOST LEAGUE POINTS IN A SEASON: 66 (First Division – Season 1993/94)(2 Points for a Win) and 68 (First Division – Season 1999/2000)(3 Points for a Win)
MOST LEAGUE GOALS SCORED BY A PLAYER IN A SEASON: Evelyn Morrison (Season 1928/29)
NO. OF GOALS SCORED: 43
RECORD ATTENDANCE: 23,100 (-v- Celtic – 21.2.1953)
RECORD VICTORY: 12-1 (-v- Laurieston – Scottish Cup, 23.3.1893)
RECORD DEFEAT: 1-11 (-v- Airdrieonians – Division 1, 28.4.1951)

The Bairns' ten year league record

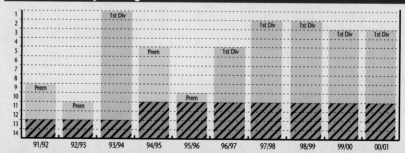

THE BAIRNS' CLUB FACTFILE 2000/2001
RESULTS… APPEARANCES… SCORERS… ATTENDANCES…

Date	Venue	Opponents	Att.	Res	Hogarth M.	Lawrie A.	McQuilken J.	Rennie S.	Christie K.	Nicholls D.	McAllister K.	Kerr M.	Roberts M.	Henry J.	Hutchison G.	Denham G.	Morris I.	Avdiu K.	McMahon D.	Pearson C.	Seaton A.	Craig S.	McStay G.	McDonald C.	Burke A.	Deuchar K.	Waddell R.
Aug 5	A	Clyde	2,706	1-3	1	2	3	4	5	6	7	8	9	10	11¹	12	14										
12	H	Morton	2,563	1-0	1	2	3	4		6	7	10	9	8¹	11	5	14	16									
19	A	Inverness Cal. Th.	2,132	3-2	1	2	3		4	6	7¹	10¹	9	8	11¹	5	15										
26	A	Ayr United	3,213	2-5	1	2¹	3		4	6		10	9¹	8	11	5					7						
Sep 9	A	Raith Rovers	2,762	2-1	1	2	3	5	4	6	15	10	9²	8	11	14				7							
16	H	Alloa Athletic	2,645	1-1	1	2	3	4		6		10¹	9	8	11	14				7	16						
23	A	Ross County	3,161	2-0	1	2¹	3	5	4	6		10	9	8	11¹	16				7							
30	H	Livingston	3,547	3-2	1	2	3	4		6¹	7		9	8¹	11	5					10	16¹		14			
Oct 7	H	Airdrieonians	2,879	2-1	1	2	3	4		6	7		9¹	8	11¹	5	15				10			14	16		
14	H	Clyde	3,003	†3-2	1	2	3	4	5	6	14¹		9	8	11¹	7				16	10						
21	A	Morton	1,503	4-0	1	2	3	4¹		6	15	7	9¹	8	11²	5		16			10	12					
28	H	Ayr United	3,783	3-0	1	2	3		4	6	15¹	7	9	8¹	11	5					10¹				16		
Nov 4	A	Raith Rovers	3,120	2-0	1	2	3	4		6	15	7	9¹	8¹	11	5					10				16		
11	H	Ross County	2,898	2-3	1	2	3	4		6¹	15	7	9¹	8	16	5					10				11		
18	A	Alloa Athletic	1,709	2-3	1	2	3	14	4	6¹	7	10	9	8		5					16¹	12			11		
25	A	Airdrieonians	2,867	0-2	1	2	3		4		15	7	9	8	11	5					10		6		16		
Dec 2	A	Livingston	4,464	1-4	1	2	3	4		6	15	7	16¹	8	9	5					10				11		
9	H	Inverness Cal. Th.	2,136	2-2	1	2¹	3	8¹	4	6	7	10	9	11	15	5					16						
16	A	Clyde	1,629	3-0	1	2	3	5	4	6¹	15	7	9	8²	10						16				11		
Jan 2	A	Alloa Athletic	2,627	2-2	1	2	3	6	4		15¹	7	9	8	10	5					16¹	12			11		
13	H	Livingston	4,914	1-0	1	2	3	5	4	6	7	10	9	8	11¹											16	
Feb 3	H	Inverness Cal. Th.	1,913	1-1	1	2¹	3	5	4	6	15	10	9	8	7		14				16				11		
24	A	Ayr United	2,668	1-2	1	2		5	4	6	7	10		8	11						3	9¹				16	14
Mar 6	A	Ayr United	2,041	0-6	1	2	3	5	4	7	15	10		8	11	6					9						
10	A	Ross County	2,620	1-4	1	2	3		4¹	6	7	8			11	5	14				12	9	10			15	
17	H	Ross County	1,955	1-1	1	2		4		6	7		9		11¹	5					3	10	8			16	
24	A	Airdrieonians	1,644	2-1	1	2	3	4		6¹	7¹	14	9		11	5						10	8			16	
27	H	Morton	1,276	1-3	1	2	3	4		6¹	7	8	16		11	5						9	14	10			
31	H	Alloa Athletic	1,186	1-0	1	2	3	4		6¹	7	14			11	5				16		10	14		9		
Apr 3	H	Raith Rovers	1,586	0-0	1	2	3	4	8	6					11	5						10	14		9		7
7	A	Airdrieonians	2,040	1-1	1	2	3	4	8	6¹		7			11	5						10			9		15
10	H	Raith Rovers	1,634	2-0	1	2	3	4	8	6		7			10¹	5						9			16		11¹
21	H	Clyde	2,200	1-1	1	2	3	4	12	15	7		8		10¹	5						9	6		16		11
24	A	Livingston	3,659	0-3	1	2	3	4		6	7				8	11	5	14				12	9	10			15
28	A	Morton	905	1-2	1	2	3	4		6		7	12	9	11	5				16¹		10	8		15		
May 5	H	Inverness Cal. Th.	2,230	2-1	1	2	3	5		6	15	7	8	14	11	4¹				9¹		10			16		
TOTAL FULL APPEARANCES					36	36	34	27	24	32	14	30	23	27	34	25	4	3	1	4	22	7			6	4	3
TOTAL SUB APPEARANCES								(1)		(1)	(14)	(2)	(3)	(1)	(2)	(1)		(12)	(1)	(4)	(5)	(5)	(3)	(1)	(5)	(8)	(2)
TOTAL GOALS SCORED						4			1	2	8	5	2	8	6	11					2	5					1

Small bold figures denote goalscorers. † denotes opponent's own goal.

Brockville Park

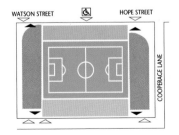

WATSON STREET · HOPE STREET · COOPERAGE LANE

CAPACITY: 7,576; Seated 1,700 Standing 5,876

PITCH DIMENSIONS: 110 yds x 71 yds

FACILITIES FOR DISABLED SUPPORTERS:
Disabled Enclosure opposite Main Stand – takes seven disabled fans in wheelchairs plus one helper each.

Team playing kits

How to get there

Brockville Park can be reached by the following routes:

TRAINS: The main Edinburgh-Glasgow railway line passes by the ground and passengers can alight at Grahamston Station. They will then have a walk of 100 yards to the ground.

BUSES: All buses departing from the city centre pass by Brockville.

CARS: Car parking facilities are available in the Meeks Road car park for coaches and cars and also in a local shopping car park which can hold 500 cars. Supporters coaches and cars will be directed to the appropriate parking area by the police on duty.

Inverness Caledonian Thistle

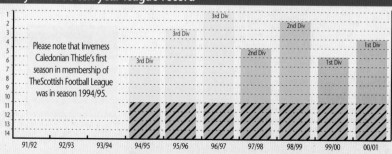

Caledonian Stadium, East Longman,
Inverness, IV1 1FF
CHAIRMAN
David F. Sutherland
VICE-CHAIRMAN
Kenneth A. Thomson
DIRECTORS
Kenneth Mackie, Ian MacDonald,
Graeme Bennett & Alexander Catto
DIRECTOR OF MANAGEMENT COMMITTEE
Ali MacKenzie
HON. LIFE PRESIDENT
John S. McDonald O.B.E.
HON. LIFE VICE-PRESIDENT
Norman H. Miller
SECRETARY
James Falconer
DIRECTOR OF FOOTBALL
Graeme Bennett
MANAGER
Steven W. Paterson
ASSISTANT MANAGER
Duncan Shearer
RESERVE TEAM COACH
John Docherty
DIRECTOR OF YOUTH DEVELOPMENT
James Jarvie
YOUTH DEVELOPMENT CO-ORDINATOR
Jackie Sutherland
YOUTH DEVELOPMENT COACH
Charlie Christie
YOUTH COACHES
John Beaton, Roddie Davidson,
Alan Johnstone, Gary Davidson,
Joe MacMillan and Graeme Thomson
COMMUNITY COACH
Michael Teasdale
CLUB DOCTOR
Dr. John N. MacAskill
ASSISTANT CLUB DOCTORS
Dr. Ian Smith, Dr. Derek MacLeod
& Dr. Donald McVicar
PHYSIOTHERAPISTS
Ian Manning & Emily Goodlad
COMMERCIAL/MARKETING
Debbie Ross
CLUB CHAPLAIN
Rev. Arthur Fraser
**FOOTBALL SAFETY OFFICERS'
ASSOCIATION REPRESENTATIVE**
John Sutherland M.B.E.
GROUNDSMAN/KIT MAN
Tommy Cumming
MEDIA LIAISON OFFICER
Ken Thomson (01343) 220550
MATCHDAY PROGRAMME EDITOR
Bryan Munro (01463) 230721
TELEPHONES
Ground (01463) 222880
Fax (01463) 715816
Sec. Home (01463) 792358
Sec. Bus. (01463) 720603
Sec. Mobile (07881) 770207
E-MAIL ADDRESS
info@caley-thistle.freeserve.co.uk
www.caley-thistle.co.uk
CLUB SHOP
Situated at Stadium. Open Mon-Fri
9.00 a.m. to 5.00 p.m. and Sat on
home match days only
OFFICIAL SUPPORTERS CLUB
Secretary, Caledonian Stadium,
East Longman, Inverness, IV1 1FF
TEAM CAPTAIN
Bobby Mann
SHIRT SPONSOR
SHARP
KIT SUPPLIER
ERREA

LIST OF PLAYERS 2001-2002

SURNAME	FIRST NAME	MIDDLE NAME	DATE OF BIRTH	PLACE OF BIRTH	DATE OF SIGNING	HEIGHT FT INS	WEIGHT ST LBS	POS. ON PITCH	PREVIOUS CLUB
Bagan	David		26/04/77	Irvine	20/06/00	5 8.0	10 7	Mid	Kilmarnock
Bavidge	Martin	Mitchell	30/04/80	Aberdeen	24/07/99	6 1.0	13 0	Fwd	Forres Mechanics
Bradshaw	Paul	Allan	25/09/79	Inverness	03/08/01	6 2.0	10 7	Def	Brora Rangers
Calder	James	Evan	29/07/60	Grantown-on-Spey	29/06/94	5 11.0	13 4	Gk	Inverness Thistle
Calder	Niall		03/09/84	Inverness	13/09/00	5 8.0	10 0	Mid	S Form
Christie	Charles		30/03/66	Inverness	05/08/94	5 8.5	11 4	Mid/Fwd	Caledonian
Duncan	Russell	Allan	15/09/80	Aberdeen	03/08/01	5 10.0	10 10	Def/Mid	Forfar Athletic
Fridge	Leslie	Francis	27/08/68	Inverness	23/05/97	5 11.0	12 0	Gk	Dundalk
Gilfillan	Bryan	James	14/09/84	Cardenden	11/10/00	5 9.0	10 7	Def/Mid	S Form
Golabek	Stuart	William	05/11/74	Inverness	27/05/99	5 10.0	11 0	Def	Ross County
Low	Anthony	Kevin	18/08/83	Glasgow	13/09/00	5 8.0	10 4	Mid/Fwd	I.C.T. Form D Under 16
MacDonald	Neil		08/01/83	Stornoway	30/03/01	5 8.0	10 5	Fwd	Fort William
Mann	Robert	Alexander	11/01/74	Dundee	05/02/99	6 3.0	14 7	Def	Forfar Athletic
McBain	Roy	Adam	07/11/74	Aberdeen	04/08/00	5 11.0	11 5	Def/Mid	Ross County
McCaffrey	Stuart	Muir	30/05/79	Glasgow	01/12/00	5 11.5	12 0	Def	Aberdeen
Munro	Grant	John	15/09/80	Inverness	21/02/00	6 0.0	12 7	Def	S Form
Ridgers	Alexander	Trevor	30/06/82	Inverness	01/01/01	6 2.0	11 7	Gk	Strathspey Thistle J.F.C.
Ritchie	Paul	Michael	25/01/69	St. Andrews	02/08/01	6 1.0	12 12	Fwd	Happy Valley A.A.
Robson	Barry	Gordon G.	07/11/78	Aberdeen	15/10/97	5 11.0	12 0	Mid/Fwd	Rangers
Stewart	Graeme	John	02/04/82	Aberdeen	02/02/01	6 1.0	10 5	Mid	Clachnacudden
Teasdale	Michael	Joseph	28/07/69	Elgin	08/12/95	6 0.0	13 0	Def/Mid	Dundee
Tokely	Ross	Norman	08/03/79	Aberdeen	03/06/96	6 3.0	13 6	Def/Mid	Huntly
Walker	Joseph	Nicol	29/09/62	Aberdeen	22/08/01	6 2.0	13 1	Gk	Aberlour Villa
Wyness	Dennis	Middleton	22/03/77	Aberdeen	14/01/00	5 10.5	12 7	Mid/Fwd	Aberdeen

Milestones

YEAR OF FORMATION: 1994
MOST LEAGUE POINTS IN A SEASON: 76 (Third Division – Season 1996/97) (3 Points for a Win)
MOST LEAGUE GOALS SCORED BY A PLAYER IN A SEASON: Iain Stewart (Season 1996/97)
NO. OF GOALS SCORED: 27
RECORD ATTENDANCE: 4,931 (-v- Ross County – 23.1.1996 - at Telford Street Park)
6,290 (-v- Aberdeen – 20.2.2000 – Scottish Cup - at Caledonian Stadium)
RECORD VICTORY: 8-1 (-v- Annan Athletic – Scottish Cup, 24.1.1998)
RECORD DEFEAT: 1-5 (-v- Morton – First Division, 12.11.1999)
(-v- Airdrieonians – First Division, 15.4.2000)

Caley Thistle's ten year league record

Please note that Inverness Caledonian Thistle's first season in membership of The Scottish Football League was in season 1994/95.

CALEY THISTLE'S CLUB FACTFILE 2000/2001
RESULTS... APPEARANCES... SCORERS... ATTENDANCES...

BELL'S SCOTTISH FOOTBALL LEAGUE

Date	Venue	Opponents	Att.	Res	Fridge L.	Tokley R.	Golabek S.	Mann R.	Hastings R.	Byers K.	Bagan D.	Xausa D.	Stewart I.	Christie C.	Wyness D.	Bavidge M.	Sheerin P.	Robson B.	McBain R.	Calder J.	McCaffrey S.	Teasdale M.	Munro G.	Graham D.	MacDonald N.	Stewart C.
Aug 5	H	Airdrieonians	2,366	2-0	1	2^1	3	4	5	6	7	8^1	9	10	11	12										
12	A	Livingston	3,838	1-3	1	2	3	4	5		7	8	12^1	10	11	9	6	15								
19	H	Falkirk	2,132	2-3	1	2	3	4	5	12	16		9	10	7	8^2	6	11	14							
26	A	Raith Rovers	1,615	1-4	1	2	3	4	5	7		8	9^1	10			6	16	11							
Sep 9	H	Clyde	1,484	1-2		2	3	4		16	7^1	8	12	10	9	14	6	11		1	5					
16	H	Ross County	4,823	0-1		7				14	12	8	9	10	16		6	11	3	1	4	2	5			
23	A	Alloa Athletic	584	4-1		7	3		5		14	8^1		16	9^1		6^1	11^1	10	1	4	2				
30	A	Ayr United	2,070	3-3		2	3	5^1			7	8^1		12	9		6^1	11	10	1	4					
Oct 7	H	Morton	1,439	4-0		2	3	4			7^1			10	9^2	6		11	8^1	1	5					
14	A	Airdrieonians	1,555	2-1		2	3	5			7	12^1		10	9		6^1	11	8	1	4					
21	H	Livingston	2,147	2-2		2	3	4			7	8		12	15	9	6^1	11	10^1	1	5	16				
28	H	Raith Rovers	1,723	1-2			3		2		7	8		10	12	9	6^1	11		1	5	4				
Nov 4	A	Clyde	935	1-1			3	5		12	7			10	8^1	9	6	11		1	4	2				
11	H	Alloa Athletic	1,384	2-1		12	3	5			7	8		10	9		6^1	11		1	4	2^1				
18	A	Ross County	5,761	3-0		12	3	5			7	14		10	8^2	9	6	11		1	4	2^1				
25	A	Morton	708	0-2			4	5	3	14	7	12		10	8	9	6	15	11	1		2				
Dec 2	H	Ayr United	1,513	7-3		14		5	3		7^2	12		10	8^3	9	6^1	15	11	1	4	2^1				
9	A	Falkirk	2,136	2-2		14		5	3		7	12		10	8^1	9	6^1	11		1	4	2				
16	H	Airdrieonians	1,570	4-0				5	3		7^1	9^1		10^1	8^1	12	6	11		1	4	2				
23	H	Clyde	1,588	2-2		14		5	3		7^1	9^1		10	8		6	16	11	1	4	2				
Jan 2	H	Ross County	5,291	3-3	1	3		5			7			10	9^2	8	6^1	12	11		4	2				
6	A	Alloa Athletic	744	1-1				5	3		7	8^1		10	9	14	6	11		1	4	2				
13	A	Ayr United	2,534	1-1	1			5	3		7	8			9^1		6	15	11		4	2		16		
Feb 3	H	Falkirk	1,913	1-1		2		5	3		7	8		10	9^1		6	11		1	4			12		
Mar 10	A	Raith Rovers	1,342	1-1		2		5	3		7	15		10	9^1	8	6	12	11	1	4					
13	H	Morton	1,016	4-2		2		5	3		7^1	8		10	9^3		6	12	11	1	4	16				
17	H	Alloa Athletic	1,613	2-0		2		5	3	16	7			10	9^1	8	6	12^1	11	1	4	14				
23	H	Raith Rovers	1,299	2-0		2		5	3	17	7			10	9^2	8	6	11	11	1	4	14				
27	A	Clyde	657	2-2		2		5	3		7^1			12	9	8	6	10	11	1	4	14				
31	A	Ross County	5,876	1-0		2		5	3		7			10	9	8	6	12	11^1	1	4	14				
Apr 3	A	Livingston	2,136	1-4		2		5	3		7			10	9^1	14	6	8	11	1	4	12				
7	A	Morton	931	3-0		2	6	5		12				10^1	9^1	8		11	14	1	4		7	3	17^1	
14	H	Ayr United	2,269	1-0		2		5^1	3		7			14	9	8	6	10	11	1	4				17	
21	A	Airdrieonians	805	1-1		11		5		12				10	9^1	17	6	15		1	4	2	3	8	7	
28	H	Livingston	2,824	2-3			3	5		15	7			10	9	8	6^2	11		1	4	2			12	14
May 5	A	Falkirk	2,230	1-2		2		5		17	7			10	9^1	8	6	11		1	4	12	3			14
TOTAL FULL APPEARANCES					7	25	16	33	21	4	29	16	4	31	28	23	33	13	30	29	31	17	4		1	1
TOTAL SUB APPEARANCES						(5)				(9)	(5)	(6)	(2)	(4)	(3)	(7)		(12)	(3)			(8)		(2)	(4)	(1)
TOTAL GOALS SCORED						1		2			8	7	2	2	24	5	11	2	3			3			1	

Small bold figures denote goalscorers. † denotes opponent's own goal.

Caledonian Stadium

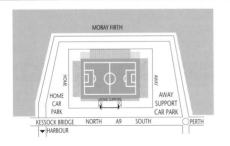

MORAY FIRTH

HOME | AWAY
HOME CAR PARK | AWAY SUPPORT CAR PARK
KESSOCK BRIDGE — NORTH — A9 — SOUTH — PERTH
HARBOUR

CAPACITY: 6,280; Seated 2,280, Standing 4,000

PITCH DIMENSIONS: 115 yds x 75 yds

FACILITIES FOR DISABLED SUPPORTERS:
By prior arrangement with the Secretary

Team playing kits

How to get there

The following routes can be used to reach Caledonian Stadium:

TRAINS: Nearest Railway Station is Inverness which is approximately one mile from the ground.

BUSES: Local services from Farraline Park Bus Station.

CARS: The Ground is located on the North side of the A9 Perth/Inverness trunk road and fans should access off the roundabout (first after Perth) before Kessock Bridge. Parking available at stadium.

Caley Thistle

email: info@sfl.scottishfootball.com • website: www.scottishfootball.com

Partick Thistle

Firhill Stadium, 80 Firhill Road, Glasgow, G20 7AL

PRESIDENT
James R. Aitken

CHAIRMAN
T. Brown McMaster

VICE-CHAIRMAN
Thomas Hughes

DIRECTORS
Allan Cowan, James Oliver,
Edward Prentice, Norman Springford
Margaret W.G. Forsyth
& Ronald S. Gilfillan

**HON. VICE-PRESIDENT/
ASSOCIATE DIRECTOR**
Robert W. Reid

ASSOCIATE DIRECTORS
Les Hope

CHIEF EXECUTIVE/SECRETARY
Alan C. Dick

MANAGER
John Lambie

ASSISTANT MANAGER
Gerry Collins

COACH
John Macdonald

YOUTH TEAM COACHES
Alan Harris (U15),
Alex Main (U13)

HONORARY MEDICAL OFFICER
Dr Alan W. Robertson

PHYSIOTHERAPIST
Walter Cannon

**STADIUM MANAGER &
CHIEF OF SECURITY**
Alan C. Dick

**FOOTBALL SAFETY OFFICERS'
ASSOCIATION REPRESENTATIVE**
Alan C. Dick (0141) 579 1971

GROUNDSMAN
George Furze

COMMERCIAL MANAGER
Amanda Stark (0141) 579 1971

LOTTERY MANAGER
Bobby Briggs

MEDIA LIAISON OFFICER
Alan C. Dick

MATCHDAY PROGRAMME EDITOR
Tom Hosie

TELEPHONES
Ground/Ticket Office/Commercial
(0141) 579 1971
Fax (0141) 945 1525
Jagsline (09068) 666474

E–MAIL AND INTERNET ADDRESS
mail@ptfc.co.uk
www.ptfc.co.uk

CLUB SHOP
80 Firhill Road, Glasgow, G20 7AL
Tel (0141) 579 1971.
Open each matchday and every
Tuesday from 12.30p.m. - 4.30p.m.
Upstairs office shop open daily from
9.00 a.m. - 4.30 p.m.

OFFICIAL SUPPORTERS CLUB
Ms. Morag McHaffie,
c/o Firhill Stadium, 80 Firhill Road,
Glasgow, G20 7AL

TEAM CAPTAIN
Danny Lennon

SHIRT SPONSOR
D.H. Morris

KIT SUPPLIER
SECCA

LIST OF PLAYERS 2001-2002

SURNAME	FIRST NAME	MIDDLE NAME	DATE OF BIRTH	PLACE OF BIRTH	DATE OF SIGNING	HEIGHT FT INS	WEIGHT ST LBS	POS. ON PITCH	PREVIOUS CLUB
Archibald	Alan	Maxwell	13/12/77	Glasgow	19/09/96	6 0.0	11 7	Def	Kilwinning Rangers
Arthur	Kenneth		07/12/78	Bellshill	01/06/97	6 3.0	13 8	Gk	Possilpark Y.M.C.A.
Brand	Andrew	Gerard	17/04/83	Glasgow	06/09/00	5 11.0	10 7	Def	Partick Thistle B.C.
Britton	Gerard	Joseph	20/10/70	Glasgow	03/07/01	6 0.0	11 11	Fwd	Livingston
Collins	Nicholas	Charles T.	29/12/83	Glasgow	10/08/00	5 9.0	10 5	Fwd	Maryhill Juniors B.C.
Connaghan	Denis		09/01/76	Glasgow	26/04/01	6 1.0	11 10	Def	Queen's Park
Craigan	Stephen	James	29/10/76	Newtonards	12/07/00	6 0.0	12 9	Def	Motherwell
Dolan	James		22/02/69	Salsburgh	07/08/01	5 8.0	10 8	Mid	Livingston
Easton	Fraser	John	23/09/82	Larbert	10/08/00	6 0.0	11 2	Def	Linlithgow Bridge B.C.
Elliot	Barry	Robert	24/10/78	Carlisle	30/03/01	5 10.0	11 5	Fwd	Dundee
Fleming	Derek	Adam	05/12/73	Falkirk	21/06/01	5 8.0	10 5	Mid	Livingston
Gibson	Andrew	Stewart	02/03/82	Glasgow	03/07/00	5 10.0	10 9	Mid	Partick Thistle B.C.
Gow	Garry	Paul	24/06/77	Glasgow	04/07/01	6 1.0	13 12	Gk	Stenhousemuir
Hardie	Martin		22/04/76	Alexandria	24/03/00	6 0.0	11 0	Mid/Fwd	East Stirlingshire
Howie	William		09/07/82	Rutherglen	21/05/99	5 9.0	10 1	Mid	Partick Thistle B.C.
Huxford	Richard	John	25/07/69	Scunthorpe	02/08/01	6 0.0	12 2	Def	Alloa Athletic
Kelly	Patrick		26/04/78	Kirkcaldy	02/08/01	6 1.0	11 6	Def	Raith Rovers
Lambie	Duncan		18/06/83	Stirling	03/07/01	5 9.0	11 2	Mid	Dunfermline Athletic
Lennon	Daniel	Joseph	06/04/70	Whitburn	24/12/99	5 7.0	10 10	Mid	Ross County
McCallum	David	John	07/09/77	Bellshill	03/07/00	5 11.0	10 10	Mid	Stirling Albion
McDowell	Murray	John L.	17/02/78	Dundee	14/08/01	5 11.0	11 11	Fwd	Cowdenbeath
McKinstrey	James		03/07/79	Glasgow	23/05/01	5 10.0	12 1	Def/Mid	Clydebank
McLean	Scott	James	17/06/76	East Kilbride	17/12/99	5 11.5	12 5	Fwd	Inverness Caledonian Thistle
Milligan	Greig	James	01/09/84	Glasgow	03/10/00	5 8.0	10 2	Def/Mid	Glasgow Perthshire B.C.
Paterson	Scott	Thomas	13/05/72	Aberdeen	25/07/01	6 2.0	13 0	Def	Morton
Perriss	Richard	Elliott	26/03/82	Glasgow	12/09/00	5 6.0	10 8	Fwd	Sauchie J.F.C.
Smith	James		11/07/78	Glasgow	31/05/00	6 3.0	12 7	Def	Stranraer
Walker	Paul		20/08/77	Kilwinning	21/08/01	5 6.0	10 1	Fwd	Stranraer

Milestones

YEAR OF FORMATION: 1876
MOST CAPPED PLAYER: Alan Rough
NO. OF CAPS: 53 (of which 51 with Partick Thistle)
MOST LEAGUE POINTS IN A SEASON: 51 (First Division - Season 1991/92) (2 Points for a Win)
    75 (Second Division - Season 2000/01)(3 Points for a Win)
MOST LEAGUE GOALS SCORED BY A PLAYER IN A SEASON: Alec Hair (Season 1926/27) (2 Points for a Win)
NO. OF GOALS SCORED: 41
RECORD ATTENDANCE: 49,838 (-v- Rangers – 18.2.1922)
RECORD VICTORY: 16-0 (-v- Royal Albert – Scottish Cup, 17.1.1931)
RECORD DEFEAT: 0-10 (-v- Queen's Park - Scottish Cup, 3.12.1881)

The Jags' ten year league record

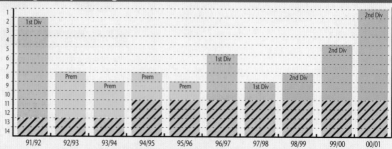

THE JAGS' CLUB FACTFILE 2000/2001
RESULTS... APPEARANCES... SCORERS... ATTENDANCES...

BELL'S — SCOTTISH FOOTBALL LEAGUE

Date	Venue	Opponents	Att.	Res	Arthur K.	McCallum D.	Stirling J.	Lennon D.	Smith J.	Archibald A.	McWilliams D.	Cameron I.	McLean S.	McCrillen P.	McKeown D.	Hardie M.	Lyle D.	Moore A.	Bottiglieri E.	Craigan S.	Lindau P.	Howie W.	Docherty S.	Brown M.	Stewart A.	Laget G.	Dunn R.	McNally M.	Shaw G.	Hamilton B.	Collins D.	Elliot B.
Aug 5	A	Arbroath	1,456	1-1	1	2	3	4	5	6	7	8	9[1]	10	11	12		15	16													
12	H	Stranraer	2,357	2-1	1		3		5	6		8	9	11	12	10[1]		15		2	4	7[1]	14									
19	A	Stenhousemuir	1,130	0-4	1	16	11		12	6		8	9	10	3	4		7		5	15		2									
26	H	Berwick Rangers	2,060	1-1	1		3		5		14		9	10	11	15[1]		16		2	6	7	8	4	1							
Sep 9	A	Queen's Park	4,019	1-0	1			8[1]	5	6	3	15	9	11	10	12				4	7		2		14							
16	H	Stirling Albion	2,251	3-1	1	16		8[1]	5	6			9[1]	11	3	7		4		10[1]	15		2		14							
23	A	Clydebank	1,379	1-2	1			8	5	6		14	9[1]	11	16	3		15		7	4		10		2							
30	H	Forfar Athletic	2,218	1-1	1			8		6		12	9[1]	11	3			7		5			14		2		4	10	16			
Oct 7	A	Queen of the South	1,499	2-1	1	11		8		6		15	9[1]	16[1]	3					5	7	14	10		2		4					
14	H	Arbroath	2,242	1-1	1	11		8		6		14	9[1]	15	3			12		4	7		10		2		5					
21	A	Stranraer	1,101	3-0	1	14		8	5	3			9[1]			10	15	7[1]		4	11[1]		2		12		6					
28	A	Berwick Rangers	1,240	2-1	1	2		8	5	3			9[2]			10	15	7		4	11		12				6					
Nov 4	H	Queen's Park	4,035	2-1	1	2		8	5	3		15	9[1]			10[1]	14	7		4	11		12				6					
11	H	Clydebank	3,101	2-0	1	2		8	5	3			9			10[1]		7		4	11[1]	16	12		15		6					
18	A	Stirling Albion	1,753	1-1	1	2		8	5	3			9	14		10[1]	16	7		4	11		12				6					
25	H	Queen of the South	2,610	2-1	1	2[1]		8	5	3		14	9[1]			10		7		4	11	16					6		12			
Dec 2	H	Forfar Athletic	1,052	1-0	1	2		8	5	3			9			10[1]		7		4	11		12				6		14			
16	A	Arbroath	1,054	1-1	1	2		8[1]	5	3			9			10		7		4	11		15				6		14	12		
26	H	Stenhousemuir	2,635	3-0	1	14		8	5	3[1]		16	9	15		10[2]				4			6						11	2	7	
30	H	Berwick Rangers	2,837	1-1	1	12		8	5	3		15				10	16			4	9		6						11[1]	2	7	
Jan 2	A	Queen's Park	3,938	2-0	1			8	5	3				12		10[1]				4	11		6						9[1]	2	7	
13	H	Stirling Albion	3,113	1-1	1			8[1]	5	3		16	9	12		10				4			6						11	2	7	
Feb 3	A	Queen of the South	2,432	3-1	1			8	5	3			9[1]	11		10[2]				4	15		6							2	7	
10	H	Forfar Athletic	3,075	4-0	1			8	5	3[1]			9[1]			10	14			4	11[1]	15					16		6	2	7[1]	
13	A	Clydebank	1,111	4-0	1	14		8	5	3			9[1]			10[1]	15			4	11[1]						6		16[1]	2	7	
17	A	Stenhousemuir	1,343	0-2	1	14		8	5				9	16		10				4	11		3				6		12	2	7	
24	H	Stranraer	2,959	3-0	1	2		8[1]	5[1]	3			9			10[1]	16			4	11	14					6				7	
Mar 3	A	Queen's Park	2,852	2-1	1	2		8	5[1]	3			9[1]			10	14			4	11						6				7	
10	A	Berwick Rangers	1,405	1-0	1	2		8	5	3			9			10[1]				4	11						6		16		7	
17	A	Clydebank	2,721	2-1	1	2		8[1]	5	3			9	16		10				4	11[1]						6		14	7	
31	A	Stirling Albion	2,748	3-0	1	2		8	5	3			9			10	15			4	11[3]	16					6			7		14
Apr 7	H	Queen of the South	3,810	0-2	1			8	5	3			9			10				4	11	2					6		16	7		14
14	A	Forfar Athletic	2,081	2-2	1	2		8	5	3			9	16[1]						4	15	11		6					14	7		10[1]
21	H	Arbroath	3,003	0-1	1	14		8		3				11			16			4	7		2	1	5		6		12	9		10
28	A	Stranraer	928	4-3	1	11		8	5	3			9[1]	15[1]						4	7		2		12		6[1]		16			10[1]
May 5	H	Stenhousemuir	4,624	4-0	1	6		8		3			15	11[2]		16		7		4[1]	10		2		5		12			9[1]		
TOTAL FULL APPEARANCES			34	18		4	33	30	34	2	3	32	11	6	27	1	12	2	35	29	2	12	2	12	1	22	4	12	12	4	
TOTAL SUB APPEARANCES						(8)		(1)			(1)	(10)		(1)	(9)	(3)		(3)	(12)	(7)		(2)	(10)		(10)			(3)		(9)	(4)	(2)
TOTAL GOALS SCORED							1		6	2	2		16	5		14		1		1	10						1		3	1	3

Small bold figures denote goalscorers.   † denotes opponent's own goal.

Firhill Stadium

Jackie Husband (East) Stand

Main (West) Stand

FIRHILL ROAD

CAPACITY: 14,538; Seated 8,397 Standing 6,141

PITCH DIMENSIONS: 110 yds x 75 yds

FACILITIES FOR DISABLED SUPPORTERS:
Covered places are available for 17 disabled supporters in front of the Main Stand (North area). Prior arrangement must be made with the Secretary and a ticket obtained.

Team playing kits

How to get there

The following routes may be used to reach Firhill Stadium:

TRAINS: The nearest railway stations are Glasgow Queen Street and Glasgow Central and buses from the centre of the city pass within 100 yards of the ground.

BUSES: The following buses from the city centre all pass near the ground: No's. 40, 61, 109 and 119 and the frequency of the buses is just under 10 minutes from Hope Street.

UNDERGROUND: The nearest Strathclyde PTE Underground station is St.George's Cross and supporters walking from here should pass through Cromwell Street into Maryhill Road and then walk up this road as far as Firhill Street. The ground is then on the right. The Kelvinbridge Underground Station is also not far from the ground and supporters from here should walk along Great Western Road as far as Napiershill Street and then follow this into Maryhill Road.

CARS: Street parking in the vicinity of the ground is somewhat limited.

The Jags

email: info@sfl.scottishfootball.com • website: www.scottishfootball.com

Left sidebar

RAITH ROVERS FOOTBALL CLUB

Stark's Park, Pratt Street,
Kirkcaldy, Fife, KY1 1SA

CHAIRMAN
Daniel Smith

DIRECTORS
Colin C. McGowan (Finance),
Eric W. Drysdale, Mario Caira,
William H. Gray, James B. Whyte
Archibald O. Smith & Turnbull Hutton

HON. PRESIDENT
John Urquhart

COMPANY SECRETARY
Eric W. Drysdale

OFFICE ADMINISTRATOR
Carrie Somerville

MANAGER
Peter Hetherston

ASSISTANT MANAGER
Kenny Black

YOUTH COACH
Graeme Robertson

YOUTH TEAM COACHES
Graeme Robertson (U18)
Jim Dempsey (U16 & U15)

CLUB DOCTOR
Dr. R. Robertson/
North Glen Medical Practice

PHYSIOTHERAPIST
Paul Greene

**FOOTBALL SAFETY OFFICERS'
ASSOCIATION REPRESENTATIVE**
Bill Brown (01592) 263514

GROUNDSMAN
John Murray

MATCHDAY PROGRAMME EDITOR
Alan Dall (01592) 205378

CLUB PHOTOGRAPHER
Tony Fimister (01592) 201645

TELEPHONES
Ground (01592) 263514
Fax (01592) 642833

E-MAIL & INTERNET ADDRESS
office@raith-rovers.co.uk
www.raith-rovers.co.uk

CLUB SHOP
South Stand Shop situated within stand.
Open during Office hours 9.00 a.m. to
5.00 p.m. and on home match days
2.00 p.m. to 5.00 p.m.

OFFICIAL SUPPORTERS CLUB
c/o Fraser Hamilton,
22 Tower Terrace, Kirkcaldy, Fife

TEAM CAPTAIN
Shaun Dennis

SHIRT SPONSOR
FIFAB

KIT SUPPLIER
TFG

LIST OF PLAYERS 2001-2002

SURNAME	FIRST NAME	MIDDLE NAME	DATE OF BIRTH	PLACE OF BIRTH	DATE OF SIGNING	HEIGHT FT INS	WEIGHT ST LBS	POS. ON PITCH	PREVIOUS CLUB
Black	Kenneth	George	29/11/63	Stenhousemuir	02/07/99	5 9.0	11 10	Mid	Airdrieonians
Blackadder	Ryan	Robert	11/10/83	Kirkcaldy	10/07/00	5 6.0	10 12	Mid	Raith Rovers Form D Under 16
Brown	Ian		16/03/84	Kirkcaldy	10/07/00	6 2.0	11 6	Def	Greig Park Rangers
Browne	Paul	Gerard	17/02/75	Glasgow	03/07/96	6 2.0	12 6	Def	Aston Villa
Caullay	Craig	Grant	04/01/84	Bellshill	10/07/00	5 7.5	12 1	Mid	Coatbridge Amateurs
Clark	Andrew	Alexander	21/04/80	Stirling	01/07/98	5 10.0	10 12	Fwd	Hutchison Vale B.C.
Clark	James	Sutherland	13/12/76	Aberdeen	06/08/01	6 1.0	13 0	Def	Falkirk
Crabbe	Scott		12/08/68	Edinburgh	07/08/01	5 8.0	11 5	Fwd	Livingston
Crumlish	Sean		31/05/84	Glasgow	09/07/01	6 1.0	11 0	Mid	Barrhead B.C.
Davidson	Alan	Martin	10/01/85	Falkirk	09/07/01	6 2.0	11 5	Def	S Form
Dennis	Shaun		22/12/69	Kirkcaldy	23/02/01	6 1.0	14 8	Def	Hibernian
Ellis	Laurence		07/11/79	Edinburgh	02/07/98	5 11.0	10 7	Def	Links United
Fennessey	Bryan		02/03/84	Bellshill	10/07/00	5 7.0	9 8	Mid	Coatbridge Amateurs
Gomez Novo	Ignacio		26/03/79	Ferrol	31/07/01	5 7.5	11 0	Fwd	S.D. Huesca
Hampshire	Paul	Christopher	20/09/81	Edinburgh	02/07/98	5 11.0	10 7	Mid	Hutchison Vale
Henderson	Darren	Ronald	12/10/66	Kilmarnock	09/07/01	5 11.0	12 7	Mid	Ross County
Matheson	Ross		15/11/77	Greenock	13/06/01	5 6.0	9 10	Mid	Morton
McCulloch	Greig		18/04/76	Girvan	24/02/96	5 8.0	10 7	Def	Aberdeen
McKenzie	Alan		12/12/84	Bellshill	09/07/01	5 10.0	11 4	Mid	S Form
Miller	Steven		21/04/84	Paisley	09/07/01	6 2.0	11 2	Def/Mid	Barrhead B.C.
Miotto	Simon	Jon	05/09/69	Tasmania	09/07/01	6 1.0	13 6	Gk	Blackpool Mechanics
Monin	Samuel		03/11/79	Dakar	06/03/01	6 2.0	12 0	Gk	A.S. Monaco
Nanou	Wilfred		16/04/79	Lyon	09/03/01	5 9.0	11 3	Mid	F.C.Vaulx/En/Velin
Nicol	Kevin	Andrew	19/01/82	Kirkcaldy	01/07/98	5 8.0	11 2	Mid	Hill O' Beath
Niven	Derek	.	12/12/83	Falkirk	10/07/00	6 1.0	11 2	Mid	Stenhousemuir
O'Boyle	George		14/12/67	Belfast	18/07/01	5 8.0	12 0	Fwd	St. Johnstone
Ross	David	Robert	01/12/84	Edinburgh	09/07/01	6 1.0	11 0	Def	Falkirk Form D Under 15
Rushford	John		09/02/82	Dunfermline	13/07/99	5 11.0	10 7	Mid	Rosyth Recreation
Scarborough	Charles	Philip	03/11/83	Kirkcaldy	10/07/00	5 10.0	11 6	Fwd	Buckhaven Colts
Slavin	Kevin		05/08/84	Bellshill	10/07/00	5 7.0	8 11	Def	Coatbridge Amateurs
Smith	Andrew	Mark	27/11/68	Aberdeen	31/03/01	6 1.0	13 10	Fwd	Kilmarnock
Smith	Christopher		04/04/84	Bellshill	10/07/00	5 8.5	10 2	Mid	S Form
Stein	Jay		13/01/79	Dunfermline	11/10/95	5 7.5	10 7	Mid	Inverkeithing United
Sweeney	Jamie		01/08/85	Edinburgh	09/07/01	5 11.0	10 10	Gk	S Form
Wheelwright	Mark	George	06/02/83	Dunfermline	10/07/00	6 2.0	11 11	Fwd	Glenrothes Strollers
Whyte	Graeme	Brand	09/04/85	Broxburn	09/07/01	6 2.0	11 4	Fwd	Gairdoch United Under 15's
Zoco	Jorge		12/07/75	Pamplona	02/08/01	6 0.0	11 7	Def/Mid	Badajoz

Milestones

YEAR OF FORMATION: 1883
MOST CAPPED PLAYER: David Morris
NO. OF CAPS: 6
MOST LEAGUE POINTS IN A SEASON: 65 (First Division - Season 1992/93)(2 Points for a Win)
69 (First Division - Season 1994/95)(3 Points for a Win)
MOST LEAGUE GOALS SCORED BY A PLAYER IN A SEASON: Norman Heywood (Season 1937/38)
NO. OF GOALS SCORED: 42
RECORD ATTENDANCE: 31,306 (-v- Heart of Midlothian – Scottish Cup, 7.2.1953)
RECORD VICTORY: 10-1 (-v- Coldstream – Scottish Cup, 13.2.1954)
RECORD DEFEAT: 2-11 (-v- Morton – Division 2, 18.3.1936)

The Rovers' ten year league record

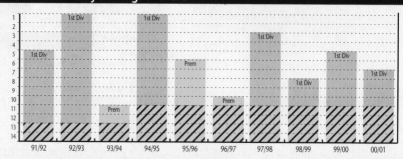

THE ROVERS' CLUB FACTFILE 2000/2001
RESULTS... APPEARANCES... SCORERS... ATTENDANCES...

Date	Venue	Opponents	Att.	Res	Van de Kamp G.	McCulloch G.	Ophiel S.	Gaughan K.	Browne P.	Javary J.	McEwan C.	Tosh S.	Clark A.	Burns A.	Stein J.	Mbaila I.	Andrews M.	Ellis L.	Black K.	Tosh P.	Creaney G.	McKinnon R.	Dennis S.	Hetherton B.	Hamilton S.	Nicol K.	Shields P.	Hampshire P.	Agnew P.	Dempsie M.	Bayne G.	Coyle C.	Inglis J.	McAnulty D.	Niven D.	Jones M.	Kelly P.	Monin S.	Nanou W.	Alfonsolobez M.	Capin Martino S.	Smith A.
Aug 5	H	Alloa Athletic	2,123	1-2	1	2	3	4	5	6	7	8	9	10	11	15¹	12																									
12	A	Airdrieonians	2,854	1-1	1	2		4	5		14	8	16	10¹	11	9			3	6	7	15																				
26	H	Inverness Cal. Th.	1,615	4-1	1	2	3	4	5			7	15	10¹	11	16			6	9¹	14¹	8¹																				
Sep 2	H	Ross County	1,759	4-1	1	2	3		5			7	15	10¹	11¹	16¹			6	9¹	14	8	4																			
9	A	Falkirk	2,762	1-2	1	2	11		5			7	15	10	12	16	4¹		6	9		8	3																			
16	A	Livingston	3,961	4-0	1	2	8		5			7	15	10¹	11		4²	12	6	9¹	14		3																			
23	H	Morton	2,078	0-1	1	2	8		5			7	15	10	11	16	4		6	9			3	14																		
30	A	Clyde	1,202	0-0	1	2			5			10		11					8	6	9		3	7	4	15	16															
Oct 7	H	Ayr United	1,858	1-3	1	2			5			10		11	15¹				8	6	9		3	12	4	7	14															
14	A	Alloa Athletic	987	1-0	1	2			5			10		11	9¹				8	6			3	7	4	12	16															
21	H	Airdrieonians	1,930	1-1	1	2			5			10		11					8	6	16		3	7	4	9¹															
28	A	Inverness Cal. Th.	1,723	2-1	1	2			5			10		11¹	9¹				8	6			3	7	4	12	16	14														
Nov 4	H	Falkirk	3,120	0-2	1	2			5			10		11	9				8	6	15		3	7	4	12		14														
11	A	Morton	742	2-1	1	2	12		5			10		11	9¹				8	16			3	7	4	6¹																
25	A	Ayr United	2,212	2-4	1	2			5			10		11	9¹				8¹	12	14		3	7	4	6		15														
Dec 2	H	Clyde	1,810	1-2	1	2						7		11	9				3	6	15		8			16			4	10¹												
5	H	Livingston	1,626	1-2	1	2			5					11¹	15				3	6	9			7	8	16			4	10												
9	A	Ross County	2,578	0-0	1	2			5			15		11	14				4	6	9		8	7		3				10												
16	H	Alloa Athletic	1,267	2-1	1	2			5			15		11	9¹				4	6	14¹		8	7		3				10												
Jan 2	A	Livingston	3,305	0-2	1	2			5			14		11	9				4	12			8	7	6	3				10												
6	H	Morton	1,721	0-0	1	4			5			9		11					3	7			14	2	8	6				10												
13	A	Clyde	1,305	1-3	1	2			5			9		11	15				3	6	4¹		14	7		8				10												
Feb 3	H	Ross County	1,380	0-4		2			4			7		9					6				11	8		3				10	1	3	15	16								
10	A	Airdrieonians	1,753	0-3					5			10		11	15		12	6					7	2	8	3					1	4	14		9							
17	H	Ayr United	1,217	1-4					5			16		11	15		4	7	10				14	8		3					1	6		9¹	2							
Mar 10	H	Inverness Cal. Th.	1,342	1-1					5					11	9		12	14	15	6			7			3				4		10¹		2	1	8						
17	A	Morton	947	1-1					5			15		11	9		6	16	14¹	4			7			3						10		2	1	8						
23	A	Inverness Cal. Th.	1,299	0-2					15			11		14	6		10	5	12	7			3			4				9				2	1	8						
31	H	Livingston	1,794	2-0					11						3		6	15	4	12			7			5				10²				1	14	2	8	9				
Apr 3	H	Falkirk	1,586	0-0					11			16					6	15	4				7			3				5				10		1	14	2	8	9			
7	A	Ayr United	2,026	0-2					5			15		16	12		6	11					7							3		4		10	8	1		2	9			
10	A	Falkirk	1,634	0-2					5			11		12			6	10	4				7			3				2				1	15			8	9			
14	H	Clyde	1,817	0-1					5			11		16			3	6	10	4										2				7	1			8	9			
21	A	Alloa Athletic	1,953	2-1					5			11		14			3	6	10¹	4			15							2				7	1		12	8	9¹			
28	A	Airdrieonians	2,186	5-0					5			11³		16			3	6	10²											2				1		7		8	9			
May 5	A	Ross County	3,004	0-4				4				11		12			3	10					16	6		8				1		7			5		2	9				
TOTAL FULL APPEARANCES					22	24	6	3	32	1	1	7	14	7	33	12	3	24	27	19	1		3	21	13	15	17	1	15		2	8	3	12		8	7	11	4	5	7	8
TOTAL SUB APPEARANCES						(1)			(1)		(12)		(2)	(19)	(1)	(4)	(3)	(10)	(5)			(6)	(3)	(5)	(6)	(3)	(1)			(2)	(1)			(3)	(1)					
TOTAL GOALS SCORED									4		6	8	3	1				9	1	1					1	1				1					4				1

Small bold figures denote goalscorers. † denotes opponent's own goal.

Stark's Park

FORTH ROAD BRIDGE ROAD
RAILWAY STAND
(HOME) (AWAY)
SOUTH STAND (HOME)
NORTH STAND (AWAY)
MAIN KINCARDINE BRIDGE ROAD
MAIN STAND
◄ To Esplanade Parking — PRATT STREET — To Railway Station ►

CAPACITY: 10,104 (All Seated)

PITCH DIMENSIONS: 113 yds x 70 yds

FACILITIES FOR DISABLED SUPPORTERS:
By prior arrangement with the Secretary.
North Stand – Away Supporters. South Stand – Home Supporters.

Team playing kits

How to get there

The following routes may be used to reach Stark's Park:
TRAINS: Kirkcaldy railway station is served by trains from Dundee, Edinburgh and Glasgow (via Edinburgh) and the ground is within walking distance of the station.
BUSES: The main bus station in Kirkcaldy is also within 15 minutes walking distance of the ground, but the Edinburgh, Dunfermline and Leven services pass close by the park.
CARS: Car parking is available in the Esplanade, which is on the south side of the ground, in Beveridge Park, which is on the north side of Stark's Road, and in ground adjacent to the railway station.

The Rovers

email: info@sfl.scottishfootball.com • website: www.scottishfootball.com

Ross County

Victoria Park Stadium, Jubilee Road,
Dingwall, Ross-shire, IV15 9QZ

CHAIRMAN
Roy J. MacGregor

VICE-CHAIRMAN
Gordon M. R. Macrae

DIRECTORS
Martin F. Mackay (Company Secretary),
Thomas A. Mackenzie,
Andrew R. Duncan
& Alexander Matheson

MANAGEMENT COMMITTEE
Donald MacBean, David R. Patience
& Calum Grant

**CHIEF EXECUTIVE/
GENERAL MANAGER**
Alastair Kennedy

SECRETARY
Donald MacBean

FOOTBALL ADMINISTRATOR
Susan Wilson (01349) 860860

PLAYER/MANAGER
Neale J. Cooper

**FIRST TEAM COACH/HEAD
DEVELOPMENT COACH**
Danny MacDonald

YOUTH DEVELOPMENT
Calum Grant

YOUTH COACHES
Ronnie Duncan & Mike Fridge (U-18)

WOMEN'S DEVELOPMENT COACH
Fiona McWilliams

CLUB DOCTOR
Dr. Colin Fettes

PHYSIOTHERAPISTS
Dougie Sim & Emily Goodlad

FACILITIES MANAGER
Brian Campbell (01349) 860862
(Mobile) 07889 644047

MARKETING EXECUTIVE
Morven MacDonald (01349) 860861

**GROUND CONVENOR AND
SAFETY OFFICER**
David R. Patience (01463) 222893

**STADIUM & GROUND
MAINTENANCE**
David Fraser

MEDIA LIAISON OFFICER
Alastair Kennedy (01349) 860860

MATCHDAY PROGRAMME EDITOR
Bryan Munro (01463) 230721

TELEPHONES
Ground/Ticket Office (01349) 860860
Fax (01349) 866277

E-MAIL & INTERNET ADDRESS
susan@rosscountyfootballclub.co.uk
www.rosscountyfootballclub.co.uk

CLUB SHOP
Official Ross County F.C. merchandising
available from MacLean Sport, 33 High
Street, Dingwall, as well as a shop
being situated at Ground (Matchdays
only) and other Sports shops in local
area

OFFICIAL SUPPORTERS CLUB
George Shiels, 4 Tulloch Place, Dingwall
(01349) 865135

TEAM CAPTAIN
Steven Ferguson

SHIRT SPONSOR
Aberdeen Asset Management

KIT SUPPLIER
XARA

LIST OF PLAYERS 2001-2002

SURNAME	FIRST NAME	MIDDLE NAME	DATE OF BIRTH	PLACE OF BIRTH	DATE OF SIGNING	HEIGHT FT INS	WEIGHT ST LBS	POS. ON PITCH	PREVIOUS CLUB
Blackley	Douglas	Michael	30/09/83	Edinburgh	23/08/00	5 7.0	9 4	Mid	Stirling Albion
Bolochoweckyj	Michael		04/05/84	Edinburgh	31/05/01	6 1.0	11 0	Def	Hearts Form D
Bone	Alexander	Syme F.	26/12/71	Stirling	02/08/00	5 9.0	11 2	Fwd	Ayr United
Boukraa	Karim		07/03/73	Le Havre	15/12/00	6 0.0	12 0	Fwd	Morton
Bullock	Antony	Brian	18/02/72	Warrington	01/08/01	6 1.0	14 10	Gk	Lincoln City
Campbell	Craig		10/12/83	Dingwall	24/08/00	5 8.0	10 5	Fwd	S Form
Canning	Martin		03/12/81	Glasgow	28/07/99	6 2.0	11 11	Mid	Clydebank
Cooper	Neale	James	24/11/63	Darjeeling	02/08/96	6 0.0	12 7	Def	Dunfermline Athletic
Cowie	Don		15/02/83	Inverness	23/08/00	5 5.0	8 5	Mid	S Form
Crilly	Paul		30/08/83	Dungannon	10/08/01	5 7.0	10 7	Def	Dungannon Swifts
Dlugonski	Bryan		18/10/82	Banff	13/09/99	6 0.0	11 0	Mid	Ross County B.C.
Duncanson	Robert		01/09/84	Inverness	31/05/01	5 0.0	10 0	Fwd	Ross County
Ferguson	Steven		18/05/77	Edinburgh	22/11/96	5 8.0	11 6	Mid	Dunfermline Athletic
Fraser	John		17/01/78	Dunfermline	29/07/99	5 10.0	11 4	Mid/Fwd	Dunfermline Athletic
Gethins	Conor		01/11/83	Lifford	04/09/00	5 7.0	9 0	Fwd	Lifford Celtic
Gilbert	Kenneth	Robert	08/03/75	Aberdeen	11/02/97	5 6.5	11 4	Mid	Hull City
Gonet	Stefan		11/11/81	Paisley	24/11/99	6 2.0	12 5	Gk	Ross County B.C.
Guild	Allan		11/09/84	Kirkcaldy	31/05/01	5 7.0	9 10	Mid	Ross County Form D
Hastings	Richard	Corey	18/05/77	Prince George, B.C.	10/08/01	6 0.0	11 8	Def	Inverness Caledonian Thistle
Hislop	Steven		14/06/78	Edinburgh	11/07/01	6 2.0	12 0	Fwd	East Stirlingshire
Holmes	Derek		18/10/78	Lanark	15/10/99	6 0.0	13 0	Fwd	Heart of Midlothian
Irvine	Brian	Alexander	24/05/65	Bellshill	27/07/99	6 2.5	13 7	Def	Dundee
Jack	Darren	James	09/08/83	Norwich	01/09/00	6 1.5	12 8	Mid/Fwd	S Form
Keldie	George	Keith	06/05/84	Kirkwall	12/10/00	5 10.0	10 8	Fwd	S Form
Lamb	Hamish	Alexander	22/01/84	Thurso	24/08/00	5 11.0	10 7	Def	Ross County B.C.
Mackay	Calum		17/09/83	Stornoway	31/05/01	5 10.0	11 0	Fwd	Point (Lewis & Harris F.A.)
Mackay	David		17/09/75	Dingwall	16/09/94	5 11.0	12 1	Def	Ross County B.C.
Mackay	Steven		26/06/81	Invergordon	10/03/00	5 11.0	10 5	Mid/Fwd	Nairn County
Maxwell	Ian		02/05/75	Glasgow	12/06/98	6 3.0	12 5	Def	Queen's Park
McCormick	Mark	Thomas	11/07/79	Bellshill	01/12/00	6 1.0	10 7	Fwd	Livingston
McQuade	John		08/07/70	Glasgow	02/08/00	5 10.0	11 10	Fwd	Stirling Albion
Millar	Marc		10/04/69	Dundee	05/08/00	5 9.0	10 12	Mid	St. Johnstone
Nicholl	Scott		30/08/83	Newcastle-upon-Tyne	31/05/01	5 7.0	10 2	Def	Ross County Form D Under 16
Perry	Mark	George	07/02/71	Aberdeen	01/12/00	6 1.0	12 8	Def	Aberdeen
Prest	Martin	Hugo	30/11/78	Mar Del Plata	26/03/01	6 1.0	12 6	Fwd	Airdrieonians
Robertson	Hugh	Scott	19/03/75	Aberdeen	02/02/01	5 9.0	13 0	Def	Dundee
Shearer	Andrew		19/10/83	Aberdeen	23/08/00	6 2.0	12 5	Gk	Brechin City
Taggart	Craig		17/01/73	Glasgow	21/03/00	5 9.0	12 2	Mid	Stirling Albion
Webb	Sean	Michael	04/01/83	Dungannon	26/09/00	6 2.0	12 5	Def	Dungannon Swifts
Wilson	David	Gavin	28/02/84	Bellshill	31/05/01	6 1.0	11 7	Fwd	Heart of Midlothian
Young	Craig		10/08/84	Edinburgh	24/08/00	5 6.0	9 8	Fwd	Stirling Albion

Milestones

YEAR OF FORMATION: 1929
MOST LEAGUE POINTS IN A SEASON: 77 (Third Division – Season 1998/99) (3 Points for a Win)
MOST LEAGUE GOALS SCORED BY A PLAYER IN A SEASON: Derek Adams (Season 1996/97)
NO. OF GOALS SCORED: 22
RECORD ATTENDANCE: 8,000 (-v- Rangers – Scottish Cup, 28.2.66)
RECORD VICTORY: 13-2 (-v- Fraserburgh – Highland League, 1965)
RECORD DEFEAT: 1-10 (-v- Inverness Thistle – Highland League)

The County's ten year league record

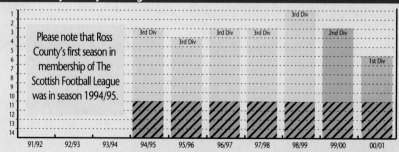

Please note that Ross County's first season in membership of The Scottish Football League was in season 1994/95.

Jarvie, Drew Busby and Paul Jonquin. It still pleases him, as well, to remember that he once played at Broomfield, thanks to a schools football tournament.

He understands the power of sport and the grip it has on people's imaginations and hearts. As a bowls player, Longmuir was good enough to represent Scotland in the early 1990's. While living in Yorkshire, it was later suggested that, through residency, he could switch allegiances and play for England. The very idea was intolerable to Longmuir.

Many others have the same depth of feeling when it comes to sport. In consequence, Bell's sponsorship is not the sort that entails only the signing of a large cheque and the pasting up of a few posters. The company's name is certainly kept in the public eye, but Bell's own employees also respond strongly to the association with the SFL.

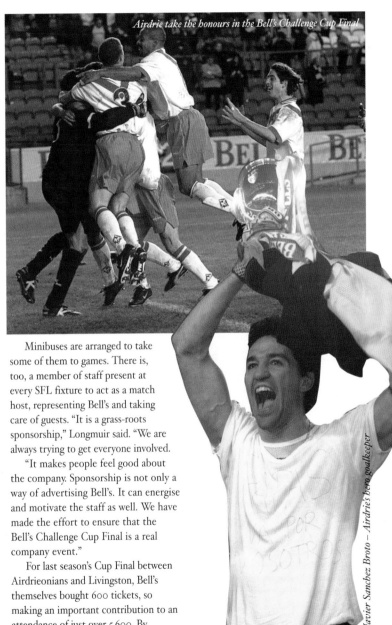

Airdrie take the honours in the Bell's Challenge Cup Final

Javier Sanchez Broto – Airdrie's hero goalkeeper

*Partick Thistle v St. Mirren...
A good start to the season*

Minibuses are arranged to take some of them to games. There is, too, a member of staff present at every SFL fixture to act as a match host, representing Bell's and taking care of guests. "It is a grass-roots sponsorship," Longmuir said. "We are always trying to get everyone involved.

"It makes people feel good about the company. Sponsorship is not only a way of advertising Bell's. It can energise and motivate the staff as well. We have made the effort to ensure that the Bell's Challenge Cup Final is a real company event."

For last season's Cup Final between Airdrieonians and Livingston, Bell's themselves bought 600 tickets, so making an important contribution to an attendance of just over 5,600. By sending people through the turnstiles and coming up with other funding of that sort, it is reckoned that Bell's add a further £700,000 or so to the agreed £2m value of the sponsorship.

Longmuir's interest in that Challenge Cup Final had a professional impartiality, but, bearing in mind his childhood

allegiance, he must have found a certain degree of satisfaction in the outcome. After needing extra-time in every round, Airdrie remained true to form by defeating Livingston in a penalty shoot-out in the Final.

That was not simply another entry

31

for the honour roll of football. There was a human drama to the victory because of the incongruity of the two clubs. Livingston, going from strength to strength, went on to take the First Division title. Airdrie, in the hands of the Interim Liquidators,

Jim Leishman

In September, 2000, Mark Kerr, then 18, was named not only Bell's Young Player of the Month, but also the overall player of the month. Nobody who had digested that remarkable achievement would have been all that surprised to find, much later, that clubs such as Leeds United were taking a serious interest in the Falkirk midfielder.

There must have been a wry smile about some of the others whose skills were marked by an award. Adam Proudlock, Bell's Player of the Month for August, was probably too prolific a scorer for Clyde's own good. He was only on loan at Broadwood and, all too soon, Wolverhampton Wanderers decided that his goals were badly needed at Molineux. The whole gamut of the game is represented on the Bell's list. The Bell's Manager of

flavour of Scottish football. On that day at Gleneagles there was much discussion about Lord Mac's "Pie of the Year Award". Lord Macfarlane, the Honorary Life President of Bell's, reported that chairmen often seemed very concerned about their position in the culinary table when he sampled the catering. East Fife's pie was judged to be supreme.

The testing of the pies was partly a bit of fun and partly a very serious matter. Football itself is rather like that. In Scotland, with its great tradition, the game itself has many facets and Bell's are reflected in all of them. Business analysts would say there was synergy in this sponsorship. To put it simply, Bell's and The Scottish Football League have been good for one another.

KEVIN McCARRA
(The Times)

Ally Dawson

must have felt a sense of relief with each week of survival that they completed.

It was proof of the bewildering fascination of football that victory should go to the club who seemed to have so little cause for hope. Their feat was recognised when Steve Archibald, then in charge at Airdrie, was voted Bell's Manager of the Month for November, 2000.

The recipient is chosen by a group of journalists, men who are always eager to identify a gripping story. That is the charm of the Bell's awards. The company is not only handing over a trophy that some football personage can display prominently in his living room. There are tales to be told and

newcomers to be introduced.

the Year awards for the First and Second Divisions went, respectively, to Jim Leishman and John Lambie, men who have shown the strength to prove themselves, time and again, over long careers.

Ally Dawson belongs to a different generation, but he, as winner of the Third Division prize, displayed the same fortitude, steering Hamilton Academical to the title, despite the fact he was in charge of a club still playing at Firhill because their own, new stadium was not quite finished.

Bell's go to great lengths to capture the

Bell's Award Winners 2000/2001

MONTHLY AWARD WINNERS

AUGUST, 2000
Player	Adam Proudlock *(Clyde)*
Young Player	Colin Stewart *(Queen's Park)*
First Division Manager	Jim Leishman *(Livingston)*
Second Division Manager	John McCormack *(Queen's Park)*
Third Division Manager	Craig Levein *(Cowdenbeath)*

SEPTEMBER, 2000
Player	Mark Kerr *(Falkirk)*
Young Player	Mark Kerr *(Falkirk)*
First Division Manager	Alex Totten *(Falkirk)*
Second Division Manager	Tommy Coyne *(Clydebank)*
Third Division Manager	Dick Campbell *(Brechin City)*

OCTOBER, 2000
Player	Scott McLean *(Partick Thistle)*
Young Player	Mark Kerr *(Falkirk)*
First Division Manager	Alex Totten *(Falkirk)*
Second Division Manager	John Lambie *(Partick Thistle)*
Third Division Manager	Ally Dawson *(Hamilton Academical)*

NOVEMBER, 2000
Player	Antonio Calderon *(Airdrieonians)*
Young Player	Steven Ferguson *(East Fife)*
First Division Manager	Steve Archibald *(Airdrieonians)*
Second Division Manager	Brian Fairley *(Stenhousemuir)*
Third Division Manager	John McVeigh *(Albion Rovers)*

DECEMBER, 2000
Player	Dennis Wyness *(Inverness Cal. Thistle)*
Young Player	Peter Weatherson *(Queen of the South)*
First Division Manager	Steve Paterson *(Inverness Cal. Thistle)*
Second Division Manager	Paul Smith *(Berwick Rangers)*
Third Division Manager	Dick Campbell *(Brechin City)*

JANUARY, 2001
Player	Glynn Hurst *(Ayr United)*
Young Player	David McFarlane *(Hamilton Academical)*
First Division Manager	Steve Paterson *(Inverness Cal. Thistle)*
Second Division Manager	John Lambie *(Partick Thistle)*
Third Division Manager	Ally Dawson *(Hamilton Academical)*

FEBRUARY, 2001
Player	Martin Hardie *(Partick Thistle)*
Young Player	Stephen Whalen *(Morton)*
First Division Manager	Neale Cooper *(Ross County)*
Second Division Manager	Brian Fairley *(Stenhousemuir)*
Third Division Manager	Tom Carson *(Dumbarton)*

MARCH, 2001
Player	Eddie Annand *(Ayr United)*
Young Player	John Bradford *(Ayr United)*
First Division Manager	Gordon Dalziel *(Ayr United)*
Second Division Manager	John Brownlie *(Arbroath)*
Third Division Manager	Dick Campbell *(Brechin City)*

SEASON AWARD WINNERS

Player of the Year
David Bingham *(Livingston)*

Young Player of the Year
Mark Kerr *(Falkirk)*

First Division Manager of the Year
Jim Leishman *(Livingston)*

Second Division Manager of the Year
John Lambie *(Partick Thistle)*

Third Division Manager of the Year
Ally Dawson *(Hamilton Academical)*

Alloa Athletic

Recreation Park,
Clackmannan Road,
Alloa, FK10 1RY

CHAIRMAN
Ewen G. Cameron

VICE-CHAIRMAN
David R. Murray

DIRECTORS
William J. McKie, Robert F. Hopkins,
Patrick Lawlor & Ian Henderson

HONORARY PRESIDENT
George Ormiston

HONORARY DIRECTOR
Ronald J. Todd

SECRETARY
Ewen G. Cameron

ADMINISTRATION OFFICER
Susan Gillon

MANAGER
Terry Christie

ASSISTANT MANAGER
Graeme Armstrong

YOUTH ADMINISTRATOR
Robert Wilson

YOUTH TEAM COACHES
Hugh McCann (U18)
Ronnie McMillan (U14)
Malcolm Gordon (U13)
Fred Stone (U12)

CLUB DOCTOR
Dr. Clarke Mullen

PHYSIOTHERAPIST
Jim Law

**FOOTBALL SAFETY OFFICERS'
ASSOCIATION REPRESENTATIVE**
Ian Love (01259) 722695

GROUNDSMAN
John Robertson

KIT MAN
Nicol Campbell

**COMMERCIAL DIRECTOR &
MEDIA LIAISON OFFICER**
William McKie
Bus. (01259) 722695
Home (01259) 730572
Mobile 07979 754979

MATCHDAY PROGRAMME EDITOR
John Glencross
Bus. (01324) 622061
Home (01786) 817362

TELEPHONES
Ground (01259) 722695
Fax (01259) 210886
Sec. Bus. (01324) 612472
Sec. Home (01259) 722696

E-MAIL & INTERNET ADDRESS
fcadmin@alloaathletic.co.uk
www.alloaathletic.co.uk

CLUB SHOP
Situated adjacent to Refreshment Kiosk

CLUB SHOP MANAGER
Peter Gibson Tel: (01259) 761417

OFFICIAL SUPPORTERS CLUB
c/o Recreation Park,
Clackmannan Road, Alloa, FK10 1RY
Contact: Ruby Shaw Tel: (01259) 217917

TEAM CAPTAIN
Craig Valentine

SHIRT SPONSOR
Alloa Advertiser

KIT SUPPLIER
Pendle

LIST OF PLAYERS 2001-2002

SURNAME	FIRST NAME	MIDDLE NAME	DATE OF BIRTH	PLACE OF BIRTH	DATE OF SIGNING	HEIGHT FT INS	WEIGHT ST LBS	POS. ON PITCH	PREVIOUS CLUB
Adamson	James	Wyper	18/05/83	Stirling	19/07/01	6 2.0	11 7	Def	East Stirlingshire
Anderson	Derek	Christopher	15/05/72	Paisley	28/06/01	6 0.0	11 0	Def	Morton
Armstrong	Graeme	John	23/06/56	Edinburgh	15/07/00	5 9.0	10 12	Def	Stenhousemuir
Cadger	Paul	Stewart	29/07/84	Edinburgh	01/08/01	6 0.0	12 0	Gk	Heart of Midlothian
Clark	Derek	Grant	24/08/76	Stirling	15/07/98	5 6.0	10 0	Mid	China Fortune
Curran	Henry		09/10/66	Glasgow	02/07/01	5 9.5	12 2	Mid	Morton
Donnachie	Stephen		16/02/82	Bellshill	03/07/01	5 10.0	10 1	Fwd	St. Mirren
Elliott	Ross	William	19/07/84	Edinburgh	13/07/01	5 10.0	10 7	Mid	Ferniside B.C.
Evans	Gareth	John	14/01/67	Coventry	02/10/00	5 7.5	11 6	Fwd	Airdrieonians
Fisher	James		14/10/67	Bridge of Allan	22/05/01	5 10.0	10 11	Mid	Stenhousemuir
Hamilton	Ross		17/06/80	Falkirk	31/07/00	5 10.0	11 0	Fwd	Stenhousemuir
Hutchison	Gareth	William McK.	04/06/72	Edinburgh	02/07/01	5 11.0	11 10	Fwd	Falkirk
Irvine	William		28/12/63	Stirling	31/05/96	5 10.0	11 3	Mid/Fwd	Berwick Rangers
Knox	Keith		06/08/64	Stranraer	13/06/01	6 0.0	12 0	Def	Stranraer
Little	Ian	James	10/12/73	Edinburgh	03/02/00	5 8.0	10 7	Mid/Fwd	Livingston
Manderson	Scott		17/02/84	Broxburn	13/07/01	6 0.0	10 12	Mid	Strathbrock Under 18's
McQueen	James		10/06/61	Edinburgh	21/08/00	6 3.0	13 10	Gk	Newtongrange Star
Mitchell	Kevin	Robert	11/01/83	Edinburgh	13/07/01	5 10.0	11 0	Def	Whitehill Welfare
Raeside	Robert		07/07/72	South Africa	28/06/01	6 2.0	13 7	Def	Morton
Seaton	Andrew	Murray	16/09/77	Edinburgh	21/07/01	5 10.0	12 6	Def	Falkirk
Sinclair	Scott	Ralph	08/05/83	Stirling	17/07/01	6 0.0	12 3	Def	Stirling Albion
Soutar	Derek	Robert J.	04/06/81	Dundee	27/07/01	6 1.5	12 0	Gk	Dundee
Stevenson	James		13/07/84	Glasgow	13/07/01	5 8.0	10 0	Mid	Aberdeen
Thomson	Steven	William	19/04/73	Glasgow	21/06/00	6 2.0	12 7	Def	Hamilton Academical
Valentine	Craig		16/07/70	Edinburgh	20/07/96	5 8.0	11 0	Def	Berwick Rangers
Walker	Richard	Alan	08/07/82	Edinburgh	13/06/01	5 11.0	11 0	Fwd	Whitehill Welfare Colts
Wallace	Edward		19/01/84	Bellshill	13/07/01	6 2.0	12 0	Mid/Fwd	Firs Park B.C.
Watson	Gregg		21/09/70	Glasgow	25/07/00	5 9.5	10 9	Def	Stenhousemuir

Milestones

YEAR OF FORMATION: 1883
MOST CAPPED PLAYER: Jock Hepburn
NO. OF CAPS: 1
MOST LEAGUE POINTS IN A SEASON: 60 (Division 2 – Season 1921/22)(2 Points for a Win)
76 (Third Division – Season 1997/98)(3 Points for a Win)
MOST LEAGUE GOALS SCORED BY A PLAYER IN A SEASON: William Crilley (Season 1921/22)
NO. OF GOALS SCORED: 49
RECORD ATTENDANCE: 13,000 (-v- Dunfermline Athletic – 26.2.1939)
RECORD VICTORY: 9-2 (-v- Forfar Athletic – Division 2, 18.3.1933)
RECORD DEFEAT: 0-10 (-v- Dundee – Division 2 and Third Lanark – League Cup)

The Wasps' ten year league record

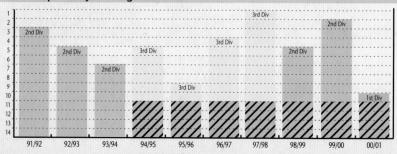

THE WASPS' CLUB FACTFILE 2000/2001
RESULTS... APPEARANCES... SCORERS... ATTENDANCES...

BELL'S — SCOTTISH FOOTBALL LEAGUE

Date	Venue	Opponents	Att.	Res	Cairns M.	Huxford R.	Clark D.	Watson G.	Conway F.	Valentine C.	Gardner R. L.	Thomson S.	Hamilton R.	Irvine W.	Little I.	Wood C.	Wilson M.	Brigain C.	Beaton D.	Davidson S.	Christie M.	Johnson I. G.	Evans G.	French H.	McQueen J.	Nish C.	Murray I.	Van de Kamp G.	McQuillan J.	McManus A.	Armstrong G.
Aug 5	A	Raith Rovers	2,123	†2-1	1	2	3^1	4	5	6	7	8	9	10	11	12	16														
12	H	Ayr United	1,274	1-1	1	2	3	4	5	6	7	8	9	10^1	11	12	16														
19	A	Morton	1,267	0-2	1	2	3	4	5	6		8	9	10	11	7					12	14									
26	H	Livingston	983	0-6	1	2	3	4	5	6	7	12	9	10	11	8					16										
Sep 9	A	Airdrieonians	1,806	2-2	1		3	4	5	6	14		7	10^1	11	9^1				2	8										
16	A	Falkirk	2,645	1-1	1		3	4	5	6	14	15	7^1	10	11	9				2	8										
23	H	Inverness Cal. Th.	584	1-4	1	2	3	4^1	5	6	14	15	9	10	11						7	8	16								
30	A	Ross County	2,775	0-1	1	2	3	4		6		5	9	12	11	10			14		8	7									
Oct 7	H	Clyde	740	3-1	16		3	4	5^1	6		2^1	9^1	12	11	15					8	7	10								
14	H	Raith Rovers	987	0-1			3	4	5	6		2	9	12	11	15					8	7	10	14							
21	A	Ayr United	2,259	1-3	16		3	2				5	7	10^1	12						8	4	9	11	20						
28	A	Livingston	3,149	0-4	16		3	4	5	6		2	7	10	11						8	15		11		9					
Nov 4	H	Airdrieonians	1,220	2-0	1	2		14		6		5	12^1	10^1	11	3					8	7	4			9					
11	A	Inverness Cal. Th.	1,384	1-2	1	2				6		5	7	10	11	3					8	15^1	12	4		9					
18	H	Falkirk	1,709	3-2	1	2	3		16^1	6		5	7^1	10	11^1						8		4	9							
25	A	Clyde	1,012	0-0	1			14	2	6		5	7	10	11	3					8	12	4			9					
Dec 2	H	Ross County	620	0-0	1			16	2	6		5	7	12	11	3					8	10	15	4		9					
9	H	Morton	704	2-1	1		3		2	6		5	7	12	11						8	10	15	4		9^2					
16	A	Raith Rovers	1,267	1-2	1		3		2	6		5	7	10	11	16					8	10	15	4		9^1					
26	A	Airdrieonians	1,427	1-2	1		3		2	6		5	7^1	10	11	4					8	14	16	12		9					
Jan 2	A	Falkirk	2,627	2-2	1	16	3	2		6		5	7		11	8				15	10	9^1	4^1								
6	H	Inverness Cal. Th.	744	1-1	1		3	2		6		5	7	12	11					16	10	14^1		9			8				
30	H	Livingston	684	0-2				2		6		5	7	12	11	9					8	10	4		1		3				
Feb 3	A	Morton	1,179	1-1				2	3	6		5^1	7	14	11						8	10	9	4				1			
24	A	Livingston	3,014	0-1			3	2	4	6		5		10	11	8					9		7					1			
Mar 10	H	Clyde	818	0-0			3	4		6		5	7	15	11	16					8	14	9	10				1	2		
13	H	Ayr United	539	0-2			3	4	16			5	7	10	12	11					8	9	6					1	2		
17	A	Inverness Cal. Th.	1,613	0-2			3	4	15			5	7	12	10	11	14				8	6	9					1	2		
24	A	Ross County	2,079	3-2			11	4	3			5	7	10^1	12						8	14	9^1	6^1				1	2		
27	H	Airdrieonians	632	6-0			11	4				5^1	7^4	10	12	14^1	15				8	6	9					1	2	3	
31	H	Falkirk	1,186	0-1			11	4				5	7	10	12	11					8	6	9	14				1	2	3	
Apr 7	A	Clyde	1,006	1-1	3			4				5		10	7	11^1					8	9	6					1	2		15
14	H	Ross County	647	1-1	3			4		14		5		10	11^1	12					8	9	16					1	2	6	
21	H	Raith Rovers	1,953	1-2	15	3		4				5	7	10^1	11	12					8	9	16					1	2	6	
28	A	Ayr United	2,234	1-4	8	3		4		6		5	8	10^1	11	14	15				12		7					1	2		
May 5	H	Morton	770	0-3			3		4	6			9	10	8	11					12		7					1	2	5	
TOTAL FULL APPEARANCES					22	12	28	27	19	28	3	31	32	24	28	19				3	25	16	16	21	1	10	2	13	11	5	
TOTAL SUB APPEARANCES					(5)	(2)	(1)	(3)	(1)	(3)	(3)	(1)	(11)	(6)	(11)	(5)	(3)	(1)		(2)	(8)	(6)	(4)	(1)						(1)
TOTAL GOALS SCORED							1	1	2			3	9	7	2	3					1	3	2			3				

Small bold figures denote goalscorers. † denotes opponent's own goal.

The Wasps

Recreation Park

CLACKMANNAN ROAD

HILTON ROAD

CAPACITY: 3,100; Seated 400, Standing 2,700

PITCH DIMENSIONS: 110 yds x 75 yds

FACILITIES FOR DISABLED SUPPORTERS:
Accommodation for wheelchairs and invalid carriages in front of Stand. Disabled toilets are also available.

Team playing kits

How to get there

Recreation Park can be reached by the following routes:

TRAINS: The nearest railway station is Stirling, which is seven miles away. Fans would have to connect with an inter-linking bus service to reach the ground from here.

BUSES: There are three main services which stop outside the ground. These are the Dunfermline-Stirling, Stirling-Clackmannan and Falkirk-Alloa buses.

CARS: Car Parking is available in the car park adjacent to the ground and this can hold 175 vehicles.

email: info@sfl.scottishfootball.com • website: www.scottishfootball.com

Berwick Rangers

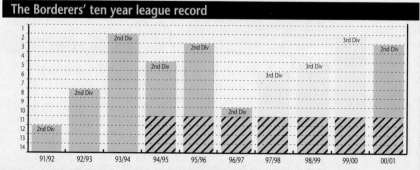

Shielfield Park,
Shielfield Terrace, Tweedmouth,
Berwick-Upon-Tweed, TD15 2EF

CHAIRMAN
James G. Curle

VICE-CHAIRMAN
W. Moray McLaren

DIRECTORS
John H. Hush, Peter McAskill,
James M.S. Rose, Robert L. Wilson,
John G. Robertson &
Robert Elliot (Commercial)

HONORARY PRESIDENT
Rt. Hon. Alan Beith M.P.

HONORARY VICE-PRESIDENT
John Thompson

CLUB SECRETARY
Dennis J. McCleary

MANAGER
Paul Smith

ASSISTANT MANAGER
David Larter

COACHING STAFF
Ian Smith, Ian Oliver,
Greg Shaw & Brian Cordery

SCHOOLS DEVELOPMENT OFFICER
Phil Rowett

KIT MAN
Ian Oliver

HON MEDICAL STAFF
Paul Ross BAEMT-P IHCD SRP
Ian Davidson BAEMT-P IHCD SRP

PHYSIO STAFF
Rev. Glyn Jones,
Ian Smith & Ian Oliver

**FOOTBALL SAFETY OFFICERS
ASSOCIATION REPRESENTATIVE**
W. Moray McLaren (01896) 754842

GROUNDSMEN
Ian Oliver & Ross Aitchison

GROUND ADVISOR
Jim Sim

COMMERCIAL MANAGER
Conrad I. Turner (01289) 307969

MEDIA LIAISON OFFICERS
Paul Smith (0131) 449 6834 &
Jamie Curle (01289) 388671

MATCHDAY PROGRAMME EDITOR
Dennis McCleary (H) (01289) 307623
& Assistant Editor Paul Smith
(Tweedmouth)

TELEPHONES
Ground/Ticket Office (01289) 307424
Fax (01289) 309424
Club Sec. Home (01289) 307623
24 Hour Hotline (09068) 800697

E-MAIL AND INTERNET ADDRESS
dennis@mccleary133.fsnet.co.uk
info@berwickrangers.com
www.berwickrangers.com

CLUB SHOP
Supporters Shop situated within
the ground. Open during first
team home matchdays.

SOCIAL CLUB
Situated in car park (01289) 305206

OFFICIAL SUPPORTERS CLUB
c/o Shielfield Park, Tweedmouth,
Berwick-Upon-Tweed, TD15 2EF
(01289) 307424

TEAM CAPTAIN
Innes Ritchie

SHIRT SPONSOR
Berwick Holiday Centre

KIT SUPPLIER
Pro Star

LIST OF PLAYERS 2001-2002

SURNAME	FIRST NAME	MIDDLE NAME	DATE OF BIRTH	PLACE OF BIRTH	DATE OF SIGNING	HEIGHT FT INS	WEIGHT ST LBS	POS. ON PITCH	PREVIOUS CLUB
Anthony	Marc		28/03/78	Edinburgh	24/07/99	5 7.0	11 0	Fwd	Celtic
Bennett	John	Neil	22/08/71	Falkirk	01/08/01	5 9.0	11 2	Mid	Stirling Albion
Bradley	Mark		10/08/76	Glasgow	14/06/01	5 8.0	10 7	Mid	Cowdenbeath
Crawford	Dale		14/09/81	Sunderland	06/08/01	6 1.0	11 8	Fwd	Horden C.W.
Duthie	Mark	James	19/08/72	Edinburgh	01/06/00	5 9.0	10 7	Mid	Ross County
Farrell	Gerard		14/06/75	Glasgow	27/07/01	5 8.0	12 0	Mid	Clydebank
Forrest	Gordon	Iain	14/01/77	Dunfermline	12/06/00	5 9.0	10 10	Def	East Fife
Glancy	Martin	Paul	24/03/76	Glasgow	27/07/01	5 8.0	10 0	Fwd	Clydebank
Gray	Dale	Ronald J.	15/02/78	Edinburgh	25/09/00	6 0.5	12 0	Def	Cowdenbeath
Lindsay	Paul	Henry R.	23/01/81	Coatbridge	19/07/01	5 11.0	11 7	Mid	East Stirlingshire
McCulloch	William		02/04/73	Baillieston	09/03/01	6 6.0	12 11	Gk	East Fife
McNicoll	Grant		07/09/77	Edinburgh	30/07/97	5 11.0	11 1	Def	Heart of Midlothian
Murie	David		02/08/76	Edinburgh	14/06/01	5 9.0	11 0	Def	Morton
Neil	Martin		16/04/70	Ashington	17/11/94	5 8.0	11 7	Mid	Bolton Wanderers
Neill	Alan	John	13/12/70	Baillieston	25/06/98	6 1.0	12 7	Def	East Stirlingshire
O'Connor	Gary		07/04/74	Newtongrange	12/09/97	6 3.0	13 7	Gk	Partick Thistle
Rae	Derek	Parlane	02/08/74	Glasgow	01/08/01	6 0.0	13 0	Mid	Stranraer
Ritchie	Innes		24/08/73	Edinburgh	25/06/99	6 0.0	12 7	Def	Clydebank
Ronald	Paul		19/07/71	Glasgow	08/06/00	6 2.0	12 7	Fwd	Stranraer
Smith	Darren		04/06/80	Edinburgh	16/10/98	5 7.0	10 2	Mid	Berwick Rangers Colts
Whelan	Jonathan		10/10/72	Liverpool	17/05/00	6 0.0	12 3	Mid	Queen's Park
Wood	Garry	Pringle G.	18/09/76	Edinburgh	18/01/00	5 11.0	12 7	Fwd	Ross County

Milestones

YEAR OF FORMATION: 1881
MOST LEAGUE POINTS IN A SEASON: 54 (Second Division – Season 1978/79) (2 Points for a Win)
66 (Third Division – Season 1999/2000) (3 Points for a Win)
MOST LEAGUE GOALS SCORED BY A PLAYER IN A SEASON: Ken Bowron (Season 1963/64)
NO. OF GOALS SCORED: 38
RECORD ATTENDANCE: 13,365 (-v- Rangers – 28.1.1967)
RECORD VICTORY: 8-1 (-v- Forfar Athletic (H) – Division 2, 25.12.1965)
8-1 (-v- Vale of Leithen – Scottish Cup at Innerleithen 17.12.1966)
RECORD DEFEAT: 1-9 (-v- Hamilton Academical – First Division, 9.8.1980)

The Borderers' ten year league record

	91/92	92/93	93/94	94/95	95/96	96/97	97/98	98/99	99/00	00/01
	2nd Div	2nd Div	2nd Div	2nd Div	2nd Div	3rd Div	3rd Div	2nd Div	3rd Div	2nd Div

THE BORDERERS' CLUB FACTFILE 2000/2001
RESULTS... APPEARANCES... SCORERS... ATTENDANCES...

Date	Venue	Opponents	Att.	Res	McLean M.	Whelan J.	Haddow L.	Ritchie I.	Neill A.	Forrest G.	McMartin G.	Neil M.	Wood G.	Findlay C.	Duthie M.	Smith D.	Ronald P.	McNicol G.	Anthony M.	Laidlaw S.	McDonald C.	Gray D.	O'Connor G.	Watt D.	Oliver N.	Magee K.	Elliot B.	Walton K.	McCulloch W.	O'Neil K.	Graham A.	Harvey J.	Elliott J.
Aug 5	A	Queen's Park	721	0-1	1	2	3	4	5	6	7	8	9	10	11	12	14	15															
12	H	Arbroath	498	2-1	1	2	3		5		14	13	8	9^{1}		7	11	10	4		6^{1}													
19	A	Stranraer	386	2-2	1	2	3	4^{1}	12	15		8^{1}	9			7	11	10	5	6	13													
26	A	Partick Thistle	2,060	1-1	1	2	3	5	12	14		8		15		7	11		4^{1}	6	9	10												
Sep 9	H	Clydebank	482	3-1	1	2	3	4		13		8^{1}	9	15^{1}	7	11			5	6^{1}	10													
16	H	Queen of the South	572	0-4	1	2	3	4		13		8	9	15	7	11			5	6	14	10												
23	A	Stenhousemuir	428	0-2	1	2		3	4	6	8	7		14	13	9	5	11		10	12													
30	H	Stirling Albion	604	2-2		13	4	3	7	2	8	9^{1}	15	14	11	10	5	6			1													
Oct 7	A	Forfar Athletic	332	5-3		3^{1}	4	5	7^{1}	2	8	9		11^{1}	10^{2}	6	15			1	13	12												
14	H	Queen's Park	514	1-1	11	3^{1}	4	5	7	2	8	9		10		6	12	1	13		15													
21	A	Arbroath	648	2-0			4	5	7	2	8	9^{1}	15^{1}	10		6	14	3	1	12	11													
28	H	Partick Thistle	1,240	1-2			4	5	7	2	8	9^{1}	15	10		6		3	1		11													
Nov 4	H	Clydebank	196	1-0			4	5^{1}	7	2	8	9	14	15	10	6		3	1	12	11													
11	H	Stenhousemuir	424	4-1	15		4	5	7^{1}	2	8	9^{1}	13		11	10^{2}		12	3	1	6													
18	A	Queen of the South	1,238	1-2	14		4	5	7^{1}	2	8	9	13		11	10		3	1	6	15													
25	H	Forfar Athletic	430	1-1	13		4	5	7	2	8	9^{1}	15		11	10		3	1	6	12													
Dec 2	A	Stirling Albion	613	1-1			4	5	7	2	8^{1}	9	12		13	10	15	3	1	6	11													
16	H	Queen's Park	690	2-0	1	6	4	5	7	2		9^{1}	10		15	8		3			11	14^{1}												
30	A	Partick Thistle	2,837	1-1	1	6	4	5	7	2		9^{1}			11	12	8	3			14	10												
Jan 2	A	Clydebank	572	1-2	1	6	4	5	7	2		9^{1}	12		11	10	8	3		14	15													
Feb 17	A	Stranraer	447	1-1	1	12	4	5		2	8	9	7^{1}	11		6		3		10	14													
Mar 10	H	Partick Thistle	1,405	0-1		7	4	5	14	2	8	9	11		6		3		10	12	1	13												
13	A	Stenhousemuir	345	2-0		2	4	5	6	8	9	11^{1}	15	14	12		3	10^{1}	1	7														
17	H	Stenhousemuir	402	1-0		7	4	5	2	8	9	13		12	3	14									11^{1}	1	10	6							
20	H	Stranraer	471	1-1		7	4^{1}	5	6	2	9	11	14	10	3	8									12	1								
25	H	Queen of the South	608	2-2		6	4	5	7	2	15	12	11	13^{1}	10^{1}	3	8^{1}								1	9								
28	H	Stirling Albion	477	4-1		6	4	5			9^{2}	12		11^{1}	13	3	8								7	1	10^{1}	2		15				
31	A	Queen of the South	984	3-3		7	4	5	2	8	9^{2}	15	12		3	6^{1}									11	1	10	14						
Apr 3	A	Forfar Athletic	413	1-0		7	4	5	15	8	9	10^{1}	11	12	3	6									1	13	2							
7	H	Forfar Athletic	480	1-0		7	4	5	14	8^{1}	12	13	11	9	3	6									1	10	2							
10	H	Clydebank	167	2-2		7	4	5	2	8	9^{1}	13	14	12	3	6^{1}									11	1	10							
14	A	Stirling Albion	525	0-1		7	4	5		8	9	12	11	10	3	6									14	1		2		15				
17	H	Arbroath	613	1-0		7	4	5^{1}	2	8	9	15	11		3	6		10							14	1								
21	H	Queen's Park	659	1-0		7	4	5	2	8	9	13	15	11	12	3	6^{1}		10						1									
28	A	Arbroath	2,124	0-2		7	4	5	2	8	9	12	14	11	6	3		10							1									15
May 5	H	Stranraer	545	0-2		6	4	5	7	8	9		3	13	10		2								15	1							12	11
TOTAL FULL APPEARANCES					11	26	9	36	31	24	20	29	29	6	12	20	20	19	27	1	4	17	10	4		5	4	4	15	6	6		1
TOTAL SUB APPEARANCES					(4)	(1)		(1)		(8)	(2)			(2)	(20)	(5)	(11)	(9)	(2)	(2)	(5)		(2)		(5)	(1)	(5)	(1)	(6)		(2)	(1)	(1)	(3)
TOTAL GOALS SCORED						2	2	2	3		5	14	3	2	2	5	1	6											2	1			1

Small bold figures denote goalscorers. † denotes opponent's own goal.

Shielfield Park

To Berwick by-pass (North and South)

Offices — Gate E

Turnstiles B (ALSO ACCESS TO STANDS)

SHIELFIELD TERRACE

Turnstiles A — Town Centre and Edinburgh North →

CAPACITY: 4,131; Seated 1,366, Standing 2,765

PITCH DIMENSIONS: 110 yds x 70 yds

FACILITIES FOR DISABLED SUPPORTERS:
Supporters should enter via gate adjacent to ground turnstiles (see ground plan above) or via official entrance.

Team playing kits

How to get there

Shielfield Park can be reached by the following routes:
The ground is approximately 1½ miles south of Berwick town centre and is situated in Shielfield Terrace, Tweedmouth. (Signposted).

BUSES: The local bus route from the town centre is the Prior Park service and the nearest stop to the ground is in Shielfield Terrace. The bus stop is only yards away from the ground.

TRAINS: The railway station is Berwick, which is situated on the East Coast line and a frequent service operates at various stages during the day. The ground is approximately 1½ miles from the station and a taxi service operates from there or alternatively, fans can take the local bus service as detailed above.

CARS: There is a large car park at the rear of the ground. (Nominal charge).

The Borderers

email: info@sfl.scottishfootball.com • website: www.scottishfootball.com

Clydebank

Cappielow Park, Sinclair Street,
Greenock, PA15 2TY

**ALL CORRESPONDENCE
SHOULD BE ADDRESSED TO:**
Nathan Higgins, c/o Planned Futures,
89 West Regent Street,
Glasgow, G2 2BA
Training Ground: Ferguslie Park,
100 Blackstoun Road,
Ferguslie, Paisley PA1

CHAIRMAN
Dr. John McK. Hall

SECRETARY
Nathan Higgins

PLAYER/MANAGER
Derek Ferguson

PLAYER LIAISON & CONSULTANT
Michael Oliver

CLUB DOCTOR
Dr David Pugh

PHYSIOTHERAPIST
Ian Cardle

KIT MANAGER
John Hardie

**FOOTBALL SAFETY OFFICERS
ASSOCIATION REPRESENTATIVE**
Michael Grana

SECURITY FIRM
Lomond Security

GROUNDSMAN
Ian Lyle

TELEPHONES
Ground (01475) 723571
(Match Days Only)
Fax (0141) 332 5959
Please Note:
All fax messages for either
press enquiries, team matters or
complimentary tickets are to be sent
to: **Nathan Higgins** (0141) 332 5959
or **Greenock Morton** (01475) 781084
(addressed to Nathan Higgins)

OFFICIAL SUPPORTERS CLUB
c/o Gordon Robertson,
Clydebank Post,
88 Dumbarton Road, Clydebank

TEAM CAPTAIN
Rab McKinnon

SHIRT SPONSOR
Viola Group

KIT SUPPLIER
Soccer Company

LIST OF PLAYERS 2001-2002

SURNAME	FIRST NAME	MIDDLE NAME	DATE OF BIRTH	PLACE OF BIRTH	DATE OF SIGNING	HEIGHT FT INS	WEIGHT ST LBS	POS. ON PITCH	PREVIOUS CLUB
Bossy	Fabian		01/10/77	Marseille	03/08/01	6 0.0	11 10	Def	Academica Viseux
Brannigan	Kenneth		08/06/65	Glasgow	04/11/99	6 2.0	13 7	Def	Partick Thistle
Burke	Alexander		11/11/77	Glasgow	17/03/01	5 7.5	10 11	Fwd	Falkirk
Ferguson	Derek		31/07/67	Glasgow	11/01/01	5 8.5	11 9	Mid	Ross County
Gilliland	James		06/10/79	Irvine	21/08/01	6 0.0	11 7	Fwd	Ardrossan Winton Rovers
Gow	Alan		09/10/82	Glasgow	03/08/01	6 0.0	11 0	Mid	Gleniffer Thistle
Graham	Alastair	Slowey	11/08/66	Glasgow	03/08/01	6 3.0	12 7	Fwd	Stirling Albion
Hamilton	Brian		05/08/67	Paisley	03/08/01	5 11.0	12 10	Mid	Partick Thistle
Kinnaird	Paul		11/11/66	Glasgow	03/08/01	5 8.0	11 11	Mid	Brechin City
McGowan	Neil	William	15/04/77	Glasgow	14/08/01	5 10.0	11 7	Def	Stranraer
McGrillen	Paul	Alexander	19/08/71	Glasgow	03/08/01	5 9.0	11 2	Fwd	Partick Thistle
McKinnon	Robert		31/07/66	Glasgow	07/11/00	5 11.5	13 7	Def	Heart of Midlothian
McNally	Mark		10/03/71	Motherwell	03/08/01	5 11.0	12 3	Def	Partick Thistle
McVey	William	Alexander	02/02/82	Glasgow	30/12/00	5 9.0	10 6	Def	Partick Thistle
Mooney	Gerard		28/08/80	Rutherglen	30/03/01	5 10.0	12 8	Mid	Coventry City
Murray	Stephen		24/08/80	Irvine	03/12/99	5 11.0	13 10	Def	Celtic
Paton	Eric	John	01/08/78	Glasgow	03/08/00	5 10.0	12 0	Mid	Partick Thistle
Robertson	Stephen		16/03/77	Glasgow	05/06/01	5 11.0	13 0	Gk	St. Johnstone
Smith	Henry	George	10/03/56	Lanark	03/08/01	6 2.0	13 13	Gk	Gretna
Whiteford	Andrew		22/08/77	Bellshill	03/08/01	5 11.0	12 0	Def	Stirling Albion

Milestones

YEAR OF FORMATION: 1965
MOST LEAGUE POINTS IN A SEASON: 58 (Division 1 – Season 1976/77)(2 Points for a Win)
60 (Second Division – Season 1997/98)(3 Points for a Win)
MOST LEAGUE GOALS SCORED BY A PLAYER IN A SEASON: Ken Eadie (Season 1990/91)
NO. OF GOALS SCORED: 29
RECORD ATTENDANCE: 14,900 (-v- Hibernian – 10.2.1965)
RECORD VICTORY: 8-1 (-v- Arbroath – Division 1, 3.1.1977)
RECORD DEFEAT: 1-9 (-v- Gala Fairydean – Scottish Cup, 15.9.1965)

The Bankies' ten year league record

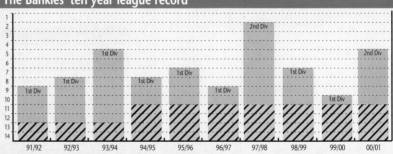

BELL'S SCOTTISH FOOTBALL LEAGUE

Date	Venue	Opponents	Att.	Res	Wylie D.	McKinstrey J.	McKinnon R.	Wishart F.	Brannigan K.	Taborda E.	Murray S.	Ferguson D.	Fal L.	Coyne T.	Hamilton B.	Rodden P.	McQuilter R.	Johnson I.G.	Walker J.	McKelvie D.	Callaghan S.	Paton E.	Conway C.	Hernandez F.	Welsh B.	McCormick S.	Jacquel R.	Racon A.	McKey W.	Murdoch S.	Burke A.	Kaak A.	Farrell G.	Glancy M.	Hutchison S.	Creaney G.	Gow A.	Smith G.	Brown P.	Mooney C.	Farrell D.	Bossy F.	Campbell J.	Milne D.
Aug 5	A	Stirling Albion	779	2-2	1	2	3	4	5	6	7	8	9[2]	10	11	16																												
12	H	Stenhousemuir	236	1-0	1	2	3		5	6	14	8	9	10[1]	11		4	7	15	16																								
19	A	Arbroath	691	0-1	1	2	3		5	6	4	11		10	8			9	15		7	14	16																					
26	H	Queen of the South	273	1-2	1	16	3	2	5	6		11	9	10			4	8	12		14		7																					
Sep 9	A	Berwick Rangers	482	1-3	1		3	2	5		12		7[1]	11		4	8	15						6	9	10	16																	
16	A	Forfar Athletic	385	2-0	1	2			5		7	11		9	8[1]			15						6	16	10[1]	12	3	4																
23	H	Partick Thistle	1,379	2-1	1	2	3	14	5		7	11			8			9						6[1]	15		12	4	10[1]																
30	A	Stranraer	551	2-0	1	2			5		7[1]			15	8			11	9[1]		14			6			3	4	10																
Oct 7	H	Queen's Park	375	2-0	1	2[1]			5		7[1]	14		16	8			11	9		15			6			3	4	10																
14	H	Stirling Albion	312	3-0	1	2		12	5		7	11		9[1]	8			15	16					6			3	4	10[2]																
21	A	Stenhousemuir	450	1-2	1	2	6		5		7	11		9	8[1]			15	16		14						3	4	10																
28	A	Queen of the South	1,156	1-1	1	2	6		5		14	11		9	8			10	7								3	4		16[1]															
Nov 4	H	Berwick Rangers	196	0-1	1		6	3	5		14	11		16	8			7	10	15							4		9	2															
11	A	Partick Thistle	3,101	0-2	1	2	6		5		7	11		9	8			16									3	4		12	10														
18	H	Forfar Athletic	153	1-1		2	6	3	5		7	11		16	8			15	9											4	10[1]	1													
25	A	Queen's Park	668	1-1	1	2	3		5			11		16			7[1]		8		6			12				4	10		9	15												
Dec 5	H	Stranraer	126	2-3	1	14	3		5		12	11		15			7		8[1]					6	4			2	10[1]		9													
16	A	Stirling Albion	534	0-0		3		6	5		14	11					15		8								12	4[1]		2	10	1	9	16	7									
23	A	Arbroath	131	1-2	1	3		6	5		7						8		9					12	4[1]			2	10			15	11	16										
Jan 2	H	Berwick Rangers	572	2-1	1	7	3	6	5		15						8		9[1]						4			2	10[1]			11												
27	A	Forfar Athletic	418	3-1	1	7	3	6	5[1]		14						8	16	9[1]						4			2	10			11[1]		15										
Feb 13	H	Partick Thistle	1,111	0-4	1	7	3	6	5		14						8	16	9						4			2	10			11												
17	A	Arbroath	537	2-4	1	7[1]	3		5		14						8	16	9[1]									2	10			11					4	6						
Mar 6	A	Stranraer	363	0-0		7	3	5			4						8		9					12				2	10			11							6	1				
10	A	Queen of the South	1,022	0-1		7	3	5			4						8		9					14	15			2	10			11							6	1				
13	H	Queen of the South	245	1-2		7	3		5		8	4							9[1]					15	14			2	10			11							6	1				
17	A	Partick Thistle	2,721	0-2		7	3		5		2	4					8		9					11	10			14	16			11							6	1				
20	H	Queen's Park	209	2-1		7	3		5		8	4							9						10[2]			2	16			11							6	1				
27	H	Stenhousemuir	256	1-0			3		5		7	4					8		15					12	2	10[1]			9			11							6	1				
31	H	Forfar Athletic	145	2-1	1	2	3		5[1]		14	4					7		9						10[1]				8	12		11							6					
Apr 7	A	Queen's Park	701	0-0	1		3		5		14	4							7					2	10			8	9			11							6		16			
10	H	Berwick Rangers	167	2-2	1	15	3		5		14	4					12		7[1]					2	10			8	9			11[1]							6					
14	H	Stranraer	159	0-0	1	15	3		5			4					16		7					2	10							11							6					
21	H	Stirling Albion	205	1-1	1	2	3		5		8	4					15		7						10[1]							11							6		9			
28	A	Stenhousemuir	404	0-0	1	14			5		12						4	9	7					3	10				8			16					2	6			11			
May 5	H	Arbroath	243	3-1	1	2			5		6						12	9[2]	7[1]						10				3	14							4	11			8			
TOTAL FULL APPEARANCES					28	27	28	12	34	4	17	26	3	10	14		3	4	16	8	1	21		1	7	1	2	13	16	15	1	20	17	2	3		16		2	1	14	6	3
TOTAL SUB APPEARANCES						(5)		(2)		(13)	(2)		(5)	(1)	(1)				(10)	(10)	(1)	(6)	(1)		(2)		(2)	(6)	(3)		(1)	(2)	(4)			(3)	(1)	(1)	(1)			(1)
TOTAL GOALS SCORED						2			2		2		2	4	2				1	3		7		1	1			1	8	1		3				2						

Small bold figures denote goalscorers. † denotes opponent's own goal.

The Bankies

Cappielow Park

SINCLAIR STREET

Limited space &♿ - Application only

CAPACITY: 7,890; Seated 5,890, Standing 2,000
PITCH DIMENSIONS: 110 yds x 71 yds
FACILITIES FOR DISABLED SUPPORTERS:
Seating facilities below Grandstand.

Team playing kits

How to get there

Cappielow Park can be reached by the following routes:

BUSES: Services from Glasgow stop just outside the park. There are also services from Port Glasgow and Gourock.

TRAINS: The nearest local station is Cartsdyke and it is a five minute walk from here to the ground. There are two to three trains every hour from Glasgow and from Gourock.

CARS: There is no official car park and fans should park in Sinclair Street beyond the railway station.

email: info@sfl.scottishfootball.com • website: www.scottishfootball.com

Cowdenbeath

Central Park, High Street,
Cowdenbeath, KY4 9QQ

CHAIRMAN
Gordon McDougall

VICE-CHAIRMAN
Albert V. Tait

DIRECTORS
Ian Fraser, Brian Watson,
Dr. Robert Brownlie, Edward Baigan,
Morris Kaplan & J. Derrick Brown

**GENERAL/COMMERCIAL
MANAGER**
Joe Macnamara

SECRETARY
Thomas Ogilvie

MANAGER
Gary Kirk

PLAYER/ASSISTANT MANAGER
Keith Wright

YOUTH TEAM COACHES
David Liddle & Ross Hamilton (U18)
John Faichney & Alan Lawrence (U16)
John Scott (U13)

FITNESS COACH
Tom Ritchie

GOALKEEPING COACH
Andy Forbes

CLUB DOCTOR
Dr. Robert Brownlie

PHYSIOTHERAPISTS
Wendy McDonald & Fiona Waite

**FOOTBALL SAFETY OFFICERS'
ASSOCIATION REPRESENTATIVE**
David Jones (H) (01383) 872074

CHIEF SCOUT
David Dair

GROUNDSMAN
Gordon McDougall Jnr.

KIT MAN
James Baxter

MATCHDAY PROGRAMME EDITOR
Andrew Mullen (01383) 611644

TELEPHONES
Ground/Ticket Office/Information
Service (01383) 610166
Sec. Home (01383) 513013
Sec. Bus (01383) 313400
Fax (01383) 512132

E-MAIL & INTERNET ADDRESS
bluebrazil@cowdenbeathfc.com
www.cowdenbeathfc.com

CLUB SHOP
Situated at Stadium. Open 10.00 a.m. –
3.00 p.m. and on Home Match Days

OFFICIAL SUPPORTERS CLUB
Central Park, High Street,
Cowdenbeath, KY4 9QQ

TEAM CAPTAIN
Craig Winter

SHIRT SPONSOR
Bernard Hunter Crane Hire

KIT SUPPLIER
Paulas Benara

LIST OF PLAYERS 2001-2002

SURNAME	FIRST NAME	MIDDLE NAME	DATE OF BIRTH	PLACE OF BIRTH	DATE OF SIGNING	HEIGHT FT INS	WEIGHT ST LBS	POS. ON PITCH	PREVIOUS CLUB
Bannatyne	Peter		13/08/82	Edinburgh	16/11/99	5 8.0	10 10	Fwd	Dundonald Bluebell
Boyle	James	Thomson	19/02/67	Glasgow	31/07/00	5 6.0	11 2	Def	Alloa Athletic
Brown	Graeme	Robert	08/11/80	Johannesburg	19/08/97	5 11.0	11 0	Fwd	Broomhall Saints B.C.
Burns	John	Paul	11/03/78	Kirkcaldy	02/08/98	5 6.0	10 9	Fwd	Heart of Midlothian
Campbell	Andrew	Mark	15/03/79	Edinburgh	06/07/01	6 0.0	12 7	Def	Easthouses Under 21's
Carnie	Grant		16/10/81	Edinburgh	26/09/00	5 10.5	13 7	Mid	Armadale Thistle
Dixon	John		05/09/83	Edinburgh		5 8.5	11 0	Fwd	Star 'A' B.C.
Duff	Steven	Robert	29/03/84	Edinburgh	24/07/01	5 10.0	11 0	Def	Hibernian
Eadie	Callum		19/08/84	Edinburgh	07/08/01	5 9.0	10 12	Mid	Hibernian
French	Hamish	Mackie	07/02/64	Aberdeen	24/07/01	5 10.5	11 7	Mid/Fwd	Alloa Athletic
Gibb	Scott		04/05/83	Edinburgh	06/07/01	5 10.0	10 7	Mid	S Form
King	Thomas	David	23/04/70	Dumbarton	13/11/00	5 9.0	11 0	Mid	Dumbarton
Knox	David		27/06/84	Edinburgh	15/08/01	5 10.0	11 7	Mid	Dalmore B.C.
Latimer	Darrell	James	26/08/84	Dunfermline	04/08/01	5 10.0	12 2	Def	S Form
Lawrence	Alan		19/08/62	Edinburgh	06/06/00	5 7.0	10 0	Fwd	Stenhousemuir
Martin	John	Galloway K.	27/10/58	Edinburgh	06/06/00	6 1.0	11 7	Gk	Preston Athletic
Mauchlen	Iain		11/06/79	Irvine	24/07/01	5 7.0	10 10	Mid/Fwd	Oakley United JFC
McBride	Ross		28/08/84	Kirkcaldy	01/08/00	5 10.0	10 2	Mid	S Form
McLean	Kenneth		14/04/83	Edinburgh	08/09/00	5 9.0	11 7	Def	Hibernian
McMaster	Ross		06/02/84	Broxburn	06/07/01	5 10.0	10 0	Mid	Livingston S Form
McMillan	Craig		04/12/81	Dunfermline	03/07/98	5 10.0	11 0	Mid	Hill of Beath Swifts
Moffat	Adam		07/05/83	Kirkcaldy	03/08/01	5 10.0	11 0	Mid	Livingston
Neeson	Craig	Patrick	06/05/81	Glasgow	06/07/01	5 9.0	11 2	Def	Heart of Midlothian
Raynes	Steven		04/09/71	Edinburgh	24/07/01	5 9.0	11 12	Def	Brechin City
Sharp	Alan		16/01/83	Falkirk	06/07/01	5 6.0	8 8	Def	Livingston
Somerville	Mark		14/07/83	Edinburgh	06/07/01	5 10.0	11 0	Fwd	X Form
Spence	Andrew		08/09/84	Dunfermline	26/09/00	5 10.0	11 3	Fwd	S Form
Swift	Stephen		21/07/80	Glasgow	03/08/01	5 11.0	11 3	Def	Livingston
Waugh	Colin		04/06/82	Dunfermline	06/12/00	6 1.0	11 7	Def/Mid	Rosyth Recreation JFC
Welsh	Brian		23/02/69	Edinburgh	03/08/01	6 3.0	13 6	Def	Clydebank
White	David	William	09/08/79	Edinburgh	09/07/99	6 1.5	11 12	Def	Motherwell
Wilson	Keith	Andrew	31/08/79	Edinburgh	06/07/01	6 3.0	15 0	Def	Coldstream
Winter	Craig	John	30/06/76	Dunfermline	19/07/94	5 9.0	10 0	Mid/Fwd	Raith Rovers
Wright	Keith	Arthur	17/05/65	Edinburgh	24/06/00	6 0.0	12 8	Fwd	Stenhousemuir
Young	Craig		02/12/81	Edinburgh	24/08/01	5 6.0	10 0	Fwd	Craigroyston

Milestones

YEAR OF FORMATION: 1881
MOST CAPPED PLAYER: Jim Paterson
NO. OF CAPS: 3
MOST LEAGUE POINTS IN A SEASON: 60 (Division 2 – Season 1938/39)(2 Points for a Win)
76 (Third Division – Season 2000/01)(3 Points for a Win)
MOST LEAGUE GOALS SCORED BY A PLAYER IN A SEASON: Rab Walls (Season 1938/39)
NO. OF GOALS SCORED: 54
RECORD ATTENDANCE: 25,586 (-v- Rangers – 21.9.1949)
RECORD VICTORY: 12-0 (-v- Johnstone – Scottish Cup, 21.1.1928)
RECORD DEFEAT: 1-11 (-v- Clyde – Division 2, 6.10.1951)

The Blue Brazil's ten year league record

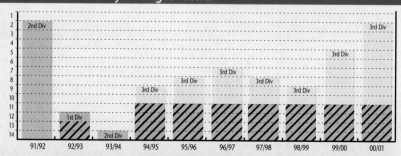

THE BLUE BRAZIL'S CLUB FACTFILE 2000/2001
RESULTS... APPEARANCES... SCORERS... ATTENDANCES...

BELL'S SCOTTISH FOOTBALL LEAGUE

Date	Venue	Opponents	Att.	Res	Martin J.	Boyle J.	McMillan C.	White D.	McCulloch K.	Lawrence A.	Winter C.	Bradley M.	McDowell M.	Wright K.	Burns J. P.	Brown G.	Allan J.	Juskowiak R.	Welsh B.	Ramsay S.	Lakie J.	Courts T.	Crabbe G.	McDonald I.	Neeson C.	Smith A.	King T.	Carnie G.	Simmons S.	Gillilan F.	Mitchell W.	Hunter M.	Barnes D.
Aug 5	A	East Stirlingshire	297	2-0	1	2	3	4	5	6	7	8¹	9	10¹	11	12	14	16															
12	H	Albion Rovers	302	5-0	1	2	3	4	5	6	7	8	9	10²	11²	12	14¹	15															
19	A	Brechin City	337	0-0	1	2	3	4		6	7	8	9		11	10	12	16	5														
26	H	Elgin City	354	3-1	1	2		4¹			7	8	9²	10	11	6				3	5	14											
Sep 9	A	East Fife	735	2-0	1	2		4	5	16	7¹	8	9	10¹	11	6					3	15											
16	H	Hamilton Academical	448	†2-0	1	2		4	5	6¹	7	8	9	10	11	12					3												
23	A	Dumbarton	348	4-2	1	2		4	5	6	7¹	8	9	10¹	11¹					14	3	16											
30	H	Montrose	378	2-0	1	2		4		5	6	7	8	9	10	11	12	14		5	3	15											
Oct 7	A	Peterhead	637	0-3	1	2		4	5	6	7	8	9	10	11	12	14				3	16											
14	H	East Stirlingshire	289	3-0	1	2		4¹	5	6	7	8	9²	10	11	12	14				3												
21	A	Albion Rovers	429	0-1	1	2		4	5	6	7	8	9	10	11	12	15				3	14											
28	A	Elgin City	836	3-2	1	2¹		4		14	7¹	8	9¹	12	6	10	11				3	5											
Nov 4	H	East Fife	626	1-0	1	2	3		5	6	7	8¹	9	12	11	10					15	4											
11	H	Dumbarton	341	1-1	1	2	3		5	6	7	8	9	14	15¹	10	12				11	4											
18	A	Hamilton Academical	598	0-0	1	2		5			7	8	12	9	6	10	16				3				4	11							
25	H	Peterhead	404	2-0	1	2		5		6		8	12	9	11¹	10					3				4¹	7							
Dec 2	H	Montrose	311	2-1	1	2		5				12	9	6	10	11²					3				4	7	8						
23	H	Brechin City	434	2-1	1	2		5		12	7	8	9¹	10	6	14					3				4	11¹							
Jan 2	H	East Fife	1,003	2-1	1	2		5		6	7	8	9¹	10	12¹						3				4	11							
Feb 17	A	Brechin City	545	0-2	1	2		5		12	7	8	9	6	10	14					3				16	4	11						
24	H	Albion Rovers	331	1-0	1	2		5		6	7	12	16¹	11	9	10					3				4	8							
Mar 7	A	Dumbarton	507	0-3	1	2		5			7	8	16	11	10	9					3				4	6		14					
10	A	Elgin City	676	2-0	1		5	2		7¹	8¹	9	15	10	11						4				6	16	4						
13	A	Peterhead	499	0-3	1		5	2		7	8	9	16	12	10	11					3				6	14	4						
17	H	Dumbarton	369	2-2	1	2		5		6	7	8	16¹	9¹	14	12					3				4	11						10	
20	H	Hamilton Academical	429	1-1	1	2		5		6	7	8	16	9	14	12					3				4	11¹						10	
25	H	Elgin City	289	1-0	1	2		5		6	7¹	8	16	9	14	12					3				4	11						10	
31	H	Hamilton Academical	666	0-0	1	2		5		6	7	8	9		12	10					3				4	11						14	
Apr 3	A	East Stirlingshire	272	2-0	1	2		5¹		6	7	8¹	9	16	10						3				4	11						12	
7	H	Peterhead	348	4-0	1	2			6¹	7	8	16	14	9¹	12					12	3				4	11²						10	
10	H	Montrose	319	2-1	1	2		5		6	7		10	14¹	9¹					4	3				11					15		8	
14	A	Montrose	407	1-0	1	2		5		6	7	8¹	12	16	14	9					3				11					4	10		
17	H	East Fife	531	3-2	1	2		5		2	7	8¹	9¹	16	6	10				4¹	3				11					12	17		
21	H	East Stirlingshire	488	1-3	1	2		5		6	7	8	9	16	12	10¹				4	3				11						10		
28	A	Albion Rovers	405	0-0	1	2		5		6	7	8	10	16	12	9					3				11								
May 5	H	Brechin City	3,448	2-1	1	2		5		12	7¹	8	14	6	9					4	3	5			11¹						10		
TOTAL FULL APPEARANCES					36	33	3	35	10	27	34	33	23	20	22	21	6	2	3	1	2	23			11	18	20	1	2		3	7	
TOTAL SUB APPEARANCES								(5)		(1)		(8)	(12)	(12)	(12)	(9)	(4)					(1)		(2)	(1)	(4)	(2)			(1)	(3)	(3)	(1)
TOTAL GOALS SCORED							1			3		2	6	8	10	7	6	4	3				1				1	5				

Small bold figures denote goalscorers. † denotes opponent's own goal.

Central Park

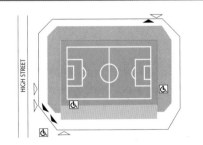

HIGH STREET

CAPACITY: 4,370; Seated 1,431, Standing 2,939

PITCH DIMENSIONS: 107 yds x 65 yds

FACILITIES FOR DISABLED SUPPORTERS:
Direct access from car park into designated area within ground. Toilet and catering facilities also provided.

Team playing kits

How to get there
You can get to Central Park by the following routes:

TRAINS: There is a regular service of trains from Edinburgh and Glasgow (via Edinburgh) which call at Cowdenbeath and the station is only 400 yards from the ground.

BUSES: A limited Edinburgh-Cowdenbeath service stops just outside the ground on matchdays and a frequent service of Dunfermline-Ballingry buses also stop outside the ground, as does the Edinburgh-Glenrothes service.

CARS: Car parking facilities are available in the public car park adjacent to the ground for 190 cars. There are also another 300 spaces at the Stenhouse Street car park, which is 200 yards from the ground.

The Blue Brazil

email: info@sfl.scottishfootball.com • website: www.scottishfootball.com

Forfar Athletic

Station Park, Carseview Road,
Forfar, DD8 3BT

CHAIRMAN
David McGregor

VICE-CHAIRMAN
Neill McK. Wilson

DIRECTORS
Alastair S. Nicoll,
Michael S. McEwan,
Gordon Menmuir (Treasurer)
& Ronald Blair

HONORARY PATRON
Rt. Hon. Lord Lyell of Kinnordy

SECRETARY
David McGregor

COMPANY SECRETARIES
McLean & Lowson

MANAGER
Neil Cooper

ASSISTANT MANAGER
Phil Bonnyman

YOUTH DEVELOPMENT CO-ORDINATOR
Peter Castle

COACHING STAFF
Donald Ritchie, Ally Taylor
& Derek Mitchell

YOUTH TEAM COACHES
Peter Castle & Ally Taylor (U18)
Donald Ritchie & Derek Mitchell (U16)

CLUB DOCTOR
Dr Peter Dick

PHYSIOTHERAPIST
Ian Barrett

GROUNDSMAN/KIT SUPERVISOR
Martin Gray

MEDIA LIAISON OFFICER
David McGregor
Tel: Home (01307) 464924
Tel: Bus (01307) 475519

MATCHDAY PROGRAMME EDITOR
John Turner
Tel: Home (01307) 460255

TELEPHONES
Ground (01307) 463576/462259
Sec. Home (01307) 464924
Sec. Bus. (01307) 475519
Sec. Bus. Fax (01307) 466956

INTERNET ADDRESS
www.forfarathletic.co.uk

OFFICIAL SUPPORTERS CLUB
c/o Mrs. Yvonne Nicoll,
7 Fyfe Jamieson, Forfar
Tel: Home (01307) 467255

TEAM CAPTAIN
Dave Bowman

SHIRT SPONSOR
Universal Telecom

KIT SUPPLIER
SPALL

LIST OF PLAYERS 2001-2002

SURNAME	FIRST NAME	MIDDLE NAME	DATE OF BIRTH	PLACE OF BIRTH	DATE OF SIGNING	HEIGHT FT INS	WEIGHT ST LBS	POS. ON PITCH	PREVIOUS CLUB
Bannon	Mark	Steven	22/08/83	Dundee	23/08/01	5 10.0	10 0	Def	S Form
Black	James		11/01/84	Dundee	31/07/01	5 6.0	9 0	Def	S Form
Bowman	David		10/03/64	Tunbridge Wells	18/07/00	5 10.0	11 4	Mid	Yee Hote Hong Kong
Bremner	Kit		07/06/84	High Wycombe	25/07/01	5 11.0	11 0	Mid	Form D Under 16
Brown	Michael		07/11/79	Stranraer	06/06/01	6 1.0	12 8	Gk	Partick Thistle
Byers	Kevin		23/08/79	Kirkcaldy	31/07/01	5 10.0	10 10	Mid	Inverness Cal. Thistle
Christie	Sean		15/07/80	Dundee	31/08/98	5 9.0	10 7	Fwd	Carnoustie Panmure
Duncan	George		26/08/83	Dundee	11/07/01	5 11.0	10 9	Def	S Form
Edmonds	Dylan		14/12/83	Dundee	11/07/01	5 7.0	9 0	Def	S Form
Farnan	Craig		07/04/71	Dundee	05/11/99	5 10.0	13 3	Mid	Montrose
Ferrie	James		23/09/83	Dundee	11/07/01	5 8.0	10 0	Def	Dundee Violet
Ferrie	Neal		23/11/81	Dundee	07/06/00	6 0.0	11 4	Gk	Dundee United
Ferrie	Ryan		02/10/83	Dundee	11/07/01	5 10.0	9 10	Mid	Monifieth B.C.
Gallazzi	Allan		26/01/84	Dundee	11/07/01	5 10.0	12 5	Fwd	Dundee Social Club U15's
Good	Iain	David	09/08/77	Glasgow	02/12/00	6 1.0	12 0	Def	Arbroath
Henry	James		07/07/75	Dundee	02/08/01	5 10.0	12 7	Mid	Stenhousemuir
Hodge	Colin	Bateman	24/12/84	Kirkcaldy	26/01/01	6 0.0	10 10	Fwd	S Form
Horn	Robert	David	03/08/77	Edinburgh	28/06/00	5 9.0	11 0	Def	Heart of Midlothian
Kerr	Craig	John	07/01/84	Dundee	31/07/01	6 0.0	11 5	Def	S Form
Kinmond	Christopher	Stuart	02/04/84	Dundee	28/07/01	5 10.0	9 5	Gk	Form D Under 16
Lunan	Paul	James	20/09/82	Dundee	04/08/01	5 10.0	10 0	Mid	Dundee Violet
McCloy	Brian		06/08/79	Pontefract	10/08/01	5 11.0	10 10	Def	East Fife
McMaster	Gregor		14/10/82	Dundee	04/08/01	6 0.0	12 0	Mid	Dundee Violet
McNicoll	Colin	R.	26/08/84	Dundee	25/07/01	5 9.0	11 5	Fwd	S Form
Milne	Kevin		27/04/81	Edinburgh	30/05/01	5 11.0	12 0	Def	Stirling Albion
Moffat	Barrie		27/12/72	Broxburn	24/05/01	5 8.0	11 7	Fwd	East Fife
Morris	Roberto		11/02/80	Dundee	30/07/99	6 1.0	10 0	Def	Dundee United Social Club
O'Rourke	Christopher	Michael	20/09/83	Dundee	11/07/01	5 9.0	10 0	Mid	Dundee Violet
Rattray	Alan	Raymond	08/06/79	Dundee	16/11/96	5 10.0	11 0	Def	Dundee Violet
Sellars	Barry	Michael	06/12/75	Arbroath	02/11/00	6 1.0	12 10	Mid	Clyde
Smeaton	Mark		13/08/84	Dundee	25/07/01	5 10.0	10 5	Mid	Form D Under 16
Stewart	William	Paul	16/04/77	Glasgow	11/08/00	5 10.0	10 2	Fwd	Cowdenbeath
Taylor	Scott	Andrew	23/01/77	Forfar	19/05/00	5 9.0	11 0	Fwd	Montrose
Thomson	Aaron		27/09/83	Dundee	25/07/01	5 10.0	10 6	Def	S Form
Tosh	Paul	James	18/10/73	Arbroath	28/06/01	6 1.0	13 4	Fwd	Raith Rovers
Walker	Dean		08/07/82	Edinburgh	03/07/01	5 10.0	10 7	Mid	Dunfermline Athletic
Williams	David		29/09/81	Glasgow	03/07/01	5 10.0	11 0	Fwd	Kilmarnock

Milestones

YEAR OF FORMATION: 1885
MOST LEAGUE POINTS IN A SEASON: 63 (Second Division – Season 1983/84) (2 Points for a Win)
80 (Third Division – Season 1994/95) (3 Points for a Win)
MOST LEAGUE GOALS SCORED BY A PLAYER IN A SEASON: Dave Kilgour (Season 1929/30)
NO. OF GOALS SCORED: 45
RECORD ATTENDANCE: 10,800 (-v- Rangers – 7.2.1970)
RECORD VICTORY: 14-1 (-v- Lindertis – Scottish Cup, 1.9.1888)
RECORD DEFEAT: 2-12 (-v- King's Park – Division 2, 2.1.1930)

The Loons' ten year league record

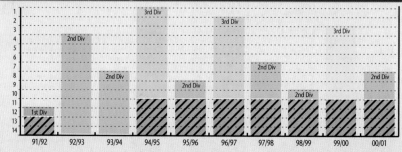

THE LOONS' CLUB FACTFILE 2000/2001
RESULTS... APPEARANCES... SCORERS... ATTENDANCES...

Date	Venue	Opponents	Att.	Res	Garden S.	McCheyne G.	Donaldson E.	Horn R.	Tully C.	Bowman D.	McPhee G.	Farnan C.	Ferguson I.	Cargill A.	Taylor S.	Rattray A.	Brand R.	Stewart W.	Morris R.	Sinclair D.	Christie S.	Craig D.	Stirling J.	Beaton D.	Ferrie N.	Farrell G.	McGraw M.	Sellars B.	Taylor A.	Good I.	Winters D.	Duncan R.	Dolan J.	Keogh L.	Moffat J.
Aug 5	A	Stranraer	397	0-2	1	2	3	4	5	6	7	8	9	10	11	12		16																	
12	H	Queen's Park	516	0-1	1	2	3	5	6	8	7	4	9	11	10			16																	
19	A	Stirling Albion	605	3-3	1	12	3	5	6		8^1	4	9^1		2	10	7^1	11	14																
26	H	Stenhousemuir	381	2-2	1	2	3	5		8	7	4	9		10	11	6^1	14^1	15															
Sep 9	A	Arbroath	876	4-3	1	2	12	5	6	8	16	4	9^2		10	7^2					3	11												
16	H	Clydebank	385	0-2	1	2	12	5	6	8		4	9	16	10	7				14	3	11												
23	A	Queen of the South	1,167	1-0	1		3	4	6	8^1		11	9		2	16	7			10	14	5												
30	A	Partick Thistle	2,218	1-1	1		3	4	6	8	15	11	9^1		2		7			10	14	5	22											
Oct 7	A	Berwick Rangers	332	†3-5			3	4	6	8	15	11	9^1		2		7^1			10		5	1	16										
14	H	Stranraer	405	0-0	1	12		5		10	8	9		2	15	7			16	3	11	6	4											
21	A	Queen's Park	741	0-0	1		4		8	5	9	10	2		7				11	3	6													
28	A	Stenhousemuir	321	0-2	1		4		8	5	9	10	2	14	7				11	3	6													
Nov 4	A	Arbroath	834	0-1	1		4		8	5		10	2	14	7		15	16	3	6				9	11									
11	H	Queen of the South	440	0-1	1	2	3	4		7	5	10			16		11		6				9	8										
18	A	Clydebank	153	1-1	1	4	3	5		15	8	10		11^1	2		14		6		9	7	16											
25	A	Berwick Rangers	430	1-1	1	11	4		15	6	14		9	10^1	2		12	3	5			7	8											
Dec 2	H	Partick Thistle	1,052	0-1	1	11	4		8	6		16	9	10	2		12		5		15	7	3											
16	A	Stranraer	419	†1-3	1	11	4		8	2	9	6			7		16		5		10	14	3											
Jan 2	A	Arbroath	1,061	1-1	1	11^1	4		8	6		8		2	10		12		5		16	7	3											
6	H	Stenhousemuir	441	7-0	1	16	11^1	4		8	6	9	15		2		12		5^1			7^2		3	10^3									
27	H	Clydebank	418	1-3	1		11^1	4		8	2	9			12		15		5^1			7		3	10	6								
Feb 10	A	Partick Thistle	3,075	0-4	1		4		8	6			2				9		5			7	14	3	10	11								
Mar 10	A	Stenhousemuir	376	1-0	1		4		8	12	9		6			2	16^1		5			7	14		3	10	11								
13	H	Queen's Park	374	3-0	1	11		8^1			16		6		15	2	10		5^1			7			3	4	9^1								
17	A	Queen of the South	974	3-2	1	11		8	12		16		6			2	10^1		5^1			7			3	4	9^1								
20	A	Stirling Albion	515	0-1	1	11				16	8		6		15	2	10		5			7			3	4	9								
31	A	Clydebank	145	1-2	1	11^1			6	12	8		16			2	10		5			7			3	4	9								
Apr 3	H	Berwick Rangers	413	0-1	1	11	4			12	8		15			2	10	6	5			7			3		9								
7	A	Berwick Rangers	480	0-1	1	3	4			9	8	6			15		11		5			7			2		10							
10	H	Stirling Albion	390	1-0		3	4			9	8	6			15		11		5			7^1			2		10	1						
14	H	Partick Thistle	2,081	2-2		3	4	11		9^1	8^1	6					16		5			7		5	2		10	1						
21	H	Stranraer	378	2-3	1	11		4			8	6					9		5			7^1		3	2		10^1							
24	H	Arbroath	1,065	1-1	1	3	4^1	11		15	9	8	6				14		12			7			2		10							
28	A	Queen's Park	951	2-0	1	3	4		7	14	9^1	8	6		15^1		11		12						5		2	10						
May 1	H	Queen of the South	522	3-1		3	4	11		14	9^1	8	6		15^1							7^1			5		2	10	1					
5	H	Stirling Albion	813	3-1		3	4	11			9	8^1	6		10^2							7			5		2		1					
TOTAL FULL APPEARANCES					31	7	28	30	9	23	9	23	24	19	2	23	7	16	11		14	7	6	25	1	1	4	21	2	12	3	16	5	13	4
TOTAL SUB APPEARANCES						(3)	(2)				(5)	(5)	(3)	(5)		(2)	(5)	(12)			(2)	(13)	(2)	(2)	(2)	(1)	(1)	(1)		(2)	(3)				
TOTAL GOALS SCORED							3	1		2	1		8	2			1	9	1		1	2						4		5		3		3	

Small bold figures denote goalscorers. † denotes opponent's own goal.

Station Park

CAPACITY: 4,640; Seated 739, Standing 3,901
PITCH DIMENSIONS: 115 yds x 69 yds
FACILITIES FOR DISABLED SUPPORTERS:
Ramp entrance via Main Stand.

(CARSEVIEW ROAD)

Team playing kits

How to get there

Station Park can be reached by the following routes:

BUSES: There is a regular service of buses departing from Dundee City Centre into Forfar. The bus station in the town is about half a mile from the ground. There is also a local service.

TRAINS: The nearest railway station is Dundee (14 miles away) and fans who travel to here should then board a bus for Forfar from the city centre. Arbroath station is also about 14 miles away.

CARS: There are car parking facilities in adjacent streets to the ground and also in the Market Muir car park.

Hamilton Academical

The Ballast Stadium,
New Douglas Park, Cadzow Avenue,
Hamilton, ML3 0FT

CHAIRMAN
Dr. Jan W. Stepek

VICE-CHAIRMAN
George McLachlan

DIRECTORS
William A. Donnelly C.A.
& William Sherry

SECRETARY
Scott A. Struthers, B.A.(Hons)

HON. LIFE PRESIDENT
Dr. Alexander A. Wilson

MANAGER
Alistair Dawson

ASSISTANT MANAGER
Robert Prytz

RESERVE TEAM COACHES
Robert Prytz & Chris Hillcoat

YOUTH DEVELOPMENT MANAGER
Bobby Jenks

YOUTH TEAM COACHES
Bobby Jenks (U18), Chris Hillcoat (U16),
Robert McMillan (U15),
Pat Savage (U14), George Muir (U13)

COMMERCIAL MANAGER
Christopher Norris
(B) (01698) 286103, (M) 07957 478468

STADIUM MANAGER
John Queen

HON. MEDICAL OFFICER
Dr. Brian Lynas

PHYSIOTHERAPIST/COACH
Jim Fallon

**FOOTBALL SAFETY OFFICERS'
ASSOCIATION REPRESENTATIVE,
MEDIA LIAISON OFFICER &
MATCHDAY PROGRAMME EDITOR**
Scott A. Struthers, B.A. (Hons)
(01698) 286103

KIT CONTROLLER
Jim Kennedy

**KIT DEPT., ADMINISTRATION
ASSISTANT, INTERNET DEPT
& PLAYER**
Gary Johnstone

ADMINISTRATION ASSISTANT
Cheryl McSeveny

TELEPHONES
Ground (01698) 368650
Club Office (01698) 286103
(Fax-Office) (01698) 285422
Information Service 09068 666492

CLUB SHOP
"The Acciesshop",
Hamilton Academical F.C.,
c/o The Ballast Stadium,
New Douglas Park, Cadzow Avenue,
Hamilton, ML3 0FT

OFFICIAL SUPPORTERS CLUB
Jim Galloway, Secretary, HAFC
Supporters Club, 3 Pitcairn Terrace,
Burnbank, Hamilton

TEAM CAPTAIN
Jim Sherry

SHIRT SPONSOR
Ballast Construction

KIT SUPPLIER
TFG

LIST OF PLAYERS 2001-2002

SURNAME	FIRST NAME	MIDDLE NAME	DATE OF BIRTH	PLACE OF BIRTH	DATE OF SIGNING	HEIGHT FT INS	WEIGHT ST LBS	POS. ON PITCH	PREVIOUS CLUB
Ajet	Wale	Kwick	27/10/77	Glasgow	02/08/01	5 11.0	11 7	Fwd	Queen's Park
Armstrong	Gareth	James	31/08/80	Irvine	06/07/01	5 11.0	11 3	Fwd	Ayr United
Bonnar	Martin	Michael	12/01/79	Bellshill	02/07/97	5 7.0	9 7	Mid	X Form
Boyle	Gerard		17/04/82	Bellshill	15/05/01	5 8.0	9 7	Fwd	Morriston Y.M.C.A.
Callaghan	Stuart		20/07/76	Calderbank	28/10/00	5 9.0	11 10	Mid	Clydebank
Cornwell	Steven		12/08/83	Motherwell	18/05/01	6 2.0	11 3	Mid	Unattached
Cunnington	Edward		12/11/69	Bellshill	05/07/01	5 8.5	12 0	Def	Ross County
Davidson	Scott	Joseph	20/08/83	Bellshill	15/05/01	5 6.0	9 7	Fwd	Albion Rovers Youth
Davidson	William	Andrew	01/12/77	Bellshill	08/08/96	5 10.0	11 5	Fwd	X Form
Dobbins	Ian	Alexander	24/08/83	Bellshill	15/05/01	6 2.0	11 7	Def	Albion Rovers
Gaughan	Paul		27/09/80	Glasgow	04/09/97	6 2.0	13 0	Def	West Park United B.C.
Graham	Alisdair		17/08/80	Lanark	19/07/01	5 10.0	10 7	Fwd	Heart of Midlothian
Grant	David		03/07/82	Bellshill	12/08/00	5 10.5	10 8	Def	X Form
Hogg	Keith	Rodger	23/01/80	Lanark	05/07/00	6 0.0	12 0	Def	Ayr United
Johnstone	Richard	Gary	29/01/82	Bellshill	15/05/01	5 5.0	10 2	Def	Queen's Park
Lurinsky	Alexander		22/07/82	Broxburn	15/05/01	5 7.0	10 2	Fwd	Ayr United
Macfarlane	Ian	John P.	05/12/68	Bellshill	06/03/99	6 2.0	13 3	Gk	Glenafton Athletic
MacLaren	Ross	Stewart	09/07/81	Bellshill	25/08/97	6 1.0	11 10	Def	S Form
Martin	Michael	Benjamin	23/05/81	Glasgow	22/10/98	5 8.0	10 7	Def	Preston North End B.C.
McCreadie	Iain	Hugh	20/01/82	Kilmarnock	04/09/99	5 8.5	10 7	Mid	Kello Rovers
McDonald	Paul	Thomas	20/04/68	Motherwell	27/07/01	5 6.5	10 2	Fwd	Morton
McFarlane	David	Thomas M.	10/04/79	Glasgow	06/08/96	5 11.0	12 2	Fwd	S Form
McShane	John		27/01/83	Bellshill	15/05/01	5 8.0	9 10	Mid	Queen's Park
Moore	Michael	Jordan	24/03/81	Paisley	16/12/98	6 0.0	11 9	Fwd	Unattached
Nelson	Mark	John	09/08/69	Bellshill	06/07/00	5 11.0	12 7	Def	Alloa Athletic
O'Neil	Kris		29/09/80	Edinburgh	19/07/01	5 7.0	10 11	Fwd	Heart of Midlothian
Oliver	Neil		11/04/67	Berwick-upon-Tweed	18/01/01	5 11.0	12 3	Def	Berwick Rangers
Potter	Graham	Joseph	04/06/79	Rutherglen	14/07/00	6 0.0	13 0	Gk	Annan Athletic
Renicks	Steven	John	28/11/75	Bellshill	01/06/94	5 8.5	10 8	Def	Hamilton Academical B.C.
Russell	Allan	John	13/12/80	Glasgow	02/07/99	6 0.0	12 1	Mid	Hibernian
Sherry	James	Cunningham	09/09/73	Glasgow	15/12/00	5 8.0	12 6	Mid	Portadown
Stewart	Colin		10/01/80	Middlesbrough	17/08/01	6 3.0	12 12	Gk	Kilmarnock
Sullivan	Nicholas		21/10/83	Lanark	15/05/01	5 11.0	11 7	Mid	Wishaw B.C.
Thomson	Stewart	Braidwood	24/12/82	Motherwell	15/05/01	5 11.0	13 4	Gk	Netherdale Community A.F.C
Vaugh	Brian	James	22/08/78	Belfast	25/07/00	6 0.0	12 0	Mid/Fwd	Cowdenbeath
Walker	John		12/12/73	Glasgow	08/06/01	5 7.0	10 6	Mid	Clydebank
Walker	Leonard	Anthony	07/09/83	Glasgow	15/05/01	5 9.0	12 0	Fwd	Leeds United Youths

Milestones

YEAR OF FORMATION: 1874
MOST CAPPED PLAYER: Colin Miller (Canada)
NO. OF CAPS: 29
MOST LEAGUE POINTS IN A SEASON: 57 (First Division – Season 1991/92)(2 Points for a Win)
        76 (Third Division – Season 2000/01)(3 Points for a Win)
MOST LEAGUE GOALS SCORED BY A PLAYER IN A SEASON: David Wilson (Season 1936/37)
NO. OF GOALS SCORED: 35
RECORD ATTENDANCE: 28,690 (-v- Heart of Midlothian – Scottish Cup 3.3.1937 at Douglas Park)
    4,280 (-v- Sunderland – Opening of The Ballast Stadium 28.7.2001)
RECORD VICTORY: 10-2 (-v- Cowdenbeath – Division 1, 15.10.1932)
RECORD DEFEAT: 1-11 (-v- Hibernian – Division 1, 6.11.1965)

The Accies' ten year league record

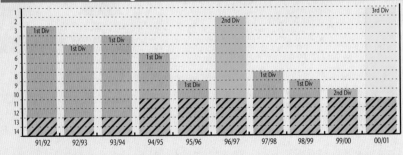

THE ACCIES' CLUB FACTFILE 2000/2001
RESULTS... APPEARANCES... SCORERS... ATTENDANCES...

BELL'S
SCOTTISH FOOTBALL LEAGUE

Date	Venue	Opponents	Att.	Res	MacFarlane I.	Nelson M.	Lynn G.	Davidson W.	Gaughan P.	Vaugh B.	Bonnar M.	Sherry J.	Eadie A.	McFarlane D.	Russell A.	Kelly R.	Clark C.	Grant D.	Moore M.	Hillcoat C.	Maclaren R.	Martin M.	Potter G.	Callaghan S.	Prytz R.	Renicks S.	Hogg K.	Thomson S.	Downs R.	Oliver N.	Kerr D.	Lumsksy A.
Aug 5	H	Dumbarton	588	2-0	1	2	3	4	5	6	7	8	9¹	10	11¹	16																
12	A	Elgin City	1,552	2-0	1	3¹	11	4	5		8		9	14¹	6	12	2	7	10	16												
19	H	Montrose	426	6-0	1	3	11			8	6	15	12³	9²		2	7	10¹	14													
26	A	East Stirlingshire	435	0-0	1	6	3	4	5	11	8		10	7	15	12	2	9														
Sep 9	H	Albion Rovers	487	0-2	1	6	3	4	5	11	8	10	15	7		14	2	9	12													
16	A	Cowdenbeath	448	0-2	1	6	3		5	11		10	8	7		12	2	9	4	15	16											
23	H	Peterhead	369	3-0	2¹			5	16	11¹	7		10			12	9	4	6		1	3	8¹	15								
30	A	East Fife	549	2-1	1	2		5¹	16	11	7		10	14			9	4	6			3¹	8	15								
Oct 7	H	Brechin City	422	4-1	1	2¹		5	11			14	10	7¹			9¹	4	6			3¹	8									
14	A	Dumbarton	368	3-2	1	2		5	11¹			14	10	7		12¹	9¹	4	6			3	8									
21	H	Elgin City	414	4-1	1	2		5	11			14	10	7			9³	4	6			3¹	8									
24	H	East Stirlingshire	344	4-0	1	2¹		5	11				10	7		12	9²	4	6			3¹	8		15							
Nov 4	H	Albion Rovers	608	1-1	1	2¹		5	11			14	10	7		12	9		6			3	8		4							
11	A	Peterhead	790	1-1	1	2		5	11			12	10	7			6		9			3	8¹		4							
18	H	Cowdenbeath	598	0-0	1	2		5	14	11			10			7	6		9		12	3	8		4							
25	H	Brechin City	483	0-0	1	2		8	5	15	11		10	12		7	6		9		14	3			4							
Dec 2	H	East Fife	518	1-1	1	2		8	5	15	11		12¹	10	7		6		9			3			4	17						
16	H	Dumbarton	485	2-0	1	2		7	5		11	8	9	10²	16		6		12			3			4							
Jan 2	H	Albion Rovers	540	3-2	1	2			5		11	8	9¹	10¹	7¹		6		12			3			4		15					
20	H	Peterhead	645	†3-0	1				5		11	8		10¹	7¹				9		2	3							4	6		
27	A	East Stirlingshire	346	4-1	1			16	5		11	8		10³	7				9		2	3¹							4	6		
Feb 3	H	Brechin City	521	†1-0	1			16	5		11	8	12	10	7				9		2	17			3				4	6		
17	H	Montrose	411	1-3	1			14	5		11	8	12	10¹	7				9		2	3							4	6	16	
Mar 10	H	East Stirlingshire	388	2-2	1			14	5	8	11			10	7				9¹		2	3¹							4	6	16	
17	A	Peterhead	710	1-2	1	14		4	5		11	8			7		12¹		9		2	3						10		6	16	
20	A	Cowdenbeath	429	1-1	1	2		4	5		6			9			8				7	11¹						10	3			
25	A	Albion Rovers	524	1-0	1	2		4	5		6			9		14	12				7	11¹						10	3			
27	A	East Fife	353	†4-1	1¹	2		4	5		6			10¹		14	9				7	11						12	3¹			
31	A	Cowdenbeath	666	0-0	1	2		4	5		6			12	9	14	8				7	11						10	3			
Apr 7	H	Brechin City	586	4-2	1	2		4	5			8	12	10²	6				9		7	11¹		2	15			14	3¹			
10	H	Elgin City	542	3-0	1			4	5	11		8		10¹	6				9²		7			2				14	3			
14	H	East Fife	507	1-1	1			5		16	8		10¹	6					9		7	11		2	4		15	3				
21	A	Dumbarton	864	2-1	1			5		6	8	14	10¹	7					9		4	11		2				3¹			
28	H	Elgin City	773	3-0	1			5		6	8¹	9	10²	7					4		17	11		2				3	15		
May 1	H	Montrose	495	2-0	14			5		6	8	9	10¹	7					4¹	12	1	11		2				3	15		
5	H	Montrose	916	4-1				5		6	8	9	10³	7					15¹		1	11		2				3			
TOTAL FULL APPEARANCES					33	23	6	15	36	3	33	20	11	30	22	7	12	5	27	7	11	13	3	29	9	7	8		4	5	17
TOTAL SUB APPEARANCES						(2)		(4)		(5)	(1)		(12)	(4)	(2)	(6)	(8)		(4)	(3)	(1)	(5)	(2)		(2)	(2)	(1)	(5)			(5)
TOTAL GOALS SCORED					1	5		1			2	1	3	24	6		2		12		1	9		2					3		

Small bold figures denote goalscorers. † denotes opponent's own goal.

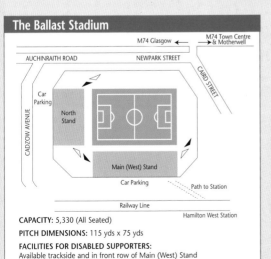

The Ballast Stadium

M74 Glasgow ←
→ M74 Town Centre & Motherwell

AUCHINRAITH ROAD
NEWPARK STREET
CAIRD STREET
Car Parking
North Stand
CADZOW AVENUE
Main (West) Stand
Car Parking
Path to Station
Railway Line
Hamilton West Station

CAPACITY: 5,330 (All Seated)

PITCH DIMENSIONS: 115 yds x 75 yds

FACILITIES FOR DISABLED SUPPORTERS:
Available trackside and in front row of Main (West) Stand

Team playing kits

How to get there

The following routes may be used to reach The Ballast Stadium:

TRAINS: Hamilton West Station is situated adjacent to the ground. Normally there are 2 trains per hour to Glasgow, Lanark (change at Motherwell) and Motherwell. A path connects the station to the ground.

BUSES: Buses from across Lanarkshire and Glasgow pass close to the ground. Buses from across Scotland and the UK call at Hamilton Bus Station 1mile away.

CARS: Exit M74 at Junction 5 (A725 Coatbridge – East Kilbride Road goes through this interchange as well). Follow signs for Hamilton Racecourse and Football Traffic. Turn right at lights at Racecourse and first right again into New Park Street. Stadium is on the left.

The Accies

email: info@sfl.scottishfootball.com • website: www.scottishfootball.com

Morton

Cappielow Park, Sinclair Street,
Greenock, PA15 2TY

CHAIRMAN
Douglas D.F. Rae

DIRECTORS
Iain Brown, Jim McColl,
Arthur Montford & James Pickett

SECRETARY
Janey Rankin

MANAGER
Peter Cormack

ASSISTANT MANAGER
David McPherson

**HEAD OF YOUTH
DEVELOPMENT/CHIEF SCOUT**
Jim Blyth

U-18 YOUTH TEAM COACH
David McPherson

CLUB DOCTOR
Dr. R. Craig Speirs

CROWD DOCTOR
Dr. Fraser Gray

PHYSIOTHERAPIST
George Hannah

GROUNDSMAN
Ian Lyle

**FOOTBALL SAFETY OFFICERS'
ASSOCIATION REPRESENTATIVE**
Michael Grana

KIT MANAGER
Andy Bryan

STADIUM MANAGER
Alex Renfrew

MATCHDAY PROGRAMME EDITOR
James Pickett (01475) 631046

TELEPHONES
Ground/Ticket Office
(01475) 723571
Fax (01475) 781084

CLUB SHOP
Morton F.C. Cappielow Park, Sinclair
Street, Greenock

OFFICIAL SUPPORTERS CLUB
Morton Supporters Club,
Regent Street, Greenock

TEAM CAPTAIN
David McPherson

SHIRT SPONSOR

KIT SUPPLIER
Pro Star

LIST OF PLAYERS 2001-2002

SURNAME	FIRST NAME	MIDDLE NAME	DATE OF BIRTH	PLACE OF BIRTH	DATE OF SIGNING	HEIGHT FT INS	WEIGHT ST LBS	POS. ON PITCH	PREVIOUS CLUB
Bannerman	Scott	John	21/03/79	Edinburgh	03/08/01	5 7.0	11 0	Def	Airdrieonians
Bottiglieri	Emilio	Hugh	13/04/79	Port Hardy, Can.	03/08/01	5 8.0	11 0	Def	East Fife
Coyle	Craig	Robert	06/09/80	Edinburgh	03/08/01	5 11.0	12 0	Gk	Raith Rovers
Frail	Stephen	Charles	10/08/69	Glasgow	03/08/01	6 0.0	11 13	Def	St. Johnstone
Gibson	John		20/04/67	Blantyre	03/08/01	5 10.0	11 3	Mid	Stenhousemuir
Greacen	Stewart		31/03/82	Lanark	03/08/01	6 2.0	13 4	Def	Livingston
Kearney	Darren		16/09/82	Coatbridge	03/08/01	5 8.0	10 0	Mid	St. Johnstone
MacGregor	David	George	09/06/81	Greenock	03/08/01	5 11.0	11 10	Mid	S Form
McAneny	Paul	James	11/11/73	Glasgow	03/08/01	5 11.0	13 0	Mid	Stenhousemuir
McPherson	David		28/01/64	Paisley	08/08/01	6 3.0	14 4	Mid	Carlton Soccer Club
Miller	Scott	Kerr	04/05/75	Glasgow	03/08/01	5 10.0	11 0	Fwd	Stenhousemuir
Moore	Allan		25/12/64	Glasgow	03/08/01	5 7.0	10 4	Fwd	Partick Thistle
O'Connor	Sean		07/07/81	Wolverhampton	03/08/01	6 3.0	13 0	Fwd	Dundee United
Redmond	Gavin	Christopher	09/11/83	Paisley	07/08/01	6 0.0	11 0	Fwd	St. Mirren B.C.
Reid	Alan		21/10/80	Paisley	03/08/01	5 8.0	10 0	Fwd	Hibernian
Ross	Keith	James W.	24/05/80	Irvine	03/08/01	6 2.0	12 7	Gk	Troon JFC
Tweedie	Garry		02/01/81	Ayr	07/08/01	5 11.0	11 7	Mid	Ayr Boswell

Milestones

YEAR OF FORMATION: 1874
MOST CAPPED PLAYER: Jimmy Cowan
NO. OF CAPS: 25
MOST LEAGUE POINTS IN A SEASON: 69 (Division 2 – Season 1966/67)
MOST LEAGUE GOALS SCORED BY A PLAYER IN A SEASON: Allan McGraw (Season 1963/64)
NO. OF GOALS SCORED: 58
RECORD ATTENDANCE: 23,500 (-v- Celtic – 1922)
RECORD VICTORY: 11-0 (-v- Carfin Shamrock – Scottish Cup, 13.11.1886)
RECORD DEFEAT: 1-10 (-v- Port Glasgow Athletic, 5.5.1884)

The Ton's ten year league record

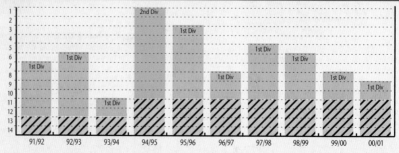

THE TON'S CLUB FACTFILE 2000/2001
RESULTS... APPEARANCES... SCORERS... ATTENDANCES...

BELL'S — SCOTTISH FOOTBALL LEAGUE

Small bold figures denote goalscorers. † denotes opponent's own goal.

Date	Venue	Opponents	Att.	Res	Boswell M.	Naylor M.	Davies D.	Anderson D.	Raeside R.	Medou-Oyte P.	Browning A.	Millen A.	Whalen S.	Boukraa K.	Curran H.	Matheson R.	McDonald P.	Murie D.	Aitken S.	Kerr B.	MacDonald S.	Tweedie G.	Carlin A.	Robb W.	Easton S.	MacGregor D.	Wingate D.	Beattie D.	James K.	McDonald K.	McConalogue S.	Paterson S.	Redmond G.	Maxwell A.	Webster S.	Broadfield G.
Aug 5	H	Livingston	1,729	0-2	1	2	3	4	5	6	7	8	9	10	11	15	14																			
12	A	Falkirk	2,563	0-1	1	2	3	4	5	6		8	16	10	7	9	11																			
19	H	Alloa Athletic	1,267	2-0	1	14	3	5	4			8	9^1	16	6	10	11^1	2	7																	
26	A	Clyde	1,480	3-0	1		3	5	4			8	9^2	16	6	10^1	11	2	7																	
Sep 9	A	Ross County	1,187	0-1	1		3	5	4			8	9	12	6	10	11	2	7	16															
16	H	Ayr United	1,308	1-1	1		3	5	4			8	9^1	10	6		11	2	12	16	7															
23	A	Raith Rovers	2,078	1-0	1	16	3	5	4			8	9^1	10	6	14	11	2			7															
30	H	Airdrieonians	1,377	1-5	1		3	14	5	4		8	9	10^1	6	7	11	2	12			16														
Oct 7	A	Inverness Cal. Th.	1,439	0-4	1		3	5				8	9	10	6	12	11	2	7		4	15														
14	A	Livingston	3,468	0-1		2		4	5			8	9	10	6	14		3	7			11	1													
21	H	Falkirk	1,503	0-4	14		3	5	4			8	9	10	6	13		2	7			11	1													
28	H	Clyde	1,051	1-1				5^1	6			9	10		7	11	2	8			4	1	3													
Nov 4	A	Ross County	2,048	1-3			3	5				8		10	6	9^1	11	2	7			4	1													
11	H	Raith Rovers	742	1-2			3	4	5			6	9	10	8	7^1	11	2			14	12	1													
18	A	Ayr United	2,256	1-1	14		3	4	5			9	12	6^1	10	11		7			2	8	1													
25	H	Inverness Cal. Th.	708	2-0			3	4^1	5	14		9	12	6	10	11	15	7^1			2	8	1													
Dec 2	A	Airdrieonians	1,643	1-1			3	4	5			6	9	14	10	11	12	7^1			2	8	1													
9	A	Alloa Athletic	704	1-2			3	4^1	5			6	9	14	10	11	12	7			2	8	1													
16	H	Livingston	888	1-2			3		5				9^1	11		7		2	8	1		4	6	10												
Jan 2	A	Ayr United	2,866	0-6	2	3						8	9	11		7		6		1	4	12	5	10												
6	A	Raith Rovers	1,721	0-0	3							8	10	11		7		4	12	1		2				5	6	9								
13	H	Airdrieonians	2,602	0-3	3	11			15			8	10			2	14	4	16	1		7				5	6	9								
Feb 3	A	Alloa Athletic	1,179	1-1			3	5				9^1	8		11	2	7	12		1		4					10	6	16							
17	A	Clyde	1,609	1-1			3	5				9^1	8			2	7	11	12	1		10				4	6	15								
24	H	Clyde	1,221	0-1	15		3	5				9	8			2	7	11		1		12				4	10	6	16							
Mar 13	A	Inverness Cal. Th.	1,016	2-4			3	5				9				7^1	11^1	2	14	6	15	1					10	4	8							
17	H	Raith Rovers	947	1-1	14		3	5				9				7^1	11	2	12	15	6						10	4^2	8			1				
27	A	Falkirk	1,276	†3-1	11		3	5				9				2	7	6	12	1						10	4	8								
31	A	Ayr United	2,111	0-3	11		3	5				9				2	7	15	6	12	1					10	4	8								
Apr 7	H	Inverness Cal. Th.	931	0-3	4		3	5				9				2	7	11	6	8	1					10		14		17						
14	A	Airdrieonians	1,331	2-0	4		3^1	5				9	12			2	7	11^1	6							10		8	15		1	16				
17	A	Ross County	1,894	2-0	4		3	5				9^2	12			2	7	11	6							10		8			1	16				
21	A	Livingston	2,727	0-2	4		3	5				9	12			2	7	11	6							10		8	16		1	15				
24	H	Ross County	812	0-3	4		3	5				9	12			2	7	11	6	15						10		8			1					
28	H	Falkirk	905	2-1			3		5			9^1	11			2^1	7^1	12	6	3		4				10		8^1								
May 5	H	Alloa Athletic	770	3-0					5			9	11^1			2^1	7^1	12	6	3		4				10		8	14	1						
TOTAL FULL APPEARANCES					9	4	20	29	33	10	1	15	21	11	21	27	23	27	27	5	24	11	20	5	15	1	1	9	2	4	11	2	1	6	
TOTAL SUB APPEARANCES					(4)	(2)	(1)				(1)	(2)	(7)		(5)	(5)	(3)	(4)	(6)	(2)	(10)				(2)							(6)	(1)	(1)	(3)
TOTAL GOALS SCORED							3	1				7	1	1		9	3	1	3	1									2			1		

Cappielow Park

SINCLAIR STREET

& Limited space – Application only

CAPACITY: 7,890; Seating 5,890, Standing 2,000
PITCH DIMENSIONS: 110 yds x 71 yds
FACILITIES FOR DISABLED SUPPORTERS:
Seating facilities below Grandstand.

Team playing kits

How to get there

Cappielow Park may be reached by the following routes:

BUSES: Services from Glasgow stop just outside the park. There are also services from Port Glasgow and Gourock.

TRAINS: The nearest local station is Cartsdyke and it is a five minute walk from here to the ground. There are two to three trains every hour from Glasgow and from Gourock.

CARS: There is no official car park and fans should park in Sinclair Street beyond the railway station.

The Ton

email: info@sfl.scottishfootball.com • website: www.scottishfootball.com

Queen of the South

Palmerston Park, Terregles Street,
Dumfries, DG2 9BA

CHAIRMAN
Ronald Bradford

VICE-CHAIRMAN
Thomas G. Harkness

DIRECTORS
Keith M. Houliston & Craig Paterson

COMPANY SECRETARY
Richard Shaw, M.B.E.

MANAGER
John Connolly

ASSISTANT MANAGER
Ian Scott

FIRST TEAM COACH
Warren Pearson

CLUB COACHES
Gordon Hyslop, Gordon Doig,
Fred Smith, George Paterson,
Tony Wilby & Tim Leighfield

YOUTH TEAM COACHES
Gordon Hyslop (U18), Tony Wilby (U15),
George Paterson (U14)

MATCH ANALYST
Iain McChesney

CLUB DOCTORS
Dr. Andrew Downie & Dr. Bill Balfour

PHYSIOTHERAPIST
Kenneth Crichton

**FOOTBALL SAFETY OFFICERS'
ASSOCIATION REPRESENTATIVE**
George Galbraith (01387) 254853

CHIEF SCOUT
Warren Pearson

GROUNDSMAN
Kevin McCormick

COMMERCIAL MANAGER
Margaret Heuchan (H) (01556) 504569
(B) (01387) 254853

COMMERCIAL DEPT.
Ian Heuchan

MEDIA LIAISON OFFICER
Bill Goldie (01387) 265569
(M) 07733 203171

MUSEUM CURATOR
Ian Black

MATCHDAY PROGRAMME EDITOR
Bruce Wright (B) (01387) 262960
(H) (01387) 252400 (F) (01387) 261112

TELEPHONES
Ground/Ticket Office/Information Service
(01387) 254853
Football Office Only (01387) 251666
Restaurant (01387) 252241
Fax (01387) 254853

E-MAIL & INTERNET ADDRESS
mail@qosfc.co.uk
www.qosfc.co.uk

CLUB SHOP
Palmerston Park, Terregles Street,
Dumfries, DG2 9BA (01387) 254853
Open 9.00am – 4.00pm Mon. to Fri.
and 1.30pm – 5.00pm on home
match days.

OFFICIAL SUPPORTERS CLUB
c/o Palmerston Park, Terregles Street,
Dumfries, DG2 9BA

TEAM CAPTAIN
Jim Thomson

SHIRT SPONSOR
Armstrong Waste Management Ltd

KIT SUPPLIER
FILA

LIST OF PLAYERS 2001-2002

SURNAME	FIRST NAME	MIDDLE NAME	DATE OF BIRTH	PLACE OF BIRTH	DATE OF SIGNING	HEIGHT FT INS	WEIGHT ST LBS	POS. ON PITCH	PREVIOUS CLUB
Aitken	Andrew	Robert	02/02/78	Dumfries	10/07/96	6 0.0	12 7	Def	Annan Athletic
Allan	Derek		24/12/74	Irvine	14/06/01	6 0.0	12 8	Def	Kingstonians
Armstrong	Graeme		28/06/83	Hexham	31/07/00	6 0.0	12 8	Mid	Haltwhistle United
Atkinson	Patrick		22/05/70	Singapore	31/07/00	5 10.0	11 10	Def	Blyth Spartans
Campbell	Jamie		02/12/80	Glasgow	30/03/01	6 5.0	15 0	Gk	Clydebank
Connell	Graham		31/10/74	Glasgow	11/01/01	5 11.0	11 7	Mid	Queen's Park
Connelly	Gordon		01/11/76	Glasgow	01/08/01	6 0.0	12 7	Mid	Carlisle United
Connolly	Stuart	Robert	05/05/78	Birmingham	11/07/01	5 10.0	12 2	Fwd	Life University U.S.A.
Crawford	Jonathan		14/10/69	Johnstone	31/05/01	6 1.0	11 7	Def	Arbroath
Davidson	Stuart	William	03/08/79	Glasgow	17/07/01	5 8.0	11 10	Mid	Airdrieonians
Feroz	Craig		24/10/77	Aberdeen	24/08/01	5 10.0	12 0	Fwd	Livingston
Gibson	William		06/08/84	Dumfries	27/09/00	5 8.0	10 0	Mid	Maxwelltown Thistle
Gray	Alan		02/05/74	Carlisle	07/06/01	6 1.0	12 3	Def	Workington A.F.C.
Hawke	Warren	Robert	20/09/70	Durham	17/12/99	5 10.5	11 4	Fwd	Morton
Hogg	Alan		27/10/77	Ashington	03/08/01	5 10.0	12 10	Fwd	Ashington
Lennox	Thomas		02/02/84	Lanark	26/07/01	5 9.0	9 5	Def	Form D Under 16
McDonald	Raymond		15/02/81	Irvine	27/07/00	5 7.0	12 4	Fwd	Bonnyton Thistle
McGhie	Gareth		22/02/82	Ashington	03/08/01	6 0.0	12 3	Mid	Sunderland
McKeown	Desmond	Michael	18/01/70	Glasgow	24/11/00	5 11.0	11 11	Def	Partick Thistle
O'Neil	John	Joseph	03/01/74	Glasgow	09/01/01	5 11.0	12 0	Mid	Ross County
Patterson	Mark		15/05/79	Consett	31/07/01	5 9.0	11 10	Mid	Brandon United
Robertson	Stuart	Eric	27/12/84	Irvine	19/07/01	6 0.0	12 0	Gk	S Form
Scott	Colin	George	19/05/70	Glasgow	03/11/00	6 2.0	14 0	Gk	Clydebank
Sloan	Steven	George	21/03/84	Dumfries	26/07/01	5 8.0	8 11	Mid	S Form
Sunderland	Jonathan		02/11/75	Newcastle-upon-Tyne	25/07/00	6 0.0	12 0	Mid	Ashington
Thomson	James		15/05/71	Stirling	23/05/01	6 1.0	12 7	Def	Arbroath
Weatherson	Peter		29/05/80	North Shields	04/08/00	6 0.0	12 3	Fwd	Newcastle Blue Star

Milestones

YEAR OF FORMATION: 1919
MOST CAPPED PLAYER: William Houliston
NO. OF CAPS: 3
MOST LEAGUE POINTS IN A SEASON: 55 (Division 2 – Season 1985/86)
MOST LEAGUE GOALS SCORED BY A PLAYER IN A SEASON: Jimmy Gray (Season 1927/28)
NO. OF GOALS SCORED: 37
RECORD ATTENDANCE: 24,500 (-v- Heart of Midlothian – Scottish Cup, 23.2.1952)
RECORD VICTORY: 11-1 (-v- Stranraer – Scottish Cup, 16.1.1932)
RECORD DEFEAT: 2-10 (-v- Dundee – Division 1, 1.12.1962)

The Doonhamers' ten year league record

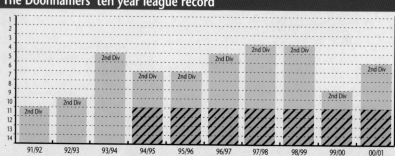

BELL'S ® SCOTTISH FOOTBALL LEAGUE

Date	Venue	Opponents	Att.	Res	Mathieson D.	Atkinson P.	Hodge S.	Aitken A.	Martin A.	Sunderland J.	Boyle D.	Nelson A.	Weatherson P.	Hawke W.	Weir M.	Muir D.	Nixon P.	Caldwell B.	Pickering S.	Young K.	Atkinson R.	Preen S.	Greacen S.	Patterson D.	Davidson S.	Suddick J.	McQuilter R.	Skinner S.	Kinnaird P.	Creaney G.	McKeown D.	Milne J.	O'Neil J.	Connell G.	Hogg A.	Angel M.	Scott C.	King S.	Hughes M.	Walkate S.	Campbell J.	Armstrong G.	Paterson G.	Gibson W.
Aug 5	A	Stenhousemuir	520	3-4	1	2	3	4¹	5¹	6¹	7	8	9	10	11	12	15	16																										
12	H	Stirling Albion	1,168	0-0	1	7	3	4	6	8	15	14	9	12	11	5	2	10																										
19	A	Queen's Park	839	0-1	1	8	3	6	5	7	9	10	11	4	14	2	16	15																										
26	A	Clydebank	273	2-1	1	8	3	6	5¹	12	16	9¹	11	4	2	15	7	10																										
Sep 9	H	Stranraer	1,630	1-4	1	2	12	5	6	8	9	7	4	15	14¹	2	11	10																										
16	A	Berwick Rangers	572	4-0	1	3	11	5	4	8	12¹	10¹	7	6¹	16	2	15	9¹																										
23	H	Forfar Athletic	1,167	0-1	1	3	11	5	14	8	12	10	15	7	6	2	9	4																										
30	A	Arbroath	667	0-2		3	5	15	16	9	8	9	8	11	10	2	7	6	4	14																								
Oct 7	A	Partick Thistle	1,499	1-2	1	11¹	5	6	9	8	12	10	2	4	3	7	15																											
14	H	Stenhousemuir	1,013	†4-2	1	11	4	6	10³	12	8	14	2	3	7	9	5																											
21	A	Stirling Albion	748	1-0	1	11	5	6	10	16¹	8	14	2	3	7	9	4																											
28	H	Clydebank	1,156	1-1	1	11	5	6	15	10¹	8	14	2	3	7	9	4	16																										
Nov 4	A	Stranraer	767	†2-3	1	11	5	6	10	8	14	2	3	7	9¹	4	16																											
11	A	Forfar Athletic	440	1-0	1	3	5	6	10	8	16¹	2	7	9	4	11																												
18	H	Berwick Rangers	1,238	2-1	1	3	5	6	10²	8	12	14	2	7	9	4	11	16																										
25	A	Partick Thistle	2,610	1-2	1	5	12	10	8¹	14	6	2	7	9	4	16	11	3																										
Dec 2	H	Arbroath	1,087	1-1	1	5	6	10	8	11¹	2	3	7	9	4	16																												
23	H	Queen's Park	1,288	1-1	1	2	5	6	9¹	8	12	7	14	15	4	10	11	3																										
Jan 2	A	Stranraer	1,643	†2-3	1	2¹	5	6	7	10	3	9	4	14	11	8	15	16																										
Feb 3	H	Partick Thistle	2,432	1-3	1	2	5	6	10	15	4	14	3	7¹	8	9	11																											
17	A	Queen's Park	711	1-2	1	2	5	6	10¹	9	14	4	3	7	8	1	11¹	15																										
24	H	Stirling Albion	1,157	†2-1	1	2	5	6	10	9	14	4	3	7	8¹	1	11																											
Mar 6	A	Stenhousemuir	250	2-1	1	2	5	10¹	9	6	4	3	7¹	8	11	12																												
10	H	Clydebank	1,022	1-0	1	2	5	6	3	10	9	14	4	7¹	8	15	11	12																										
13	A	Clydebank	245	2-1	1	2	5	6	11	12	9	15	4	3	7¹	8¹	10																											
17	H	Forfar Athletic	974	2-3	1	2	5	6	12	10¹	9	16	4	3	7¹	8	11	14																										
20	A	Arbroath	698	2-5	1	5	11	10	9	12	2	4	3	7	8	14¹	6¹	15																										
25	A	Berwick Rangers	608	2-2		5	10¹	9	6	4	3	7¹	8	14	1	11	2																											
31	H	Berwick Rangers	984	3-3	2	5	6	9¹	12	4	7¹	8	10	11	3	115¹																												
Apr 3	A	Stranraer	600	0-2	2	5	6	9	14	4	12	7	8	11	10	3	1																											
7	A	Partick Thistle	3,810	2-0	2	5	10	9	11	6	14	4	3	7²	8	1																												
14	H	Arbroath	1,141	1-0	2	5	10	9	11	6	15¹	4	12	7	8	3	1																											
21	H	Stenhousemuir	1,111	1-3	2	5	10	11	6	9	12	4	3	7¹	15	8	1																											
28	A	Stirling Albion	587	1-1	2	5	6	10¹	9	4	2	3	7	8	12	16	14	1	11																									
May 1	A	Forfar Athletic	522	1-3		5	6	9¹	10	2	3	7	8	4	1	11																												
5	H	Queen's Park	1,176	0-1	2	5	15	9	4	3	7	8	14	6	1	10	11	16																										
TOTAL FULL APPEARANCES					25	29	7	35	7	26	4	43	31	29	4	12	7	5	20	1	3	4	3	7	9	9	24	1	5		16		17	16	2	4	3	6	3	6	8	1	3
TOTAL SUB APPEARANCES					(1)		(5)	(3)	(3)	(3)	(1)	(7)	(11)	(5)	(7)	(2)	(1)			(2)		(2)		(5)	(1)	(1)	(2)	(1)	(1)		(6)	(1)		(5)	(1)		(1)		(1)		
TOTAL GOALS SCORED						2		1	2	1		16	3			2	3			1					1						10	2	1	1		1				1	

Small bold figures denote goalscorers. † denotes opponent's own goal.

Palmerston Park

PORTLAND DRIVE

NEW EAST STAND

TERREGLES STREET

CAPACITY: 6,412; Seated 3,509, Standing 2,903

PITCH DIMENSIONS: 112 yds x 73 yds

FACILITIES FOR DISABLED SUPPORTERS: Situated in East Stand.

Team playing kits

How to get there

Palmerston Park can be reached by the following routes:

TRAINS: There is a reasonable service to Dumfries Station from Glasgow on Saturdays, but the service is more limited in midweek. The station is about ¾ mile from the ground.

BUSES: Buses from Glasgow, Edinburgh, Ayr and Stranraer all pass within a short distance of the park.

CARS: The car park may be reached from Portland Drive or King Street and has a capacity for approximately 174 cars.

The Doonhamers

email: info@sfl.scottishfootball.com • website: www.scottishfootball.com

Stenhousemuir

Ochilview Park, Gladstone Road,
Stenhousemuir, FK5 4QL
CHAIRMAN
A. Terry Bulloch
DIRECTORS
David O. Reid, John Rolland (Treasurer),
James S. B. Gillespie, Martin I. McNairney,
Graeme Mackie, Jack T. Gammie
& Michael R. Laing
SECRETARY
David O. Reid
GENERAL MANAGER
George W. Peat C.A.
MANAGER
Brian Fairley
ASSISTANT MANAGER
Alan McGonigal
FOOTBALL DEVELOPMENT OFFICER
Gordon Buchanan
YOUTH INITIATIVE DIRECTOR
Martin I. McNairney
YOUTH DEVELOPMENT OFFICER
Tom Elliott
**YOUTH DEVELOPMENT INITIATIVE
ADMINISTRATOR**
Bill Darroch
YOUTH TEAM COACHES
Gordon Buchanan (U18), Tom Elliott (U16),
James Gordon (U15) & Brian Glasgow (U14)
GOALKEEPING COACH
Alan Banner
CLUB DOCTOR
Dr. Steven Brown
PHYSIOTHERAPIST
Mrs. Lee Campbell
COMMERCIAL MANAGER
John Rolland (01324) 562992
CHIEF SCOUT
Alan Fraser
GROUNDSMAN
James Cuthill
**FOOTBALL SAFETY OFFICERS'
ASSOCIATION REPRESENTATIVE**
Jack T. Gammie (01786) 819920
MEDIA LIAISON OFFICER
David Reid (0141) 566 8231
MATCHDAY PROGRAMME EDITOR
Margaret Kilpatrick (01324) 562992
TELEPHONES
Ground (01324) 562992
Fax (01324) 562980
Sec. Home (01324) 714833
Sec. Bus. (0141) 566 8231
E-MAIL & INTERNET ADDRESS
stenhousemuir.fc@talk21.com
CLUB SHOP
Ochilview Park, Gladstone Road,
Stenhousemuir, FK5 4QL.
(01324) 562992.
Open during first team home
match days between 2.00pm until
5.00pm & Mon to Fri 9.00am till
5.00pm. Contact Mrs M. Kilpatrick
OFFICIAL SUPPORTERS CLUB
Ochilview Park, Gladstone Road,
Stenhousemuir, FK5 4QL
SUPPORTERS CLUB CHAIRMAN
Harry Larkin
WARRIORS ABROAD
contact Alan McNeil
TEAM CAPTAIN
Jimmy Sandison
SHIRT SPONSOR
Butts of Stroud
KIT SUPPLIER
SECCA

LIST OF PLAYERS 2001-2002

SURNAME	FIRST NAME	MIDDLE NAME	DATE OF BIRTH	PLACE OF BIRTH	DATE OF SIGNING	HEIGHT FT INS	WEIGHT ST LBS	POS. ON PITCH	PREVIOUS CLUB
Abbott	Gordon	Thomas K.	24/02/79	Edinburgh	02/03/01	5 11.0	11 7	Mid	Linlithgow Rose Ath. JFC
Alexander	Andrew		01/08/83	Edinburgh	14/08/00	6 3.0	13 7	Gk	Crammond B.C.
Black	Gregor		07/10/83	Falkirk	14/08/00	5 10.0	10 7	Fwd	Stenhousemuir B.C. U'16s
Cormack	Peter	Robert	08/06/74	Liverpool	14/07/00	6 1.0	12 2	Def	Ross County
Davidson	Graeme		18/01/68	Edinburgh	21/08/98	5 10.0	11 4	Def	Livingston
Donald	Barry		24/12/78	Glasgow	13/01/01	6 1.0	12 0	Mid	Campsie Black Watch
Donald	Graeme	Still	14/04/74	Stirling	25/05/01	6 0.0	12 7	Def	Stirling Albion
Donaldson	Euan	Gordon	20/08/75	Falkirk	24/05/01	5 10.0	11 0	Mid	Forfar Athletic
English	Isaac		12/11/71	Paisley	06/07/00	5 9.5	11 7	Mid/Fwd	Partick Thistle
Ferguson	Ian		05/08/68	Dunfermline	14/06/01	6 1.0	13 7	Fwd	Forfar Athletic
Forrest	Fraser	Wilson	14/09/83	Galashiels	14/08/00	6 1.5	12 0	Def	Berwick Rangers
Graham	David		02/06/83	Stirling	06/07/01	5 9.0	10 12	Fwd	Dunipace JFC
Graham	Marc	John	15/07/77	Kirkcaldy	17/07/01	6 3.0	13 4	Gk	Hill of Beath Hawthorn
Graham	Steven		03/08/83	Falkirk	01/08/00	5 11.0	11 4	Def	Heart of Midlothian
Jackson	Christopher	Robert	29/10/73	Edinburgh	08/02/01	5 7.0	11 0	Mid	East Fife
Johnston	Steven		27/01/83	Livingston	14/08/00	5 8.0	9 5	Def	Albion Rovers
Manson	Robert		16/01/83	Edinburgh	27/06/00	5 9.0	10 0	Mid	Crammond B.C.
McColl	Dean	Aron W.	12/07/83	Falkirk	09/08/01	5 8.0	12 2	Mid	Pumpherston JFC
McGurk	Ryan		06/06/81	Edinburgh	03/07/01	6 4.0	11 7	Gk	Oakley United JFC
Miller	Paul		14/05/83	Falkirk	26/06/99	5 9.0	10 4	Fwd	Gairdoch United
Mooney	Martin	James	25/09/70	Alexandria	31/07/99	5 7.5	11 0	Fwd	Dumbarton
Murphy	Scott		01/12/83	Bellshill	20/08/00	5 8.0	10 4	Mid	Cumbernauld United
O'Rourke	Ryan		01/06/83	Glasgow	14/08/00	5 11.0	10 7	Mid	Cumbernauld United
Sandison	James	William	22/06/65	Edinburgh	08/02/01	5 10.5	12 2	Def	Airdrieonians
Shanks	Paul		01/03/84	Dunfermline	24/05/01	6 0.0	11 2	Mid	Stenhousemuir Form D U16
Shearer	Gary		26/06/80	Paisley	26/07/01	5 9.0	11 2	Mid	Eadie Star Juveniles
Stacey	Steve		21/04/83	Edinburgh	27/06/00	6 1.0	11 7	Fwd	Crammond B.C.
Stone	Michael		15/01/79	Stirling	24/07/01	6 1.0	13 7	Def	Doncaster Rovers
Storrar	Andrew	David	06/10/77	Stirling	11/08/00	5 6.0	11 4	Def	East Stirlingshire
Vella	Simon		19/09/79	London	24/08/01	6 2.0	13 5	Def	Sutton United
Wood	Christopher	Alan	29/09/79	Stirling	20/07/01	5 11.0	12 12	Fwd	Alloa Athletic

Milestones

YEAR OF FORMATION: 1884
MOST LEAGUE POINTS IN A SEASON: 50 (Division 2 – Season 1960/61) (2 Points for a Win)
64 (Third Division – Season 1998/99) (3 Points for a Win)
MOST LEAGUE GOALS SCORED BY A PLAYER IN A SEASON: Evelyn Morrison (Season 1927/28) and
Robert Murray (Season 1936/37)
NO. OF GOALS SCORED: 31
RECORD ATTENDANCE: 12,500 (-v- East Fife – 11.3.1950)
RECORD VICTORY: 9-2 (-v- Dundee United – Division 2, 16.4.1937)
RECORD DEFEAT: 2-11 (-v- Dunfermline Athletic – Division 2, 27.9.1930)

The Warriors' ten year league record

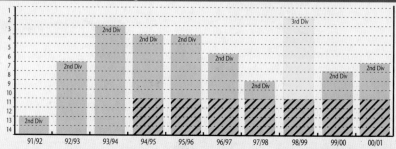

THE WARRIORS' CLUB FACTFILE 2000/2001
RESULTS... APPEARANCES... SCORERS... ATTENDANCES...

BELL'S — SCOTTISH FOOTBALL LEAGUE

Date	Venue	Opponents	Att.	Res	Cow G.	Davidson G.	Fisher J.	McAneny P.	Cormack P.	Ferguson P.	Mooney M.	McKinnon C.	English I.	Menelaws D.	Wood D.	Lorimer D.	McLauchlan M.	Gibson L.	Donald B.	Storrar A.	Pittman S.	Duncan G.	Miller S.	Graham T.	Gibson J.	Smith C.	Henderson N.	Blaikie A.	Fallon S.	Mensing S.	Sandison J.	McColligan B.	Jackson C.	Abbott G.	Henry J.	McGurk R.	Murphy S.
Aug 5	H	Queen of the South	520	4-3	1	2	3	4	5	6	7	8	9[1]	10[2]	11[1]	12	14	16																			
12	A	Clydebank	236	0-1	1	2	3	4	5			8	15	9	10	11	12	16	6	7																	
19	H	Partick Thistle	1,130	4-0	1	2	3	4	5[1]		7	8[1]	9[1]	10	11	14	16[1]		6	12																	
26	A	Forfar Athletic	381	2-2	1	2	3	4	5		12	8[1]	11[1]	10	14	9	15		6	7	3																
Sep 9	H	Stirling Albion	594	0-2	1					7	8	9	10	11	14	6	3		2	10	16																
16	A	Arbroath	541	0-3	1	2			5			8	9	14	11	16	15	3	7	10	4	6															
23	H	Berwick Rangers	428	2-0	1			2	5	6[1]	8[1]	12	9	11		7	14		10	4	3																
30	A	Queen's Park	793	0-2	1			2	5	6	8	12	9	11		7	14		10	4	3	16															
Oct 7	H	Stranraer	277	1-2	1			4	5	7	8	14	11	15[1]	9	6	3	2	10	16																	
14	A	Queen of the South	1,013	2-4	1			4	16	14	8	12				6	3	2	10[1]	5	9	7	11[1]														
21	H	Clydebank	450	2-1	1	6		4	16		8	12[2]				10	2	9	5	3	7	11															
28	H	Forfar Athletic	321	2-0	1	6		4			8	11[1]				10	15	2	9[1]	5	3	7	12														
Nov 4	H	Stirling Albion	645	3-2	1	6		4	3	15	8	11[2]	16			10	2	9	5		7	12[1]															
11	A	Berwick Rangers	424	1-4	1	6		4	3	6	8	11[1]	15			10	14	2	9	5	7	12															
18	H	Arbroath	369	3-1	1	6		4	3	7		10[2]	15	16	8		2	9[1]	5	12	11																
25	A	Stranraer	454	4-1	1	6		4[1]	3	7	8	11[2]	15		10		2	9[1]	5																		
Dec 2	H	Queen's Park	492	1-1	1	6		4	3	7	8	11			10		2	9[1]	5																		
26	A	Partick Thistle	2,635	0-3	1	6		4	3	7	8	11	16		10		2	9	5					15	14												
Jan 2	H	Stirling Albion	573	1-1	1	6	11	4	3	7	12[1]		10	15	8		2	9	5					15	16												
6	A	Forfar Athletic	441	0-7	1	6	11	4	3	14	8	10	15	12			2	9	5					7													
13	A	Arbroath	575	0-5	1	11	12	6	7	16	8	10	15				2	4	9	5					3												
Feb 3	H	Stranraer	351	2-2	1	4		12		14	11	15		8	2	9[1]		7	10[1]		3	5	6														
10	A	Queen's Park	704	2-1	1	4			10[1]					8	2	15	9[1]		7	14	3	5	6	11	16												
17	H	Partick Thistle	1,343	2-0	1	4				8[1]	11[1]	15		2	14	9		10		5	6	3	7														
Mar 6	H	Queen of the South	250	1-2	1	4		11				11	12	8	2	14	9		10	16	5	6	3[1]	7	16												
10	A	Forfar Athletic	376	0-1	1	4						11	12	8	2		9		10	16	5	6	3	14	7												
13	H	Berwick Rangers	345	0-2	1	4						10	11	8	2	15	9		12		5	6	3	7	14												
17	A	Berwick Rangers	402	0-1	1	4				8		10	11		2	14	9		12		5	6	3	7	15												
27	A	Clydebank	256	0-1	1		11			8		12	9	4	2	14	15				5	6	3	7	10												
31	H	Arbroath	475	0-1	1	4	15					11	12	8	2						5	6	3	7	9	10											
Apr 3	H	Stirling Albion	390	0-0	1	6	3						11	8	2	9	16				5	4	12		7	10											
7	A	Stranraer	365	1-2	1	4	14					11[1]	8	2	9	15				5	6	3	16	7	10											
14	A	Queen's Park	519	2-0	1	4	3		16	11		8	2	9[1]	10				5[1]	6		7														
21	A	Queen of the South	1,111	3-1	1	4[1]	3		16	11[2]	8	2	9	10			5	6		7	15																
28	H	Clydebank	404	0-0	4	3					15	11		2	9	10	5	6	8	7	14	1	16														
May 5	H	Partick Thistle	4,624	0-4	4	12					10		11		8	2	9		15	5	6	3	7	1													
TOTAL FULL APPEARANCES					34	27	11	19	19	9	9	19	28	11	8			2	2	26	20	3	16	30	15	6	1	14	3	3	15	15	11	10	5	3	2
TOTAL SUB APPEARANCES						(3)	(1)	(2)	(4)	(5)	(3)	(5)	(14)	(1)	(3)	(3)	(7)	(2)	(5)		(5)	(1)	(1)		(2)	(9)	(7)			(1)	(3)	(5)				(1)
TOTAL GOALS SCORED						1			1	1		1	5	18	2	1	1			1					8				1	2		1		1		

Small bold figures denote goalscorers.   † denotes opponent's own goal.

Ochilview Park

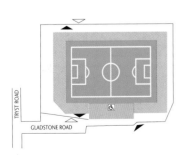

TRYST ROAD
GLADSTONE ROAD

CAPACITY: 2,396; Seated 626, Standing 1,770
PITCH DIMENSIONS: 110 yds x 72 yds
FACILITIES FOR DISABLED SUPPORTERS:
Accommodation for disabled in new Stand. Toilet facilities also provided.

Team playing kits

How to get there

Ochilview Park can be reached by the following routes:

TRAINS: The nearest station is Larbert, which is about 1 mile away from the ground.

BUSES: There are regular bus services from Falkirk.

CARS: There is a large car park on the north side of the ground.

email: info@sfl.scottishfootball.com • website: www.scottishfootball.com

Stranraer

Stair Park, London Road,
Stranraer, DG9 8BS

CHAIRMAN
Robert J. Clanachan

VICE-CHAIRMAN
James Bark

COMMITTEE
George F. Compton, James T. Robertson,
Thomas Rice, James Hannah,
Leo R. Sprott, Alexander McKie,
Nigel C. Redhead,
Thomas L. Sutherland &
R. A. Graham Rodgers

SECRETARY
R. A. Graham Rodgers

MATCH SECRETARY
James T. Robertson

MANAGER
William McLaren

GOALKEEPER COACH/KIT MAN
John Taylor

YOUTH COACHES
Barney Duffy, John Pollock,
Nish Walker & Seamus Donnelly

CLUB DOCTORS
Dr. R. Spicer & Dr. N. Balmer

PHYSIOTHERAPIST
Alan Anderson

**FOOTBALL SAFETY OFFICERS'
ASSOCIATION REPRESENTATIVE**
David Kirkwood

GROUNDSMAN
Murray Gibson

COMMERCIAL MANAGER
Thomas L. Sutherland
Bus (01776) 889000

MATCHDAY PROGRAMME EDITOR
R.A. Graham Rodgers
(01776) 702194

TELEPHONES
Ground (01776) 703271
Sec. Home/Ticket Office/
Information Service (01776) 702194
Fax (01776) 702194

CLUB SHOP
Situated at Ground.
Open 2.30pm – 3.00pm
and at half-time on home matchdays

SFC SOCIAL CLUB
Situated in North Strand Street,
Stranraer
(01776) 704121

TEAM CAPTAIN
Billy Macdonald

SHIRT SPONSOR
Stena Line

KIT SUPPLIER
ICIS

LIST OF PLAYERS 2001-2002

SURNAME	FIRST NAME	MIDDLE NAME	DATE OF BIRTH	PLACE OF BIRTH	DATE OF SIGNING	HEIGHT FT INS	WEIGHT ST LBS	POS. ON PITCH	PREVIOUS CLUB
Aitken	Stephen	Smith	25/09/76	Glasgow	10/07/01	5 8.0	11 1	Mid	Morton
Blair	Paul		05/07/76	Greenock	12/02/00	5 9.0	11 8	Mid/Fwd	Morton
Farrell	David	John	29/10/69	Glasgow	06/03/01	5 9.0	11 4	Def	Airdrieonians
Finlayson	Kevin	Charles	07/12/79	Glasgow	10/07/01	5 9.0	10 10	Fwd	Queen's Park
Gallagher	Mark	Andrew	06/12/74	Irvine	07/06/01	6 2.0	12 10	Fwd	Queen's Park
Gaughan	Kevin		06/03/78	Glasgow	28/07/01	6 1.0	12 9	Def	Stirling Albion
George	Duncan	Henry	04/12/67	Paisley	01/08/97	5 10.0	10 7	Mid	Ayr United
Grace	Alexander		20/03/74	Vale of Leven	20/01/01	5 7.0	11 6	Mid	Dumbarton
Harty	Ian	McGuinness	08/04/78	Bellshill	02/07/98	5 8.0	10 7	Fwd	Albion Rovers
Hodge	Sandy	George	04/10/80	Lanark	11/11/00	6 3.0	13 0	Def	Queen of the South
Jenkins	Allan	David	07/10/81	Stranraer	03/09/98	6 1.0	12 4	Mid	Ayr Boswell
Johnstone	Douglas	Iain	12/03/69	Irvine	30/01/98	6 2.0	12 8	Def	Morton
Macdonald	William	James	17/09/76	Irvine	26/11/99	5 8.0	11 0	Mid	Clydebank
McGeown	Mark		10/05/70	Paisley	30/07/99	5 10.5	12 0	Gk	Stirling Albion
O'Neill	Stephen		30/06/75	Paisley	30/07/99	6 0.0	13 0	Gk	Renfrew Juniors
Paterson	Andrew		05/05/72	Glasgow	10/07/00	5 9.5	11 12	Def	Stirling Albion
Shaw	George		10/02/69	Glasgow	18/08/01	5 7.0	11 6	Fwd	Partick Thistle
Sherry	Mark		11/01/82	Glasgow	04/08/01	5 8.0	10 7	Mid	Clyde
Weir	Mark	John	30/03/80	Lanark	22/12/00	5 9.0	12 0	Mid	Queen of the South
Wingate	Derek		26/09/75	Glasgow	10/07/01	6 2.0	13 0	Def	Benburb JFC
Wright	Fraser		23/12/79	East Kilbride	03/09/98	5 10.0	11 10	Def	St. Mirren B.C.

Milestones

YEAR OF FORMATION: 1870
MOST LEAGUE POINTS IN A SEASON: 56 (Second Division – 1993/94)(2 Points for a Win)
61 (Second Division – 1997/98)(3 Points for a Win)
MOST LEAGUE GOALS SCORED BY A PLAYER IN A SEASON: Derek Frye (Season 1977/78)
NO. OF GOALS SCORED: 27
RECORD ATTENDANCE: 6,500 (-v- Rangers – 24.1.1948)
RECORD VICTORY: 7-0 (-v- Brechin City – Division 2, 6.2.1965)
RECORD DEFEAT: 1-11 (-v- Queen of the South – Scottish Cup, 16.1.1932)

The Blues' ten year league record

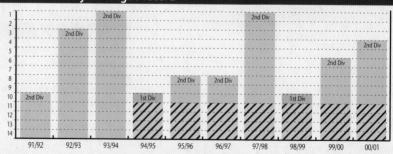

THE BLUES' CLUB FACTFILE 2000/2001
RESULTS... APPEARANCES... SCORERS... ATTENDANCES...

BELL'S SCOTTISH FOOTBALL LEAGUE

Date	Venue	Opponents	Att.	Res	McGeown M.	Paterson A.	Johnstone D.	Knox K.	McDonald G.	George D.	Walker P.	Macdonald W.	Harty I.	Geraghty M.	Blaikie A.	Blair P.	Wright F.	McCormick S.	Hughes M.	Rae D.	Bryce T.	McMillan A.	Edgar S.	McQuilter R.	McLauchlan M.	Stewart P.	Hodge S.	Stirling J.	Jenkins A.	O'Neill S.	Weir M.	Grace A.	Farrell D.	McGowan N.
Aug 5	H	Forfar Athletic	397	2-0	1		3	4	5	6	7	8	9[1]	10[1]	11	12																		
12	A	Partick Thistle	2,357	1-2	1	2		5	4	7	6	9[1]	8	15	11	3		10	14															
19	H	Berwick Rangers	386	2-2	1	2		4	3	6[1]	11[1]	8	9	10	12	7		5	16															
26	H	Arbroath	426	2-1	1	2			5	4	6	11[1]	8	9[1]		14	7	3		10														
Sep 9	A	Queen of the South	1,630	4-1	1	11		2	4	3	8	7[2]		9	10[1]	14[1]		6	5															
16	H	Queen's Park	587	3-0	1		3	2	4	5	6[1]	7[2]	10	9	11		14	8								12	16							
23	A	Stirling Albion	763	0-2	1	2		4	5		6	7	9	10	14	11	3											8	12	15				
30	A	Clydebank	551	0-2	1			5	4	12	6	8	9	10	11	7	3			14										2	15			
Oct 7	A	Stenhousemuir	277	2-1	1		2	3			8	10[1]	5	9[1]	11		7	6								15			4					
14	A	Forfar Athletic	405	0-0	1		2	4		5	7	6	9			8	3		14	10										11	17			
21	H	Partick Thistle	1,101	0-3	1		2	3	5	6	8	4	9	10		7	11		14	16														
28	A	Arbroath	528	1-1	1		2	4	5	8		6	9[1]		11	7	3		15	10										12	17			
Nov 4	H	Queen of the South	767	3-2	1		2	5[1]	4	6	11[1]	7[1]	9			10	3		8															
11	H	Stirling Albion	441	1-1	1			3	2	5[1]	8	6	9	14		7	4		10	12										11				
18	A	Queen's Park	753	2-1	1			2			5	10	8	9		7	4			6									3	11[2]				
25	H	Stenhousemuir	454	1-4	1			2		5	7	6[1]	9	10		4			8									15	3	11				
Dec 5	H	Clydebank	126	3-2	1			2[1]		5[1]	7	6	9	16[1]		4			10	8								15	3	11	14			
16	H	Forfar Athletic	419	3-1	1			5	3	4	10[1]	6	9	12		7[1]	2		8[1]									15		11				
Jan 2	A	Queen of the South	1,643	3-2	1			6	2	3	11[1]	8	9[2]			5			10										4	7	17			
13	H	Queen's Park	556	0-1	1			4	2	5	6		9	10		7	3										12		11	8	1	14		
Feb 3	A	Stenhousemuir	351	2-2	1			4	2		5	8	9			7	3		12										11	6[2]	17	10		
17	H	Berwick Rangers	447	1-1	1			2		5	7	6	9	14		3												4	10[1]	11	8		
24	A	Partick Thistle	2,959	0-3	1			4	2		5	14	8	9		3			12	17								7		11	6			
Mar 6	H	Clydebank	363	0-0	1	7		2		5	14	6	9			3			10									8		11		4		
10	A	Arbroath	670	1-2	1	7	2	5[1]		8	14	6	9			3			10	16										11	12	4		
13	A	Stirling Albion	448	1-0	1		2	5		8	10	6	9[1]	14		3												11		12	7	4		
17	H	Stirling Albion	446	0-3	1			2	4	8	10		9	12		3		14										11			6	5		
20	A	Berwick Rangers	471	1-1	1	2	5			8	7	6	9[1]			3												11		10	7	4		
25	A	Arbroath	394	0-1	1	7	2	5		8		6	9	14		3			16						10					1	17	8	4	11
31	A	Queen's Park	619	0-1	1	7	3	2		6	12		9	14		5									10					1	17	8	4	11
Apr 3	A	Queen of the South	600	2-0	1			2		5	8	7	9[2]			3			14						10					1		6	4	11
7	H	Stenhousemuir	365	2-1	1			2		5	7	8	9			3			14						10				17[1]	1		6	4[1]	11
14	A	Clydebank	159	0-0	1		2			5	7	10	9	17		3												8	1	11		4	6	
21	A	Forfar Athletic	378	3-2	1		2	6	3		7	8				17	5[1]		14									9		1	10	12	4[1]	11[1]
28	H	Partick Thistle	928	3-4				3	2		7[2]					8	5		14									17		1	8	6	4	11
May 5	A	Berwick Rangers	545	2-0				3	2		10		9[1]			7	5[1]		12											1	8	6	4	11
TOTAL FULL APPEARANCES					28	11	23	34	15	32	27	29	35	13	2	18	35	1	8	6	1			1	5	8	7	11	8	8	10	13	7	
TOTAL SUB APPEARANCES						(1)		(4)			(10)	(5)	(3)			(1)	(2)	(8)	(9)	(2)	(2)					(5)	(3)		(4)	(1)	(4)	(2)	
TOTAL GOALS SCORED							3			4	12	2	13	3	1	1	2			1								2	4			2	1

Small bold figures denote goalscorers. † denotes opponent's own goal.

Stair Park

LONDON ROAD — ENTRY FOR VISITING SUPPORTERS

NORTH STAND

SOUTH STAND

ENTRY TO SOUTH STAND FOR VISITING SUPPORTERS

CAPACITY: 5,600; Seated 1,830, Standing 3,770

PITCH DIMENSIONS: 110 yds x 70 yds

FACILITIES FOR DISABLED SUPPORTERS:
By prior arrangement with Club Secretary.

Team playing kits

How to get there

Stair Park can be reached by the following routes:

TRAINS: There is a regular service of trains from Ayr and the station is only 1 mile from the ground.

BUSES: Two services pass the park. These are the buses from Glenluce to Portroadie and the Dumfries-Stranraer service.

CARS: Car parking is available in the Public Park at the ground, where there is space for approximately 50 vehicles and also in the side streets around the park. Signs for away supporters will be displayed and parking situated at Stranraer Academy, McMasters Road.

The Blues

ALLOA ATHLETIC
SEASON TICKET INFORMATION

SEATED	ADULT	£150
	JUVENILE/OAP	£80
STANDING	ADULT	£140
	JUVENILE/OAP	£70

LEAGUE ADMISSION PRICES

SEATED	ADULT	£10
	JUVENILE/OAP	£6
STANDING	ADULT	£9
	JUVENILE/OAP	£5

COWDENBEATH
SEASON TICKET INFORMATION

SEATED	ADULT	£130
	(including all cup ties)	
	JUVENILE/OAP	£60

LEAGUE ADMISSION PRICES

SEATED	ADULT	£9
	JUVENILE/OAP	£4.50
STANDING	ADULT	£8
	JUVENILE/OAP	£4

BERWICK RANGERS
SEASON TICKET INFORMATION

	BELL'S SECOND DIV GAMES ONLY	PRE-SEASON FRIENDLIES & BELL'S SECOND DIVISION
SEATED AND STANDING		
ADULT	£120	£135
CONCESSIONS	£60	£70
(Includes Juvenile/OAP/Unemployed with UB40/Registered Disabled)		
FAMILY TICKET (1 ADULT/2 JUVENILES)		
	£150	£170
PLUS £10 FOR EACH ADDITIONAL JUVENILE		
OR £30 EACH ADDITIONAL ADULT.		
JUVENILE TICKETS ON REQUEST		

LEAGUE ADMISSION PRICES
SEATED AND STANDING

ADULT	£8
CONCESSIONS	£4
PRESIDENT'S BOX	
PRICES ON APPLICATION	

N.B. All fans for Stand enter via either Ground 'A', 'B' or 'E' and transfer to Stand.

FORFAR ATHLETIC
SEASON TICKET INFORMATION

SEATED	ADULT	£130
	JUVENILE/OAP	£65
	JUVENILE (U-12)	£40
STANDING	ADULT	£120
	JUVENILE/OAP	£60
	JUVENILE (U-12)	£40

LEAGUE ADMISSION PRICES

SEATED	ADULT	£8.50
	JUVENILE/OAP	£4.50
STANDING	ADULT	£8
	JUVENILE/OAP	£4

CLYDEBANK

SEASON TICKET INFORMATION

NO SEASON TICKETS WILL BE SOLD UNTIL FURTHER NOTICE

LEAGUE ADMISSION PRICES
SEATED

ADULT	£10
JUVENILE/OAP	£5
2 PARENTS & JUVENILE (U-11)	£15
1 PARENT & 1 JUVENILE (U-11)	£10

Queen of the South's Palmerston Park

Hamilton Academical's Ballast Stadium

HAMILTON ACADEMICAL
SEASON TICKET INFORMATION
SEATED

ADULT	£150
JUVENILE /OAP	£75
JUVENILE (U-14)	£40
ADULT AND JUVENILE (U-14)	£160

LEAGUE ADMISSION PRICES
SEATED
WEST (MAIN) STAND

ADULT	£10
JUVENILE (U-16)/OAP	£5

NORTH STAND

ADULT	£9
JUVENILE (U-16)/OAP	£4

MORTON
SEASON TICKET INFORMATION
SEATED

GRANDSTAND (Sections A & B)	
ADULT	£120
CONCESSIONS (Excluding Unemployed)	£60
PARENT & JUVENILE	£150
GRANDSTAND (Sections C & D Numbered Seats)	
ADULT	£140
CONCESSIONS	£70
PARENT & JUVENILE	£180
FAMILY	£320

STANDING

ADULT	£80
CONCESSIONS	£40

LEAGUE ADMISSION PRICES
SEATED

GRANDSTAND (Sections A,B,E & F)	
ADULT	£9.00
CONCESSIONS (OAP, Unemployed & Juveniles U15)	£4.50
PARENT & JUVENILE	£11.00

STANDING

ADULT	£7.00
CONCESSIONS	£3.50
PARENT & JUVENILE	£8.50

STENHOUSEMUIR
SEASON TICKET INFORMATION
SEATED

ADULT	£130
JUVENILE/OAP/STUDENT	£65
FAMILY FLEXI - ADD £30 FOR EACH ADDITIONAL FAMILY MEMBER (UP TO 4 PERSONS) TO A FULL PRICE SEASON TICKET	

STANDING

ADULT	£100
JUVENILE/OAP/STUDENT	£50

LEAGUE ADMISSION PRICES
SEATED

ADULT	£9
JUVENILE/OAP	£5

STANDING

ADULT	£8
JUVENILE/OAP	£4

QUEEN OF THE SOUTH
SEASON TICKET INFORMATION

SEATED	ADULT	£140
	JUVENILE (EAST STAND)	£30
	JUVENILE (WEST STAND)	£70
	OAP	£90
STANDING	ADULT	£140
	OAP	£90
	SCHOOL CHILDREN	£30

LEAGUE ADMISSION PRICES

SEATED	ADULT	£9
	SCHOOL CHILDREN/OAP	£6
STANDING	ADULT	£9
	UNEMPLOYED (WITH UB40)/ OAP/FAMILY SUPPLEMENT	£6
	SCHOOL CHILDREN	£3

STRANRAER
SEASON TICKET INFORMATION
SEATED

ADULT	£120
JUVENILE/OAP	£60
FAMILY	£40

STANDING

ADULT	£100
JUVENILE/OAP	£50

LEAGUE ADMISSION PRICES
SEATED

ADULT	£8
JUVENILE/OAP	£4

STANDING

ADULT	£6
JUVENILE/OAP	£3

A True Venue of Legends

Even legends have to move with the times. Alfredo di Stefano and Hampden Park may be inextricably linked with one of football's priceless moments, but neither is willing to halt the path of progress. Even at 75, di Stefano remains the heart and soul of Real Madrid, where he is Honorary President, just as he did on that May evening 41 years ago when Hampden was graced by a European Cup Final dubbed the greatest club match ever seen.

His hat-trick in the 7-3 defeat of Eintracht Frankfurt sealed Real's place in

history, giving the Spanish club the trophy for the fifth successive time. This summer, Real used di Stefano's birthday to announce the capture of Zinedine Zidane from Juventus and the world-record signing of £47.2million was handed his fabled white shirt by none other than the silver-haired legend himself.

Like Hampden, di Stefano is keeping the flame alive. It may come wrapped up in a more expensive garment, but underneath the modern 21st century look is an unquenchable spirit of the past that makes both so special. How fitting it would be if Hampden and di Stefano - with Zidane, of course – could meet for could meet for a

reunion on 15th May, 2002.

The Champions League Final 2002 will mark Hampden's return to the world football stage. It would be fitting if Real were there, though you can catch di Stefano at the stadium almost any time you want. The man feted as one of the greatest players ever is celebrated - along with the others from that 1960 European Cup Final - in the new Scottish Football Museum.

However, while the Champions League Final will undoubtedly be THE special date in Hampden's calendar this season, this is a venue which comes to life on 365 days a year. Rock concerts, conferences, corporate entertaining, American football and even rugby are just some of the reasons Hampden never shuts its doors now. Yet with all of Scotland's football bodies setting up home there and the opening of the museum last May, Hampden remains the place where football comes alive.

Hampden's latest star attraction - which sits underneath the cavernous BT Scotland Stand - cost £6million. Ironically, that brought the bill for the magnificent south stand project to around £48million.........the price of a Zidane.

Being awarded the prestigious Final by UEFA is the icing on the cake for a stadium that has had £70million spent on it. It may no longer be the world's largest ground - as it once was until the Maracana was built in Rio - but it is undoubtedly one of the best.

The 52,046 seats which will be filled next May is a modest total, compared to the 149,547 who saw Scotland play England at the old lady in 1937 when the attendance record was set. But, unlike other old arenas, Hampden has moved with the times and given itself a future.

Part of that future is the museum. A National Stadium can no longer be something that is dusted down and used several times a year, it is a seven-days a week operation. The whole of Scottish football is under one roof, with The Scottish Football Association, The

56

flooding into the ground in 1937 for that remarkable crowd against England.

Having seen other museums around the world, such as Barcelona's Nou Camp, I can only testify that Hampden eclipses them all.

"We are the first national football museum in the world," proclaims the man behind it, Project Director Ged O'Brien. "We are helping to make sense of the heritage of Scotland, and we hope proving Scotland's status as the world's most important football country."

O'Brien's team have recreated the old press box, which for years clung to the roof of the old South Stand, to depict it as it was on the night of the Real-Eintracht game. "Over 250 journalists from around Europe were crammed in there," he observes.

Which brings us neatly back to the Champions League Final. Hampden has already acquitted itself superbly by hosting the last three Tennents Scottish Cup Finals and two CIS Insurance Cup Finals, but knowing that an entire continent nurses dreams of being in the south side of Glasgow next May simply gives David Kells a buzz of anticipation.

"This is going to put Hampden back on the map," he declares. "It is a major event not only for the stadium, but also the city. A lot of football fans from around Europe will come here, generating business for hotels, bars and restaurants.

"There was a lot of criticism about Hampden initially. But we have been running the stadium for a year and staged four concerts, the Mike Tyson fight, the Claymores and, of course, the two domestic Cup Semi-Final and Final ties as well as Scotland international matches. We are always learning.

"Hampden Park Limited has a 20-year lease on Hampden which allows people to be confident when booking events in advance with us," continued Kells.

No doubt that would appeal to Sir Alex Ferguson. Nothing would suit Manchester United's manager more than a Champions League Final in his native Glasgow as a swansong before retiring.

Scottish Football League and The Scottish Premier League all on the sixth floor of the BT Scotland Stand, while the Amateur, Junior, Youth, Women's and Schools' Associations are all down on the third floor.

Hampden, though, no longer just caters for footballers. Rock stars Robbie Williams, Bon Jovi and the Eagles had sell-out 50,000 concerts scheduled at the venue, while the American footballers of the Scottish Claymores also set up home there. The SNP also used the stadium's facilities to stage a conference.

David Kells, the Managing Director of Hampden Park Limited, the company which runs the stadium, feels that many of the football non-believers who have crossed the doors in the last year - whether for concerts or corporate lunches - will be the ones who spread the gospel best about Hampden's resurrection.

"The perception of Hampden is changing," said Kells. "Because of the variety of events we have had here, we have brought a new audience to Hampden who can see what we have to offer.

"The general public's memories and impressions of football grounds are often different to the reality they see at Hampden. Our facilities are second to none."

That is a view shared by David Thomson, The Scottish Football League Assistant Secretary, who guided me around Hampden with the kind of missionary zeal that can only come from

a man who remembers every nook and cranny of the famous old ground. The panoramic view from the SFL's new offices overlooks what was once the red-ash pitches behind the old South Stand where Thomson and many other Glasgow kids came to train with Queen's Park, the club which still remains at the core of Hampden.

"There is not a single seat with a restricted sightline," he says proudly. Indeed, the most expensive ones in the house have a view to die for. The 26 executive boxes in the BT Scotland Stand each have ten seats, a dining table for pre-match meals and a television to catch those replays.

There are 10 lounges - named after Scottish inventors such as Alexander Graham Bell and John Logie Baird - for silver and gold debenture holders, while the North Stand has two equally impressive lounges behind the VIP gantry's 220 padded seats. Ordinary ticket holders are not left out, with more food outlets and toilets than many modern stadia.

All of that, as older fans will testify, is a complete contrast to the way Hampden was. Founded in 1903, it was the third home of Queen's Park but it was for national Cup Finals and Scotland matches that the old grey ground became synonymous.

Those days are wonderfully captured in the Museum - which is covered at greater length elsewhere in this book - with a scene recreating the hordes

PHIL GORDON

57

Albion Rovers

Cliftonhill Stadium, Main Street,
Coatbridge, ML5 3RB

CHAIRMAN
Andrew Dick, M.Sc., B.Sc., C.Eng.

VICE-CHAIRMAN
David T. Shanks, B.Sc.

DIRECTORS
Edward P. Hagerty, Alan M. Brown,
Robert Watt & David Wright

GENERAL MANAGER
John Reynolds

SECRETARY
David T. Shanks, B.Sc.

MANAGER
John McVeigh

ASSISTANT MANAGER
Andy Smith

**YOUTH DEVELOPMENT OFFICER/
U18 YOUTH TEAM COACH**
Jimmy Lindsay

U16 YOUTH TEAM COACH
Paul Smith

U13 YOUTH TEAM COACH
John Bell

PHYSIOTHERAPIST
Dan Young

CHIEF SCOUT
Robert Watt

STADIUM DIRECTOR
Andrew Dick, M.Sc., B.Sc., C.Eng.

**FOOTBALL SAFETY OFFICERS'
ASSOCIATION REPRESENTATIVE**
Edward P. Hagerty (01236) 427671

GROUNDSMAN
Hugh McBride

COMMERCIAL MANAGERS
Denis Newall & Chris Fahey
(01236) 606334

MEDIA LIAISON OFFICER
John Reynolds (01236) 606334

MATCHDAY PROGRAMME EDITOR
Maxwell Crichton (01236) 602552

CLUB STEWARD
Chic Young

HOUSEKEEPER
Wilma McBride

TELEPHONES
Ground (01236) 606334/607041
Telefax (01236) 606334
Sec. Home (01236) 421686
Sec. Bus. (01236) 762775

CLUB SHOP
Cliftonhill Stadium, Main Street,
Coatbridge, ML5 3RB. Open one hour
prior to kick-off at first team home
matches.

OFFICIAL SUPPORTERS CLUB
John Smith, 45 Blair Road, Coatbridge
(01236) 420417

TEAM CAPTAIN
Steven Hamilton

SHIRT SPONSOR
Reigart Demolition

KIT SUPPLIER
SECCA

LIST OF PLAYERS 2001-2002

SURNAME	FIRST NAME	MIDDLE NAME	DATE OF BIRTH	PLACE OF BIRTH	DATE OF SIGNING	HEIGHT FT INS	WEIGHT ST LBS	POS. ON PITCH	PREVIOUS CLUB
Bonar	Paul		28/12/76	Glasgow	27/07/01	6 0.0	11 8	Def	Kirkintilloch Rob Roy
Booth	Mark		07/03/80	Coatbridge	06/07/00	5 9.5	12 0	Mid	Cumbernauld United
Buchanan	John		25/05/84	Edinburgh	18/07/01	5 8.0	11 0	Mid	Hibernian
Carr	David		23/09/83	Bellshill	10/08/01	5 6.0	9 10	Mid	Albion Rovers B.C.
Coulter	James		29/01/83	Bellshill	27/07/01	6 1.0	11 5	Mid	Stonehouse Violet
Cusack	Ryan		15/07/84	Bellshill	07/07/00	5 8.0	9 8	Def	Motherwell B.C.
Diack	Iain	Gordon	17/02/81	Glasgow	21/10/98	5 11.0	10 8	Fwd	Celtic B.C.
Easton	Stewart		10/10/81	Coatbridge	10/01/01	5 9.0	11 2	Mid	Airdrieonians
Fahey	Christopher		28/06/78	Coatbridge	06/07/00	6 1.0	11 12	Gk	Larkhall
Fulton	Michael		25/04/84	Greenock	17/05/00	5 8.0	10 8	Mid	Gourock Y.A.C.
Hamilton	Steven	James	19/03/75	Baillieston	03/08/01	5 9.0	12 5	Mid	Raith Rovers
Harty	Martin	John	11/07/82	Bellshill	21/10/98	5 11.0	10 8	Fwd	Albion Rovers B.C.
Hughes	John	Ronald	15/09/83	Glasgow	17/05/00	5 8.0	10 6	Mid	Heart of Midlothian
Hutcheson	Ceiran		24/03/83	Bellshill	17/05/00	5 6.0	11 0	Def	Heart of Midlothian
Ingram	Stuart		07/11/79	Stockton	23/02/01	6 1.0	12 5	Fwd	Airdrieonians
Lumsden	Todd		06/02/78	Consett	10/08/99	6 2.0	12 10	Def	Stirling Albion
McCaul	Graeme		05/10/84	Edinburgh	30/07/01	5 9.0	10 0	Mid	Heart of Midlothian
McCormick	Steven	Walter	10/11/75	Bellshill	09/12/00	5 6.0	10 0	Fwd	Hamilton Academical
McGhee	Kevin		07/12/84	Bellshill	18/07/01	6 2.0	10 6	Gk	Airdrie B.C.
McGuinness	Mark	Alexander	06/11/83	Glasgow	07/07/00	5 6.0	10 9	Fwd	Heart of Midlothian
McKenna	Gerard		02/02/77	Bellshill	23/02/01	5 9.0	11 4	Mid	Maryhill
McKenzie	James		29/11/80	Bellshill	31/03/00	5 7.5	11 4	Mid/Fwd	Raith Rovers
McKenzie	James		25/02/84	Glasgow	08/09/00	5 10.0	11 0	Gk	Motherwell
McLean	Charles	Crossan N.	08/11/73	Glasgow	27/07/01	5 10.0	11 7	Fwd	Larkhall Thistle
McLees	James	Edward	30/08/80	Coatbridge	21/10/98	5 8.0	10 4	Mid	Lenzie Youth Club
McMillan	James		24/01/84	Bellshill	07/07/00	5 6.0	10 2	Mid	S Form
McMullan	Ryan		26/11/81	Bellshill	14/04/00	5 7.0	9 0	Mid/Fwd	Dundee United
McNab	William		21/01/84	Bellshill	20/05/00	5 9.0	10 10	Def	Albion Rovers B.C.
Murray	Steven		05/07/84	Glasgow	14/03/01	5 4.0	9 5	Def	Motherwell
Rankin	Ian		05/09/79	Bellshill	06/07/00	5 5.5	10 0	Fwd	Airdrieonians
Richardson	Mark		23/02/84	Paisley	18/07/01	5 10.0	11 0	Def	Hibernian
Rodden	Paul	Andrew	12/08/82	Glasgow	12/03/01	5 4.0	11 0	Fwd	Clydebank
Shearer	Scott		15/02/81	Glasgow	06/07/00	6 2.5	11 8	Gk	Tower Hearts
Silvestro	Christopher		16/03/79	Bellshill	15/04/99	5 7.0	10 4	Mid	Glenboig
Smith	Jordan		02/02/82	Bellshill	29/07/99	6 2.0	12 0	Def	S Form
Stewart	Christopher David		21/10/84	Motherwell	22/01/01	5 10.0	10 0	Fwd	S Form
Stirling	Jered		13/10/76	Stirling	12/03/01	5 11.0	12 4	Def	Stranraer
Struthers	William		04/12/81	Bellshill	24/08/01	6 0.0	12 0	Mid	Airdrieonians
Sutherland	David		21/08/82	Glasgow	02/02/00	6 0.0	10 5	Def	X Form
Tait	Thomas		08/09/67	Ayr	29/07/99	5 11.0	12 7	Def	Hamilton Academical
Waldie	Colin		06/02/81	Lanark	06/07/00	5 8.0	11 0	Mid	Raith Rovers
Weir	Mark		04/10/84	Bellshill	22/01/01	5 10.0	10 6	Fwd	S Form

Milestones

YEAR OF FORMATION: 1882
MOST CAPPED PLAYER: John White
NO. OF CAPS: 1
MOST LEAGUE POINTS IN A SEASON: 54 (Division 2 – Season 1929/30)
MOST LEAGUE GOALS SCORED BY A PLAYER IN A SEASON: John Renwick (Season 1932/33)
NO. OF GOALS SCORED: 41
RECORD ATTENDANCE: 27,381 (-v- Rangers 8.2.1936)
RECORD VICTORY: 12-0 (-v- Airdriehill – Scottish Cup, 3.9.1887)
RECORD DEFEAT: 1-11 (-v- Partick Thistle – League Cup, 11.8.1993)

The Wee Rovers' ten year league record

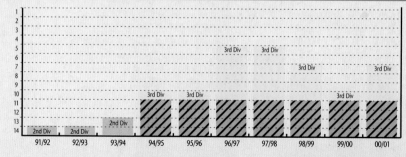

BELL'S SCOTTISH FOOTBALL LEAGUE

Date	Venue	Opponents	Att	Res	Fahey C.	Smith J.	Lumsden T.	Clyde B.	Clark S.	Booth M.	Waldie C.	McKenzie J.	Begue Y.	Rankin I.	Silvestro C.	Diack I.	Martin A.	McLees J.	Tait T.	McMullan R.	Harty M.	Grosset W.	McBride K.	Shields P.	McCormick S.	Easton S.	McKenna G.	Ingram S.	Stirling J.	Coyne T.	Rodden P.	McMillan A.	Deegan C.	Carr D.	Shearer S.
Aug 5	H	East Fife	465	0-1	1	2	3	4	5	6	7	8	9	10	11	15																			
12	A	Cowdenbeath	302	0-5	1	2	3	4	5	6	7	8	9	10	11	14	12	16																	
19	H	Elgin City	412	1-1	1	2	3	4¹		6	8	12	9	16	11		10		5	7															
26	H	Dumbarton	343	0-1	1	2	3	4		6	12	8		13	11	10	9		5	7	16														
Sep 9	A	Hamilton Academical	487	2-0	1	2	3	4		6¹	7	8	9¹	12	11				15	5	10		16												
16	H	Brechin City	254	1-3	1	2	2	4		6¹	7	8	9	12	11				15	5	10		16												
23	A	East Stirlingshire	271	1-1	1	12	3		4	6	2	8	9¹	14	7				10	5				11	16											
30	H	Peterhead	358	0-0	1		3	4	2	6	7	8	9	16	11				12	5				10											
Oct 7	A	Montrose	230	2-0	1		3	4	2	6	7	8		12		16		14¹	5	9	11¹		10												
14	A	East Fife	445	0-0	1		3	4	2	6	7		15	8				11	5	9			10												
21	H	Cowdenbeath	429	1-0	1		3	4	2	6	7			8				11	5	10				9¹											
28	A	Dumbarton	277	1-0	1	12	3	4	2	6	7			14	8			11	5	10			15	9¹											
Nov 4	H	Hamilton Academical	608	1-1	1	12	3	4	2	6	7	16¹		14	8			11	5	10				9											
11	H	East Stirlingshire	334	2-1	1		3	4	2		7	8			16			6¹	5	10	15	11		9¹											
18	A	Brechin City	337	1-2	1		3	4	2		7	8		6	15¹			11	5	10	16			9											
25	H	Montrose	311	3-2	1		3	4	2	6¹	7¹	8			11	15			5	14				9¹	10										
Dec 2	A	Peterhead	516	2-1	1		3	4	2	6¹	7	8			11	16			5	15				9¹	10										
23	H	East Fife	372	1-2	1		2¹	3	4		7		10	16	8				11	5	14				9	15									
Jan 2	A	Hamilton Academical	540	2-3	1		4	3			6	2		15	10	11			5	7	12¹		14¹		9	8									
27	H	Dumbarton	369	1-3	1	4¹			3	6	2			12	15	14		5	10	11					7	8	9								
Feb 3	A	Montrose	244	1-0	1	4			6	2		10			16			11	5	7	12	3			8	15¹	9								
17	H	Elgin City	287	0-1	1			5		6	2	10						4	7					8	11	15	3	9							
24	A	Cowdenbeath	331	0-1	1	2	4			6	7						14	5	10					8	11	9	3	16							
Mar 10	A	Dumbarton	808	4-1	1			2¹		6	7							5	11¹	14²			10		8	9	3				4	16			
13	A	East Stirlingshire	196	0-1	1			2		6	7							5	11	9			10		8		3	16	4						
17	H	East Stirlingshire	248	2-2	1			2		6	7	14						5	11	9			10¹		12	8	3¹	4							
20	H	Peterhead	272	0-1	1			5		6	2	8							7	9			10		12	11	3	16	4						
25	H	Hamilton Academical	524	0-1	1					4	6	2	8						12	9			10		7	11	3		5						
28	A	Elgin City	268	2-1	1			5		2	6¹	7	8					15		14	11		10¹		12		3	9	4						
Apr 7	H	Montrose	213	2-1	1			5		2	6¹	7	12						15	9¹			10		8	11	3	16	4						
10	H	Brechin City	283	1-1	1			5		2	5	9							11	9			10¹		8		3	16	4						
14	A	Peterhead	526	1-1	1			5¹		2	6	7	14		16				11	9					8	15	3	10	4						
17	H	Brechin City	369	2-1	1			5		2	6	7								9			10¹		8¹	11	3		4					16	17
21	A	East Fife	333	1-2	1			5		2	6	7	14		15				16	9			10¹		8	11	3		4						1
28	H	Cowdenbeath	405	0-0	1		2		14	6	7		9	16				5		15			10		8	11	3		4						
May 5	A	Elgin City	487	0-1	16		2			7	6			11	9			5	15	14			10		8		3		4						1
TOTAL FULL APPEARANCES					34	11	33	17	21	33	35	16	11	3	18	3	1	9	26	22	10	3	2	11	15	13	12	4	15	1	2	13			2
TOTAL SUB APPEARANCES					(4)		(1)		(1)	(6)	(1)	(11)	(3)	(10)	(1)	(8)			(7)	(9)	(3)	(2)		(1)	(3)	(2)		(5)		(1)	(1)	(1)		
TOTAL GOALS SCORED						2	2	1		6	1	1	2		1			2		1	4	1	1	5	5	1	1		1					

Small bold figures denote goalscorers. † denotes opponent's own goal.

Cliftonhill Stadium

CAPACITY: 2,496; Seated 538, Standing 1,958
PITCH DIMENSIONS: 110 yds x 72 yds
FACILITIES FOR DISABLED SUPPORTERS:
Access from East Stewart Street with toilet facilities and space for wheelchairs, cars etc. Advanced contact with club advised – this area is uncovered.

Team playing kits

How to get there

The following routes can be used to reach Cliftonhill Stadium:

BUSES: The ground is conveniently situated on the main Glasgow-Airdrie bus route and there is a stop near the ground. Local buses serving most areas of Coatbridge and Airdrie pass by the stadium every few minutes.

TRAINS: The nearest railway station is Coatdyke on the Glasgow-Airdrie line and the ground is a ten minute walk from there. The frequency of service is 15 minutes.

CARS: Vehicles may park in Hillcrest Avenue, Albion Street and East Stewart Street, which are all adjacent to the ground.

The Wee Rovers

email: info@sfl.scottishfootball.com • website: www.scottishfootball.com

Brechin City

Glebe Park, Trinity Road,
Brechin, Angus, DD9 6BJ
CHAIRMAN
David H. Birse
VICE-CHAIRMAN
Hugh A. Campbell Adamson
DIRECTORS
Martin G. Smith (Treasurer),
Calum I. McK. Brown,
Kenneth W. Ferguson,
Stephen D. Mitchell, Henry
G. Stewart & Martin D. Smith
HON. LIFE PRESIDENT
David H. Will
HON. LIFE MEMBERS
David K. Lindsay &
George C. Johnston
SECRETARY
Kenneth W. Ferguson
MANAGER
Richard M. Campbell
ASSISTANT MANAGER
Ian Campbell
U16 YOUTH TEAM COACH
George Shields
CHIEF SCOUT
Frank McGuiness
CLUB DOCTOR
Dr. Archie McInnes
SPORTS THERAPIST
Tom Gilmartin
TRAINER
Alan Grieve
**FOOTBALL SAFETY OFFICERS'
ASSOCIATION REPRESENTATIVE**
Calum Brown (01307) 461222
GROUNDSMAN
Alex Laing
BACKROOM STAFF
Norman Ross & Paul Ross
**COMMERCIAL MANAGER/
MEDIA LIAISON OFFICER**
Steve Mitchell (01356) 626336
MATCHDAY PROGRAMME EDITOR
Martin D. Smith
TELEPHONES
Ground (Matchdays Only) (01356) 622856
Fax (01356) 622856
Sec. Home (01356) 625691
Sec. Bus. (01356) 625285/
(01674) 678910
Sec. Mobile 07803 089060
Sec. Home Fax (01356) 625667
Sec. Bus. Faxes (01356) 625524/
(01674) 678345
E-MAIL/INTERNET ADDRESS
bcfc@glebepk.demon.co.uk
www.brechincity.co.uk
CLUB SHOP
Glebe Park, Brechin, Angus, DD9 6BJ
Open during home match days.
OFFICIAL SUPPORTERS CLUB
c/o Glebe Park, Brechin,
Angus, DD9 6BJ
TEAM CAPTAIN
Harry Cairney
SHIRT SPONSOR
A.P. Jess Scottish Food Group
KIT SUPPLIER
SPALL

LIST OF PLAYERS 2001-2002

SURNAME	FIRST NAME	MIDDLE NAME	DATE OF BIRTH	PLACE OF BIRTH	DATE OF SIGNING	HEIGHT FT INS	WEIGHT ST LBS	POS. ON PITCH	PREVIOUS CLUB
Bain	Kevin		19/09/72	Kirkcaldy	29/07/98	6 0.0	11 9	Def	Stirling Albion
Black	Roddy		22/02/78	Dundee	10/09/95	5 10.0	12 8	Mid	Carnoustie Panmure
Boylan	Paul		04/12/80	Dundee	05/03/99	5 11.0	12 4	Def	Dundee United
Cairney	Henry		01/09/61	Holytown	12/02/92	5 7.0	11 10	Def	Stenhousemuir
Cairns	Mark	Henry	25/09/69	Edinburgh	25/07/01	6 0.0	13 2	Gk	Alloa Athletic
Campbell	Paul	Richard	18/03/80	Kirkcaldy	23/08/00	5 10.0	11 8	Mid	Victoria Rovers
Craig	Douglas	Ewing	30/01/71	London	03/08/01	5 10.0	13 0	Def	Montrose
Dewar	Gary		02/09/81	Dunfermline	12/09/00	5 9.0	10 2	Fwd	Rangers
Donachie	Barry	James T.	21/12/79	Dundee	04/11/99	5 8.0	11 11	Def	Arbroath
Fotheringham	Kevin	George	13/08/75	Dunfermline	15/02/01	5 10.0	12 4	Def/Mid	Arbroath
Grant	Roderick	John	16/09/66	Gloucester	18/01/01	5 11.0	12 7	Fwd	Ayr United
Harris	Paul	Michael	22/01/83	Dundee	03/11/00	5 10.0	10 0	Fwd	S Form
Henderson	Robbie		02/09/81	Perth	18/07/01	5 11.0	11 3	Fwd	Scone Thistle
Honeyman	Ben		14/02/77	Adelaide	29/10/99	5 9.0	12 0	Fwd	East Fife
King	Charles	Alexander	15/11/79	Edinburgh	18/07/01	5 7.0	10 2	Fwd	Livingston
Leask	Moray	Stuart	02/10/79	Edinburgh	04/08/00	5 9.0	10 12	Fwd	Berwick Rangers
McAllister	Steven		17/05/82	Perth	03/08/01	5 9.0	10 4	Mid	St. Johnstone
McKeown	Kevin		12/10/67	Glasgow	21/08/01	6 1.0	13 6	Gk	Coleraine
Miller	Greg	Allan	01/04/76	Glasgow	12/01/01	5 8.0	10 10	Mid	Vasteras
Riley	Paul	John	07/08/75	Edinburgh	31/03/99	5 9.0	11 0	Mid	Hibernian
Smith	Daryn	Andrew M.	09/10/80	Dundonald	18/08/00	5 7.0	9 7	Mid	St. Johnstone
Templeman	Christopher		12/01/80	Kirkcaldy	18/07/01	6 5.0	15 2	Fwd	Stirling Albion

Milestones

YEAR OF FORMATION: 1906
MOST LEAGUE POINTS IN A SEASON: 55 (Second Division – Season 1982/83)(2 Points for a Win)
72 (Third Division – Season 2000/01)(3 Points for a Win)
MOST LEAGUE GOALS SCORED BY A PLAYER IN A SEASON: Ronald McIntosh (Season 1959/60)
NO. OF GOALS SCORED: 26
RECORD ATTENDANCE: 8,122 (-v- Aberdeen – 3.2.1973)
RECORD VICTORY: 12-1 (-v- Thornhill – Scottish Cup, 28.1.1926)
RECORD DEFEAT: 0-10 (-v- Airdrieonians, Albion Rovers and Cowdenbeath – Division 2, 1937/38)

The City's ten year league record

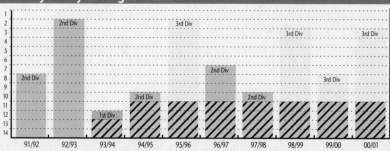

THE CITY'S CLUB FACTFILE 2000/2001
RESULTS... APPEARANCES... SCORERS... ATTENDANCES...

BELL'S SCOTTISH FOOTBALL LEAGUE

Date	Venue	Opponents	Att.	Res	Soutar D.	Riley P.	Raynes S.	Bain K.	Smith G.	Nairn J.	Coulston D.	Bailey L.	Grant R.	Black R.	McKeith J.	Williamson K.	Hutcheon A.	Leask M.	Honeyman B.	O'Sullivan L.	Cairney H.	Sturrock B.	Christie G.	Smith D.	Dewar G.	Donachie B.	Campbell P.	Gardner R.L.	Mackay D.	Miller G.	Fotheringham K.	Kinnaird P.	Parkyn M.
Aug 5	H	Elgin City	509	2-1	1	2	3	4^1	5	6	7	8	9^1	10	11	15	14	16															
12	A	Dumbarton	370	2-0	1		8	6		2	12	15	9	10						7^1	3	4	5	11	16^1								
19	H	Cowdenbeath	337	0-0	1		8	3	12		6	11		10	7		14	16			5		9	2	4									
26	A	Peterhead	563	2-1	1		8	3	4		6	11	9^2	10	15					12			5	7		2							
Sep 9	H	Montrose	465	6-1	1			3	4		6	7^1	14^1	9^1						10^1	11		5		2^1	8	12^1	16					
16	A	Albion Rovers	254	3-1	1		8	6	4		10		15	9						7	3^1		5	11		2	12^1	14					
23	H	East Fife	403	3-1	1		8	6	4^1		7	2	9							12	11		5	10^2		2	14	3	16				
30	H	East Stirlingshire	343	4-1	1	15	6	4			8^1	3^1	14	9^1						12	11^1		5	7		2	10						
Oct 7	A	Hamilton Academical	422	1-4	1	7	6	4			8	3	12	9^1			14			11			5	10		16	2						
14	A	Elgin City	835	2-2	1	8	6	5	4	12	3		9^2							10	7		14			2	11	13					
21	H	Dumbarton	455	3-1	1		6	4^1		16	3^1	14	9							11^1	7	5				2	10	12	8				
28	H	Peterhead	469	3-2	1		6	4			7	3	14^1	9						10^1	16	5				2	11	12	8				
Nov 4	A	Montrose	622	1-1	1		6	4	17		8	3	12	9^1	16					10		5				2	11		7				
11	A	East Fife	549	0-1	1		6			4	8	3	10	9	16					11		5				2	14	12	7				
18	H	Albion Rovers	337	2-1	1		6	8^1	4	14	3	9		11						10^1		5	17		2		12	7					
25	H	Hamilton Academical	483	0-0	1		6	8	4		3	12	9	11						10		5			2		17	14	7				
Dec 2	A	East Stirlingshire	249	1-0	1		6	8^1	4	12	3	17	9	10						11		5			2		16	7					
16	H	Elgin City	333	2-1	1	7		4	6	8	3		9^1	11						10		5	17		2^1		14	16					
23	A	Cowdenbeath	434	1-2	1	11	3^1	4	6	8		14	9	10						7		5	16		2							
30	A	Peterhead	889	2-0	1	7	6	8	4	12	3^1	9^1		10					16			5	11		2							
Feb 3	H	Hamilton Academical	521	0-1	1	4			3		10	7	9							5	11		12	17		6	4			2	8		
17	H	Cowdenbeath	545	2-0	1	4			6		3	11	9^2	10						5	17		7	12		14				2	8		
24	A	Dumbarton	722	0-1	1	7		12	5	6		3	8	9	10					17							4	2	11			
Mar 17	A	East Fife	416	4-1	1	17	3	4			11		9^1		16					5	10^1		14		8^1		2		6^1	7			
20	H	Montrose	526	3-0	1	16	3	4			7		9^1		17					5	10^2		12		8		2		6	11			
24	H	East Stirlingshire	351	5-1	1	16	3	4^1			11		9^3		17					5	10^1		12		8		2		6	7			
27	H	Peterhead	396	1-1	1			3	4	14	7		9		16					5	10						2	8	6^1	11			
Apr 3	H	East Fife	407	1-0	1			3	4		7		9^1	16	17					5	10		12				2	8	6	11			
7	H	Hamilton Academical	586	3-4				3	4		7		9^1	16	17					5	10		14^1				2	8	6^1	11	1		
10	A	Albion Rovers	283	1-1			6		4	3^1	12		9	8	11						10		5				2	14	7	17	1		
14	A	East Stirlingshire	253	2-0					4^1		11		9	6			10^1			5	17		16			8	2	12	3	7	1		
17	H	Albion Rovers	369	1-2			14		4^1		7		9	6			10			5	17				8		2	12	3	11	1		
21	A	Elgin City	570	3-0			16		4^2		7		6^1				10			5	9		8	17	3		2	12		11	1		
24	A	Montrose	544	3-1	1	8			4	16	7^1		6^1				10			5	9				3	14	2^1	12					
28	H	Dumbarton	510	1-0	1	8			4	12	11		9^1	6			10			5	10						2	14	3	7			
May 5	A	Cowdenbeath	3,448	1-2	1	8			4	14	7		9	6			17			5	10		12^1				2		3	11		
TOTAL FULL APPEARANCES					31	18	26	31	13	13	32	7	32	19	1		14	12	1	32	20	1	14	7	9	5	7	16	6	12	12	5
TOTAL SUB APPEARANCES					(6)	(1)	(1)	(6)	(6)	(1)	(10)		(4)	(2)	(1)	(1)	(11)	(4)		(7)	(2)	(9)	(5)	(5)	(13)		(6)		(1)			
TOTAL GOALS SCORED						1	11		1	5	3	22	2				5	3			6	1	4	1	1	1		1		3		

Small bold figures denote goalscorers. † denotes opponent's own goal.

Glebe Park

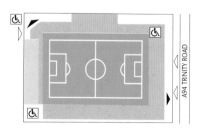

A94 TRINITY ROAD

CAPACITY: 3,060; Seated 1,518, Standing 1,542
PITCH DIMENSIONS: 110 yds x 67 yds
FACILITIES FOR DISABLED SUPPORTERS:
Section of Terracing designated for disabled supporters.

Team playing kits

How to get there

The following routes may be used to reach Glebe Park:

TRAINS: The nearest railway station is Montrose, which is eight miles away. There is a regular Inter-City service from all parts of the country and fans alighting at Montrose can then catch a connecting bus service to Brechin.

BUSES: Brechin bus station is only a few hundred yards from the ground and buses on the Aberdeen-Dundee and Montrose-Edzell routes stop here.

CARS: Car parking is available in the Brechin City car park, which is capable of holding 50 vehicles. There are also a number of side streets which may be used for this purpose.

email: info@sfl.scottishfootball.com • website: www.scottishfootball.com

Strathclyde Homes Stadium,
Castle Road, Dumbarton, G82 1JJ

CHAIRMAN
Douglas S. Dalgleish, M.A., LL.B.

MANAGING DIRECTOR
Neil Rankine

DIRECTORS
David O. Stark,
John G. MacFarlane &
Colin J. Hosie

HON. PRESIDENTS
Ian A. Bell, J.P. &
R. Campbell Ward, C.A.

CLUB SECRETARY
Colin J. Hosie

ASSISTANT CLUB SECRETARY
J. David Prophet

COMPANY SECRETARY
John Benn M.Sc.

ADMINISTRATION MANAGER
Freida McMahon

MANAGER
Tom Carson

ASSISTANT MANAGER
Stephen Morrison

COACH
George Clark

CLUB DOCTOR
Neil MacKay, MBC, HB

SPORTS THERAPIST
Linda McIlwraith,
Diploma Sports Therapy

CHIEF SCOUT
Willie Hughes

**PUBLIC RELATIONS EXECUTIVE/
COMMERCIAL MANAGER**
Ian MacFarlane (01389) 762569

**FOOTBALL SAFETY OFFICER'S
ASSOCIATION REPRESENTATIVE**
David Douglas

MEDIA LIAISON OFFICER
Ian MacFarlane (01389) 762569

MATCHDAY PROGRAMME EDITOR
Graeme Robertson (0131) 441 5451

TELEPHONES
Ground (01389) 762569
Sec. Bus. (0141) 309 2288
Sec. Home (01389) 841996
Sec. Mobile (07770) 831490
Fax (01389) 762629
Sec. Fax (01389) 842080

E-MAIL & INTERNET ADDRESS
www.dumbartonfc.com

CLUB SHOP
Situated in ground –
open on home matchdays and
10.00 a.m. – 4.00 p.m. Mon-Fri

OFFICIAL SUPPORTERS CLUB
c/o Dumbarton FC,
Strathclyde Homes Stadium,
Castle Road, Dumbarton, G82 1JJ

TEAM CAPTAIN
David Stewart

SHIRT SPONSOR
Methode Electronics Europe

KIT SUPPLIER
XARA

LIST OF PLAYERS 2001-2002

SURNAME	FIRST NAME	MIDDLE NAME	DATE OF BIRTH	PLACE OF BIRTH	DATE OF SIGNING	HEIGHT FT INS	WEIGHT ST LBS	POS. ON PITCH	PREVIOUS CLUB
Bonar	Steven	Andrew	20/05/79	Glasgow	30/03/00	5 9.5	10 6	Mid	Albion Rovers
Brittain	Craig		10/01/74	Glasgow	14/06/97	5 5.0	9 7	Def	Ashfield Juniors
Brown	Andrew	Stewart	11/10/76	Edinburgh	21/07/99	6 4.0	14 0	Fwd	Clydebank
Bruce	Jamie	Ross	29/08/76	East Kilbride	01/02/99	6 0.0	11 4	Def	East Kilbride Thistle
Dickie	Michael	John	05/05/79	Vale of Leven	11/06/99	5 8.0	10 0	Def	Dundee
Dillon	John	Peter	16/12/78	Vale of Leven	30/07/99	5 7.0	10 0	Mid	Clyde
Flannery	Patrick	Martin F.	23/07/76	Glasgow	27/12/97	6 1.0	11 9	Fwd	Morton
Hillcoat	John	George	16/12/70	Paisley	15/07/00	5 11.5	12 6	Gk	Queen of the South
Jack	Stephen	John	27/03/71	Bellshill	25/02/98	5 11.0	10 0	Mid	Cowdenbeath
Lynes	Craig		07/02/81	Edinburgh	22/03/01	6 4.0	12 0	Mid	East Stirlingshire
McCann	Kevin		17/12/80	Bellshill	02/06/00	6 1.0	11 8	Def	Partick Thistle
McKelvie	Daniel		06/06/80	Paisley	05/07/01	5 9.0	10 7	Fwd	Clydebank
McKeown	John	Paton	21/04/81	Glasgow	08/06/01	6 4.5	13 5	Def	Ayr United
Melvin	Martin		12/06/77	Glasgow	31/03/00	5 7.0	10 7	Mid/Fwd	Beith Juniors
Murdoch	Scott	McKenzie	27/02/69	Glasgow	09/06/01	5 9.0	11 4	Mid	Clydebank
O'Neill	Martin		17/06/75	Glasgow	29/01/01	5 8.0	11 6	Mid	East Fife
Ritchie	John	Joseph	08/07/79	Vale of Leven	05/02/01	5 11.0	11 8	Mid	Dumbarton Under 21's
Robertson	Joseph		12/04/77	Glasgow	14/08/98	5 8.0	11 5	Fwd	Clydebank
Stewart	David		14/08/78	Irvine	01/12/99	6 1.0	12 4	Def	Clydebank
Wight	John	Campbell	11/12/73	Alexandria	04/08/00	6 0.0	13 0	Gk	Beith Juniors

Milestones

YEAR OF FORMATION: 1872
MOST CAPPED PLAYERS: J. Lindsay and J. McAulay
NO. OF CAPS: 8 each
MOST LEAGUE POINTS IN A SEASON: 53 (First Division – Season 1986/87) (2 Points for a Win)
        60 (Second Division – Season 1994/95) (3 Points for a Win)
MOST LEAGUE GOALS SCORED BY A PLAYER IN A SEASON: Kenneth Wilson (Season 1971/72)
NO. OF GOALS SCORED: 38
RECORD ATTENDANCE: 18,001 (-v- Raith Rovers – 2.3.1957 at Boghead Park)
        1,876 (-v- Elgin City – 2.12.2000 at Strathclyde Homes Stadium)
RECORD VICTORY: 13-2 (-v- Kirkintilloch – Scottish Cup)
RECORD DEFEAT: 1-11 (-v- Ayr United/Albion Rovers)

The Sons' ten year league record

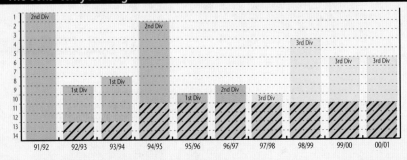

BELL'S — SCOTTISH FOOTBALL LEAGUE

Date	Venue	Opponents	Att.	Res	Hillcoat J.	Dickie M.	Dillon J.	Bruce J.	Jack S.	Stewart D.	Wilson W.	King T.	Brown Andrew	Smith C.	Robertson J.	Bonar S.	Melvin M.	McCann K.	Dempsey G.	McGinty B.	Brittain C.	Flannery P.	Grace A.	Gentile C.	McCormick S.	Wight J.	Wilson S.	Brown Alan	O'Neill M.	Robinson R.	Ritchie J.	Lynes C.
Aug 5	A	Hamilton Academical	588	0-2	1	2	3	4	5	6	7	8	9	10	11	14	15															
12	H	Brechin City	370	0-2	1	2	3	5	4			7	8	9	10	11		14	6	16	15											
19	A	Peterhead	630	0-2	1	2	11		5			7	6	10				8	16	4	3	9	12									
26	A	Albion Rovers	343	1-0	1	2			12	4				11	14	15	5				3	9¹		8									
Sep 9	H	East Stirlingshire	259	1-2	1		11			5	8	7	6	10	12	15	2		4		3	9¹		14									
16	A	Montrose	317	2-2	1					5	8	7	6	10¹	12	11	2		4		3	9¹	14										
23	H	Cowdenbeath	348	2-4	1				8	4	2	6¹	10¹		11	14		5			3	12	7	16	9								
30	A	Elgin City	752	0-2	1	2			14	5	7	6	10		11			4			3	9		8	12								
Oct 7	A	East Fife	256	2-3	1	2	7¹		5	6		8¹	10		11			4			3	9		14	16								
14	H	Hamilton Academical	368	2-3				5					10		11¹	16		4			3	9¹	7			1	8						
21	A	Brechin City	455	1-3		2		5	8	6			10	12	11			4¹			3	9	7			1							
28	A	Albion Rovers	277	0-1		2	15	4	5	6	7		10		11	12	16				3	9	8			1							
Nov 4	A	East Stirlingshire	246	1-1	1	15	16	5		4	2		10		11	6					3	9¹	8					7					
11	H	Cowdenbeath	341	1-1	1	2		5¹	16	6			10		11	7		4			3	8	8										
18	H	Montrose	238	1-0	1	2		5		6			10		11	7	14	4			3	9	8¹										
25	A	East Fife	465	0-1	1	2		5		6			10	12	11	7	14	4			3	9	8										
Dec 2	H	Elgin City	1,876	3-0	1	2		4		6			10¹		11	7		5			3¹	9¹	8										
16	H	Hamilton Academical	485	0-2	1	2	6	4					10	12	11	7		5			3	9	8										
23	H	Peterhead	821	1-3	1	2	6	4		7			10¹	12	11		15	5			3	9	8										
Jan 2	H	East Stirlingshire	658	+3-0	1	2	14	5		7			10	12¹	11	8		6			3	9¹	9	16									
27	A	Albion Rovers	369	3-1	1	2	11	4	5	6			10¹			7	12				3	9²						8					
Feb 3	H	East Fife	711	2-0	1	2	3	4	5	6¹			10¹		12	7	14					9¹						8	11				
24	A	Brechin City	722	1-1	1	2	3	4	5	6			10¹		12	7	16	14				9¹						8	11				
Mar 7	H	Cowdenbeath	507	3-0	1	2	3¹	4	5	6			10¹		12	7	17	14				9¹						8	11				
10	H	Albion Rovers	808	1-4	1	2	3	4	5	6			10		11	7	17					9¹			15			8					
13	A	Elgin City	424	3-0		2	3¹	4¹	5	6			10¹		12	7	17	14				9¹			1			8	11				
17	A	Cowdenbeath	369	2-2		2	3	4	5	6			10		11	7	16	14			12	9²			1					8			
20	A	East Stirlingshire	209	0-0		2	3	4	5	6					10	7		11			12	9			1			8					
24	A	Peterhead	432	1-0			3	4	5	6					11¹	7		2				9			1			8			10		
27	A	Montrose	165	2-1			3	4	5	6					11	7¹		2			12	9¹			1			8			10		
31	H	Montrose	751	1-2			3	4	5	6				12	11		17	2			7	9¹			1			8			10		
Apr 7	A	East Fife	313	1-0	1	2	3	4	5	6				10		15	7				11				1			8	12		9¹		
14	H	Elgin City	685	2-0	1	2	3	4	5	6			10¹	14	11			7			16							8¹			17	9	
21	H	Hamilton Academical	864	1-2	1	2		4	5	6			10	3	11	7					17							8			14	9¹	
28	A	Brechin City	510	0-1	1	2	16	4	5	6			10		11	7	14				17	9						8					3
May 5	H	Peterhead	715	2-2	1	2	14	4	5	6¹			10		12	7					3	9¹	8					8					11
TOTAL FULL APPEARANCES					27	29	20	29	25	32	11	9	31	4	27	23		23			22	30	12	2	1	9	1	15	4	1	8
TOTAL SUB APPEARANCES					(1)	(5)		(3)						(9)	(6)	(6)	(17)	(4)	(1)	(1)	(6)	(1)	(2)	(4)	(2)	(1)			(1)	(2)	
TOTAL GOALS SCORED							3	2		2		2	9	1	2	1		1			1	17	1					1			2

Small bold figures denote goalscorers. † denotes opponent's own goal.

Strathclyde Homes Stadium

CAR PARK · CAR PARK · CAR PARK · CASTLE ROAD · COACH PARK

CAPACITY: 2,020 (All Seated)

PITCH DIMENSIONS: 114 yds x 75 yds

FACILITIES FOR DISABLED SUPPORTERS:
20 Wheelchair spaces are accommodated at the front of the stand. Contact the Club Secretary in advance regarding availability.

Team playing kits

How to get there

Strathclyde Homes Stadium can be reached by the following routes:

TRAINS: The train service from Glasgow Queen Street and Glasgow Central Low Level both pass through Dumbarton East Station (fans best choice) situated just under a ten minute walk from the ground.

BUSES: There are two main services which pass close to the ground. These are bound for Helensburgh and Balloch from Glasgow.

CARS: Follow A82 then A814 Helensburgh/Dumbarton sign post. Follow Road for about 1 mile. Pass under Dumbarton East Railway Bridge and take second right – Victoria Street (also signposted Dumbarton Castle). The car park at the new stadium holds 500 cars and 10 coaches.

The Sons

63

email: info@sfl.scottishfootball.com • website: www.scottishfootball.com

East Fife

Bayview Stadium, Harbour View,
Methil, Leven, Fife, KY8 3RW

CHAIRMAN
W. Bruce Black

DIRECTORS
Julian S. Danskin, Kenneth R. MacKay,
David Hamilton, A. Ronald Lindsay,
Robert Moreland &
David McK. Stevenson

ASSOCIATE DIRECTORS
Douglas Briggs, James Stewart &
James Taylor

HONORARY VICE-PRESIDENT
John Fleming

SECRETARY
Kenneth R. MacKay

OFFICE SECRETARY
Ms. Leona Guidi

STADIUM CONTROLLER
Robert M. Scott

MANAGER
David Clarke

ASSISTANT MANAGER
Mike Marshall

**YOUTH DEVELOPMENT
COACH/CHIEF SCOUT/
U18 YOUTH TEAM COACH**
Danny Hendry

U16 YOUTH TEAM COACH
Alex Brown

CLUB DOCTORS
Dr. William McCrossan
& Dr. Robert Dunn

SURGEON
Ivan Brenkell, M.B., Ch.B., F.R.C.S.

PHYSIOTHERAPIST
Neil Bryson

**FOOTBALL SAFETY OFFICERS'
ASSOCIATION REPRESENTATIVE**
James Dick (01333) 426323

GROUNDSMAN
Adam Porteous

KIT PERSON
Leanne Hamilton

CATERING MANAGER
Marc Dryburgh

MATCHDAY PROGRAMME EDITOR
Jim Stewart

TELEPHONES
Ground/Commercial (01333) 426323
Fax (01333) 426376

E-MAIL & INTERNET ADDRESS
admin@eastfife.org
www.eastfife.org

CLUB SHOP
A Supporters' Club Shop is situated
within the Ground

TEAM CAPTAIN
John Gallagher

SHIRT SPONSOR
First Choice Playing Kit: Timber Center
Second Choice Playing Kit: XARA Soccer

KIT SUPPLIER
First Choice: ACA Sport
Second Choice: XARA

LIST OF PLAYERS 2001-2002

SURNAME	FIRST NAME	MIDDLE NAME	DATE OF BIRTH	PLACE OF BIRTH	DATE OF SIGNING	HEIGHT FT INS	WEIGHT ST LBS	POS. ON PITCH	PREVIOUS CLUB
Allan	James		21/09/79	Glasgow	28/06/01	5 9.0	12 0	Mid	Cowdenbeath
Brown	Steven	Alexander	20/07/84	Kirkcaldy	28/06/01	5 6.5	11 4	Mid	East Fife U'16s
Brown	Steven	Anthony	21/02/83	Kirkcaldy	01/08/01	5 10.0	10 4	Fwd	Lochgelly Albert U'18
Cassells	Gary		29/08/83	Kirkcaldy	28/06/01	6 0.0	12 0	Mid	S Form
Coulston	Douglas		12/08/71	Glasgow	25/05/01	5 10.0	11 0	Mid/Fwd	Brechin City
Courts	Conrad		13/07/83	Kirkcaldy	22/11/00	5 9.0	10 5	Mid	Bluebell Colts U'16
Cunningham	Grant		24/07/79	Kirkcaldy	25/07/01	5 9.0	11 0	Mid	Glenrothes Strollers
Gallagher	John		02/06/69	Glasgow	30/05/00	5 9.0	12 4	Def/Mid	Queen of the South
Garvie	Colin		07/04/83	Edinburgh	23/03/01	5 11.0	11 5	Gk	Newtongrange Star 'A' U18
Gibson	Keith		01/05/81	Dundee	13/07/01	5 11.0	9 13	Mid	Dundee
Godfrey	Ross		21/01/77	Edinburgh	31/05/01	6 0.0	13 0	Gk	Cowdenbeath
Graham	James	Ross	03/06/71	Baillieston	25/07/01	6 1.0	14 0	Fwd	Kirrie Thistle
Herkes	James		28/02/78	Kirkcaldy	31/07/01	5 11.0	12 0	Mid	St. Andrews United
Johnstone	Craig		15/11/84	Kirkcaldy	28/06/01	5 7.0	9 1	Def	East Fife U'16s
Kirk	Andrew		30/07/83	Kirkcaldy	28/06/01	5 11.0	11 5	Fwd	East Fife S Form
Lofting	Aaron	Paul	15/04/82	Leicester	17/11/00	5 9.0	11 7	Mid	Forfar West End JFC
MacDonald	Arran		14/08/83	Kirkcaldy	19/05/01	5 11.0	13 0	Def	S Form
McGovern	Steven		20/02/82	Glasgow	23/08/01	6 2.0	12 6	Gk	Airdrieonians
McManus	Paul		26/12/82	Kirkcaldy	27/01/01	5 8.0	10 7	Mid	West Park United U'18
Mortimer	Paul		14/02/80	Falkirk	03/08/00	6 2.0	12 5	Mid	Stirling Albion
Motion	Kevin		27/11/83	Edinburgh	01/08/01	5 9.0	9 10	Mid	Newtongrange Star 'A' U'18
Munro	Kenneth	Neil	08/08/77	Edinburgh	20/09/97	5 11.0	12 7	Def/Mid	Cowdenbeath
Murray	Steven		03/06/84	Kirkcaldy	28/06/01	6 0.0	11 0	Mid	East Fife Form D
Nairn	James		25/08/72	Kirkcaldy	27/03/01	5 10.0	13 7	Mid	Brechin City
Ovenstone	John	William	07/10/82	Kirkcaldy	27/01/01	6 0.0	11 7	Def	Bayview Y.C. U'18
Rae	James	Alexander	21/10/83	Kirkcaldy	01/08/01	6 1.0	11 7	Mid	Buckhaven Colts U18s
Wilson	William	Stewart	19/08/72	Glasgow	30/01/01	5 8.0	10 2	Mid	Dumbarton

Milestones

YEAR OF FORMATION: 1903
MOST CAPPED PLAYER: George Aitken
NO. OF CAPS: 5
MOST LEAGUE POINTS IN A SEASON: 57 (Division 2 – Season 1929/30)(2 Points for a Win)
67 (Second Division – Season 1995/96)(3 Points for a Win)
MOST LEAGUE GOALS SCORED BY A PLAYER IN A SEASON: Henry Morris (Season 1947/48)
NO. OF GOALS SCORED: 41
RECORD ATTENDANCE: 22,515 (-v- Raith Rovers – 2.1.1950 at Bayview Park – old Stadium)
1,819 (-v- Livingston – 27.1.2001 at Bayview Stadium – new Stadium)
RECORD VICTORY: 13-2 (-v- Edinburgh City – Division 2, 11.12.1937)
RECORD DEFEAT: 0-9 (-v- Heart of Midlothian – Division 1, 5.10.1957)

The Fifers' ten year league record

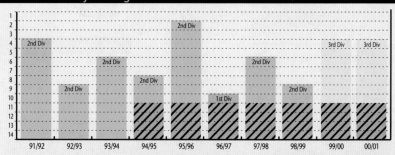

THE FIFERS' CLUB FACTFILE 2000/2001
RESULTS... APPEARANCES... SCORERS... ATTENDANCES...

Date	Venue	Opponents	Att.	Res	Stewart A.	Munro K.	Gallagher J.	McCloy B.	Sharp R.	Allison J.	Hunter M.	Mortimer P.	Simpson P.	Kerrigan S.	Mackay S.	Moffat B.	Logan R.	Ferguson S.	Gibb R.	Agostini D.	Tinley G.	O'Neill M.	Wright D.	Devine C.	McCulloch W.	Shannon R.	McWilliams D.	Bottiglieri E.	McKinnon R.	McManus P.	Wilson W.	Reid A.	Lofting A.	Beith G.	Wood D.	Mair L.	Magee K.	Nairn J.
Aug 5	A	Albion Rovers	465	†1-0	1	2	3	4	5	6	7	8	9	10	11	12		14		16																		
12	H	Peterhead	619	1-1	1	2	3	4	5	6	7	8	9	12	11¹	10		14		16																		
19	H	East Stirlingshire	310	5-2	1	2	3	4		6	14	8	12¹	9¹	11¹	10²		7		15	5																	
26	A	Montrose	355	1-0	1	2	3	4		6		8	12	9	7¹	10	15			11	5	16																
Sep 9	H	Cowdenbeath	735	0-2	1	2	3	4		6	15	8	12	9	7	10				11	5	14																
16	H	Elgin City	444	1-1	1	2	11	4		6			5	9		10				3	15	8	7¹	12														
23	A	Brechin City	403	1-3		11		4	16	2		8		9	7	10¹				3	5	6	12	1														
30	H	Hamilton Academical	549	1-2		2	11¹	4		6	14		12	7		10	16			3	5	8	9	1														
Oct 7	A	Dumbarton	256	3-2		2	16	4		6	11	8¹		9	7	10²	14			3	5			1														
14	H	Albion Rovers	445	0-0		2	10	4	16	6	7	8	12	9			14			3	5			1														
21	A	Peterhead	637	0-0		2	16	4		8	15	7		9		10	11			3	5		14	1		6												
28	H	Montrose	375	3-1		2	16	4	6	8	14			11²	10	12				9¹	3	5		1				7										
Nov 4	A	Cowdenbeath	626	0-1		2	16		6	8	14	4			11	10				9	3	5		12	1			7										
11	H	Brechin City	549	1-0		2	8	4	5	6	15	7		11	14	10				9¹	3			12	1													
18	A	Elgin City	730	3-1		11		4	3	6		7¹		10	16	12				9²	5			1					2	8								
25	H	Dumbarton	465	1-0		14	3	4		6		7		10	11	12				9¹	5			16	1				2	8								
Dec 2	A	Hamilton Academical	518	1-1			3	4		8	15			10	11					9¹	5			1			6		2	7								
23	A	Albion Rovers	372	2-1	12	11				6	8	4		9¹	7	10¹				3	5			1					2									
26	H	East Stirlingshire	492	3-1	7	11			6¹	9¹	4			8¹		10				3	5			1					2	16								
Jan 2	H	Cowdenbeath	1,003	1-2	16	15	2	3	6	11	4			9	8¹	10					5			1				7										
Feb 3	A	Dumbarton	711	0-2	1			4	6			8		11	7	10				3	5		9		2							14	12	16				
17	A	East Stirlingshire	286	0-1	1			4	3			8		9	7	10					5		12		2							14	16		6	11		
24	A	Peterhead	380	2-1	1		11¹	4	3¹			9		8	10						5		12		2							14	7	16	6		2	
Mar 10	H	Montrose	407	1-0	1			3	4			8		9	6	10							12							7	15¹		16	11		2	
13	A	Montrose	249	1-1	1		9	4	3			8¹		11	7	10							14		2								6	5			
17	A	Brechin City	416	1-4	1			4	5			8		9	7	10				3¹			12								14	2	11	6			
20	H	Elgin City	223	1-1	1			4	3			8		9¹	7	10							14		2							6		5	11		
27	H	Hamilton Academical	353	1-4	1			4	3		14	9					12			10					2				7		6¹		5	11	8		
31	A	Elgin City	512	3-1	1			4	3			9¹				14				7¹	6				2				15		10		5¹	11	8		
Apr 3	A	Brechin City	407	0-1	1			4	3			16		9		14				8			2				12	7		10	5	11	6				
7	H	Dumbarton	313	0-1	1			4	3			16		9		12				7	6		2				14		10	5	11	8					
14	H	Hamilton Academical	507	1-1	1	15		3				8		9	7				5				12			14		10¹	2		6	4	11				
17	A	Cowdenbeath	531	2-3	1		3		4			8¹		9	7	15										14		10	2		6	5	11¹				
21	H	Albion Rovers	333	2-1	1		3	12	4			8¹		9¹	7													10	2	16	6	5	11				
28	A	Peterhead	511	1-2	1	6	3	14	4			8		9¹		12												10	2	15	11	5	12				
May 5	H	East Stirlingshire	356	†4-1	1	7	3	6				4		9	10²	14				12								8	2	15	11	5¹					
TOTAL FULL APPEARANCES					22	16	22	29	22	19	8	28	32	27	22	1	7	16	19	3	6	14	4	2	11	4	6	11	1	15	1	13	8	4			
TOTAL SUB APPEARANCES					(3)	(6)	(2)	(2)		(7)	(4)	(4)	(2)	(2)	(6)	(3)		(4)	(6)		(2)	(1)		(12)				(2)		(8)	(3)	(2)	(6)				(1)
TOTAL GOALS SCORED						2		1	1	1	5	1	8	7	6			6	1				1	1						1	1		1		2	1

Small bold figures denote goalscorers.   † denotes opponent's own goal.

Bayview Stadium

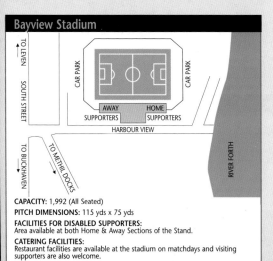

TO LEVEN · SOUTH STREET · CAR PARK · CAR PARK · AWAY SUPPORTERS · HOME SUPPORTERS · HARBOUR VIEW · TO BUCKHAVEN · TO METHIL DOCKS · RIVER FORTH

CAPACITY: 1,992 (All Seated)

PITCH DIMENSIONS: 115 yds x 75 yds

FACILITIES FOR DISABLED SUPPORTERS:
Area available at both Home & Away Sections of the Stand.

CATERING FACILITIES:
Restaurant facilities are available at the stadium on matchdays and visiting supporters are also welcome.

Team playing kits

How to get there

Bayview Park can be reached by the following routes:

TRAINS: The nearest railway station is Kirkcaldy (8 miles away), and fans will have to catch an inter-linking bus service from just outside the station to the ground.

BUSES: A regular service from Kirkcaldy to Leven passes close to the ground, as does the Leven to Dunfermline service. The Leven bus terminus is approximately $^2/_3$ mile from the ground (5 minutes walk).

CARS: There are Car Parking facilities available for both Home and Away fans at the ground.

email: info@sfl.scottishfootball.com • website: www.scottishfootball.com

East Stirlingshire

EST. 1881

Firs Park, Firs Street,
Falkirk, FK2 7AY

CHAIRMAN
Alan J. Mackin

VICE-CHAIRMAN
Alexander S.H. Forsyth

DIRECTORS
Alexander M. McCabe,
John M. D. Morton,
& Douglas W. Morrison

HON. PRESIDENT
James Middlemass

CHIEF EXECUTIVE/SECRETARY
Leslie G. Thomson

MANAGER
Brian Ross

U18 YOUTH TEAM COACHES
Thomas Beattie & Ian Campbell

U16 YOUTH TEAM COACH
Archie Morrison

U14 YOUTH TEAM COACHES
Jack Martin & Ian Black

PHYSIOTHERAPIST
Laura Gillogley

**FOOTBALL SAFETY OFFICERS'
ASSOCIATION REPRESENTATIVE**
Robert Goldie (01324) 634154

CHIEF SCOUT
Sandy Craig

STADIUM DIRECTOR
John Morton

GROUNDSMAN/KITMAN
James Wilson

COMMERCIAL MANAGER
Miss Collette Morton (01324) 623583

MEDIA LIAISON OFFICER
Leslie G. Thomson (01324) 623583

TELEPHONES
Ground (01324) 623583
Fax (01324) 637862
Sec. Home (01324) 551099
Sec. Mobile (07887) 883753
Manager (at Ground) (01324) 679796

E-MAIL & INTERNET ADDRESS
lest@theshire.madasafish.com
chaletom@aol.com
www.east-stirlingshire-fc.co.uk

CLUB SHOP
Situated at ground. Open Mon-Fri
10.00 a.m. till 3.00 p.m. (except
Wednesday) and on all home
matchdays

CLUB CAPTAIN
Gordon Russell

SHIRT SPONSOR
Finewood Joinery Products Ltd

KIT SUPPLIER
SECCA

LIST OF PLAYERS 2001-2002

SURNAME	FIRST NAME	MIDDLE NAME	DATE OF BIRTH	PLACE OF BIRTH	DATE OF SIGNING	HEIGHT FT INS	WEIGHT ST LBS	POS. ON PITCH	PREVIOUS CLUB
Aitchison	Cameron		08/11/84	Bellshill	21/07/01	5 5.0	9 0	Mid	Airdrie B.C.
Aitken	Alan	Alexander	04/09/82	Stirling	20/07/01	5 8.0	11 2	Fwd	Stirling Albion
Connelly	David		22/03/83	Broxburn	21/07/01	5 7.0	10 10	Mid	East Stirlingshire Under 16's
Cormack	Scott		12/12/82	Edinburgh	03/08/01	5 9.0	10 10	Mid	Hibernian
Ferguson	Alexander	Brown	04/06/81	Falkirk	26/07/99	5 10.0	11 8	Def	S Form
Gordon	Kevin	Mervyn	01/05/77	Tranent	14/07/99	5 8.0	10 7	Mid	Easthouses U'21
Hall	Michael		11/12/74	Edinburgh	01/06/00	6 2.0	12 6	Def	Stenhousemuir
Hay	David	Alexander	02/01/80	Edinburgh	13/07/01	6 3.0	12 12	Gk	Dunfermline Athletic
Lorimer	David	James	26/01/74	Bellshill	03/11/00	5 9.0	12 0	Mid	Stenhousemuir
Lyle	Derek		13/02/81	Glasgow	03/08/01	5 8.0	10 5	Fwd	Partick Thistle
Maughan	Roderick	Edward A.	18/12/80	Edinburgh	21/07/01	5 11.0	11 5	Mid	Arbroath
McAuley	Sean		27/02/80	Edinburgh	30/03/01	5 8.0	10 10	Mid	Clyde
McCheyne	Graeme		21/12/73	Bellshill	02/08/01	6 1.0	12 8	Def	Forfar Athletic
McCulloch	Gary		15/01/84	Dechmont	21/07/01	5 8.0	9 7	Mid	Livingston
McDonald	Ian		07/03/78	Newcastle	03/11/00	6 0.5	13 8	Mid	Cowdenbeath
McGhee	Graham		24/09/81	Coatbridge	03/01/01	6 1.0	12 6	Def	Clyde
McKechnie	Gregor	Alistair	04/06/74	Stirling	10/06/00	5 11.0	12 7	Fwd	Alloa Athletic
McLaren	Graeme		08/09/83	Stirling	21/07/01	5 10.0	10 2	Mid	Carse Thistle
McLaughlin	Paul		10/10/84	Rutherglen	03/08/01	5 7.0	8 8	Def	Stenhousemuir
McPherson	David		15/06/84	Bellshill	21/07/01	5 7.0	9 2	Def	Zeneca Juveniles
Menelaws	David		14/04/78	Chorley	23/05/01	5 8.0	10 7	Fwd	Stenhousemuir
O'Hear	David		16/12/83	Glasgow	21/07/01	5 9.0	10 7	Mid	Tower Hearts
Oates	Stephen		02/01/84	Falkirk	31/07/01	6 0.0	9 7	Mid	Zeneca Juveniles
Reid	Craig	Andrew	08/09/83	Falkirk	21/07/01	5 10.0	11 9	Def	Falkirk
Russell	Gordon	Alan	03/03/68	Falkirk	23/09/95	5 9.5	10 0	Def	Stenhousemuir
Scott	Andrew	McKean	11/03/81	Glasgow	14/07/99	5 9.0	10 0	Fwd	S Form
Simpson	Ross		02/10/83	Glasgow	21/07/01	6 2.0	11 0	Def	Cumbernauld United U18's
Sproule	Christopher	Steven	11/07/84	Edinburgh	21/07/01	5 7.0	9 4	Mid	Burnvale
Sutherland	Michael		30/12/81	Edinburgh	24/03/00	5 11.5	11 7	Fwd	Links United
Todd	Christopher	James	01/07/82	Stirling	21/07/01	5 11.0	12 0	Gk	Kilsyth B.C.
Todd	Douglas		07/07/70	Stirling	06/07/00	5 9.0	12 0	Mid	Bo'ness United Juniors
Wilson	John	Kerr T.	29/04/83	Broxburn	21/07/01	5 6.0	10 5	Mid	East Stirlingshire B.C.
Wood	David	Wilson	30/12/75	Broxburn	17/08/01	5 11.0	11 1	Mid	Stenhousemuir

Milestones

YEAR OF FORMATION: 1881
MOST CAPPED PLAYER: Humphrey Jones
NO. OF CAPS: 5 (for Wales)
MOST LEAGUE POINTS IN A SEASON: 55 (Division 2 – Season 1931/32) (2 Points for a Win)
59 (Third Division – Season 1994/95) (3 Points for a Win)
MOST LEAGUE GOALS SCORED BY A PLAYER IN A SEASON: Malcolm Morrison (Season 1938/39)
NO. OF GOALS SCORED: 36
RECORD ATTENDANCE: 11,500 (-v- Hibernian – 10.2.1969)
RECORD VICTORY: 10-1 (-v- Stenhousemuir – Scottish Cup, 1.9.1888)
RECORD DEFEAT: 1-12 (-v- Dundee United – Division 2, 13.4.1936)

The Shire's ten year league record

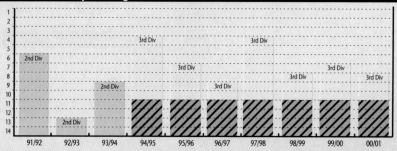

THE SHIRES' CLUB FACTFILE 2000/2001
RESULTS... APPEARANCES... SCORERS... ATTENDANCES...

BELL'S
SCOTTISH FOOTBALL LEAGUE

Date	Venue	Opponents	Att.	Res	Butter J.	Russell G.	McPherson D.	Hall M.	Quinn C.	Todd D.	Scott A.	Gordon K.	Higgins G.	Hislop S.	Stewart S.	McKechnie G.	Ferguson A.	Carlow R.	Tortolano J.	McKenzie C.	Lynes C.	Spence J.	Clarke J.	Allison C.	McWilliams D.	McDonald I.	Lorimer D.	Wood D.	McGhee G.	Lindsay P.	McAuley S.	Wilson J.
Aug 5	H	Cowdenbeath	297	0-2	1	2	3	4	5	6	7	8	9	10	11	12	16				15											
12	A	Montrose	304	1-0	1	4	6^1	3	5			8	12	9	7	10	2		11	16	14											
19	H	East Fife	310	2-5	1	4	6	3	2	5		10	12	9^1	7	8^1			11		15											
26	H	Hamilton Academical	435	0-0	1	5	6	3	2	4		10	16	9	7	8	14		11		15											
Sep 9	A	Dumbarton	259	2-1	1	4	14	3	2	5		10		8^1	7^1	9	15		11	12	6											
16	A	Peterhead	614	4-2	1	4		3	2	5		7		8^2	10	9^1	16		11	12	6^1											
23	H	Albion Rovers	271	1-1	1	4	14	3	2	5			15^1	10		9	8		11	6	7											
30	A	Brechin City	343	1-4	1	4	11	3	2	8			10^1	5	9	15	16	6		7	14											
Oct 7	H	Elgin City	248	0-2	1	4	6	3	2	5			9	7	10	8	11	14														
14	A	Cowdenbeath	289	0-3	1	4		3	14	5	15		9	7		10	6					2	8	11								
21	H	Montrose	258	1-2	1	2	16	5	4	3	11		9	6	8^1	10	15	12			7											
24	A	Hamilton Academical	344	0-4	1	4	14	3	2		8		10	7	9	15	11	5				12	6									
Nov 4	H	Dumbarton	246	1-1	1	2	14	6		4	11		9	7		15						5	10		3	8^1						
11	A	Albion Rovers	334	1-2	1	2		5		6	11		9^1	7								4	10		3	8						
18	A	Peterhead	262	1-3	1	2	12	5		6			9^1	7	16							4	10		3	8	11					
25	H	Elgin City	634	2-1	1	2		4		6			10	7	15^2							5	9		3	8	11					
Dec 2	H	Brechin City	249	0-1	1	2	16	4		6			10	7	15	12						4	9		3	8	11					
26	A	East Fife	492	1-3	1	3		5	2	6	11	16	9^1	7		15					12	4	10			8						
Jan 2	A	Dumbarton	658	0-3	1	6		3	2	5	7	8	9	11							14	4	12			10		15				
13	A	Peterhead	606	2-1	1	5		6	2	4	10	11	9^2	7	12											8		3				
27	A	Hamilton Academical	346	1-4	1	2	15	5	4	6	11	12	9^1	7	10							14				8		3				
Feb 3	H	Elgin City	240	1-0	1	4	6		6	8	11		9^1	7	10	2					12					3						
17	H	East Fife	286	1-0	1	4	6	5			11		9	7	10^1	2					8					3						
24	A	Montrose	305	1-1	1	4	6	5		14	8		9	11	10^1	2					7					3						
Mar 10	A	Hamilton Academical	388	2-2	1	4			6		11		9	12	10^2	2					8		16			3			5	7		
13	H	Albion Rovers	196	1-0	1	4			6		11	16	9^1	12	10	2					8					3			5	7		
17	A	Albion Rovers	248	2-2	1	4	16	2		6		8	12	9^1	11	10^1					7		14			3			5			
20	H	Dumbarton	209	0-0	1	2	7	16		8		11		9	6	10	5									3		4	14			
24	A	Brechin City	351	1-5	1	4	7			6		8	12	9^1	11	10	2									3		5				
31	H	Peterhead	190	1-0	1	4	8			6			7	10	9^1		12	2								3		5			11	
Apr 3	H	Cowdenbeath	272	0-2	1	4	6			8			10	9	7		2					15				3		5	11	14	16	
7	A	Elgin City	405	2-4	1	4	6	5		8		11	12	9	16^1	10^1	2									3		14		7		
14	H	Brechin City	253	0-2	1	5				8		7	10	9	11		2									3		4		6		
21	A	Cowdenbeath	488	3-1	1	4				8		7		9	15	10^2	2									3	6^1	5		11		
28	H	Montrose	186	0-1	1	4				8	15	11		9		10	2									3	6	5	16	7		
May 5	A	East Fife	356	1-4	1		16			8	15	14		9	4	10	2									3	11	5	7^1	6		
TOTAL FULL APPEARANCES					36	35	13	26	14	30	13	21	4	36	29	23	15	4	10	2	9	8	8	2	20	9	6	13	4	6	
TOTAL SUB APPEARANCES						(10)	(2)	(1)	(1)	(3)	(3)	(8)		(4)	(5)	(5)	(6)	(1)	(5)	(7)	(1)		(6)						(2)	(2)	(1)	(1)
TOTAL GOALS SCORED							1					1	16	2	11	2					1						1	1		1

Small bold figures denote goalscorers.   † denotes opponent's own goal.

Firs Park

Visiting Players and Directors Entrance

1,2 &3 Terracings closed to spectators except for access

Emergency Exit

FIRS ST.

Main Gate Vehicle Access — Turnstiles

THORNHILL ROAD

CAPACITY: 781; Seated 245, Standing 536

PITCH DIMENSIONS: 108 yds x 71 yds

FACILITIES FOR DISABLED SUPPORTERS:
By prior arrangement with Secretary.

Team playing kits

How to get there

The following routes may be used to reach Firs Park:

TRAINS: Passengers should alight at Grahamston Station and the ground is then five minutes walk.

BUSES: All buses running from the town centre pass close by the ground. The Grangemouth via Burnbank Road and Tamfourhill via Kennard Street services both stop almost outside the ground.

CARS: Car parking is available in the adjacent side streets. There are also spaces available in the car park adjacent to the major stores around the ground.

---

email: info@sfl.scottishfootball.com • website: www.scottishfootball.com

Borough Briggs, Borough Briggs Road, Elgin, IV30 1AP

CHAIRMAN
Denis J. Miller

DIRECTORS
Martyn Hunter, Ronald W. McHardy,
Ewen C. Menzies, John R. Meichan,
John A. Milton & William Arif

CHIEF EXECUTIVE
Martyn Hunter

SECRETARY
John A. Milton

GENERAL MANAGER
Harry McFadden

MANAGER
Alexander Caldwell

FIRST TEAM COACH
Neil McLennan

GOALKEEPER COACH
Gary Watt

HEAD YOUTH COACH
Graeme Porter

U18 YOUTH COACHES
Graeme Porter, Ian Morrison &
Ally Grant

U15 YOUTH COACHES
Gordon Shanks, Willie McInnes &
David Kerr

CLUB DOCTOR
Dr. Alan Rodger, MB, ChB

PHYSIOTHERAPIST
Maurice O'Donnell

**FOOTBALL SAFETY OFFICERS'
ASSOCIATION REPRESENTATIVE**
Steven Hamilton Tel: (07773) 525375

HEAD GROUNDSMAN
Steven Dunn

KIT MAN
Ricky Graham

COMMERCIAL DEPARTMENT
Audrey Fanning, Kaye Sutherland
& James Falconer

MATCHDAY PROGRAMME EDITOR
Bill McKenzie

TELEPHONES
Ground (01343) 551114
Ground Fax (01343) 547921
Sec. Bus. (01343) 822541
Sec. Home (01343) 546312

CLUB SHOP
Situated at Stadium (01343) 551114
Mon – Fri 9.30a.m.-12.30p.m.
& 1.30p.m.-4.30p.m.
Sat – 10.00a.m.-12noon
Matchday – 1.00p.m.-5.00p.m.

OFFICIAL SUPPORTERS CLUB
Borough Briggs, Borough Briggs Road,
Elgin, IV30 1AP
President: Cecil Jack;
Secretary: Mrs. June Jack

ECFC SOCIAL CLUB
Situated within the Main Stand
Tel: (01343) 542710

TEAM CAPTAIN
Willie Furphy

SHIRT SPONSOR
J. Gordon Williamson

KIT SUPPLIER
ERREA

LIST OF PLAYERS 2001-2002

SURNAME	FIRST NAME	MIDDLE NAME	DATE OF BIRTH	PLACE OF BIRTH	DATE OF SIGNING	HEIGHT FT INS	WEIGHT ST LBS	POS. ON PITCH	PREVIOUS CLUB
Burchell	Kieran		21/06/84	Elgin	21/08/01	5 10.0	10 0	Fwd	Fochabers Juniors
Campbell	Connor		26/01/80	Inverness	28/09/00	5 6.0	10 7	Fwd	Ross County
Craig	David	Alexander MacL.	22/01/80	Inverness	13/02/01	5 10.0	12 0	Mid	Inverness Caledonian Th.
Craig	Richard	Gary	27/04/80	Aberdeen	13/07/01	5 8.0	11 7	Mid/Fwd	Formartine United
Furphy	William		07/05/66	London	17/10/00	5 11.0	12 4	Def	Stranraer
Gilzean	Ian	Roger	10/12/69	Enfield	06/07/01	6 2.0	13 0	Fwd	St. Patricks Athletic
Hind	David	Scott	15/02/82	Inverness	30/03/01	6 1.0	11 7	Def	Inverness Caledonian Th.
MacDonald	Jordan		07/09/82	Inverness	26/07/00	5 11.0	11 6	Def	Inverness Caledonian Th.
MacDonald	Steven		07/12/75	Inverness	16/06/01	6 2.0	12 7	Def	Forres Mechanics
Mailer	Craig	James	27/09/67	Perth	27/07/01	6 0.0	13 4	Def	Montrose
McBride	Russell	Edward	29/09/78	Glasgow	03/08/01	5 10.0	12 4	Def/Mid	Fraserburgh
McConnachie	Darren	Scott	25/11/83	Elgin	04/08/01	5 10.0	11 0	Gk	Fochabers Juniors
McGlashan	Colin	James	17/03/64	Perth	04/06/01	5 7.0	11 6	Fwd	Arbroath
Milne	Colin	Richard	23/10/74	Aberdeen	27/07/00	6 2.0	13 10	Fwd	Peterhead
Milne	Craig	David	01/04/81	Perth	26/07/00	5 10.0	12 0	Def	Forfar Athletic
Morrison	Michael	Ian	21/10/79	Elgin	26/07/00	6 2.0	14 0	Def	S Form
Pirie	Martin	James	01/06/72	Aberdeen	26/07/00	6 2.0	14 0	Gk	Peterhead
Rae	Michael	Allan	19/05/81	Inverness	06/08/00	6 1.0	12 0	Gk	Fort William
Ross	David		30/06/70	Inverness	07/10/00	6 2.0	12 9	Fwd	Ross County
Rutherford	Ryan		16/10/82	Kirkcaldy	06/07/01	5 9.0	11 0	Fwd	Ross County
Shanks	Lee	Fraser	09/07/84	Elgin	04/08/01	6 2.0	13 7	Fwd	S Form
Sim	Mark	Gordon	16/08/83	Elgin	04/08/01	6 1.0	10 7	Def	Bishopmill United
Sim	Steven		20/11/84	Elgin	09/08/01	6 0.0	10 3	Def	Elgin City B.C.
Smith	Andrew	Brown	12/03/84	Fochabers	09/08/01	6 3.0	11 0	Def	Elgin City B.C.
Strathdee	Stuart		26/04/83	Elgin	09/08/01	6 0.0	12 0	Fwd	Bishopmill United
Tully	Craig		07/01/76	Stirling	14/02/01	6 0.0	12 0	Def	Forfar Athletic

Milestones

YEAR OF FORMATION: 1893
MOST CAPPED PLAYER: Douglas Grant
MOST LEAGUE POINTS IN A SEASON: 55 (Highland League - Season 1967/68) (2 Points for a Win))
81 (Highland League - Season 1989/90) (3 Points for a Win))
22 (SFL Third Division - Season 2000/01) (3 Points for a Win))
MOST LEAGUE GOALS SCORED BY A PLAYER IN A SEASON: Colin Milne (Season 2000/01)
NO. OF GOALS SCORED: 7
RECORD ATTENDANCE: 12,608 (-v- Arbroath – 17.2.1968)
RECORD VICTORY: 18-1 (-v- Brora Rangers – North of Scotland Cup – 6.2.1960)
RECORD DEFEAT: 1-14 (-v- Heart of Midlothian – Scottish Cup – 4.2.1939)

The Black and Whites' ten year league record

Please note that Elgin City's first season in membership of The Scottish Football League was in season 2000/01.

3rd Div

91/92 92/93 93/94 94/95 95/96 96/97 97/98 98/99 99/00 00/01

THE BLACK AND WHITES' CLUB FACTFILE 2000/2001
RESULTS... APPEARANCES... SCORERS... ATTENDANCES...

BELL'S SCOTTISH FOOTBALL LEAGUE

Date	Venue	Opponents	Att.	Res	Pirie M.	Milne Craig	MacDonald J.	Morris A.	O'Brien L.	Russell G.	Whyte N.	Cameron S.	Milne Colin	Slythe M.	Clinton S.	Noble S.	Maguire P.	Morrison M.	Ellis S.	Green R.	Campbell C.	Green M.	Peters S.	Furphy W.	Craig R.	Ross D.	Mackay S.	Edwards S.	Duncan R.	Irvine D.	Munro G.	Tully C.	Craig D.	Shanks L.	Hind D.	McMullan M.	Rae M.
Aug 5	A	Brechin City	509	1-2	1	2	3	4	5	6	7	8	9	10¹	11	14	15																				
12	H	Hamilton Academical	1,552	0-2	1	2	3	5	15	4		12	9	10	11		16	6	7	8																	
19	A	Albion Rovers	412	1-1	1	2	3	5	15	4	7	14	9	10	6¹					8	11	12															
26	A	Cowdenbeath	354	1-3	1	2	3		6	12	8	15	9	10¹	11					5	7		4														
Sep 9	H	Peterhead	1,135	1-3	1	2	3	5		12	8		9¹	14	6			11		10	7		4														
16	A	East Fife	444	1-1	1	2	3			8	7		9	12	6			5¹		10	11		4														
23	H	Montrose	817	1-1	1	2	3	14		6	7		9	10	12			5¹		11	8		4														
30	H	Dumbarton	752	2-0	1	2	3	14		8	12		9		6¹			5		10	7¹			4	11												
Oct 7	A	East Stirlingshire	248	2-0	1	2	3				8		9¹		6¹			5		10	11			4		7											
14	H	Brechin City	835	2-2	1	2	3				8		9	15	6			5¹		10	11			4		7¹											
21	A	Hamilton Academical	414	†1-4	1	2	3				8		9	16	6			5		10	11			4		7	12	14									
28	H	Cowdenbeath	836	2-3	1	2	3				12		9¹		6			5			14			4		10	11	7¹	8								
Nov 4	A	Peterhead	850	0-1	1		3				8		9					5		12	11			4		7	6	2	10								
11	A	Montrose	459	0-0	1		3				8		9	15	6			5		4	11					7	10	2									
18	H	East Fife	730	1-3	1		3	15			8		9		11			5	16	4	12					7¹	10	2	6								
25	H	East Stirlingshire	634	1-2	1	2	3				8		9¹	12	6			5		11	7					4			10								
Dec 2	A	Dumbarton	1,876	0-3	1		3				8		9	12	11			5		6	7					4		2	10	16							
16	A	Brechin City	333	1-2	1	2	3				7		9		15			5		14	11					8¹		12	10	6	4						
Feb 3	A	East Stirlingshire	240	0-1	1	2	3				14		9					5	8	6	11			4		7		15			10						
17	A	Albion Rovers	287	1-0	1		3						9¹						8		10			4		7		2		14	5	6	11				
Mar 6	H	Peterhead	524	0-1	1		3				14		9						8		10			4		7		2			5	6	11	15			
10	H	Cowdenbeath	676	0-2	1		3				12				14			5			10			4		7		2			8	6	11	9			
13	H	Dumbarton	424	0-3	1		3				10		9					5		15	12			4		7		2			8	6	11				
17	A	Montrose	366	1-2	1	14	3				8		9¹		15			5		10	13					7		2			6	4	11				
20	A	East Fife	223	1-1	1	2	3				8							5		9	10					7¹		11			6	4					
25	A	Cowdenbeath	289	0-1	1	2	3				8		9					5		12	10					7		11				4	6				
28	H	Albion Rovers	268	1-2	1	2	3				8							5	12	4	10					7		9¹		6			11				
31	H	East Fife	512	1-3	1	2	3				8							5	14	10¹						7		9		12		4	11		6		
Apr 3	H	Montrose	385	0-2	1	2	3				8							5	12	10						7		9				4	11		6		
7	H	East Stirlingshire	405	4-2		2	3				8							5		12				4		7²						6	11¹		9¹	10	1
10	H	Hamilton Academical	542	0-3		2	3				8		16					5	12	11				4		7						6			9	10	1
14	A	Dumbarton	685	0-2	1	2	3				8		9					5	15	12				4		7		14				6			11	10	
21	H	Brechin City	570	0-3	1	2	3				8		9					5	14	12						7		11		4			10		6	15	
28	A	Hamilton Academical	773	0-3	1	2	3				8		9							12				4		7		15				6	11		5	9	
May 1	A	Peterhead	475	1-1	1		3				8		9							11¹				4		7		10				6			5	2	
5	H	Albion Rovers	487	1-0	1	2	3						9						7	8¹				4				10				6	11			5	
TOTAL FULL APPEARANCES					34	26	36	4	2	6	28	1	29	5	15			28	5	23	21		4	17	1	27	4	18	6	3	8	15	13	1	8	6	2
TOTAL SUB APPEARANCES						(1)		(3)	(2)	(2)	(5)	(3)	(1)	(7)	(4)	(1)	(2)		(7)	(8)	(4)	(1)					(1)	(5)		(3)				(1)		(1)	
TOTAL GOALS SCORED													6	2	3			3		3	1					6		2					1		1		

Small bold figures denote goalscorers. † denotes opponent's own goal.

Borough Briggs Stadium

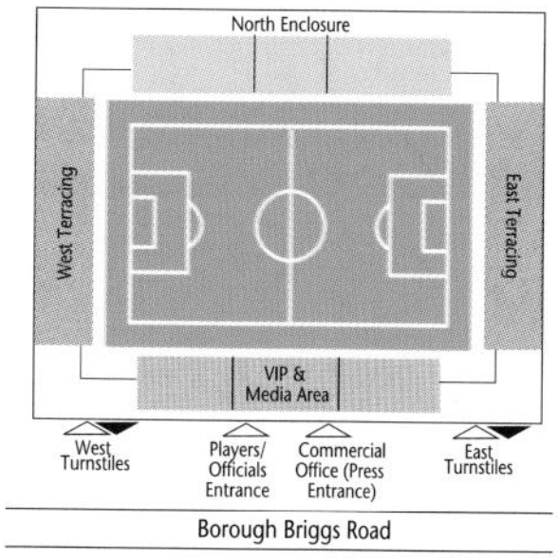
North Enclosure
West Terracing
East Terracing
VIP &
Media Area
West
Turnstiles
Players/
Officials
Entrance
Commercial
Office (Press
Entrance)
East
Turnstiles
Borough Briggs Road

CAPACITY: 4,962; Seated 480, Standing 4,482

PITCH DIMENSIONS: 111 yds x 72 yds

FACILITIES FOR DISABLED SUPPORTERS:
An area is designated in the south east enclosure.

Team playing kits

How to get there

Borough Briggs can be reached by the following routes:
TRAINS: – Elgin Railway Station is situated approximately one mile south of the stadium.
BUSES: – Elgin bus station is situated in the town centre, which is only half a mile from Borough Briggs.
CARS: – Elgin is situated on the A96, 38 miles east of Inverness and 67 miles west of Aberdeen. From the south, leave A9 at Aviemore and take the A95 as far as Craigellachie then take A941 to Elgin.

Links Park Stadium,
Wellington Street,
Montrose, DD10 8QD

**ALL CORRESPONDENCE
SHOULD BE ADDRESSED TO:**
Malcolm J. Watters Esq.,
133 Murray Street, Montrose, DD10 8JQ

CHAIRMAN
John F. Paton

VICE-CHAIRMAN
Malcolm J. Watters

DIRECTORS
John D. Crawford & David I. Tait

ASSOCIATE DIRECTORS
Arthur Forsyth & David G. Skene

HON. PRESIDENT
William Johnston, M.B.E., J.P.

SECRETARY
Malcolm J. Watters

ASSISTANT SECRETARY
Andrew Stephen

MATCHDAY SECRETARY
Iain Gordon

MANAGER
John Sheran

ASSISTANT MANAGER
Malcolm Lowe

RESERVE/GOALKEEPING COACH
James Butter

YOUTH COACH/U18 COACH
Derek Armstrong

YOUTH CO-ORDINATOR
John Crawford

COMMERCIAL EXECUTIVE
Mrs Glynis Crawford
(B) (01674) 673200 (H) (01674) 673758

PHYSIOTHERAPIST
Allan Borthwick

**FOOTBALL SAFETY OFFICERS'
ASSOCIATION REPRESENTATIVE/
HEAD OF SECURITY**
Wilson Patrick (H) (01674) 676917

GROUNDSMAN
Ron Marquis

KIT MANAGER
Brian Leiper

KIT MEN
George Ferris & Ron Marquis

MATCHDAY PROGRAMME EDITOR
Andrew Stephen
(B) (01356) 626766 (H) (01674) 672314

TELEPHONES
Ground/Commercial (01674) 673200
Sec. Home (01674) 674838
Sec. Bus. (01674) 674941
Sec. Fax (01674) 677830
Ground Fax (01674) 677311

INTERNET ADDRESS
www.montrosefc.co.uk

CLUB SHOP
Situated at Stadium (01674) 674941.
Open 10.30 a.m. – 5.00 p.m. Fri.
and on home matchdays

OFFICIAL SUPPORTERS CLUB
c/o Links Park, Wellington Street,
Montrose, DD10 8QD

TEAM CAPTAIN
Mark Craib

SHIRT SPONSOR
Bon Accord Glass

KIT SUPPLIER
SPALL

LIST OF PLAYERS 2001-2002

SURNAME	FIRST NAME	MIDDLE NAME	DATE OF BIRTH	PLACE OF BIRTH	DATE OF SIGNING	HEIGHT FT INS	WEIGHT ST LBS	POS. ON PITCH	PREVIOUS CLUB
Adam	Ronald	George	22/09/82	Dundee	07/10/00	5 9.0	10 7	Gk	Forfar West End
Allison	John		05/06/70	Dunfermline	08/06/01	5 8.0	11 3	Mid	East Fife
Brand	Ralph		17/07/70	Dundee	30/05/01	5 9.0	12 0	Fwd	Forfar Athletic
Butter	James	Ross	14/12/66	Dundee	14/07/01	6 1.0	12 12	Gk	East Stirlingshire
Christie	Graeme		01/01/71	Dundee	20/10/00	6 3.0	12 6	Def	Brechin City
Conway	Francis	Joseph	29/12/69	Dundee	30/05/01	6 0.0	12 4	Def	Alloa Athletic
Craib	Mark		08/02/70	St. Andrews	17/07/92	5 10.0	11 12	Def	Dundee
Ferguson	Stuart		09/11/80	Broxburn	03/08/00	5 10.0	10 5	Def/Mid	Forfar Athletic
Hutcheon	Andrew	John	16/05/79	Aberdeen	17/11/00	5 8.0	11 7	Fwd	Brechin City
Johnson	Ian	Grant	24/03/72	Dundee	30/05/01	5 11.0	11 10	Mid	Alloa Athletic
Kerrigan	Steven	Paul	29/09/70	Wolverhampton	30/05/01	5 10.0	11 7	Fwd	East Fife
Laidlaw	Steven	James	17/06/73	Edinburgh	11/12/00	6 0.0	13 0	Fwd	Berwick Rangers
Lowe	Bradley		16/07/81	Dundee	24/05/00	6 0.0	11 2	Mid	Forfar Athletic
Magee	Kevin		10/04/71	Livingston	08/06/01	5 10.0	12 0	Mid	East Fife
McGlynn	Gary	Dominic	24/11/77	Falkirk	30/07/99	5 11.0	12 5	Gk	Dundee
McHattie	Keith		23/12/80	Aberdeen	15/03/99	5 10.0	10 8	Mid	Parkvale Juniors
McKellar	James	Robert	29/12/76	Bellshill	24/05/00	5 8.0	11 0	Mid	Forfar Athletic
McKenzie	Michael	Stanley	22/06/79	Aberdeen	03/08/00	6 1.0	13 7	Fwd	Lossiemouth
McQuillan	John		20/07/70	Stranraer	03/08/01	5 10.0	11 7	Def	Dundee United
Mitchell	Jonathan	Andrew	22/06/81	Dundee	24/05/00	5 10.0	10 4	Fwd	Forfar Athletic
Muirhead	David		16/02/78	Stirling	24/05/00	6 0.0	13 0	Mid	East Stirlingshire
Sharp	Raymond		16/11/69	Stirling	30/05/01	5 11.0	13 7	Def	East Fife
Stewart	Steven	Alexander	15/12/72	Dundee	31/07/01	5 11.0	12 7	Mid	East Stirlingshire
Young	John		11/03/81	Aberdeen	30/03/01	6 1.0	12 5	Def	Dyce JFC

Milestones

YEAR OF FORMATION: 1879
MOST CAPPED PLAYER: Sandy Keiller
NO. OF CAPS: 6 (2 whilst with Montrose)
MOST LEAGUE POINTS IN A SEASON: 53 (Division 2 – 1974/75 and Second Division 1984/85) (2 Points for a Win)
67 (Third Division – Season 1994/95) (3 Points for a Win)
RECORD ATTENDANCE: 8,983 (-v- Dundee – 17.3.1973)
RECORD VICTORY: 12-0 (-v- Vale of Leithen – Scottish Cup, 4.1.1975)
RECORD DEFEAT: 0-13 (-v- Aberdeen, 17.3.1951)

The Gable Endies' ten year league record

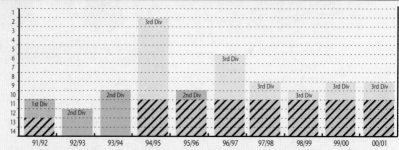

THE GABLE ENDIES' CLUB FACTFILE 2000/2001
RESULTS... APPEARANCES... SCORERS... ATTENDANCES...

Date	Venue	Opponents	Att	Res	McClymn G.	Young J.	Black K.	Marwick S.	Niddrie K.	Craib M.	Robertson S.	Harrison T.	McIlravey P.	McKenzie M.	Dailly G.	Mailer C.	Mitchell J.	McWilliam R.	Ferguson S.	McKellar J.	O'Driscoll J.	Snedden S.	Ogboke C.	Lowe B.	Muirhead D.	Scott W.D.	Gillillan F.	Thompson B.	Joy I.	Zahani-Oni L.	Catto P.	Christie G.	Shand M.	Hutcheson A.	Laidlaw S.	Byers K.	Craig D.	Fox R.
Aug 5	A	Peterhead	745	0-2	1	2	3	4	5	6	7	8	9	10	11	14	15	12																				
12	H	East Stirlingshire	304	0-1	1	2				4		6	10	11	9	3	8	14	7	5	12	15																
19	A	Hamilton Academical	426	0-6	1	2		4		6		8		9	7	16	10	3	11	5	15																	
26	H	East Fife	355	0-1	1	2				6	7	8	12	9	4		10	3	11	14	5		15															
Sep 9	A	Brechin City	465	1-6	1	2		7		6		8	9[1]		12		16	3	11	10			15		4	5												
16	H	Dumbarton	317	2-2	1	2		7		6		8	9[1]		5			3	11	10[1]					4			16										
23	A	Elgin City	817	1-1	1	2		7		6		8	9[1]		5	16	15	3	11	10					4			12										
30	A	Cowdenbeath	378	0-2			3	4		6	2		9		5							14	7		8	1	10	11										
Oct 7	A	Albion Rovers	230	0-2			5	7		6	2	16			4	12				8			10	1	3	11	15											
14	H	Peterhead	409	0-2	1		5	4		6	2		12	9	7	14		3		10		11	15		8													
21	A	East Stirlingshire	258	2-1	1			16		6		8		12	2	9[2]	14		7	10		4			3			11	5									
28	A	East Fife	375	1-3	1			7		6		8		14	2[1]	9			12	10		4			3			11	5	15								
Nov 4	H	Brechin City	622	1-1	1			7		6		8		12[1]	2	9			14	10		4			3			11	5									
11	H	Elgin City	459	0-0	1			7		6		8		10	2	9		15				4			3			11	5	16								
18	A	Dumbarton	238	0-1	1			7		6	4	8		12	2	15				10					3			11	5	9								
25	A	Albion Rovers	311	2-3	1			7[1]		6	4	8		9[1]	2		11								3				5	10								
Dec 2	H	Cowdenbeath	311	1-2	1			7		6	2		9	8	14[1]	3						12	4		11				5	10								
Feb 3	H	Albion Rovers	244	0-1						6	8				2	15	12	3	7			16	4	1				5	10	9	11							
17	A	Hamilton Academical	411	3-1	1			2		6		16	10		8	14						4			11			5		9[3]	7	3						
24	H	East Stirlingshire	305	1-1	1			2		6	15		10		8	12						4	7		11[1]			5		9		3						
Mar 10	A	East Fife	407	0-1	1					6		8	10		2	14		15				7	4		11			5		12	9	3						
13	H	East Fife	249	1-1	1					6		8	10		2	14	12					7	4		11			5		15	9	3[1]						
17	H	Elgin City	366	†2-1	1					6		8[1]	10		2		12	16				7	4		11			5		15	9	3						
20	A	Brechin City	526	0-3	1					6		8	12	16		15			11	7			4					2	5	10	9	3						
27	H	Dumbarton	165	1-2	1					6			9		2	12	16	11	7				4		15			8	5	10[1]		3						
31	A	Dumbarton	751	2-1	1					6	8				2	9[1]	15	7					4		11				5	10[1]		3		16				
Apr 3	A	Elgin City	385	2-0	1					6	8		12		2	9	15	7[1]					4		11[1]					10		3	5					
7	A	Albion Rovers	213	1-2	1					6	8	14	12		2	9[1]	15	7					4		11					10		3	5					
10	A	Cowdenbeath	319	1-2	1			2		6	8		14	10		12			3	7			4		11					5	9[1]							
14	H	Cowdenbeath	407	0-1	1			2		6	8		14	10	15	12			3	7			4		11					5	6							
17	A	Peterhead	325	1-1	1					6	4[1]		9	12		10			8	7			2		11					5						3		
21	H	Peterhead	369	2-2	1					6	4	15	9[1]		14	10[1]			8	7			2		11					5						3		
24	H	Brechin City	544	1-3	1					6	4	10	9	14	8[1]	12	15	11	7				2							5						3		
28	A	East Stirlingshire	186	1-0	1					8			14	6	10[1]		3	7		15		4			11					5	9						2	
May 1	H	Hamilton Academical	495	0-2	1					6	8		16	12	2	10		3	7			4			11					5	9							
5	H	Hamilton Academical	916	1-4	1	2				6	16	14	5		10			4	7			15	8		11						9[1]					3		
TOTAL FULL APPEARANCES					33	8	4	19	1	35	8	24	7	22	5	28	12	3	23	17	8	2	1	11	22	1	2	3	24	2	8	23	14	7	2	14	3
TOTAL SUB APPEARANCES								(1)			(3)	(5)	(11)	(5)		(4)	(18)	(10)	(2)	(6)	(2)			(5)	(4)		(2)		(1)		(1)		(1)	(4)		(1)
TOTAL GOALS SCORED								1				1	1	6		2	7		1		1						2					4	3		1

Small bold figures denote goalscorers. † denotes opponent's own goal.

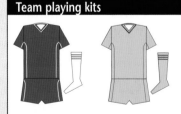

Links Park Stadium

WELLINGTON PARK
WELLINGTON STREET
UNION ROW

CAPACITY: 3,292; Seated 1,334, Standing 1,958
PITCH DIMENSIONS: 110 yds x 70 yds
FACILITIES FOR DISABLED SUPPORTERS:
Area set aside for wheelchairs and designated area in new stand.

Team playing kits

How to get there

Links Park can be reached by the following routes:

TRAINS: Montrose is on the Inter-City 125 route from London to Aberdeen and also on the Glasgow-Aberdeen route. There is a regular service and the station is about 15 minutes walk from the ground.

BUSES: An hourly service of buses from Aberdeen and Dundee stop in the town centre and it is a 15 minute walk from here to the ground.

CARS: Car parking is available in the car park at the ground and there are numerous side streets all round the park which can be used if necessary.

---

email: info@sfl.scottishfootball.com • website: www.scottishfootball.com

Peterhead

Balmoor Stadium, Lord Catto Park,
Balmoor Terrace, Peterhead, AB42 1EU
ALL CORRESPONDENCE
SHOULD BE ADDRESSED TO:
George Moore, 23 Willowbank Road,
Peterhead, AB42 2FG

CHAIRMAN
Roger Taylor

VICE-CHAIRMAN
Roger G. Morrison

DIRECTORS
Colin Grant, George Watson,
Gerry Gaffney, A. Gordon MacGregor

MANAGEMENT COMMITTEE
Dave Watson, Arthur Duncan &
George Moore

SECRETARY
George Moore

GENERAL MANAGER
Dave Watson

MANAGER
Ian Wilson

ASSISTANT MANAGER
Alan Lyons

YOUTH DEVELOPMENT OFFICER
Derek Robertson

CLUB DOCTOR
Dr. Ian Small

PHYSIOTHERAPIST
Jennifer Johnson

ACCOUNTS
Shona Aird

FOOTBALL SAFETY OFFICERS'
ASSOCIATION REPRESENTATIVE
Arthur Duncan (01779) 873171

STADIUM & GROUND MAINTENANCE
Jack Wilson

COMMERCIAL MANAGER
Colin Grant Bus. (01358) 724270

KIT MAN
Allan Park

MEDIA LIAISON OFFICERS
Dave Watson (01224) 771100 &
George Moore (01224) 820851

MATCHDAY PROGRAMME EDITOR
Billy Youngson
c/o Club (01779) 478256

TELEPHONES
Ground (01779) 478256
Fax (01779) 490682
Sec. Bus. (01224) 820851
Sec. Home (01779) 476870

OFFICIAL SUPPORTERS CLUB
c/o Balmoor Stadium,
Peterhead, AB42 1EU

TEAM CAPTAIN
Steve King

SHIRT SPONSOR
ASCO

KIT SUPPLIER
RIVA

LIST OF PLAYERS 2001-2002

SURNAME	FIRST NAME	MIDDLE NAME	DATE OF BIRTH	PLACE OF BIRTH	DATE OF SIGNING	HEIGHT FT INS	WEIGHT ST LBS	POS. ON PITCH	PREVIOUS CLUB
Bisset	Kevin		09/01/81	Aberdeen	27/07/01	6 1.0	12 7	Mid	Longside
Brown	Scott	Edward A.	19/02/68	Aberdeen	03/08/00	5 6.0	11 0	Mid	Montrose
Buchanan	Ross	Alexander	20/10/80	Aberdeen	01/08/00	6 1.0	15 0	Gk	Buchanhaven Hearts JFC
Clark	Gary		01/11/71	Aberdeen	03/08/00	5 10.0	12 3	Fwd	Lossiemouth
Clark	Scott	Norman	24/04/72	Aberdeen	01/08/00	5 8.0	11 2	Def/Mid	Fraserburgh
Cooper	Craig	Brian	17/01/73	Arbroath	14/09/00	5 10.0	11 0	Mid/Fwd	Arbroath
Duffy	John		22/08/81	Paisley	27/07/01	6 0.0	12 0	Def	Dundee United
Findlay	Craig		22/09/80	Broxburn	02/08/01	6 1.0	13 0	Fwd	Berwick Rangers
Gibson	Andrew	Mitchell	02/02/69	Broxburn	01/08/00	5 9.0	11 12	Mid	Forfar Athletic
Johnston	Martin	Alan	24/06/78	Aberdeen	03/08/00	6 2.0	12 0	Mid/Fwd	Cove Rangers
King	Steven	Charles	06/04/67	Aberdeen	03/08/00	5 11.0	12 7	Def	Montrose
Livingstone	Richard		10/04/74	Aberdeen	01/08/00	5 11.0	12 4	Fwd	Burnley
Mackay	Stuart	John	03/03/75	Inverness	23/05/01	5 10.0	12 7	Mid	East Fife
Murray	Ian		29/09/75	Aberdeen	17/11/00	5 5.0	10 8	Mid	Fraserburgh
Pirie	Ivor	Douglas L.	30/06/64	Inverurie	01/08/00	6 0.0	13 0	Gk	Lossiemouth
Simpson	Mark	James	04/11/75	Aberdeen	01/08/00	5 11.0	12 6	Def	Morton
Slater	Mark	Andrew	02/04/79	Buckie	07/08/01	5 11.0	12 0	Def	Dundee
Smith	Greig	Robert	26/03/76	Aberdeen	22/06/01	6 0.0	12 8	Def	Brechin City
Stewart	Iain	Angus	23/10/69	Dundee	12/10/00	5 7.0	10 5	Fwd	Inverness Caledonian Th.
Tindal	Kevin	Douglas	11/04/71	Arbroath	14/09/00	5 8.0	12 4	Mid	Arbroath
Yeats	Craig		28/09/69	Aberdeen	18/08/00	5 9.0	12 9	Mid	Montrose

Milestones

YEAR OF FORMATION: 1891
MOST CAPPED PLAYER:
MOST LEAGUE POINTS IN A SEASON: 89 (Highland League – Season 1989/90 (3 Points for a Win))
49 (SFL Third Division – Season 2000/01 (3 Points for a Win))
MOST LEAGUE GOALS SCORED BY A PLAYER IN A SEASON: Craig Yeats (Season 2000/01)
NO. OF GOALS SCORED: 11
RECORD ATTENDANCE: 6,310 (-v- Celtic – 1948 at Recreation Park)
1,647 (-v- Morton – 27.1.2001 – at Balmoor Stadium)
RECORD VICTORY: 17-0 (-v- Fort William – Season 1998/99)
RECORD DEFEAT: 0-13 (-v- Aberdeen, Scottish Cup, Season 1923/24)

The Blue Toon's ten year league record

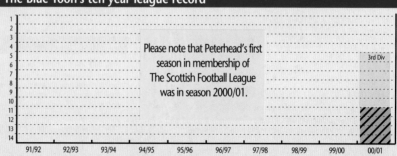

Please note that Peterhead's first season in membership of The Scottish Football League was in season 2000/01.

3rd Div

91/92 92/93 93/94 94/95 95/96 96/97 97/98 98/99 99/00 00/01

THE BLUE TOON'S CLUB FACTFILE 2000/2001
RESULTS... APPEARANCES... SCORERS... ATTENDANCES...

BELL'S SCOTTISH FOOTBALL LEAGUE

Date	Venue	Opponents	Att.	Res	Pirie I.	Craig D.	King S.	Herd W.	Simpson M.	Paterson S.	Cooper C.	Johnston M.	Clark G.	Brown S.	Livingstone R.	De-Barros M.	Smith D.	Gibson A.	Keddie J.	Clark S.	O'Connor G.	Yeats C.	Tindal K.	Stewart I.	Watson C.	Bett B.	Murray I.	Buchanan R.	Smith G.	Huggon R.	Clark P.	Duffy J.
Aug 5	H	Montrose	745	2-0	1	2	3	4¹	5	6	7	8¹	9	10	11	12																
12	A	East Fife	619	1-1	1	2	3	4	5	6¹	7	8	9	10	11		16	15														
19	H	Dumbarton	630	2-0	1	2	3	4	5	6	7¹	8¹			11	16	10	9	15	12												
26	H	Brechin City	563	1-2	1	2	3	4	5	6	7	8			11	15	10¹		14		9											
Sep 9	A	Elgin City	1,135	†3-1	1	2	3	4				8		10	11	6	7	15		5	9¹	12¹										
16	H	East Stirlingshire	614	2-4	1	2	3	4							15						9	14¹										
23	A	Hamilton Academical	369	0-3	1	2	3	4		6	7	8			11				16		12		9	10								
30	A	Albion Rovers	358	0-0	1			4	5	6		8			11	15	12	7		2	9	10	3									
Oct 7	H	Cowdenbeath	637	†3-0	1	16	3	4	5	6					11	7	10¹	14		2	9¹	8										
14	A	Montrose	409	2-0	1		3		5	14	15	12			11	7	10	6		4	8	2	9²									
21	H	East Fife	637	0-0	1		3	4	5	16	15	14			11	7				2	8	6	9									
28	A	Brechin City	469	2-3	1		3	4	5		7	12			11		10¹			2	8	6	9¹	16	15							
Nov 4	H	Elgin City	850	1-0	1		3	4	5¹		7	11				14	10	16		2	8	6	9	15								
11	H	Hamilton Academical	790	1-1	1		3	4	5		7	8				14	10	16		2	9¹	6		12	11							
18	A	East Stirlingshire	262	3-1	1		3	4	5			8¹			11	16	10	12		2	9¹			6¹	7							
25	A	Cowdenbeath	404	0-2	1		3	4	5			8			11		10			2	9		14	6	7	17						
Dec 2	H	Albion Rovers	516	1-2	1		3	4	5			8			11		10	15		2	9¹	14	12	6	7	1						
23	A	Dumbarton	821	3-1	1		3			16¹		10			11		12	6		2	9¹	5	8¹	4	15	7						
30	H	Brechin City	889	0-2			3		5		15	12			11		16	10		2	9	6	8	4	7							
Jan 13	H	East Stirlingshire	606	1-2			3	4			7	10			11	15¹	12			2	9	6	8	5	14							
20	A	Hamilton Academical	645	0-3			3				12	10			11		6			2	14	5	8	15	7	9						
Feb 24	A	East Fife	380	1-2			3					12			11	14			7		10	2	8¹		16		9	6				
Mar 6	H	Elgin City	524	1-0			3	4	5	11¹	10					14			2		12	6	8			9	7	15				
13	H	Cowdenbeath	499	3-0			3		5		7	10¹		16				6	11	9¹	2	8¹			15				14			4
17	H	Hamilton Academical	710	2-1			3		5		7	10		14	11	6				9¹	2	8¹	16						15			4
20	A	Albion Rovers	272	1-0			3		5			10		7	11	6		14		9	2	8¹										4
24	H	Dumbarton	432	0-1			3	12	5			10		7	11	6		15			8	16										4
27	A	Brechin City	396	1-1			3	6	5			10¹			11			7		9	2	8	14									4
31	A	East Stirlingshire	190	0-1			3	6	5			10		15	11	7				9	2	8							12			4
Apr 7	A	Cowdenbeath	348	0-4			3		5			10		11	14	6				9	2	8					15	16	7			4
14	H	Albion Rovers	526	1-1			3	4	5			10		15	9¹	6				7	2	8					11					
17	H	Montrose	325	1-1			3		5	16	10¹			11	9	4				6	2	8					7		15	12		
21	A	Montrose	369	2-2			3	4	5	11	10		15		6					14¹		8					7		9¹			2
28	H	East Fife	511	2-1			3	4	5		7	10¹		14	11	6¹				9	12	8					15					2
May 1	H	Elgin City	475	1-1			3		5	12	10			11	15	6		16		9¹		7										2
5	A	Dumbarton	715	2-2			3			11¹	10¹		8	16	15	6		2		9	5		14		7							4
TOTAL FULL APPEARANCES					35	7	35	25	31	8	16	30	2	6	25	4	17	16	24	4	27	25	22	3	4	11	1	4	3	11		
TOTAL SUB APPEARANCES						(1)		(1)		(2)	(7)	(5)		(2)	(4)	(8)	(11)	(10)	(2)	(5)		(5)	(2)	(2)	(8)	(3)	(5)	(1)	(2)	(5)	(1)
TOTAL GOALS SCORED							1		1	1	5	8			5	1				1	11		8			1			1		

Small bold figures denote goalscorers. † denotes opponent's own goal.

Balmoor Stadium

BALMOOR ROAD

CAR PARK

CAR PARK

CAPACITY: 3,250; Seated 990, Standing 2,260
PITCH DIMENSIONS: 105 yds x 70 yds
FACILITIES FOR DISABLED SUPPORTERS:
Designated area in new stand

Team playing kits

How to get there

Balmoor Stadium can be reached by the following routes:
TRAINS: The nearest train station is Aberdeen. From Aberdeen you would have to travel by bus to Peterhead. Travel time 1 hour.
BUSES: Buses leave Aberdeen City every hour for Peterhead. Travel time 1 hour.
CARS: From Aberdeen City: Take A90 to Peterhead, at first roundabout approaching Peterhead take a left at McDonalds to St. Fergus (still on A90). Continue on this road to next roundabout - go straight on to the next T-junction. Take right A980 back into Peterhead - continue on A980 through next roundabout and Balmoor Stadium is about ½ mile past the roundabout on the right hand side.

The Blue Toon

email: info@sfl.scottishfootball.com • website: www.scottishfootball.com

The National Stadium,
Hampden Park, Mount Florida,
Glasgow, G42 9BA

HON. PATRON
The Lord Macfarlane of Bearsden KT
PRESIDENT
A. Kenneth C. Harvey
COMMITTEE
David Gordon, B.Acc., A.C.M.A. (Treasurer),
Malcolm D. Mackay, David McNeil,
Garry M. Templeman, James M. Hastie LL.B,
Dr. Alan S. Hutchison B.Sc., M.B., ChB.,
F.R.C.P. Glas, F.R.C., P.A.T.H., David B. Stirling,
Ross Caven MBA, M.Sc, B.Sc &
James Nicholson
SECRETARY
Alistair MacKay
OFFICE STAFF
Mrs. Janice Balmain & Mrs. Margaret Dunlop
TEAM COACH
John McCormack
RESERVE TEAM COACH
David Hunter
COACHING STAFF
Keith MacKenzie, Robert Kelly,
Bobby Dickson, Graham Ogg,
Michael Jamieson, Steve Adam &
Archie Stormonth
GOALKEEPING COACH
Ronnie Cant
YOUTH DEVELOPMENT OFFICER
Frank Reilly
YOUTH ADVISOR
Tommy Wilson
YOUTH TEAM COACHES
U18 – Keith MacKenzie, Robert Kelly
& Michael Jamieson,
U16 – Bobby Dickson, Steve Adam
& Graham Ogg
U15 – Craig Mulholland, Barry McNab
& Willie Neil
U14 – Michael O'Halloran, Michael Gillespie
& David White
U13 – Andy Gilmartin, Chic McGarry
& Gordon Smith
CLUB DOCTOR
Alan S. Hutchison
PHYSIOTHERAPIST
Robert C. Findlay
CHIEF SCOUT
Jack Jolly
GROUNDSMEN
Dougie Imrie & Scott McCreadie
**FOOTBALL SAFETY OFFICERS'
ASSOCIATION REPRESENTATIVE**
Alistair MacKay (0141) 632 1275
PAVILION ATTENDANT & KIT MANAGER
William Neil
COMMERCIAL DIRECTOR
Garry M. Templeman (0141) 632 1275
MEDIA LIAISON OFFICER
Alistair MacKay
MATCHDAY PROGRAMME EDITORS
David B. Stirling & Logan Taylor
TELEPHONES
Office (0141) 632 1275
Stadium Operations (0141) 620 4000
Fax (0141) 636 1612
E-MAIL/INTERNET ADDRESS
d.mcneil@queensparkfc.co.uk
www.queensparkfc.co.uk
CLUB SHOP
Home matches only – Hampden Park (Kiosk
within BT Scotland Stand).
Open 2.15p.m. – 3.00p.m. and
4.45pm – 5.00pm on home match days.
Mail Orders may be obtained through the
Secretary of the
Official Supporters Club.
OFFICIAL SUPPORTERS CLUB
c/o Secretary, Keith McAllister,
58 Brunton Street,
Glasgow, G44 3NQ
TEAM CAPTAIN
Danny Ferry
SHIRT SPONSOR
Barr Irn Bru - Original and Best
KIT SUPPLIER
FILA

LIST OF PLAYERS 2001-2002

SURNAME	FIRST NAME	MIDDLE NAME	DATE OF BIRTH	PLACE OF BIRTH	DATE OF SIGNING	HEIGHT FT INS	WEIGHT ST LBS	POS. ON PITCH	PREVIOUS CLUB
Borland	Paul	Joseph	28/06/79	Rutherglen	27/08/99	5 9.0	9 8	Def	Celtic
Brown	James	Paul	24/09/77	Greenock	26/11/98	5 11.0	12 7	Mid	Gourock Y.A.C.
Bruce	Gordon		10/07/75	Edinburgh	22/08/00	6 2.0	14 0	Gk	Stranraer
Bruce	James		03/12/82	Rutherglen	01/08/01	6 0.0	12 10	Def	Dundee United
Canning	Steven		06/05/83	Glasgow	31/07/01	5 10.0	11 0	Mid	X Form
Carberry	Andrew	Alexander W.	27/06/81	Glasgow	29/06/01	5 10.0	11 7	Fwd	Knightswood Juveniles
Carson	Kevin		30/08/81	Bellshill	03/08/01	6 0.0	12 7	Def	Rutherglen Glencairn
Caven	Ross		04/08/65	Glasgow	12/08/82	6 0.0	12 0	Def/Mid	Possil Y.M.C.A.
Clark	Ross		07/02/83	Rutherglen	31/07/01	5 9.0	11 0	Mid	X Form
Collins	Neill		02/09/83	Irvine	29/06/01	6 2.0	12 7	Def	S Form
Cunningham	John		28/10/79	Glasgow	19/07/00	6 2.0	13 0	Def	Knightswood U'21
Ewing	Christopher	Gordon	12/10/78	Glasgow	03/08/01	6 4.0	13 0	Fwd	Pollok
Ferry	Daniel		31/01/77	Glasgow	23/06/95	5 7.0	11 4	Mid/Fwd	Queen's Park U'18s
Fisher	Christopher	Alexander	30/06/83	Glasgow	29/06/01	5 9.0	12 0	Fwd	Queen's Park B.C.
Gallagher	Patrick	Joseph D.	28/12/74	Glasgow	26/06/01	5 10.0	12 0	Fwd	St. Mungo's U'21s
Jackson	Ross	Douglas	28/10/79	Vale of Leven	30/11/00	5 10.0	12 0	Fwd	St. Mungo's U'21s
Marshall	Stephen		30/04/80	Glasgow	25/05/00	5 10.0	10 8	Mid	Clyde
Martin	William	McLean	21/08/81	Glasgow	25/05/00	6 1.0	13 0	Mid/Fwd	Kilmarnock
McKee	Chris		20/10/79	Glasgow	26/06/01	5 8.0	10 7	Mid	Viewfield Rovers U'21s
McPhee	Gary		01/10/79	Glasgow	31/07/01	5 10.0	110	Mid	Forfar Athletic
Miller	Brian		15/08/79	Glasgow	29/06/01	5 10.0	12 0	Mid	Kilbirnie Ladeside
Miller	Greg		23/02/77	Glasgow	26/07/00	5 11.0	12 0	Fwd	Neilston Juniors
Mitchell	Anthony	Martin	10/01/79	Glasgow	03/08/01	6 1.0	13 8	Gk	Larkhall Thistle
Orr	Stewart	John	05/11/80	Glasgow	05/06/99	5 11.5	11 7	Mid	St. Johnstone
Quinn	Anthony	Thomas P.	09/09/81	Glasgow	26/06/01	6 0.0	12 7	Def	Kirkintilloch Rob Roy
Sinclair	Richard		20/05/82	Glasgow	25/05/00	5 10.0	12 0	Def	S Form
Smith	Graham		03/10/82	Bellshill	03/08/01	6 1.0	12 7	Gk	Kilmarnock
White	James		05/06/80	Glasgow	26/06/01	6 0.0	11 6	Def	Chryston U'21s

Milestones

YEAR OF FORMATION: 1867
MOST CAPPED PLAYER: Walter Arnott
NO. OF CAPS: 14
MOST LEAGUE POINTS IN A SEASON: 57 (Division 2 – Season 1922/23) (2 points for a win)
69 (Third Division – Season1999/2000) (3 points for a win)
MOST LEAGUE GOALS SCORED BY A PLAYER IN A SEASON: William Martin (Season 1937/38)
NO. OF GOALS SCORED: 30
GROUND RECORD ATTENDANCE: 149,547 (Scotland v England – 17.4.1937)
CLUB RECORD ATTENDANCE: 95,772 (-v- Rangers – 18.01.1930)
RECORD VICTORY: 16-0 (-v- St. Peters – Scottish Cup, 29.8.1885)
RECORD DEFEAT: 0-9 (-v- Motherwell – Division 1, 29.4.1930)

The Spiders' ten year league record

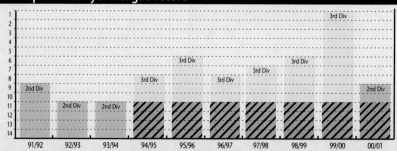

THE SPIDERS' CLUB FACTFILE 2000/2001
RESULTS... APPEARANCES... SCORERS... ATTENDANCES...

BELL'S®
SCOTTISH FOOTBALL LEAGUE

Date	Venue	Opponents	Att.	Res	Stewart C.	Ferry D.	Marshall S.	Duncan G.	Connaghan D.	Sinclair R.	Finlayson K.	Connell G.	Gallagher M.	Brown J.	Carroll F.	Ajet W.	Flannigan C.	Miller G.	Martin P.	Scobie R.	Orr S.	Caven A.	Borland P.	Smith A.	Christie F.	Fisher C.	Travers M.	Bruce G.	MacFarlane N.	Jackson R.	Cunningham J.	Canning S.	Herve M.	Corr R.	Martin W.	Clark R.	Collins N.
Aug 5	H	Berwick Rangers	721	1-0	1	2	3[1]	4	5	6	7	8	9	10	11																							
12	A	Forfar Athletic	516	1-0	1	2	3	4	5	6	7	8	9	10	11[1]	15	14	12																				
19	H	Queen of the South	839	1-0	1	2	3	4	5	6	7[1]	8	9	12	11	14	16	10																				
26	A	Stirling Albion	753	1-0	1	2	3	4	5	6	7	8	9	10	11[1]			16	14	15																		
Sep 9	H	Partick Thistle	4,019	0-1	1	2	3	4	5	6	7		9	10	11		8	14	12	15																		
16	A	Stranraer	587	0-3	1	2	3	4	5		7		9	12	11		10	14	8	6	15																	
23	H	Arbroath	721	0-0		2	3	4	5		7		9					11	10	6	8	1	15	16	14													
30	H	Stenhousemuir	793	2-0	1	2	10	4	5		7		9					11		8	6[1]	3[1]																
Oct 7	A	Clydebank	375	0-2		2	10	4	5	16	7	14	9	12				11		8	6					3	1											
14	A	Berwick Rangers	514	1-1		2	10	4	5	6	7[1]	8	9	15	11			12	16							3												
21	A	Forfar Athletic	741	0-0		2	10	4	5	6	7	8	9	16	11			12								3												
28	H	Stirling Albion	920	3-0		2	6	4	5		7[1]	8	9[1]		10[1]			12								16	14	3	1									
Nov 4	A	Partick Thistle	4,035	1-2		2	6	4	5		7	8	9[1]		11			10		12						16	14	3	1									
11	A	Arbroath	573	†2-2		2	8	4	5	14	7		9[1]					10		11	12	6					16	3	1									
18	H	Stranraer	753	1-2		2	8	4	5	12	7		9[1]	15	14			10		11	6							3	1									
25	H	Clydebank	668	1-1			10	4	5	6	7	8	9		14			12	16	11		1						3[1]		2								
Dec 2	H	Stenhousemuir	492	1-1			10		5	6	7	8	9		11			14		4[1]	15	1					3			2	16							
16	H	Berwick Rangers	690	1-1		2	10	15	5		2	7	8	9				16			6	3						4	11									
23	H	Queen of the South	1,288	1-1			10		5	2	7[1]	8	12	9				14		6	3						11	4	16									
Jan 2	H	Partick Thistle	3,938	0-2			10		5	7	12	9	15	2						6	3						8	11	4	16								
13	A	Stranraer	556	1-0	1		10		5	6		9	7	11				8	14	12[1]							4	15	2									
20	H	Arbroath	1,148	1-1	1		10		5	6	7		9	11	14			8			3[1]						4	15	2									
Feb 10	H	Stenhousemuir	704	1-2	14	10		5	4	7			12[1]					8		15		1					3	6	11			2	9					
17	H	Queen of the South	711	1-2		3		5		7			11	12				8		10	6					1	4	15			2[1]	9						
Mar 3	A	Partick Thistle	2,852	1-2		2	10[1]		5	4	7							8		14	16	6	3								11	12	1	9			
10	H	Stirling Albion	822	†1-1		2	4		5	7				12	10	8		16		6	3					14					11		1	9			
13	A	Forfar Athletic	374	0-3		2	4		5	7				14	10	8		16		6	3										11	15	1	9			
17	A	Arbroath	605	0-2		2	4		5				11			8		7	16	6						12	3	10	14	1	9						
20	A	Clydebank	209	1-2		2			5			9		12		8		14	10[1]								3	7	4	6	1	11	15					
24	A	Stirling Albion	568	2-0		2			5		7		9[1]			8			10[1]	6	3								4	11	1	16	15	14			
31	H	Stranraer	619	1-0		2			5		7		9[1]		12	8			10	6	3								4	11	1	16	15				
Apr 7	H	Clydebank	701	0-0		2			5		7		9		12	8			10	6									4	11	1	16	15				
14	A	Stenhousemuir	519	0-2		2	11		5		7		9		12	8			10	6									4	3	1	16			14		
21	A	Berwick Rangers	659	0-1		2	11			5	7		9	10		8			12	6									4	3	1	15			14		
28	H	Forfar Athletic	951	0-2		2	3				4	7		9	12	8			10	15								16	5	11	1						6
May 5	A	Queen of the South	1,176	1-0		2	10				7		9[1]	14	16	8				6	3								5	11			1	12			4
TOTAL FULL APPEARANCES					13	28	31	16	33	17	33	12	26	12	13		2	26	4	12	21	16	4			9	7	8	5	11	16	2	12	5			2
TOTAL SUB APPEARANCES						(1)	(1)	(3)		(1)		(2)	(7)	(15)	(2)	(2)	(7)	(1)	(9)	(11)	(3)	(2)	(2)	(3)	(1)		(7)	(2)	(3)					(6)	(4)	(3)
TOTAL GOALS SCORED							2				4		7	1	2			1		2	3	2						1		1					

Small bold figures denote goalscorers. † denotes opponent's own goal.

The National Stadium, Hampden Park

SOMERVILLE DRIVE
PURPLE CAR PARK
CARMUNNOCK ROAD
Lesser Hampden
WEST STAND
NORTH STAND
C — D
EAST STAND
AIKENHEAD ROAD
BT SCOTLAND STAND
Letherby Drive
Exit 46 (West Roadway)
MAIN ENTRANCE
Exit 33 (East Roadway)
RED CAR PARK
YELLOW CAR PARK
MOUNT ANNAN DRIVE
Kinghorn Drive

CAPACITY: 52,046 (All Seated)
PITCH DIMENSIONS: 115 yds x 75 yds
FACILITIES FOR DISABLED SUPPORTERS:
Disabled facilities are situated in the BT Scotland Stand as follows:
West Front (44 places & 44 helpers), West Section A (21 places & 21 helpers),
Ambulant/Blind (55 places), East Front (44 places & 44 helpers),
East Section G (21 places & 21 helpers), Ambulant/Blind (55 places)

Team playing kits

How to get there

The following routes may be used to reach The National Stadium, Hampden Park:
TRAINS: There are two stations within five minutes walk of the ground. Mount Florida Station, on the Cathcart Circle, and King's Park Station. A 15 minute service runs from Glasgow Central.
BUSES: Services to approach Mount Florida end of Stadium: From City Centre: 5, 5A, 5B, MS, M14, 31, 37, 66, 66A, 66B, 66C; From Govan Cross; 34; From Drumchapel: 96, 97, Circular Service: 89, 90; G.C.T. Service: 1; Services to approach King's Park end of Stadium; From City Centre: 12, 12A, 74; Circular Service: 89, 90; G.C.T. Service: 19.
CARS: Car and Coach parking facilities are available in the car park in Letherby Drive, which is capable of holding 200 vehicles. Side streets can also be used.

email: info@sfl.scottishfootball.com • website: www.scottishfootball.com

Stirling Albion

Forthbank Stadium, Springkerse, Stirling, FK7 7UJ

CHAIRMAN
Peter McKenzie

VICE-CHAIRMAN
Peter Gardiner, C.A.

DIRECTORS
Duncan B. MacGregor
& John L. Smith

SECRETARY
Mrs. Marlyn Hallam

MANAGER
Raymond Stewart

ASSISTANT MANAGER
Jim Moffat

YOUTH DEVELOPMENT OFFICER
Raymond Ross

U18 YOUTH TEAM COACH
Andy Gould

U16 YOUTH TEAM COACH
Raymond Ross

U14 YOUTH TEAM COACH
Paul Donnelly

U13 YOUTH TEAM COACH
Mike Kerr

CLUB DOCTOR
Dr. Gordon Mackay

PHYSIOTHERAPIST
George Cameron

FOOTBALL SAFETY OFFICERS' ASSOCIATION REPRESENTATIVE
Nick Sabo (01786) 442953

CHIEF SCOUT
Ian Miller

GROUND MAINTENANCE
Greentech, Bannockburn

COMMERCIAL MANAGER
Mrs. Marlyn Hallam
Tel (01786) 450399

TEAM ADMIN/KIT MAN
Scott McLean

MATCHDAY PROGRAMME EDITOR
Allan Grieve (01259) 751152
email: ADGrieve@aol.com

TELEPHONES
Ground/Ticket Office
(01786) 450399
Fax (01786) 448400

INTERNET ADDRESS
www.stirlingalbionfc.co.uk

CLUB SHOP
Situated at Forthbank Stadium.
Open Mon. – Fri. and
Home Match Days.

OFFICIAL SUPPORTERS CLUB
Stephen Torrance, Secretary,
Forthbank Stadium, Springkerse,
Stirling, FK7 7UJ

TEAM CAPTAIN
Graeme Morrison

SHIRT SPONSOR
Scottish Amicable

KIT SUPPLIER
VIRMA

LIST OF PLAYERS 2001/2002

SURNAME	FIRST NAME	MIDDLE NAME	DATE OF BIRTH	PLACE OF BIRTH	DATE OF SIGNING	HEIGHT FT INS	WEIGHT ST LBS	POS. ON PITCH	PREVIOUS CLUB
Bailey	Lee		10/07/72	Edinburgh	23/03/01	5 7.0	11 2	Fwd	Brechin City
Beveridge	Ross		24/08/84	Dunfermline	23/07/01	5 8.5	9 7	Fwd	Rangers
Butler	David	R.	04/04/83	Glasgow	15/07/00	5 6.0	9 6	Mid	Stirling Albion Youth
Devine	Stewart		11/04/84	Edinburgh	13/07/00	5 10.0	9 11	Mid	Stirling Albion Youth
Edwards	Christopher	Peter	09/02/82	Glasgow	29/09/00	5 11.0	11 7	Def	Partick Thistle
Geraghty	Michael	John	30/10/70	Glasgow	26/07/01	5 11.0	11 9	Fwd	Stranraer
Goldie	Darren		25/02/81	Glasgow	25/08/01	5 9.5	11 8	Def	Heart of Midlothian
Hay	Paul		14/11/80	Glasgow	16/03/01	5 10.0	11 2	Def	Clyde
Henderson	Nicholas	Sinclair	08/02/69	Edinburgh	26/07/01	6 0.0	12 0	Mid	Stenhousemuir
Higgins	Gary		15/09/72	Stirling	26/07/01	5 11.0	12 5	Fwd	East Stirlingshire
Hutchison	Steven		01/08/85	Stirling	23/07/01	5 11.0	9 0	Fwd	Rangers
Johnston	Ross	William	16/02/84	Stirling	22/09/00	6 1.0	10 8	Def	Form D Under 15
Kelly	Gary	Patrick	01/09/81	Falkirk	25/08/00	5 11.0	10 7	Def/Mid	Sauchie JFC
McCallion	Kevin		23/07/82	Bellshill	31/07/98	5 10.0	11 6	Mid	Mill United B.C.
McLellan	Kenneth	John	08/09/83	Stirling	15/07/00	5 10.0	10 7	Def	Falkirk Youth
Moffat	James		27/01/60	Dunfermline	20/07/01	6 0.0	13 0	Gk	Forfar Athletic
Moriarty	Tadg	Lee	28/09/80	Edinburgh	03/08/01	5 11.0	11 0	Mid	Celtic
Morrison	Graeme	George	29/10/76	Falkirk	03/08/01	6 1.0	13 7	Def	Morton
Munro	Gareth	Ross	13/10/82	Stirling	05/07/99	5 10.0	11 2	Mid	Cumbernauld Hearts B.C.
O'Brien	David		24/01/84	Stirling	20/07/01	5 10.0	9 7	Def	Denny
Ramage	Michael	George	04/11/83	Stirling	23/05/01	6 1.0	12 0	Fwd	Stirling Albion Youth
Reid	Christopher	Thomas	04/11/71	Edinburgh	03/06/00	6 2.0	13 2	Gk	Hamilton Academical
Reilly	Steven	James	29/08/81	Glasgow	03/08/01	6 0.0	12 0	Def	Heart of Midlothian
Ross	David	Malcolm	13/10/77	Stirling	06/08/01	6 1.0	13 10	Fwd	Camelon Juniors
Scott	Greig		21/07/83	Stirling	13/07/00	6 0.0	12 0	Mid	St. Johnstone Youth
Stuart	William	Gibb	28/01/83	Paisley	05/07/99	5 6.0	8 13	Def	West Park United
Turner	Iain	Robert	26/01/84	Stirling	29/09/00	6 3.0	12 0	Gk	Riverside B.C.
Williams	Alexander	Boyd	15/01/83	Glasgow	27/08/99	5 10.5	10 7	Fwd	West Park Under 15's
Wilson	Douglas	John	27/05/84	Stirling	20/07/01	5 5.0	8 7	Mid	Stirling Albion Under 16
Wilson	Stephen		28/01/82	Bellshill	24/08/01	6 1	13 0	Gk	Airdrieonians

Milestones

YEAR OF FORMATION: 1945
MOST LEAGUE POINTS IN A SEASON: 59 (Division 2 – Season 1964/65)(2 Points for a Win)
81 (Second Division – Season 1995/96)(3 Points for a Win)
MOST LEAGUE GOALS SCORED BY A PLAYER IN A SEASON: Joe Hughes (Season 1969/70)
NO. OF GOALS SCORED: 26
RECORD ATTENDANCE: 26,400 (-v- Celtic – Scottish Cup, 11.3.1959 at Annfield Park)
3,808 (-v- Aberdeen – Scottish Cup, 17.02.1996 at Forthbank Stadium)
RECORD VICTORY: 20-0 (-v- Selkirk – Scottish Cup, 8.12.1984)
RECORD DEFEAT: 0-9 (-v- Dundee United – Division 1, 30.12.1967)

The Albion's ten year league record

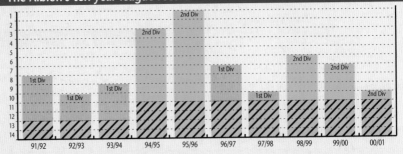

THE SCOTTISH PREMIER LEAGUE

ABERDEEN

League Champions:
Division I: 1954/55
Premier Division: 1979/80, 1983/84, 1984/85
League Cup Winners:
1955/56, 1976/77, 1985/86, 1989/90, 1995/96
Scottish Cup Winners: 1947, 1970, 1982, 1983, 1984, 1986, 1990
European Cup Winners' Cup:
1982/83
European Super Cup: 1983
Drybrough Cup Winners:
1970/71, 1980/81

CELTIC

League Champions:
Division I: 1892/93, 1893/94, 1895/96, 1897/98, 1904/05, 1905/06, 1906/07, 1907/08, 1908/09, 1909/10, 1913/14, 1914/15, 1915/16, 1916/17, 1918/19, 1921/22, 1925/26, 1935/36, 1937/38, 1953/54, 1965/66, 1966/67, 1967/68, 1968/69, 1969/70, 1970/71, 1971/72, 1972/73, 1973/74
Premier Division: 1976/77, 1978/79, 1980/81, 1981/82, 1985/86, 1987/88, 1997/98,
SPL: 2000/01
League Cup Winners:
1956/57, 1957/58, 1965/66, 1966/67, 1967/68, 1968/69, 1969/70, 1974/75, 1982/83, 1997/98, 1999/2000, 2000/01
Scottish Cup Winners:
1892, 1899, 1900, 1904, 1907, 1908, 1911, 1912, 1914, 1923, 1925, 1927, 1931, 1933, 1937, 1951, 1954, 1965, 1967, 1969, 1971, 1972, 1974, 1975, 1977, 1980, 1985, 1988, 1989, 1995, 2001
European Cup Winners: 1966/67
Runners-up: 1969/70
Empire Exhibition Cup Winners: 1938
Coronation Cup Winners: 1953
Drybrough Cup Winners: 1974/75

DUNDEE

League Champions:
Division I: 1961/62
Division II: 1946/47
First Division: 1978/79, 1991/92, 1997/98
League Cup Winners:
1951/52, 1952/53, 1973/74
Scottish Cup Winners: 1910
B&Q Centenary Cup: 1990/91

DUNDEE UNITED

League Champions:
Division II: 1924/25, 1928/29
Premier Division: 1982/83
League Cup Winners:
1979/80, 1980/81
Scottish Cup Winners: 1993/94
UEFA Cup Runners-up: 1986/87

DUNFERMLINE ATHLETIC

League Champions:
Division II: 1925/26
First Division: 1988/89, 1995/96
Second Division: 1985/86
Scottish Cup Winners: 1961, 1968
Scottish Qualifying Cup: 1911/12

HEART OF MIDLOTHIAN

League Champions:
Division I: 1894/95, 1896/97, 1957/58, 1959/60
First Division: 1979/80
League Cup Winners: 1954/55, 1958/59, 1959/60, 1962/63
Scottish Cup Winners: 1891, 1896, 1901, 1906, 1956, 1998

HIBERNIAN

League Champions:
Division I: 1902/03, 1947/48, 1950/51, 1951/52
Division II: 1893/94, 1894/95, 1932/33
First Division: 1980/81, 1998/99
League Cup Winners: 1972/73, 1991/92
Scottish Cup Winners: 1887, 1902
Drybrough Cup Winners:
1972/73, 1973/74

KILMARNOCK

League Champions:
Division I: 1964/65
Division II: 1897/98, 1898/99
Scottish Cup Winners:
1920, 1929, 1997
Scottish Qualifying Cup Winners:
1896/97

LIVINGSTON

(Formerly Meadowbank Thistle)
League Champions:
First Division: 2000/01
Second Division: 1986/87, 1998/99
Third Division: 1995/96

MOTHERWELL

League Champions:
Division I: 1931/32
First Division: 1981/82, 1984/85
Division II: 1953/54, 1968/69
League Cup Winners: 1950/51
Scottish Cup Winners: 1952, 1991

RANGERS

League Champions:
Division I: 1890/91 (shared), 1898/99, 1899/1900, 1900/01, 1901/02, 1910/11, 1911/12, 1912/13, 1917/18, 1919/20, 1920/21, 1922/23, 1923/24, 1924/25, 1926/27, 1927/28, 1928/29, 1929/30, 1930/31, 1932/33, 1933/34, 1934/35, 1936/37, 1938/39, 1946/47, 1948/49, 1949/50, 1952/53, 1955/56, 1956/57, 1958/59, 1960/61, 1962/63, 1963/64, 1974/75
Premier Division: 1975/76, 1977/78, 1986/87, 1988/89, 1989/90, 1990/91, 1991/92, 1992/93, 1993/94, 1994/95, 1995/96, 1996/97
SPL: 1998/99, 1999/2000
League Cup Winners:
1946/47, 1948/49, 1960/61, 1961/62, 1963/64, 1964/65, 1970/71, 1975/76, 1977/78, 1978/79, 1981/82, 1983/84, 1984/85, 1986/87, 1987/88, 1988/89, 1990/91, 1992/93, 1993/94, 1996/97, 1998/99
Scottish Cup Winners:
1894, 1897, 1898, 1903, 1928, 1930, 1932, 1934, 1935, 1936, 1948, 1949, 1950, 1953, 1960, 1962, 1963, 1964, 1966, 1973, 1976, 1978, 1979, 1981, 1992, 1993, 1996, 1999, 2000
European Cup Winners' Cup:
1971/72
Runners-up: 1960/61, 1966/67
Drybrough Cup Winners:
1979/80

ST. JOHNSTONE

League Champions:
First Division: 1982/83, 1989/90, 1996/97
Division II: 1923/24, 1959/60, 1962/63

S.P.L. Club Honours

S.F.L. and S.P.L. – Final Tables 2000/2001

BELL'S S.F.L. FIRST DIVISION

	P	W	L	D	F	A	PTS
LIVINGSTON	36	23	6	7	72	31	76
AYR UNITED	36	19	5	12	73	41	69
FALKIRK	36	16	12	8	57	59	56
INVERNESS CAL. THISTLE	36	14	10	12	71	54	54
CLYDE	36	11	11	14	44	46	47
ROSS COUNTY	36	11	15	10	48	52	43
RAITH ROVERS	36	10	18	8	41	55	38
AIRDRIEONIANS	36	8	14	14	49	67	38
MORTON	36	9	19	8	34	61	35
ALLOA ATHLETIC	36	7	18	11	38	61	32

BELL'S S.F.L. SECOND DIVISION

	P	W	L	D	F	A	PTS
PARTICK THISTLE	36	22	5	9	66	32	75
ARBROATH	36	15	8	13	54	38	58
BERWICK RANGERS	36	14	10	12	51	44	54
STRANRAER	36	15	12	9	51	50	54
CLYDEBANK	36	12	13	11	42	43	47
QUEEN OF THE SOUTH	36	13	16	7	52	59	46
STENHOUSEMUIR	36	12	18	6	45	63	42
FORFAR ATHLETIC	36	10	16	10	48	52	40
QUEEN'S PARK	36	10	16	10	28	40	40
STIRLING ALBION	36	5	14	17	34	50	32

BELL'S S.F.L. THIRD DIVISION

	P	W	L	D	F	A	PTS
HAMILTON ACADEMICAL	36	22	4	10	75	30	76
COWDENBEATH	36	23	6	7	58	31	76
BRECHIN CITY	36	22	8	6	71	36	72
EAST FIFE	36	15	13	8	49	46	53
PETERHEAD	36	13	13	10	46	46	49
DUMBARTON	36	13	17	6	46	49	45
ALBION ROVERS	36	12	15	9	38	43	45
EAST STIRLINGSHIRE	36	10	19	7	37	69	37
MONTROSE	36	6	22	8	31	65	26
ELGIN CITY	36	5	24	7	29	65	22

BANK OF SCOTLAND SCOTTISH PREMIER LEAGUE

	P	W	L	D	F	A	PTS
CELTIC	38	31	3	4	90	29	97
RANGERS	38	26	8	4	76	36	82
HIBERNIAN	38	18	8	12	57	35	66
KILMARNOCK	38	15	14	9	44	53	54
HEART OF MIDLOTHIAN	38	14	14	10	56	50	52
DUNDEE	38	13	17	8	51	49	47
ABERDEEN	38	11	15	12	45	52	45
MOTHERWELL	38	12	19	7	42	56	43
DUNFERMLINE ATHLETIC	38	11	18	9	34	54	42
ST. JOHNSTONE	38	9	16	13	40	56	40
DUNDEE UNITED	38	9	21	8	38	63	35
ST. MIRREN	38	8	24	6	32	72	30

S.F.L. RESERVE LEAGUE EAST

	P	W	L	D	F	A	PTS
ROSS COUNTY	10	6	2	2	18	16	20
INVERNESS CAL. THISTLE	10	5	4	1	31	19	16
MONTROSE	10	4	4	2	21	15	14
BRECHIN CITY	10	4	4	2	20	22	14
ARBROATH	10	3	4	3	18	23	12
FORFAR ATHLETIC	10	3	7	0	19	32	9

S.F.L. RESERVE LEAGUE WEST

	P	W	L	D	F	A	PTS
LIVINGSTON	15	15	0	0	50	15	45
AYR UNITED	15	9	5	1	30	17	28
HAMILTON ACADEMICAL	15	7	6	2	25	28	23
CLYDE	15	6	9	0	20	32	18
FALKIRK	15	4	8	3	27	36	15
QUEEN'S PARK	15	0	13	2	10	34	2

AIRDRIEONIANS F.C. AND MORTON F.C. WERE BOTH GIVEN PERMISSION TO WITHDRAW FROM THE RESERVE LEAGUE WEST COMPETITION BY THE LEAGUE MANAGEMENT COMMITTEE AND THEREFORE BOTH CLUBS' POINTS WERE EXPUNGED FROM THE RECORDS.

S.F.L. UNDER 18 YOUTH DIVISION

	P	W	L	D	F	A	PTS
AYR UNITED	18	14	2	2	59	18	44
FALKIRK	18	12	5	1	48	32	37
EAST FIFE	18	10	5	3	48	30	33
QUEEN'S PARK	18	9	3	6	34	19	33
STENHOUSEMUIR	18	8	2	8	44	18	32
CLYDE	18	9	5	4	43	35	31
ARBROATH	18	8	5	5	40	25	29
STIRLING ALBION	18	9	7	2	31	24	29
FORFAR ATHLETIC	18	8	8	2	39	41	26
HAMILTON ACADEMICAL	18	7	7	4	38	28	25
PARTICK THISTLE	18	7	8	3	38	35	24
RAITH ROVERS	18	6	7	5	42	33	23
COWDENBEATH	18	5	5	8	26	19	23
ALBION ROVERS	18	6	7	5	36	37	23
BERWICK RANGERS	18	5	6	7	34	35	22
MORTON	18	4	10	4	19	30	16
EAST STIRLINGSHIRE	18	2	11	5	23	48	11
ALLOA ATHLETIC	18	2	14	2	18	65	8
BRECHIN CITY	18	2	16	0	13	101	6

Champions since 1890

SEASON	DIVISION ONE	POINTS	DIVISION TWO	POINTS
1952/53	Rangers*	43	Stirling Albion	44
1953/54	Celtic	43	Motherwell	45
1954/55	Aberdeen	49	Airdrieonians	46
1955/56	Rangers	52	Queen's Park	54
1956/57	Rangers	55	Clyde	64
1957/58	Heart of Midlothian	62	Stirling Albion	55
1958/59	Rangers	50	Ayr United	60
1959/60	Heart of Midlothian	54	St. Johnstone	53
1960/61	Rangers	51	Stirling Albion	55
1961/62	Dundee	54	Clyde	54
1962/63	Rangers	57	St. Johnstone	55
1963/64	Rangers	55	Morton	67
1964/65	Kilmarnock*	50	Stirling Albion	59
1965/66	Celtic	57	Ayr United	53
1966/67	Celtic	58	Morton	69
1967/68	Celtic	63	St. Mirren	62
1968/69	Celtic	54	Motherwell	64
1969/70	Celtic	57	Falkirk	56
1970/71	Celtic	56	Partick Thistle	56
1971/72	Celtic	60	Dumbarton¥	52
1972/73	Celtic	57	Clyde	56
1973/74	Celtic	53	Airdrieonians	60
1974/75	Rangers	56	Falkirk	54

SEASON	PREMIER DIVISION	POINTS	FIRST DIVISION	POINTS	SECOND DIVISION	POINTS	THIRD DIVISION	POINTS
1975/76	Rangers	54	Partick Thistle	41	Clydebank¥	40		
1976/77	Celtic	55	St. Mirren	62	Stirling Albion	55		
1977/78	Rangers	55	Morton¥	58	Clyde¥	53		
1978/79	Celtic	48	Dundee	55	Berwick Rangers	54		
1979/80	Aberdeen	48	Heart of Midlothian	53	Falkirk	50		
1980/81	Celtic	56	Hibernian	57	Queen's Park	50		
1981/82	Celtic	55	Motherwell	61	Clyde	59		
1982/83	Dundee United	56	St. Johnstone	55	Brechin City	55		
1983/84	Aberdeen	57	Morton	54	Forfar Athletic	63		
1984/85	Aberdeen	59	Motherwell	50	Montrose	53		
1985/86•	Celtic¥	50	Hamilton Academical	56	Dunfermline Athletic	57		
1986/87•	Rangers	69	Morton	57	Meadowbank Thistle	55		
1987/88•	Celtic	72	Hamilton Academical	56	Ayr United	61		
1988/89§	Rangers	56	Dunfermline Athletic	54	Albion Rovers	50		
1989/90§	Rangers	51	St. Johnstone	58	Brechin City	49		
1990/91§	Rangers	55	Falkirk	54	Stirling Albion	54		
1991/92§	Rangers	72	Dundee	58	Dumbarton	52		
1992/93	Rangers	73	Raith Rovers	65	Clyde	54		
1993/94	Rangers	58	Falkirk	66	Stranraer	56		
1994/95†	Rangers	69	Raith Rovers	69	Greenock Morton	64	Forfar Athletic	80
1995/96†	Rangers	87	Dunfermline Athletic	71	Stirling Albion	81	Livingston	72
1996/97†	Rangers	80	St. Johnstone	80	Ayr United	77	Inverness Caledonian Thistle	76
1997/98†	Celtic	74	Dundee	70	Stranraer	61	Alloa Athletic	76

SEASON	SCOTTISH PREMIER LEAGUE	POINTS	S.F.L. FIRST DIVISION	POINTS	S.F.L. SECOND DIVISION	POINTS	S.F.L. THIRD DIVISION	POINTS
1998/99	Rangers	77	Hibernian	89	Livingston	77	Ross County	77
1999/2000	Rangers	90	St. Mirren >	76	Clyde >	65	Queen's Park >	69
2000/01	Celtic	97	Livingston>	76	Partick Thistle>	75	Hamilton Academical>	76 (on goal difference)

Champions on goal average.   •*Competition known as Fine Fare League.*   †*Competition known as Bell's League Championship.*
¥*Champions on goal difference.*   §*Competition known as B&Q League.*   >*Competition known as Bell's Scottish Football League Championship.*

FIRST ROUND
Tuesday, 8th August, 2000

QUEEN OF THE SOUTH 2   **FORFAR ATHLETIC 1**
S. Hodge, P. Weatherson,   S. Taylor
Queen of the South: D. Mathieson, D. Muir, (S. Pickering),
S. Hodge, A. Aitken, A. Martin, P. Nixon, P. Atkinson, J. Sunderland,
(D. Boyle), P. Weatherson, B. Caldwell, (W. Hawke), M. Weir
Substitutes not used: D. Boyle, R. McColm
Forfar Athletic: S. Garden, A. Ramsay, E. Donaldson, D. Bowman, (C. Farnan),
R. Horn, C. Tully, G. McPhee, A. Cargill, I. Ferguson, R. Brand, S. Taylor
Substitutes not used: D. Craig, R. Morris, S. Christie, N. Ferrie
Referee: Brian McGarry
Attendance: 1,187

PETERHEAD 2   **INVERNESS CAL. THISTLE 3**
C. Cooper (2)   I. Stewart, D. Xausa, R. Mann
Peterhead: I. Pirie, D. Craig, S. King, W. Herd, M. Simpson, S. Paterson,
C. Cooper, M. Johnston, G. Clark, S. Brown, R. Livingstone
Substitutes not used: S. Clark, D. Smith, C. Watson, J. Keddie, R. Buchanan
Inverness Caledonian Thistle: L. Fridge, R. Tokely, S. Golabek, (R. McBain),
R. Mann, R. Hastings, K. Byers, D. Bagan, (P. Sheerin), D. Xausa, I. Stewart,
(M. Bavidge), C. Christie, D. Wyness
Substitutes not used: B. Robson, A. Ridgers
Referee: Alan Freeland
Attendance: 1,001

EAST STIRLINGSHIRE 2   **HAMILTON ACADEMICAL 1**
G. McKechnie, K. Gordon   A. Russell
East Stirlingshire: J. Butter, C. Quinn, M. Hall, G. Russell, D. Todd,
D. McPherson, S. Stewart, K. Gordon, G. Hislop, G. Higgins,
(G. McKechnie), J. Tortolano
Substitutes not used: C. Lynes, A. Scott, J. Clarke, C. Todd
Hamilton Academical: I. Macfarlane, M. Nelson, G. Lynn, W. Davidson,
P. Gaughan, B. Vaugh, (M. Moore), M. Bonnar, J. Sherry, A. Eadie,
D. McFarlane, (R. Kelly), A. Russell
Substitutes not used: D. Grant, G. Clark, G. Potter
Referee: Bobby Orr
Attendance: 504

QUEEN'S PARK 2   **STRANRAER 0**
J. Brown, M. Gallagher
Queen's Park: A. Smith, D. Ferry, S. Marshall, (M. Travers), G. Duncan,
D. Connaghan, R. Sinclair, K. Finlayson, G. Connell, M. Gallagher,
(C. Flannigan), J. Brown, (G. Miller), F. Carroll
Substitutes not used: R. Scobie, T. Magennis
Stranraer: M. McGeown, A. Paterson, D. Johnstone, K. Knox, G. McDonald,
(M. Hughes), D. George, P. Walker, W. Macdonald, I. Harty, M. Geraghty,
(F. Wright), A. Blaikie, (S. Edgar)
Substitutes not used: D. Rae, S. O'Neill
Referee: Dougie Smith
Attendance: 566

COWDENBEATH 3   **ELGIN CITY 0**
M. McDowell, K. Wright, J.P. Burns
Cowdenbeath: J. Martin, J. Boyle, C. McMillan, D. White, J. Lakie,
A. Lawrence, (J. Allan), C. Winter, M. Bradley, M. McDowell, (G. Brown),
K. Wright, (R. Juskowiak), J.P. Burns
Substitutes not used: I. McDonald, R. Godfrey
Elgin City: M. Pirie, Craig Milne, J. MacDonald, A. Morris, L. O'Brien,
G. Russell, N. Whyte, (M. Green), R. Green, Colin Milne, M. Slythe,
(P. Maguire), S. Clinton
Substitutes not used: S. Cameron, S. Ellis, M. Rae
Referee: Eric Martindale
Attendance: 234

STIRLING ALBION 0   **STENHOUSEMUIR 1**
M. McLauchlan
Stirling Albion: C. Reid, A. McStea, (M. McGraw), J.N. Bennett, (P. Jack),
K. Milne, G. Hunter, J. Millar, C. King, G. Donald, A. Graham, C. Feroz,
I. McAulay, (J. Gardner)
Substitutes not used: M. O'Neill, A. Buchanan
Stenhousemuir: G. Gow, G. Davidson, J. Fisher, P. McAneny, T. Graham,
B. Donald, L. Gibson, D. Lorimer, (P. Ferguson), M. McLauchlan,
D. Menelaws, (I. English), D. Wood, (P. Cormack)
Substitutes not used: M. Mooney, A. Banner
Referee: Tom Brown
Attendance: 605

PARTICK THISTLE 1   **AIRDRIEONIANS 2**
(AET -1-1 After 90 Minutes)
S. McLean   M. Alfonso, H.A. McCann
Partick Thistle: M. Brown, J. Smith, J. Stirling, D. Lennon, S. Craigan,
A. Archibald, (D. McKeown), D. McCallum, (A. Moore), I. Cameron,
S. McLean, P. Lindau, (R. McGrillen), M. Hardie
Substitutes not used: D. Lyle, K. Arthur
Airdrieonians: S. Wilson, S. Boyce, (S. Capin), H.A. McCann, M. Alfonso,
(R. Coulter), E. Forrest, F. Moreau, G. Evans, J. Sanjuan, D. McGuire,
D. Fernandez, (D. Brady), S. Taylor
Substitutes not used: S. Easton, S. McGovern
Referee: John Underhill
Attendance: 2,652

ROSS COUNTY 1   **ALBION ROVERS 0**
D. Holmes
Ross County: J.N. Walker, K. Gilbert, E. Cunnington, I. Maxwell, B. Irvine,
C. Taggart, G. Shaw, D. Henderson, (D. Holmes), A. Bone, M. Millar,
(F. Escalon), P. Kinnaird, (D. Ross)
Substitutes not used: D. Mackay, G. Hamilton
Albion Rovers: C. Fahey, J. Smith, T. Lumsden, R. Clyde, S. Clark, M. Booth,
C. Waldie, (A. Martin), J. McKenzie, Y. Begue, (I. Diack), I. Rankin,
(M. Harty), C. Silvestro
Substitutes not used: K. McBride, S. Shearer
Referee: Garry Mitchell
Attendance: 777

CLYDE 5   **MORTON 1**
A. Proudlock, J. Ross, A. Grant,   D. Anderson
M. McLaughlin, A. Kane
Clyde: B. Halliwell, D. Murray, M. McLaughlin, B. Smith, C. Cranmer,
J. Ross, (N. Henderson), S. Convery, (R. McCusker), B. Sellars,
A. Proudlock, (A. Kane), P. Keogh, A. Grant
Substitutes not used: G. Greer, D. Hanley
Morton: M. Boswell, M. Naylor, D. Davies, D. Anderson, R. Raeside,
P. Medou-Otye, A. Brownrigg, (P. McDonald), A. Millen, R. Matheson,
K. Boukraa, H. Curran
Substitutes not used: S. Aitken, S. MacDonald, D. Murie, A. Carlin
Referee: Kenny Clark
Attendance: 1,048

EAST FIFE 1   **RAITH ROVERS 2**
B. Moffat   P. Tosh, J. Stein
East Fife: A. Stewart, K. Munro, J. Gallacher, B. McCloy, R. Sharp,
J. Allison, M. Hunter, R. Logan, P. Simpson, (S. Ferguson), B. Moffat,
(S. Kerrigan), S. Mackay
Substitutes not used: D. Agostini, R. Gibb, W. McCulloch
Raith Rovers: G. Van De Kamp, G. McCulloch, L. Ellis, M. Andrews,
P. Browne, K. Black, P. Tosh, (A. Clark), S. Tosh, I. Mballa, (D. Shields),
A. Burns, J. Stein
Substitutes not used: K. Gaughan, C. McEwan, C. Coyle
Referee: Alan Gemmill
Attendance: 1,540

MONTROSE 1   **BERWICK RANGERS 0**
G. Dailly
Montrose: G. McGlynn, J. Young, G. Dailly, S. Marwick, S. Ferguson,
M. Craib, R. McWilliam, C. Mailer, M. McKenzie, (J. Mitchell), T. Harrison,
(J. McKellar), P. McIlravey
Substitutes not used: J. O'Driscoll, P. Catto, B. Thompson
Berwick Rangers: M. McLean, J. Whelan, (C. Findlay), L. Haddow,
I. Ritchie, G. McNicoll, M. Anthony, G. McMartin, (M. Duthie), M. Neil,
P. Ronald, G. Wood, (S. Laidlaw), D. Smith
Substitutes not used: N. Oliver, C. Weir
Referee: John Rowbotham
Attendance: 282

CLYDEBANK 0   **ALLOA ATHLETIC 2**
C. Wood (2)
Clydebank: D. Wylie, J. McKinstrey, R. McKinnon, F. Wishart,
K. Brannigan, E. Taborda, S. Murray, (P. Rodden), D. Ferguson, L. Fal,
T. Coyne, B. Hamilton, (I.G. Johnson)
Substitutes not used: E. Paton, S. Murdoch, S. Hutchison
Alloa Athletic: M. Cairns, R. Huxford, (G. Farrell), D. Clark, G. Watson,
F. Conway, C. Valentine, R.L. Gardner, S. Thomson, R. Hamilton,
W. Irvine, (M. Wilson), I. Little, (C. Wood)
Substitutes not used: D. Beaton, G. Armstrong
Referee: Kevin Toner
Attendance: 216

ARBROATH 2   **BRECHIN CITY 0**
J. Mercer, C. McGlashan
Arbroath: C. Hinchcliffe, T. King, K. Fotheringham, (K. Tindal), J. Thomson,
J.G. Rowe, I. Good, J. Cusick, T. Bryce, (S. Florence), C. McGlashan,
S. Mallan, J. Mercer, (P. Brownlie)
Substitutes not used: J. Crawford, C. Wight
Brechin City: D. Soutar, G. Smith, S. Raynes, K. Bain, H. Cairney, J. Nairn,
J. McKeith, (M. Leask), P. Riley, L. Bailey, (K. Williamson), R. Grant,
D. Coulston, (B. Honeyman)
Substitutes not used: D. Riley, A. Hutcheon
Referee: Ian Fyfe
Attendance: 686

Wednesday, 9th August, 2000

DUMBARTON 0   **AYR UNITED 0 (AET)**
Dumbarton won 5-4 on Kicks from the Penalty Mark
Dumbarton: J. Hillcoat, M. Dickie, J. Dillon, J. Bruce, S. Jack, K. McCann,
W. Wilson, T. King, Andrew Brown, (A. Grace), C. Smith, (P. Flannery), J. Robertson
Substitutes not used: S. Bonar, C. Gentile, J. Wight
Ayr United: C. Nelson, (M. Rovde), M. Renwick, P. Lovering, P. McGinlay,
J. Hughes, C. Duffy, G. Hurst, M. Wilson, E. Annand, G. Teale,
(N. Scally), M. Reynolds
Substitutes not used: M. Crilly, G. Burns, J. Bradford
Referee: Willie Young
Attendance: 421

SECOND ROUND
Tuesday, 22nd August, 2000

ST. JOHNSTONE 3   **COWDENBEATH 1**
P. Hartley, N. Dasovic, G. Bollan   J. Allan
St. Johnstone: A. Main, M. Sylla, G. Bollan, D. Dods, J. Weir, (J.P. McBride), M. O'Neill, (M. McCulloch), N. Dasovic, P. Hartley, K. Parker, (C. Russell), T. Lovenkrands, G. Jones
Substitutes not used: B. Crozier, S. Robertson
Cowdenbeath: J. Martin, J. Boyle, C. McMillan, (S. Ramsay), D. White, J. Lakie, A. Lawrence, (J. Allan), C. Winter, M. Bradley, M. McDowell, G. Brown, (K. Wright), J.P. Burns
Substitutes not used: W. Mitchell, R. Godfrey
Referee: Tom Brown
Attendance: 2,139

CLYDE 1   **KILMARNOCK 2**
(AET–0-0 After 90 Minutes)
A. Kane   F. Dindeleux, A. McCoist
Clyde: B. Halliwell, D. Murray, M. McLaughlin, B. Smith, C. Cranmer, (G. Greer), J. Ross, J. Mitchell, (A. Kane), N. Henderson, (B. Sellars), A. Proudlock, P. Keogh, A. Grant
Substitutes not used: C. McPherson, D. Hanley
Kilmarnock: C. Meldrum, A. MacPherson, M. Baker, F. Dindeleux, S. Hessey, A. Mahood, A. McLaren, G. Holt, P. Wright, (A. McCoist), J. Vareille, (J. Fowler), A. Mitchell
Substitutes not used: P. Canero, G. Hay, G. Smith
Referee: Bobby Orr
Attendance: 2,018

ROSS COUNTY 1   **ST. MIRREN 3**
(AET–1-1 After 90 Minutes)
G. Shaw   H. Murray, S. Walker, T. Brown
Ross County: J.N. Walker, K. Gilbert, E. Cunnington, I. Maxwell, B. Irvine, C. Taggart, (J. McQuade), G. Shaw, S. Ferguson, (F. Escalon), A. Bone, M. Millar, (J. Fraser), D. Holmes
Substitutes not used: D. Mackay, G. Hamilton
St. Mirren: L. Roy, C. Drew, J. McGowan, P. Rudden, S. Walker, H. Murray, I. Nicolson, (S. MacKenzie), R. Gillies, J. Paeslack, (M. Yardley), S. McGarry, (T. Brown), J. Quitongo
Substitutes not used: S. Baltacha, D. Scrimgour
Referee: Willie Young
Attendance: 1,115

RAITH ROVERS 2   **ARBROATH 1**
A. Burns (2)   P. Brownlie
Raith Rovers: G. Van de Kamp, G. McCulloch, S. Opinel, M. Andrews, (K. Gaughan), P. Browne, K. Black, S. Tosh, (A. Clark), R. McKinnon, P. Tosh, (G. Creaney), A. Burns, J. Stein
Substitutes not used: I. Mballa, C. Coyle
Arbroath: C. Hinchcliffe, T. King, (C. McGlashan), I. Good, J. Thomson, J.G. Rowe, S. Florence, J. Cusick, (J. Mercer), J. McGlashan, S. Mallan, P. Brownlie, K. Fotheringham
Substitutes not used: J. McAulay, T. Bryce, J. Crawford
Referee: Eric Martindale
Attendance: 1,354

QUEEN'S PARK 0   **MOTHERWELL 3**
G. Strong, P. Harvey, L. McCulloch
Queen's Park: A. Smith, D. Ferry, S. Marshall, G. Duncan, D. Connaghan, R. Sinclair, K. Finlayson, G. Connell, M. Gallagher, (W. Ajet), J. Brown, (C. Flannigan), F. Carroll, (G. Miller)
Substitutes not used: P. Martin, G. Bruce
Motherwell: A. Goram, M. Corrigan, S. McMillan, G. Strong, S. Hammell, A. Oueifio, (M. Wood) D. Townsley, D. Goodman, D. Adams, (J. Davies), L. McCulloch, S. Elliott, (P. Harvey)
Substitutes not used: S. Nicholas, S. Woods
Referee: Michael McCurry
Attendance: 1,845

INVERNESS CAL. THISTLE 0   **AIRDRIEONIANS 2**
J. Elliott, D. Fernandez
Inverness Caledonian Thistle: L. Fridge, R. Tokely, S. Golabek, R. Mann, R. Hastings, (K. Byers), P. Sheerin, D. Bagan, (D. Xausa), M. Bavidge, I. Stewart, C. Christie, B. Robson (R. McBain)
Substitutes not used: D. Wyness, J. Calder
Airdrieonians: J.S. Broto, S. Boyce, H.A. McCann, R. Coulter, E. Forrest, F. Moreau, D. Brady, J. Sanjuan, J. Elliott, (M. Prest), A. Calderon, D. Fernandez, (G. Evans)
Substitutes not used: S. Taylor, P. Clark, S. Wilson
Referee: Hugh Dallas
Attendance: 867

ALLOA ATHLETIC 0   **DUNDEE UNITED 3**
S. McConalogue (3)
Alloa Athletic: M. Cairns, R. Huxford, D. Clark, G. Watson, F. Conway, C. Valentine, R.L. Gardner, S. Thomson, (C. Wood), R. Hamilton, W. Irvine, (C. Brigain), I. Little
Substitutes not used: D. Beaton, G. Farrell, J. McQueen
Dundee United: A. Combe, S. Wright, (J. McQuillan), D. Partridge, J. De Vos, H. Aljofree, M.J. Buchan, (J. Fernandez), D. Hannah, A. Mathie, J. Hamilton, H. Davidson, S. McConalogue, (A. Smith)
Substitutes not used: P. Onstad, D. McCracken
Referee: Stuart Dougal
Attendance: 1,088

FALKIRK 3   **QUEEN OF THE SOUTH 1**
D. Nicholls, K. McAllister, M. Roberts   W. Hawke
Falkirk: M. Hogarth, A. Lawrie, J. McQuilken, K. Christie, G. Denham, D. Nicholls, K. McAllister, J. Henry, M. Roberts, M. Kerr, G. Hutchison
Substitutes not used: A. Seaton, S. Rennie, K. Avdiu, C. McDonald, D. Hill
Queen of the South: D. Mathieson, K. Robison, S. Hodge, R. Atkinson, A. Martin, A. Aitken, S. Pickering, (B. Caldwell), J. Sunderland, P. Weatherson, (S. Preen), W. Hawke, M. Weir, (A. Nelson)
Substitutes not used: K. Young, R. McColm
Referee: John Underhill
Attendance: 1,696

STENHOUSEMUIR 1   **HIBERNIAN 2**
C. McKinnon   T. McManus, D. Lehmann
Stenhousemuir: G. Gow, G. Davidson, S. Pittman, P. McAneny, P. Cormack, J. Fisher, (B. Donald), L. Gibson, C. McKinnon, I. English, (D. Menelaws), M. Mooney, (A. Storrar), D. Wood
Substitutes not used: M. McLauchlan, A. Banner
Hibernian: N. Colgan, T. Smith, P. Fenwick, D. Collins, S. Lovell, M. McIntosh, G. Brebner, L. Andrews, (H. Sar-Temsoury), D. Lehmann, G. Smith, T. McManus, (D. Agathe)
Substitutes not used: I. Westwater, S. Bannerman, J. O'Neil
Referee: Dougie Smith
Attendance: 1,723

DUNFERMLINE ATHLETIC 1   **EAST STIRLINGSHIRE 0**
S. Boyle
Dunfermline Athletic: M. Ruitenbeek, J. Dair, S. Boyle, J. Skinner, A. Skerla, S.M. Thomson, J. Mendes, (E. May), I. Ferguson, S. Crawford, D. Moss, B. Nicholson
Substitutes not used: R. Mattinea, B. Reid, G. Fotheringham, S.Y. Thomson
East Stirlingshire: J. Butter, C. Quinn, J. Tortolano, S. Stewart, (C. Lynes), G. Russell, M. Hall, K. Gordon, R. Carlow, S. Hislop, D. McPherson, G. McKechnie, (G. Higgins)
Substitutes not used: C. McKenzie, J. Clarke, C. Todd
Referee: George Clyde
Attendance: 2,691

DUMBARTON 0   **LIVINGSTON 4**
D. Bingham (2), D. Hagen (2)
Dumbarton: J. Hillcoat, M. Dickie, C. Brittain, K. McCann, S. Jack, T. King, W. Wilson, A. Grace, (C. Gentile), P. Flannery, (C. Smith), Andrew Brown, J. Robertson, (D. Stewart)
Substitutes not used: S. Bonar, J. Wight
Livingston: N. Alexander, A. McManus, D. Fleming, J. Dolan, (P. Kelly), G. Coughlan, (S. Sweeney), J. Anderson, B. McPhee, (M. McCormick), Grant Smith, D. Bingham, G. Britton, D. Hagen
Substitutes not used: Gordon Smith, I. McCaldon
Referee: Kevin Toner
Attendance: 357

Wednesday, 23rd August, 2000

DUNDEE 3   **MONTROSE 0**
L. Wilkie,
F. Caballero (2)
Dundee: R. Douglas, B. Smith, M. Marrocco, (S. McSkimming), L. Wilkie, S. Tweed, (C. Coyne), M. Yates, G. Nemsadze, (J. Sara), G. Rae, P. Billio, F. Caballero, W. Falconer
Substitutes not used: J. Langfield, S. Milne
Montrose: G. McGlynn, J. Young, S. Ferguson, C. Mailer, S. Snedden, M. Craib, S. Marwick, T. Harrison, M. McKenzie, (P. McIlravey), S. Robertson, (R. McWilliam), J. McKellar, (J. O'Driscoll)
Substitutes not used: J. Mitchell, B. Thompson
Referee: Alan Freeland
Attendance: 2,635

87

THIRD ROUND

Tuesday, 5th September, 2000

DUNDEE UNITED 0   AIRDRIEONIANS 0 (AET)
Dundee United won 4-3 on Kicks from the Penalty Mark
Dundee United: A. Combe, S. Wright, D. Partridge,
J. McQuillan, H. Aljofree, M.J. Buchan, J. Paterson,
(S. Thompson), K. McDonald, (J. De Vos),
N. Heaney, (D. Hannah), A. Tchami, S. McConalogue
Substitutes not used: A. Venetis, P. Onstad
Airdrieonians: J.S. Broto, S. Boyce, (S. Taylor), H.A. McCann, M. Alfonso,
E. Forrest, F. Moreau, J. Elliott, (M. Pacífico), J. Sanjuan, B. Elliot, (P. Clark),
A. Calderon, D. Fernandez
Substitutes not used: D. Brady, S. Wilson
Referee: John Rowbotham
Attendance: 5,018

ST. MIRREN 3   DUNDEE 0
S. Walker, T. Brown, J. Paeslack
St. Mirren: L. Roy, B. McLaughlin, J. McGowan, (P. Rudden), (S. MacKenzie),
T. Turner, S. Walker, H. Murray, R. Gillies, I. Nicolson, J. Paeslack, S. McGarry,
(T. Brown), J. Quitongo
Substitutes not used: M. Yardley, D. Scrimgour
Dundee: R. Douglas, B. Smith, M. Marrocco, S. Tweed, L. Wilkie, I. Bonetti,
A. Romano, (C. Coyne), J. Artero, P. Billio, J. Sara, (G. Rae), F. Caballero,
(G. Nemsadze)
Substitutes not used: W. Falconer, J. Langfield
Referee: Tom Brown
Attendance: 3,571

CELTIC 4   RAITH ROVERS 0
C. Sutton, T. Johnson (2), A. Thompson
Celtic: S. Kerr, T. Boyd, S. Mahe, J. Valgaeren, J. McNamara, B. Petta, (O. Tebily),
(R. Scheidt), C. Healy, A. Thompson, M. Burchill, T. Johnson, C. Sutton, (E. Berkovic)
Substitutes not used: J. Gould, H. Larsson
Raith Rovers: G. Van de Kamp, G. McCulloch, S. Dennis, M. Andrews,
P. Browne, K. Black, S. Tosh, R. McKinnon, (A. Clark), P. Tosh, (I. Mballa),
A. Burns, J. Stein, (G. Creaney)
Substitutes not used: L. Ellis, C. Coyle
Referee: Douglas McDonald
Attendance: 30,753

ST. JOHNSTONE 0   KILMARNOCK 1
A. McCoist
St. Johnstone: A. Main, M. Sylla, G. Bollan, J. Weir, A. Kernaghan, M. McCulloch,
J.P. McBride, P. Kane, P. Hartley, (K. Parker), T. Lovenkrands, (C. Russell), G. Jones
Substitutes not used: D. Dods, B. Crozier, S. Robertson
Kilmarnock: G. Marshall, A. MacPherson, G. Hay, F. Dindeleux, C. Innes,
A. Mahood, G. Holt, A. Mitchell, A. McLaren, (J. Fowler), A. McCoist,
(C. Cocard), P. Wright, (I. Durrant)
Substitutes not used: P. Canero, C. Meldrum
Referee: Stuart Dougal
Attendance: 3,231

Wednesday, 6th September, 2000

DUNFERMLINE ATHLETIC 2   MOTHERWELL 0
S.M. Thomson, D. Moss
Dunfermline Athletic: M. Ruitenbeek, M. Doesburg, J. Dair, J. Skinner,
A. Skerla, S.M. Thomson, (R. Matthaei), J. Mendes, (L. Bullen), I. Ferguson,
S. Crawford, B. Nicholson, D. Moss
Substitutes not used: E. May, S. Boyle, S.Y. Thomson
Motherwell: A. Goram, M. Corrigan, S. McMillan, A. Oueifio, S. Hammell,
S. Leitch, J. Davies, (G. Brannan), D. Townsley, D. Goodman, L. McCulloch,
(S. Elliott), J. Spencer
Substitutes not used: B. Kemble, M. Wood, S. Woods
Referee: Alan Freeland
Attendance: 3,428

LIVINGSTON 0   HEART OF MIDLOTHIAN 2
C. Cameron, G. Naysmith
Livingston: N. Alexander, A. McManus, D. Fleming, J. Anderson, G. Coughlan,
(G. Britton), S. Sweeney, B. Wilson, (M. Keith), M. McCulloch, B. McPhee,
(M. McCormick), D. Bingham, D. Hagen
Substitutes not used: Grant Smith, I. McCaldon
Heart of Midlothian: A. Niemi, S. Pressley, G. Naysmith, G. Locke, (K. O'Neil),
G. Murray, L. Makel, (D. Jackson), G. McSwegan, (A. Kirk), S. Fulton, Juanjo,
C. Cameron, T. Flögel
Substitutes not used: K. James, R. McKenzie
Referee: Michael McCurry
Attendance: 5,549

RANGERS 4   ABERDEEN 2
G. Van Bronckhorst, R. Wallace,   Derek Young, R. Winters
W. Dodds, L. Amoruso
Rangers: S. Klos, F. Ricksen, S. Wilson, (T. Kerimoglu), L. Amoruso, A. Numan,
B. Ferguson, G. Van Bronckhorst, R. Wallace, W. Dodds, R. De Boer,
N. McCann, (A. Johnston)
Substitutes not used: A. Kanchelskis, T. Vidmar, L. Charbonnier
Aberdeen: R. Esson, P. McGuire, K. McNaughton, (C. Clark), D. Whyte,
D. Rowson, Darren Young, C. Guntveit, D. Mackie, R. Belabed, R. Winters,
Derek Young, (J. McAllister)
Substitutes not used: M. Perry, R. O'Donoghue, D. Preece
Referee: Willie Young
Attendance: 37,026

FALKIRK 1   HIBERNIAN 2
D. McMahon   R. Latapy (2)
Falkirk: M. Hogarth, A. Lawrie, J. McQuilken, K. Christie, G. Denham,
D. Nicholls, D. McMahon, (K. McAllister), J. Henry, M. Roberts, M. Kerr,
(I. Morris), G. Hutchison
Substitutes not used: A. Seaton, S. Rennie, D. Hill
Hibernian: N. Colgan, T. Smith, P. Fenwick, M. Jack, M. McIntosh, D. Collins,
F. Sauzee, G. Brebner, (R. Latapy), J. O'Neil, D. Lehmann, (H. Sar-Temsoury),
D. Zitelli, (M-M. Paatelainen)
Substitutes not used: S. Bannerman, I. Westwater
Referee: Kenny Clark
Attendance: 4,344

FOURTH ROUND

Tuesday, 31st October, 2000

KILMARNOCK 2   HIBERNIAN 1
A. McLaren, C. Dargo   R. Latapy
Kilmarnock: G. Marshall, A. MacPherson, G. Hay, F. Dindeleux, C. Innes,
A. Mahood, G. Holt, (C. Dargo), I. Durrant, A. McLaren, C. Cocard,
(P. Wright), A. Mitchell
Substitutes not used: J. Vareille, K. McGowne, C. Meldrum
Hibernian: N. Colgan, U. Luarsen, G. Smith, P. Fenwick, (D. Collins),
M. McIntosh, M. Jack, S. Lovell, R. Latapy, J. Andrews, (T. Smith),
M-M. Paatelainen, (D. Lehmann), J. O'Neil,
Substitutes not used: T. McManus, M. Franks
Referee: Hugh Dallas
Attendance: 7,879

RANGERS 2   DUNDEE UNITED 0
K. Miller, B. Ferguson
Rangers: J. Christiansen, S. Porrini, L. Amoruso, S. Wilson, A. Numan, F. Ricksen,
T. Kerimoglu, B. Ferguson, N. McCann, W. Dodds, K. Miller, (P. Lovenkrands)
Substitutes not used: B. Konterman, J. Gibson, M. Brown
Dundee United: A. Combe, J. Licina, D. Partridge, (M. Atangana), J. De Vos,
H. Aljofree, J. McQuillan, J. Lauchlan, M.J. Buchan, A. Venetis, (S. Leoni),
C. Easton, S. Thompson, (S. McConalogue)
Substitutes not used: H. Davidson, P. Onstad
Referee: Michael McCurry
Attendance: 30,966

ST. MIRREN 2   DUNFERMLINE ATHLETIC 1
S. McGarry, R. Gillies   B. Nicholson
St. Mirren: D. Scrimgour, B. McLaughlin, J. McGowan, T. Turner, S. Walker,
I. Nicolson, H. Murray, (S. MacKenzie), R. Gillies, G. Fenton, (L. Sharp),
S. McGarry, M. Yardley
Substitutes not used: J. Paeslack, J. Quitongo, L. Roy
Dunfermline Athletic: M. Ruitenbeek, C. McGroarty, J. Dair, J. Skinner,
A. Skerla, S.M. Thomson, B. Nicholson, I. Ferguson, D. Moss, S. Crawford,
O. Coyle, (S. Hampshire)
Substitutes not used: D. Graham, R. Matthaei, M. McGarty, S.Y. Thomson
Referee: Douglas McDonald
Attendance: 4,045

Wednesday, 1st November, 2000

HEART OF MIDLOTHIAN 2   CELTIC 5
(AET–2-2 After 90 Minutes)
C. Cameron (2)   S. Crainey, J. Smith, C. Healy,
                        L. Moravcik, J. McNamara
Heart of Midlothian: A. Niemi, S. Pressley, S. Severin, G. Petric, G. Locke,
(R. Neilson), G. Murray, R. Tomaschek, S. Fulton, (K. Milne), T. Flögel, (Juanjo),
C. Cameron, A. Kirk
Substitutes not used: K. O'Neil, R. McKenzie
Celtic: J. Gould, V. Riseth, J. Smith, (S. Petrov), J. Valgaeren, J. McNamara,
A. Stubbs, C. Healy, A. Thompson, T. Johnson, (T. Boyd), L. Moravcik,
S. Crainey, (B. Petta)
Substitutes not used: J. Mjallby, S. Kerr
Referee: Kenny Clark
Attendance: 12,922

SEMI-FINALS

Tuesday, 6th February, 2001
The National Stadium, Hampden Park, Glasgow

ST. MIRREN 0   KILMARNOCK 3
                        A. McLaren, C. Dargo, P. Canero
St. Mirren: L. Roy, S. Baltacha, P. Rudden, T. Turner, S. Walker, G. Bowman,
(H. Murray), C. Kerr, R. Gillies, S. MacKenzie, (J. Quitongo), G. Fenton,
(S. McGarry), M. Yardley
Substitutes not used: I. Nicolson, D. Scrimgour
Kilmarnock: G. Marshall, A. MacPherson, M. Baker, F. Dindeleux, K. McGowne,
G. Holt, A. Mitchell, (M. Reilly), C. Dargo, (J. Fowler), P. Wright, (C. Cocard),
P. Canero, A. McLaren
Substitutes not used: C. Stewart, G. Hay
Referee: Kenny Clark
Attendance: 9,203

Wednesday, 7th February, 2001
The National Stadium, Hampden Park, Glasgow

CELTIC 3   RANGERS 1
C. Sutton, H. Larsson (2)   J. Albertz
Celtic: J. Gould, T. Boyd, J. Mjallby, R. Vega, A. Thompson, J. McNamara,
(B. Petta), N. Lennon, P. Lambert, S. Petrov, H. Larsson, (L. Moravcik),
C. Sutton, (T. Johnson)
Substitutes not used: D. Kharine, O. Tebily
Rangers: S. Klos, C. Reyna, S. Wilson, B. Konterman, A. Numan, R. Malcolm,
T. Kerimoglu, (A. Johnston), B. Ferguson, J. Albertz, T.A. Flo, N. McCann, (M. Mols)
Substitutes not used: F. Ricksen, K. Miller, M. Brown
Referee: Willie Young
Attendance: 50,019

FINAL

Sunday, 18th March, 2001

The National Stadium, Hampden Park, Glasgow

KILMARNOCK 0   CELTIC 3

Kilmarnock: G. Marshall, A. MacPherson, K. McGowne, F. Dindeleux, (P. Canero), C. Innes, G. Hay, G. Holt, I. Durrant, (M. Reilly), A. Mahood, C. Cocard, (A. McLaren), C. Dargo
Substitutes not used: A. McCoist, C. Meldrum

Celtic: J. Gould, J. Mjallby, J. Valgaeren, R. Vega, B. Petta, (S. Crainey), (T. Boyd), C. Healy, N. Lennon, P. Lambert, L. Moravcik, (J. Smith), H. Larsson, C. Sutton,
Substitutes not used: T. Johnson, D. Kharine

Scorer: H. Larsson (3)

Referee: Hugh Dallas

Attendance: 48,830

THE CIS INSURANCE CUP
SEASON 2000/01

ROUND BY ROUND
GOALS ANALYSIS

	No. of Goals Scored	Ties Played	Average Per Game
First Round	35	14	2.5
Second Round	37	12	3.1
Third Round	21	8	2.6
Fourth Round	15	4	3.75
Semi-Finals	7	2	3.5
Final	3	1	3
Total No. of Goals Scored:	118		
Total No. of Ties Played	41		
Average Goals per Game:	2.9		

SEASON 1946/47

5th April, 1947 at Hampden Park;
Attendance 82,584; Referee: Mr R. Calder (Rutherglen)

RANGERS 4   **ABERDEEN 0**
Gillick, Williamson,
Duncanson (2)

SEASON 1947/48

25th October, 1947 at Hampden Park;
Attendance 52,781; Referee: Mr P. Craigmyle (Aberdeen)

EAST FIFE 0   **FALKIRK 0**
After Extra Time

REPLAY
1st November, 1947 at Hampden Park;
Attendance 30,664; Referee: Mr. P. Craigmyle (Aberdeen)

EAST FIFE 4   **FALKIRK 1**
Duncan (3), Adams   Aikman

SEASON 1948/49

12th March, 1949 at Hampden Park; Attendance 53,359;
Referee: Mr W. G. Livingstone (Glasgow)

RANGERS 2   **RAITH ROVERS 0**
Gillick, Paton

SEASON 1949/50

29th October, 1949 at Hampden Park;
Attendance 38,897; Referee: Mr W. Webb (Glasgow)

EAST FIFE 3   **DUNFERMLINE ATHLETIC 0**
Fleming, Duncan, Morris

SEASON 1950/51

28th October, 1950 at Hampden Park;
Attendance 63,074; Referee: Mr J. A. Mowat (Glasgow)

MOTHERWELL 3   **HIBERNIAN 0**
Kelly, Forrest, Watters

SEASON 1951/52

27th October, 1951 at Hampden Park;
Attendance 91,075; Referee: Mr J. A. Mowat (Glasgow)

DUNDEE 3   **RANGERS 2**
Flavell, Pattillo, Boyd Findlay, Thornton

SEASON 1952/53

25th October, 1952 at Hampden Park;
Attendance 51,830; Referee: Mr J. A. Mowat (Glasgow)

DUNDEE 2   **KILMARNOCK 0**
Flavell (2)

SEASON 1953/54

24th October, 1953 at Hampden Park;
Attendance 88,529; Referee: Mr J. S. Cox (Rutherglen)

EAST FIFE 3   **PARTICK THISTLE 2**
Gardiner, Fleming, Christie Walker, McKenzie

SEASON 1954/55

23rd October, 1954 at Hampden Park;
Attendance 55,640; Referee: Mr J. A. Mowat (Glasgow)

HEART OF MIDLOTHIAN 4 **MOTHERWELL 2**
Bauld (3), Wardhaugh   Redpath (pen), Bain

SEASON 1955/56

22nd October, 1955 at Hampden Park;
Attendance 44,103; Referee: Mr H. Phillips (Wishaw)

ABERDEEN 2   **ST. MIRREN 1**
Mallan (og), Leggat   Holmes

SEASON 1956/57

27th October, 1956 at Hampden Park;
Attendance 58,973; Referee: Mr J. A. Mowat (Glasgow)

CELTIC 0   **PARTICK THISTLE 0**

REPLAY
31st October, 1956 at Hampden Park;
Attendance 31,126; Referee: Mr J. A. Mowat (Glasgow)

CELTIC 3   **PARTICK THISTLE 0**
McPhail (2), Collins

SEASON 1957/58

19th October, 1957 at Hampden Park;
Attendance 82,293; Referee: Mr J. A. Mowat (Glasgow)

CELTIC 7   **RANGERS 1**
Mochan (2), McPhail (3), Simpson
Wilson, Fernie (pen)

SEASON 1958/59

25th October, 1958 at Hampden Park;
Attendance 59,960; Referee: Mr R. H. Davidson (Airdrie)

HEART OF MIDLOTHIAN 5 **PARTICK THISTLE 1**
Murray (2), Bauld (2), Hamilton Smith

SEASON 1959/60

24th October, 1959 at Hampden Park;
Attendance 57,974; Referee: Mr R. H. Davidson (Airdrie)

HEART OF MIDLOTHIAN 2 **THIRD LANARK 1**
Hamilton, Young   Gray

SEASON 1960/61

29th October, 1960 at Hampden Park;
Attendance 82,063; Referee: Mr T. Wharton (Glasgow)

RANGERS 2   **KILMARNOCK 0**
Brand, Scott

SEASON 1961/62

28th October, 1961 at Hampden Park;
Attendance 88,635; Referee: Mr R. H. Davidson (Airdrie)

RANGERS 1   **HEART OF MIDLOTHIAN 1**
Millar   Cumming (pen)

REPLAY
18th December, 1961 at Hampden Park;
Attendance 47,552; Referee: Mr R. H. Davidson (Airdrie)

RANGERS 3   **HEART OF MIDLOTHIAN 1**
Millar, Brand, McMillan Davidson

SEASON 1962/63

27th October, 1962 at Hampden Park;
Attendance 51,280; Referee: Mr T. Wharton (Glasgow)

HEART OF MIDLOTHIAN 1 **KILMARNOCK 0**
Davidson

SEASON 1963/64

26th October, 1963 at Hampden Park;
Attendance 105,907; Referee: Mr H. Phillips (Wishaw)

RANGERS 5   **MORTON 0**
Forrest (4), Willoughby

SEASON 1964/65

24th October, 1964 at Hampden Park;
Attendance 91,000; Referee: Mr H. Phillips (Wishaw)

RANGERS 2   **CELTIC 1**
Forrest (2)   Johnstone

SEASON 1965/66

23rd October, 1965 at Hampden Park;
Attendance 107,609; Referee: Mr H. Phillips (Wishaw)

CELTIC 2   **RANGERS 1**
Hughes (2 (2 pen))   Young (o.g.)

SEASON 1966/67

29th October, 1966 at Hampden Park;
Attendance 94,532; Referee: Mr T. Wharton (Glasgow)

CELTIC 1   **RANGERS 0**
Lennox

SEASON 1967/68

28th October, 1967 at Hampden Park;
Attendance 66,660; Referee: Mr R. H. Davidson (Airdrie)

CELTIC 5
Chalmers (2), Hughes,
Wallace, Lennox

DUNDEE 3
G. McLean (2), J. McLean

SEASON 1968/69

5th April, 1969 at Hampden Park;
Attendance 74,000; Referee: Mr W. M. M. Syme (Airdrie)

CELTIC 6
Lennox (3), Wallace, Auld, Craig

HIBERNIAN 2
O'Rourke, Stevenson

SEASON 1969/70

25th October, 1969 at Hampden Park;
Attendance 73,067; Referee: Mr J. W. Paterson (Bothwell)

CELTIC 1
Auld

ST. JOHNSTONE 0

SEASON 1970/71

24th October, 1970 at Hampden Park;
Attendance 106,263; Referee: Mr T. Wharton (Glasgow)

RANGERS 1
Johnstone

CELTIC 0

SEASON 1971/72

23rd October, 1971 at Hampden Park;
Attendance 62,740; Referee: Mr W. J. Mullan (Dalkeith)

PARTICK THISTLE 4
Rae, Lawrie, McQuade, Bone

CELTIC 1
Dalglish

SEASON 1972/73

9th December, 1972 at Hampden Park;
Attendance 71,696; Referee: Mr A. MacKenzie (Larbert)

HIBERNIAN 2
Stanton, O'Rourke

CELTIC 1
Dalglish

SEASON 1973/74

15th December, 1973 at Hampden Park;
Attendance 27,974; Referee: Mr R. H. Davidson (Airdrie)

DUNDEE 1
Wallace

CELTIC 0

SEASON 1974/75

26th October, 1974 at Hampden Park;
Attendance 53,848;
Referee: Mr J. R. P. Gordon (Newport on Tay)

CELTIC 6
Johnstone, Deans (3), Wilson, Murray

HIBERNIAN 3
Harper (3)

SEASON 1975/76

25th October, 1975 at Hampden Park;
Attendance 58,806; Referee: Mr W. Anderson (East Kilbride)

RANGERS 1
MacDonald

CELTIC 0

SEASON 1976/77

6th November, 1976 at Hampden Park;
Attendance 69,268; Referee: Mr J. W. Paterson (Bothwell)

ABERDEEN 2
Jarvie, Robb

CELTIC 1
Dalglish (pen.)

After extra-time – 1-1 After 90 Minutes

SEASON 1977/78

18th March, 1978 at Hampden Park;
Attendance 60,168; Referee: Mr D. F. T. Syme (Rutherglen)

RANGERS 2
Cooper, Smith

CELTIC 1
Edvaldsson

After extra-time – 1-1 After 90 Minutes

SEASON 1978/79

31st March, 1979 at Hampden Park;
Attendance 54,000; Referee: Mr I. M. D. Foote (Glasgow)

RANGERS 2
McMaster (o.g.), Jackson

ABERDEEN 1
Davidson

SEASON 1979/80 – BELL'S LEAGUE CUP

8th December, 1979 at Hampden Park;
Attendance 27,299; Referee: Mr B. R. McGinlay (Balfron)

DUNDEE UNITED 0
After extra-time

ABERDEEN 0

REPLAY

12th December, 1979 at Dens Park;
Attendance 28,984; Referee: Mr B. R. McGinlay (Balfron)

DUNDEE UNITED 3
Pettigrew (2), Sturrock

ABERDEEN 0

SEASON 1980/81 – BELL'S LEAGUE CUP

6th December, 1980 at Dens Park;
Attendance 24,466; Referee: Mr R. B. Valentine (Dundee)

DUNDEE UNITED 3
Dodds, Sturrock (2)

DUNDEE 0

SEASON 1981/82

28th November, 1981 at Hampden Park;
Attendance 53,795;
Referee: Mr E. H. Pringle (Edinburgh)

RANGERS 2
Cooper, Redford

DUNDEE UNITED 1
Milne

SEASON 1982/83

4th December, 1982 at Hampden Park;
Attendance 55,372; Referee: Mr K. J. Hope (Clarkston)

CELTIC 2
Nicholas, MacLeod

RANGERS 1
Bett

SEASON 1983/84

25th March, 1984 at Hampden Park;
Attendance 66,369; Referee: Mr R. B. Valentine (Dundee)

RANGERS 3
McCoist 3 (1 pen)

CELTIC 2
McClair, Reid (pen)

After extra-time – 2-2 After 90 Minutes

SEASON 1984/85 – SKOL CUP

28th October, 1984 at Hampden Park;
Attendance 44,698; Referee: Mr B. R. McGinlay (Balfron)

RANGERS 1
Ferguson

DUNDEE UNITED 0

SEASON 1985/86 – SKOL CUP

27th October, 1985 at Hampden Park;
Attendance 40,065; Referee: Mr R. B. Valentine (Dundee)

ABERDEEN 3
Black (2), Stark

HIBERNIAN 0

SEASON 1986/87 – SKOL CUP

26th October, 1986 at Hampden Park;
Attendance 74,219; Referee: Mr D. F. T. Syme (Rutherglen)

RANGERS 2
Durrant, Cooper (pen)

CELTIC 1
McClair

SEASON 1987/88 – SKOL CUP

25th October, 1987 at Hampden Park;
Attendance 71,961; Referee: Mr R. B. Valentine (Dundee)

RANGERS 3   **ABERDEEN 3**
Cooper, Durrant, Fleck   Bett, Falconer, Hewitt
After extra-time – 3-3 After 90 Minutes
Rangers won 5-3 on Kicks from the Penalty Mark

SEASON 1988/89 – SKOL CUP

23rd October, 1988 at Hampden Park;
Attendance 72,122; Referee: Mr G. B. Smith (Edinburgh)

RANGERS 3   **ABERDEEN 2**
McCoist (2), I. Ferguson   Dodds (2)

SEASON 1989/90 – SKOL CUP

22nd October, 1989 at Hampden Park;
Attendance 61,190; Referee: Mr G. B. Smith (Edinburgh)

ABERDEEN 2   **RANGERS 1**
Mason (2)   Walters (pen)
After extra-time – 1-1 after 90 minutes

SEASON 1990/91 – SKOL CUP

28th October, 1990 at Hampden Park;
Attendance 62,817; Referee: Mr J. McCluskey (Stewarton)

RANGERS 2   **CELTIC 1**
Walters, Gough   Elliott

SEASON 1991/92 – SKOL CUP

27th October, 1991 at Hampden Park;
Attendance 40,377; Referee: Mr B. R. McGinlay (Balfron)

HIBERNIAN 2   **DUNFERMLINE ATHLETIC 0**
McIntyre (pen), Wright

SEASON 1992/93 – SKOL CUP

25th October, 1992 at Hampden Park;
Attendance 45,298; Referee: Mr D. D. Hope (Erskine)

RANGERS 2   **ABERDEEN 1**
McCall, Smith (o.g.)   Shearer
After extra-time – 1-1 after 90 minutes

SEASON 1993/94

24th October, 1993 at Celtic Park;
Attendance 47,632; Referee: Mr J. McCluskey (Stewarton)

RANGERS 2   **HIBERNIAN 1**
Durrant, McCoist   McPherson (o.g.)

SEASON 1994/95 – COCA-COLA CUP

27th November, 1994 at Ibrox Stadium;
Attendance 45,384; Referee: Mr J. McCluskey (Stewarton)

RAITH ROVERS 2   **CELTIC 2**
S. Crawford, G. Dalziel   C. Nicholas, A. Walker
After extra-time – 2-2 after 90 minutes
Raith Rovers won 6-5 on Kicks from the Penalty Mark

SEASON 1995/96 – COCA-COLA CUP

26th November, 1995 at Hampden Park;
Attendance 33,099; Referee: Mr L.W. Mottram (Forth)

ABERDEEN 2   **DUNDEE 0**
D. Shearer, W. Dodds

SEASON 1996/97 – COCA-COLA CUP

24th November, 1996 at Celtic Park;
Attendance 48,559; Referee: Mr H. Dallas (Motherwell)

RANGERS 4   **HEART OF MIDLOTHIAN 3**
P. Gascoigne (2),A. McCoist (2)   D. Weir, S. Fulton, J. Robertson

SEASON 1997/98 – COCA-COLA CUP

30th November, 1997 at Ibrox Stadium, Glasgow;
Attendance 49,305; Referee: Mr J. McCluskey (Stewarton)

CELTIC 3   **DUNDEE UNITED 0**
M. Rieper, H. Larsson, C. Burley

SEASON 1998/99

29th November, 1998 at Celtic Park, Glasgow;
Attendance 45,533; Referee: Mr H. Dallas (Motherwell)

RANGERS 2   **ST. JOHNSTONE 1**
S. Guivarc'h, J. Albertz   N. Dasovic

SEASON 1999/2000 – CIS INSURANCE CUP

19th March, 2000 at The National Stadium, Hampden Park,
Glasgow; Attendance 50,073; Referee: Mr K. Clark (Paisley)

CELTIC 2   **ABERDEEN 0**
V. Riseth, T. Johnson

SEASON 2000/01 – CIS INSURANCE CUP

18th March, 2001 at The National Stadium, Hampden Park,
Glasgow; Attendance 48,830; Referee: Mr H. Dallas (Motherwell)

CELTIC 3   **KILMARNOCK 0**
H. Larsson (3)

WINNERS AT A GLANCE

RANGERS	21
CELTIC	12
ABERDEEN	5
HEART OF MIDLOTHIAN	4
DUNDEE	3
EAST FIFE	3
DUNDEE UNITED	2
HIBERNIAN	2
MOTHERWELL	1
PARTICK THISTLE	1
RAITH ROVERS	1

APPEARANCES IN FINALS

(Figures do not include replays)

RANGERS	27
CELTIC	24
ABERDEEN	12
HIBERNIAN	7
DUNDEE	6
HEART OF MIDLOTHIAN	6
DUNDEE UNITED	5
PARTICK THISTLE	4
EAST FIFE	3
KILMARNOCK	4
DUNFERMLINE ATHLETIC	2
MOTHERWELL	2
RAITH ROVERS	2
ST. JOHNSTONE	2
FALKIRK	1
MORTON	1
ST. MIRREN	1
THIRD LANARK	1

FIRST ROUND

Saturday, 9th December, 2000

STENHOUSEMUIR 1 **BERWICK RANGERS 4**
Menelaws Watt, Anthony, Wood, Ronald
Stenhousemuir: Gow, Duncan, Cormack, McAneny, Graham, (Menelaws), Davidson, Ferguson, (Blaikie), McKinnon, (Henderson), S. Miller, Donald, English
Substitutes not used: Storrar, Banner
Berwick Rangers: McLean, McMartin, Gray, Ritchie, A. Neill, Anthony, Forrest, Watt, Wood, (Whelan), Ronald, (Findlay), Magee, (Smith)
Substitutes not used: McNicoll, O'Connor
Referee: Dougie Smith
Attendance: 303

*MONTROSE 0 **ARBROATH 1**
  Mercer
Montrose: McGlynn, Mailer, Ferguson, Muirhead, Christie, Craib, Marwick, (McKellar), Harrison, McKenzie, J. Mitchell, (Hutcheon), Dailly, (Catto)
Substitutes not used: Lowe, Thompson
Arbroath: Hinchcliffe, Rowe, McInally, McAulay, (Heenan), J. Thomson, Crawford, (Mercer), Cunningham, Webster, C. McGlashan, (Kirk), Mallan, J. McGlashan
Substitutes not used: Steele, Wight
Referee: Calum Murray
Attendance: 1,038
***Match ordered to be replayed as a result of Arbroath having played two players whilst under SFA suspension.**

ALBION ROVERS 1 **EAST FIFE 1**
Shields Ferguson
Albion Rovers: Fahey, Clark, Lumsden, Clyde, Tait, Booth, Waldie, McKenzie, Shields, (Diack), R. McMullan, (Rankin), Silvestro, (McLees)
Substitutes not used: Smith, Shearer
East Fife: McCulloch, Bottiglieri, Sharp, (Gibb), McCloy, Agostini, Allison, McKinnon, Mackay, Ferguson, (Devine), Kerrigan, Hunter
Substitutes not used: Moffat, Shannon, Stewart
Referee: Charlie Richmond
Attendance: 360

DUMBARTON 1 **EAST STIRLINGSHIRE 1**
Flannery Hislop
Dumbarton: Hillcoat, (Wight), Dickie, Brittain, Bruce, McCann, Stewart, Bonar, (Dillon), Grace, Flannery, (Smith), Brown, Robertson
Substitutes not used: Jack, Gentile
East Stirlingshire: Butter, Ferguson, Russell, Clarke, Hall, Scott, Stewart, Lorimer, (D. Todd), Allison, Hislop, (McKechnie), Wood
Substitutes not used: Quinn, McPherson, C. Todd
Referee: Iain Brines
Attendance: 834

Tuesday, 12th December, 2000

BRECHIN CITY 3 **FORFAR ATHLETIC 0**
Leask, Black, Bain
Brechin City: Soutar, D. Smith, Coulston, Bain, Cairney, G. Smith, Leask, (Bailey), Nairn, Grant, (Sturrock), Riley, (Donachie), Black
Substitutes not used: Parkyn, Campbell
Forfar Athletic: Garden, Morris, Tully, (McGraw), Horn, Beaton, Farnan, A. Taylor, Bowman, (Cargill), I. Ferguson, (Brand), Stewart, Donaldson
Substitutes not used: McCheyne, Ferrie
Referee: Colin Hardie
Attendance: 447

Saturday, 16th December, 2000

WHITEHILL WELFARE 0 **PETERHEAD 0**
Whitehill Welfare: Cantley, McLaren, Gowrie, Martin, Steel, (Cunningham), Bennett, Jardine, Samuel, Bird, Hope, (Black), Manson, (Bailey)
Substitutes not used: Devine, Malcolm
Peterhead: Pirie, S. Clark, King, Herd, Simpson, Tindal, Murray, Yeats, Stewart, D. Smith, Livingstone
Substitutes not used: Gibson, Johnston, Bett, Watson, Buchanan
Referee: George Thomson
Attendance: 237

Monday, 18th December, 2000

QUEEN OF THE SOUTH 2 **CLYDEBANK 0**
Weatherson (2)
Queen of the South: Mathieson, P. Atkinson, McKeown, McQuilter, Aitken, Sunderland, (Nixon), Muir, Hawke, Weatherson, (Suddick), Skinner, (Caldwell), Kinnaird
Substitutes not used: Patterson, Scott
Clydebank: Hutchison, Mackay, McKinstrey, Murdoch, Brannigan, Wishart, Murray, Paton, Coyne, Glancy, McVey, (Morrison),
Substitute not used: Wylie
Referee: Brian McGarry
Attendance: 1,017

Wednesday, 20th December, 2000

EDINBURGH CITY 0 **BUCKIE THISTLE 1**
  Rowley
Edinburgh City: Mackintosh, Burrell, Ferry, Scott, Foster, Edgar, (Rennie), Salton, (Blair), Summerville, O'Donnell, Hartley, Seeley
Substitutes not used: Miller, Irving, Ewart
Buckie Thistle: Rae, Grant, Lamberton, Anderson, McPherson, Rattray, Rowley, Stephen, Thomson, (Reid), Bruce, (Stewart), Craik, (Milne)
Substitutes not used: Matheson, Davidson
Referee: Craig Thomson
Attendance: 246

REPLAYED TIE

Saturday, 6th January, 2001

MONTROSE 0 **ARBROATH 0**
Montrose: McGlynn, Marwick, Ferguson, Lowe, Christie, Craib, Muirhead, Mailer, McKenzie, McIlravey, (Hutcheon), (McWilliam), Joy, (Catto)
Substitutes not used: J. Mitchell, Thompson
Arbroath: Hinchcliffe, Rowe, McInally, Cusick, (Heenan), Thomson, Webster, Steele, Mercer, C. McGlashan, (Brownlie), J. McGlashan, (Cunningham), Florence
Substitutes not used: Wight, Henslee
Referee: Calum Murray
Attendance: 1,250

FIRST ROUND REPLAYS

Tuesday, 12th December, 2001

EAST STIRLINGSHIRE 0 **DUMBARTON 1**
  Robertson
East Stirlingshire: Butter, Ferguson, Russell, Clarke, Hall, Scott, (D. Todd), Stewart, (McPherson), Lorimer, Hislop, Allison, Wood
Substitutes not used: Quinn, McKechnie, C. Todd
Dumbarton: Hillcoat, Dickie, Brittain, (Dillon), Bruce, McCann, Stewart, Bonar, Jack, Flannery, Andrew Brown, Robertson
Substitutes not used: Smith, Gentile, Wilson, Wight
Referee: Iain Brines
Attendance: 170

EAST FIFE 2 **ALBION ROVERS 0**
Ferguson (2)
East Fife: McCulloch, Bottiglieri, Gibb, McCloy, Agostini, Allison, McKinnon, Mackay, Ferguson, (Moffat), Kerrigan, Hunter, (Mortimer)
Substitutes not used: Munro, Devine, Stewart
Albion Rovers: Fahey, Clark, Lumsden, Smith, Tait, Booth, Waldie, J. McKenzie, Shields, Begue, (Diack), Silvestro, (R. McMullan)
Substitutes not used: McLees, Rankin, Shearer
Referee: Charlie Richmond
Attendance: 398

Monday, 18th December, 2000

PETERHEAD 3 **WHITEHILL WELFARE 0**
King, Livingstone, Tindal
Peterhead: Pirie, S. Clark, King, Herd, Simpson, Tindal, Murray, (Bett), Stewart, (De-Barros), Yeats, (Gibson), Johnston, Livingstone
Substitutes not used: Cooper, Buchanan
Whitehill Welfare: Cantley, McLaren, (Temple), Gowrie, Malcolm, Martin, (Steele), Bennett, Jardine, Samuel, Bird, Baillie, (Black), Manson
Substitutes not used: Cunningham, Tulloch
Referee: John Gilmour
Attendance: 465

Saturday, 9th January, 2001

ARBROATH 1   MONTROSE 2
Cusick   McKenzie (2)

Arbroath: Hinchcliffe, Rowe, McInally, (Steele), Florence, (Cunningham), Webster, Cusick, Heenan, (Brownlie), Mercer, C. McGlashan, J. McGlashan, Fotheringham
Substitutes not used: Henslee, Wight

Montrose: McGlynn, Mailer, Ferguson, Lowe, (Harrison), Christie, Craib, McWilliam, (Joy), Muirhead, McIlravey (J. Mitchell), McKenzie, Catto
Substitutes not used: McKellar, Thompson

Referee: Calum Murray
Attendance: 1,225

SECOND ROUND

Saturday, 6th January, 2001

SPARTANS 1   STIRLING ALBION 3
Hughes   Donald, Graham, Williams

Spartans: Brown, Robertson, (B. Quinn), Rae, Hughes, M. Thomson, McKeating, Watson, (Wilson), S. Thomson, Hoggins, McGovern, M. Quinn, (Ford)
Substitutes not used: Ewing, Burns

Stirling Albion: Reid, Kelly, Milne, Devine, Gaughan, McAulay, Feroz, Donald, Graham, (Williams), Templeman, (McCallion), Millar
Substitutes not used: Hunter, Munro, Buchanan

Referee: Brian Cassidy
Attendance: 709

STRANRAER 2   DUMBARTON 0
Walker, Harty

Stranraer: McGeown, Knox, Wright, Johnstone, George, Macdonald, Blair, Walker, Harty, Rae (Geraghty), Stirling
Substitutes not used: McLauchlan, Hodge, Paterson, O'Neill

Dumbarton: Hillcoat, Dickie, Brittain, (Melvin), Bruce, Jack, Stewart, (Smith), Bonar, Grace, Flannery, Andrew Brown, Dillon
Substitutes not used: Wilson, Gentile, Wight

Referee: Ian Frickleton
Attendance: 595

BERWICK RANGERS 3   COWDENBEATH 3
A. Neill (2), Anthony   Bradley (2), Winter

Berwick Rangers: McLean, McMartin, Gray, Ritchie, A. Neill, Watt, Forrest, Anthony, Wood, Elliot, (Findlay), Smith
Substitutes not used: Oliver, Whelan, Magee, Pucko

Cowdenbeath: Martin, Boyle, Courts, (Neeson), Smith, White, Lawrence, Winter, Bradley, McDowell, Brown, King, (Allan)
Substitutes not used: Wright, McCulloch, Barnes

Referee: Cammy Melville
Attendance: 505

BUCKIE THISTLE 2   HAMILTON ACADEMICAL 0
Stephen, Stewart

Buckie Thistle: Rae, G. Grant, Lamberton, Anderson, McPherson, Rattray, Rowley, Stephen, Thomson, (Reid), Bruce (Craik), Stewart, (Milne)
Substitutes not used: Matheson, Duncan

Hamilton Academical: Macfarlane, Nelson, (Downs) Callaghan, Hogg, Gaughan, Clark, Russell, Sherry, Eadie, (Moore), McFarlane, Bonnar
Substitutes not used: Martin, Prytz, Potter

Referee: Alan Gemmill
Attendance: 1,028

PETERHEAD 3   COVE RANGERS 0
Johnstone, Herd, Stewart

Peterhead: Pirie, S. Clark, King, Herd, Simpson, Tindal, Cooper, (Murray), Stewart, (Gibson), Yeats, (Smith), Johnston, Livingstone
Substitutes not used: Watson, Buchanan

Cove Rangers: Coull, Mullen, McGinlay, Alexander, Murphy, Baxter, Adam, (Summers), Yule, Coutts, (Taylor), Beattie, Brown
Substitutes not used: K. Coull, Pilichos, Henderson

Referee: Mike Ritchie
Attendance: 1,425

COLDSTREAM 2   BRECHIN CITY 6
Hutchison, Dishington   Grant (2), Bailey (4)

Coldstream: Weir, Hutchison, Finlay, O'Connor, Wilson, Keenan, (Dishington), Evans, Cummings, (McLeod), Shennan, (Cowie), Cockburn, Tait
Substitutes not used: Cowe, Walker

Brechin City: Soutar, G. Smith, Coulston, (D. Smith), Bain, Cairney, Raynes, (Nairn), Dewar, (Black), Bailey, Grant, P. Riley, Sturrock
Substitutes not used: Parkyn, Leask

Referee: Eddie Mack
Attendance: 393

EAST FIFE 1   QUEEN'S PARK 0
Moffat

East Fife: McCulloch, Bottigilieri, Sharp, McCloy, Agostini, Allison, Munro, (Stewart), Mortimer, (Gibb), Kerrigan, Moffat, (Hunter), Mackay
Substitutes not used: Devine, Gallagher

Queen's Park: Smith, Canning, Travers, Duncan, (Jackson), Connaghan, Sinclair, Finlayson, Miller, Gallagher, Brown, Carroll, (Scobie)
Substitutes not used: Cunningham, Caven, Bruce

Referee: John Fleming
Attendance: 759

PARTICK THISTLE 3   DEVERONVALE 0
Hardie (2), Collins

Partick Thistle: Arthur, Hamilton, Archibald, (McCallum), Craigan, Smith, McNally, (Stewart), Collins, Lennon, Shaw, Hardie, Lindau, (McGrillen)
Substitutes not used: Brown, Cameron

Deveronvale: Speirs, Dolan, Kinghorn, Chisholm, Henderson, Montgomery, More, (Singer), Brown, (McAllister), Cadger, Watt, (Nicol), Urquhart
Substitutes not used: Phimister, Craigie

Referee: Garry Mitchell
Attendance: 3,160

Saturday, 13th January, 2001

MONTROSE 1   KEITH 1
Harrison   Still

Montrose: Thompson, Marwick, (McKellar), Ferguson, Mailer, Muirhead, Craib, Byers, Harrison, McKenzie, Laidlaw, Catto, (McWilliam)
Substitutes not used: McIlravey, Joy, Adams

Keith: Rodd, Darcy, (Hendry), Simmers, Maver, Watt, Gibson, Still, Presslie, Robertson, (Stewart), Nicol, McPherson, (Brown)
Substitutes not used: McKenzie, Green

Referee: Steven Kaney
Attendance: 1,150

Saturday, 27th January, 2001

ELGIN CITY 0   QUEEN OF THE SOUTH 1
                               Weatherson

Elgin City: Pirie, Craig Milne, MacDonald, (Green), Furphy, Morrison, Munro, Campbell, N. Whyte, (Clinton), Colin Milne, Edwards, (Irvine), Ross
Substitutes not used: Ellis, Rae

Queen of the South: Mathieson, P. Atkinson, McKeown, McQuilter, Aitken, Sunderland, Muir, (Nixon), Boyle, Skinner, (Hogg), Weatherson, Paterson, (Kinnaird)
Substitutes not used: Pickering, Scott

Referee: Craig MacKay
Attendance: 1,035

SECOND ROUND REPLAYS

Wednesday, 24th January, 2001

COWDENBEATH 0   BERWICK RANGERS 1
                               Elliot

Cowdenbeath: Martin, Boyle, Courts, D. White, Smith, Lawrence, Winter, Bradley, McDowell, Brown, Neeson, (Burns)
Substitutes not used: Wright, Allan, Reilly, Barnes

Berwick Rangers: McLean, McMartin, (Elliot), Gray, Ritchie, A. Neill, Anthony, Forrest, M. Neil, Wood, Ronald, Smith, (Duthie)
Substitutes not used: Pucko, Findlay, Whelan

Referee: Cammy Melville
Attendance: 544

KEITH 0   MONTROSE 1 (AET)
                               Mitchell

Keith: Thain, Darcy, Simmers, Maver, Watt, Gibson, Stewart, (Hendry), Presslie, (Green), Robertson, Nicol, McPherson, (McKenzie)
Substitutes not used: Brown Robb

Montrose: McGlynn, McWilliam, (McKellar), Ferguson, Mailer, Christie, Craib, Byers, Muirhead, M. McKenzie, (Harrison), Laidlaw, (J. Mitchell), Joy
Substitutes not used: Thompson, Marwick

Referee: Mike Ritchie
Attendance: 489

THIRD ROUND

Saturday, 27th January, 2001

ST. JOHNSTONE 0 **DUNFERMLINE ATHLETIC 0**

St. Johnstone: Main, Dods, Bollan, Weir, Frail, McBride, (Lovenkrands), Dasovic, O'Neill, (Kane), Sylla, Parker, Connolly, (Lowndes)
Substitutes not used: Cuthbert, McCluskey
Dunfermline Athletic: Ruitenbeek, Doesburg, S.M. Thomson, Skinner, Skerla, McGroarty, Nicholson, (Mason), I. Ferguson, Hampshire, (Dair), Crawford, Moss, (Dijkhuizen)
Substitutes not used: S.Y. Thomson, Tod
Referee: Bobby Orr
Attendance: 5,026

BERWICK RANGERS 0 **HEART OF MIDLOTHIAN 0**

Berwick Rangers: McLean, McMartin, Gray, Ritchie, A. Neill, Anthony, Forrest, M. Neil, Wood, (Neil), Elliot, (Findlay), Smith, (Duthie)
Substitutes not used: Watt, Pucko
Heart of Midlothian: Niemi, Pressley, Flögel, Petric, Murray, Tomaschek, (Makel), Boyack, Fulton, (Juanjo), Cameron, Durie, (McSwegan), Kirk
Substitutes not used: McKenzie, Severin
Referee: John Rowbotham
Attendance: 3,139

STIRLING ALBION 2 **RAITH ROVERS 0**
Graham, Templeman

Stirling Albion: Reid, Kelly, (McCallion), Milne, Devine, (Aitken), Gaughan, McAulay, (Williams), Feroz, Donald, Graham, Templeman, Martin
Substitutes not used: Millar, Buchanan
Raith Rovers: Van de Kamp, McCulloch, Hampshire, Ellis, (Hetherston), Browne, Black, Tosh, Nicol, Bayne, (Mballa), Clark, Stein
Substitutes not used: Hamilton, Niven, Coyle
Referee: Hugh Dallas
Attendance: 1,389

KILMARNOCK 1 **PARTICK THISTLE 0**
Mitchell

Kilmarnock: Marshall, Dindeleux, Baker, Innes, Mahood, Canero, Holt, Mitchell, McLaren, (Hay), Cocard, (Vareille), Dargo, (Wright)
Substitutes not used: Stewart, Reilly
Partick Thistle: Arthur, Hamilton, Archibald, Craigan, Docherty, (Stewart), McNally, Collins, Lennon, McLean, (McGrillen), Hardie, Shaw
Substitutes not used: Brown, Lindau, McCallum
Referee: Ian Fyfe
Attendance: 3,836

ALLOA ATHLETIC 0 **ABERDEEN 3**
Rowson, Winters, Mackie

Alloa Athletic: Cairns, (McQueen), Huxford, (Watson), Clark, French, Thomson, Valentine, Hamilton, Christie, Little, (Evans), Irvine, Wood
Substitutes not used: Johnston, Armstrong
Aberdeen: Preece, McNaughton, Whyte, McGuire, Solberg, Belabed, Rowson, Darren Young, Winters, (Derek Young), Stavrum, (Mackie), Dow
Substitutes not used: Esson, McAllister, Rutkiewicz
Referee: Tom Brown
Attendance: 2,877

ROSS COUNTY 2 **BUCKIE THISTLE 1**
Henderson, Cunnington Rowley

Ross County: Walker, Perry, Cunnington, Maxwell, Irvine, Fraser, McCormick, (Bone), S. Ferguson, Coyle, Boukraa, Henderson
Substitutes not used: Hamilton, Holmes, Gilbert, Zahana-Oni
Buckie Thistle: Rae, Grant, Lamberton, Anderson, McPherson, Rattray, (Milne), Rowley, (Reid), Stephen, Thompson, Bruce, Craik, (Stewart)
Substitutes not used: Duncan, Davidson
Referee: Steve Kaney
Attendance: 2,461

MONTROSE 0 **DUNDEE UNITED 2**
Lauchlan (2)

Montrose: McGlynn, Mailer, Joy, Muirhead, Christie, Craib, McKellar, (Lowe), Harrison, (McWilliam), McKenzie, (Mitchell), Laidlaw, Byers
Substitutes not used: Marwick, Thompson
Dundee United: Gallacher, McCunnie, Partridge, De Vos, Lauchlan, Griffin, Aljofree, (Buchan), Miller, (Heaney), Easton, Hamilton, (Thompson), Lilley
Substitutes not used: McCracken, Onstad
Referee: John Underhill
Attendance: 2,592

INVERNESS CAL. TH. 4 **AYR UNITED 3**
Sheerin, Mann, Xausa, Annand, Campbell,
Wyness, Wilson

Inverness Caledonian Thistle: Fridge, Teasdale, (Tokely), Hastings, McCaffrey, Mann, Sheerin, Bagan, Xausa, (Graham), Wyness, Christie, McBain
Substitutes not used: Bavidge, Golabek, Calder
Ayr United: Rovde, Renwick, (Reynolds), Lovering, McGinlay, Hughes, Campbell, Teale, (Craig), Wilson, Hurst, Annand, (Grady), Scally
Substitutes not used: Nelson, Sharp
Referee: Eric Martindale
Attendance: 2,257

DUNDEE 0 **FALKIRK 0**

Dundee: Roccati, Smith, Marrocco, Coyne, Tweed, (McSkimming), Milne, (Falconer), Nemsadze, Artero, (Romano), Rae, Caniggia, Carranza
Substitutes not used: Langfield, Del Rio
Falkirk: Hogarth, Lawrie, McQuilken, Christie, Rennie, Nicholls, McAllister, (Burke), Henry, Roberts, Kerr, Hutchison, (Craig)
Substitutes not used: Seaton, Morris, Hill
Referee: Michael McCurry
Attendance: 6,395

HIBERNIAN 6 **CLYDE 1**
Laursen, Jack, Sauzee, McLaughlin
Paatelainen, Lehmann (2)

Hibernian: Colgan, Fenwick, Smith, Sauzee, Jack, (Brebner), Laursen, Lovell, (Zitelli), Latapy, (Andrews), O'Neil, Paatelainen, Lehmann
Substitutes not used: Franks, Dennis
Clyde: Halliwell, Murray, McLaughlin, Smith, Greer, Ross, Crawford, (Cranmer), Millen, Keogh, McClay, (Henry), Grant, (Kane)
Substitutes not used: Cook, Bingham
Referee: Alan Freeland
Attendance: 9,494

PETERHEAD 4 **MORTON 1**
G. Smith, Carlin (o.g.), Matheson
Cooper, Simpson

Peterhead: Pirie, Tindal, King, Herd, Simpson, Gibson, Murray, (S. Clark), Stewart, (D. Smith), G. Smith, Yeats, Cooper, (Livingstone)
Substitutes not used: Johnston, Buchanan
Morton: Carlin, Murie, (MacGregor), Davies, (K. McDonald), S. MacDonald, James, Aitken, (Raeside), Matheson, Curran, Whalen, D. Anderson, P. McDonald
Substitutes not used: Tweedie, Maxwell
Referee: Douglas McDonald
Attendance: 1,647

EAST FIFE 1 **LIVINGSTON 4**
Moffat Bingham, Wilson (2), Britton

East Fife: Stewart, Bottiglieri, Sharp, McCloy, Agostini, Allison, Mackay, (Gallagher), Mortimer, Kerrigan, Moffat, Devine, (McManus)
Substitutes not used: Gibb, Munro, Garvie
Livingston: Alexander, McManus, Deas, McCulloch, Andrews, Anderson, McPhee, (Crabbe), Tosh, Wilson, (Britton), Bingham, Hagen, (Fleming)
Substitutes not used: Hart, McEwan
Referee: Kevin Toner
Attendance: 1,819

RANGERS 2 **BRECHIN CITY 0**
Johnston, Miller

Rangers: Klos, Ricksen, Konterman, Vidmar, Numan, B. Ferguson, Johnston, Reyna, (Wallace), Miller, De Boer, (Mols), Albertz, (Kerimoglu)
Substitutes not used: Brown, Porrini
Brechin City: Soutar, D. Smith, (Campbell), Coulston, (Sturrock), Bain, Cairney, Raynes, Bailey, P. Riley, Grant, Black, (Donachie), G. Smith
Substitutes not used: Nairn, Parkyn
Referee: David Somers
Attendance: 22,606

ST. MIRREN 1 **MOTHERWELL 2**
Quitongo McCulloch, Spencer

St. Mirren: Roy, Kerr, Rudden, Turner, Walker, Baltacha, Murray, Gillies, MacKenzie, (Yardley), Fenton, (Quitongo), Renfurm, (McGarry)
Substitutes not used: Nellis, Nicolson
Motherwell: Goram, Corrigan, Kemble, Hammell, Strong, Leitch, Brannan, Townsley, Adams, (Spencer), McCulloch, (Twaddle), Goodman
Substitutes not used: Woods, Lasley, Oueifio
Referee: Willie Young
Attendance: 5,002

Sunday, 28th January, 2001

STRANRAER 1   CELTIC 4
Harty   Valgaeren, McNamara,
                         Knox (o.g.), Moravcik

Stranraer: McGeown, Johnstone, Wright, Knox, George, Hodge, Blair, Macdonald, Harty, Jenkins, (Bryce), Walker
Substitutes not used: Stirling, Geraghty, Rae, O'Neill
Celtic: Douglas, Boyd, Valgaeren, (Mjallby), Vega, Thompson, McNamara, Lennon, Petta, (Lambert), Agathe, Larsson (Moravcik), Sutton
Substitutes not used: Gould, Smith
Referee: Stuart Dougal
Attendance: 5,660

Monday, 12th February, 2001

QUEEN OF THE SOUTH 1   AIRDRIEONIANS 3
Hawke   Moreau, Pilvi, Sanjuan

Queen of the South: Scott, P. Atkinson, McKeown, McQuilter, Aitken, Sunderland, O'Neil, Connell, Hawke, Weatherson, Patterson, (Hogg)
Substitutes not used: Nixon, Hughes, Pickering, Mathieson
Airdrieonians: Broto, Armstrong, McAlpine, Brady, Capin, Alfonso, Moreau, Sanjuan, Pilvi, (McGuire), Calderon, Fernandez
Substitutes not used: Gonzalez, Elliot, Prest, Boyce
Referee: Colin Hardie
Attendance: 2,216

THIRD ROUND REPLAYS

Wednesday, 7th February, 2001

HEART OF MIDLOTHIAN 2   BERWICK RANGERS 1
McSwegan, Juanjo   Elliot

Heart of Midlothian: Niemi, Pressley, Flögel, Petric, Murray, (Neilson), Tomaschek, Boyack, (Severin), Juanjo, Cameron, McSwegan, Kirk, (Adam)
Substitutes not used: McKenzie, Makel
Berwick Rangers: McLean, McMartin, Gray, Ritchie, A. Neill, Anthony, Forrest, (Whelan), M. Neil, Wood, (Findlay), Elliot, Duthie, (Smith)
Substitutes not used: Pucko, Ronald
Referee: Eric Martindale
Attendance: 7,502

Monday, 12th February, 2001

FALKIRK 0   DUNDEE 2
               Sara, Caniggia

Falkirk: Hogarth, Lawrie, McQuilken, (Craig), Christie, Rennie, Nicholls, McAllister, Henry, Roberts, (Burke), Kerr, Hutchison
Substitutes not used: Hill, Seaton, Morris
Dundee: Roccati, Smith, Romano, Coyne, Tweed, Carranza, (Russo), Nemsadze, Artero, Rae, Caniggia, (Milne), Sara, (Falconer)
Substitutes not used: Langfield, Del Rio
Referee: Michael McCurry
Attendance: 5,156

Tuesday, 13th February, 2001

DUNFERMLINE ATHLETIC 3   ST. JOHNSTONE 2
S.M. Thomson, Dijkhuizen, Moss   Russell, Lowndes

Dunfermline Athletic: Ruitenbeek, Dair, S.M. Thomson, Skinner, (Mason), Skerla, Nicholson, Rossi, Dijkhuizen, (Matthaei), Moss, Bullen, Petrie, (Tod)
Substitutes not used: S.Y. Thomson, McGroarty
St. Johnstone: Main, Dods, Bollan, Weir, Frail, McBride, Dasovic, Kane, Russell, (Parker), Sylla, (Lovenkrands), Lowndes
Substitutes not used: Cuthbert, McCluskey, O'Neill
Referee: Bobby Orr
Attendance: 4,748

FOURTH ROUND

Saturday, 17th February, 2001

HEART OF MIDLOTHIAN 1   DUNDEE 1
Juanjo   Sara

Heart of Midlothian: Niemi, Pressley, Flögel, McCann, Severin, Tomaschek, (McAnespie), Boyack, Juanjo, Cameron, McSwegan, (Wales), (Murray), Adam
Substitutes not used: McKenzie, Makel
Dundee: Roccati, Smith, Marrocco, Coyne, Tweed, Carranza, Nemsadze, Artero, Rae, Caniggia, Sara, (Milne)
Substitutes not used: Langfield, Del Rio, Yates, Falconer
Referee: Hugh Dallas
Attendance: 9,970

MOTHERWELL 0   DUNDEE UNITED 2
                  Miller, Easton

Motherwell: Goram, Corrigan, (Dempsie), Oueifio, Townsley, Hammell, Leitch, Lasley, Adams, (McFadden), Twaddle, (Nicholas), Spencer, Elliott
Substitutes not used: Woods, Ramsay
Dundee United: Gallacher, McCunnie, Lauchlan, De Vos, Aljofree, Griffin, Hannah, (Smith), Miller, Easton, Hamilton, (Thompson), Lilley, (Naveda)
Substitutes not used: Onstad, Buchan
Referee: Stuart Dougal
Attendance: 6,186

*AIRDRIEONIANS v PETERHEAD
Tie Awarded to Peterhead after Airdrieonians withdrew.

INVERNESS CALEDONIAN THISTLE 1   KILMARNOCK 1
Robson   Hay

Inverness Caledonian Thistle: Calder, Mann, McCaffrey, Hastings, Tokely, Christie, Sheerin, Bagan, (Robson), McBain, Xausa, Wyness, (Graham)
Substitutes not used: Golabek, Bavidge, Fridge
Kilmarnock: Marshall, MacPherson, Baker, McGowne, (Fowler), Dindeleux, Canero, Holt, Mitchell, McLaren, Wright, (Cocard), Dargo, (Hay)
Substitutes not used: Stewart, Reilly
Referee: Douglas McDonald
Attendance: 5,294

STIRLING ALBION 2   HIBERNIAN 3
Templeman, Graham   Sauzee, O'Neil, McManus

Stirling Albion: Reid, Kelly, (Stuart), Milne, Gaughan, Martin, McCallion, (Gardner), Donald, Templeman, Millar, Feroz, (Aitken), Graham
Substitutes not used: Williams, Buchanan
Hibernian: Colgan, Fenwick, Smith, Sauzee, Jack, Laursen, Murray, (McManus), Latapy, O'Neil, Paatelainen, Zitelli
Substitutes not used: Franks, Andrews, Brebner, Lehmann
Referee: John Rowbotham
Attendance: 3,673

DUNFERMLINE ATHLETIC 2   CELTIC 2
Skerla, Nicholson   Larsson (2)

Dunfermline Athletic: Ruitenbeek, Tod, S.M. Thomson, Skinner, Skerla, Mason, (Dair), Nicholson, I. Ferguson, Rossi, Dijkhuizen, (Bullen), Moss, (McGroarty)
Substitutes not used: S.Y. Thomson, Petrie
Celtic: Douglas, Boyd, Valgaeren, (Tebily), Vega, Thompson, Petta, (Petrov), Lennon, Lambert, Agathe, Larsson, Sutton
Substitutes not used: Gould, Johnson, Moravcik
Referee: Willie Young
Attendance: 11,222

LIVINGSTON 0   ABERDEEN 0

Livingston: Alexander, Brinquin, (McManus), Deas, Andrews, Anderson, McCulloch, Jackson, (Britton), McPhee, (Fleming), Wilson, Burns, Bingham
Substitutes not used: Crabbe, McCaldon
Aberdeen: Preece, McNaughton, (Derek Young), McAllister, (Darren Young), Whyte, (McGuire), Rowson, Solberg, Guntveit, Belabed, Winters, Stavrum, Mackie
Substitutes not used: Clark, Esson,
Referee: Kenny Clark
Attendance: 6,288

Sunday, 18th February, 2001

ROSS COUNTY 2   RANGERS 3
Bone (2)   Flo (2), Ferguson

Ross County: Walker, Perry, Robertson, Maxwell, Irvine, Ferguson, McCormick, (Fraser), Coyle, Bone, Boukraa, (Holmes), Henderson, (Mackay)
Substitutes not used: Hamilton, Cunnington
Rangers: Klos, Ricksen, Malcolm, Konterman, Wilson, Ferguson, Reyna, Kerimoglu, McCann, Miller, (Johnston), Flo
Substitutes not used: Moore, Carson, Christiansen, McHale
Referee: Michael McCurry
Attendance: 5,972

FOURTH ROUND REPLAYS

Wednesday, 28th February, 2001

KILMARNOCK 0   INVERNESS CALEDONIAN THISTLE 0
Match Abandoned after 28 Minutes due to Frozen Pitch
Kilmarnock: Marshall, MacPherson, McGowne, Dindeleux, Baker, Canero, Holt, Reilly, McLaren, Dargo, Cocard
Substitutes not used: Stewart, Wright, Innes, Hay, Di Giacomo

Inverness Caledonian Thistle: Calder, Tokely, Hastings, McCaffrey, Mann, Bagan, Sheerin, Christie, McBain, Xausa, Bavidge, Teasdale, Fridge
Referee: Douglas McDonald
Attendance: 5,000

Tuesday, 6th March, 2001

ABERDEEN 0	LIVINGSTON 1
	Crabbe

Aberdeen: Esson, McGuire, McAllister, Solberg, Rowson, Darren Young, (Clark), Guntveit, Belabed, (Lilley), Winters, Stavrum, Dow, (Derek Young)
Substitutes not used: Peat, O'Donaghue
Livingston: Alexander, Brinquin, Andrews, Anderson, Deas, McCulloch, Tosh, Jackson, (McPhee), Burns, (Crabbe), Wilson, Bingham
Substitutes not used: McManus, Hagen, McCaldon
Referee: Robert Orr
Attendance: 9,959

KILMARNOCK 2	INVERNESS CALEDONIAN THISTLE 1
McGowne, Wright	Xausa

Kilmarnock: Marshall, MacPherson, McGowne, Dindeleux, Baker, Canero, Holt, Mahood, (Hay), Reilly, Cocard, Wright, (McCoist)
Substitutes not used: Stewart, Innes, Di Giacomo
Inverness Caledonian Thistle: Calder, Tokely, Hastings, Mann, McCaffrey, Bagan, (Robson), Sheerin, (Bavidge), Christie, McBain, Xausa, Wyness
Substitutes not used: Teasdale, Golabek, Fridge
Referee: Douglas McDonald
Attendance: 6,528

Wednesday, 7th March, 2001

DUNDEE 0	HEART OF MIDLOTHIAN 1
	Tomaschek

Dundee: Roccati, Smith, Marrocco, (Carranza), Coyne, Tweed, de Marchi, Nemsadze, Artero, Rae, Caniggia, Sara
Substitutes not used: Langfield, Del Rio, Russo, Falconer
Heart of Midlothian: Niemi, Pressley, Flögel, McCann, Severin, (Juanjo), Tomaschek, Makel, Boyack, (Neilson), Cameron, Durie, Kirk
Substitutes not used: McKenzie, Murray, McAnespie
Referee: John Underhill
Attendance: 6,947

CELTIC 4	DUNFERMLINE ATHLETIC 1
Vega (2), Larsson (2)	S.M. Thomson

Celtic: Douglas, Mjallby, Valgaeren, Vega, Thompson, McNamara, (Petrov), Lennon, Agathe, Moravcik, Larsson, (Crainey), Johnson, (Lambert)
Substitutes not used: Gould, Boyd
Dunfermline Athletic: Ruitenbeek, Doesburg, (Bullen), S.M. Thomson, McGroarty, Skerla, Dair, (Dijkhuizen), Nicholson, Ferguson, Rossi, Crawford, Hampshire
Substitutes not used: S.Y. Thomson, Skinner, Moss
Referee: Willie Young
Attendance: 33,900

FIFTH ROUND

Saturday, 10th March, 2001

KILMARNOCK 0	HIBERNIAN 1
	McManus

Kilmarnock: Marshall, MacPherson, (Canero), Baker, McGowne, (McCoist), Innes, Dindeleux, Holt, Mahood, Reilly, Cocard, Wright, (McLaren)
Substitutes not used: Meldrum, Hay
Hibernian: Colgan, Fenwick, Smith, Sauzee, (Murray), Laursen, (Paatelainen), Brebner, Lovell, Latapy, O'Neil, Libbra, Zitelli, (McManus)
Substitutes not used: Franks, Andrews
Referee: Michael McCurry
Attendance: 8,288

LIVINGSTON 3	PETERHEAD 1
Anderson (2), Bingham	Johnston

Livingston: McCaldon, Brinquin, Deas, McCulloch, Andrews, (Fleming), Anderson, Crabbe, (McPhee), Tosh, Wilson, Jackson, (Burns), Bingham
Substitutes not used: Hart, McEwan
Peterhead: Pirie, Tindal, King, Herd, (S. Clark), Simpson, Gibson, Cooper,(Murray), I. Stewart, (Livingstone), Yeats, Johnston, (D. Smith)
Substitutes not used: Watson, Buchanan
Referee: John Rowbotham
Attendance: 3,552

Sunday, 11th March, 2001

CELTIC 1	HEART OF MIDLOTHIAN 0
Larsson	

Celtic: Douglas, Mjallby, (Boyd), Valgaeren, Vega, Thompson, Petrov, Lennon, Lambert, Moravcik, (Johnson), Larsson, Agathe
Substitutes not used: Gould, McNamara, Crainey
Heart of Midlothian: Niemi, Pressley, McCann, Flögel, Makel, (McSwegan), Severin, Tomaschek, Boyack, (Murray), Cameron, Juanjo, Kirk
Substitutes not used: McKenzie, McAnespie, Neilson
Referee: Kenny Clark
Attendance: 34,529

DUNDEE UNITED 1	RANGERS 0
Hannah	

Dundee United: Gallacher, McCunnie, Lauchlan, De Vos, Buchan, Griffin, Hannah, Miller, Easton, Hamilton, (Thompson), Lilley
Substitutes not used: Combe, Venetis, Naveda, Smith
Rangers: Klos, Moore, (Malcolm), Porrini, Konterman, Amorosu, Ricksen, (Carson), Wilson, Ferguson, Johnston, (Miller), Flo, Dodds
Substitutes not used: Christiansen, Kauppila
Referee: John Underhill
Attendance: 11,793

SEMI-FINALS

Saturday, 14th April, 2001
The National Stadium, Hampden Park, Glasgow

HIBERNIAN 3	LIVINGSTON 0
O'Neil (2), Zitelli	

Hibernian: Colgan, Fenwick, G. Smith, Sauzee, Laursen, Jack, (Brebner), Murray, Latapy, O'Neil, Paatelainen, (Libbra), Zitelli, (McManus)
Substitutes not used: Westwater, Arpinon
Livingston: McCaldon, Brinquin, Fleming, Anderson, Andrews, Deas, (Jackson), Tosh, McCulloch, (Hagen), Wilson, Burns, (Britton), Bingham
Substitutes not used: Hart, McEwan
Referee: Willie Young
Attendance: 24,658

Sunday, 15th April, 2001
The National Stadium, Hampden Park, Glasgow

CELTIC 3	DUNDEE UNITED 0
Larsson (2), McNamara	

Celtic: Douglas, Mjallby, (Boyd), Valgaeren, Vega, Thompson, Agathe, Lennon, Lambert, Moravcik, (McNamara), Larsson, Sutton, (Johnson)
Substitutes not used: Gould, Healy
Dundee United: Gallacher, Lauchlan, McCunnie, (Partridge), De Vos, Buchan, Griffin, Hannah, Miller, Easton, (Hamilton), Thompson, Lilley
Substitutes not used: Combe, Venetis, Winters
Referee: Hugh Dallas
Attendance: 38,699

FINAL

Saturday, 26th May, 2001
The National Stadium, Hampden Park, Glasgow

CELTIC 3   HIBERNIAN 0

Celtic: Douglas, Mjallby, Valgaeren, Vega, Thompson, (Johnson), Agathe, Lennon, Lambert, (Boyd), Moravcik, (McNamara), Larsson, Sutton
Substitutes not used: Stubbs, Gould
Hibernian: Colgan, Fenwick, G. Smith, Sauzee, Jack, Laursen, Murray, Brebner, (Arpinon), (Lovell), O'Neil, Paatelainen, (Zitelli), Libbra
Substitutes not used: Lehmann, Westwater
Scorers: Celtic: McNamara, Larsson (2)
Referee: Kenny Clark
Attendance: 51,284

SEASON 1873/74
21st March, 1874 at First Hampden; Attendance 2,500

QUEEN'S PARK 2   CLYDESDALE 0
W. McKinnon, Leckie

SEASON 1874/75
10th April, 1875 at First Hampden; Attendance 7,000

QUEEN'S PARK 3   RENTON 0
A. McKinnon, Highet,
W. McKinnon

SEASON 1875/76
11th March, 1876 at Hamilton Crescent; Attendance 10,000

QUEEN'S PARK 1   THIRD LANARK 1
Highet   Drinnan

REPLAY
18th March, 1876 at Hamilton Crescent; Attendance 6,000

QUEEN'S PARK 2   THIRD LANARK 0
Highet (2)

SEASON 1876/77
17th March, 1877 at Hamilton Crescent; Attendance 12,000

VALE OF LEVEN 1   RANGERS 1
Paton   McDougall (o.g.)

REPLAY
7th April, 1877 at Hamilton Crescent; Attendance 15,000

VALE OF LEVEN 1   RANGERS 1 (AET)
McDougall   Dunlop

SECOND REPLAY
13th April, 1877 at First Hampden; Attendance 8,000

VALE OF LEVEN 3   RANGERS 2
Watson (o.g.),   P. Campbell, W. McNeil
Baird, Paton

SEASON 1877/78
30th March, 1878 at First Hampden; Attendance 5,000

VALE OF LEVEN 1   THIRD LANARK 0
McDougall

SEASON 1878/79
19th April, 1879 at First Hampden; Attendance 6,000

VALE OF LEVEN 1   RANGERS 1
Ferguson   Struthers

*VALE OF LEVEN WERE AWARDED CUP AFTER RANGERS
FAILED TO TURN UP FOR A REPLAY ON 26TH APRIL, 1879.*

SEASON 1879/80
21st February, 1880 at First Cathkin; Attendance 7,000

QUEEN'S PARK 3   THORNLIEBANK 0
Highet (2,) Kerr

SEASON 1880/81
26th March, 1881 at Kinning Park; Attendance 10,000

QUEEN'S PARK 2   DUMBARTON 1
McNeil, Kay   McAulay

AFTER A PROTEST BY DUMBARTON, A REPLAY WAS ORDERED.

REPLAY
9th April, 1881 at Kinning Park; Attendance 10,000

QUEEN'S PARK 3   DUMBARTON 1
Smith (2), Kerr   Meikleham

SEASON 1881/82
18th March, 1882 at First Cathkin; Attendance 12,000

QUEEN'S PARK 2   DUMBARTON 2
Harrower (2)   Brown, Meikleham

REPLAY
1st April, 1882 at First Cathkin; Attendance 15,000

QUEEN'S PARK 4   DUMBARTON 1
Richmond, Kerr,   J. Miller
Harrower, Kay

SEASON 1882/83
31st March, 1883 at First Hampden; Attendance 15,000

DUMBARTON 2   VALE OF LEVEN 2
Paton, McArthur   Johnstone, McCrae

REPLAY
7th April, 1883 at First Hampden; Attendance 8,000

DUMBARTON 2   VALE OF LEVEN 1
Anderson, R. Brown   Friel

SEASON 1883/84
23rd February, 1884 at First Cathkin

VALE OF LEVEN   QUEEN'S PARK
*VALE OF LEVEN FAILED TO TURN UP FOR THE FINAL WITH
QUEEN'S PARK AND IT WAS LATER DECIDED TO AWARD
THE CUP TO QUEEN'S PARK.*

SEASON 1884/85
21st February, 1885 at Second Hampden; Attendance 2,500

RENTON 0   VALE OF LEVEN 0

REPLAY
28th February, 1885 at Second Hampden; Attendance 3,500

RENTON 3   VALE OF LEVEN 1
J. McCall, McIntyre (2) Gillies

SEASON 1885/86
13th February, 1886 at First Cathkin; Attendance 7,000

QUEEN'S PARK 3   RENTON 1
Hamilton, Christie,   Kelso
Somerville

SEASON 1886/87
12th February, 1887 at Second Hampden; Attendance 10,000

HIBERNIAN 2   DUMBARTON 1
Smith, Groves   Aitken

SEASON 1887/88
4th February, 1888 at Second Hampden; Attendance 10,000

RENTON 6   CAMBUSLANG 1
D. Campbell,   H. Gourlay
McCallum, McNee,
McCall (2), J. Campbell

SEASON 1888/89
2nd February, 1889 at Second Hampden; Attendance 17,000

THIRD LANARK 3   CELTIC 0
Oswald Jun. (2),
Hannah

*A REPLAY WAS ORDERED AFTER PROTESTS CONCERNING
GROUND CONDITIONS.*

REPLAY
9th February, 1889 at Second Hampden; Attendance 16,000

THIRD LANARK 2   CELTIC 1
Marshall, Oswald Jun. McCallum

SEASON 1889/90
15th February, 1890 at First Ibrox; Attendance 10,000

QUEEN'S PARK 1   VALE OF LEVEN 1
Hamilton   McLachlan

REPLAY
22nd February, 1890 at First Ibrox; Attendance 14,000

QUEEN'S PARK 2   VALE OF LEVEN 1
Hamilton Stewart   Bruce

SEASON 1890/91
7th February, 1891 at Second Hampden; Attendance 14,000

HEART OF MIDLOTHIAN 1   DUMBARTON 0
Russell

SEASON 1891/92
12th March, 1892 at First Ibrox; Attendance 40,000

CELTIC 1   QUEEN'S PARK 0
Campbell

*CROWD ENCROACHMENT OCCURRED AT THE ABOVE GAME
AND AS A RESULT THE GAME WAS CONSIDERED A FRIENDLY.*

REPLAY
9th April, 1892 at First Ibrox; Attendance 20,000

CELTIC 5   QUEEN'S PARK 1
Campbell (2),   Waddell
McMahon (2),
Sillars (o.g.)

SEASON 1892/93
25th February, 1893 at First Ibrox; Attendance 20,000

CELTIC 1   QUEEN'S PARK 0
Towie

*A REPLAY WAS ORDERED BECAUSE OF GROUND CONDITIONS
AND THE ABOVE GAME WAS CONSIDERED A FRIENDLY.*

REPLAY
11th March, 1893 at First Ibrox; Attendance 15,000

QUEEN'S PARK 2   CELTIC 1
Sellar (2)   Blessington

SEASON 1893/94
17th February, 1894 at Second Hampden; Attendance 15,000

RANGERS 3   CELTIC 1
H. McCreadie, Barker, W. Maley
McPherson

SEASON 1894/95
20th April, 1895 at First Ibrox; Attendance 13,500

ST. BERNARD'S 2   RENTON 1
Clelland (2)   Duncan

SEASON 1895/96
14th March, 1896 at Logie Green; Attendance 16,034

HEART OF MIDLOTHIAN 3   HIBERNIAN 1
Baird, Walker, Michael   O'Neill

SEASON 1896/97
20th March, 1897 at Second Hampden; Attendance 15,000

RANGERS 5   DUMBARTON 1
Miller (2), Hyslop,   W. Thomson
McPherson, A. Smith

SEASON 1897/98
26th March, 1898 at Second Hampden; Attendance 14,000

RANGERS 2   KILMARNOCK 0
A. Smith, Hamilton

SEASON 1898/99
22nd April, 1899 at Second Hampden; Attendance 25,000

CELTIC 2   RANGERS 0
McMahon, Hodge

SEASON 1899/1900
14th April, 1900 at Second Hampden; Attendance 25,000

CELTIC 4   QUEEN'S PARK 3
McMahon,   Christie, W. Stewart,
Divers (2), Bell   Battles (o.g.)

SEASON 1900/01
6th April, 1901 at Ibrox; Attendance 15,000

HEART OF MIDLOTHIAN 4   CELTIC 3
Walker, Bell (2), Thomson   McOustra (2),
                              McMahon

SEASON 1901/02
26th April, 1902 at Celtic Park; Attendance 16,000

HIBERNIAN 1   CELTIC 0
McGeachan

SEASON 1902/03
11th April, 1903 at Celtic Park; Attendance 28,000

RANGERS 1   HEART OF MIDLOTHIAN 1
Stark   Walker

REPLAY
18th April, 1903 at Celtic Park; Attendance 16,000

RANGERS 0   HEART OF MIDLOTHIAN 0

SECOND REPLAY
25th April, 1903 at Celtic Park; Attendance 32,000

RANGERS 2   HEART OF MIDLOTHIAN 0
Mackie, Hamilton

SEASON 1903/04
16th April, 1904 at Hampden Park; Attendance 64,323

CELTIC 3   RANGERS 2
Quinn (3)   Speedie (2)

SEASON 1904/05
8th April, 1905 at Hampden Park; Attendance 55,000

THIRD LANARK 0   RANGERS 0

REPLAY
15th April, 1905 at Hampden Park; Attendance 40,000

THIRD LANARK 3   RANGERS 1
Wilson (2), Johnstone   Smith

SEASON 1905/06
28th April, 1906 at Ibrox; Attendance 30,000

HEART OF MIDLOTHIAN 1   THIRD LANARK 0
G. Wilson

SEASON 1906/07
20th April, 1907 at Hampden Park; Attendance 50,000

CELTIC 3   HEART OF MIDLOTHIAN 0
Orr (Pen), Somers (2)

SEASON 1907/08
18th April, 1908 at Hampden Park; Attendance 55,000

CELTIC 5   ST. MIRREN 1
Bennett (2), Hamilton,   Cunningham
Somers, Quinn

SEASON 1908/09
10th April, 1909 at Hampden Park; Attendance 70,000

CELTIC 2   RANGERS 2
Quinn, Munro   Gilchrist, Bennett

REPLAY
17th April, 1909 at Hampden Park; Attendance 60,000

CELTIC 1   RANGERS 1
Quinn   Gordon

CUP WITHHELD AFTER RIOT FOLLOWING REPLAY.

SEASON 1909/10
9th April, 1910 at Ibrox; Attendance 60,000

DUNDEE 2   CLYDE 2
Blair (o.g.), Langlands   Chalmers, Booth

REPLAY
16th April, 1910 at Ibrox; Attendance 20,000

DUNDEE 0   CLYDE 0 (A.E.T.)

SECOND REPLAY
20th April, 1910 at Ibrox; Attendance 24,000

DUNDEE 2   CLYDE 1
Bellamy, Hunter   Chalmers

SEASON 1910/11
8th April, 1911 at Ibrox; Attendance 45,000

CELTIC 0   HAMILTON ACADEMICAL 0

REPLAY
15th April, 1911 at Ibrox; Attendance 25,000

CELTIC 2   HAMILTON ACADEMICAL 0
Quinn, McAteer

SEASON 1911/12
6th April, 1912 at Ibrox; Attendance 45,000

CELTIC 2   CLYDE 0
McMenemy, Gallagher

SEASON 1912/13
12th April, 1913 at Celtic Park; Attendance 45,000

FALKIRK 2   RAITH ROVERS 0
Robertson, T. Logan

SEASON 1913/14
11th April, 1914 at Ibrox; Attendance 55,000

CELTIC 0   HIBERNIAN 0

REPLAY
16th April, 1914 at Ibrox; Attendance 36,000

CELTIC 4   HIBERNIAN 1
McColl (2),   Smith
Browning (2)

SEASONS 1914/15 TO 1918/19
NO COMPETITIONS DUE TO FIRST WORLD WAR

SEASON 1919/20
17th April, 1920 at Hampden Park; Attendance 95,000;
Referee: Mr W. Bell (Hamilton)

KILMARNOCK 3   ALBION ROVERS 2
Culley, Shortt, J. Smith   Watson, Hillhouse

SEASON 1920/21
16th April, 1921 at Celtic Park; Attendance 28,294;
Referee: Mr H. Humphreys (Greenock)

PARTICK THISTLE 1   RANGERS 0
Blair

SEASON 1921/22
15th April, 1922 at Hampden Park; Attendance 75,000
Referee: Mr T. Dougray (Bellshill)

MORTON 1   RANGERS 0
Gourlay

SEASON 1922/23
31st March, 1923 at Hampden Park;
Attendance 80,100; Referee: Mr T. Dougray (Bellshill)

CELTIC 1   HIBERNIAN 0
Cassidy

SEASON 1923/24
19th April, 1924 at Ibrox Stadium; Attendance 59,218;
Referee: Mr T. Dougray (Bellshill)

AIRDRIEONIANS 2   HIBERNIAN 0
Russell (2)

SEASON 1924/25
11th April, 1925 at Hampden Park;
Attendance 75,137; Referee: Mr T. Dougray (Bellshill)

CELTIC 2   DUNDEE 1
Gallacher, McGrory   McLean

SEASON 1925/26
10th April, 1926 at Hampden Park; Attendance 98,620;
Referee: Mr P. Craigmyle (Aberdeen)

ST. MIRREN 2   CELTIC 0
McCrae, Howieson

SEASON 1926/27
16th April, 1927 at Hampden; Attendance 80,070;
Referee: Mr T. Dougray (Bellshill)

CELTIC 3   EAST FIFE 1
Robertson (o.g.),   Wood
McLean, Connolly

SEASON 1927/28
14th April, 1928 at Hampden Park; Attendance 118,115;
Referee: Mr W. Bell (Motherwell)

RANGERS 4   CELTIC 0
Meiklejohn (pen),
Archibald (2), McPhail

SEASON 1928/29
6th April, 1929 at Hampden Park; Attendance 114,708;
Referee: Mr T. Dougray (Bellshill)

KILMARNOCK 2   RANGERS 0
Aitken, Williamson

SEASON 1929/30
12th April, 1930 at Hampden Park; Attendance 107,475;
Referee: Mr W. Bell (Motherwell)

RANGERS 0   PARTICK THISTLE 0

REPLAY
16th April, 1930 at Hampden Park; Attendance 103,686;
Referee: Mr W. Bell (Motherwell)

RANGERS 2   PARTICK THISTLE 1
Marshall, Craig   Torbet

SEASON 1930/31
11th April, 1931 at Hampden Park; Attendance 104,803;
Referee: Mr P. Craigmyle (Aberdeen)

CELTIC 2   MOTHERWELL 2
McGrory, Craig (o.g.)   Stevenson, McMenemy

REPLAY
15th April, 1931 at Hampden Park; Attendance 98,579;
Referee: Mr P. Craigmyle (Aberdeen)

CELTIC 4   MOTHERWELL 2
R. Thomson (2),   Murdoch, Stevenson
McGrory (2)

SEASON 1931/32
16th April, 1932 at Hampden Park; Attendance 111,982;
Referee: Mr P. Craigmyle (Aberdeen)

RANGERS 1   KILMARNOCK 1
McPhail   Maxwell

REPLAY
20th April, 1932 at Hampden Park; Attendance 110,695;
Referee: Mr P. Craigmyle (Aberdeen)

RANGERS 3   KILMARNOCK 0
Fleming, McPhail, English

SEASON 1932/33
15th April, 1933 at Hampden Park; Attendance 102,339;
Referee: Mr T. Dougray (Bellshill)

CELTIC 1   MOTHERWELL 0
McGrory

SEASON 1933/34
21st April, 1934 at Hampden Park; Attendance 113,430;
Referee: Mr M. C. Hutton (Glasgow)

RANGERS 5   ST. MIRREN 0
Nicholson (2),
McPhail, Main, Smith

SEASON 1934/35
20th April, 1935 at Hampden Park; Attendance 87,286;
Referee: Mr H. Watson (Glasgow)

RANGERS 2   HAMILTON ACADEMICAL 1
Smith (2)   Harrison

SEASON 1935/36
18th April 1936 at Hampden Park; Attendance 88,859;
Referee: Mr J. M. Martin (Ladybank)

RANGERS 1   **THIRD LANARK 0**
McPhail

SEASON 1936/37
24th April, 1937 at Hampden Park; Attendance 147,365;
Referee: Mr M. C. Hutton (Glasgow)

CELTIC 2   **ABERDEEN 1**
Crum, Buchan   Armstrong

SEASON 1937/38
23rd April, 1938 at Hampden Park; Attendance 80,091;
Referee: Mr H. Watson (Glasgow)

EAST FIFE 1   **KILMARNOCK 1**
McLeod   McAvoy

REPLAY
27th April, 1938 at Hampden Park; Attendance 92,716;
Referee: Mr H. Watson (Glasgow)

EAST FIFE 4   **KILMARNOCK 2**
McKerrell (2),   Thomson (pen), McGrogan
McLeod, Miller
After extra–time

SEASON 1938/39
22nd April, 1939 at Hampden Park; Attendance 94,799;
Referee: Mr W. Webb (Glasgow)

CLYDE 4   **MOTHERWELL 0**
Wallace, Martin (2), Noble

SEASONS 1939/40 TO 1945/46
NO COMPETITIONS DUE TO SECOND WORLD WAR

SEASON 1946/47
19th April, 1947 at Hampden Park; Attendance 82,140;
Referee: Mr R. Calder (Glasgow)

ABERDEEN 2   **HIBERNIAN 1**
Hamilton, Williams   Cuthbertson

SEASON 1947/48
17th April, 1948 at Hampden Park; Attendance 129,176;
Referee: Mr J. M. Martin (Blairgowrie)

RANGERS 1   **MORTON 1**
Gillick   Whyte
After extra–time

REPLAY
21st April, 1948 at Hampden Park; Attendance 131,975;
Referee: Mr J. M. Martin (Blairgowrie)

RANGERS 1   **MORTON 0**
Williamson
After extra–time

SEASON 1948/49
23rd April, 1949 at Hampden Park; Attendance 108,435;
Referee: Mr R. G. Benzie (Irvine)

RANGERS 4   **CLYDE 1**
Young (2 (2 pens)),   Galletly
Williamson, Duncanson

SEASON 1949/50
22nd April, 1950 at Hampden Park; Attendance 118,262
Referee: Mr J. A. Mowat (Burnside)

RANGERS 3   **EAST FIFE 0**
Findlay, Thornton (2)

SEASON 1950/51
21st April, 1951 at Hampden Park; Attendance 131,943
Referee: Mr J. A. Mowat (Burnside)

CELTIC 1   **MOTHERWELL 0**
McPhail

SEASON 1951/52
19th April, 1952 at Hampden Park; Attendance 136,304;
Referee: Mr J. A. Mowat (Burnside)

MOTHERWELL 4   **DUNDEE 0**
Watson, Redpath,
Humphries, Kelly

SEASON 1952/53
25th April, 1953 at Hampden Park; Attendance 129,861;
Referee: Mr J. A. Mowat (Burnside)

RANGERS 1   **ABERDEEN 1**
Prentice   Yorston

REPLAY
29th April, 1953 at Hampden Park; Attendance 112,619;
Referee: Mr J. A. Mowat (Burnside)

RANGERS 1   **ABERDEEN 0**
Simpson

SEASON 1953/54
24th April, 1954 at Hampden Park; Attendance 129,926;
Referee: Mr C. E. Faultless (Giffnock)

CELTIC 2   **ABERDEEN 1**
Young (o.g.), Fallon   Buckley

SEASON 1954/55
23rd April, 1955 at Hampden Park; Attendance 106,111;
Referee: Mr C. E. Faultless (Giffnock)

CLYDE 1   **CELTIC 1**
Robertson   Walsh

REPLAY
27th April, 1955 at Hampden Park; Attendance 68,735;
Referee: Mr C. E. Faultless (Giffnock)

CLYDE 1   **CELTIC 0**
Ring

SEASON 1955/56
21st April, 1956 at Hampden Park; Attendance 133,399;
Referee: Mr R. H. Davidson (Airdrie)

HEART OF MIDLOTHIAN 3   **CELTIC 1**
Crawford (2), Conn   Haughney

SEASON 1956/57
20th April, 1957 at Hampden Park; Attendance 81,057;
Referee: Mr J. A. Mowat (Burnside)

FALKIRK 1   **KILMARNOCK 1**
Prentice (pen)   Curlett

REPLAY
24th April, 1957 at Hampden Park; Attendance 79,785;
Referee: Mr J. A. Mowat (Burnside)

FALKIRK 2   **KILMARNOCK 1**
Merchant, Moran   Curlett
After extra–time

SEASON 1957/58
26th April, 1958 at Hampden Park; Attendance 95,123;
Referee: Mr J. A. Mowat (Burnside)

CLYDE 1   **HIBERNIAN 0**
Coyle

SEASON 1958/59
25th April 1959 at Hampden Park; Attendance 108,951;
Referee: Mr J. A. Mowat (Burnside)

ST. MIRREN 3   **ABERDEEN 1**
Bryceland, Miller, Baker Baird

SEASON 1959/60
23rd April, 1960 at Hampden Park; Attendance 108,017;
Referee: Mr R. H. Davidson (Airdrie)

RANGERS 2   **KILMARNOCK 0**
Millar (2)

SEASON 1960/61
22nd April, 1961 at Hampden Park; Attendance 113,618;
Referee: Mr H. Phillips (Wishaw)

DUNFERMLINE ATHLETIC 0   **CELTIC 0**

REPLAY
26th April, 1961 at Hampden Park; Attendance 87,866;
Referee: Mr H. Phillips (Wishaw)

DUNFERMLINE ATHLETIC 2   **CELTIC 0**
Thomson, Dickson

SEASON 1961/62
21st April, 1962 at Hampden Park; Attendance 126,930;
Referee: Mr T. Wharton (Clarkston)

RANGERS 2   **ST. MIRREN 0**
Brand, Wilson

SEASON 1962/63
4th May, 1963 at Hampden Park; Attendance 129,527;
Referee: Mr T. Wharton (Clarkston)

RANGERS 1   **CELTIC 1**
Brand   Murdoch

REPLAY
15th May, 1963 at Hampden Park; Attendance 120,263;
Referee: Mr T. Wharton (Clarkston)

RANGERS 3   **CELTIC 0**
Brand (2), Wilson

SEASON 1963/64
25th April, 1964 at Hampden Park; Attendance 120,982
Referee: Mr H. Phillips (Wishaw)

RANGERS 3   **DUNDEE 1**
Millar (2), Brand   Cameron

SEASON 1964/65
24th April, 1965 at Hampden Park; Attendance 108,800;
Referee: Mr H. Phillips (Wishaw)

CELTIC 3   **DUNFERMLINE ATHLETIC 2**
Auld (2), McNeill   Melrose, McLaughlin

SEASON 1965/66
23rd April, 1966 at Hampden Park; Attendance 126,559;
Referee: Mr T. Wharton (Clarkston)

RANGERS 0   **CELTIC 0**

REPLAY
27th April, 1966 at Hampden Park; Attendance 96,862;
Referee: Mr T. Wharton (Clarkston)

RANGERS 1   **CELTIC 0**
Johansen

SEASON 1966/67
29th April, 1967 at Hampden Park; Attendance 127,117;
Referee: Mr W. M. M. Syme (Glasgow)

CELTIC 2   **ABERDEEN 0**
Wallace (2)

SEASON 1967/68
27th April, 1968 at Hampden Park; Attendance 56,365;
Referee: Mr W. Anderson (East Kilbride)

DUNFERMLINE ATH. 3   **HEART OF MIDLOTHIAN 1**
Gardner (2), Lister (pen)   Lunn (o.g.)

SEASON 1968/69
26th April, 1969 at Hampden Park; Attendance 132,870;
Referee: Mr J. Callaghan (Glasgow)

CELTIC 4   **RANGERS 0**
McNeill, Lennox,
Connelly, Chalmers

SEASON 1969/70
11th April, 1970 at Hampden Park; Attendance 108,434;
Referee: Mr R. H. Davidson (Airdrie)

ABERDEEN 3   **CELTIC 1**
Harper (pen), McKay (2)   Lennox

SEASON 1970/71
8th May, 1971 at Hampden Park; Attendance 120,092;
Referee: Mr T. Wharton (Glasgow)

CELTIC 1   **RANGERS 1**
Lennox   D. Johnstone

REPLAY
12th May, 1971 at Hampden Park; Attendance 103,332;
Referee: Mr T. Wharton (Glasgow)

CELTIC 2	RANGERS 1
Macari, Hood (pen)	Callaghan (o.g.)

SEASON 1971/72
6th May, 1972 at Hampden Park; Attendance 106,102;
Referee: Mr A. MacKenzie (Larbert)

CELTIC 6	HIBERNIAN 1
McNeill, Deans (3),	Gordon
Macari (2)	

SEASON 1972/73
5th May, 1973 at Hampden Park; Attendance 122,714;
Referee: Mr J. R. P. Gordon (Newport–on–Tay)

RANGERS 3	CELTIC 2
Parlane, Conn, Forsyth	Dalglish, Connelly (pen)

SEASON 1973/74
4th May, 1974 at Hampden Park; Attendance 75,959;
Referee: Mr W. S. Black (Glasgow)

CELTIC 3	DUNDEE UNITED 0
Hood, Murray, Deans	

SEASON 1974/75
3rd May, 1975 at Hampden Park; Attendance 75,457;
Referee: Mr I. M. D. Foote (Glasgow)

CELTIC 3	AIRDRIEONIANS 1
Wilson (2),	McCann
McCluskey (pen)	

SEASON 1975/76
1st May 1976 at Hampden Park; Attendance 85,354;
Referee: Mr R. H. Davidson (Airdrie)

RANGERS 3	HEART OF MIDLOTHIAN 1
Johnstone (2),	Shaw
MacDonald	

SEASON 1976/77
7th May, 1977 at Hampden Park; Attendance 54,252;
Referee: Mr R. B. Valentine (Dundee)

CELTIC 1	RANGERS 0
Lynch (pen)	

SEASON 1977/78
6th May, 1978 at Hampden Park; Attendance 61,563;
Referee: Mr B. R. McGinlay (Glasgow)

RANGERS 2	ABERDEEN 1
MacDonald, Johnstone	Ritchie

SEASON 1978/79
12th May, 1979 at Hampden Park; Attendance 50,610;
Referee: Mr B. R. McGinlay (Glasgow)

RANGERS 0	HIBERNIAN 0

REPLAY
16th May, 1979 at Hampden Park; Attendance 33,504;
Referee: Mr B. R. McGinlay (Glasgow)

RANGERS 0	HIBERNIAN 0
After extra–time

SECOND REPLAY
28th May, 1979 at Hampden Park; Attendance 30,602;
Referee: Mr I. M. D. Foote (Glasgow)

RANGERS 3	HIBERNIAN 2
Johnstone (2),	Higgins, MacLeod (pen)
Duncan (o.g.)	
After extra–time – 2-2 After 90 Minutes

SEASON 1979/80
10th May, 1980 at Hampden Park; Attendance 70,303;
Referee: Mr G. B. Smith (Edinburgh)

CELTIC 1	RANGERS 0
McCluskey	
After extra–time

SEASON 1980/81
9th May, 1981 at Hampden Park; Attendance 53,000;
Referee: Mr I. M. D. Foote (Glasgow)

RANGERS 0	DUNDEE UNITED 0
After extra–time

REPLAY
12th May, 1981 at Hampden Park; Attendance 43,099;
Referee: Mr I. M. D. Foote (Glasgow)

RANGERS 4	DUNDEE UNITED 1
Cooper, Russell,	Dodds
MacDonald (2)	

SEASON 1981/82
22nd May, 1982 at Hampden Park; Attendance 53,788;
Referee: Mr B. R. McGinlay (Balfron)

ABERDEEN 4	RANGERS 1
McLeish, McGhee,	MacDonald
Strachan, Cooper	
After extra–time – 1-1 after 90 minutes

SEASON 1982/83
21st May, 1983 at Hampden Park; Attendance 62,979;
Referee: Mr D. F. T. Syme (Rutherglen)

ABERDEEN 1	RANGERS 0
Black	
After extra–time

SEASON 1983/84
19th May 1984 at Hampden Park; Attendance 58,900;
Referee: Mr R. B. Valentine (Dundee)

ABERDEEN 2	CELTIC 1
Black, McGhee	P. McStay
After extra–time – 1-1 after 90 minutes

SEASON 1984/85
18th May, 1985 at Hampden Park; Attendance 60,346;
Referee: Mr B. R. McGinlay (Balfron)

CELTIC 2	DUNDEE UNITED 1
Provan, McGarvey	Beedie

SEASON 1985/86
10th May, 1986 at Hampden Park; Attendance 62,841;
Referee: Mr H. Alexander (Irvine)

ABERDEEN 3	HEART OF MIDLOTHIAN 0
Hewitt (2), Stark	

SEASON 1986/87
16th May, 1987 at Hampden Park; Attendance 51,782;
Referee: Mr K. J. Hope (Clarkston)

ST. MIRREN 1	DUNDEE UNITED 0
Ferguson	
After extra–time

SEASON 1987/88
14th May, 1988 at Hampden Park; Attendance 74,000;
Referee: Mr G. B. Smith (Edinburgh)

CELTIC 2	DUNDEE UNITED 1
McAvennie (2)	Gallacher

SEASON 1988/89
20th May, 1989 at Hampden Park; Attendance 72,069;
Referee: Mr R. B. Valentine (Dundee)

CELTIC 1	RANGERS 0
Miller	

SEASON 1989/90
12th May, 1990 at Hampden Park; Attendance 60,493;
Referee: Mr G. B. Smith (Edinburgh)

ABERDEEN 0	CELTIC 0
After extra–time. Aberdeen won 9–8 on Kicks from the Penalty Mark

SEASON 1990/91
18th May, 1991 at Hampden Park; Attendance 57,319;
Referee: Mr D. F. T. Syme (Rutherglen)

MOTHERWELL 4	DUNDEE UNITED 3
Ferguson, O'Donnell,	Bowman, O'Neil, Jackson
Angus, Kirk	
After extra–time - 3-3 after 90 minutes

SEASON 1991/92
9th May 1992 at Hampden Park; Attendance 44,045;
Referee: Mr D. D. Hope (Erskine)

RANGERS 2	AIRDRIEONIANS 1
Hateley, McCoist	Smith

SEASON 1992/93
29th May, 1993 at Celtic Park; Attendance 50,715;
Referee: Mr J. McCluskey (Stewarton)

RANGERS 2	ABERDEEN 1
Murray, Hateley	Richardson

SEASON 1993/94
21st May, 1994 at Hampden Park; Attendance 37,709;
Referee: Mr D. D. Hope (Erskine)

DUNDEE UNITED 1	RANGERS 0
Brewster	

SEASON 1994/95
27th May, 1995 at Hampden Park; Attendance 38,672;
Referee: Mr L. W. Mottram (Forth)

CELTIC 1	AIRDRIEONIANS 0
Van Hooijdonk	

SEASON 1995/96
18th May, 1996 at Hampden Park; Attendance 37,760;
Referee: Mr H. Dallas (Motherwell)

RANGERS 5	HEART OF MIDLOTHIAN 1
Laudrup (2), Durie (3)	Colquhoun

SEASON 1996/97
24th May, 1997 at Ibrox Stadium; Attendance 48,953;
Referee: Mr H. Dallas (Motherwell)

KILMARNOCK 1	FALKIRK 0
Wright	

SEASON 1997/98
16th May, 1998 at Celtic Park; Attendance 48,946;
Referee: Mr W. Young (Clarkston)

HEART OF MIDLOTHIAN 2	RANGERS 1
Cameron, Adam	McCoist

SEASON 1998/99
29th May, 1999 at The National Stadium, Hampden Park;
Attendance 51,746; Referee: Mr H. Dallas (Motherwell)

RANGERS 1	CELTIC 0
Wallace	

SEASON 1999/2000
27th May, 2000 at The National Stadium, Hampden Park;
Attendance 50,685; Referee: Mr J. McCluskey

RANGERS 4	ABERDEEN 0
Van Bronckhorst,	
Vidmar, Dodds, Albertz	

SEASON 2000/01
26th May, 2001 at The National Stadium, Hampden Park;
Attendance 51,284; Referee: Mr K. Clark

CELTIC 3	HIBERNIAN 0
McNamara, Larsson (2)	

FIRST ROUND

Tuesday, 15th August, 2000

BELL'S CHALLENGE CUP

| COWDENBEATH 2 | FALKIRK 1 |

(AET–1-1 After 90 Minutes)

G. Brown, R. Juskowiak   G. Hutchison

Cowdenbeath: J. Martin, J. Boyle, C. McMillan, D. White, K. McCulloch, (J. Lakie), A. Lawrence, (I. McDonald), C. Winter, M. Bradley, M. McDowell, (R. Juskowiak), G. Brown, J. Allan
Substitutes not used: W. Mitchell, R. Godfrey
Falkirk: M. Hogarth, A. Lawrie, A. Seaton, (J. McQuilken), K. Christie, G. Denham, D. Nicholls, I. Morris, G. Hutchison, C. McDonald, K. Avdiu, (M. Roberts), R. Waddell, (M. Kerr)
Substitutes not used: S. Rennie, D. Hill
Referee: John Fleming
Attendance: 544

| AIRDRIEONIANS 2 | QUEEN OF THE SOUTH 1 |

(AET–1-1 After 90 Minutes)

A. Calderon, P. Clark   P. Atkinson

Airdrieonians: J.S. Broto, D. Brady, H.A. McCann, (J. McAlpine), M. Alfonso, R. Coulter, F. Moreau, S. Capin, J. Sanjuan, M. Prest, (P. Clark), A. Calderon, (S. Taylor), G. Evans
Substitutes not used: P. Armstrong, S. Wilson
Queen of the South: D. Mathieson, D. Muir, (S. Pickering), S. Hodge, P. Nixon, A. Martin, A. Aitken, P. Atkinson, J. Sunderland, P. Weatherson, B. Caldwell, (W. Hawke), M. Weir, (A. Nelson)
Substitutes not used: R. Atkinson, R. McColm
Referee: Eric Martindale
Attendance: 1,936

| RAITH ROVERS 0 | MORTON 4 |

S. Whalen (2), R. Matheson, B. Kerr

Raith Rovers: G. Van de Kamp, G. McCulloch, L. Ellis, (J. Stein), K. Gaughan, P. Browne, K. Black, (B. Hetherston), C. McEwan, S. Tosh, A. Clark, A. Burns, G. Creaney, (I. Mballa)
Substitutes not used: P. Tosh, C. Coyle
Morton: M. Boswell, D. Murie, D. Anderson, P. Medou-Otye, R. Raeside, H. Curran, S. Aitken, A. Millen, (A. Brownrigg), S. Whalen, R. Matheson, (B. Kerr), P. McDonald
Substitutes not used: M. Naylor, S. MacDonald, A. Carlin
Referee: Bobby Orr
Attendance: 1,160

| FORFAR ATHLETIC 1 | PETERHEAD 1 |

(AET–1-1 After 90 Minutes)
Peterhead won 4-2 on Kicks from the Penalty Mark

G. McPhee   G. Clark

Forfar Athletic: S. Garden, D. Bowman, (R. Morris), E. Donaldson, C. Farnan, R. Horn, C. Tully, W. Stewart, G. McPhee, I. Ferguson, (R. Brand), S. Taylor, A. Cargill, (G. McCheyne)
Substitutes not used: D. Craig, N. Ferrie
Peterhead: I. Pirie, D. Craig, S. King, W. Herd, M. Simpson, M. Paterson, M. De-Barros, (S. Clark), (A. Gibson), M. Johnston, G. Clark, (D. Smith), S. Brown, R. Livingstone
Substitutes not used: C. Watson, R. Buchanan
Referee: Alan Gemmill
Attendance: 407

| STRANRAER 4 | BERWICK RANGERS 2 |

F. Wright, P. Walker,   N. Oliver, G. McMartin
I. Harty, M. Geraghty

Stranraer: S. O'Neill, A. Paterson, F. Wright, K. Knox, G. McDonald, (S. Abbott), D. George, P. Walker, W. Macdonald, I. Harty, P. Blair, (A. Blaikie), M. Geraghty
Substitute not used: D. Rae
Berwick Rangers: G. O'Connor, N. Oliver, M. Duthie, (S. Anderson), G. McNicoll, A. Neill, K. Rafferty, G. McMartin, G. Forrest, S. Laidlaw, C. Findlay, (J. Harvey), D. Smith, (K. Magee)
Substitutes not used: M. Neil, C. Weir
Referee: Colin Hardie
Attendance: 285

| BRECHIN CITY 3 | AYR UNITED 1 |

B. Sturrock, R. Grant, C. Duffy (o.g.)   P. McGinlay

Brechin City: D. Soutar, G. Christie, S. Raynes, J. Nairn, H. Cairney, P. Riley, (B. Donachie), J. McKeith, (B. Honeyman), R. Black, B. Sturrock, M. Leask, (R. Grant), D. Coulston
Substitutes not used: K. Williamson, A. Hutcheon
Ayr United: M. Rovde, M. Renwick, P. Lovering, (M. Reynolds), P. McGinlay, (M. Crilly), J. Hughes, C. Duffy, N. Scally, M. Wilson, E. Annand, (G. Hurst), G. Teale, J. Bradford
Substitutes not used: G. Burns, J. Dodds
Referee: Craig MacKay
Attendance: 276

| ALBION ROVERS 0 | CLYDEBANK 1 |

T. Coyne

Albion Rovers: C. Fahey, C. Waldie, T. Lumsden, J. Smith, R. Clyde, M. Booth, R. McMullan, C. Silvestro, I. Diack, I. Rankin, (Y. Begue), J. McLees, (J. McKenzie)
Substitutes not used: A. Martin, S. Clark, S. Shearer
Clydebank: D. Wylie, J. McKinstrey, F. Wishart, R. McQuilter, (S. Murdoch), K. Brannigan, E. Taborda, I.G. Johnson, B. Hamilton, D. McKelvie, (L. Fal), T. Coyne, D. Ferguson
Substitutes not used: S. Callaghan, J. Walker, S. Hutchison
Referee: Cammy Melville
Attendance: 212

| ROSS COUNTY 2 | CLYDE 1 |

A. Bone, D. Henderson   P. Cannie

Ross County: J.N. Walker, D. Mackay, E. Cunnington, I. Maxwell, B. Irvine, F. Escalon, (S. Ferguson), G. Shaw, J. Fraser, (D. Henderson), A. Bone, M. Millar, D. Holmes
Substitutes not used: J. McQuade, D. Ross, G. Hamilton
Clyde: D. Hanley, G. Greer, C. McPherson, P. Hay, G. McGhee, J. Henry, (C. Aitken), C. Bingham, D. Dunn, (Sean McAuley), J. Barrett, (Stephen McAuley), R. McCusker, P. Cannie
Substitutes not used: S. Cringean, B. Halliwell
Referee: Steve Kaney
Attendance: 521

| EAST STIRLINGSHIRE 3 | EAST FIFE 0 |

S. Hislop, G. McKechnie, C. Lynes

East Stirlingshire: J. Butter, C. Quinn, M. Hall, G. Russell, D. Todd, (C. Lynes), D. McPherson, S. Stewart, G. McKechnie, S. Hislop, (G. Higgins), C. McKenzie, (K. Gordon), J. Tortolano
Substitutes not used: R. Carlow, C. Todd
East Fife: A. Stewart, K. Munro, J. Gallagher, R. Logan, D. Agostini, R. Sharp, (S. Mackay), S. Ferguson, (J. Allison), P. Mortimer, S. Kerrigan, B. Moffat, M. Hunter
Substitutes not used: P. Simpson, R. Gibb, W. McCulloch
Referee: Tom Brown
Attendance: 201

| QUEEN'S PARK 2 | MONTROSE 0 |

M. Gallagher (2)

Queen's Park: C. Stewart, G. Miller, S. Marshall, G. Duncan, P. Martin, R. Sinclair, K. Finlayson, G. Connell, (S. Canning), M. Gallagher, J. Brown, (M. Travers), F. Carroll, (W. Ajet)
Substitutes not used: C. Flannigan, A. Smith
Montrose: G. McGlynn, J. Young, S. Ferguson, S. Marwick, (S. Robertson), S. Snedden, M. Craib, J. McKellar, T. Harrison, (C. Mailer), M. McKenzie, P. McIlravey, (J. Mitchell), R. McWilliam
Substitutes not used: J. O'Driscoll, B. Thompson
Referee: Brian Cassidy
Attendance: 482

| STIRLING ALBION 2 | ARBROATH 3 |

M. O'Neill, I. McAulay   A. Webster, C. McGlashan (2)

Stirling Albion: C. Reid, A. Whiteford, I. Joy, G. Hunter, K. Milne, J. Millar, C. King, I. McAulay, M. McGraw, (A. Aitken), C. Feroz, (A. Graham), G. Donald, (M. O'Neill)
Substitutes not used: K. McCallion, A. Buchanan
Arbroath: C. Hinchliffe, T. King, S. Florence, A. Webster, (J. Cusick), J.G. Rowe, I. Good, P. Brownlie, (S. Mallan), J. McGlashan, C. McGlashan, J. Mercer, (K. Tindal), K. Fotheringham
Substitutes not used: T. Bryce, C. Wight
Referee: Kevin Toner
Attendance: 424

PARTICK THISTLE 0 **LIVINGSTON 2**

B. Wilson, G. Britton

Partick Thistle: M. Brown, S. Docherty, (J. Smith), D. McKeown, W. Howie, (I. Cameron), S. Craigan, A. Archibald, A. Moore, D. Lyle, R. Dunn, (P. Lindau), D. McCallum, J. Stirling

Substitutes not used: E. Bottiglieri, K. Arthur

Livingston: N. Alexander, A. McManus, D. Fleming, J. Dolan, (Grant Smith), G. Coughlan, J. Anderson, B. Wilson, M. McCulloch, S. Crabbe, (G. Britton), D. Bingham, D. Hagen, (M. McCormick)

Substitutes not used: S. Sweeney, I. McAldon

Referee: Brian McGarry

Attendance: 1,805

ELGIN CITY 2 **DUMBARTON 4**

R. Green (2) P. Flannery (3), Andrew Brown

Elgin City: M. Pirie, Craig Milne, J. MacDonald, G. Russell, L. O'Brien, M. Green, S. Ellis, (M. Morrison), R. Green, Colin Milne, M. Slythe, S. Clinton, (S. Cameron)

Substitutes not used: P. Maguire, S. Noble, M. Rae

Dumbarton: J. Hillcoat, M. Dickie, S. Bonar, K. McCann, S. Jack, D. Stewart, (C. Brittain), A. Grace, (W. Wilson), T. King, P. Flannery, Andrew Brown, (C. Gentile), J. Robertson

Substitutes not used: C. Smith, J. Wight

Referee: Garry Mitchell

Attendance: 828

ALLOA ATHLETIC 2 **INVERNESS CALEDONIAN THISTLE 3**

R. Hamilton (2) M. Bavidge, I. Stewart (2)

Alloa Athletic: M. Cairns, G. Farrell, (C. Brigain), D. Clark, G. Watson, F. Conway, C. Valentine, R.L. Gardner, S. Thomson, R. Hamilton, M. Wilson, (R. Huxford), C. Wood, (W. Irvine)

Inverness Caledonian Thistle: L. Fridge, R. Tokely, S. Golabek, R. Mann, G. Munro, P. Sheerin, D. Wyness, (D. Hind), M. Bavidge, I. Stewart, R. McBain, B. Robson, (C. Christie)

Substitutes not used: K. Byers, A. Allan, A. Ridgers

Referee: Dougie Smith

Attendance: 597

SECOND ROUND

Tuesday, 29th August, 2000

COWDENBEATH 1 **STENHOUSEMUIR 2**

M. McDowell L. Gibson, D. Menelaws

Cowdenbeath: J. Martin, J. Boyle, T. Courts, D. White, J. Lakie, J. Allan, (I. McDonald), C. Winter, M. Bradley, M. McDowell, K. Wright, J.P. Burns

Substitutes not used: A. Lawrence, A. Spence, S. Ramsay, R. Godfrey

Stenhousemuir: G. Gow, G. Duncan, L. Gibson, T. Graham, P. Cormack, P. Ferguson, (C. McKinnon), A. Storrar, D. Lorimer, M. McLauchlan, (I. English), M. Mooney, (D. Menelaws), D. Wood

Substitutes not used: P. McAneny, A. Banner

Referee: John Underhill

Attendance: 223

ROSS COUNTY 0 **LIVINGSTON 3**

D. Bingham, G. Britton (2)

Ross County: J.N. Walker, K. Gilbert, E. Cunnington, I. Maxwell, B. Irvine, F. Escalon, (A. Bone), G. Shaw, J. Fraser, S. Ferguson, M. Millar, P. Kinnaird, (S. King)

Substitutes not used: D. Mackay, J. McQuade, G. Hamilton

Livingston: N. Alexander, A. McManus, D. Fleming, Grant Smith, (G. Britton), G. Coughlan, J. Anderson, B. McPhee, (M. McCormick), M. McCulloch, B. Wilson, (P. Kelly), D. Bingham, D. Hagen

Substitutes not used: S. Sweeney, I. McCaldon

Referee: Alan Freeland

Attendance: 825

EAST STIRLINGSHIRE 3 **MORTON 2**

C. Lynes, D. Todd, K. Gordon K. Boukraa, R. Matheson

East Stirlingshire: J. Butter, C. Quinn, M. Hall, C. Lynes, G. Russell, D. Todd, S. Stewart, G. Higgins, (S. Hislop), G. McKechnie, K. Gordon, J. Tortolano

Substitutes not used: C. McKenzie, D. McPherson, R. Carlow, C. Todd

Morton: M. Boswell, D. Murie, D. Anderson, P. Medou-Otye, R. Raeside, H. Curran, S. Aitken, A. Millen, K. Boukraa, (B. Kerr), R. Matheson, P. McDonald, (D. Davies)

Substitutes not used: A. Brownrigg, M. Naylor, A. Carlin

Referee: David Somers

Attendance: 427

BRECHIN CITY 1 **QUEEN'S PARK 1**

(AET–1-1 After 90 Minutes)

Brechin City won 4-2 on Kicks from the Penalty Mark

B. Sturrock K. Finlayson

Brechin City: D. Soutar, P. Riley, (K. Williamson), B. Donachie, (M. Leask), K. Bain, H. Cairney, J. Nairn, D. Smith, J. McKeith, (B. Honeyman), R. Grant, B. Sturrock, D. Coulston

Substitutes not used: D. Reilly, M. Parkyn

Queen's Park: S. Stewart, R. Caven, S. Marshall, G. Duncan, D. Connaghan, P. Martin, K. Finlayson, G. Connell, M. Gallagher, (R. Scobie), J. Brown, (S. Orr), F. Carroll, (C. Flannigan)

Substitutes not used: M. Travers, G. Bruce

Referee: Tom Brown

Attendance: 328

Saturday, 2nd September, 2000

HAMILTON ACADEMICAL 0 **AIRDRIEONIANS 1**

(AET) M. Pacifico

Hamilton Academical: I. Macfarlane, D. Grant, G. Lynn, W. Davidson, (C. Hillcoat), P. Gaughan, M. Nelson, A. Russell, (A. Eadie), J. Sherry, M. Moore, D. McFarlane, M. Bonnar, (R. Prytz)

Substitutes not used: G. Clark, G. Potter

Airdrieonians: J.S. Broto, S. Boyce, H.A. McCann, M. Alfonso, E. Forrest, F. Moreau, D. Brady, (S. Taylor), J. Sanjuan, J. Elliott, (M. Pacifico), A. Calderon, D. Fernandez, (M. Prest)

Substitutes not used: P. Armstrong, S. Wilson

Referee: Michael McCurry

Attendance: 1,108

ARBROATH 2 **DUMBARTON 0**

P. Brownlie, S. Mallan

Arbroath: C. Hinchcliffe, S. Florence, K. Fotheringham, J. McAulay, J.G. Rowe, A. Webster, J. Cusick, (K. Tindal), T. Bryce, (S. Mallan), C. McGlashan, (J. Mercer), P. Brownlie, J. McGlashan

Substitutes not used: C. Devine, J. Crawford

Dumbarton: J. Hillcoat, S. Bonar, C. Brittain, K. McCann, S. Jack, T. King, W. Wilson, D. Stewart, P. Flannery, Andrew Brown, J. Dillon

Substitutes not used: C. Smith, C. Gentile, M. Melvin, A. Grace, J. Wight

Referee: Bobby Orr

Attendance: 459

INVERNESS CAL. THISTLE 1 **STRANRAER 2**

M. Bavidge D. Rae, I. Harty

Inverness Caledonian Thistle: J. Calder, D. Hind, (K. Byers), R. McBain, R. Mann, R. Tokely, P. Sheerin, D. Bagan, M. Bavidge, I. Stewart, C. Christie, B. Robson, (D. Wyness)

Substitutes not used: S. Golabek, L. Fridge

Stranraer: M. McGeown, A. Paterson, F. Wright, K. Knox, G. McDonald, D. George, P. Blair, W. Macdonald, (D. Johnstone), I. Harty, D. Rae, (M. Hughes), (A. Blaikie), P. Walker

Substitutes not used: S. Edgar, S. O'Neill

Referee: John Rowbotham

Attendance: 664

CLYDEBANK 1 **PETERHEAD 0**

S. McCormick

Clydebank: D. Wylie, J. McKinstrey, R. McKinnon, R. McQuilter, K. Brannigan, B. Welsh, P. Rodden, (T. Coyne), E. Paton, S. McCormick, (D. McKelvie), R. Jacquel, J. Walker, (I.G. Johnson)

Substitutes not used: S. Murray, S. Hutchison

Peterhead: I. Pirie, D. Craig, (A. Gibson), S. King, W. Herd, M. Simpson, S. Paterson, (M. De-Barros), C. Cooper, C. Johnston, G. O'Connor, D. Smith, (S. Clark), R. Livingstone

Substitutes not used: J. Keddie, R. Buchanan

Referee: George Clyde

Attendance: 202

THIRD ROUND

Tuesday, 12th September, 2000

EAST STIRLINGSHIRE 4   EAST STENHOUSEMUIR 0
B. Ferguson, S. Hislop (2),
G. Davidson (o.g.)
East Stirlingshire: J. Butter, B. Ferguson, (R. Carlow),
M. Hall, G. Russell, D. Todd, K. Gordon, S. Stewart, C. Lynes, (D.
McPherson), G. McKechnie, (C. McKenzie), S. Hislop, J. Tortolano
Substitutes not used: J. Spence, C. Todd
Stenhousemuir: G. Gow, G. Duncan, A. Storrar, P. McAneny, (T. Graham),
P. Cormack, G. Davidson, L. Gibson, (B. Donald), C. McKinnon, I. English,
D. Menelaws, D. Wood, (D. Lorimer)
Substitutes not used: P. Ferguson, A. Banner
Referee: John Rowbotham
Attendance: 251

STRANRAER 3   ARBROATH 2
I. Harty (2), M. Geraghty   J. Mercer, C. McGlashan
Stranraer: M. McGeown, D. Johnstone, F. Wright, G. McDonald, K. Knox,
W. Macdonald, (P. Blair), A. Paterson, D. George, I. Harty, M. Geraghty,
(A. Blaikie), P. Walker
Substitutes not used: A. McMillan, S. Edgar, S. O'Neill
Arbroath: C. Hinchcliffe, T. King, S. Florence, J. McAulay, (K. Heenan),
J.G. Rowe, I. Good, J. Mercer, J. McGlashan, C. McGlashan, P. Brownlie,
(T. Bryce), K. Fotheringham
Substitutes not used: J. Cusick, J. Crawford, C. Wight
Referee: Kevin Toner
Attendance: 230

LIVINGSTON 3   BRECHIN CITY 1
G. Britton, M. McCormick,   M. Leask
M. Keith
Livingston: N. Alexander, A. McManus, (S. Greacen), D. Fleming,
M. McCulloch, G. Coughlan, S. Sweeney, B. Wilson, B. McPhee,
(M. Keith), G. Britton, (D. Hagen), D. Bingham, M. McCormick
Substitutes not used: Grant Smith, I. McCaldon
Brechin City: D. Soutar, B. Donachie, (G. Smith), D. Coulston, K. Bain,
H. Cairney, S. Raynes, D. Smith, J. Nairn, (G. Dewar), R. Grant, M. Leask,
(B. Sturrock), B. Honeyman
Substitutes not used: L. Bailey, M. Parkyn
Referee: Eric Martindale
Attendance: 873

Tuesday, 19th September, 2000

AIRDRIEONIANS 1   CLYDEBANK 1
(AET–1-1 After 90 Minutes)
Airdrieonians won 4-3 on Kicks from the Penalty Mark
M. Prest   R. Jacquel
Airdrieonians: J.S. Broto, S. Boyce, J. McAlpine, (H.A. McCann),
M. Alfonso, E. Forrest, F. Moreau, D. Brady, J. Sanjuan, M. Prest,
A. Calderon, (J. Elliott), D. Fernandez, (S. McKeown)
Substitutes not used: S. Taylor, S. Wilson
Clydebank: H. Smith, J. McKinstrey, W. McVey, S. Murdoch, (J. Walker),
K. Brannigan, F. Wishart, S. Murray, B. Hamilton, (E. Paton), T. Coyne,
R. Jacquel, (S. McCormick), A. Burke
Substitutes not used: A. Racon, D. Milne
Referee: Bobby Orr
Attendance: 979

SEMI-FINALS

Tuesday, 26th September, 2000

LIVINGSTON 2   EAST STIRLINGSHIRE 1
D. Bingham, J. Anderson   G. McKechnie
Livingston: N. Alexander, M. Hart, (A. McManus), D. Fleming, J. Dolan,
J. Anderson, P. Deas, B. Wilson, (B. McPhee), M. McCulloch, S. Crabbe,
(D. Hagen), D. Bingham, M. Keith
Substitutes not used: G. Britton, I. McCaldon
East Stirlingshire: J. Butter, C. Quinn, M. Hall, G. Russell, D. Todd,
(B. Ferguson), C. Lynes, S. Stewart, G. Higgins, (D. McPherson), S. Hislop,
G. McKechnie, J. Tortolano
Substitutes not used: R. Carlow, C. McKenzie, C. Todd
Referee: Michael McCurry
Attendance: 789

STRANRAER 2   AIRDRIEONIANS 4
(AET–2-2 After 90 Minutes)
I. Harty, D. George   M. Prest, D. Fernandez,
       S. Taylor, S. McKeown
Stranraer: M. McGeown, D. Johnstone, (S. Edgar), A. McMillan, K. Knox,
F. Wright, A. Paterson, (G. McDonald), P. Blair, D. George, I. Harty,
W. Macdonald, (A. Blaikie), M. Geraghty
Substitutes not used: M. Hughes, S. O'Neill
Airdrieonians: J.S. Broto, P. Armstrong, J. McAlpine, (S. McKeown),
S. Taylor, E. Forrest, F. Moreau, D. Brady, J. Sanjuan, M. Prest, (M. Pacifico),
J. Elliott, (B. Elliot), D. Fernandez
Substitutes not used: R. Coulter, S. Wilson
Referee: Kenny Clark
Attendance: 528

FINAL

Sunday, 19th November, 2000

LIVINGSTON 2   AIRDRIEONIANS 2
(AET–2-2 After 90 Minutes)
Airdrieonians won 3-2 on Kicks from the Penalty Mark
J. Anderson, S. Crabbe   M. Prest, D. McGuire

Livingston: N. Alexander, A. McManus, D. Fleming, J. Anderson,
G. Coughlan, P. Deas, B. Wilson, (M. Hart), M. McCulloch, M. Keith,
(B. McPhee), S. Crabbe, D. Bingham, (D. Hagen)
Substitutes not used: M. McCormick, D. McEwan

Airdrieonians: J.S. Broto, P. Armstrong, (S. Capin), H.A. McCann,
D. Brady, E. Forrest, C. Ireland, J. Elliott, (D. McGuire), F. Moreau,
M. Prest, A. Calderon, (J. Sanjuan), D. Fernandez
Substitutes not used: S. Boyce, T. Phillips

Referee: John Rowbotham
Attendance: 5,623

ROUND BY ROUND GOALS ANALYSIS

	No. of Goals Scored	Ties Played	Average Per Game
First Round	49	14	3.5
Second Round	20	8	2.5
Third Round	15	4	3.75
Semi-Finals	9	2	4.5
Final	4	1	4
Total No. of Goals Scored			97
Total No. of Ties Played			29
Average Goals per Game			3.3

Player of the Year Awards

Scottish Professional Footballers' Association

1992/93
Premier Division — **Andy Goram** *(Rangers)*
First Division — **Gordon Dalziel** *(Raith Rovers)*
Second Division — **Alexander Ross** *(Brechin City)*
Young Player of the Year — **Eoin Jess** *(Aberdeen)*

1993/94
Premier Division — **Mark Hateley** *(Rangers)*
First Division — **Richard Cadette** *(Falkirk)*
Second Division — **Andrew Thomson** *(Queen of the South)*
Young Player of the Year — **Philip O'Donnell** *(Motherwell)*

1994/95
Premier Division — **Brian Laudrup** *(Rangers)*
First Division — **Stephen Crawford** *(Raith Rovers)*
Second Division — **Derek McInnes** *(Greenock Morton)*
Third Division — **David Bingham** *(Forfar Athletic)*
Young Player of the Year — **Charlie Miller** *(Rangers)*

1995/96
Premier Division — **Paul Gascoigne** *(Rangers)*
First Division — **George O'Boyle** *(St. Johnstone)*
Second Division — **Stephen McCormick** *(Stirling Albion)*
Third Division — **Jason Young** *(Livingston)*
Young Player of the Year — **Jackie McNamara** *(Celtic)*

1996/97
Premier Division — **Paolo Di Canio** *(Celtic)*
First Division — **Roddy Grant** *(St. Johnstone)*
Second Division — **Paul Ritchie** *(Hamilton Academical)*
Third Division — **Iain Stewart** *(Inverness Cal. Thistle)*
Young Player of the Year — **Robbie Winters** *(Dundee United)*

1997/98
Premier Division — **Jackie McNamara** *(Celtic)*
First Division — **James Grady** *(Dundee)*
Second Division — **Paul Lovering** *(Clydebank)*
Third Division — **Willie Irvine** *(Alloa Athletic)*
Young Player of the Year — **Gary Naysmith** *(Heart of Midlothian)*

1998/99
Scottish Premier League — **Henrik Larsson** *(Celtic)*
First Division — **Russell Latapy** *(Hibernian)*
Second Division — **David Bingham** *(Livingston)*
Third Division — **Neil Tarrant** *(Ross County)*
Young Player of the Year — **Barry Ferguson** *(Rangers)*

1999/2000
Scottish Premier League — **Mark Viduka** *(Celtic)*
First Division — **Stevie Crawford** *(Dunfermline Athletic)*
Second Division — **Brian Carrigan** *(Clyde)*
Third Division — **Steven Milne** *(Forfar Athletic)*
Young Player of the Year — **Kenny Miller** *(Hibernian)*

2000/01
Scottish Premier League — **Henrik Larsson** *(Celtic)*
First Division — **David Bingham** *(Livingston)*
Second Division — **Scott McLean** *(Partick Thistle)*
Third Division — **Steve Hislop** *(East Stirlingshire)*
Young Player of the Year — **Stilian Petrov** *(Celtic)*

Scottish Football Writers' Association

1965 **Billy McNeill** *(Celtic)*
1966 **John Greig** *(Rangers)*
1967 **Ronnie Simpson** *(Celtic)*
1968 **Gordon Wallace** *(Raith Rovers)*
1969 **Bobby Murdoch** *(Celtic)*
1970 **Pat Stanton** *(Hibernian)*
1971 **Martin Buchan** *(Aberdeen)*
1972 **Dave Smith** *(Rangers)*
1973 **George Connelly** *(Celtic)*
1974 **World Cup Squad**
1975 **Sandy Jardine** *(Rangers)*
1976 **John Greig** *(Rangers)*
1977 **Danny McGrain** *(Celtic)*
1978 **Derek Johnstone** *(Rangers)*
1979 **Andy Ritchie** *(Morton)*
1980 **Gordon Strachan** *(Aberdeen)*
1981 **Alan Rough** *(Partick Thistle)*
1982 **Paul Sturrock** *(Dundee United)*
1983 **Charlie Nicholas** *(Celtic)*
1984 **Willie Miller** *(Aberdeen)*
1985 **Hamish McAlpine** *(Dundee United)*
1986 **Sandy Jardine** *(Heart of Midlothian)*
1987 **Brian McClair** *(Celtic)*
1988 **Paul McStay** *(Celtic)*
1989 **Richard Gough** *(Rangers)*
1990 **Alex McLeish** *(Aberdeen)*
1991 **Maurice Malpas** *(Dundee United)*
1992 **Alistair McCoist** *(Rangers)*
1993 **Andy Goram** *(Rangers)*
1994 **Mark Hateley** *(Rangers)*
1995 **Brian Laudrup** *(Rangers)*
1996 **Paul Gascoigne** *(Rangers)*
1997 **Brian Laudrup** *(Rangers)*
1998 **Craig Burley** *(Celtic)*
1999 **Henrik Larsson** *(Celtic)*
2000 **Barry Ferguson** *(Rangers)*
2001 **Henrik Larsson** *(Celtic)*

JULY

- **Celtic break the Scottish transfer record when they sign striker Chris Sutton from Chelsea for £6 million.**

- Former Scotland international defender Allan Evans is named as the new Manager of Morton.

- Gary Mackay is dismissed as Manager of Airdrieonians as former Scotland striker Steve Archibald is given preferred bidder status of the Lanarkshire club.

Steve Archibald

- St. Johnstone sign Guinea international utility player Mohammed Sylla from French club Le Havre on a free transfer.

- Rangers defeat Lithuanian champions Zalgiris Kaunas 4–1 at Ibrox in the first leg of their Champions League Second Qualifying Round tie.

- Celtic sign Belgian international defender Joos Valgaeren from Dutch club Roda £3.5 million.

- Rangers sell Finnish international striker Jonatan Johansson to Charlton Athletic for £3.3 million.

- Other transfers this month include: Lyndon Andrews (Joe Public to

John O'Neil

Hibernian), Fabian Caballero (Sol de America to Dundee), Marco de Marchi (Vitesse Arnhem to Dundee), Georgi Nemsadze (Reggiana to Dundee), Juan Sara (Cerro Portino to Dundee), Danny Griffin (St. Johnstone to Dundee United), Andrius Skerla (PSV Eindhoven to Dunfermline Athletic), Marco Ruitenbeek (Go Ahead Eagles to Dunfermline Athletic), Junior Mendes (St. Mirren to Dunfermline Athletic), Rob Matthaei (Motherwell to Dunfermline Athletic), Paul Fenwick (Raith Rovers to Hibernian), Ulrich Laursen (Odense to Hibernian), John O'Neil (St. Johnstone to Hibernian), Gary Smith (Aberdeen to Hibernian), Andy McLaren (Reading to Kilmarnock), Stuart Elliott (Glentoran to Motherwell), Alex Neil (Airdrieonians to Barnsley), Mark Roberts (Kilmarnock to Falkirk), Martin Cameron (Alloa Athletic to Bristol Rovers), Craig Feroz (Livingston to Stirling Albion), Stephen Mallan (Queen of the South to Arbroath), Ross Hamilton (Stenhousemuir to Alloa Athletic).

AUGUST

- Rangers advance to the Third Qualifying Round of the Champions League after a 0–0 draw against Zalgiris Kaunas in Lithuania completes a 4–1 aggregate win in the Second

Qualifying Round.

- Gordon Bennett resigns as Chief Executive of Aberdeen.

- Paul Sturrock resigns as Manager of Dundee United in the wake of a 3–0 defeat by Hibernian at Easter Road. He is replaced by Alex Smith.

- Rangers record an impressive 3–0 away win against Danish champions Herfolge in the first leg of their Champions League Third Qualifying Round tie.

- In the first leg of the UEFA Cup Qualifying Round, Celtic defeat Jeunesse Esch 4–0 in Luxembourg, Heart of Midlothian win 2–0 against Vestmannaeyjar in Iceland but Aberdeen suffer a shock 2–1 defeat at home to Irish club Bohemians.

- Rangers sell Scotland defender Paul Ritchie to Manchester City for £500,000 less than three months after signing him.

- Dundee United sign Cameroon striker Alphonse Tchami from Al Wasl and former Scotland defender Stephen Wright from Bradford City.

- Rangers beat Herfolge 3–0 at Ibrox for a 6–0 aggregate success in the Champions League Third Qualifying Round and a place in the First Group Stage of the competition.

- Two out of three Scottish clubs reach the First Round proper of the UEFA Cup. Celtic crush Jeunesse Esch 7–0 at Parkhead for an 11–0 aggregate win and

Heart of Midlothian beat Vestmannaeyjar 3–0 at Tynecastle for a 5–0 overall success but Aberdeen lose their Qualifying Round tie on away goals to Bohemians despite a 1–0 second leg win in Dublin.

- The first Old Firm League fixture of the

Celtic's Stilian [...] scores again[...] Jeunesse Esc[...]

Scotland suffered last minute agony against Belgium at Hampden

- Partick Thistle secure promotion to the Bell's First Division with a 3–0 win over Stirling Albion at Forthbank Stadium.

- Other transfers this month include: Don Goodman (Motherwell to Walsall), Antonio Calderon (Airdrieonians to Kilmarnock), Jesus Sanjuan (Airdrieonians to Kilmarnock), Colin McKinnon (Stenhousemuir to Arbroath), Willie McCulloch (East Fife to Berwick Rangers), Davide Xausa (Inverness Caledonian Thistle to Livingston), Craig Lynes (East Stirlingshire to Dumbarton), James Henry (Clyde to Stenhousemuir), Andy Webster (Arbroath to Heart of Midlothian).

APRIL

- The Scottish Football Association's Appeals Committee overturns the decision of the SPL appointed Independent Commission and backs St. Johnstone's decision to dismiss George O'Boyle and Kevin Thomas.

- Celtic clinch the SPL title with five games to spare when a Tommy Johnson goal earns them a 1–0 win over St. Mirren at Parkhead.

- Hibernian win the first of the Tennent's Scottish Cup Semi-Finals when they defeat First Division Livingston 3–0 at Hampden.

- Celtic beat Dundee United 3–1 in the second Tennent's Scottish Cup Semi-Final to remain on course for the domestic 'treble'.

- Scottish football mourns the death of former Rangers and Scotland midfielder Jim Baxter at the age of 61.

- Scott Booth marks his return to the Scotland side with the equaliser as they draw 1–1 with Poland in a friendly in Bydgoszcz. No fewer than seven players make their full international debut for the Scots.

- Scotland captain Colin Hendry is handed a six-match suspension by FIFA for elbowing San Marino's Nicola Albani at Hampden in March. The SFA appeal against the decision.

- Livingston clinch the Bell's First Division title and promotion to the SPL for the first time with a game to spare as they defeat Inverness Caledonian Thistle 3–2 at Caledonian Stadium. Morton and Alloa Athletic are

2001 saw a sad farewell to 'Slim' Jim Baxter

111

Celtic win the Tennent's Scottish Cup....

- Rangers appoint former Ajax Manager Jan Wouters as their new First Team Coach.

- Alan Stubbs makes his first team return for Celtic after winning his cancer battle and marks it with a goal in a 5–2 win over Hibernian at Easter Road.

- Tommy McLean returns to Ibrox when he is named as Director of Football Development by Rangers.

- Henrik Larsson is named Player of the Year by the Scottish Football Writers Association. Martin O'Neill makes it a double for Celtic when he lifts the Manager of the Year award.

- Ian Welsh resigns as Chief Executive of Kilmarnock and the Rugby Park club announce Sir John Orr will become their new Chairman in July.

- Trinidad and Tobago international Russell Latapy is dismissed by Hibernian after a serious breach of club discipline.

relegated to the Second Division.

- Arbroath claim the second promotion place from the Bell's Second Division with a 2–0 win over fellow promotion challengers Berwick Rangers at Gayfield. Stirling Albion are relegated to the Bell's Third Division.

- Celtic win the final SPL Old Firm fixture of the season with Henrik Larsson claiming his 50th goal of the season in the 3–0 defeat of Rangers at Ibrox.

- Henrik Larsson is named Player of the Year by The Scottish Professional Footballers Association. His Celtic team-mate Stilian Petrov becomes the first non-Scot to win the Young Player of the Year award.

MAY

- A hectic final day of the Bell's Scottish Football League season sees Hamilton Academical win the Bell's Third Division title with a 4–1 win over Montrose at Links Park. Cowdenbeath

are also promoted as they beat nearest rivals Brechin City 2–1 at Central Park.

- Despite a 1–0 win at Queen of the South on the final day, Queen's Park are relegated to the Bell's Third Division. Rivals Forfar Athletic survive thanks to a 3–1 win over Stirling Albion at Station Park.

club discipline.

- Scottish football mourns the death of Bobby Murdoch at the age of 56. The former Scotland midfielder is the first of Celtic's famous 1967 European Cup winning side to pass away.

- FIFA reduce Scotland captain Colin Hendry's ban from six games to three,

......as Larsson and O'Neill collect more awards

Russell Latapy

2001/02 with a 1-0 win over Celtic at Rugby Park on the final day of the SPL season. They edge out Heart of Midlothian who beat Dundee 2-0 at Tynecastle.

- St. Mirren are relegated to the First Division after a 3-3 draw with Motherwell as Dundee United secure their survival with a 2-1 win over Aberdeen at Pittodrie.

- Jorg Albertz and Tugay Kerimoglu leave Rangers to join Hamburg and Blackburn Rovers for £4 million and £1.3 million respectively.

- Livingston's Jim Leishman is named the Bell's First Division Manager of the Year. John Lambie of Partick Thistle collects the Second Division award and Hamilton Academical Manager Ally Dawson takes the Third Division honour. Livingston's David Bingham receives the Bell's Player of the Year award whilst Falkirk teenager Mark Kerr is named the Young Player of the Year.

ruling him out of the three remaining World Cup group qualifying fixtures.

- Kilmarnock clinch Scotland's final UEFA Cup place for season

Kilmarnock claim a place in the UEFA Cup

- Celtic complete their first domestic treble since season 1968/69 when they defeat Hibernian 3-0 in the Tennent's Scottish Cup Final at Hampden with goals from Jackie McNamara and a Henrik Larsson double.

- Clyde's Gordon Greer moves to Premiership new boys Blackburn Rovers in a deal that could land the Cumbernauld club in excess of £½million.

JUNE

- Ramon Vega turns down Celtic's offer of a new contract to sign for English First Division side Watford.

- Arsenal sign Rangers' Dutch midfielder Giovanni van Bronckhorst for a fee of £8.5 million.

- Hibernian sign Ecuador international Ulises de la Cruz for £600,000.

- Alan Stubbs leaves Celtic under Freedom of Contract to sign for Everton.

- Rangers sign Argentine striker Claudio Caniggia from Dundee for £900,000.

- Henrik Larsson ends speculation surrounding his future when he signs an extension to his contract at Celtic until 2004.

- German international midfielder Christian Nerlinger joins Rangers from Borussia Dortmund for £1.9 million.

Sadness in the middle of Celtic success. Lisbon Lion Bobby Murdoch passes away

STEPHEN HALLIDAY
(The Scotsman)

THE SCOTTISH FOOTBALL LEAGUE

FIRST DIVISION

AIRDRIEONIANS
IAN McCALL
Player: Queen's Park, Dunfermline Athletic, Rangers, Bradford City, Dunfermline Athletic, Dundee, Falkirk, Hamilton Academical, Happy Valley (Hong Kong), Hamilton Academical, Partick Thistle
Manager: Clydebank, Morton, Airdrieonians

ARBROATH
JOHN BROWNLIE
Player: Hibernian, Newcastle United, Middlesbrough, Hartlepool United, Berwick Rangers, Scotland
Manager: Cowdenbeath, East Stirlingshire, Arbroath

AYR UNITED
GORDON DALZIEL
Player: Rangers, Manchester City, Partick Thistle, East Stirlingshire, Raith Rovers, Ayr United
Manager: Ayr United

CLYDE
ALLAN MAITLAND
Player: Did Not Play at Senior Level.
Manager: Clyde

FALKIRK
ALEX TOTTEN
Player: Liverpool, Dundee, Dunfermline Athletic, Falkirk, Queen of the South, Alloa Athletic
Manager: Alloa Athletic, Falkirk, Dumbarton, St. Johnstone, East Fife, Kilmarnock, Falkirk

INVERNESS CALEDONIAN THISTLE
STEVE PATERSON
Player: Manchester United, Sheffield United, Hong Kong Rangers, Sydney Olympic, Yorniuri Tokyo
Manager: Inverness Caledonian Thistle

PARTICK THISTLE
JOHN LAMBIE
Player: Falkirk, St. Johnstone
Manager: Hamilton Academical, Partick Thistle, Hamilton Academical, Partick Thistle, Falkirk, Partick Thistle

RAITH ROVERS
PETER HETHERSTON
Player: Falkirk (twice), Sheffield United, Watford, Raith Rovers, Aberdeen, Airdrieonians, Partick Thistle
Manager: Raith Rovers

ROSS COUNTY
NEALE COOPER
Player: Aberdeen, Aston Villa, Rangers, Reading, Dunfermline Athletic, Ross County
Manager: Ross County

ST. MIRREN
THOMAS HENDRIE
Player: Meadowbank Thistle, Berwick Rangers
Manager: Berwick Rangers, Alloa Athletic, St. Mirren

SECOND DIVISION

ALLOA ATHLETIC
TERRY CHRISTIE
Player: Dundee, Raith Rovers, Stirling Albion
Manager: Meadowbank Thistle, Stenhousemuir, Alloa Athletic

BERWICK RANGERS
PAUL SMITH
Player: Dundee, Dundee United, Raith Rovers, Motherwell, Dunfermline Athletic, Falkirk, Dunfermline Athletic, Heart of Midlothian, Ayr United, Berwick Rangers
Manager: Berwick Rangers

CLYDEBANK
DEREK FERGUSON
Player: Rangers, Dundee (loan), Heart of Midlothian, Sunderland, Falkirk, Dunfermline Athletic, Portadown, Partick Thistle, Adelaide Force, Ross County, Clydebank, Scotland
Manager: Clydebank

COWDENBEATH
GARY KIRK
Player: Did Not Play at Senior Level
Manager: Cowdenbeath

FORFAR ATHLETIC
NEIL COOPER
Player: Grimsby Town, St. Mirren, Hibernian, Aberdeen
Manager: Forfar Athletic

HAMILTON ACADEMICAL
ALLY DAWSON
Player: Rangers, Blackburn Rovers, Airdrieonians, St. Andrews (Malta), Scotland
Manager: St. Andrews (Malta), Hamilton Academical

MORTON
PETER CORMACK
Player: Hibernian, Nottingham Forest, Liverpool, Bristol City, Hibernian, Scotland
Manager: Partick Thistle, Morton

QUEEN OF THE SOUTH
JOHN CONNOLLY
Player: St. Johnstone, Everton, Birmingham City, Newcastle United, Hibernian, Scotland
Manager: Queen of the South

STENHOUSEMUIR
BRIAN FAIRLEY
Player: Hibernian, Cowdenbeath
Manager: Stenhousemuir

STRANRAER
BILLY McLAREN
Player: Queen of the South (twice), Morton (twice), East Fife, Cowdenbeath, Dunfermline Athletic, Hibernian, Partick Thistle
Manager: Queen of the South, Hamilton Academical, Albion Rovers, Queen of the South, Albion Rovers, Stranraer

THIRD DIVISION

ALBION ROVERS
JOHN McVEIGH
Player: Airdrieonians, Clyde, Hamilton Academical, Kilmarnock, Falkirk
Manager: Partick Thistle, Raith Rovers, Albion Rovers

BRECHIN CITY
DICK CAMPBELL
Player: Brechin City, East Stirlingshire
Manager: Dunfermline Athletic, Brechin City

DUMBARTON
TOM CARSON
Player: Dumbarton, Dundee, Hibernian (loan), Partick Thistle (loan), Queen of the South (loan), Dunfermline Athletic (loan), Ipswich Town (loan), Dumbarton (loan), Raith Rovers, Kilmarnock
Manager: Dumbarton

EAST FIFE
DAVID CLARKE
Player: East Fife
Manager: East Fife, Falkirk, East Fife

EAST STIRLINGSHIRE
BRIAN ROSS
Player: Airdrieonians, Ayr United, East Stirlingshire
Manager: East Stirlingshire

ELGIN CITY
ALEXANDER CALDWELL
Player: St. Johnstone, Dundee
Manager: Elgin City

MONTROSE
JOHN SHERAN
Player: Montrose
Manager: Montrose

PETERHEAD
IAN WILSON
Player: Aberdeen, Dundee, Leicester City, Everton, Derby County, Wigan Athletic, Bury, Besiktas, Scotland
Manager: Peterhead

QUEEN'S PARK
JOHN McCORMACK
Player: Clydebank, St. Mirren, Dundee, Airdrieonians, Partick Thistle
Coach: Dundee (Manager), Queen's Park

STIRLING ALBION
RAY STEWART
Player: Dundee United, West Ham United, St. Johnstone, Stirling Albion, Scotland
Manager: Livingston, Stirling Albion

THE SCOTTISH PREMIER LEAGUE

ABERDEEN
EBBE SKOVDAHL
Player: Van Loes, Brondby, Hvalsoe
Manager: Hvalsoe, Glostrop BC, Bronshoi, Brondby IF, Benfica, Brondby IF, Vejle, Brondby IF, Aberdeen

CELTIC
MARTIN O'NEILL
Player: Distillery, Derry City, Nottingham Forest, Norwich City, Manchester City, Norwich City, Notts County, Northern Ireland
Manager: Wycombe Wanderers, Leicester City, Celtic

DUNDEE
IVANO BONETTI
Player: Torino, Brescia, Bologna, Sampdoria, Atalanta, Genoa, Tranmere Rovers, Grimsby Town
Manager: Dundee

DUNDEE UNITED
ALEX SMITH
Player: Stirling Albion, East Stirlingshire, Albion Rovers, Stenhousemuir
Manager: Stenhousemuir, Stirling Albion, St. Mirren, Aberdeen, Clyde, Dundee United

DUNFERMLINE ATHLETIC
JAMES CALDERWOOD
Player: Birmingham City, Cambridge United (loan), Sparta Rotterdam, Willem II, Roda JC, SC Heracles
Manager: Rietvogels, FC Zwolle, SC Cambuur, Leeuwarden, Willem II, NEC Nijmegan, Dunfermline Athletic

HEART OF MIDLOTHIAN
CRAIG LEVEIN
Player: Cowdenbeath, Heart of Midlothian, Scotland
Manager: Cowdenbeath, Heart of Midlothian

HIBERNIAN
ALEX McLEISH
Player: Aberdeen, Motherwell, Scotland
Manager: Motherwell, Hibernian

KILMARNOCK
BOBBY WILLIAMSON
Player: Clydebank, Rangers, West Bromwich Albion, Rotherham United, Kilmarnock
Manager: Kilmarnock

LIVINGSTON
JAMES LEISHMAN
Player: Dunfermline Athletic, Cowdenbeath
Manager: Dunfermline Athletic, Inverness Thistle, Montrose, Livingston (Formerly Meadowbank Thistle), Livingston

MOTHERWELL
BILLY DAVIES
Player: Rangers, St. Mirren, Leicester City, IF Elsborg, Dunfermline Athletic, Motherwell
Manager: Motherwell

RANGERS
DICK ADVOCAAT
Player: Den Haag, Breda Kerkrod, Berlow, Chicago Sting
Manager: Harlem, Dordrecht, Holland, PSV Eindhoven, Rangers

ST. JOHNSTONE
SANDY CLARK
Player: Airdrieonians, West Ham United, Rangers, Heart of Midlothian, Partick Thistle, Dunfermline Athletic, Heart of Midlothian
Manager: Partick Thistle, Heart of Midlothian, Hamilton Academical, St. Johnstone

INFORMATION COMPILED BY JIM JEFFREY

OFFICIAL LIST OF REFEREES 2001/02

BELL'S
SCOTTISH FOOTBALL LEAGUE

CLASS 1

Iain Brines
Tom Brown
Brian Cassidy
Kenny Clark
George Clyde
Steve Conroy
Hugh Dallas
Stuart Dougal
John Fleming
Alan Freeland
Ian Frickleton
Ian Fyfe
Alan Gemmill
John Gilmour
Colin Hardie
Andrew Hunter
Michael McCurry
Douglas McDonald
Brian McGarry
Craig MacKay
Eddie Mack
Eric Martindale
Cammy Melville
Garry Mitchell
Calum Murray
Bobby Orr
Charlie Richmond
Mike Ritchie
John Rowbotham
Dougie Smith
David Somers
Craig Thomson
George Thomson
Kevin Toner
John Underhill
Willie Young

CLASS 1 SPECIALIST ASSISTANT REFEREES

Graeme Alison
Francis Andrews
Neil Brand
Roddy Cobb
Peter Crilley
Frank Cole
Martin Cryans
Alan Cunningham
Andy Davis
Willie Dishington
David Doig
Martin Doran
Jim Dunne
Gordon Hunter
Wilson Irvine
Robert Johnston
Stuart Logan
Jim Lyon
Stuart Macaulay
Gordon McBride
Jim McBride
Joe McDowall
Brian McDuffie
Robert McKendry
Derek Mason
Gordon Middleton
Ricky Mooney
Tom Murphy
Andrew Seymour
Stewart Shearer
Ricky Smith
Allen Thurston

CLASS 1 REFEREES (CATEGORY 2)

Crawford Allan
James Bee
Alan Boyd
Jim Boyd
Chris Boyle
Kevin Carter
Derek Clark
Jamie Downie
George Drummond
Steven Duff
Stephen Finnie
Joe Heggie
Willie Hornby
Scott MacDonald
John McKendrick
Alan Muir
Willie Murray
Stevie O'Reilly
Martin Sproule
Gary Sweeney
Mike Tumilty
Brian Winter

CLASS 1 ASSISTANT REFEREES

Jeff Banks
Stuart Bennett
John Brady
Colin Brown
Scott Brown
John Campbell
Graham Chambers
Craig Charleston
Gary Cheyne
Paul Cheyne
William Collum
Martin Conroy
Steven Craven
Hugh Dalgetty
David Davidson
Mark Doyle
Ian Elmslie
Andrew Gault
William Gilfillan
Kevin Grant
Keith Hadden
Andy Halliday
Jason Hasson
David Hodgson
Tommy Johnston
Steve Kaney
Lawrence Kerrigan
Gary Kirkwood
Anthony Law
Derek Lowe
Steve McGeouch
Gordon MacKay
Cameron McKay
Jim McNeil
Craig Marshall
Brian Martin
Michael Monaghan
Neil Mooney
Steven Nicholls
Euan Norris
Steve Pullar
Eric Robertson
Scott Robertson
Thomas Robertson
Charlie Smith
Eddie Smith
Keith Sorbie
Steve Todd
Paul Watson
Willie Weir
Rod Williamson
Chris Young
Ewan Young

WORLD CUP 2002 - Qualifying Competition and International Friendly Matches Played by Scotland during Season 2000/01

WORLD CUP 2002 - QUALIFYING COMPETITION

Saturday, 2nd September, 2000 - Skonto Stadium, Riga

LATVIA 0   **SCOTLAND 1**
                      N. McCann

Latvia: Kolinko, Stepanovs, Astafjevs, Laizans, Lobanovs, Blagonadezdins, Ivanovs, Bleidelis, Pahars, Rubins, Stolcers

Substitutes not used: Vanins, Vucans, Miholaps, Zakresevskis, Poljakovs, Pelcis, Troitskis

Scotland: N. Sullivan, D. Weir, (C. Cameron), C. Dailly, M. Elliott, C. Hendry, C. Davidson, (G. Naysmith), T. Boyd, B. Ferguson, W. Dodds, D. Hutchison, (G. Holt), N. McCann

Substitutes not used: J. Gould, J. McNamara, B. O'Neil, A. Johnston

Referee: Andreas Schluchter (Switzerland)

Attendance: 9,200

Saturday, 7th October, 2000 - Olimpico Stadium, Serravalle

SAN MARINO 0   **SCOTLAND 2**
                      M. Elliott, D. Hutchison

San Marino: F. Gasperoni, Gennari, Marani, Gobbi, Matteoni, (Valentini), Bacciocchi, Zonzini, (Della Valle), Manzaroli, Montagna, (Deluigi), R. Muccioli, B. Gasperoni

Substitutes not used: S. Muccioli, Selva, Mularoni, Gualtieri

Scotland: N. Sullivan, J. McNamara, G. Naysmith, M. Elliott, C. Hendry, C. Dailly, (D. Weir), W. Dodds, C. Cameron, K. Gallacher, (P. Dickov), D. Hutchison, N. McCann, (A. Johnston)

Substitutes not used: J. Gould, T. Boyd, G. Holt, C. Davidson

Referee: Gylfi Thor Orrason (Iceland)

Attendance: 4,377

Wednesday, 11th October, 2000 - Maksimir Stadium, Zagreb

CROATIA 1   **SCOTLAND 1**
Boksic   K. Gallacher

Croatia: Pavlovic, R. Kovac, Jarni, Soldo, (Biscan), Stimac, Simic, Saric, Prosinecki, Balaban, N. Kovac, (Zivkovic), Boksic, (Vugrinec)

Substitutes not used: Pletikosa, Tudor, Cvitanovic, Jurcic

Scotland: N. Sullivan, D. Weir, G. Naysmith, M. Elliott, C. Hendry, T. Boyd, A. Johnston, (P. Dickov), (G. Holt), C. Burley, K. Gallacher, D. Hutchison, C. Cameron

Substitutes not used: J. Gould, P. Ritchie, B. O'Neil, S. Pressley, M. Burchill

Referee: Gilles Veissiere (France)

Attendance: 17,995

Saturday, 24th March, 2001 - The National Stadium, Hampden Park, Glasgow

SCOTLAND 2   **BELGIUM 2**
W. Dodds (2)   Wilmots, van Buyten

Scotland: N. Sullivan, D. Weir, T. Boyd, P. Lambert, C. Hendry, M. Elliott, B. Ferguson, C. Burley, W. Dodds, (K. Gallacher), D. Hutchison, D. Matteo

Substitutes not used: R. Douglas, S. Pressley, G. Holt, A. Johnston, S. Gemmill, C. Cameron

Belgium: De Vlieger, Deflandre, Valgaeren, (van Buyten), de Boeck, Dheedene, Vanderhaeghe, Wilmots, Goor, Mpenza, Baseggio, (Vermant), Hendrikx, (Peeters)

Substitutes not used: Gaspercic, Boffin, Simons, Goossens

Referee: Kim Milton Nielsen (Denmark)

Attendance: 37,480

Wednesday, 28th March, 2001 - The National Stadium, Hampden Park, Glasgow

SCOTLAND 4   **SAN MARINO 0**
C. Hendry (2), W. Dodds,
C. Cameron

Scotland: N. Sullivan, D. Weir, A. Johnston, P. Lambert, C. Hendry, M. Elliott, (T. Boyd), C. Cameron, (S. Gemmill),C. Burley, W. Dodds, D. Hutchison, D. Matteo, (K. Gallacher)

Substitutes not used: R. Douglas, S. Pressley, G. Holt, G. Rae

San Marino: F. Gasperoni, Della Balda, (Albani), Marani, Bacciocchi, Matteoni, Gobbi, Muccioli, Zonzini, A. Selva, Vannucci, (Bugli), Manzaroli, (R. Selva)

Substitutes not used: Ceccoli, Deluigi, Montagna, C. Selva

Referee: Petteri Kari (Finland)

Attendance: 27,313

GROUP SIX TABLE

	P	W	D	L	F	A	PTS
BELGIUM	6	4	2	0	23	5	14
CROATIA	5	3	2	0	10	2	11
SCOTLAND	5	3	2	0	10	3	11
LATVIA	7	1	1	5	4	14	4
SAN MARINO	7	0	1	6	3	26	1

FULL INTERNATIONAL FRIENDLY MATCHES

Wednesday, 15th November, 2000 - The National Stadium, Hampden Park, Glasgow

SCOTLAND 0   **AUSTRALIA 2**
                         Emerton, Zdrilic

Scotland: J. Gould, D. Weir, (M. Elliott), T. Boyd, C. Dailly, B. O'Neil, (C. Hendry), B. Ferguson, W. Dodds, C. Burley, (P. Dickov), C. Cameron, (N. McCann), D. Hutchison, D. Matteo
Substitutes not used: R. Douglas, P. Ritchie, S. Pressley
Australia: Schwarzer, Muscat, Murphy, Okon, Popovic, Skoko, (Wehrman), Tiatto, (Burns), Lazaridis, Zdrilic, (Zane), Emerton, Agostino, (Sterjovski)
Substitutes not used: Filan, Laybutt, Casserly
Referee: Pascal Garibian (France)
Attendance: 30,985

Wednesday, 25th April, 2001 – WKS Zawisza Stadium, Bydgoszcz

POLAND 1   **SCOTLAND 1**
Kaluzny   S. Booth

Poland: Dudek, Klos, Zielinski, (Kaluzny), Michal Zewlakow, (Zajac), Waldoch, Hajto, Kozminski, Iwan, Kryszalowicz, (Zurawski), Zdebel, (Swierczewski), Marcin Zewlakow, (Mieciel)
Substitutes not used: Majdan, Krzynowek
Scotland: N. Sullivan, B. Nicholson, C. Davidson, (D. Weir), T. Boyd, C. Dailly, J. O'Neil, (S. Gemmill), C. Miller, (S. Caldwell), G. Rae, W. Dodds, (S. Crawford), C. Cameron, (A. McLaren), S. Booth, (K. Miller)
Substitutes not used: R. Douglas
Referee: Juan Roca (Spain)
Attendance: 18,000

EUROPEAN "UNDER 21" CHAMPIONSHIP

Friday, 1st September, 2000 - Daugava Stadium, Riga

LATVIA 1   **SCOTLAND 3**
Kolesnicenko   R. Hughes, M. Burchill, C. Easton

Latvia: Vanins, Pasins, Lasko, Soleicuks, Mihadjuks, J. Romanovs, Kacanovs, (Sergejevs), Solonicins, Morozs, (Karlsons), Kolesnicenko, (Grebis), Verpakovskis
Substitutes not used: Pavlovs, A. Romanovs, Bezzubovs, Sokolskis
Scotland: R. Esson, S. Fraser, W. Cummings, L. Wilkie, S. Caldwell, C. Doig, M. Stewart, (P. Canero), S. Severin, (C. Easton), M. Burchill, R. Hughes, A. Notman, (K. Kyle)
Substitutes not used: J. Langfield, A. Jordan, J. Paterson, T. McManus
Referee: Kristinn Jakobsson (Iceland)
Attendance: 1,200

Tuesday, 10th October, 2000 - FC Slaven Belupo Stadium, Koprivnica

CROATIA 3   **SCOTLAND 1**
Mikic (2), Olic   A. Notman

Croatia: Maric, Sabolcki, Seric, Miladin, Mijatovic, Neretljak, Mikic, (Lovrek), Banovic, (Bilic), Bosnjak, Vranjes, Olic, (Balatinac)
Substitutes not used: Sunara, Polovanec, Sklepic, Skocibusic

Scotland: R. Esson, S. Fraser, W. Cummings, L. Wilkie, S. Caldwell, C. Doig, (Derek Young), M. Stewart, C. Easton, K. Miller, (K. Kyle), R. Hughes, (P. Canero), A. Notman
Substitutes not used: J. Langfield, A. Jordan, R. Neilson, K. McAnespie
Referee: Jack van Hulten (Holland)
Attendance: 2,910

Friday 23rd March, 2001 - East End Park, Dunfermline

SCOTLAND 0   **BELGIUM 1**
                         Theunis

Scotland: R. Esson, P. Canero, W. Cummings, S. Severin, (Derek Young), S. Caldwell, G. Caldwell, M. Stewart, (I. Murray), C. Easton, K. Miller, M. Burchill, (T. McManus), R. Hughes
Substitutes not used: P. Gallacher, R. Malcolm, C. McGroarty, J. Smith
Belgium: Gillet, Theunis, Hayen, Vandenbroeck, Vlaminck, Vrancken, Van Dessel, Dufer, Smoulders, (Dever), Soetaers, (Claes), Chatelle, (Imschoot)
Substitutes: Renard, Delorge, De Roeck, Teelen
Referee: Paulo Gomes Costa (Portugal)
Attendance: 5,856

GROUP TABLE

	P	W	D	L	F	A	PTS
BELGIUM	4	4	0	0	8	1	12
CROATIA	4	2	1	1	7	5	7
SCOTLAND	3	1	0	2	4	5	3
LATVIA	5	0	1	4	3	11	1

"UNDER-21" INTERNATIONAL FRIENDLIES

Tuesday, 24th April, 2001 – Osir Stadium, Wloclawek

POLAND 1   **SCOTLAND 0**
Rasiak

Poland: Szazko, Sznaucner, (Dziewicki), Nowak, (Kowalski), Ciesielski, Lewandowski, Glowacki, Wasilewski, Kolendowicz, (Nuszalik), Rasiak, (Labedzki), Snolarek, (Mierzejewski), Lawa
Substitutes not used: Melcarz
Scotland: R. Esson, J. McCunnie, W. Cummings, (S. Hammell), R. Malcolm, C. Doig, H. Murray, P. Canero, (K. Kyle), G. Caldwell, M. Burchill, (K. Parker), Derek Young, (M. Kerr), M. Stewart, (T. McManus)
Substitutes not used: C. Stewart, J. Langfield
Referee: Jacek Granat (Poland)
Attendance: 2,500

UEFA CHAMPIONS LEAGUE

Second Qualifying Round - First Leg

Wednesday, 26th July, 2000, Ibrox Stadium, Glasgow

RANGERS 4   **ZALGIRIS KAUNAS 1**
Johnston, Albertz, Dodds (2)   Zuta

Rangers: Klos, Ricksen, Moore, Wilson, (McCann), Vidmar, (Miller), Ferguson, Johnston, Reyna, Johansson, (Dodds), Wallace, Albertz
Substitutes not used: Brown, Kanchelskis, Porrini, Ritchie,

Zalgiris Kaunas: Poskus, Barasa, Kancelskis, Juodeikis, Bezykornovas, (Gelgota), Zuta, (Danilicevas), Regelskis, (Mika), Ksanavicius, Petrenko, Dedura, Zelmikas
Substitutes not used: Padimanskas, Puotkalis, Velicka, Kunevicius
Referee: Emanuel Zammit (Malta)
Attendance: 45,974

Second Qualifying Round - Second Leg

Wednesday, 2nd August, 2000, S Darius & S. Girenas SC, Kaunas

ZALGIRIS KAUNAS 0   **RANGERS 0**

Zalgiris Kaunas: Padimanskas, Kancelskis, Danilicevas, (Velicka), Juodeikis, Bezykornovas, (Puotkalis), Zuta, Mika, Regelskis, (Gelgota), Ksanavicius, Dedura, Zelmikas
Substitutes not used: Kurskis, Kunevicius
Rangers: Klos, Ricksen, (Kanchelskis), Konterman, Amoruso, Vidmar, (Porrini), Ferguson, Reyna, Van Bronckhorst, Dodds, Wallace, (Johnston), Kerimoglu
Substitutes not used: Brown, Miller, Ritchie
Referee: Franck De Bleeckere (Belgium)
Attendance: 4,000
(Rangers won 4-1 on Aggregate)

Third Qualifying Round - First Leg

Wednesday, 9th August, 2000, Herfolge Stadium, Herfolge

HERFOLGE 0   **RANGERS 3**
                        Albertz, Wallace, Amoruso

Herfolge: Mikkelsen, Lustu, L. Jakobsen, Lykke, K. Jensen, (J. Jakobsen), Hoyer, Falck, Hermansen, (Knudsen), Kastrup, Thomsen, Schram, (Heyde)
Substitutes not used: Udengaard, J. Jensen, Henriksen, Abel
Rangers: Klos, Porrini, Konterman, Amoruso, Reyna, Ferguson, McCann, (Johnston), Van Bronckhorst, Dodds, (Kanchelskis), Wallace, (Miller), Albertz
Substitutes not used: Brown, Kerimoglu, Ricksen, Vidmar
Referee: Lubomir Pucek (Czech Republic)
Attendance: 3,523

Third Qualifying Round - Second Leg

Wednesday, 23rd August, 2000, Ibrox Stadium, Glasgow

RANGERS 3   **HERFOLGE 0**
Wallace, Johnston, Kanchelskis

Rangers: Klos, Ricksen, (Kanchelskis), Konterman, Amoruso, Reyna, Ferguson, McCann, Van Bronckhorst, Dodds, (Johnston), Wallace, Albertz, (Vidmar)
Substitutes not used: Brown, Kerimoglu, Porrini, Wilson
Herfolge: Mikkelsen, Lustu, L. Jakobsen, (Knudsen), Lykke, Hoyer, Falck, J. Jakobsen, (Hermansen), Kastrup, Lubbers, Schram, (J. Jensen), Heyde
Substitutes not used: Udengaard, Henriksen, Avnskjold, Abel
Referee: Dani Koran (Israel)
Attendance: 34,141
(Rangers won 6-0 on Aggregate)

FIRST GROUP MATCH STAGE

Tuesday, 12th September, 2000, Ibrox Stadium, Glasgow

RANGERS 5   **STURM GRAZ 0**
Mols, De Boer, Albertz,
Van Bronckhorst, Dodds

Rangers: Klos, Amoruso, Numan, Ferguson, Van Bronckhorst, Mols, (Dodds), Albertz, Reyna, De Boer, (McCann), Konterman, Johnston, (Kanchelskis)
Substitutes not used: Charbonnier, Ricksen, Kerimoglu, Vidmar
Sturm Graz: Schicklgruber, Foda, Strafner, Schupp, Reinmayr, (Mahlich), Korsos, Prilasnig, Mamedov, Schopp, Yuran, (Szabics), Fleurquin
Substitutes not used: Baruwa, Popovic, Koutsoupias
Referee: Lucillo Cortez-Baptista (Portugal)
Attendance: 49,317

Wednesday, 20th September, 2000, Stade Louis II, Monaco

MONACO 0   **RANGERS 1**
                        Van Bronckhorst

Monaco: Porato, Riise, (Prso), Marquez, Djetou, Giuly, Simone, Nonda, (Courville), Bonnal, (Gravelaine), Irles, Abidal, Rodriguez,
Substitutes not used: Aubry, Di Tommaso, Farnerud, Givet
Rangers: Klos, Amoruso, Numan, Ferguson, Van Bronckhorst, Mols, (McCann), Reyna, (Vidmar), De Boer, Konterman, Kerimoglu, Johnston
Substitutes not used: Charbonnier, Ricksen, Kanchelskis, Albertz, Dodds
Referee: Atanas Ouzounov (Bulgaria)
Attendance: 18,000

Wednesday, 27th September, 2000, Ali Sami Yen Stadium, Istanbul

GALATASARAY 3   **RANGERS 2**
Bulent, Haken, Jardel   Kanchelskis, Van Bronckhorst

Galatasaray: Taffarel, K. Bulent, Popescu, B. Emre, (Faruk), Jardel, Hasan, (Ahmet), Fatih, Umit, A. Bulent, Hakan, Ergun,
Substitutes not used: Kerem, Serkan, A. Emre, Marcio
Rangers: Klos, Amoruso, Numan, Ferguson, Van Bronckhorst, Mols, (Dodds), Reyna, De Boer, Konterman, Kerimoglu, Johnston, (Kanchelskis)
Substitutes not used: Brown, Ricksen, Albertz, McCann, Vidmar
Referee: Pierluigi Collina (Italy)
Attendance: 22,000

Tuesday, 17th October, 2000, Ibrox Stadium, Glasgow

RANGERS 0   **GALATASARAY 0**

Rangers: Klos, Ferguson, Kanchelskis, Albertz, Reyna, De Boer, Konterman, Kerimoglu, Porrini, Vidmar, (Wilson), Lovenkrands, (McCann)
Substitutes not used: Brown, Dodds, Miller, Negri, Ross
Galatasaray: Taffarel, K. Bulent, Popescu, Jardel, (Marcio), Hagi, (Okan), Hasan, Fatih, Umit, A. Bulent, Hakan, Ergun
Substitutes not used: Kerem, Serkan, Faruk, A. Emre, Capone
Referee: Merk Markus (Germany)
Attendance: 49,603

Wednesday, 25th October, 2000,
Arnold Schwarsenegger Stadium, Graz

STURM GRAZ 2   **RANGERS 0**
Yuran, Prilasnig

Sturm Graz: Schicklgruber, Neukirchner, Schupp, Reinmayr, (Minavandchal), Korsos, Prilasnig, Mamedov, (Feldhofer), Kocijan, Popovic, Yuran, (Strafner), Fleurquin
Substitutes not used: Baruwa, Foda, Atangana, Koutsoupias
Rangers: Christiansen, Amoruso, Numan, Ferguson, Kanchelskis, Van Bronckhorst, (McCann), Wallace, (Dodds), De Boer, Konterman, Kerimoglu, Porrini, (Negri)
Substitutes not used: Brown, Ricksen, Wilson, Ross
Referee: Antonio Lopez-Nieto (Spain)
Attendance: 15,400

Tuesday, 7th November, 2000, Ibrox Stadium, Glasgow

RANGERS 2
Miller, Mols

MONACO 2
Da Costa, Simone

Rangers: Christiansen, Ricksen, Amoruso, Numan, Ferguson, Mols, (Kerimoglu), Albertz, (McCann), De Boer, (Wallace), Wilson, Miller, Vidmar
Substitutes not used: Brown, Kanchelskis, Dodds, Porrini
Monaco: Porato, Contreras, Christanval, Da Costa, Giuly, (Eloi), Gallardo, (Gravelaine), Simone, Dabo, Nonda, (Prso), Bonnal, Irles
Substitutes not used: Biancarelli, Riise, Leonard, Rodriguez
Referee: Lubos Michel (Slovakia)
Attendance: 50,228

GROUP TABLE

	P	W	D	L	F	A	PTS
STURM GRAZ	6	3	1	2	9	12	10
GALATASARAY	6	2	2	2	10	13	8
RANGERS	6	2	2	2	10	7	8
MONACO	6	2	1	3	13	10	7

Kenny Miller scores against Monaco at Ibrox

UEFA CUP

First Qualifying Round - First Leg
Thursday, 10th August, 2000, Pittodrie Stadium, Aberdeen

ABERDEEN 1
Winters

BOHEMIANS 2
Maher, Molloy

Aberdeen: Esson, Jess, Winters, Stavrum, (Clark), Zerouali, (Derek Young), Dow, (Belabed), Rowson, Darren Young, McGuire, Perry, McNaughton
Substitutes not used: Preece, McAllister, O'Donaghue, Inglis
Bohemians: Russell, Bowman, Webb, Hunt, Maher, Hill, Morrison, (O'Connor), O'Brien, (Crowe), Molloy, O'Keefe, M. Dempsey
Substitutes not used: M. Dempsey, Doyle, O'Neill, Williamson, Caffrey
Referee: Kristinn Jakobsson (Iceland)
Attendance: 13,638

Josy Barthel Stadium, Luxembourg

JEUNESSE ESCH. 0

CELTIC 4
Moravcik (2), Larsson, Lambert

Jeunesse Esch: Van Rijswijck, Thill, Schaack, Lamborelle, Scuto, Amodio, Schauls, Betis, (Dillman), Kurtz, (Neis), Borbiconi, Wagner, (Meylender)
Substitutes not used: Logelin, Sabotic, Laruell, Muller

Celtic: Gould, Mahe, McNamara, (Healy), Valgaeren, Larsson, (Johnson), Sutton, Lambert, (Scheidt), Petta, Moravcik Riseth, Mjallby
Substitutes not used: Kerr, Berkovic, Tebily, Burchill
Referee: Georgios Kaznaferis (Greece)
Attendance: 3,587

Laugardalsvollur Stadium, Reykjavik

VESTMANNAEYJAR 0

HEART OF MIDLOTHIAN 2
Severin, Jackson

Vestmannaeyjar: Kristinsson, P. Gudmundsson, Aleksic, Stefansson, I. Sigurdsson, (Thorvaldsson), Bragason, Johannesson, Vidarsson, (M. Sigurdsson), Jonsson, (Moller), Mileta, Almarsson
Substitutes not used: K. Gudmundsson, Antonsson, Johannsson, Olafsson
Heart of Midlothian: Niemi, Pressley, Naysmith, Flögel, Severin, Tomaschek, Makel, (Locke), Fulton, McSwegan, (O'Neil), Cameron, Jackson, (Kirk)
Substitutes not used: Rousset, Murray, Juanjo, Simpson
Referee: Stephane Moulin (France)
Attendance: 861

First Qualifying Round - Second Leg
Thursday, 24th August, 2000 Tolka Park, Dublin

BOHEMIANS 0

ABERDEEN 1
Morrison (o.g.)

Bohemians: Russell, Bowman, (O'Connor), Webb, Hunt, Maher, Hill, Morrison, Caffrey, Molloy, O'Keeffe, M. Dempsey,
Substitutes not used: M. Dempsey, Crowe, O'Neill, Williamson, O'Brien, Doyle
Aberdeen: Esson, Whyte, (Belabed), Guntveit, Winters, Zerouali, Dow, (Rutkiewicz), Bernard, (Mackie), Rowson, Young, McGuire, McNaughton
Substitutes not used: Preece, McAllister, Perry, Inglis
Referee: Leif Sundell (Sweden)
Attendance: 7,450
(Bohemians won 2-1 on Aggregate)

Celtic Park, Glasgow

CELTIC 7
Burchill (3), Berkovic (2),
Riseth, Petrov

JEUNESSE ESCH. 0

Celtic: Gould, Berkovic, Lambert, (Miller), Petta, Tebily, Healy, Burchill, (Boyd), Riseth, Scheidt, Lynch, (Petrov), Mjallby,
Substitutes not used: Corr, Valgaeren, Larsson, Sutton
Juenesse Esch: Van Rijswijck, Schaack, Meylender, Lamborelle, Sabotic, Amodio, Schauls, Betis, (Dillmann), Kurtz, (Neis), Borbiconi, Wagner, (Thill)
Substitutes not used: Logelin, Laruell, Peiffer, Muller
Referee: Phillipe Leuba (Switzerland)
Attendance: 40,519
(Celtic won 11-0 on Aggregate)

Tynecastle Stadium, Edinburgh

HEART OF MIDLOTHIAN 3
McSwegan, Tomaschek, O'Neil

VESTMANNAEYJAR 0

Heart of Midlothian: Niemi, Pressley, Naysmith, Locke, (Murray), Severin, Tomaschek (Flögel), Juanjo, Fulton, McSwegan, (Kirk), Makel, O'Neil
Substitutes not used: McKenzie, James, Cameron, Simpson
Vestmannaeyjar: Kristinsson, P. Gudmundsson, Aleksic, Stefansson, I. Sigurdsson, (Moller), Bragason, Johannesson, M. Sigurdsson, (Johannsson), Jonsson, Mileta, (Vidarsson) Almarsson
Substitutes not used: K. Gudmundsson, Olafsson, Egilsson, Thorvaldsson
Referee: Antonio Almeida Costa (Portugal)
Attendance: 8,720
(Heart of Midlothian won 5-0 on Aggregate)

Henrik Larsson heads in the first goal against HJK Helsinki

First Round - First Leg
Thursday, 14th September, 2000, Celtic Park, Glasgow

CELTIC 2   **HJK HELSINKI 0**
Larsson (2)
Celtic: Gould, Boyd, Mahe, (Healy), McNamara, Valgaeren, Larsson, Sutton, Lambert, Petrov, Moravcik, (Berkovic), Mjallby
Substitutes not used: Kerr, Burchill, Riseth, Scheidt, Miller
HJK Helsinki: Viander, Turpeinen, Nylund, Eremenko, (Haarala), Kallio, Saarinen, Heikkinen, Hakanpaa, Kuivasto, Pires Vieira, (Moraes), Yla-Jussila, (Roiha)
Substitutes not used: Wallen, Kunnas, Kokkonen, Kopteff
Referee: Dietmar Drabek (Austria)
Attendance: 40,544

Gottlieb-Daimler Stadium, Stuttgart

VfB STUTTGART 1   **HEART OF MIDLOTHIAN 0**
Balakov
VfB Stuttgart: Hildebrand, Meissner, Thiam, Balakov, Carnell, Seitz, (Pinto), Soldo, Endress, (Schneider), Lisztes, Hosny, Dundee, (Ganea)
Substitutes not used: Trautner, Blank, Todt, Gleb
Heart of Midlothian: Niemi, Pressley, Naysmith, Severin, (Makel), Murray, Petric, Juanjo, Flögel, Jackson, (McSwegan), Cameron, (Neilson), Simpson
Substitutes not used: McKenzie, O'Neil, Kirk, James
Referee: Cosimo Bolognino (Italy)
Attendance: 9,845

First Round - Second Leg
Thursday, 28th September, 2000, Finnair Stadium, Helsinki

HJK HELSINKI 2   **CELTIC 1 (AET -2-0 After 90 Minutes)**
Roiha (2)   Sutton
HJK Helsinki: Viander, Turpeinen, Nylund, Eremenko, (Moraes), Kallio, Roiha, Saarinen, Heikkinen, Hakanpaa, (Yla-Jussila), Kuivasto, Kopteff, (Haarala)
Substitutes not used: Kunnas, Saastamoinen, Wallen, Kokkonen
Celtic: Gould, Boyd, (Riseth), McNamara, (Moravcik), Valgaeren, Larsson, Sutton, Berkovic, (Healy), Lambert, Petta, Petrov, Mjallby
Substitutes not used: Kerr, Tebily, Agathe, Smith
Referee: Ladislav Gadosi (Slovakia)
Attendance: 6,530
(Celtic won 3-2 on Aggregate)

Tynecastle Stadium, Edinburgh

HEART OF MIDLOTHIAN 3   **VfB STUTTGART 2**
Naysmith, Petric, Cameron   Hosny, Bordon
Heart of Midlothian: Niemi, Pressley, Naysmith, Murray, James, Petric, Juanjo, Flögel, Kirk, (McSwegan), Cameron, Locke, (Neilson)
Substitutes not used: Rousset, Jackson, Adam, O'Neil, Simpson
VfB Stuttgart: Hildebrand, Meissner, Bordon, Thiam, Balakov, (Blank), Schneider, Carnell, Seitz, (Pinto), Lisztes, (Todt), Hosny, Dundee
Substitutes not used: Trautner, Ganea, Gleb, Amanatidis
Referee: Bruno Derrien (France)
Attendance: 14,448
124 ***(Aggregate: 3-3 - VfB Stuttgart won on Away Goals Rule)***

Second Round - First Leg
Thursday, 26th October, 2000, Chaban-Delmas Stadium, Bordeaux

BORDEAUX 1   **CELTIC 1**
Dugarry   Larsson
Bordeaux: Rame, Roche, (Saveljic), Laslandes, (Bugnet), Legwinski, (Battles), Grenet, Sommeil, Diabate, Basto, Carreiro Resendes, Dugarry, Feindouno
Substitutes not used: Roux, Jemmali, Afanou, Alicarte
Celtic: Gould, Boyd, McNamara, Valgaeren, Larsson, Lambert, Petta, (Healy), Agathe, Petrov, Moravcik, Mjallby
Substitutes not used: Kerr, Stubbs, Berkovic, Johnson, Riseth, Smith
Referee: Tom Henning Ovrebo (Norway)
Attendance: 20,717

Second Round - Second Leg
Thursday, 9th November, 2000, Celtic Park, Glasgow

CELTIC 1   **BORDEAUX 2**
(AET - 1-1 After 90 Minutes)
Petta   Laslandes (2)
Celtic: Gould, Boyd, McNamara, (Healy), Valgaeren, Larsson, Sutton, Petta, (Berkovic), Agathe, Petrov, Moravcik, (Johnson), Mjallby
Substitutes not used: Kerr, Stubbs, Smith, Crainey
Bordeaux: Rame, Jemmali, (Saveljic), Bonnissel, Roche, Laslandes, Legwinski, Sommeil, Diabate, (Afanou), Battles, (Basto), Carreiro Resendes, Dugarry
Substitutes not used: Roux, Grenet, Alicarte, Bugnet
Referee: Sergey Shmolik (Belarus)
Attendance: 51,242
(Bordeaux won 3-2 on Aggregate)

Third Round - First Leg
Thursday, 30th November, 2000, Ibrox Stadium, Glasgow

RANGERS 1   **KAISERLAUTERN 0**
Albertz
Rangers: Klos, Amoruso, Numan, Ferguson, Mols, (Wallace), Albertz, Reyna, De Boer, (McCann), Konterman, Wilson, Miller, Vidmar
Kaiserlautern: G. Koch, Yakin, Ramzy, Hristov, Grammozis, Pettersson, Lokvenc, (Klose) Komljenovic, Djorkaeff, (Strasser), Buck, (Reich), H. Koch
Substitutes not used: Weidenfeller, Schjonberg, Marschall, Adzic
Referee: Gilles Veissiere (France)
Attendance: 47,279

Third Round - Second Leg
Tuesday, 7th December, 2000, Fritz-Walter Stadium, Kaiserlautern

KAISERLAUTERN 3   **RANGERS 0**
Klose, Buck, Lovenc
Kaiserlautern: G. Koch, Yakin, Ramzy, Hristov, (Basler), Grammozis, Lokvenc, Komljenovic, (Strasser), Djorkaeff, Buck, H. Koch, Klose, (Marschall)
Substitutes not used: Weidenfeller, Schjonberg, Reich, Adzic
Rangers: Klos, Ricksen, (McCann), Amoruso, Numan, Wallace, Albertz, Reyna, Konterman, Kerimoglu, (Dodds), Wilson, Miller, (Mols)
Substitutes not used: Christiansen, De Boer, Porrini, Vidmar
Referee: Knud Erik Fisker (Denmark)
Attendance: 25,757
(Kaiserlautern won 3-1 on Aggregate)

Saturday, August 4th, 2001
BELL'S SCOTTISH LEAGUE FIRST DIVISION
Airdrieonians v. Raith Rovers
Clyde v. Inverness Cal. Th.
Falkirk v. Ayr United
Partick Thistle v. St. Mirren
Ross County v. Arbroath
BELL'S SCOTTISH LEAGUE SECOND DIVISION
Berwick Rangers v. Alloa Athletic
Forfar Athletic v. Clydebank
Hamilton Academical v. Queen of the South
Morton v. Stenhousemuir
Stranraer v. Cowdenbeath
BELL'S SCOTTISH LEAGUE THIRD DIVISION
Dumbarton v. Brechin City
East Fife v. Albion Rovers
Elgin City v. East Stirlingshire
Montrose v. Queen's Park
Stirling Albion v. Peterhead

Saturday, August 11th, 2001
BELL'S SCOTTISH LEAGUE FIRST DIVISION
Arbroath v. Airdrieonians
Ayr United v. Ross County
Inverness Cal. Th. v. Falkirk
Raith Rovers v. Partick Thistle
St. Mirren v. Clyde
BELL'S SCOTTISH LEAGUE SECOND DIVISION
Alloa Athletic v. Morton
Clydebank v. Hamilton Academical
Cowdenbeath v. Berwick Rangers
Queen of the South v. Forfar Athletic
Stenhousemuir v. Stranraer
BELL'S SCOTTISH LEAGUE THIRD DIVISION
Albion Rovers v. Stirling Albion
Brechin City v. East Fife
East Stirlingshire v. Montrose
Peterhead v. Dumbarton
Queen's Park v. Elgin City

Saturday, August 18th, 2001
BELL'S SCOTTISH LEAGUE FIRST DIVISION
Airdrieonians v. Ayr United
Clyde v. Arbroath
Falkirk v. St. Mirren
Partick Thistle v. Inverness Cal. Th.
Ross County v. Raith Rovers
BELL'S SCOTTISH LEAGUE SECOND DIVISION
Berwick Rangers v. Clydebank
Forfar Athletic v. Stenhousemuir
Hamilton Academical v. Cowdenbeath
Morton v. Queen of the South
Stranraer v. Alloa Athletic
BELL'S SCOTTISH LEAGUE THIRD DIVISION
Dumbarton v. Queen's Park
East Fife v. East Stirlingshire
Elgin City v. Albion Rovers
Montrose v. Peterhead
Stirling Albion v. Brechin City

Saturday, August 25th, 2001
BELL'S SCOTTISH LEAGUE FIRST DIVISION
Arbroath v. Partick Thistle
Ayr United v. Raith Rovers
Falkirk v. Clyde
Ross County v. Airdrieonians
St. Mirren v. Inverness Cal. Th.
BELL'S SCOTTISH LEAGUE SECOND DIVISION
Cowdenbeath v. Alloa Athletic
Hamilton Academical v. Forfar Athletic
Morton v. Stranraer
Queen of the South v. Clydebank
Stenhousemuir v. Berwick Rangers

BELL'S SCOTTISH LEAGUE THIRD DIVISION
Brechin City v. Albion Rovers
Dumbarton v. Montrose
East Fife v. Peterhead
Elgin City v. Stirling Albion
Queen's Park v. East Stirlingshire

Sunday, September 2nd, 2001
BELL'S SCOTTISH LEAGUE SECOND DIVISION
Berwick Rangers v. Morton
Forfar Athletic v. Alloa Athletic
Queen of the South v. Stenhousemuir

Saturday, September 8th, 2001
BELL'S SCOTTISH LEAGUE FIRST DIVISION
Airdrieonians v. St. Mirren
Clyde v. Ross County
Inverness Cal. Th. v. Arbroath
Partick Thistle v. Ayr United
Raith Rovers v. Falkirk
BELL'S SCOTTISH LEAGUE SECOND DIVISION
Alloa Athletic v. Stenhousemuir
Berwick Rangers v. Hamilton Academical
Clydebank v. Morton
Forfar Athletic v. Cowdenbeath
Stranraer v. Queen of the South
BELL'S SCOTTISH LEAGUE THIRD DIVISION
Albion Rovers v. Queen's Park
East Stirlingshire v. Dumbarton
Montrose v. Brechin City
Peterhead v. Elgin City
Stirling Albion v. East Fife

Saturday, September 15th, 2001
BELL'S SCOTTISH LEAGUE FIRST DIVISION
Airdrieonians v. Falkirk
Ayr United v. St. Mirren
Partick Thistle v. Clyde
Raith Rovers v. Arbroath
Ross County v. Inverness Cal. Th.
BELL'S SCOTTISH LEAGUE SECOND DIVISION
Alloa Athletic v. Clydebank
Cowdenbeath v. Queen of the South
Morton v. Forfar Athletic
Stenhousemuir v. Hamilton Academical
Stranraer v. Berwick Rangers
BELL'S SCOTTISH LEAGUE THIRD DIVISION
Dumbarton v. Albion Rovers
East Stirlingshire v. Peterhead
Elgin City v. East Fife
Montrose v. Stirling Albion
Queen's Park v. Brechin City

Tuesday, September 18th, 2001
BELL'S SCOTTISH LEAGUE FIRST DIVISION
Arbroath v. Ayr United
Clyde v. Airdrieonians
Falkirk v. Partick Thistle
St. Mirren v. Ross County
BELL'S SCOTTISH LEAGUE SECOND DIVISION
Hamilton Academical v. Stranraer
BELL'S SCOTTISH LEAGUE THIRD DIVISION
Albion Rovers v. East Stirlingshire
Brechin City v. Elgin City
East Fife v. Montrose

Wednesday, September 19th, 2001
BELL'S SCOTTISH LEAGUE FIRST DIVISION
Inverness Cal. Th. v. Raith Rovers
BELL'S SCOTTISH LEAGUE SECOND DIVISION
Clydebank v. Cowdenbeath
BELL'S SCOTTISH LEAGUE THIRD DIVISION
Stirling Albion v. Dumbarton

Saturday, September 22nd, 2001
BELL'S SCOTTISH LEAGUE FIRST DIVISION
Airdrieonians v. Inverness Cal. Th.
Arbroath v. Falkirk
Raith Rovers v. St. Mirren
Ross County v. Partick Thistle
BELL'S SCOTTISH LEAGUE SECOND DIVISION
Alloa Athletic v. Hamilton Academical
Berwick Rangers v. Queen of the South
Morton v. Cowdenbeath
Stenhousemuir v. Clydebank
Stranraer v. Forfar Athletic
BELL'S SCOTTISH LEAGUE THIRD DIVISION
Dumbarton v. Elgin City
East Stirlingshire v. Stirling Albion
Montrose v. Albion Rovers
Peterhead v. Brechin City
Queen's Park v. East Fife

Sunday, September 23rd, 2001
BELL'S SCOTTISH LEAGUE FIRST DIVISION
Ayr United v. Clyde

Saturday, September 29th, 2001
BELL'S SCOTTISH LEAGUE FIRST DIVISION
Clyde v. Raith Rovers
Falkirk v. Ross County
Inverness Cal. Th. v. Ayr United
Partick Thistle v. Airdrieonians
St. Mirren v. Arbroath
BELL'S SCOTTISH LEAGUE SECOND DIVISION
Clydebank v. Stranraer
Cowdenbeath v. Stenhousemuir
Forfar Athletic v. Berwick Rangers
Hamilton Academical v. Morton
Queen of the South v. Alloa Athletic
BELL'S SCOTTISH LEAGUE THIRD DIVISION
Albion Rovers v. Peterhead
Brechin City v. East Stirlingshire
East Fife v. Dumbarton
Elgin City v. Montrose
Stirling Albion v. Queen's Park

Saturday, October 6th, 2001
BELL'S SCOTTISH LEAGUE THIRD DIVISION
Peterhead v. Queen's Park

Saturday, October 13th, 2001
BELL'S SCOTTISH LEAGUE FIRST DIVISION
Arbroath v. Ross County
Ayr United v. Falkirk
Inverness Cal. Th. v. Clyde
Raith Rovers v. Airdrieonians
St. Mirren v. Partick Thistle
BELL'S SCOTTISH LEAGUE SECOND DIVISION
Alloa Athletic v. Berwick Rangers
Clydebank v. Forfar Athletic
Cowdenbeath v. Stranraer
Queen of the South v. Hamilton Academical
Stenhousemuir v. Morton
BELL'S SCOTTISH LEAGUE THIRD DIVISION
Albion Rovers v. East Fife
Brechin City v. Dumbarton
East Stirlingshire v. Elgin City
Peterhead v. Stirling Albion
Queen's Park v. Montrose

Saturday, October 20th, 2001
BELL'S SCOTTISH LEAGUE FIRST DIVISION
Airdrieonians v. Arbroath
Clyde v. St. Mirren
Falkirk v. Inverness Cal. Th.
Partick Thistle v. Raith Rovers
Ross County v. Ayr United

BELL'S SCOTTISH LEAGUE SECOND DIVISION
Berwick Rangers v. Cowdenbeath
Forfar Athletic v. Queen of the South
Hamilton Academical v. Clydebank
Morton v. Alloa Athletic
Stranraer v. Stenhousemuir
BELL'S SCOTTISH LEAGUE THIRD DIVISION
Dumbarton v. Peterhead
East Fife v. Brechin City
Elgin City v. Queen's Park
Montrose v. East Stirlingshire
Stirling Albion v. Albion Rovers

Saturday, October 27th, 2001
BELL'S SCOTTISH LEAGUE FIRST DIVISION
Arbroath v. Inverness Cal. Th.
Ayr United v. Partick Thistle
Falkirk v. Raith Rovers
Ross County v. Clyde
St. Mirren v. Airdrieonians
BELL'S SCOTTISH LEAGUE SECOND DIVISION
Cowdenbeath v. Forfar Athletic
Hamilton Academical v. Berwick Rangers
Morton v. Clydebank
Queen of the South v. Stranraer
Stenhousemuir v. Alloa Athletic
BELL'S SCOTTISH LEAGUE THIRD DIVISION
Brechin City v. Montrose
Dumbarton v. East Stirlingshire
East Fife v. Stirling Albion
Elgin City v. Peterhead
Queen's Park v. Albion Rovers

Saturday, November 3rd, 2001
BELL'S SCOTTISH LEAGUE FIRST DIVISION
Airdrieonians v. Ross County
Clyde v. Falkirk
Inverness Cal. Th. v. St. Mirren
Partick Thistle v. Arbroath
Raith Rovers v. Ayr United
BELL'S SCOTTISH LEAGUE SECOND DIVISION
Alloa Athletic v. Cowdenbeath
Berwick Rangers v. Stenhousemuir
Clydebank v. Queen of the South
Forfar Athletic v. Hamilton Academical
Stranraer v. Morton
BELL'S SCOTTISH LEAGUE THIRD DIVISION
Albion Rovers v. Brechin City
East Stirlingshire v. Queen's Park
Montrose v. Dumbarton
Peterhead v. East Fife
Stirling Albion v. Elgin City

Saturday, November 10th, 2001
BELL'S SCOTTISH LEAGUE FIRST DIVISION
Airdrieonians v. Clyde
Ayr United v. Arbroath
Partick Thistle v. Falkirk
Raith Rovers v. Inverness Cal. Th.
Ross County v. St. Mirren
BELL'S SCOTTISH LEAGUE SECOND DIVISION
Berwick Rangers v. Stranraer
Clydebank v. Alloa Athletic
Forfar Athletic v. Morton
Hamilton Academical v. Stenhousemuir
Queen of the South v. Cowdenbeath
BELL'S SCOTTISH LEAGUE THIRD DIVISION
Albion Rovers v. Dumbarton
Brechin City v. Queen's Park
East Fife v. Elgin City
Peterhead v. East Stirlingshire
Stirling Albion v. Montrose

Saturday, November 17th, 2001
BELL'S SCOTTISH LEAGUE FIRST DIVISION
Arbroath v. Raith Rovers
Clyde v. Partick Thistle
Falkirk v. Airdrieonians
Inverness Cal. Th. v. Ross County
St. Mirren v. Ayr United

Saturday, November 24th, 2001
BELL'S SCOTTISH LEAGUE FIRST DIVISION
Airdrieonians v. Partick Thistle
Arbroath v. St. Mirren
Ayr United v. Inverness Cal. Th.
Raith Rovers v. Clyde
Ross County v. Falkirk
BELL'S SCOTTISH LEAGUE SECOND DIVISION
Alloa Athletic v. Forfar Athletic
Cowdenbeath v. Clydebank
Morton v. Berwick Rangers
Stenhousemuir v. Queen of the South
Stranraer v. Hamilton Academical
BELL'S SCOTTISH LEAGUE THIRD DIVISION
Dumbarton v. Stirling Albion
East Stirlingshire v. Albion Rovers
Elgin City v. Brechin City
Montrose v. East Fife
Queen's Park v. Peterhead

Saturday, December 1st, 2001
BELL'S SCOTTISH LEAGUE FIRST DIVISION
Clyde v. Ayr United
Falkirk v. Arbroath
Inverness Cal. Th. v. Airdrieonians
Partick Thistle v. Ross County
St. Mirren v. Raith Rovers
BELL'S SCOTTISH LEAGUE SECOND DIVISION
Clydebank v. Stenhousemuir
Cowdenbeath v. Morton
Forfar Athletic v. Stranraer
Hamilton Academical v. Alloa Athletic
Queen of the South v. Berwick Rangers
BELL'S SCOTTISH LEAGUE THIRD DIVISION
Albion Rovers v. Montrose
Brechin City v. Peterhead
East Fife v. Queen's Park
Elgin City v. Dumbarton
Stirling Albion v. East Stirlingshire

Saturday, December 8th, 2001
BELL'S SCOTTISH LEAGUE FIRST DIVISION
Arbroath v. Clyde
Ayr United v. Airdrieonians
Inverness Cal. Th. v. Partick Thistle
Raith Rovers v. Ross County
St. Mirren v. Falkirk

Saturday, December 15th, 2001
BELL'S SCOTTISH LEAGUE FIRST DIVISION
Airdrieonians v. Raith Rovers
Clyde v. Inverness Cal. Th.
Falkirk v. Ayr United
Partick Thistle v. St. Mirren
Ross County v. Arbroath
BELL'S SCOTTISH LEAGUE SECOND DIVISION
Alloa Athletic v. Queen of the South
Berwick Rangers v. Forfar Athletic
Morton v. Hamilton Academical
Stenhousemuir v. Cowdenbeath
Stranraer v. Clydebank
BELL'S SCOTTISH LEAGUE THIRD DIVISION
Dumbarton v. East Fife
East Stirlingshire v. Brechin City
Montrose v. Elgin City
Peterhead v. Albion Rovers
Queen's Park v. Stirling Albion

Saturday, December 22nd, 2001
BELL'S SCOTTISH LEAGUE FIRST DIVISION
Inverness Cal. Th. v. Arbroath
BELL'S SCOTTISH LEAGUE SECOND DIVISION
Alloa Athletic v. Stranraer
BELL'S SCOTTISH LEAGUE THIRD DIVISION
Peterhead v. Montrose

Wednesday, December 26th, 2001
BELL'S SCOTTISH LEAGUE FIRST DIVISION
Airdrieonians v. St. Mirren
Clyde v. Ross County
Partick Thistle v. Ayr United
Raith Rovers v. Falkirk
BELL'S SCOTTISH LEAGUE SECOND DIVISION
Clydebank v. Berwick Rangers
Cowdenbeath v. Hamilton Academical
Queen of the South v. Morton
Stenhousemuir v. Forfar Athletic
BELL'S SCOTTISH LEAGUE THIRD DIVISION
Albion Rovers v. Elgin City
Brechin City v. Stirling Albion
East Stirlingshire v. East Fife
Queen's Park v. Dumbarton

Saturday, December 29th, 2001
BELL'S SCOTTISH LEAGUE FIRST DIVISION
Arbroath v. Partick Thistle
Ayr United v. Raith Rovers
Falkirk v. Clyde
Ross County v. Airdrieonians
St. Mirren v. Inverness Cal. Th.
BELL'S SCOTTISH LEAGUE SECOND DIVISION
Berwick Rangers v. Alloa Athletic
Forfar Athletic v. Clydebank
Hamilton Academical v. Queen of the South
Morton v. Stenhousemuir
Stranraer v. Cowdenbeath
BELL'S SCOTTISH LEAGUE THIRD DIVISION
Dumbarton v. Brechin City
East Fife v. Albion Rovers
Elgin City v. East Stirlingshire
Montrose v. Queen's Park
Stirling Albion v. Peterhead

Wednesday, January 2nd, 2002
BELL'S SCOTTISH LEAGUE FIRST DIVISION
Airdrieonians v. Falkirk
Ayr United v. St. Mirren
Partick Thistle v. Clyde
Raith Rovers v. Arbroath
Ross County v. Inverness Cal. Th.
BELL'S SCOTTISH LEAGUE SECOND DIVISION
Alloa Athletic v. Stenhousemuir
Berwick Rangers v. Hamilton Academical
Clydebank v. Morton
Forfar Athletic v. Cowdenbeath
Stranraer v. Queen of the South
BELL'S SCOTTISH LEAGUE THIRD DIVISION
Albion Rovers v. Queen's Park
East Stirlingshire v. Dumbarton
Montrose v. Brechin City
Peterhead v. Elgin City
Stirling Albion v. East Fife

Saturday, January 12th, 2002
BELL'S SCOTTISH LEAGUE FIRST DIVISION
Arbroath v. Ayr United
Clyde v. Airdrieonians
Falkirk v. Partick Thistle
Inverness Cal. Th. v. Raith Rovers
St. Mirren v. Ross County
BELL'S SCOTTISH LEAGUE SECOND DIVISION
Cowdenbeath v. Alloa Athletic
Hamilton Academical v. Forfar Athletic
Morton v. Stranraer
Queen of the South v. Clydebank
Stenhousemuir v. Berwick Rangers
BELL'S SCOTTISH LEAGUE THIRD DIVISION
Brechin City v. Albion Rovers
Dumbarton v. Montrose
East Fife v. Peterhead
Elgin City v. Stirling Albion
Queen's Park v. East Stirlingshire

Saturday, January 19th, 2002
BELL'S SCOTTISH LEAGUE FIRST DIVISION
Airdrieonians v. Inverness Cal. Th.
Arbroath v. Falkirk
Ayr United v. Clyde
Raith Rovers v. St. Mirren
Ross County v. Partick Thistle
BELL'S SCOTTISH LEAGUE SECOND DIVISION
Berwick Rangers v. Morton
Clydebank v. Cowdenbeath
Forfar Athletic v. Alloa Athletic
Hamilton Academical v. Stranraer
Queen of the South v. Stenhousemuir
BELL'S SCOTTISH LEAGUE THIRD DIVISION
Albion Rovers v. East Stirlingshire
Brechin City v. Elgin City
East Fife v. Montrose
Queen's Park v. Peterhead
Stirling Albion v. Dumbarton

Saturday, January 26th, 2002
BELL'S SCOTTISH LEAGUE SECOND DIVISION
Alloa Athletic v. Clydebank
Cowdenbeath v. Queen of the South
Morton v. Forfar Athletic
Stenhousemuir v. Hamilton Academical
Stranraer v. Berwick Rangers
BELL'S SCOTTISH LEAGUE THIRD DIVISION
Dumbarton v. Albion Rovers
East Stirlingshire v. Peterhead
Elgin City v. East Fife
Montrose v. Stirling Albion
Queen's Park v. Brechin City

Saturday, February 2nd, 2002
BELL'S SCOTTISH LEAGUE FIRST DIVISION
Clyde v. Raith Rovers
Falkirk v. Ross County
Inverness Cal. Th. v. Ayr United
Partick Thistle v. Airdrieonians
St. Mirren v. Arbroath
BELL'S SCOTTISH LEAGUE SECOND DIVISION
Clydebank v. Stranraer
Cowdenbeath v. Stenhousemuir
Forfar Athletic v. Berwick Rangers
Hamilton Academical v. Morton
Queen of the South v. Alloa Athletic
BELL'S SCOTTISH LEAGUE THIRD DIVISION
Albion Rovers v. Peterhead
Brechin City v. East Stirlingshire
East Fife v. Dumbarton
Elgin City v. Montrose
Stirling Albion v. Queen's Park

Saturday, February 9th, 2002
BELL'S SCOTTISH LEAGUE FIRST DIVISION
Airdrieonians v. Ayr United
Clyde v. Arbroath
Falkirk v. St. Mirren
Partick Thistle v. Inverness Cal. Th.
Ross County v. Raith Rovers
BELL'S SCOTTISH LEAGUE SECOND DIVISION
Alloa Athletic v. Hamilton Academical
Berwick Rangers v. Queen of the South
Morton v. Cowdenbeath
Stenhousemuir v. Clydebank
Stranraer v. Forfar Athletic
BELL'S SCOTTISH LEAGUE THIRD DIVISION
Dumbarton v. Elgin City
East Stirlingshire v. Stirling Albion
Montrose v. Albion Rovers
Peterhead v. Brechin City
Queen's Park v. East Fife

Saturday, February 16th, 2002
BELL'S SCOTTISH LEAGUE FIRST DIVISION
Arbroath v. Airdrieonians
Ayr United v. Ross County
Inverness Cal. Th. v. Falkirk
Raith Rovers v. Partick Thistle
St. Mirren v. Clyde

BELL'S SCOTTISH LEAGUE SECOND DIVISION
Alloa Athletic v. Morton
Clydebank v. Hamilton Academical
Cowdenbeath v. Berwick Rangers
Queen of the South v. Forfar Athletic
Stenhousemuir v. Stranraer
BELL'S SCOTTISH LEAGUE THIRD DIVISION
Albion Rovers v. Stirling Albion
Brechin City v. East Fife
East Stirlingshire v. Montrose
Peterhead v. Dumbarton
Queen's Park v. Elgin City

Saturday, February 23rd, 2002
BELL'S SCOTTISH LEAGUE SECOND DIVISION
Berwick Rangers v. Clydebank
Forfar Athletic v. Stenhousemuir
Hamilton Academical v. Cowdenbeath
Morton v. Queen of the South
Stranraer v. Alloa Athletic
BELL'S SCOTTISH LEAGUE THIRD DIVISION
Dumbarton v. Queen's Park
East Fife v. East Stirlingshire
Elgin City v. Albion Rovers
Montrose v. Peterhead
Stirling Albion v. Brechin City

Saturday, March 2nd, 2002
BELL'S SCOTTISH LEAGUE FIRST DIVISION
Airdrieonians v. Ross County
Clyde v. Falkirk
Inverness Cal. Th. v. St. Mirren
Partick Thistle v. Arbroath
Raith Rovers v. Ayr United
BELL'S SCOTTISH LEAGUE SECOND DIVISION
Alloa Athletic v. Cowdenbeath
Berwick Rangers v. Stenhousemuir
Clydebank v. Queen of the South
Forfar Athletic v. Hamilton Academical
Stranraer v. Morton
BELL'S SCOTTISH LEAGUE THIRD DIVISION
Albion Rovers v. Brechin City
East Stirlingshire v. Queen's Park
Montrose v. Dumbarton
Peterhead v. East Fife
Stirling Albion v. Elgin City

Saturday, March 9th, 2002
BELL'S SCOTTISH LEAGUE FIRST DIVISION
Arbroath v. Inverness Cal. Th.
Ayr United v. Partick Thistle
Falkirk v. Raith Rovers
Ross County v. Clyde
St. Mirren v. Airdrieonians
BELL'S SCOTTISH LEAGUE SECOND DIVISION
Cowdenbeath v. Forfar Athletic
Hamilton Academical v. Berwick Rangers
Morton v. Clydebank
Queen of the South v. Stranraer
Stenhousemuir v. Alloa Athletic
BELL'S SCOTTISH LEAGUE THIRD DIVISION
Brechin City v. Montrose
Dumbarton v. East Stirlingshire
East Fife v. Stirling Albion
Elgin City v. Peterhead
Queen's Park v. Albion Rovers

Saturday, March 16th, 2002
BELL'S SCOTTISH LEAGUE FIRST DIVISION
Airdrieonians v. Clyde
Ayr United v. Arbroath
Partick Thistle v. Falkirk
Raith Rovers v. Inverness Cal. Th.
Ross County v. St. Mirren
BELL'S SCOTTISH LEAGUE SECOND DIVISION
Berwick Rangers v. Stranraer
Clydebank v. Alloa Athletic
Forfar Athletic v. Morton
Hamilton Academical v. Stenhousemuir
Queen of the South v. Cowdenbeath

BELL'S SCOTTISH LEAGUE THIRD DIVISION
Albion Rovers v. Dumbarton
Brechin City v. Queen's Park
East Fife v. Elgin City
Peterhead v. East Stirlingshire
Stirling Albion v. Montrose

Saturday, March 23rd, 2002
BELL'S SCOTTISH LEAGUE FIRST DIVISION
Arbroath v. Raith Rovers
Clyde v. Partick Thistle
Falkirk v. Airdrieonians
Inverness Cal. Th. v. Ross County
St. Mirren v. Ayr United
BELL'S SCOTTISH LEAGUE SECOND DIVISION
Alloa Athletic v. Forfar Athletic
Cowdenbeath v. Clydebank
Morton v. Berwick Rangers
Stenhousemuir v. Queen of the South
Stranraer v. Hamilton Academical
BELL'S SCOTTISH LEAGUE THIRD DIVISION
Dumbarton v. Stirling Albion
East Stirlingshire v. Albion Rovers
Elgin City v. Brechin City
Montrose v. East Fife
Peterhead v. Queen's Park

Saturday, March 30th, 2002
BELL'S SCOTTISH LEAGUE FIRST DIVISION
Clyde v. Ayr United
Falkirk v. Arbroath
Inverness Cal. Th. v. Airdrieonians
Partick Thistle v. Ross County
St. Mirren v. Raith Rovers
BELL'S SCOTTISH LEAGUE SECOND DIVISION
Clydebank v. Stenhousemuir
Cowdenbeath v. Morton
Forfar Athletic v. Stranraer
Hamilton Academical v. Alloa Athletic
Queen of the South v. Berwick Rangers
BELL'S SCOTTISH LEAGUE THIRD DIVISION
Albion Rovers v. Montrose
Brechin City v. Peterhead
East Fife v. Queen's Park
Elgin City v. Dumbarton
Stirling Albion v. East Stirlingshire

Saturday, April 6th, 2002
BELL'S SCOTTISH LEAGUE FIRST DIVISION
Airdrieonians v. Partick Thistle
Arbroath v. St. Mirren
Ayr United v. Inverness Cal. Th.
Raith Rovers v. Clyde
Ross County v. Falkirk
BELL'S SCOTTISH LEAGUE SECOND DIVISION
Alloa Athletic v. Queen of the South
Berwick Rangers v. Forfar Athletic
Morton v. Hamilton Academical
Stenhousemuir v. Cowdenbeath
Stranraer v. Clydebank
BELL'S SCOTTISH LEAGUE THIRD DIVISION
Dumbarton v. East Fife
East Stirlingshire v. Brechin City
Montrose v. Elgin City
Peterhead v. Albion Rovers
Queen's Park v. Stirling Albion

Saturday, April 13th, 2002
BELL'S SCOTTISH LEAGUE FIRST DIVISION
Arbroath v. Ross County
Ayr United v. Falkirk
Inverness Cal. Th. v. Clyde
Raith Rovers v. Airdrieonians
St. Mirren v. Partick Thistle
BELL'S SCOTTISH LEAGUE SECOND DIVISION
Alloa Athletic v. Berwick Rangers
Clydebank v. Forfar Athletic
Cowdenbeath v. Stranraer
Queen of the South v. Hamilton Academical
Stenhousemuir v. Morton

BELL'S SCOTTISH LEAGUE THIRD DIVISION
Albion Rovers v. East Fife
Brechin City v. Dumbarton
East Stirlingshire v. Elgin City
Peterhead v. Stirling Albion
Queen's Park v. Montrose

Saturday, April 20th, 2002
BELL'S SCOTTISH LEAGUE FIRST DIVISION
Airdrieonians v. Arbroath
Clyde v. St. Mirren
Falkirk v. Inverness Cal. Th.
Partick Thistle v. Raith Rovers
Ross County v. Ayr United
BELL'S SCOTTISH LEAGUE SECOND DIVISION
Berwick Rangers v. Cowdenbeath
Forfar Athletic v. Queen of the South
Hamilton Academical v. Clydebank
Morton v. Alloa Athletic
Stranraer v. Stenhousemuir
BELL'S SCOTTISH LEAGUE THIRD DIVISION
Dumbarton v. Peterhead
East Fife v. Brechin City
Elgin City v. Queen's Park
Montrose v. East Stirlingshire
Stirling Albion v. Albion Rovers

Saturday, April 27th, 2002
BELL'S SCOTTISH LEAGUE FIRST DIVISION
Arbroath v. Clyde
Ayr United v. Airdrieonians
Inverness Cal. Th. v. Partick Thistle
Raith Rovers v. Ross County
St. Mirren v. Falkirk
BELL'S SCOTTISH LEAGUE SECOND DIVISION
Alloa Athletic v. Stranraer
Clydebank v. Berwick Rangers
Cowdenbeath v. Hamilton Academical
Queen of the South v. Morton
Stenhousemuir v. Forfar Athletic
BELL'S SCOTTISH LEAGUE THIRD DIVISION
Albion Rovers v. Elgin City
Brechin City v. Stirling Albion
East Stirlingshire v. East Fife
Peterhead v. Montrose
Queen's Park v. Dumbarton

© The Scottish Football League 2001
The copyrighted fixtures may not
be reproduced in whole or in
part, stored in a retrieval system,
or transmitted in any form, or by
any means, electronic,
mechanical, photocopying,
recording, via the internet or
otherwise without the prior
permission of The Scottish
Football League.
The Scottish Football League
reserves the right to change any
of these fixtures, or the date of
any of these fixtures, without
notice and without liability.

The CIS Insurance
Cup Draw Season 2001/02

1st Round

Berwick Rangers	-v-	Partick Thistle
Raith Rovers	-v-	Montrose
Stirling Albion	-v-	Cowdenbeath
Alloa Athletic	-v-	Peterhead
Forfar Athletic	-v-	Falkirk
East Stirlingshire	-v-	Queen of the South
Clyde	-v-	Stenhousemuir
Queen's Park	-v-	Hamilton Academical
East Fife	-v-	Arbroath
Airdrieonians	-v-	Morton
Elgin City	-v-	Stranraer
Albion Rovers	-v-	Inverness Caledonian Thistle
Dumbarton	-v-	Clydebank
Ross County	-v-	Brechin City

Above ties to be played on Tuesday, 11th September, 2001 or Wednesday, 12th September 2001

2nd Round

....	-v-	....
....	-v-	....
....	-v-	....
....	-v-	....
....	-v-	....
....	-v-	....
....	-v-	....
....	-v-	....
....	-v-	....
....	-v-	....

Ties to be played on Tuesday, 25th or Wednesday, 26th September, 2001

3rd Round

......	-v-	......
......	-v-	......
......	-v-	......
......	-v-	......
......	-v-	......
......	-v-	......
......	-v-	......
......	-v-	......

Ties to be played on Tuesday, 9th or Wednesday, 10th October, 2001

4th Round

......	-v-	......
......	-v-	......
......	-v-	......
......	-v-	......

Ties to be played on Tuesday, 27th or Wednesday, 28th November, 2001

Semi–Finals

......	-v-	......
......	-v-	......

Ties to be played on Tuesday, 5th and Wednesday, 6th February, 2002

THE CIS INSURANCE CUP FINAL

......	-v-	......

To be played on Sunday, 17th March, 2002

In the event of a draw after normal time in all rounds, extra time of 30 minutes (i.e. 15 minutes each way) will take place and thereafter, if necessary, Kicks from the Penalty Mark in accordance with the Rules laid down by The International Football Association Board will be taken.

The Bell's Challenge Cup Draw
Season 2001/02

1st Round

BELL'S
CHALLENGE
CUP

Airdrieonians	-v-	Queen of the South
Cowdenbeath	-v-	Ross County
Falkirk	-v-	Arbroath
East Fife	-v-	Raith Rovers
Berwick Rangers	-v-	Elgin City
Stenhousemuir	-v-	Stranraer
East Stirlingshire	-v-	Alloa Athletic
Morton	-v-	Clyde
Brechin City	-v-	Stirling Albion
Peterhead	-v-	Hamilton Academical
St. Mirren	-v-	Ayr United
Inverness Caledonian Thistle	-v-	Forfar Athletic
Albion Rovers	-v-	Montrose
Partick Thistle	-v-	Queen's Park

Byes: Dumbarton and Clydebank

Above ties to be played on Tuesday, 7th August, 2001

2nd Round

-v-
-v-
-v-
-v-
-v-
-v-
-v-
-v-

Ties to be played on Tuesday, 14th August, 2001

3rd Round

-v-
-v-
-v-
-v-

Ties to be played on Tuesday, 21st August, 2001

Semi-Finals

-v-
-v-

Ties to be played on Tuesday, 28th August, 2001

THE BELL'S CHALLENGE CUP FINAL

-v-

To be played on Sunday, 14th October, 2001

In the event of a draw after normal time in all rounds, extra time of 30 minutes (i.e. 15 minutes each way) will take place and thereafter, if necessary, Kicks from the Penalty Mark in accordance with the Rules laid down by The International Football Association Board will be taken.

ALLOCATION OF SPONSORSHIP MONIES
DURING 2001/02

DISTRIBUTION OF BELL'S SCOTTISH FOOTBALL LEAGUE CHAMPIONSHIP MONIES

First Division	£17,000 per club
Second Division	£10,000 per club
Third Division	£8,500 per club

DISTRIBUTION OF CIS INSURANCE CUP MONIES

1st Round Losers	14 x £7,000
2nd Round Losers	12 x £9,500
3rd Round Losers	8 x £16,500
4th Round Losers	4 x £26,000
Semi-Final Losers	2 x £32,000
Runner-up	£60,000
Winner	£80,000

DISTRIBUTION OF BELL'S CHALLENGE CUP MONIES

1st Round Losers	14 x £3,000
2nd Round Losers	8 x £4,000
3rd Round Losers	4 x £5,000
Semi-Final Losers	2 x £6,000
Runner-up	£12,000
Winner	£16,000

When you turn the pages of your glossy, colourful, immaculately produced matchday programme, you will see no evidence of the blood, sweat and tears that went into producing its pristine pages. Such are the skills and dedication of the programme producers, that those stains of strife fall everywhere but the final pages.

A slightly melodramatic – if not entirely exaggerated – description of the process of producing a matchday programme, but one that will be more familiar to beleaguered editors, burning the midnight oil before a printer's deadline, than the casual acceptance of the fortnightly offering by programme-buying fans.

A match programme is like a football referee – an essential part of the fabric of the game, but only noticed when something goes wrong. The little faux pas which sometimes escalate into major issues, fuelled by an eager media for once grateful to be judge rather than judged, are rare slip-ups in a rigorous process of ensuring that the pearls of wisdom cast amongst us each Saturday are accurate and inoffensive.

Contrasting images of the programme editor were illustrated in the early 1960s by two clubs formerly resident in Glasgow's South Side. The Clyde programme editor was seen to be dictating his copy at a leisurely pace, a luxury afforded to only the elite of programme compilers, and on rare occasions during a season at that.

In the aftermath of a glorious victory, or a long run of good results, a match

programme is a positive joy to write. There is only good news to impart, after all. Players and managers are falling over themselves to be quoted; laughter and humour fills the pavilion; and the fan-with-the-typewriter who writes the programme is full of the joys of success.

Contrast that with six straight defeats, not a hint of a goal scored, and turmoil on and off the park. Having put off the evil moment to the very last, the editor switches on his computer screen on a Tuesday night – and stares at a blank screen. Perspiration compensates for the absent inspiration, and by 1 a.m. ,

In a previous, programme editing existence, this writer sat with a contented smile as a Cup tie drew to a conclusion, his team comfortably nursing a one-goal lead. Ten minutes from time, an equaliser. "Bang goes the rest of my weekend" as the benumbed brain started to plan a programme for Tuesday's replay. A late winner for the opposition brought somewhat conflicting emotions. Out of the Cup perhaps, but at least the night out with the wife (and domestic harmony) survived.

Holidays, eagerly anticipated by the majority, are dreaded by editors. They

The Perils of Programme Production

he bears a close resemblance to the Third Lanark programme editor, labouring over a sweat-lashed keyboard.

For every loser, there has to be a winner, a truism which serves as little comfort to an editor starved of good news with a deadline looming, every second week. He must be the only person at a football club praying for an away draw in a cup tie – but then there is always the possibility of a replay in the Scottish Cup, and that means another programme.

have to plan family holidays around the fixture card ; and the traditional Christmas/New Year and Easter shut-downs in the printing industry may require two or three programmes to be compiled in the space of a few days – and up to a couple of weeks in advance of the fixtures. Try explaining to the missus that you can't accompany her for some last minute Christmas shopping because you are struggling to identify the latest South Americans to be signed by the team visiting three weeks hence.

Much of the pressure involved in programme editing is self-inflicted, with pride in the final product setting high standards which are only appreciated by readers on the few occasions they fall short. There is also the worst kind of peer group pressure. A season of flawless programmes will pass unremarked, but the smallest typographical error, or factual inaccuracy, will be pounced upon with glee.

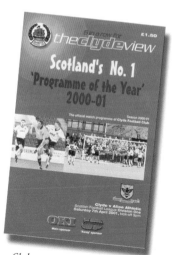

Clyde -
Programme of the Year 2000/01

The occasional slip-up remains tattooed on the memory of the programme editor on the receiving end of the resulting approbation, and inspires the rest not to make the same mistakes.

That is why a great deal of time is spent by the editor in checking facts, ensuring that nothing slips between his hands and the printers, and the unremitting grind of proof reading. Everything, but everything, has to be checked. A St. Johnstone programme editor of the early 1980s still has nightmares about a front cover photo, when shorts were shorts and a high-kicking defender revealed more than his limited ball control.

In the days of using photographic negatives, the editor prayed that a photo with the back view of players would be printed the right way up, otherwise the numbers on the back of jerseys would be in mirror image. In front view, the shirt-sponsors logo would appear to be in Cyrillic.

Modern technology has increased, rather than reduced, the incidence of errors. Page designs are now stored on computer, and merely updated from one week to the next. It is therefore not unknown to find the name of the previous week's opponents above a

different set of team lines (or vice versa) ; or a club badge of the previous visitors ; or last week's League tables and/or fixtures haven't been updated.

League tables and match statistics are an invitation for nit-picking analysis – why don't these critics get a life? Or become a programme editor? Spell-checking on modern computers may help eliminate the toe-curling typographical errors that can occur when typing Aldershot and Fulham at two-in-the-morning, but their americanese suggested alternatives have to be handled with great care.

Sometimes – no, make that often – well intentioned attempts to improve the

Partick Thistle
Second Division Programme of the Year
2000/01

programme backfire on the ambitious editor. There is a fine line between making articles more interesting and readable (ie sensational and scurrilous) and offending someone. Getting managers and players to digress from their "game of two halves" "boy done well" mantras and actually say something that people want to read, runs the risk of straying into controversy.

Both the SFA and SFL in their regulations specifically prohibit criticism of match officials and fellow clubs, but what may pass for harmless banter and

joshing humour on one side, can induce po-faced disapproval on the receiving end.

Nowhere is this the case more than in the visitors coverage. Everyone criticises this page, no matter the chosen format. Reproducing pen pictures and a well-trodden club history, both usually provided by the Club itself, is safe, deadly boring and instantly recognised as repetitive by visiting supporters, who read no further and dismiss the entire programme as worthless hack-work.

A number of editors have tried to enliven this page by taking a more jocular view of the opposition, often inviting ex-players, fanzine editors or guest writers to share their humour in describing the physical and technical foibles of their favourites. The result, you can guarantee, is a howl of protest, and the inevitable mention in a tabloid newspaper. You can't win.

Programme editors have long memories, and at times a keen sense of retribution. One was incensed at the pen pictures of his favourites in a local derby programme, the rivals suggesting that their visitors were uniformly overweight. His patience was rewarded by a rare trophy success and, for the next local

Montrose
Third Division Programme of the Year
2000/01

131

derby, he casually mentioned that each and every opponent "would not be playing in Europe next season". Not everyone shared his sense of humour and it was back to the bland leading the bland.

Contrary to popular belief, programme editors have been fighting a losing battle against boring issues for years, but it seems as if their every effort is thwarted by touchy officialdom and selective sense-of-humour by-pass. A Hibs programme editor enlivened his match reports with graphical illustrations, only to suffer the ire of the manager for showing where the penalty kicker placed his shots. No-one ever discovered whether that afternoon's visiting goalkeeper actually read the programme before the game, or just guessed luckily.

In much the same way as satire succeeds where a full-blooded attack fails, perhaps a subtle approach to humour is required. Unfortunately, not every club has the opportunity to include a cartoon of the quality of "Super Saint" in the St. Johnstone programme, to poke fun in a way that would not be accepted were it in written form.

It's not just a questionable sense of humour that a programme editor has to guard against. Tight deadlines do nothing to deaden the critical faculties, and a raging injustice over refereeing decisions, opponents tactics or the behaviour of opposing players, officials or fans can sometimes find their way into print. The programme editor's golden rule is – never editorialise immediately after a

controversial match. It may let off steam, but it only causes problems on publication date.

There are many other pitfalls. The influx of foreign players and managers may have added an exotic flavour to our game, but it doesn't make interviews any easier, nor career profiles in programmes. Where Rothmans Football Yearbook and The Scottish Football League Review were once all that was needed, now a mastery of foreign languages is a necessity. One editor was heard to wail : "I can handle it when we sign a player I haven't heard of. I can just about take it when I haven't heard of his previous team. But when I have to ask him to spell the name of his country, it's time to find another hobby."

Manager's Notes are a constant

minefield. "I want you to print this" is the precursor to a deranged rant which would have the programme scrutinized by everyone from the Disciplinary Committee to the Lord Chancellor's Department. On other occasions, try making 400 words out of "We were a disgrace. The referee was a homer. The opposition were a shower of dirty *****" and a clunk as the manager's phone is smashed back on its cradle.

Every January the editors vote amongst themselves to decide on the Programme of the Year in each of the divisions. Someone gets to walk a little taller when the results are announced in late March ; some are encouraged by an improvement in their ratings. Most mutter about the injustice of it all.

In many cases, the hardest working editors – those from smaller clubs with scant resources to devote to the appearance and presentation of their matchday programmes – gain little recognition for their efforts. They compensate by putting a great deal of effort into articles, features and interviews – then watch as inferior work is voted above them because it looks better in colour and on glossy paper.

Why do we do it ? The highs may not outnumber the lows, but they are much more memorable. In much the same way as fans turn up, week in, week out, in the belief that at some point they will witness a great victory, or a memorable goal, programme editors know that occasionally they will be allowed to bask in the reflected glory of a rare golden moment in their club's history. They don't want to miss it when it happens.

So pause awhile, as you contemplate the glossy brochure you buy at the match, and think of the hours of torture that have gone in to producing the matchday programme. Just as much time has been spent on ensuring that some things DON'T appear in print, as has been expended in conjuring up the words and images which entertain and enlighten you on a Saturday afternoon.

JOHN LITSTER
(Programme Monthly)

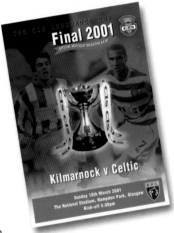

Scottish Programme Awards

SCOTTISH PREMIER LEAGUE

00/01	(99/00)	CLUB
1.	(1 (FD))	Dunfermline Athletic
2.	(1)	Dundee United
3.	(3)	Dundee
4.	(5)	Aberdeen
5.	(4)	Heart of Midlothian
6.	(2)	Rangers
7.	(6)	Hibernian
8.	(7)	Kilmarnock
9.	(8)	Celtic
10.	(3 (FD))	St. Mirren
11.	(9)	St. Johnstone
12.	(10)	Motherwell

SFL FIRST DIVISION

00/01	(99/00)	CLUB
1.	(1 (SD))	Clyde
2.	(2)	Falkirk
3.	(6)	Ayr United
4.	(5)	Livingston
5.	(7 (SD))	Ross County
6.	(7)	Raith Rovers
7.	(8)	Inverness Cal. Thistle
8.	(5 (SD))	Alloa Athletic
9.	(4)	Morton
10.	(9)	Airdrieonians

SFL SECOND DIVISION

00/01	(99/00)	CLUB
1.	(2)	Partick Thistle
2.	(1 (TD))	Queen's Park
3.	(9)	Stenhousemuir
4.	(3)	Stirling Albion
5.	(4)	Queen of the South
6.	(4 (TD))	Forfar Athletic
7.	(10)	Arbroath
8.	(6 (TD))	Berwick Rangers
9.	(6)	Stranraer
10.	(10 (FD))	Clydebank

SFL THIRD DIVISION

00/01	(99/00)	CLUB
1.	(2)	Montrose
2.	(8 (SD))	Hamilton Academical
3.	(5)	Brechin City
4.	(3)	Cowdenbeath
5.	(7)	Albion Rovers
6.	(10)	East Stirlingshire
7.	(-)	Peterhead
8.	(-)	Elgin City
9.	(9)	Dumbarton
10.	(8)	East Fife

SCOTTISH PROGRAMMES OF THE YEAR - PREVIOUS WINNERS

1973/74	Ayr United
1974/75	Hamilton Academical
1975/76	Heart of Midlothian
1976/77	Motherwell
1977/78	Hamilton Academical
1978/79	Hamilton Academical
1979/80	Berwick Rangers
1980/81	Aberdeen
1981/82	Hamilton Academical
1982/83	Dundee
1983/84	Dundee United
1984/85	Aberdeen
1985/86	Celtic
1986/87	Rangers
1987/88	Rangers
1988/89	Rangers
1989/90	Aberdeen
1990/91	Celtic
1991/92	Aberdeen
1992/93	Rangers
1993/94	Rangers
1994/95	Rangers
1995/96	Clyde
1996/97	Clyde
1997/98	Clyde
1998/99	Clyde
1999/2000	Clyde
2000/01	Clyde

PREMIER LEAGUE PROGRAMME OF THE YEAR

as above, except for ...)

1974/75	Motherwell (old Div.One)
1975/76	Heart of Midlothian
1976/77	Motherwell
1977/78	Rangers
1978/79	Morton
1979/80	Morton
1995/96	Kilmarnock
1996/97	Dundee United
1997/98	Dundee United
1998/99	Dundee United
1999/2000	Dundee United
2000/01	Dunfermline Athletic

FIRST DIVISION PROGRAMME OF THE YEAR

1975/76	Hamilton Academical
1976/77	Hamilton Academical
1977/78	Hamilton Academical
1978/79	Hamilton Academical
1979/80	Berwick Rangers
1980/81	Hamilton Academical
1981/82	Hamilton Academical
1982/83	Queen's Park
1983/84	Hamilton Academical
1984/85	Clyde
1985/86	Clyde
1986/87	Clyde

1987/88	Hamilton Academical & Clydebank
1988/89	Dunfermline Athletic
1989/90	Airdrieonians
1990/91	Dundee
1991/92	Partick Thistle
1992/93	Kilmarnock
1993/94	Dunfermline Athletic
1994/95	Dunfermline Athletic
1995/96	Dundee United
1996/97	Partick Thistle
1997/98	St. Mirren
1998/99	Hibernian
1999/2000	Dunfermline Athletic
2000/01	Clyde

SECOND DIVISION PROGRAMME OF THE YEAR

1973/74	Hamilton Academical
1974/75	Hamilton Academical
1975/76	Berwick Rangers
1976/77	Albion Rovers
1977/78	Meadowbank Thistle
1978/79	Berwick Rangers
1979/80	Albion Rovers
1980/81	Clyde
1981/82	Clyde
1982/83	Stirling Albion
1983/84	Stirling Albion
1984/85	Stirling Abion
1985/86	Stirling Albion
1986/87	Raith Rovers
1987/88	Stirling Albion
1988/89	Stirling Albion
1989/90	Kilmarnock
1990/91	Stirling Albion
1991/92	Clyde
1992/93	Clyde
1993/94	Forfar Athletic
1994/95	Clyde
1995/96	Clyde
1996/97	Clyde
1997/98	Clyde
1998/99	Clyde
1999/2000	Clyde
2000/01	Partick Thistle

THIRD DIVISION PROGRAMME OF THE YEAR

1994/95	Forfar Athletic
1995/96	Livingston
1996/97	Inverness Cal. Thistle
1997/98	Montrose
1998/99	Queen's Park
1999/2000	Queen's Park
2000/01	Montrose

Information supplied by John Litster (Editor of "Programme Monthly & Football Collectable" Magazine)

Take your Step into History

Hampden Park has long been the spiritual home of Scottish Football and since May 2001, the Scottish Football Museum has been welcoming fans from across the country to their new purpose built facility in the South Stand of the historic stadium.

"It's very important for us to make the Museum appealing to fans of clubs, regardless of their size, or how many championships they have won. To this end, we have always focussed a lot of our work on going out and meeting clubs across the country." says Clare Illand, the Curator of the world's first National Museum of Football.

"As we made our way across Scotland, it became very apparent that each of Scotland's clubs has its own unique story to tell. For this reason, we will soon begin work on a new gallery looking at each club in isolation - how it was founded, the character of the club and the major figures in the club's history."

The Museum has already entrusted fans of Clydebank, Greenock Morton, St. Mirren and Kilmarnock with the task of producing home-made video diaries illustrating what it is like to be a supporter of their team.

"Obviously, with the constantly changing circumstances at clubs like

Morton, video diaries are a great way to document an era in a club's history. We couldn't pretend to know what it is like for ordinary fans of these clubs, so it is much more meaningful to allow them to tell the story in their own words."

As well as the 'Clubs Gallery', the Museum will expand in a number of other ways over the next 18 months. Plans are well under way for a 'Technical Football Gallery' which will examine the development of training, tactics and management in Scottish Football from the first international match in 1872 (when Scotland played a 2-2-6 formation) through to the present day. Curators are also working on a Hall of Fame, where the greats of Scottish Football will be honoured, with an annual ceremony inducting new members.

For the moment though, visitors are still treated to a vast array of Scottish Football memorabilia. Within the first 15 feet of the Museum are some of the most valuable football objects in the world:-

Ged O'Brien; The Man at the heart of the Museum

• The Scottish Cup: the world's oldest major trophy has been given 'semi-retirement' status in the new Museum after 128 years of active service. The Cup will now only be used for the presentation on Cup Final day, before being returned to the security of the Museum.

• The World Championship Trophy: won by Renton in 1888. As Scottish Champions, the Dunbartonshire side organised a match against the English Cup Champions, West Bromwich Albion. The game took place at Hampden in front of 6,000 spectators with Renton winning 4-1. After beating Preston North End two weeks later, a sign was hung on the Renton clubhouse door. It read "Renton F.C. – Champions of the World." This silver-plated trophy was made to celebrate the success.

• Match Ticket and Cap, Scotland v England, 1872: Surprisingly few Scots are aware that the world's first official international match took place in Glasgow. While the match itself ended in a 0-0 draw, its importance in historical terms is huge. It was during this game that the Scotland team (made up entirely of Queen's Park players) first demonstrated their passing and running style of football to a wider audience.

It's a good day out... why not come along and visit us.
ANNIE McGUIRE *(Media Officer)*

The Scottish Football Museum is open from 10am - 5pm from Monday – Saturday and from 11am - 5pm Sundays.

Admission costs are £5 for adults and £2.50 for children and concessions. Stadium Tours are also available. Please call (0141) 616 6139 for details.

135

Useful Football Addresses

FIFA:

General Secretary: M. Zen-Ruffinen,
P.O. Box 85, 8030 Zurich,Switzerland.
Tel: 00 411 384 9595 **Fax:** 00 411 384 9696
Website: www.fifa.com

UEFA:

Chief Executive: G. Aigner, Route de Genève 46, CH-1260,
Nyon 2, Switzerland.
Tel: 00 41 22 994 4444 **Fax:** 00 41 22 994 4488
Website: www.uefa.com

LEAGUES IN MEMBERSHIP OF THE
INTERNATIONAL FOOTBALL LEAGUE BOARD

THE SCOTTISH FOOTBALL LEAGUE:

Secretary: P. Donald, Hampden Park, Glasgow, G42 9EB.
Tel: 0141 620 4160 **Fax:** 0141 620 4161
e-mail: info@sfl.scottishfootball.com **Website:** www.scottishfootball.com

THE SCOTTISH PREMIER LEAGUE:

Chief Executive: R. Mitchell, Hampden Park, Glasgow, G42 9DE.
Tel: 0141 620 4140 **Fax:** 0141 620 4141
Website: www.scotprem.com

THE F.A. PREMIER LEAGUE:

Secretary: M. Foster, 11 Connaught Place, London, W2 2ET.
Tel: 0207 298 1600 **Fax:** 0207 298 1601
e-mail: general@.fapl.co.uk

THE FOOTBALL LEAGUE:

Chief Executive: D.C. Burns, Edward VII Quay, Navigation Way,
Preston, PR2 2YF.
Tel: 01772 325800 **Fax:** 01772 325801
e-mail: fl@football-league.co.uk **Website:** www.football-league.co.uk

THE IRISH FOOTBALL LEAGUE:

Secretary: H. Wallace, 96 University Street, Belfast, BT7 1HE.
Tel: 02890 242888 **Fax:** 02890 330773
e-mail: irishleague@talk21.com

NATIONAL ASSOCIATIONS WITHIN
THE UNITED KINGDOM

THE SCOTTISH FOOTBALL ASSOCIATION:

Chief Executive: D. Taylor, The National Stadium,
Hampden Park, Glasgow, G42 9AY.
Tel: 0141 616 6000 **Fax:** 0141 616 6001
e-mail: info@scottishfa.co.uk
Website: www.scottishfa.co.uk

THE FOOTBALL ASSOCIATION:

Chief Executive: A. Crozier, 25 Soho Square, London, W1D 4FA.
Tel: 0207 745 4545 **Fax:** 0207 745 4546
e-mail: info@the-fa.org **Website:** www.the-fa.org

THE IRISH FOOTBALL ASSOCIATION:

Secretary: D.I. Bowen, 20 Windsor Avenue, Belfast, BT9 6EG.
Tel: 02890 669458 **Fax:** 02890 667620
e-mail: enquiries@irishfa.com **Website:** www.irishfa.com

THE FOOTBALL ASSOCIATION OF WALES:

Secretary: D.G. Collins, 3 Westgate Street, Cardiff, CF10 1DP.
Tel: 02920 372325 **Fax:** 02920 343961
e-mail: dcollins@faw.co.uk **Website:** www.faw.org.uk

OTHER LEAGUES IN SCOTLAND

THE HIGHLAND FOOTBALL LEAGUE:

Secretary: J.H. Grant, 35 Hamilton Drive, Elgin, IV30 4NN.
Tel/Fax: 01343 544995
e-mail: hfleague@globalnet.co.uk

EAST OF SCOTLAND LEAGUE:

Secretary: J.M. Greenhorn, 2 Babberton Mains Court,
Edinburgh, EH14 3ER
Tel/Fax: (B) 0131 442 1402 (H) 0131 538 0289
e-mail: john.greenhorn@tesco.net

SOUTH OF SCOTLAND LEAGUE:

Secretary: R. Shaw M.B.E., 8 Kirkland Road, Heathhall,
Dumfries, DG1 3RN.
Tel/Fax: (B) 01387 254853 (H) 01387 261736

AFFILIATED NATIONAL ASSOCIATIONS OF THE
SCOTTISH FOOTBALL ASSOCIATION

THE SCOTTISH JUNIOR FOOTBALL ASSOCIATION:

Secretary: T. Johnston, Hampden Park, Glasgow, G42 9DD.
Tel: 0141 620 4560 **Fax:** 0141 620 4561

THE SCOTTISH AMATEUR FOOTBALL ASSOCIATION:

Secretary: H. Knapp, Hampden Park, Glasgow, G42 9DB.
Tel: 0141 620 4550 **Fax:** 0141 620 4551
e-mail: hughknapp@scottishamateurfa.co.uk
Website: www.scottishamateurfa.co.uk

THE SCOTTISH YOUTH FOOTBALL ASSOCIATION:

Secretary: D. Little, Hampden Park, Glasgow, G42 9BF.
Tel: 0141 620 4590 **Fax:** 0141 620 4591
e-mail: info@scottishyouthfa.co.uk
Website: www.scottishyouthfa.co.uk

THE SCOTTISH WELFARE FOOTBALL ASSOCIATION:

Secretary: D. McNair, 14 Yair Drive, Glasgow, G52 2JX.
Tel: 0141 883 5008 **Fax:** 01324 813527

THE SCOTTISH SCHOOLS FOOTBALL ASSOCIATION:

Secretary: J.C. Watson, Hampden Park, Glasgow, G42 9AZ.
Tel: 0141 620 4570 **Fax:** 0141 620 4571
e-mail: jcwatson@lineone.net

SCOTTISH WOMEN'S FOOTBALL:

Executive Administrator: Mrs. M. McGonigle, Hampden Park,
Glasgow, G42 9DF.
Tel: 0141 620 4580/4582 **Fax:** 0141 620 4581
e-mail: swfa@supanet.com

PLAYER'S UNION

THE SCOTTISH PROFESSIONAL
FOOTBALLERS ASSOCIATION:

Secretary: T. Higgins, Fountain House, 1/3 Woodside Crescent,
Charing Cross, Glasgow, G3 7UJ.
Tel: 0141 332 8641 **Fax:** 0141 332 4491
e-mail: SPFA@gmb.org.uk

THE HIGHLAND FOOTBALL LEAGUE
DIRECTORY OF CLUBS

BRORA RANGERS F.C.

Secretary:	Kevin MacKay
Manager:	Keith Ferries
Club Address:	Dudgeon Park, Dudgeon Drive, Brora, KW9 6QN.
Ground Tel:	01408 621231
Sec Bus:	01408 623005
Sec Home/Fax:	01408 621114
E-Mail:	kevinamackay/operations/uk/udv@udv
Year of Formation:	1879
Capacity:	4,000 (250 Seated 3,750 Standing)
Pitch Dimensions:	112yds x 70yds

Playing Kits: 1st Choice

Shirt:	Red
Shorts:	White
Stockings:	Red

2nd Choice

Shirt:	White
Shorts:	Red
Stockings:	White

3rd Choice

Shirt:	Scarlet & Royal Blue Stripes
Shorts:	Royal Blue
Stockings:	Scarlet

BUCKIE THISTLE F.C.

Secretary:	Stewart Sandison
Manager:	Alan Scott
Club Address:	Victoria Park, Midmar Street, Buckie, AB56 1BT.
Ground Tel No:	01542 836468 (Matchdays Only)
Sec Bus:	01542 833352
Sec Home:	01542 839192
Website:	www.buckiethistle.com
E-Mail:	bl@sbmia.co.uk **OR** bill@buckiethistle.com
Year of Formation:	1889
Capacity:	5,400 (400 Seated 5,000 Standing)
Pitch Dimensions:	109yds x 73yds

Playing Kits: 1st Choice

Shirt:	Green & White Hoops
Shorts:	Green & White Flashings
Stockings:	White

2nd Choice

Shirt:	White
Shorts:	Green
Stockings:	White

CLACHNACUDDIN F.C. (1990) LTD.

Secretary:	Gilbert Skinner
Manager:	Robert Williamson
Club Address:	Grant Street Park, Wyvis Place, Inverness, IV3 6DR.
Ground Tel No:	01463 238825
Ticket Information:	01463 710707
Sec Home:	01463 235339
Fax No:	01463 718261
Year of Formation:	1886
Capacity:	3,000 (154 Seated 2,846 Standing)
Pitch Dimensions:	108yds x 70yds

Playing Kits: 1st Choice

Shirt:	White
Shorts:	Black
Stockings:	White

2nd Choice

Shirt:	Yellow
Shorts & Stockings:	Yellow

COVE RANGERS F.C.

Secretary:	Duncan Little
Manager:	Robert Summers
Club Address:	Allan Park, Loirston Road, Cove, Aberdeen, AB12 3NR.
Ground Tel No:	01224 890433
Sec Bus:	01224 854990
Sec Home:	01224 896282
Fax No:	01224 879023/895199
E-Mail:	duncanl@coverangersfc.freeserve.co.uk
Year of Formation:	1922
Capacity:	2,300 (200 Seated 2,100 Standing)
Pitch Dimensions:	104yds x 65yds

Playing Kits: 1st Choice

Shirt:	Blue & White
Shorts:	Blue & White
Stockings:	White & Blue

2nd Choice

Shirt:	Yellow & Blue
Shorts & Stockings:	Yellow & Blue

DEVERONVALE F.C.

Secretary:	Stewart McPherson
Manager:	Gregg Carrol
Club Address:	Princess Royal Park, 56 Eirlie Gardens, Banff, AB45 1AZ.
Ground Tel No:	01261 818489/818303
Sec Home/Bus:	07813 733617
Fax No:	01261 833736
Website:	www.deveronvale.co.uk
Year of Formation:	1938
Capacity:	2,600 (300 Seated 2,300 Standing)
Pitch Dimensions:	109yds x 78yds

Playing Kits: 1st Choice

Shirt:	Red with White Trim
Shorts:	White
Stockings:	Black with Red Tops

2nd Choice

Shirt:	Sky Blue
Shorts:	Navy Blue
Stockings:	Sky Blue

FORRES MECHANICS F.C.

Secretary:	David Macdonald
Manager:	Gordon Connelly
Club Address:	Mosset Park, Lea Road, Forres, Moray, IV36 0AU.
Ground Tel/Fax No:	01309 675096
Sec Bus:	01309 672277
Sec Home:	01343 544294
E-Mail:	d-w-macdonald@hotmail.com
Year of Formation:	1884
Capacity:	6,540 (540 Seated 6,000 Standing)
Pitch Dimensions:	106yds x 69yds

Playing Kits: 1st Choice

Shirt:	Yellow & Maroon Stripes
Shorts:	Maroon
Stockings:	Yellow

2nd Choice

Shirt:	White
Shorts & Stockings:	White

FORT WILLIAM F.C.

Secretary:	James Campbell
Manager:	Danny Conlon
Club Address:	Claggan Park, Fort William
Sec Home:	01397 700246
Sec Fax:	01397 772298
Website:	www.fortwilliamfc.org.uk
E-Mail:	info@fortwilliamfc.org.uk
Year of Formation:	1984
Capacity:	4,600 (400 Seated 4,200 Standing)
Pitch Dimensions:	102yds x 80yds

Playing Kits: 1st Choice

Shirt:	Gold
Shorts:	Black
Stockings:	Gold

2nd Choice

Shirt:	White
Shorts:	Navy Blue
Stockings:	Black

FRASERBURGH F.C.

Secretary:	Finlay M. Noble
Manager:	Charles Duncan
Club Address:	Bellslea Park, Seaforth Street, Fraserburgh, AB43 9BD.
Ground Tel No:	01346 518444
Fax No:	01346 516414
Sec Bus:	07747 003806
Sec Home:	01346 513474
Website:	www.burghfc.demon.co.uk
E-Mail:	ffc@burghfc.demon.co.uk
Year of Formation:	1910
Capacity:	4,500 (480 Seated 4,020 Standing)
Pitch Dimensions:	106yds x 66yds

Playing Kits: 1st Choice

Shirt:	Black and White Verticle Stripes
Shorts:	Black
Stockings:	Red

2nd Choice

Shirt:	Red
Shorts & Stockings:	White

HUNTLY F.C.

Secretary:	Peter Morrison
Co-Managers:	William Lawson & Kevin Will
Club Address:	Christie Park, East Park Street, Huntly, AB54 8JE.
Ground Tel No:	01466 793548
Sec Bus:	01466 793286
Sec Home:	01466 793269
Fax No:	01466 792157
Website:	www.huntlyfc.co.uk
E-Mail:	bob@longtechnology.com
Year of Formation:	1928
Capacity:	4,500 (270 Seated 4,230 Standing)
Pitch Dimensions:	105yds x 72yds
Playing Kits:	**1st Choice**
Shirt:	Gold & Black Stripes
Shorts:	Black with Gold Trim
Stockings:	Black with Gold Trim
	2nd Choice
Shirt:	White
Shorts & Stockings:	White

INVERURIE LOCO WORKS F.C.

Secretary:	Gordon Park
Manager:	John Gardiner
Club Address:	Harlaw Park, Harlaw Road, Inverurie, AB51 4SG.
Ground Tel No:	01467 622168
Sec Bus:	01467 624500
Sec Home:	01467 621347
E-Mail:	inverurielocos@teamdiscovery.com
Year of Formation:	1903
Capacity:	1,925, (125 Seated, 1,800 Standing)
Pitch Dimensions:	103 yds x 71 yds
Playing Kits:	**1st Choice**
Shirt:	Red & Black
Shorts:	Black
Stockings:	Red
	2nd Choice
Shirt:	White & Black
Shorts:	Black
Stockings:	White

KEITH F.C.

Secretary:	Alexander Rutherford
Manager:	Martin Allan
Club Address:	Kynoch Park, Balloch Road, Keith, AB55 5EN.
Ground Tel No:	01542 882629
Sec Bus/Fax:	01542 882629
Sec Mobile:	07811 155789
Website:	www.keith-fc.co.uk
Year of Formation:	1919
Capacity:	4,500 (450 Seated 4,050 Standing)
Pitch Dimensions:	110yds x 75yds
Playing Kits:	**1st Choice**
Shirt:	Maroon with Sky Blue Facings
Shorts:	Maroon and Sky Blue Stripe
Stockings:	Maroon
	2nd Choice
Shirt:	White with Yellow and Navy Blue
Shorts & Stockings:	Navy Blue

LOSSIEMOUTH F.C.

Secretary:	Alan McIntosh
Manager:	Graham Tatters
Club Address:	Grant Park, Kellas Avenue, Lossiemouth, IV31 6JG.
Ground Tel No:	01343 813717
Sec Home:	01343 813328
Sec Mobile:	07967 519384
Fax No:	01343 815440
Year of Formation:	1945
Capacity:	3,500 (250 Seated 3,250 Standing)
Pitch Dimensions:	110yds x 60yds
Playing Kits:	**1st Choice**
Shirt:	Red with White Trim
Shorts:	Red with White Trim
Stockings:	Red with White Hoops
	2nd Choice
Shirt:	Yellow with Blue Trim
Shorts:	Blue with Yellow Trim
Stockings:	Blue with Yellow Hoops

NAIRN COUNTY F.C.

Secretary:	John McNeill
Manager:	Ronald Sharp
Club Address:	Station Park, Balblair Road, Nairn, IV12 5LT.
Ground Tel No:	01667 454298
Sec Bus:	01463 792424
Sec Home/Fax:	01667 462510
Year of Formation:	1914
Capacity:	3,800 (250 Seated 3,550 Standing)
Pitch Dimensions:	110yds x 62yds
Playing Kits:	**1st Choice**
Shirt:	Yellow with Black Chest Band
Shorts & Stockings:	Yellow
	2nd Choice
Shirt:	Red
Shorts:	Black
Stockings:	White

ROTHES F.C.

Secretary:	Neil McKenzie
Manager:	Graham McBeath
Club Address:	Mackessack Park, Station Street, Rothes, Aberlour
Ground Tel No:	01340 831972
Sec Bus:	07802 773695
Sec Home:	01340 831344
E-Mail:	neil.r.mckenzie@btinternet.com
Year of Formation:	1938
Capacity:	2,650 (160 Seated 2,490 Standing)
Pitch Dimensions:	108yds x 74yds
Playing Kits:	**1st Choice**
Shirt:	Tangerine with Black Trim
Shorts:	Black
Stockings:	Tangerine with Three Black Hoops
	2nd Choice
Shirt:	Black with Tangerine Trim
Shorts:	Black
Stockings:	Black with Three Tangerine Hoops
	3rd Choice
Shirt:	White with Blue
Shorts & Stockings:	Blue

WICK ACADEMY F.C.

Secretary:	Andrew Carter
Manager:	Pat Miller
Club Address:	Harmsworth Park, South Road, Wick, KW1 5NH.
Ground Tel/Fax No:	01955 602446
Sec Bus/Fax:	01847 802277
Sec Home:	01955 604275
Year of Formation:	1893
Capacity:	2,000 (433 Seated 1,567 Standing)
Pitch Dimensions:	106yds x 76yds
Playing Kits:	**1st Choice**
Shirt:	Black & White Stripes
Shorts & Stockings:	Black
	2nd Choice
Shirt:	Sky Blue and White Stripes
Shorts:	Navy Blue
Stockings:	Sky Blue

PRESS & JOURNAL LEAGUE
FINAL TABLE – SEASON 2000/2001

	P	W	D	L	F	A	Pts
Cove Rangers	26	20	3	3	74	32	63
Huntly	26	19	2	5	61	29	59
Buckie Thistle	26	13	7	6	46	33	46
Clachnacuddin	26	13	5	8	47	35	44
Keith	26	11	9	6	54	43	42
Deveronvale	26	11	8	7	40	32	41
Forres Mechanics	26	10	10	6	44	39	40
Fraserburgh	26	12	3	11	47	38	39
Nairn County	26	8	7	11	44	58	31
Wick Academy	26	8	5	13	39	43	29
Rothes	26	6	5	15	30	45	23
Lossiemouth	26	6	4	16	27	60	22
Brora Rangers	26	4	3	19	42	78	15
Fort William	26	3	5	18	27	57	14

THE EAST OF SCOTLAND LEAGUE DIRECTORY OF CLUBS

ANNAN ATHLETIC F.C.

Secretary: Alan T. Irving
Manager: David Irons
Club Address: Galabank, North Street, Annan, Dumfries & Galloway.
Ground Tel/Fax No: 01461 204108
Sec Bus: 01461 207218
Sec Home: 01461 203702
Website: www.members.synup.com/annanathletic
E-Mail: annanathletic@synup.net
Year of Formation: 1942
Capacity: 2,000 (All Standing)
Pitch Dimensions: 110 yds x 65 yds
Playing Kits:
1st Choice: Shirt: Black and Gold Broad Vertical Stripes; Shorts: Black; Stockings: Black with Two Gold Rings
2nd Choice: Shirt: Blue; Shorts: White; Stockings: White with Blue Tops

CIVIL SERVICE STROLLERS F.C.

Secretary: Edward S. Turnbull
Manager: Steven Torrance
Club Address: Muirhouse Civil Service Sports Ground, Marine Drive, Edinburgh.
Ground Tel No: 0131 332 1175 (Matchdays Only)
Sec Bus: 0131 314 4220
Sec Home: 0131 539 0171
Fax No: 0131 314 4344
Website: www.strollers.org.uk
E-Mail: eddie.turnbull@gro-scotland.gov.uk
Year of Formation: 1908
Capacity: 500 (All Standing)
Pitch Dimensions: 100 yds x 60 yds
Playing Kits:
1st Choice: Shirt: White; Shorts: Black; Stockings: Red
2nd Choice: Shirt: Red; Shorts: Black; Stockings: Red

COLDSTREAM F.C.

Secretary: Ms. Morag Evans
Manager: Stuart Robertson
Club Address: Home Park, Coldstream, Berwickshire.
Ground Tel/Fax No: 01890 883085
Sec Home: 01890 883352
Year of Formation: 1895
Capacity: 1,500 (All Standing)
Pitch Dimensions: 100 yds x 60 yds
Playing Kits:
1st Choice: Shirt: Royal Blue with Black Trim; Shorts: Black; Stockings: Royal Blue
2nd Choice: Shirt: Red; Shorts: Red; Stockings: Red

CRAIGROYSTON F.C.

Secretary: Jim Sivewright
Manager: Alan Whyte
Club Address: St. Mark's Park, Warriston, Edinburgh
Sec Bus: 0131 346 5753
Sec Home: 0131 228 1803
Year of Formation: 1976
Capacity: 1,000, (All Standing)
Pitch Dimensions: 106 yds x 76 yds
Playing Kits:
1st Choice: Shirt: Yellow; Shorts: Yellow; Stockings: Yellow
2nd Choice: Shirt: Royal Blue; Shorts: White; Stockings: Royal Blue

DALBEATTIE STAR F.C.

Secretary: Robert Geddes
Manager: Brian Aitchison
Club Address: Islecroft Stadium, Dalbeattie.
Ground Tel: 01556 611151
Sec Bus/Home: 01556 610563
Fax No: 01556 611747
E-Mail: bob@solwaypressservices.co.uk
Year of Formation: 1905 (approx)
Capacity: 4,000 (All Standing)
Pitch Dimensions: 110 yds x 70 yds
Playing Kits:
1st Choice: Shirt: Red and Black Stripes; Shorts: Black; Stockings: Red
2nd Choice: Shirt: Maroon/Sky Blue; Shorts: Maroon; Stockings: Maroon

EASTHOUSES LILY MINERS WELFARE F.C.

Secretary: R. Paul
Manager: Keith Jancyzk
Club Address: Mayfield Park, Newbattle, Easthouses
Sec Home: 0131 663 9768
Year of Formation: 1969
Capacity: 1,000 (All Standing)
Pitch Dimensions: 110 yds x 67 yds
Playing Kits:
1st Choice: Shirt: Red; Shorts: White; Stockings: Red
2nd Choice: Shirt: Blue; Shorts: Blue; Stockings: Blue

EDINBURGH ATHLETIC F.C.

Secretary: I. Gracie
Manager: Davide DeGaetano
Club Address: Civil Service Sports Ground, Marine Drive, Edinburgh.
Ground Tel No: 0131 332 0650
Sec Home: 01875 340983
Website: www.edinburghathletic.com
Year of Formation: 1968
Capacity: 500 (All Standing)
Pitch Dimensions: 100 yds x 60 yds
Playing Kits:
1st Choice: Shirt: Navy Blue; Shorts: Navy Blue; Stockings: Navy Blue
2nd Choice: ; Shirt: Green; Shorts: Green; Stockings: Green

EDINBURGH CITY F.C.

Secretary: Kevin Hogg
Manager: Charles Kivlin
Club Address: Meadowbank Stadium, London Road, Edinburgh, EH7 6AE.
Ground Tel No: 0131 661 5351
Sec Bus: 0131 245 6882
Sec Home: 0131 228 1882
Website: www.edinburghcityfc.com
Year of Formation: 1928
Capacity: 13,841 (All Seated)
Pitch Dimensions: 105 yds x 72 yds
Playing Kits:
1st Choice: Shirt: White; Shorts: Black; Stockings: Black
2nd Choice: Shirt: Yellow; Shorts: Black; Stockings: Yellow

EDINBURGH UNIVERSITY ASSOCIATION F.C.

Secretary: Ian Lunan
Manager: Neil Orr
Club Address: Peffermill Playing Fields, Peffermill Road, Edinburgh.
Ground Tel No: 0131 667 7541
Sec Bus: 0131 650 2346
Sec Home: 0131 446 0731
Website: www.ed.ac.uk/euafc
E-Mail: s.c.whyte@sms.ed.ac.uk
Year of Formation: 1878
Capacity: 1,012; 12 Seated, 1000 Standing
Pitch Dimensions: 115 yds x 66 yds
Playing Kits:
1st Choice: Shirt: Blue and Green; Shorts: Blue; Stockings: Blue
2nd Choice: Shirt: Black and White Stripes; Shorts: Black; Stockings: Black
3rd Choice: Shirt: Red; Shorts: Red; Stockings: Red

EYEMOUTH UNITED F.C.

Secretary: I. Thomson
Manager: Tom Brown
Club Address: Gunsgreen Park, Johns Road, Eyemouth
Sec Home: 01890 751301
Year of Formation: 1949
Capacity: 1,000 (All Standing)
Pitch Dimensions: 110 yds x 70 yds
Playing Kits:
1st Choice: Shirt: Maroon; Shorts: Maroon; Stockings: Maroon
2nd Choice: Shirt: White; Shorts: Maroon; Stockings: Sky Blue

GALA FAIRYDEAN F.C.

Secretary: John Clayton
Manager: John Clark
Club Address: Netherdale, Galashiels.
Ground Tel No: 01896 753554
Sec Bus: 01896 754797
Sec Home: 01896 753797
Fax: 01896 754412
E-Mail: john.clayton@sepa.org.uk
Year of Formation: 1907
Capacity: 5,500, 495 Seated, 5,005 Standing
Pitch Dimensions: 110 yds x 72 yds
Playing Kits:
1st Choice: Shirt: Black and White; Shorts: Black; Stockings: Black with White Tops
2nd Choice: Shirt: Yellow; Shorts: Yellow; Stockings: Yellow
3rd Choice: Shirt: Yellow; Shorts: Black; Stockings: Black with White Tops

HAWICK ROYAL ALBERT F.C.

Secretary: Douglas J. Purves
Club Address: Albert Park, Mansfield Road, Hawick.
Ground Tel No: 01450 374231
Sec Bus: 0131 537 9241
Sec Home: 01450 371261
Year of Formation: 1947
Capacity: 2,000, 500 Seated, 1,500 Standing
Pitch Dimensions: 100 yds x 68 yds
Playing Kits:
1st Choice: Shirt: Royal Blue with Red and White Stripe; Shorts: Royal Blue; Stockings: Royal Blue
2nd Choice: Shirt: Red with Black Detail; Shorts: Black; Stockings: Black with Red and White Detail

HERIOT-WATT UNIVERSITY F.C.

Secretary: A. Matheson
Manager: J. Glover
Club Address: Heriot-Watt University Riccarton Campus, Riccarton, Edinburgh
Ground Tel No: 0131 451 3000
Sec Bus: 01786 467106
Sec Home: 01506 848012
Website: www.gosports.to/hwufc/
E-Mail: overtoun@cliché.co.uk

Year of Formation: 1945
Capacity: 1,000 (All Standing)
Pitch Dimensions: 116 yds x 79 yds
Playing Kits:
1st Choice: Shirt: Yellow, Blue trim; Shorts: Yellow; Stockings: Blue
2nd Choice: Shirt: Green & White Hoops; Shorts: White; Stockings: White

KELSO UNITED F.C.

Secretary: A. Douglas
Manager: Brian Lough
Club Address: Woodside Park, Kelso.
Ground Tel No: 01573 223780
Sec Home: 01573 225314
Year of Formation: 1924
Capacity: 1,000 (All Standing)
Pitch Dimensions: 107 yds x 70 yds
Playing Kits:
1st Choice: Shirt: Black and White Stripes; Shorts: Black; Stockings: Black & White
2nd Choice: Shirt: Red; Shorts: Navy Blue; Stockings: Red

LOTHIAN THISTLE F.C.

Secretary: Tom Allison
Manager: George Bowmaker
Club Address: Saughton Enclosure, Edinburgh.
Ground Tel No: 0131 444 0422 (Matchdays Only)
Sec Bus: 0131-333-1976
Sec Home: 0131 336 1751
Website: www.lothianthistlefc.co.uk
E-Mail: secretary@lothianthistlefc.co.uk
Year of Formation: 1969
Capacity: 1,000 (All Standing)
Pitch Dimensions: 112 yds x 74 yds
Playing Kits:
1st Choice: Shirt: Maroon; Shorts: White; Stockings: White
2nd Choice: Shirt: White; Shorts: White; Stockings: White

PEEBLES ROVERS F.C.

Secretary: C. Morrish
Manager: N. Nisbet
Club Address: Whitestone Park, Peebles.
Sec Bus: 0131 478 5050
Sec Home: 01721 720543
Website: www.memberstripod.com/peeblesrovers
E-Mail: cmorrish@btclick.com
Year of Formation: 1893
Capacity: 1,000, 200 Seated, 800 Standing
Pitch Dimensions: 110 yds x 75 yds
Playing Kits:
1st Choice: Shirt: Red; Shorts: Red; Stockings: Red
2nd Choice: Shirt: Yellow/Black stripe; Shorts: Black; Stockings: Yellow/Black hoops

PENCAITLAND & ORMISTON F.C.

Secretary: John M. Greenhorn
Manager: Walter Borthwick
Club Address: Recreation Park, Ormiston.
Sec Bus: 0131 453 5252
Sec Home: 0131 538 0289
E-Mail: john.greenhorn@tesco.net
Year of Formation: 1884
Capacity: 1,000 (All Standing)
Pitch Dimensions: 108 yds x 68 yds
Playing Kits:
1st Choice: Shirt: Maroon and White; Shorts: Maroon; Stockings: White
2nd Choice: Shirt: Blue/White Broad stripe; Shorts: Blue; Stockings: Blue

PRESTON ATHLETIC F.C.

Secretary: Robert McNeil
Manager: Stephen Myatt
Club Address: Pennypitt Park, Rope Walk, Prestonpans, East Lothian.
Ground Tel No: 01875 815221
Sec Bus: 01698 413129
Sec Home: 01875 611830
Fax: 01698 413099
E-Mail: preston.athletic@ondigital.com

Year of Formation: 1945
Capacity: 4,000, 313 Seated, 3,687 Standing
Pitch Dimensions: 110 yds x 72 yds
Playing Kits:
1st Choice: Shirt: Blue; Shorts: White with Blue Stripe; Stockings: Black with Red Top
2nd Choice: Shirt: Red with White Stripe; Shorts: White with Red Stripe; Stockings: Red with White Top

SELKIRK F.C.
Secretary/Manager: Derek Kerr
Club Address: Yarrow Park, Selkirk
Sec Bus: 01896 755379
Sec Home: 01750 23060
Fax: 01896 754837
Year of Formation: 1880
Capacity: 1,000 (All Standing)
Pitch Dimensions: 108 yds x 70 yds
Playing Kits:
1st Choice:
Shirt: Half Blue and Half White; Shorts: Blue; Stockings: Blue
2nd Choice: Shirt: White; Shorts: Blue; Stockings: Blue
3rd Choice: Shirt: White with Blue Vertical Stripe, Shorts: Blue
Stockings: Blue

SPARTANS F.C.
Secretary: James Murray
Manager: Sam Lynch
Club Address: City Park, Ferry Road, Edinburgh.
Sec Bus/Fax: 0131 667 9923
Sec Home: 0131 668 2188
Year of Formation: 1951
Capacity: 3,000 (All Standing)
Pitch Dimensions: 108 yds x 65 yds
Playing Kits:
1st Choice: Shirt: White with Red Trim; Shorts: Red; Stockings: White with Red Tops
2nd Choice: Shirt: Blue; Shorts: Blue; Stockings: Blue

THREAVE ROVERS F.C.
Secretary: Robert McCleary
Manager: William C. Sim
Club Address: Meadow Park, Castle Douglas, Dumfries & Galloway.
Ground Tel No: 01556 504536
Sec Bus: 01556 502119
Sec Home/Fax: 01556 503512
Sec Mobile: 07752 322221
E-Mail: bobbymccleary@threaverovers.fsnet.co.uk
Year of Formation: 1953
Capacity: 5,000 (All Standing)
Pitch Dimensions: 110 yds x 75 yds
Playing Kits:
1st Choice: Shirt: Black and White Vertical Stripes; Shorts: Black; Stockings: Black with White Trim
2nd Choice: Shirt: Blue; Shorts: White; Stockings: White
3rd Choice: Shirt: White; Shorts: White; Stockings: White

TOLLCROSS UNITED F.C.
Secretary: Alistair Wilkie
Manager: R. Dignan
Club Address: Fernieside Recreation Park, Fernieside Avenue, Edinburgh.
Sec Bus: 0131 467 5555
Sec Home: 0131 622 1148
Year of Formation: 1971
Capacity: 1,000 (All Standing)
Pitch Dimensions: 115 yds x 76 yds
Playing Kits:
1st Choice: Shirt: Red and White Sleeves; Shorts: White; Stockings: White
2nd Choice: Shirt: White; Shorts: Black; Stockings: White

VALE OF LEITHEN F.C.
Secretary: Ian Haggarty
Manager: William Hume
Club Address: Victoria Park, Innerleithen.
Sec Bus: 0131 244 2524

Sec Home/Fax: 01896 830995
Fax No: 0131 244 2326
Year of Formation: 1891
Capacity: 1,500 (All Standing)
Pitch Dimensions: 108 yds x 70 yds
Playing Kits:
1st Choice: Shirt: Navy Blue with White Sleeves; Shorts: Navy Blue; Stockings: White
2nd Choice: Shirt: Red ; Shorts: Red; Stockings: Red

WHITEHILL WELFARE F.C.
Secretary: Peter McGauley
Manager: David Smith
Club Address: Ferguson Park, Carnethie Street, Rosewell, Midlothian.
Ground Tel No: 0131 440 0115
Sec Home: 0131 440 3417
Website: www.whitehillwelfare.com
E-Mail: w.welfare@aol.com
Year of Formation: 1953
Capacity: 4,000 (All Standing)
Pitch Dimensions: 108 yds x 70 yds
Playing Kits:
1st Choice: Shirt: Claret Body with Sky Blue Sleeves; Shorts: White; Stockings: White
2nd Choice: Shirt: Sky Blue and Navy Blue; Shorts: Navy Blue; Stockings: Navy Blue
3rd Choice: Shirt: Sky Blue with Claret Trim; Shorts: Sky Blue with Broad Claret Stripes; Stockings: Sky Blue

EAST OF SCOTLAND LEAGUE

FINAL TABLES – SEASON 2000/2001

PREMIER DIVISION

	P	W	D	L	F	A	Pts
Annan Athletic	22	13	6	3	48	26	45
*Whitehill Welfare	22	13	5	4	47	18	41
Threave Rovers	22	11	6	5	39	28	39
Spartans	22	10	8	4	45	31	38
Craigroyston	22	9	5	8	30	28	32
Edinburgh City	22	8	6	8	37	40	30
Lothian Thistle	22	7	6	9	30	30	27
Vale of Leithen	22	7	3	12	34	42	24
Coldstream	22	7	3	12	28	42	24
Gala Fairydean	22	7	3	12	29	45	24
Civil Service Strollers	22	7	2	13	35	43	23
Easthouses Lily	22	5	3	14	21	50	18

*Whitehill Welfare Deducted 3 Points

FIRST DIVISION

	P	W	D	L	F	A	Pts
Pencait. & Ormiston	20	13	4	3	43	16	43
Edinburgh University	20	12	6	2	35	11	42
Peebles Rovers	20	9	7	4	44	26	34
Hawick Royal Albert	20	8	5	7	41	40	29
Edinburgh Athletic	20	9	2	9	28	33	29
Preston Athletic	20	8	4	8	33	29	28
Eyemouth United	20	8	3	9	30	47	27
Tollcross United	20	5	7	8	25	28	22
Kelso United	20	6	3	11	32	38	21
Selkirk	20	5	2	13	30	49	17
Heriot-Watt University	20	3	5	12	23	47	14

THE SOUTH OF SCOTLAND LEAGUE
DIRECTORY OF CLUBS

ABBEY VALE F.C.

Secretary:	David Morton
Manager:	James Neil
Club Address:	Maryfield Park, New Abbey
Sec Bus:	07881 704151
Sec Home:	01387 256004
Year of Formation:	1974
Playing Kits:	**1st Choice**
	Shirt: Black/Gold
	Shorts & Stockings: Black
	2nd Choice
	Shirt: Red
	Shorts & Stockings: Black

ANNAN ATHLETIC F.C.

Secretary:	Alan T. Irving
Manager:	David Irons
Club Address:	Galabank, North Street, Annan, Dumfries & Galloway.
Ground Tel/Fax No:	01461 204108
Sec Bus:	01461 207218
Sec Home:	01461 203702
Website:	www.members.synup.com/annanathletic
E-Mail:	annanathletic@synup.net
Year of Formation:	1942
Capacity:	2,000 (All Standing)
Pitch Dimensions:	110 yds x 65 yds
Playing Kits:	**1st Choice**
	Shirt: Black and Gold Broad Vertical Stripes
	Shorts: Black
	Stockings: Black with Two Gold Rings
	2nd Choice
	Shirt: Blue
	Shorts: White
	Stockings: White with Blue Tops

CREETOWN F.C.

Secretary:	Andrew Ward
Manager:	James McCrossan
Club Address:	Castlecary Park, Creetown.
Sec Home:	01671 820251
Year of Formation:	1894
Pitch Dimensions:	110yds x 66yds
Playing Kits:	**1st Choice**
	Shirt: Yellow & Black
	Shorts: Yellow & Black
	Stockings: Yellow & Black Hoops
	2nd Choice
	Shirt: Burgandy & White
	Shorts & Stockings: Burgandy

CRICHTON F.C.

Secretary:	Kenny Cameron
Manager:	Neil Currie
Club Address:	Crichton Park, Dumfries
Sec Home:	01387 265930
Sec Bus:	01387 258462
E-Mail:	kenny-ac.cameron@gbr.dupont.com
Year of Formation:	1970 (as Blackwood Dynamos)
Capacity:	2,500 (All Standing)
Pitch Dimensions:	106yds x 67yds
Playing Kits:	**1st Choice**
	Shirt: Blue & White
	Shorts & Stockings: Blue
	Stockings: Blue
	2nd Choice
	Shirt: Red & White
	Shorts: Black
	Stockings: Red

DALBEATTIE STAR F.C.

Secretary:	Robert Geddes
Manager:	Brian Aitchison
Club Address:	Islecroft Stadium, Dalbeattie.
Ground Tel:	01556 611151
Sec Bus/Home:	01556 610563
Fax No:	01556 611747
E-Mail:	bob@solwaypressservices.co.uk
Year of Formation:	1905 (approx)
Capacity:	4,000 (All Standing)
Pitch Dimensions:	110yds x 70yds
Playing Kits:	**1st Choice**
	Shirt: Red and Black Stripes
	Shorts: Black
	Stockings: Red
	2nd Choice
	Shirt: Maroon/Sky Blue
	Shorts & Stockings: Maroon

DUMFRIES F.C.

Secretary:	Tommy Parker
Manager:	Colin Lennox
Club Address:	Norfolk Park, Dumfries
Sec Home:	01387 263285
Sec Bus:	07710 679794
Website:	www.dumfriesfc.co.uk
E-Mail:	tommyparker3659@aol.com
Year of Formation:	2000
Capacity:	500 (All Standing)
Pitch Dimensions:	105yds x 63yds
Playing Kits:	**1st Choice**
	Shirt: Navy & Yellow
	Shorts & Stockings: Navy
	2nd Choice
	Shirt: Yellow & Green
	Shorts: Green
	Stockings: Yellow

GIRVAN F.C.

Secretary:	John M. Irvine
Manager:	James Miller
Club Address:	Hamilton Park, Girvan.
Sec Bus:	01465 714440
Sec Home:	01465 712702
Capacity:	700 (Approx) (200 Seated 500 Standing)
Pitch Dimensions:	104.5yds x 70 yds
Playing Kits:	**1st Choice**
	Shirt: Azure Blue with Black Vertical Stripe
	Shorts: Azure Blue
	Stockings: Black
	2nd Choice
	Shirt: Purple with White Pinstripe
	Shorts: Purple
	Stockings: Purple with White Flash

GRETNA F.C.

Secretary:	Ron McGregor
Manager:	Stuart Rome
Club Address:	Raydale Park, Gretna.
Ground Tel:	01461 337602
Fax No:	01461 338047
Sec Home/Fax:	01387 811820
Year of Formation:	1946
Capacity:	2,200 (1,500 Seated 700 Standing)
Playing Kits:	**1st Choice**
	Shirt: Black & White Hoops
	Shorts: Black
	Stockings: Black with White Tops
	2nd Choice
	Shirt: Claret & Grey
	Shorts & Stockings: Claret

NEWTON STEWART F.C.

Secretary:	John R. McNaught
Manager:	Alan Groves
Club Address:	Blairmount Park, Newton Stewart
Sec Bus:	01671 402776
Sec Home:	01671 403066
Playing Kits:	**1st Choice**

Shirt:	Black and White Vertical Stripes
Shorts:	Black
Stockings:	Black with White Tops
2nd Choice	
Shirt:	Yellow and Black
Shorts & Stockings:	Black and Yellow

NITHSDALE WANDERERS F.C.

Secretary:	Sam MacFarlane
Sec Home:	01659 50546
Treasurer:	William Watson
Treasurer's Home:	01659 58312
Club Address:	Lorimer Park, Sanquhar
Coaches:	Sam MacFarlane, Iain Mitchell, George Bain
Playing Kits:	**1st Choice**

Shirt:	Blue and White
Shorts:	Blue
2nd Choice	
Shirt:	Black and White
Short:	White

ST. CUTHBERT WANDERERS F.C.

Secretary:	Brian Mellon
Manager:	James Thompson
Club Address:	St. Mary's Park, Kirkcudbright.
Sec Bus/Home/Fax:	01557 500233
Pitch Dimensions:	100yds x 56yds
Playing Kits:	**1st Choice**

Shirt:	Blue with White Hoops
Shorts:	Blue with White Narrow Band
Stockings:	Blue with White Band on Tops
2nd Choice	
Shirt:	Yellow
Shorts:	Blue
Stockings:	Blue with White Band on Tops

STRANRAER ATHLETIC F.C.

Secretary:	Yvonne Lees
Manager:	Ivan White
Club Address:	Stranraer Academy, Stranraer.
Sec Home:	01776 707273
Playing Kits:	Shirt, Shorts & Stockings: Blue & White

TARFF ROVERS F.C.

Secretary:	Gavin McCleary
Manager:	Toby Paterson
Club Address:	Balgreen Park, Kirkcowan
Sec Bus:	01671 403603
Sec Home/Fax:	01671 830340
E-Mail:	tarffroversfc@aol.com
Year of Formation:	1874
Capacity:	4,070 (50 Seated 4,020 Standing)
Pitch Dimensions:	106yds x 63yds
Playing Kits:	**1st Choice**

Shirt:	Jade with Black Trim
Shorts:	Black
Stockings:	Jade and Black
2nd Choice	
Shirt:	Azure Blue and Black
Shorts:	Black
Stockings:	Black and Blue

THREAVE ROVERS F.C.

Secretary:	Robert McCleary
Manager:	William C. Sim
Club Address:	Meadow Park, Castle Douglas, Dumfries & Galloway.
Ground Tel No:	01556 504536
Sec Bus:	01556 502119
Sec Home/Fax:	01556 503512
E-Mail:	bobbymcleary@threaverovers.fsnet.co.uk
Year of Formation:	1953
Capacity:	5,000 (All Standing)
Pitch Dimensions:	110yds x 75yds
Playing Kits:	**1st Choice**

Shirt:	Black and White Vertical Stripes
Shorts:	Black
Stockings:	Black with White Trim
2nd Choice	
Shirt:	Blue
Shorts & Stockings:	White
3rd Choice	
Shirt:	White
Shorts & Stockings:	White

WIGTOWN AND BLADNOCH F.C.

Secretary:	Ian Bodle
Manager:	Andrew Kiltie
Club Address:	Trammondford Park, Wigtown.
Sec Home:	01988 500772
Year of Formation:	1880
Capacity:	1,500 (All Standing)
Pitch Dimensions:	110yds x 74yds
Playing Kits:	**1st Choice**

Shirt:	Red with White Trim
Shorts & Stockings:	Red
2nd Choice	
Shirt:	Blue with Yellow Trim
Shorts & Stockings:	Blue and Yellow

SOUTH OF SCOTLAND LEAGUE

FINAL TABLE – SEASON 2000/2001

	P	W	D	L	F	A	Pts
Queen of the South	14	13	0	1	59	16	39
Tarff Rovers	13	9	2	2	38	19	29
Dalbeattie Star	14	9	1	4	46	24	28
Crichton	13	7	4	2	29	21	25
St. Cuthbert Wanderers	13	6	4	3	33	26	22
Dumfries	14	6	2	6	31	32	20
Creetown	14	6	2	6	36	39	20
Annan Athletic	14	6	0	8	33	30	18
Girvan	19	3	6	10	30	63	15
Newton Stewart	9	4	1	4	22	20	13
Threave Rovers	11	3	0	8	17	33	9
Wigtown & Bladnoch	14	2	2	10	21	46	8
Stranraer Athletic	14	1	2	11	18	44	5

League Championship abandoned due to Foot and Mouth crisis.

Aberdeen

Pittodrie Stadium, Pittodrie Street,
Aberdeen, AB24 5QH

CHAIRMAN
Stewart Milne

VICE-CHAIRMAN
Ian R. Donald

DIRECTORS
Gordon A. Buchan,
Martin J. Gilbert
& Hugh Little

**COMPANY
SECRETARY/ACCOUNTANT**
Roy Johnston

FOOTBALL GENERAL MANAGER
David Johnston

MANAGER
Ebbe Skovdahl

ASSISTANT MANAGER
Gardner Spiers

U-21 & U-18 MANAGER
Drew Jarvie

YOUTH DEVELOPMENT MANAGER
Chic McLelland

FITNESS COACH
Stuart Hogg

KIT MANAGERS
Teddy Scott & Jim Warrender

CLUB DOCTORS
Dr. Derek Gray &
Dr. Stephen Wedderburn

PHYSIOTHERAPISTS
David Wylie & John Sharp

COMMUNITY COACHES
Neil Simpson & Jim Crawford

COMMUNITY OFFICERS
Bill Gordon & Sandy Finnie

CHIEF SCOUT
John Kelman

**FOOTBALL SAFETY OFFICERS'
ASSOCIATION REPRESENTATIVE**
John Morgan (01224) 650400

GROUNDSMAN
Paul Fiske

MARKETING & SALES MANAGER
Ian Riddoch (01224) 650400

HOSPITALITY MANAGER
Paul Quick

BUSINESS DEVELOPMENT MANAGER
Alan Dinnett

PROMOTIONS MANAGER
Jim Whyte

**SALES & MARKETING
CO-ORDINATOR**
Elaine Brainwood

CUSTOMER SERVICES MANAGER
Alan Stables

**PUBLIC RELATIONS MANAGER/
MATCHDAY PROGRAMME EDITOR**
Dave Macdermid

TELEPHONES
Ground/General Enquiries
(01224) 650400
Ticket Office (01224) 631903
Fax (01224) 644173
Dons Clubcall (09068) 121551
(AFC Events) (01224) 650420

E-Mail & Internet Address
davidj@afc.co.uk
feedback@afc.co.uk
www.afc.co.uk

CLUB SHOPS
AFC Direct, 19 Bridge Street,
Aberdeen, Tel (01224) 405305,
Fax (01224) 592250
Pittodrie Superstore,
Pittodrie Stadium, Aberdeen
Tel (01224 452003)

OFFICIAL SUPPORTERS CLUB
Association Secretary:
Mrs. Susan Scott, 'Aldon',
Wellington Road,
Aberdeen, AB12 4BJ
susan.scottone@virgin.net

TEAM CAPTAIN
Derek Whyte

SHIRT SPONSOR
A-FAB

KIT SUPPLIER
Le Coq Sportif

LIST OF PLAYERS 2001-2002

Squad No.	Name	Place & Date of Birth	Previous Club	Lge Career Apps	Gls
2	Russell Anderson	Aberdeen 25.10.78	Dyce Juniors	81 (9)	1
16	Rachid Belabed	Brussels, Belgium 20.10.80	RWD Molenbeek	11 (29)	1
27	Calum Bett	Reykjavik, Iceland 3.10.81	Aberdeen B.C.	– (2)	–
7	Roberto Bisconti	Brussels, Belgium 21.7.73	Charleroi	–	–
18	Chris Clark	Aberdeen 15.9.80	Hermes	14 (12)	–
19	Eugene Dadi	France 20.8.73	Toulouse	–	–
26	Robert Duncan	Peterhead 8.3.83	'S' Form	–	–
23	Ryan Esson	Aberdeen 19.3.80	Parkvale	37	–
4	Cato Guntveit	Drammen, Norway 6.8.75	Brann Bergen	48 (2)	4
15	David Lilley	Bellshill 31.10.77	Queen of the South	16 (8)	–
6	Jamie McAllister	Glasgow 26.4.78	Queen of the South	50 (9)	–
14	Philip McGuire	Glasgow 4.3.80	Dyce Juniors	26 (6)	–
17	Kevin McNaughton	Dundee 28.8.82	'S' Form	30 (3)	–
22	Darren Mackie	Inverurie 5.1.82	'S' Form	14 (11)	2
28	Scott Michie	Aberdeen 22.8.83	'S' Form	– (1)	–
24	Ross O'Donoghue	Glasgow 9.2.83	'S' Form	– (2)	–
13	Mark Peat	Bellshill 13.3.82	'S' Form	–	–
30	David Preece	Sunderland 26.8.76	Darlington	11 (1)	–
20	Kevin Rutkiewicz	Glasgow 10.5.80	Larkhall Thistle	1 (12)	–
5	Thomas Solberg	Oslo, Norway 25.1.70	Viking Stavanger	46 (2)	4
12	Ben Thornley	Bury 21.4.75	Huddersfield Town	–	–
25	Fergus Tiernan	Helensburgh 3.1.82	'S' Form	– (2)	–
3	Derek Whyte	Glasgow 31.8.68	Middlesbrough	102 (1)	–
9	Robbie Winters	East Kilbride 4.11.74	Dundee United	88 (10)	28
8	Darren Young	Glasgow 13.10.78	Crombie Sports	68 (8)	2
10	Derek Young	Glasgow 27.5.80	Lewis United	35 (13)	6
11	Hicham Zerouali	Morocco 17.1.77	Fus Rabat	8 (11)	3

Milestones

YEAR OF FORMATION: 1903
MOST CAPPED PLAYER: Alex McLeish
NO. OF CAPS: 77
MOST LEAGUE POINTS IN A SEASON: 64 (Premier Division - Season 1992/93) (44 games)(2 Points for a Win)
MOST LEAGUE GOALS SCORED BY A PLAYER IN A SEASON: Benny Yorston (Season 1929/30)
NO. OF GOALS SCORED: 38
RECORD ATTENDANCE: 45,061 (-v- Heart of Midlothian – 13.3.1954)
RECORD VICTORY: 13-0 (-v- Peterhead – Scottish Cup, 9.2.1923)
RECORD DEFEAT: 0-8 (-v- Celtic - Division 1, 30.1.65)

The Dons' ten year league record

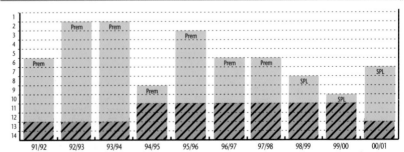

RESULTS... APPEARANCES... SCORERS... ATTENDANCES...

Date	Venue	Opponents	Att.	Res	Esson R.	Perry M.	McAllister J.	Solberg T.	Dow A.	Young Darren	Rowson D.	Jess E.	Winters R.	Stavrum A.	Young Derek	McGuire P.	Zerouali H.	Rutkiewicz K.	McNaughton K.	Guntveit C.	Clark C.	Belabed R.	Mackie D.	Whyte D.	Bernard P.	Mayer A.	Di Rocco A.	Lilley D.	Preece D.	Bett C.	O'Donoghue R.	Tiernan F.	Michie S.
July 29	A	Dunfermline Athletic	7,381	0-0	1	2	3	4	5	6	7	8	9	10	11	12	13	14															
Aug 5	A	St. Mirren	11,996	2-1	1	2[1]	3		5	6	7	8	9	10[1]		4	11		12	13	14												
	13	H	Heart of Midlothian	11,139	1-1	1	2		12		6	5	8	9	10	11[1]	4	13		3	7	14		8										
	19	H	Hibernian	12,450	0-2	1	2	13			6	5		9	10	11	4	12		3	7			8										
	27	A	Motherwell	6,009	1-1	1				14	6	5		9[1]		11	2	10		3	8		13	12	4	7								
Sep 9	H	St. Johnstone	10,464	1-1	1				10	6	5		9[1]			2			3	8	12	13	11	4	7								
	16	A	Kilmarnock	6,876	0-1	1					6	5	10	9			2			3	8	11	12	13	4	7	14							
	23	A	Dundee United	7,699	5-3	1	14				6	5	8[1]	9[3]		11[1]	2			3	7	10	13	12	4									
Oct 1	H	Celtic	17,580	1-1	1					5	8	9[1]		11	2			3	6	10	12	7	4										
	14	H	Dundee	15,332	0-2	1				13	5	8	9		11	2			3	6	10	12	7	4										
	21	H	Dunfermline Athletic	11,195	0-0	1	2			13	6	5	8	9	12				3	7	10		11	4										
	28	A	St. Mirren	5,763	0-2	1	2				6	5	8	9		11			3	7	10		12	4		13								
Nov 4	A	Heart of Midlothian	12,744	0-3	1	2	3			7	6	8	9	12	11			5		10	14	4		13									
	12	H	Rangers	16,798	1-2	1		13	2		6	5		9	10[1]	11			3	7	8			4		14	12							
	18	A	Hibernian	10,995	2-0	1	14		2		6	5	12	9	10[1]				3	7	11			4		13[1]	8							
	25	H	Motherwell	11,502	3-3	1			2		6	5	12	9	10[1]	11			3	7	13			4			8[2]							
	28	A	St. Johnstone	4,897	0-0	1			12		6	5	8	9	10	13	2		3	7	14			4		11								
Dec 2	H	Kilmarnock	11,584	1-2	1		13	4		6	5	8	9	10[1]	12	2		3	7					14	11								
	13	A	Rangers	45,285	1-3	1		3	4	13		5		9	10[1]	11	2		6	7	8				12	14								
	16	A	Celtic	59,677	0-6	1		3	4	12		5		9	10	11	2		7	8		14			13	6								
	23	A	Dundee	9,093	2-2	1		3	6	12		5		9	10[1]	11	2				8	13		4		7[1]								
	26	A	Dunfermline Athletic	6,880	2-3	1		3	6	7[1]		5[1]		9	10	11	2		23			12	24	4		8								
Jan 2	H	Heart of Midlothian	12,760	1-0	1		3	6	12	7	5[1]		9	10	11	2		13				4		8									
	31	A	Rangers	45,621	0-1	1		14	6		7	5		9	23	11	2		3	8		10	22	4						1				
Feb 10	H	Motherwell	6,680	1-0	1		3	2			5		9	10	12[1]		6	7		8	11	4		13	1								
	21	H	St. Mirren	9,457	3-0	1		3	4		7	5		9	10[3]	11	2		6	12	14	8			13									
Mar 3	A	Kilmarnock	6,577	0-0	1		3	4	12	6	5		9	10	11	2			7	14		8		13									
	13	H	Hibernian	8,799	1-0	1		3			7	5		9	10	11	2	12	6	8[1]				4										
	17	A	Dundee United	8,472	1-1	1		3			7	5		9[1]	10	11	2		6	8	12			4		13								
	27	H	St. Johnstone	8,496	3-3	1		3			7[1]	5		9[1]	10	11[1]	2		6		8	12		4		13								
Apr 1	H	Celtic	16,064	0-1	1		3	14		7	5		9	10	11	2		6		22	23	8	4										
	4	A	Dundee United	9,562	4-1	1			3	12		7	5		9	10[3]	11[1]	2	14		8	13		6										
	7	H	Dundee	12,005	0-2	1		3	6	14	7	5		9	10	11	2			8		22	23	4										
	21	H	Dunfermline Athletic	8,613	1-0	1		3	6		7	5		9	10[1]			2	8	11		13	4		12	14								
	28	A	St. Johnstone	3,611	3-0	1		3	6		7	5			10[1]			2	8	9	14	11[2]	4					12	13					
May 5	H	Motherwell	3,905	2-0	1		3	5		6			9[1]	10[1]	12	13	2	8	14	7	11	4											
	12	A	St. Mirren	5,780	1-2	1		3	5		7			9	10	11[1]	14	2	6	12		8	4					13						
	20	H	Dundee United	11,683	1-2	1		3			7			9	10[1]	11	2		5	6		8	4					12	23	24				
TOTAL FULL APPEARANCES					36	7	21	20	4	31	35	12	37	28	27	26	2		30	28	14	5	12	29	3		7	2	2				
TOTAL SUB APPEARANCES						(2)	(4)	(2)	(11)			(2)	(3)	(4)	(3)	(3)	(3)		(3)	(2)	(10)	(14)	(10)		(7)	(3)	(6)		(2)	(2)	(2)	(1)
TOTAL GOALS SCORED						1			1	1	2	1	9	17	6				1				2			1	3					

Small bold figures denote goalscorers. † denotes opponent's own goal.

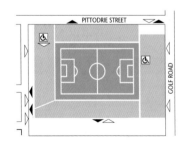

Pittodrie Stadium

PITTODRIE STREET

GOLF ROAD

CAPACITY: 21,662 (All Seated)

PITCH DIMENSIONS: 109 yds x 72 yds

FACILITIES FOR DISABLED SUPPORTERS:
Wheelchair section in front of Merkland Stand and in front row of Richard Donald Stand and also front row of Main Stand Section F.
(Please telephone Ticket Office and reserve place(s) in advance).

Team playing kits

FIRST CHOICE
Shirt: Red with White Trim.
Shorts: Red with White Trim.
Stockings: Red with White Trim.

SECOND CHOICE
Shirt: White with Red Trim.
Shorts: White with Red Trim.
Stockings: White with Red Trim.

How to get there

You can reach **Pittodrie Stadium** by these routes:

BUSES: The following buses all depart from the city centre to within a hundred yards of the ground: Nos. 1, 2, 3 and 11.

TRAINS: The main Aberdeen station is in the centre of the city and the above buses will then take fans to the ground.

CARS: Motor vehicles coming from the city centre should travel along Union Street, then turn into King Street and the park will be on your right, about half a mile further on.
Parking on Beach Boulevard and Beach Esplanade.

The Dons

Aberdeen F.C. is a member of The Scottish Premier League

Celtic

Celtic Park, Glasgow, G40 3RE

CELTIC PLC DIRECTORS
Brian Quinn, C.B.E. (Chairman),
Ian J.W. McLeod (Chief Executive),
Dermot F. Desmond, Eric J. Riley,
Sir Patrick Sheehy & Kevin Sweeney

CELTIC F.C. DIRECTORS
John S. Keane,
Michael A. McDonald
& James P. Hone

COMPANY SECRETARY
Robert M. Howat

FOOTBALL MANAGER
Martin O'Neill

FOOTBALL ASSISTANT MANAGER
John Robertson

FIRST TEAM COACH
Steve Walford

YOUTH DEVELOPMENT MANAGER
Tommy Burns

HEAD YOUTH COACH
Willie McStay

UNDER 21 COACH
Kenny McDowall

CLUB DOCTOR
Roddy McDonald

PHYSIOTHERAPIST
Brian Scott

**FOOTBALL SAFETY OFFICERS'
ASSOCIATION REPRESENTATIVE**
George E. Douglas
(0141) 556 2611/(0141) 551 4256

GROUNDSMAN
John Hayes

KIT CONTROLLER
John Clark

PUBLIC RELATIONS MANAGER
Kate Cunningham
(0141) 551 4276

CORPORATE SERVICES MANAGER
Frank McNally
(0141) 551 4278

MANAGING DIRECTOR CELTIC POOLS
John Maguire
(0141) 551 9922

MATCHDAY PROGRAMME EDITOR
Paul Cuddihy

TELEPHONES
Ground (0141) 556 2611
Fax (0141) 551 8106
Ticket Services (0141) 551 4223
Credit Card Hotline (0141) 551 8653/4
Celtic ClubCall (09066) 555561
Celtic View (0141) 551 4218
Walfrid Restaurant (0141) 551 9955
Mail Order Hotline (0141) 550 1888

CELTIC WORLD WIDE WEBSITE
www.celticfc.co.uk

CLUB SHOPS
Superstore, Celtic Park, Glasgow, G40 3RE
Tel (0141) 554 4231
(9.00 a.m. to 6.00 p.m. Mon-Sat,
10.00a.m. to 5.00p.m. Sunday),
40 Dundas Street, Glasgow G1 2AQ
Tel (0141) 332 2727
(9.00 a.m. to 5.00 p.m. Mon-Sat) and
21 High Street, Glasgow, G1 1LX
Tel (0141) 552 7630
(9.30 a.m. to 5.30 p.m. Mon-Sat,
11.30 a.m. to 4.30 p.m. Sunday)

OFFICIAL SUPPORTERS CLUB
Celtic Supporters Association,
1524 London Road, Glasgow G40 3RJ
Tel (0141) 556 1882/554 6250/554 6342

CLUB CAPTAIN
Tom Boyd

TEAM CAPTAIN
Paul Lambert

SHIRT SPONSOR
NTL

KIT SUPPLIER
Umbro

LIST OF PLAYERS 2001-2002

Squad No.	Name	Place & Date of Birth	Previous Club	Lge Career Apps	Gls
17	Didier Agathe	Saint Pierre, France 16.8.75	Hibernian	26 (1)	3
6	Dianbobo Balde	Marseille, France 10.5.75	Toulouse	–	–
22	Stephane Bonnes	France 26.2.78	FC Mulhouse	–	–
2	Tom Boyd	Glasgow 24.11.65	Chelsea	287 (10)	2
33	John Convery	Newtonards 1.4.80	Glenavon	– (1)	–
38	Barry John Corr	Glasgow 13.1.81	Celtic B.C.	–	–
40	Stephen Crainey	Glasgow 22.6.81	Celtic B. C.	5 (6)	–
20	Robert Douglas	Lanark 24.4.72	Dundee	22	–
34	Mark Fotheringham	Dundee 22.10.83	Celtic B. C	2 (1)	–
42	James Goodwin	Waterford 20.11.81	Tramore	1	–
1	Jonathan Gould	London 18.7.68	Bradford City	106 (1)	–
30	Steve Guppy	Winchester 29.3.69	Leicester City	–	–
10	John Hartson	Swansea 5.4.75	Coventry City	–	–
24	Colin Healy	Cork 14.3.80	Wilton United	14 (11)	1
41	John Kennedy	Lanark 18.8.83	'S' Form	1 (4)	–
37	Liam Keogh	Aberdeen 6.9.81	Celtic B.C.	–	–
21	Stewart Kerr	Lanark 13.11.74	Celtic B.C.	33 (1)	–
23	Dimitre Kharine	Moscow, Russia 16.8.68	Chelsea	5	–
14	Paul Lambert	Glasgow 7.8.69	Borussia Dortmund	110 (1)	5
7	Henrik Larsson	Helsingborg, Sweden 20.9.71	Feyenoord	114 (2)	87
18	Neil Lennon	Lurgan, 25.6.71	Leicester City	17	1
32	Simon Lynch	Montreal 19.5.82	Celtic Youth Initiative	1 (1)	1
28	Ryan McCann	Bellshill 21.9.81	Celtic B. C.	1	–
4	Jackie McNamara	Glasgow 24.10.73	Dunfermline Athletic	141 (16)	7
29	Shaun Maloney	Malaysia 24.1.83	Celtic Youth Initiative	1 (3)	–
43	Liam Miller	Cork 13.2.81	Celtic B.C.	– (1)	–
35	Johan Mjallby	Sweden 9.2.71	AIK Stockholm	73 (9)	7
25	Lubomir Moravcik	Slovakia 22.6.65	MSV Duisburg	59 (12)	23
15	Bobby Petta	Rotterdam, Holland 6.8.74	Ipswich Town	22 (10)	–
19	Stilian Petrov	Bulgaria 5.7.79	CSKA Sofia	47 (7)	8
31	Rafael Scheidt	Brazil 10.2.76	Gremio Porto Alegrens	1 (2)	–
26	Paul Shields	Dunfermline 15.8.81	Raith Rovers	– (1)	–
39	James Smith	Alexandria 20.11.80	Celtic B. C.	2 (5)	–
9	Chris Sutton	Nottingham 10.3.73	Chelsea	24	11
3	Mohammed Sylla	Bouakake, Ivory Coast 13.3.77	St. Johnstone	–	–
16	Olivier Tebily	Abidjan, Ivory Coast 19.12.75	Sheffield United	21 (6)	–
8	Alan Thompson	Newcastle 22.12.73	Aston Villa	29 (1)	3
5	Joos Valgaeren	Louvain, Belgium 3.3.76	Roda JC	35	3
11	Morten Wieghorst	Glostrup, Denmark 25.2.71	Dundee	58 (25)	10

Milestones

YEAR OF FORMATION: 1888
MOST CAPPED PLAYER: Paul McStay
NO. OF CAPS: 76
MOST LEAGUE POINTS IN A SEASON: 72 (Premier Division – Season 1987/88) (2 Points for a Win)
97 (Scottish Premier League – Season 2000/01) (3 Points for a Win)
MOST LEAGUE GOALS SCORED BY A PLAYER IN A SEASON: Jimmy McGrory (Season 1935/36)
NO. OF GOALS SCORED: 50
RECORD ATTENDANCE: 92,000 (-v- Rangers – 1.1.1938)
RECORD VICTORY: 11-0 (-v- Dundee – Division 1, 26.10.1895)
RECORD DEFEAT: 0-8 (-v- Motherwell – Division 1, 30.4.1937)

The Bhoys' ten year league record

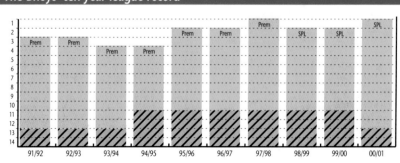

Date	Venue	Opponents	Att.	Res	Gould J.	Valgaeren J.	Mahe S.	Boyd T.	Stubbs A.	McNamara J.	Petrov S.	Lambert P.	Berkovic E.	Larsson H.	Sutton C.	Johnson T.	Tebily O.	Mjallby J.	Petta B.	Moravcik L.	Burchill M.	Thompson A.	Healy C.	Agathe D.	Riseth V.	Douglas R.	Lennon N.	Vega R.	Smith J.	Crainey S.	Maloney S.	Kharine D.	Fotheringham M.
July 30	A	Dundee United	11,761	2-1	1	2	3	4	5	6	7	8	9	10[1]	11[1]	12																
Aug 5	H	Motherwell	59,057	1-0	1	2	3	4		6	7	8	9[1]	10	11		5	12														
13	H	Kilmarnock	57,258	2-1	1	2	3	4	5		7	8		10[1]	11[1]	12		6	9														
19	A	Heart of Midlothian	16,744	4-2	1	2	3	13	5	4	7	8		10[1]	11[2]	12		6	9[1]														
27	H	Rangers	59,476	6-2	1	2	3	13	5	4	7[1]	8[1]		10[2]	11[2]	12		6	9	14													
Sep 9	H	Hibernian	60,040	3-0	1	2		3	5	4	7	8		10[2]	11	12			9	13[1]	6												
18	A	Dunfermline Athletic	9,493	2-1	1	2	3	4		6	7	8		10[2]	11		5	12		9													
23	H	Dundee	59,524	1-0	1		3		4	13	5	7[1]	8	14	10	11		2	9	6	12												
Oct 1	A	Aberdeen	17,580	1-1			3	12	4		5	7	8	10[1]	11			2	6	13		9	14										
14	H	St. Mirren	59,788	2-0			3		4		7	8		10[1]	11[1]			2	9		5	13	6	12									
17	A	St. Johnstone	8,946	2-0	1		3[1]		4		7	8		10[1]	11			2	6		5	12	9										
21	H	Dundee United	59,323	2-1	1		3		4	12	7	8		10[1]	11			2	6		5[1]		9										
29	A	Motherwell	12,421	3-3	1		3[1]		4	12	5[1]	7	8	10				2[1]	6	13		9		11									
Nov 5	A	Kilmarnock	13,412	1-0	1		3		4		5	7	8	10	11			2	6		9[1]	13	12										
12	H	St. Johnstone	56,952	4-1			3		4		7		23	10[2]	11[1]	24		2	6	9[1]		5	12	8			1						
18	H	Heart of Midlothian	59,849	6-1			3[1]		4		13	7[1]		10[2]	11	12	14	2[1]	6	9[1]		5		8			1						
26	A	Rangers	50,083	1-5			3	23	4		22	7		10[1]	11	14		2	6		5		8			1							
29	A	Hibernian	14,939	0-0			3	12	4		5	7		10	11			2	6	13			9	8			1						
Dec 2	H	Dunfermline Athletic	59,196	3-1			3		4		12	7		10[1]		11[1]		2	6	9[1]		5		8			1						
10	H	Dundee	10,763	2-1			3		4		13	7[1]		10		12		2	6	9		5	11[1]		1	8							
16	H	Aberdeen	59,677	6-0			3			12	7		10[3]		11		2	6			5		9		1	8	4[2]	13[1]					
23	A	St. Mirren	9,487	2-0			3			12	7		10[1]	11			2	6			5		9[1]		1	8	4						
26	A	Dundee United	12,306	4-0			3				5	7[1]		10[1]	11[2]	22		2	6	23			9		1	8	4	24					
Jan 2	H	Kilmarnock	59,103	6-0			3				5	7		10[4]	11[2]			2	6	23		12	9		1	8	4	24					
Feb 4	A	Heart of Midlothian	13,077	3-0			3	12			5		8	10[3]	11			2		24		6	9		1	7	4	23					
11	H	Rangers	59,496	1-0			3				8		10	11		12	2	5			6[1]	9		1	7	4							
21	H	Motherwell	58,736	1-0			3		13		12	8		10	11			2	5	14[1]		6	9		1	7	4						
25	H	Hibernian	59,791	1-1			3				5	8		10	11			2[1]		12		6	9		1	7	4						
Mar 4	A	Dunfermline Athletic	8,779	3-0			3				5[1]	8		10[1]	11	12		2				6	9		1	7[1]	4		13				
14	A	St. Johnstone	8,993	2-1			3			12	5	8		10[1]	11[1]			2				6	9		1	7	4		13				
Apr 1	A	Aberdeen	16,064	1-0			3			13		8		10	11			2	12			5	9	6[1]	1	7	4						
4	H	Dundee	59,190	2-1			3	13		12		8		10	11[1]			2[1]	9			5	6		1	7	4						
7	H	St. Mirren	60,102	1-0			3	13		12		8		10	11[1]			2	9			5	14	6	1	7	4						
22	A	Heart of Midlothian	58,708	1-0			3	14		5		8		10	11			2	12[1]			6	9	7	1		4	13					
29	A	Rangers	50,057	3-0			3	14		5		8		10[1]	11			2	9[2]			5	6		1	7	4			12			
May 6	A	Hibernian	8,879	5-2			3		2	22[1]	5[1]		8	10[1]					9[1]			6[1]	11			7	4			23	1	14	
13	H	Dundee	58,967	0-2	1		3	22	14	5		8		10				2	9			6				7	4	11	23				
20	A	Kilmarnock	12,578	0-1		6	3	5	7								2				9					1	4	11	10				8
TOTAL FULL APPEARANCES					15	35	7	21	7	18	27	27	2	37	24	9	2	30	20	16		29	4	26	22	17	18	2	1	1		1	1
TOTAL SUB APPEARANCES					(3)	(9)		(4)	(12)	(1)		(2)				(7)	(2)	(5)		(11)	(2)	(1)	(7)	(1)	(1)				(5)	(2)	(3)		(1)
TOTAL GOALS SCORED							3		1	2	6	1	1	35	11	5		4		9		1	4	3				1	2	1		

Small bold figures denote goalscorers. † denotes opponent's own goal.

Celtic Park

NORTH STAND (JANEFIELD STREET)

JOCK STEIN STAND

EAST STAND

MAIN SOUTH STAND (KERRYDALE STREET)

CAPACITY: 60,506 (All Seated)

PITCH DIMENSIONS: 115 yds x 74 yds

FACILITIES FOR DISABLED SUPPORTERS:
There is provision for 142 wheelchair positions for disabled supporters and their helpers. These are split into 87 in the North Stand, at the front of the lower terracing, 10 in the East Stand, lower terracing and 37 in the South Stand, lower terracing. Celtic fans should contact the club for availability. There is also a provision for 6 away positions in the lower East Stand.

Team playing kits

FIRST CHOICE
Shirt: Green and White Hoops. Collar White with Two Green Stripes.
Shorts: White.
Stockings: White with Green Tops and Two Green Leg Bands.

SECOND CHOICE
Shirt: Gold with Petrol Green Trim.
Shorts: Petrol Green with Gold Waistband.

Stockings: Petrol Green with Two Gold Hoops on Turnover.

THIRD CHOICE
Shirt: White with Green Shoulder and Collar Stripe and Black Trim.
Shorts: Black with White and Green Piping.
Stockings: Black with White and Green Piping.

How to get there

The following routes may be used to reach Celtic Park:

BUSES: The following buses all leave from the city centre and pass within 50 yards of the ground. Nos. 61, 62, and 64.

TRAINS: There is a frequent train service from Glasgow Central Low Level station to Bridgeton Cross Station and this is only a ten minute walk from the ground. There is also a train from Queen Street Station (lower level) to Bellgrove Rail Station, approximately 1 1/2 miles from the ground.

CARS: From the city centre, motor vehicles should travel along London Road and this will take you to the ground. Parking spaces are available in various areas close to the ground. On matchdays all car parking is strictly limited and is only available to those in possession of a valid car park pass.

Celtic F.C. is a member of The Scottish Premier League

Dens Park Stadium,
Sandeman Street, Dundee, DD3 7JY

CHAIRMAN
James M. Marr

DIRECTORS
James H. C. Connor, Peter Marr
& A. Ritchie Robertson

CHIEF EXECUTIVE
Peter Marr

COMPANY SECRETARY
A. Ritchie Robertson

FINANCIAL MANAGER
Michael G. Craig

MANAGER
Ivano Bonetti

ASSISTANT MANAGER
Dario Bonetti

CLUB CO-ORDINATOR
Dario Magri

UNDER 21 COACH
Ray Farningham

YOUTH TEAM COACH
Stevie Campbell

GOALKEEPER COACH
Claudio Bozzini

FITNESS COACH
Harry Hay

MASSEUR
Jack Cashley

CLUB DOCTORS
Dr. Phyllis Windsor, M.D., FRCR.,
Dr. John Vernon & Dr. Alan Dawson

PHYSIOTHERAPIST
Giovanni Grassi

FOOTBALL SAFETY OFFICERS'
ASSOCIATION REPRESENTATIVE
John Malone (01382) 313612

YOUTH DEVELOPMENT
CO-ORDINATOR
Kenny Cameron

COMMUNITY COACH
Kevin Lee

MANAGER'S SECRETARY
Mrs Laura Hayes

OPERATIONS MANAGER
Jim Thomson

TICKET OFFICE MANAGER
Neil Cosgrove

GROUNDSMAN
Brian Robertson

KIT MANAGER
Brian Duncan

COMMERCIAL DIRECTOR
Jim Connor Tel (01382) 884450
Fax (01382) 858963

COMMERCIAL MANAGER
Ian Reilly Tel (01382) 884450

MARKETING MANAGER
Brian Gray

MATCHDAY PROGRAMME EDITOR/
DENS PROMOTIONS MANAGER
Dave Forbes (07767) 214520

TELEPHONES
Football/Manager (01382) 826104
Administration/Accounts/
Youth Development (01382) 889966
Commercial/ Marketing
(01382) 884450
Ticket Office (01382) 204777
Stadium Manager (01382) 815250
Fax (01382) 832284
Commercial Fax (01382) 858963

E-MAIL & INTERNET ADDRESS
www.dundeefc.co.uk
dfc@dundeefc.co.uk
laura@dundeefc.co.uk

CLUB SHOP
Dundee F.C. Shop, situated between
Main Stand and Bobby Cox Stand

OFFICIAL SUPPORTERS CLUB
Contact: Norrie Price (01224) 639967

TEAM CAPTAIN
Barry Smith

SHIRT SPONSOR
Ceramic Tile Warehouse

KIT SUPPLIER
XARA

LIST OF PLAYERS 2001-2002

Squad No.	Name	Place & Date of Birth	Previous Club	Lge Career Apps	Gls
18	Javier Artero	Madrid, Spain 16. 4.75	San Lorenzo	38 (6)	4
7	Fabian Caballero	Misiones, Argentina 31.1.78	Sol de America	12 (3)	6
5	Alberto Carranza	Quilmes, Argentina 15.6.72	San Lorenzo	15 (7)	3
6	Chris Coyne	Brisbane, Australia 20.12.78	West Ham United	16 (2)	–
17	Walter Del Rio	Argentina 16.6.76	Crystal Palace	7 (2)	–
20	Umberto Fatello	Rome, Italy 21.1.83	Lodigiani	–	–
14	Alberto Garrido	Argentina 26.9.74	Pristina	8 (2)	–
13	Zurab Khizanishvili	Georgia 6.10.81	Lokomotiv Tiblisi	5 (1)	–
1	Jamie Langfield	Paisley 22.12.79	Glasgow City BC	10 (2)	–
4	Marcello Marrocco	Modena, Italy 7.6.69	Modena	24	–
40	Paul Mathers	Aberdeen 17.1.70	Linfield	112	–
15	Steven Milne	Dundee 5.5.80	Downfield	6 (17)	4
10	Giorgi Nemsadze	Georgia 10.5.72	Reggiani	33 (2)	2
8	Gavin Rae	Aberdeen 28.11.77	Hermes Juniors	104 (21)	11
21	Alessandro Romano	Rome, Italy 29.6.69	Verona	14 (2)	–
11	Mark Robertson	Sydney, Australia 6.4.77	Walsall	2 (2)	–
9	Juan Sara	Argentina 13.10.76	Cerro Portino	25 (6)	15
2	Barry Smith	Paisley 19.2.74	Celtic	187 (4)	1
23	Lee Wilkie	Dundee 20.4.80	Downfield Juniors	26 (7)	–

Milestones

YEAR OF FORMATION: 1893
MOST CAPPED PLAYER: Alex Hamilton
NO. OF CAPS: 24
MOST LEAGUE POINTS IN A SEASON: 58 (First Division – Season 1991/92) (2 Points for a Win)
70 (First Division – Season 1997/98) (3 Points for a Win)
MOST LEAGUE GOALS SCORED BY A PLAYER IN A SEASON: Alan Gilzean (Season 1963/64)
NO. OF GOALS SCORED: 32
RECORD ATTENDANCE: 43,024 (-v- Rangers – 1953)
RECORD VICTORY: 10-0 (-v- Fraserburgh, 1931; -v- Alloa, 1947; -v- Dunfermline Athletic, 1947; -v- Queen of the South, 1962)
RECORD DEFEAT: 0-11 (-v- Celtic – Division 1, 26.10.1895)

The Dark Blues' ten year league record

THE DARK BLUES' CLUB FACTFILE 2000/2001
RESULTS... APPEARANCES... SCORERS... ATTENDANCES...

Date	Venue	Opponents	Att	Res	Douglas R.	Smith B.	Marrocco M.	de Marchi M.	Tweed S.	Bonetti I.	Nemsadze G.	Artero J.	Billio P.	Caballero F.	Sara J.	McSkimming S.	Falconer W.	Robertson H.	Yates M.	Milne S.	Coyne C.	Rae G.	Wilkie L.	Romano A.	Caniggia C.	Carranza A.	Langfield J.	Roccati M.	del Rio W.	Russo M.	Garrido A.	Khizanishvili Z.	Robertson M.	Vargiu M.
July 29	A	Motherwell	5,961	2-0	1	2	3	4	5	6	7	8¹	9¹	10	11	12	13																	
Aug 5	H	Dunfermline Athletic	9,507	†3-0	1	2	3	4	5		7	8	9	10¹	11¹				22	6	23	14												
12	A	Hibernian	12,730	1-5	1	2	3	4	5	6	7	8	9	10¹	11		12	13																
19	A	St. Mirren	5,165	1-2	1	2	3		5		7	8		11¹			10	6	12		4	9												
27	H	Heart of Midlothian	6,779	1-1	1	2			5	12	7	8	6	10¹	11	9			13				3	4										
Sep 9	H	Rangers	10,439	1-1	1	2	3	4	5	6	7	8		10	12¹						9	13	11											
16	A	St. Johnstone	5,055	0-0	1	2	3	4	5	6	7	8	9	10	13	12			11															
20	H	Dundee United	9,838	3-0	1	2			4	5	6	7¹	13		10	11²	9				8	12	3											
23	A	Celtic	59,524	0-1	1	2			5	6	7	8		11	10	12	14		13		9	3	4											
30	H	Kilmarnock	6,170	0-0	1	2			5		7	8	9		11	10			12	13	6	3	4											
Oct 14	A	Aberdeen	15,332	2-0	1	2	3	4	5	6¹	13	8		11					10		9			7	12¹	14								
21	H	Motherwell	7,344	1-2		2	3	4		6	12	8	9	11							12		5	7	10¹	13	1							
28	A	Dunfermline Athletic	5,925	0-1		2	3	4	5	6	7	8							12		9		11	10	13		1						
Nov 5	H	Hibernian	6,602	1-2		2	3	4	5¹		7	8	6	12		11					9			10			1						
11	A	Dundee United	11,454	2-0		2	3	4	5	6	7¹	8		12		11					9			10¹	13		1						
18	H	St. Mirren	6,393	5-0		2	3	4	5	6	7	8¹		23		11			22¹		9¹		14	10²			1						
25	A	Heart of Midlothian	11,539	1-3		2	3	4	5	6		8		12	11				13		9			10	7¹		1						
Dec 2	H	St. Johnstone	7,014	1-1		2	3	4	5	6	7	8		11¹					14		9	12		10	13		1						
10	H	Celtic	10,763	†1-2		2	3	4	5		7	8		11	13				14	12	9			10	6		1						
16	A	Kilmarnock	6,573	3-2		2	3		5	6¹	7	12		11		13			10²	4	9			8			1						
23	H	Aberdeen	9,093	2-2		2	3	4	5		7	8		11¹	12				13		9			10	6¹		1						
26	A	Motherwell	6,183	3-0		2	3		5	12	7	13		11²	9	14			10		8¹				6		1		4				
Jan 2	H	Hibernian	12,381	0-3		2			5	6	7			11	3				12		9			10	8	15	1		4				
31	H	Dundee United	11,724	2-3		2			5	12	7	8		3	11¹				4		9	10¹		6		1		13				
Feb 3	A	St. Mirren	4,085	1-2		2			5		7	8		11¹					13	4	9		3	10	6		1		12				
21	H	Dunfermline Athletic	6,113	0-1		2	3				8				11		23	9	4	7	22			10	6		1		5	14			
24	H	Rangers	9,778	0-1		2		4	5		7	8		11					3	9				10			1			6			
Mar 3	A	St. Johnstone	5,065	3-2		2		4	5		7	8¹		11¹			13		3	9¹				10			1		12	6			
14	A	Rangers	45,035	2-0		2	3		5		7	8		11					12¹	4	9			10¹			1	13	6				
18	H	Heart of Midlothian	7,327	0-0		2	3				7	8		11					13	4	9			10	12		1	5	6				
31	H	Kilmarnock	6,719	2-2		2	3		5		7	8	12	11¹					4	9¹				10	6		1						
Apr 4	H	Celtic	59,190	1-2		2	3		5		7	8	12	11¹					4	9			10	13	1				6	14			
7	A	Aberdeen	12,005	2-0			3		5		7¹	8	10¹	11					4	9				6	1				12	2			
21	H	Rangers	10,687	0-3					5		7	8	13	11				10	4	9	12			6	1		14		3	2			
29	A	Hibernian	6,659	0-2		2			5		7		11							9	8	10		1		4		6	3	12			
May 5	H	Kilmarnock	6,261	2-1		2					7	8	10	11¹				13	4	9	5		6¹	1				3	12	14			
13	A	Celtic	58,967	2-0		2					8	10²						13	4	9	6		7	1		5		12	3	11			
20	A	Heart of Midlothian	13,554	0-2		2				7		10	12					13	4	14	3	6	9	1		5		8		11			
TOTAL FULL APPEARANCES					11	36	24	18	32	15	33	32	8	12	25	7	8	2	5	16	31	5	14	20	15	8	19	7			8	5	2	
TOTAL SUB APPEARANCES								(3)	(2)	(3)		(3)	(6)	(5)	(6)	(1)	(6)	(16)		(2)	(1)	(4)	(2)	(1)	(7)	(1)			(2)	(4)	(2)	(1)	(2)	(1)
TOTAL GOALS SCORED								1	2	3	3	1	6	14			1			4			4			7	3						

Small bold figures denote goalscorers. † denotes opponent's own goal.

Dens Park Stadium

SANDEMAN STREET — TANNADICE STREET
PROVOST ROAD
DENS ROAD

CAPACITY: 11,850 (All Seated)

PITCH DIMENSIONS: 113 yds x 74 yds

FACILITIES FOR DISABLED SUPPORTERS:
There is provision for disabled supporters in both the East and West Stands.

Team playing kits

	FIRST CHOICE	SECOND CHOICE
Shirt:	Navy Blue with White Piping.	Four Sky Blue and White Vertical Stripes.
Shorts:	White with Navy Blue Piping.	Navy Blue with Sky Blue Piping.
Stockings:	Navy Blue with Two White Bands on Tops.	White with Two Navy Blue Bands on Tops.

How to get there

You can reach Dens Park Stadium by the following routes:

BUSES: There is a frequent service of buses from the city centre. Nos. 1A and 1B leave from Albert Square and Nos. 18, 19 and 21 leave from Commercial Street.

TRAINS: Trains from all over the country pass through the mainline Dundee station and fans can then proceed to the ground by the above buses from stops situated close to the station.

CARS: Cars may be parked in the car park (Densfield Park) and local streets adjacent to the ground.

The Dark Blues

Dundee F.C. is a member of The Scottish Premier League

Dundee United

Tannadice Park, Tannadice Street,
Dundee, DD3 7JW

CHAIRMAN
Douglas B. Smith

DIRECTORS
A. Bruce Robertson,
William M. Littlejohn &
Donald T. Ridgway

MANAGING DIRECTOR
William M. Littlejohn

CLUB SECRETARY
Spence Anderson

ASSISTANT CLUB SECRETARY
Mrs. Elisabeth Leslie

MANAGER
Alexander N. Smith

ASSISTANT MANAGER
John Blackley

COACHING STAFF
Maurice Malpas, Paul Hegarty,
Graham Lowe & Graeme Liveston

CLUB DOCTOR
Dr. Derek J. McCormack

PHYSIOTHERAPISTS
David Rankine & Eric Ferguson

CHIEF SCOUT
Graeme Liveston

GROUNDSMAN
Peter Fox

**FOOTBALL SAFETY OFFICERS'
ASSOCIATION REPRESENTATIVE**
David Anderson (01382) 833166

**COMMUNITY
DEVELOPMENT OFFICER**
John Holt

COMMERCIAL MANAGER
Bill Campbell (01382) 832202

MATCHDAY PROGRAMME EDITOR
Peter Rundo

TELEPHONES
Ground (01382) 833166
Fax (01382) 889398

E-MAIL & INTERNET ADDRESS
dundee.united.fc@cableinet.co.uk
www.dundeeunitedfc.co.uk

CLUB SHOP
The United Shop, Unit 2,
5 Victoria Road, Dundee
Tel/Fax (01382) 204066 -
Open 9.00 a.m. to 5.30 p.m.
Mon-Fri, 9.00a.m. to 5.00 p.m. Sat.
Souvenir shops are also situated
within the ground in the East and
George Fox Stands and are open
on home matchdays.

OFFICIAL SUPPORTERS CLUB
Norrie Boath
Tel: (07711) 363104
E-Mail: federationdufc@hotmail.com

TEAM CAPTAIN
Danny Griffin

SHIRT SPONSOR
Telewest Communications

KIT SUPPLIER
TFG

LIST OF PLAYERS 2001-2002

Squad No.	Name	Place & Date of Birth	Previous Club	Lge Career Apps	Gls
14	Hasney Aljofree	Manchester 11.7.78	Bolton Wanderers	24 (2)	2
15	Jamie Buchan	Manchester 3.4.77	Aberdeen	33 (2)	1
1	Alan Combe	Edinburgh 3.4.74	St. Mirren	68	–
27	Stephen Carson	Ballymoney 6.10.80	Rangers	–	–
20	Hugh Davidson	Dundee 3.8.80	Dundee United BC	23 (11)	1
7	Craig Easton	Bellshill 26.2.79	Dundee United BC	99 (28)	8
10	Jamie Fullarton	Bellshill 20.7.74	Crystal Palace	3 (2)	–
13	Paul Gallacher	Glasgow 16.8.79	Lochee United	16	
16	Danny Griffin	Belfast 10.8.77	St. Johnstone	18	–
17	Jim Hamilton	Aberdeen 9.2.76	Aberdeen	22 (11)	3
4	David Hannah	Coatbridge 4.8.73	Celtic	115 (20)	16
6	Jim Lauchlan	Glasgow 2.2.77	Kilmarnock	23	1
9	Derek Lilley	Paisley 9.2.74	Oxford United	18	6
22	Jim McIntyre	Alexandria 24.5.72	Reading	–	–
25	Stephen McConalogue	Glasgow 16.6.81	Dundee United BC	12 (16)	1
32	David McCracken	Glasgow 16.10.81	Dundee United BC	8 (3)	–
12	Jamie McCunnie	Bellshill 15.4.83	Dundee United BC	15	–
8	Charlie Miller	Glasgow 18.3.76	Watford	24	5
21	David Partridge	London 26.11.78	West Ham United	46 (3)	–
11	Jim Paterson	Bellshill 25.9.79	Dundee United BC	21 (8)	2
19	Stephen Thompson	Paisley 14.10.78	Dundee United BC	42 (40)	6
18	Anastasios Venetis	Larissa, Greece 24.3.80	Larissa	15 (16)	1
3	Stephen Wright	Bellshill 27.8.71	Bradford City	5	–
23	David Winters	Paisley 7.3.82	Dundee United BC	– (5)	

Milestones

YEAR OF FORMATION: 1923 (1909 as Dundee Hibs)
MOST CAPPED PLAYER: Maurice Malpas
NO. OF CAPS: 55
MOST LEAGUE POINTS IN A SEASON: 60 (Premier Division - Season 1986/87) (2 Points for a Win)
67 (First Division - Season 1995/96) (3 Points for a Win)
MOST LEAGUE GOALS SCORED BY A PLAYER IN A SEASON: John Coyle (Season 1955/56)
NO. OF GOALS SCORED: 41
RECORD ATTENDANCE: 28,000 (-v- Barcelona – 16.11.1966)
RECORD VICTORY: 14-0 (-v- Nithsdale Wanderers – Scottish Cup, 17.1.1931)
RECORD DEFEAT: 1-12 (-v- Motherwell – Division 2, 23.1.1954)

The Terrors' ten year league record

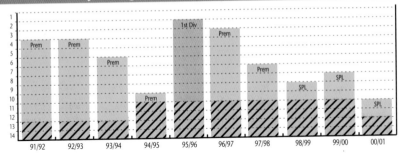

150

THE TERRORS' CLUB FACTFILE 2000/2001
RESULTS... APPEARANCES... SCORERS... ATTENDANCES...

Date	Venue	Opponents	Att.	Res	Combe A.	McCracken D.	Buchan M.J.	De Vos J.	Alljofree H.	Paterson J.	Easton C.	Hannah D.	Heaney N.	Thompson S.	Mathie A.	Venetis A.	Hamilton J.	McConalogue S.	McQuillan J.	Partridge D.	Fernandez J.	Davidson H.	Smith A.	Wright S.	Tchami A.	Leoni S.	Atangana M.	Licina J.	McDonald K.	Caloppo M.	Fuentes G.	Marcora C.	Ramirez F.	Lauchlan J.	Miller C.	Naveda A.	Fullarton J.	O'Connor S.	Lilley D.	Griffin D.	Winters D.	McCunnie J.	Gallacher P.	Robinson P.	Brady D.
July 30	H	Celtic	11,761	1-2	1	2¹	3	4	5	6	7	8	9	10	11	12	13	14																											
Aug 5	A	Hibernian	9,613	0-3	1		8	4	5	6	7	12	11	10	13	9	14			2	3																								
12	H	Motherwell	6,201	1-1	1	3	7	4	5	6¹	12	8	14	10	11			13	2		9																								
19	H	St. Johnstone	6,636	1-2	1	3	6	4	5¹		9	10	11				2	12		13	14																								
26	A	Dunfermline Athletic	4,980	0-1	1		7	4	5	6	14	8	12	13			10		3		9		2	11																					
Sep 9	A	Kilmarnock	6,380	0-1	1		3	4	5	6	7		12	10		14			8				2	11	9	13																			
16	H	St. Mirren	5,943	0-0	1		3	4	5		13	8		10					7	14			2	6	9	11	12																			
20	A	Dundee	9,838	0-3	1	14	3	4	5		12	8		10					7	9				6	11	2	13																			
23	A	Aberdeen	7,699	3-5	1	14	3				12¹	8¹							13¹	5			7	9			4		6	11	2															
Oct 1	A	Rangers	44,324	0-3	1	3		4	5		9	8		14	13				2					6	11	12		7	10																	
14	H	Heart of Midlothian	7,016	0-4	1		6	4	5			10		23					12	3	7		2		9			8	11	24																
21	A	Celtic	59,323	†1-2	1		8	4	5		9			10					7		6	3			13	12	2		11		14															
28	H	Hibernian	8,042	0-1	1		8	4	5		9			10		13		12	6	3			11	7								2														
Nov 4	A	Motherwell	6,864	1-2	1		7	4	5		9	12		13					6	3			11							2	8	10¹		14												
11	H	Dundee	11,454	0-2	1		6		5		9	8		14					12	4	3		11	2							7	10	13													
18	A	St. Johnstone	4,295	0-1	1		2		5		11	8	12					13	6	4											4	9	10	7												
25	H	Dunfermline Athletic	6,012	3-2	1		3	4	5		7¹	13	12					11	14												2	8¹	10	6	9¹											
28	H	Kilmarnock	5,497	0-1	1		3	4	5			7	9	12		13		11					14								2	8	10	6												
Dec 5	A	St. Mirren	4,685	1-1	1		3	4	5			7	9	13			10	14	6	12											2	8	11¹													
17	H	Rangers	10,750	1-1	1		5	7	4	6			9				14	12	13		3										2	8	11		10¹											
23	A	Heart of Midlothian	12,128	1-3	1	3	7	4	6¹		12		9				10		13	2		14									8			11	5											
26	H	Celtic	12,306	0-4	1	13	7	4	6		9			10			11		2	3		12									8					5	14									
30	A	Hibernian	10,197	0-1	1		4	6			9			10			12		3	13											5	8			11	7	14	2								
Jan 2	H	Motherwell	6,311	2-0			4	6			9¹			12			10¹		3												5	8			11	7		2	1							
31	A	Dundee	11,724	3-2			6	4			9¹			12			10			7¹											3¹	8	13		11	5		2	1							
Feb 3	H	St. Johnstone	6,482	1-1			6	4	12		9			13			10			7											3	8¹	14		11	5		2	1							
10	A	Dunfermline Athletic	4,899	1-3			6	4	12		9			13			10			7											3	8	14		11¹	5		2	1							
24	A	Kilmarnock	6,289	0-0			6	4			9	7					10					14									3	8	13		11	5		2	1	12						
Mar 3	H	St. Mirren	8,334	4-0			6	4			9	7¹					12	10¹													3	8¹	13		11¹	5		2	1	14						
17	H	Aberdeen	8,472	1-1			2	4			9			14			12	10			6										3	8¹			11	5		7	1	13						
31	A	Rangers	48,382	2-0			2	4			9			12¹			10														3	8			11	5		7	1	6						
Apr 4	A	Aberdeen	9,562	1-4			2	4			9	12		10																	3	8			11	5¹		7	1	6						
7	H	Heart of Midlothian	7,242	1-1			2	4			9	6		10¹		12															3	8	14		11	5		7	1	13						
23	A	St. Mirren	6,473	1-2			6	4			7	8		9¹			10			2											3				11	5				1						
28	H	Motherwell	5,928	1-0			4¹				9	6		12			13	10		2											3	8			11	5	14	7	1							
May 6	A	Dunfermline Athletic	6,679	1-0			13	4			9	6		10¹			12			2											3	8			11	5	14	7	1							
12	H	St. Johnstone	6,497	3-2			12	4			9¹	6		10			13			2											3	8¹			11¹	5	14	7	1							
20	A	Aberdeen	11,683	2-1			2		6	13	9			4¹	10																3	8	14		11¹	5		7	1	12						
TOTAL FULL APPEARANCES					23	6	33	33	24	5	27	20	7	18	3	3	14	3	12	17	6	6	1	5	3	5	8	5			2	3	23	24	7	3	1	18	18			15	15	2
TOTAL SUB APPEARANCES						(3)	(2)		(2)	(1)	(6)	(4)	(5)	(13)	(1)	(11)	(6)	(8)	(3)	(2)			(5)	(2)			(1)	(3)	(2)	(1)		(1)	(1)				(6)	(2)	(1)		(5)		(4)	(1)
TOTAL GOALS SCORED					1	1		2	1	5	2		4		1	2	1			1														1	5	2		1	6	1					

Small bold figures denote goalscorers.   † denotes opponent's own goal.

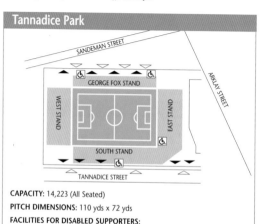

Tannadice Park

SANDEMAN STREET

GEORGE FOX STAND

WEST STAND · EAST STAND

SOUTH STAND

TANNADICE STREET

ARKLAY STREET

CAPACITY: 14,223 (All Seated)

PITCH DIMENSIONS: 110 yds x 72 yds

FACILITIES FOR DISABLED SUPPORTERS:
George Fox Stand – Lower Tier – Home Supporters.
East Stand – Lower Tier – Home Supporters.
West Stand – Away Supporters.

Team playing kits

FIRST CHOICE
Shirt: Tangerine with Black Trim on 'V' Neck and Black Cuffs.
Shorts: Black with Tangerine Piping on both Sides.
Stockings: White with Black Band. Black Trim on Turnover.

SECOND CHOICE
Shirt: White with Black Trim on 'V' Neck and Black Cuffs.
Shorts: White with Black Piping on both Sides.
Stockings: White with Black Band. Black Trim on Turnover.

THIRD CHOICE
Shirt: Green 'V' Neck with Black Collar, White Trim and Tangerine Piping from Shoulder to Underarm.
Shorts: White with Two Sets of Tangerine Piping down both Sides.
Stockings: White with Tangerine and Green Trim on Turnover.

How to get there

Tannadice Park can be reached by the following routes:
BUSES: The following buses leave from the city centre at frequent intervals:- Nos. 1a, 18, 19 and 21 from Meadowside and No. 20 from Littlewoods High Street.
TRAINS: Trains from all over the country pass through the main Dundee station and fans can then proceed to the ground by the above bus services from stops situated within walking distance of the station.
CARS: There is parking in the streets adjacent to the ground.

Dundee United F.C. is a member of The Scottish Premier League

East End Park, Halbeath Road,
Dunfermline, Fife, KY12 7RB

CHAIRMAN
John W. Yorkston

DIRECTORS
C. Roy Woodrow, William M. Rennie,
Gavin G. Masterton, C.B.E., F.I.B. (Scot),
Andrew T. Gillies, John Meiklem,
W. Brian Robertson, W.S.,
Graham A Thomson &
Francis M. McConnell, SSC.

**FOOTBALL SECRETARY/
GENERAL MANAGER**
Paul A. M. D'Mello

COMPANY SECRETARY
Elaine Cromwell

HEAD COACH
James Calderwood

ASSISTANT HEAD COACH
James Nicholl

PRINCIPAL COACHING STAFF
Hamish French & Joe Nelson

**COMMUNITY PROGRAMME
DIRECTOR**
Robert Paton

**COMMUNITY PROGRAMME
MANAGER**
John Glancy

CLUB DOCTOR
Dr. Gerry D. Gillespie

PHYSIOTHERAPIST
Philip Yeates, M.C.S.P.

**YOUTH DEVELOPMENT
MANAGER**
John B. Ritchie

**FOOTBALL SAFETY OFFICERS'
ASSOCIATION REPRESENTATIVE/
SECURITY ADVISOR**
David Dickson (01383) 724295

STADIUM MANAGER
Brian Gallagher (01383) 725557

HEAD GROUNDMAN
John Wilson

KIT CO-ORDINATOR
Andrew Hutton

ACTING COMMERCIAL MANAGER
Paul D'Mello

CLUB SHOP MANAGER
Kevin Gillespie

MATCHDAY PROGRAMME EDITOR
Duncan Simpson

TELEPHONES
Ground/Secretary/Manager/
Commercial/Ticket Office
(01383) 724295/721749
Fax (01383) 723468
Clubcall (09066) 555060

E-MAIL & INTERNET ADDRESS
pars@dunfermline-athletic.com
www.dunfermline-athletic.com

CLUB SHOP
Situated at Ground
Open 9.00 a.m. – 5.00 p.m.
Mon to Sat. Tel: (01383) 626737

OFFICIAL SUPPORTERS CLUB
c/o Mrs. Joan Malcolm, Secretary,
Dunfermline Athletic Supporters Club,
13 South Knowe, Crossgates, KY4 8AW

TEAM CAPTAIN
Ian Ferguson

SHIRT SPONSOR
RAC Auto Windscreens

KIT SUPPLIER
TFG

LIST OF PLAYERS 2001-2002

Squad No.	Name	Place & Date of Birth	Previous Club	Lge Career Apps	Gls
27	Steven Boyle	Edinburgh 11.12.80	Ratho Colts	2 (6)	2
21	Lee Bullen	Edinburgh 29.3.71	PAE Kalamata	25 (12)	11
9	Stephen Crawford	Dunfermline 9.1.74	Hibernian	62	25
3	Jason Dair	Dunfermline 15.6.74	Raith Rovers	56 (11)	6
2	Michel Doesburg	Beverwyk 10.8.68	Motherwell	26 (6)	–
8	Ian Ferguson	Glasgow 15.3.67	Rangers	40	2
28	George Fotheringham	Rutherglen 13.3.81	Raith Rovers	2	–
10	Jack de Gier	Schijendel 29.7.68	NEC Nijmegen	–	–
12	Steven Hampshire	Edinburgh 17.10.79	Chelsea	22 (16)	5
29	Mark McGarty	Fauldhouse 3.8.82	Unattached	1 (3)	–
16	Chris McGroarty	Bellshill 6.2.81	Rosyth Rec U–18	36 (11)	1
18	Angus MacPherson	Glasgow 11.10.68	Kilmarnock	–	–
15	Gary Mason	Edinburgh 15.10.79	Manchester City	8 (2)	–
24	Rob Matthaei	Amsterdam 20.9.66	Motherwell	11 (5)	–
22	Junior Mendes	London 15.9.76	St. Mirren	7 (6)	–
25	David Moss	Doncaster 15.11.68	Falkirk	36 (14)	12
19	David Nicholls	Bellshill 5.4.72	Falkirk	–	–
7	Barry Nicholson	Dumfries 24.8.78	Rangers	36	3
26	Colin Nish	Edinburgh 7.3.81	Rosyth Rec U–18	– (8)	–
11	Stewart Petrie	Dundee 27.2.70	Forfar Athletic	194 (37)	43
17	John Potter	Dunfermline 15.12.79	Celtic	17 (4)	1
14	Youssef Rossi	Morocco 28.6.73	NEC Nijmegen	11	1
1	Marco Ruitenbeek	Weesp 12.5.68	Go Ahead Eagles	36	–
5	Andrius Skerla	Vilnius 29.4.77	PSV Eindhoven	34	–
4	Justin Skinner	London 30.1.69	Hibernian	60 (5)	–
6	Scott M Thomson	Aberdeen 29.1.72	Raith Rovers	82 (2)	5
20	Scott Y Thomson	Edinburgh 8.11.66	Airdrieonians	2	–
23	Andrew Tod	Dunfermline 4.11.71	Kelty Hearts	211 (15)	34

Milestones

YEAR OF FORMATION: 1885
MOST CAPPED PLAYER: Istvan Kozma
NO. OF CAPS: Hungary 29 (13 whilst with Dunfermline Athletic)
MOST LEAGUE POINTS IN A SEASON: 65 (First Division – Season 1993/94) (2 Points for a Win)
      71 (First Division – Seasons 1995/96 and 1999/2000) (3 Points for a Win)
MOST LEAGUE GOALS SCORED BY A PLAYER IN A SEASON: Bobby Skinner (Season 1925/26)
NO. OF GOALS SCORED: 53
RECORD ATTENDANCE: 27,816 (-v- Celtic – 30.4.1968)
RECORD VICTORY: 11-2 (-v- Stenhousemuir – Division 2, 27.9.1930)
RECORD DEFEAT: 0-10 (-v- Dundee – Division 2, 22.3.1947)

The Pars' ten year league record

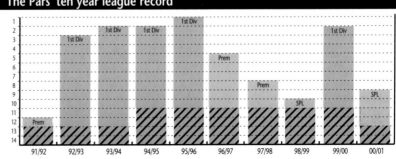

THE PARS' CLUB FACTFILE 2000/2001
RESULTS... APPEARANCES... SCORERS... ATTENDANCES...

Date	Venue	Opponents	Att.	Res	Ruitenbeek M.	Doesburg M.	Thomson S. M.	Skinner J.	Skerla A.	Dair J.	May E.	Ferguson I.	Mendes J.	Crawford S.	Petrie S.	Coyle O.	Matthaei R.	Nicholson B.	Nish C.	Moss D.	Templeman C.	Reid B.	Boyle S.	Bullen L.	Thomson S. Y.	Tod A.	McGroarty C.	Graham D.	McGarty M.	Hampshire S.	Rossi Y.	Dijkhuizen M.	Mason G.	Danilevicius T.	Fotheringham G.
July 29	H	Aberdeen	7,381	0-0	1	2	3	4	5	6	7	8	9	10	11	12	13																		
Aug 5	A	Dundee	9,507	0-3	1	2	3	4	5	12	7	8	9	10	11				6	13															
12	H	St. Johnstone	3,477	1-1	1	2	3	4	5	6		8	9	10^1	11	12					7	13	14												
16	A	Motherwell	5,257	1-0	1	2	3	4		6		8	9	10			14	5		7			11^1		12	13									
19	A	Rangers	47,452	1-4	1		3	4		6	13	8		10		12	5	7					11		2	9^1									
26	H	Dundee United	4,980	1-0	1	2	3	4	5	6		8	9	10^1				7					11				12								
Sep 9	A	Heart of Midlothian	11,811	0-2		2	3	4	5	6		8	12	10			23	7					11		24	9	1								
18	H	Celtic	9,493	1-2	1	2	3	4	5	12		8	11	10^1			6	7							13	9									
23	H	Hibernian	8,275	1-1	1	2	3	4	5	12		8		10			6	7	13	11^1					9	14									
30	A	St. Mirren	5,002	1-2	1	2	3	4	5	12^1		8	6	10			7	13	11^1						9										
Oct 14	A	Kilmarnock	6,454	1-2	1	2	3	4	5	6		14		10^1			9	7					12			13			8	11					
21	A	Aberdeen	11,195	0-0	1		3	4	5	2	12			10				8	7				11				6	9	13	14					
28	H	Dundee	5,925	1-0	1		3	4	5	2		8		10			13	7					11^1				6	9		12					
Nov 4	A	St. Johnstone	4,287	2-0	1		3	4	5	2^1		8		10			9	13	7^1				11				6			12					
11	H	Motherwell	4,146	1-2	1		3	4	5	2			12	10			9	8	7				11^1				6			13					
18	H	Rangers	10,706	0-0	1		3	4	5	6	12			10				7					9				8		13	2					
25	A	Dundee United	6,012	2-3	1		3	4	5	6		8		10				9	11^1				13	12^1			7			2					
29	H	Heart of Midlothian	5,281	1-0	1		3	4	5	2^1	9			10			8	7				12	11				6		13						
Dec 2	A	Celtic	59,196	1-3	1		3	4	5	2^1	6			10			8	7		11		12	9						14	13					
9	A	Hibernian	10,078	0-3	1		3	4	5			12		10			6	8		11							13	7	9						
16	H	St. Mirren	4,538	2-0	1	13	3^1	4	5			8		10				7	11				12			6^1			9	2					
23	H	Kilmarnock	5,337	1-0	1	22	3	4	5			8		10^1				7	11				6				9	2	23						
26	H	Aberdeen	6,880	3-2	1	13	3	4	5	14		8		10^1				7^1	11				6				9	2^1	12						
Jan 2	H	St. Johnstone	6,117	0-0	1	2	3		5	12				10				7	13				14				6		11		4	9			
31	A	Motherwell	4,601	1-1	1	2	3	4	5	12				10				7					11^1				6			13	9				
Feb 3	A	Rangers	46,302	0-2	1	2	3	4	5	6				10	11		7						9			22	3	14	23						
10	H	Dundee United	4,899	3-1	1	2	9	4	5	6		8		10				7	13^1				12				11^1	3	14^1						
21	A	Dundee	6,113	1-0	1	13	9	4	5	2		8		10				7^1	11				12	3	6										
24	A	Heart of Midlothian	11,251	1-7	1		6	11	4	5	2^1	8		10				7	14				22	3	9				23						
Mar 4	H	Celtic	8,779	0-3	1		9	4	5	6		8		10				7	11				14	12			13	2	3						
17	H	Hibernian	7,154	2-1	1	2	4	12	3	5		8		10^1	14			7	13				9^1					6	11						
31	A	St. Mirren	5,371	1-1	1	2	7	4	5	6				10^1					12				3	14			9		13	8	11				
Apr 7	A	Kilmarnock	6,529	1-2	1	2	9	4	5	6								7	12				13^1				14	10	3		8	11			
21	A	Aberdeen	8,613	0-1	1	2		12	5	14		8		10	11			6	13				9				3		7		4				
28	H	St. Mirren	4,669	1-2	1	14		4	5	2		8	12	10	13			7					11^1					9	3	6					
May 6	A	Dundee United	6,679	0-1	1	12		4		2		8	14	10	11		13	7					9				5	6		3					
12	H	Motherwell	2,437	1-2	1	2	13		5			8		10^1	11		4	7					9				14	3				12		6	
20	H	St. Johnstone	4,084	0-0			3	4				8		10	11		13	7					12	1	5	2				6		9			
TOTAL FULL APPEARANCES					36	21	34	34	34	25	4	28	7	37	8	2	11	36		18	1	1	14	2	5	19	3	1	11	11	2	8	3	2
TOTAL SUB APPEARANCES						(6)		(3)		(8)	(3)		(6)		(2)	(4)	(6)		(4)	(8)	(1)	(1)	(6)	(10)		(3)	(3)	(1)	(3)	(8)		(7)	(2)	
TOTAL GOALS SCORED							1			5				9				3		6			1			4			1			2	1	1

Small bold figures denote goalscorers. † denotes opponent's own goal.

East End Park

CAPACITY: 12,565 (All Seated)

PITCH DIMENSIONS: 115 yds x 70 yds

FACILITIES FOR DISABLED SUPPORTERS:
12 spaces in East Stand for Away Supporters. 12 spaces in the Norrie McCathie Stand for Home Supporters. 24 seats for helpers.

Team playing kits

	FIRST CHOICE	SECOND CHOICE
Shirt:	Black and White Vertical Stripes.	Red.
Shorts:	White with Black Piping on Sides.	Red with White Piping on Sides.
Stockings:	White with Black Band Round Top.	Red with White Tops.

How to get there

East End Park may be reached by the following routes:

TRAINS: Dunfermline Station is served by trains from both Glasgow and Edinburgh and the ground is a 15 minute walk from here.

BUSES: Buses destined for Kelty, Perth, St. Andrews and Kirkcaldy all pass close to East End Park.

CARS: Car Parking is available in a large car park adjoining the east end of the ground and there are also facilities in various side streets. Multi-storey car parking approximately 10 minutes walk from the ground.

Dunfermline Athletic F.C. is a member of The Scottish Premier League

Heart of Midlothian

Tynecastle Stadium, Gorgie Road,
Edinburgh, EH11 2NL

CHAIRMAN
Douglas A. Smith

DIRECTORS
Christopher P. Robinson,
Stewart Fraser, Brian J. Duffin
& Andrew Flanagan

CHIEF EXECUTIVE
Christopher P. Robinson

P.A. to CHIEF EXECUTIVE
Irene McPhee (0131) 200 7245

**FINANCE DIRECTOR/
COMPANY SECRETARY**
Stewart Fraser (0131) 200 7270

HEAD COACH
Craig Levein

ASSISTANT HEAD COACH
Peter Houston

FITNESS COACH
Tom Ritchie

YOUTH COACH
John McGlynn

CLUB DOCTOR
Dr. Dewar Melvin

PHYSIOTHERAPIST
Alan Rae

KIT CONTROLLER
Norrie Gray

S.F.A. COMMUNITY OFFICER
Alan White (0131) 200 7242

DIRECTOR OF YOUTH DEVELOPMENT
John Murray

PITCH MAINTENANCE
Souters of Stirling

RETAIL MANAGER
Clare Sargent (0131) 200 7206

**CORPORATE HOSPITALITY/
BANQUETING**
Graeme Pacitti (0131) 200 7240

COMMUNICATIONS MANAGER
Douglas Dalgleish (0131) 200 7260

SALES & MARKETING MANAGER
Kenny Wittmann (0131) 200 7205/7207

CUSTOMER SERVICES MANAGER
Colin Sked (0131) 200 7272

**FOOTBALL SAFETY OFFICERS'
ASSOCIATION REPRESENTATIVE**
Tom Purdie (0131) 200 7258

STADIUM MANAGER
John Boag (0131) 200 7254

TICKET MANAGER
Neil Hunter (0131) 200 7201

MATCHDAY PROGRAMME EDITOR
Douglas Dalgleish

TELEPHONES
Ground (0131) 200 7200
Fax (0131) 200 7222
Ticket Office (0131) 200 7201
Information Service (0131) 200 7255
Sales & Marketing (0131) 200 7205
Credit Card Bookings (0131) 200 7209
Superstore (0131) 200 7211
Clubcall (09068) 121183

E-MAIL & INTERNET ADDRESS
hearts@homplc.co.uk
www.heartsfc.co.uk

CLUB SHOP
Heart of Midlothian Superstore,
Tynecastle Stadium, Gorgie Road,
Edinburgh. Tel (0131) 200 7211
Open 9.30 a.m. – 5.30 p.m.
Mon. to Sat. and matchdays.

OFFICIAL SUPPORTERS CLUB
Heart of Midlothian Federation,
John N. Borthwick, 21/9 Festival
Gardens, Edinburgh, EH11 1RB
Tel: (0131) 337 3782

TEAM CAPTAIN
Steven Pressley

SHIRT SPONSOR
Strongbow

KIT SUPPLIER
Errea

LIST OF PLAYERS 2001-2002

Squad No.	Name	Place & Date of Birth	Previous Club	Lge Career Apps	Gls
9	Stephane Adam	Lille, France 15.5.69	Metz	79 (11)	25
12	Steven Boyack	Edinburgh 4.9.76	Dundee	9 (3)	–
29	Ryan Davidson	Irvine 22.4.82	Heart of Midlothian B. C.	–	–
7	Thomas Flögel	Vienna, Austria 7.6.71	Austria Vienna	81 (22)	9
16	Stephen Fulton	Greenock 10.8.70	Falkirk	153 (15)	12
31	Craig Gordon	Balerno 31.12.82	Heart of Midlothian B. C.	–	–
34	Neil Janczyk	Edinburgh 7.4.83	Heart of Midlothian B. C.	–	–
20	Juanjo	Barcelona, Spain 4.5.77	Barcelona	26 (38)	7
33	Paul Kaczan	Bellshill 3.2.83	Hibernian B.C.	– (1)	–
14	Andrew Kirk	Belfast 29.5.79	Glentoran	28 (13)	13
18	Austin McCann	Clydebank 21.1.80	Airdrieonians	10	–
5	Kevin McKenna	Calgary, Canada 20.1.80	Energie Cottbus	7 (1)	–
13	Roddy McKenzie	Bellshill 8.8.75	Stenhousemuir	21 (2)	–
19	Gary McSwegan	Glasgow 24.9.70	Dundee United	53 (23)	26
3	Stephane Mahe	Puteaux, France 23.9.68	Celtic	–	–
17	Kenny Milne	Stirling 26.8.79	Edinburgh United	3 (5)	–
21	Robbie Neilson	Paisley 19.6.80	Rangers B. C.	16 (2)	–
26	Antti Niemi	Oulu, Finland 31.5.72	Rangers	54	–
36	Paul Parkin	Edinburgh 18.10.83	Heart of Midlothian B. C.	–	–
4	Steven Pressley	Elgin 11.10.73	Dundee United	101 (1)	1
6	Scott Severin	Stirling 15.2.79	Musselburgh Juniors	49 (10)	6
28	Stephen Simmons	Glasgow 27.2.82	Celtic B. C.	– (3)	–
35	Robert Sloan	Paisley 14.7.83	Heart of Midlothian B. C.	–	–
24	Anthony Smith	Perth 28.7.81	Celtic B. C.	–	–
30	Barry Smith	Dublin 16.3.82	Manortown	–	–
37	Elliot Smith	Edinburgh 23.12.83	Hutchison Vale B. C.	–	–
8	Robert Tomaschek	Nitra, Slovakia 25.8.72	Slovan Bratislava	35 (7)	4
15	Gary Wales	East Calder 4.1.79	Hamilton Academical	19 (13)	7
23	Andrew Webster	Dundee 23.4.82	Arbroath	3 (1)	–

Milestones

YEAR OF FORMATION: 1874
MOST CAPPED PLAYER: Bobby Walker
NO. OF CAPS: 29
MOST LEAGUE POINTS IN A SEASON: 63 (Premier Division - Season 1991/92)(2 Points for a Win)
67 (Premier Division - Season 1997/98)(3 Points for a Win)
MOST LEAGUE GOALS SCORED BY A PLAYER IN A SEASON: Barney Battles (Season 1930/31)
NO. OF GOALS SCORED: 44
RECORD ATTENDANCE: 53,396 (-v- Rangers – 13.2.1932)
RECORD VICTORY: 21-0 (-v- Anchor – EFA Cup, 1880)
RECORD DEFEAT: 1-8 (-v- Vale of Leven – Scottish Cup, 1883)

The Jam Tarts' ten year league record

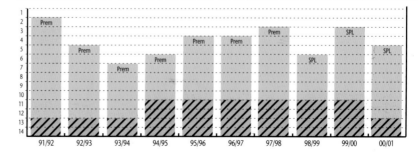

THE JAM TARTS' CLUB FACTFILE 2000/2001
RESULTS... APPEARANCES... SCORERS... ATTENDANCES...

Date	Venue	Opponents	Att.	Res	Niemi A.	Pressley S.	Naysmith G.	Petric G.	Flögel T.	Severin S.	Tomaschek R.	Fulton S.	Cameron C.	Juanjo	Kirk A.	McSwegan G.	Simpson F.	Jackson D.	Makel L.	O'Neil K.	Locke G.	Murray G.	Neilson R.	James K.	Durie G.	Adam S.	Milne K.	Simmons S.	Goldie D.	Boyack S.	McAnespie K.	McKenzie R.	McCann H. A.	Kaczan P.	McKenna K.	Wales G.
July 30	H	Hibernian	17,132	0-0	1	2	3	4	5	6	7	8	9	10	11	12	13																			
Aug 6	A	St. Johnstone	6,165	2-2	1	2		4	3	6	7¹	8	9	10		22		5	11	23	14¹																
13	A	Aberdeen	11,139	1-1	1	2	3	4		6	7	8	9	12		10¹		11	5	14	13																
19	H	Celtic	16,744	2-4	1	2		4	6¹	7	8	9	22¹	10				11	5	23																	
27	A	Dundee	6,779	1-1	1	2	3	4	6		8	9¹	11	10				5	7																		
Sep 9	H	Dunfermline Athletic	11,811	2-0	1	2	3	4		7	9	11¹	10¹	13	8	12		5	6																		
17	A	Rangers	47,496	0-1	1	2	3	4	6	8	9	11	10	7	13	12		5																			
20	A	St. Mirren	10,524	2-0	1	2	3	4	6	7	9	11¹	13	10¹	12	8		5																			
24	H	Kilmarnock	10,379	0-2	1	2	3	4	6	9	11	10	7	8	14	22	5	23																			
Oct 1	H	Motherwell	10,460	3-0	1	2	3	4	6	9	11	8¹	24	12	7	5	10²	23																			
14	A	Dundee United	7,016	4-0	1	2		4	12	6¹	7	9	11	8²	14	13	3	5¹	10																		
22	A	Hibernian	12,926	2-6	1	2		4	3	6	7	9¹	11	8¹	22	23	14	5	10																		
28	H	St. Johnstone	10,883	0-3	1	2		12	6	13	7	9	11	8	14	4	5	10	3																		
Nov 4	H	Aberdeen	12,744	3-0	1	2		4	7¹	12	8	9¹	11	10¹	6	5	3																				
11	A	St. Mirren	5,234	2-1	1	2		4	7¹	12	8	9¹	11	10	13	6	5	3	14																		
18	A	Celtic	59,849	1-6	1	2		4	14	7	8	9¹	11	10	13	6	5	3	12																		
25	H	Dundee	11,539	3-1	1	2		4	6	13	7	9²	11	12	8¹	5	3	10																			
29	A	Dunfermline Athletic	5,281	0-1	1	2		4	5	12	7	9	11	8	13	6	3	14	10																		
Dec 3	H	Rangers	16,710	0-1	1	2		4	6	13	7	9	11	8		5	3	10	12																		
9	A	Kilmarnock	6,828	3-0	1	2			5	6	7¹	9	11	8²	14	12	4	3	10	13																	
16	A	Motherwell	5,440	0-2	1	2			5	6	7	9	11	8	13	14	4	3	10	12																	
23	H	Dundee United	12,128	†3-1	1	2		4	7	6	8	9¹	12	11	10¹		5											3	13								
26	H	Hibernian	17,619	1-1	1	2		4	7	6	8	9	13	11	10¹	12	5											3	14								
30	H	St. Johnstone	5,173	2-2	1	2		4	6	7	9	11	8¹	10	5	3	12¹																				
Jan 2	A	Aberdeen	12,760	0-1	1	2			12	6	7	9	11	13	8	5	4	10										14	3								
31	H	St. Mirren	10,164	1-0	1	2		4	5	14	6	9¹	13	8	10	12	3											7	11								
Feb 4	H	Celtic	13,077	0-3	1	2		4	7	5	6	9	13	8	14	3	10											12	11								
24	H	Dunfermline Athletic	11,251	7-1	1	2		3	4	6¹	9²	12	11¹	8	5	13	10³											7	14								
Mar 3	A	Rangers	49,003	0-2		2		3	5	6	9	12	11	8	10													7	13	1	4					
14	A	Kilmarnock	9,195	3-0	1	2		3¹	6¹	7	10¹	11	13	5	8	12												9		4	14						
18	A	Dundee	7,327	0-0	1	2		8	7	9	10	11	13	6	5												12		4		3						
31	H	Motherwell	11,581	3-0	1	2		10	7¹	9	13	11²	6	3	8												8		4		5	12					
Apr 7	A	Dundee United	7,242	1-1	1	2		10	13	7	9	14	11	6	3	8											8		4		5	12¹					
22	A	Celtic	58,708	0-1	1	2		3	7	9	12	11	6	13	8												8		4		5	10					
27	A	Kilmarnock	6,867	1-1	1	2		7	9	14	11¹	6	5	10	8												8		4		12	13					
May 5	H	Rangers	15,315	1-4	1	2		3	7	6	9	12	11	13	10¹												8		4		5	14					
13	A	Hibernian	8,512	0-0	1		3	7	8	9	14	13	12	2	10												10¹		4		5	11					
20	H	Dundee	13,554	2-0	1		7	6	13	9¹	11	14	2	10¹	8												10¹		4		5	12					
TOTAL FULL APPEARANCES					37	36	9	19	22	26	22	23	37	23	27	13	3	6	10		7	22	16	4	12	5	3		1	9	3	1	10		7	2
TOTAL SUB APPEARANCES						(3)	(3)	(6)	(1)					(14)	(4)	(13)	(3)	(4)	(3)	(6)	(6)	(3)	(2)		(4)	(1)	(4)	(3)			(3)	(2)		(1)	(1)	(5)
TOTAL GOALS SCORED									1	4	4	1	12	4	12	6			1				1	3	5									1

Small bold figures denote goalscorers. † *denotes opponent's own goal.*

Tynecastle Stadium

WHEATFIELD ROAD

WHEATFIELD STAND

GORGIE STAND — ROSEBURN STAND

GORGIE ROAD

MAIN STAND

McLEOD STREET

RUSSELL ROAD

CAPACITY: 17,700 (All Seated)

PITCH DIMENSIONS: 107 yds x 74 yds

FACILITIES FOR DISABLED SUPPORTERS:
There are 15 spaces for visiting fans at the Roseburn Stand. Regarding facilities for home supporters, fans should contact the club in advance for availability.

Team playing kits

FIRST CHOICE
Shirt: Maroon with White 'V' Neck.
Shorts: White.
Stockings: Maroon with White Tops.

SECOND CHOICE
Shirt: White with Maroon Piping.
Shorts: Maroon with White Piping.
Stockings: White with Maroon Band.

How to get there

Tynecastle Stadium can be reached by the following routes:
BUSES: A frequent service of buses leaves from the city centre, Nos. 1, 2, 3, 4, 33, 34, 35 and 44 all pass the ground.
TRAINS: Haymarket Station is about half a mile from the ground.
CARS: Car Parking facilities exist in the adjacent side streets in Robertson Avenue and also the Westfield area.

Heart of Midlothian F.C. is a member of The Scottish Premier League

Hibernian

Easter Road Stadium,
12 Albion Place,
Edinburgh, EH7 5QG

CHAIRMAN
Malcolm H. McPherson

MANAGING DIRECTOR
Rod M. Petrie

DIRECTORS
Stephen W. Dunn, Erick Davidson
& Kenneth Lewandowski

SECRETARY
Graeme Johnston

MANAGER
Alexander McLeish

ASSISTANT MANAGER
Andy Watson

COACH
Donald Park

CLUB DOCTOR
Dr. Tom Schofield

PHYSIOTHERAPIST
Malcolm Colquhoun

S.F.A. COMMUNITY COACH
Malcolm J. Thomson

**YOUTH DEVELOPMENT
OFFICER/CHIEF SCOUT**
John Park

**COMMERCIAL DEVELOPMENT
MANAGER**
Tony Mitchell (0131) 656 7080

CATERING MANAGER
Craig Samson

**SALES MANAGER
CONFERENCE & BANQUETING**
Frances Crolla
(0131) 656 7075

SALES EXECUTIVE
Amanda Vatesse

**STADIUM MANAGER/
FOOTBALL SAFETY OFFICERS'
ASSOCIATION REPRESENTATIVE**
Garry O'Hagen (0131) 656 7077

HEAD GROUNDSMAN
Tam McCourt

MATCHDAY PROGRAMME EDITOR
James Alexander

TELEPHONES
Ground (0131) 661 2159
Fax (0131) 659 6488/652 1907
Ticket Office (0131) 661 1875

E-MAIL & INTERNET ADDRESS
club@hibernianfc.co.uk
www.hibernianfc.co.uk

CLUB SHOP
12 Albion Place, Edinburgh
Open Tue.-Sat.: 9.00a.m. - 5.00p.m.,
Home matchdays:
9.30a.m. - 3.00p.m.
Away First Team matchdays:
9.00a.m. - 5.00p.m.
Tel (0131) 656 7078

OFFICIAL SUPPORTERS CLUB
11 Sunnyside Lane, Off Easter Road,
Edinburgh, EH7

TEAM CAPTAIN
Franck Sauzee

SHIRT SPONSOR
Carlsberg

KIT SUPPLIER
Le Coq Sportif

156

LIST OF PLAYERS 2001-2002

Squad No.	Name	Place & Date of Birth	Previous Club	Lge Career Apps	Gls
15	Lyndon Andrews	Trinidad & Tobago 20.1.76	Joe Public	4 (7)	–
10	Frederic Arpinon	Nimes, France 9.5.69	Troyes	6 (1)	–
8	Grant Brebner	Edinburgh 6.12.77	Reading	47 (1)	1
9	Craig Brewster	Dundee 13.12.66	Ionikos	–	–
25	Leslie Byle	Glasgow 29.8.82	Chelsea	–	–
31	Tony Caig	Whitehaven 11.4.74	Charlton Athletic	–	–
1	Nick Colgan	Drogheda 19.9.73	Bournemouth	61	–
2	Ulises de la Cruz	Ecuador 8.2.74	Deportivo Universatario	–	–
29	Allan Dempsie	Bellshill 5.11.82	Hibernian B. C.	–	–
22	Mark Dempsie	Bellshill 19.10.80	Hibernian B. C.	13 (4)	–
14	Paul Fenwick	London 25.8.69	Raith Rovers	31	1
19	Mathias Jack	Leipzig, Germany 15.2.69	Fortuna Dusseldorf	57 (2)	1
3	Ulrick Laursen	Denmark 28.2.76	OB Odense	29	2
7	Francisco Luna	Spain 23.9.71	Monterrey	–	–
24	Martin McIntosh	East Kilbride 19.3.71	Stockport County	13	–
17	Thomas McManus	Glasgow 28.2.81	'S' Form	4 (15)	2
6	Ian Murray	Edinburgh 20.3.81	Dundee United	19 (11)	1
27	Garry O'Connor	Edinburgh 7.5.83	Salvesen B. C.	– (1)	–
11	John O'Neil	Bellshill 6.7.71	St. Johnstone	33	4
23	Alen Orman	Bosnia 31.5.78	Royal Antwerp	–	–
26	Liam O'Sullivan	Edinburgh 28.10.81	Hutchison Vale B. C.	–	–
30	Derek Riordan	Edinburgh 16.1.83	Hutchison Vale B. C.	–	–
4	Franck Sauzee	Aubenas, France 28.10.65	Montpellier	66 (1)	9
18	Gary Smith	Glasgow 25.3.71	Aberdeen	37	–
12	Derek Townsley	Carlisle 21.3.73	Motherwell	–	–
13	Ian Westwater	Loughborough 8.11.63	Dunfermline Athletic	–	–
20	David Zitelli	France 3.10.68	Strasbourg	24 (7)	10

Milestones

YEAR OF FORMATION: 1875
MOST CAPPED PLAYER: Lawrie Reilly
NO. OF CAPS: 38
MOST LEAGUE POINTS IN A SEASON: 57 (First Division – Season 1980/81)(2 Points for a Win)
89 (First Division – Season 1998/99)(3 Points for a Win)
MOST LEAGUE GOALS SCORED BY A PLAYER IN A SEASON: Joe Baker (Season 1959/60)
NO. OF GOALS SCORED: 42
RECORD ATTENDANCE: 65,860 (-v- Heart of Midlothian – 2.1.1950)
RECORD VICTORY: 22-1 (-v- 42nd Highlanders 3.9.1881)
RECORD DEFEAT: 0-10 (-v- Rangers – 24.12.1898)

The Hibees' ten year league record

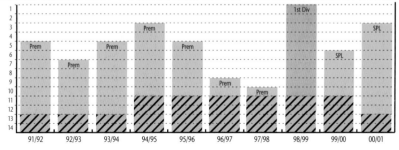

THE HIBEES' CLUB FACTFILE 2000/2001
RESULTS... APPEARANCES... SCORERS... ATTENDANCES...

Note: Small bold figures (shown here in brackets, e.g. 10[1]) denote the number of goals scored. † denotes opponent's own goal.

Date	Ven	Opponents	Att.	Res	Colgan N.	Laursen U.	Smith T.	Smith G.	Fenwick P.	Jack M.	Sauzee F.	Latapy R.	O'Neill J.	Paatelainen M-M.	Agathe D.	McManus T.	Lehmann D.	Murray I.	Lovell S.	McIntosh M.	Bannerman S.	Zitelli D.	Brebner G.	Sar Temsoury H.	Andrews L.	Franks M.	Libbra M.	Dempsie M.	Arpinon F.	O'Connor G.
Jul 30	A	Heart of Midlothian	17,132	0-0	1	2	3	4	5	6	7	8	9	10	11	12														
Aug 5	A	Dundee United	9,613	3-0	1	2	3	4	5	6	7	8	9	10	11[2]	14[1]	12	13												
Aug 12	H	Dundee	12,730	5-1	1	2	3	4	5	6	7	8	9	10	11[2]		13[2]	14	12[1]											
Aug 16	A	Kilmarnock	8,672	1-0	1	2	3	4		6	7	8	9	10[1]	11		12			5										
Aug 19	A	Aberdeen	12,450	2-0	1	2	5	3		6	7	8[1]	9	10[1]	11		14			4	12	13								
Aug 26	H	St. Mirren	11,814	2-0	1		2	3	4	5	7	8	9	10		12	11		6[2]											
Sep 9	A	Celtic	60,040	0-3	1	5		3	2	6	7	8	9	10		12			7			11	13							
Sep 16	H	Motherwell	9,868	2-0	1	5		3	2	6	4	8	9	10[2]	11				7			12								
Sep 23	A	Dunfermline Athletic	8,275	1-1	1	5		3	2	6	4	8[1]	9	10	11	12			7			13								
Sep 30	A	St. Johnstone	5,464	3-0	1	5		3	2	6	4[1]	8[1]	9	10					7			11[1]					12			
Oct 14	A	Rangers	14,524	1-0	1	5		3	2	6	4	8	9	10		12			7			11[1]								
Oct 22	H	Heart of Midlothian	12,926	6-2	1	5		3	2	6	4	8[1]	9[1]	10[3]					7			11[1]					12			
Oct 28	A	Dundee United	8,042	1-0	1	5		3	2	6	4	8	9	10		13[1]	12		7			11								
Nov 5	A	Dundee	6,602	2-1	1	5		3	2	6	4	8	9[1]	10		12			7			11[1]								
Nov 11	H	Kilmarnock	12,588	1-1	1	5		3	2	6	4	8	9	10[1]		13	12		7			11								
Nov 18	H	Aberdeen	10,995	0-2	1	5		3	2	6	4	8	9			13	10		7			11	12							
Nov 25	A	St. Mirren	5,225	1-1	1	4		3	2	5	6	8	9[1]	10		12	13		7			11								
Nov 29	H	Celtic	14,939	0-0	1	5		3	2	6	4	8	9	10		13			7			11		15						
Dec 3	A	Motherwell	5,715	†3-1	1	5		3	2	6	4	8	9	10		14	23	22	7			11[2]			1					
Dec 9	H	Dunfermline Athletic	10,078	3-0	1	5[1]		3	2	6	4	8	9	10[1]		22	23		7			11[1]			14					
Dec 16	H	St. Johnstone	10,374	2-0	1	5		3	2	6	4	8	9	10[1]			7[1]					11			12					
Dec 23	A	Rangers	49,993	0-1	1	5		3	2	6	4	8	9	10		12	13		7			11			14					
Dec 26	A	Heart of Midlothian	17,619	1-1	1	5		3	2	6	4	8		10		12			7[1]			11	9							
Dec 30	H	Dundee United	10,197	1-0	1	5		3	2	6	4	8[1]	9	10		12	13		7			11								
Jan 2	H	Dundee	12,381	3-0	1	5		3	2[1]	6	4	8	9[1]	10[1]		14	13		7			11	12							
Jan 30	A	Kilmarnock	6,385	1-1	1	5[1]		3	2		4	8		10		11			7		13	12	6	9						
Feb 10	H	St. Mirren	8,799	4-2	1	5		3	2	6	4[1]	8[1]	9	10		12			7			11[2]								
Feb 25	A	Celtic	59,791	1-1	1	5		3	2	6	4		9	10		12			7			11	8				13[1]			
Mar 4	H	Motherwell	8,225	1-1	1	5		3	2	4		8[1]	9	10	14	6	7					11	13				12			
Mar 13	A	Aberdeen	8,799	0-1	1			3	2		12	9	10	13	14	5	7	4				8			6		11			
Mar 17	A	Dunfermline Athletic	7,154	1-2	1			3	2		9	10	11	5[1]	7						13	8			6		12	4		
Apr 1	A	St. Johnstone	4,346	0-2	1	5		3	2	6	8	12	10		14	4						11	13				9		7	
Apr 8	H	Rangers	9,704	0-0	1	5		3	2	6	4	8	10		13	7						11	12				14		9	
Apr 21	H	Kilmarnock	8,113	1-1	1			3	2	5	4	9	12	10	13	6	7					14					11[1]		8	
Apr 29	A	Dundee	6,659	2-0	1			3	5	4	12	13	10	2	7							11[1]	8				9[1]		6	14
May 6	H	Celtic	8,879	2-5	1			3	5	4	8	9	10	11	2	7						12					6[2]		13	
May 13	H	Heart of Midlothian	8,512	0-0	1			3	5	4	9	10	11	2	7		13					12					8		6	
May 20	A	Rangers	47,023	0-4	1	5		2	3	4	9	13		14	6	7						11	12				10		8	
TOTAL FULL APPEARANCES					37	29	8	37	31	37	33	31	33	32	5	3	9	11	30	4		24	5		4	1	7	1	7	6
TOTAL SUB APPEARANCES												(2)		(4)		(13)	(21)	(10)	(1)		(2)	(7)	(6)	(1)	(7)	(1)	(4)		(1)	(1)
TOTAL GOALS SCORED						2		1			2	7	4	11	4	2	2	1	5			10					5			

Small bold figures denote goalscorers. † denotes opponent's own goal.

Easter Road Stadium

(Stadium plan showing the pitch, seating areas, disabled-access points, ALBION PLACE and ALBION RD.)

CAPACITY: 17,500 (All Seated)

PITCH DIMENSIONS: 115 yds x 69 yds

FACILITIES FOR DISABLED SUPPORTERS:
Area in South Seated Enclosure and North Stand.

Team playing kits

FIRST CHOICE
Shirt: Green with White Sleeves. White Round Neck Collar.
Shorts: White.
Stockings: White.

SECOND CHOICE
Shirt: Purple.
Shorts: Purple.
Stockings: Purple.

How to get there

Easter Road Stadium can be reached by the following routes:

BUSES: The main bus station in the city is served by buses from all over the country and the following local buses departing from Princes Street all stop near the ground:- Nos. 4, 15, 42 and 44.

TRAINS: Edinburgh Waverley Station is served by trains from all parts of the country and the above buses all stop near the ground.

Hibernian F.C. is a member of The Scottish Premier League

Kilmarnock

Rugby Park, Rugby Road,
Kilmarnock, KA1 2DP

CHAIRMAN
Sir John Orr, O.B.E.

JOINT VICE-CHAIRMEN
William Costley & James T. Moffat

DIRECTORS
James H. Clark, Robert Wyper,
Brian J. Sage & Jim Murdoch

CHIEF EXECUTIVE
David Heath

SECRETARY
Kevin D. Collins

MANAGER
Robert Williamson

ASSISTANT MANAGERS
Jim Clark & Gerry McCabe

YOUTH COACHES
Paul Clarke & Stuart McLean

YOUTH DEVELOPMENT COACH
Alan Robertson

CLUB DOCTORS
Dr. Masood Zaidi & Dr. Brian Syme

PHYSIOTHERAPISTS
Alistair Macfie, B.Sc. (Hons),
M.C.S.P., S.R.P. &
Hugh Allan, M.B.E.

S.F.A. COMMUNITY OFFICER
Eric Young

**COMMERCIAL MANAGER/
PRESS OFFICER**
James McSherry (01563) 545305

COMMERCIAL ASSISTANT
Anne Clark

STADIUM MANAGER
Angus Hollas

**FOOTBALL SAFETY OFFICERS'
ASSOCIATION REPRESENTATIVE**
Kevin D. Collins (01563) 545306

MATCHDAY PROGRAMME EDITOR
Richard Cairns

TELEPHONES
Ground (01563) 545300
Fax (01563) 522181
Matchday/Ticket Information
(09068) 633249

E-MAIL & INTERNET ADDRESS
kevin.collins@kilmarnockfc.co.uk
kfc@sol.co.uk
www.kilmarnockfc.co.uk

CLUB SHOP
Situated in the Commercial Centre
at the ground. Tel (01563) 545310.
Open Mon to Fri
9.00 a.m.–5.00 p.m.
Saturday home matchdays
10.00 a.m.–5.30 p.m.
Saturday away matchdays
10.00 a.m.–2.00 p.m.

OFFICIAL SUPPORTERS CLUB
c/o Rugby Park, Kilmarnock, KA1 2DP

CLUB CAPTAIN
Ian Durrant

TEAM CAPTAIN
Frederic Dindeleux

SHIRT SPONSOR
Seriously Strong

KIT SUPPLIER
TFG

LIST OF PLAYERS 2001-2002

Squad No.	Name	Place & Date of Birth	Previous Club	Lge Career Apps	Gls
16	Martin Baker	Glasgow 8.6.74	St. Mirren	60 (1)	1
22	Kris Boyd	Irvine 18.8.83	Kilmarnock Youth	– (1)	–
33	Chris Boyle	Irvine 10.6.82	Kilmarnock Youth	–	–
25	Antonio Calderon	Cadiz, Spain 2.6.67	Airdrieonians	7	–
23	Mark Canning	Bellshill 12.9.83	Kilmarnock Youth	–	–
4	Peter Canero	Glasgow 18.1.81	Kilmarnock Youth	22 (17)	1
6	Christophe Cocard	Bernay, France 23.11.67	Olympic Lyon	40 (18)	12
19	Craig Dargo	Edinburgh 3.1.78	Raith Rovers	16 (9)	7
30	Paul Di Giacomo	Glasgow 30.6.82	Kilmarnock Youth	2 (8)	–
17	Frederic Dindeleux	Lille, France 16.1.74	Lille Olympic SC	63	3
10	Ian Durrant	Glasgow 29.10.66	Rangers	80 (2)	8
26	James Fowler	Stirling 26.10.80	Gairdoch BC	4 (15)	1
24	Garry Hay	Irvine 7.9.77	Kilmarnock BC	35 (6)	4
31	Robbie Henderson	Bellshill 11.10.82	Leeds United	–	–
9	Sean Hessey	Liverpool 19.9.78	Huddersfield Town	13 (4)	–
21	Chris Innes	Broxburn 13.7.76	Stenhousemuir	32 (1)	1
34	James Lundie	Irvine 2.8.82	Kilmarnock Youth	–	–
27	Gary McCutcheon	Dumfries 8.10.78	Kilmarnock BC	2 (14)	2
28	Gary McDonald	Irvine 10.4.82	Kilmarnock Youth	–	–
5	Kevin McGowne	Kilmarnock 16.12.69	St. Johnstone	112 (6)	5
20	Andy McLaren	Glasgow 5.6.73	Reading	30 (2)	6
14	Alan Mahood	Kilwinning 26.3.73	Morton	55 (24)	6
1	Gordon Marshall	Edinburgh 19.4.64	Celtic	93	–
12	Colin Meldrum	Kilmarnock 26.11.75	Kilwinning Rangers	4 (1)	–
13	David Merdy	Brest, France 19.12.75	Beziers	–	–
11	Alistair Mitchell	Kirkcaldy 3.12.68	East Fife	283 (36)	42
32	Ross Moffat	Glasgow 17.1.82	Kilmarnock Youth	–	–
18	Michel Ngonge	Huy, Belgium 10.1.67	Queens Park Rangers	–	–
2	Mickael Pizzo	Paris 26.3.79	Red Star Paris	–	–
7	Mark Reilly	Bellshill 30.3.69	Reading	246 (20)	11
8	Jesus Sanjuan	Zaragoza, Spain 22.8.71	Airdrieonians	3	–
15	Jerome Vareille	Vernoux, France 1.6.74	FC Mulhouse	59 (30)	12

Milestones

YEAR OF FORMATION: 1869
MOST CAPPED PLAYER: Joe Nibloe
NO. OF CAPS: 11
MOST LEAGUE POINTS IN A SEASON: 58 (Division 2 - Season 1973/74)
MOST LEAGUE GOALS SCORED BY A PLAYER IN A SEASON: Harry "Peerie" Cunningham (Season 1927/28) and
Andy Kerr (Season 1960/61)
NO. OF GOALS SCORED: 34
RECORD ATTENDANCE: 34,246 (-v- Rangers – August, 1963)
RECORD VICTORY: 13-2 (-v- Saltcoats – Scottish Cup, 12.9.1896)
RECORD DEFEAT: 0-8 (-v- Rangers and Hibernian - Division 1)

Killie's ten year league record

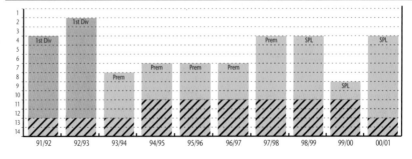

KILLIE'S CLUB FACTFILE 2000/2001
RESULTS... APPEARANCES... SCORERS... ATTENDANCES...

Date	Venue	Opponents	Att.	Res	Marshall G.	MacPherson A.	Baker M.	McGowne K.	Dindeleux F.	Mahood A.	Holt G.	Durrant I.	McLaren A.	Cocard C.	Vareille J.	Canero P.	Wright P.	Di Giacomo P.	Hay G.	McCoist A.	Hessey S.	Fowler J.	Mitchell A.	Dargo C.	Innes C.	Reilly M.	Davidson S.	Meldrum C.	Sanjuan J.	Canning M.	Calderon A.	Boyd K.
July 29	A	St. Mirren	7,388	1-0	1	2	3	4	5	6	7^1	8	9	10	11	12	13	14														
Aug 5	H	Rangers	14,680	2-4	1	2	3	4	5	6	7		9^2	10	11	8			14	12	13											
13	A	Celtic	57,258	1-2	1	2	3		5	6	7		11^1	14	12	9	13			10		4	8									
16	H	Hibernian	8,672	0-1	1	2		4	5	22	7		11	9			6	23		10		3		8	14							
19	H	Motherwell	6,533	3-2	1	2	3		5^1	6	7		9			23	8	22^1		10		4	14		11^1							
26	A	St. Johnstone	3,773	1-1	1	2			5	6	7	12	9^1			13	11			3	10			8		4						
Sep 9	H	Dundee United	6,380	1-0	1	2			5	6	7	24	9	23		12	11			3	10			8^1		4						
16	H	Aberdeen	6,876	1-0	1	2			5	6		8	9	12		14	11			3	10		13	7^1		4						
24	A	Heart of Midlothian	10,379	2-0	1	2			5^1	6	7	8	11	12			10^1			3		14	9	13		4						
30	A	Dundee	6,170	0-0	1	2			5	6	7	8	13				11			3	10		9	12		4						
Oct 14	H	Dunfermline Athletic	6,454	2-1	1	2			5	6	7^1	8	11	13		14	10^1			3		12		9		4						
21	A	St. Mirren	7,839	2-1	1	2			5	6^1	7	8	11^1	13		14	10^1			3				9		4						
28	A	Rangers	49,659	†3-0	1	2			5	6	7^1	8	11	10^1	12					3			13	9	14	4						
Nov 5	H	Celtic	13,412	0-1	1	2			5	6		8	11	10		12	14			3		7	9	13	4							
11	A	Hibernian	12,588	1-1	1	2			5	6		8	11	10			7	13^1		3			9	12	4							
18	A	Motherwell	6,571	2-1	1	2		4	5	6		8	9	13^1		12	10^1			3			7	11								
25	A	St. Johnstone	6,330	0-2	1	2		4	5	6			9	13	14	10				3			12	7	11							
28	A	Dundee United	5,497	†1-0	1	2		4	5	6		8	9	13			14			3		5	12	7	11							
Dec 2	A	Aberdeen	11,584	2-1	1			2		6			9^1	10	13	8				3		4	12^1	7	11		5					
9	H	Heart of Midlothian	6,828	0-3	1	2	5			6			9	10	13	12	14			3		4	8	11		7						
16	H	Dundee	6,573	2-3	1	3^1		2	5	6			9^1	12		8	10		14				13	11	4	7						
23	A	Dunfermline Athletic	5,337	0-1	1	3		2	5	6			11	10		8	14		12				13	4	7	9						
26	A	St. Mirren	5,649	3-1	1	2		4		6	7		9	12		8	10^3			3			11		5							
Jan 2	A	Celtic	59,103	0-6	1	2		4		6	7		9	8		5	10			3	12		11	13	14							
30	H	Hibernian	6,385	1-1	1	2	3		5	6	7		11			8			13	12^1		9	10	4								
Feb 3	H	Motherwell	6,018	1-2	1	2	6		5		7		11	13		8	14			3		12	9	10^1	4							
11	A	St. Johnstone	6,627	2-1	1	2	3	4	5		7		9	12		6^1	10					8	11^1									
24	H	Dundee United	6,289	0-0	1	2	3	4	5		7			12		9			10			8	11									
Mar 3	A	Aberdeen	6,577	0-0	1	2	3	4	5	6			10	9	13		12					8	11	7								
14	A	Heart of Midlothian	9,195	0-3	1		2		5	8	7		11	13		6	10	14		3			4	8		12						
31	A	Dundee	6,719	2-2		2		4	5	7^1			14							3	10		8	11^1	6	12		1	9	13		
Apr 7	H	Dunfermline Athletic	6,529	2-1		2^1		4	5	7			11	14		12			13	3	10^1			6	8		1			9		
11	H	Rangers	14,585	1-2		2		4	5	7			11	12		14	3^1	10					13	6	8		1			9		
21	H	Hibernian	8,113	1-1		2		4	5	7			11	10^1			3	12	13	8			6				1			9		
27	H	Heart of Midlothian	6,867	1-1		2		4^1	5	7			11	10			3	12		8			6	13			1			9		
May 5	A	Dundee	6,261	1-2	1	2		4	5				11	10			3	13		8	12^1	6	7		1			9				
12	A	Rangers	46,577	1-5		2			5	7			12			13	3			8	10^1	4	6		1		11	9				
20	A	Celtic	12,578	1-0	1	2		4	5	7^1			12			13				6					8		9	14				
TOTAL FULL APPEARANCES					31	32	14	20	35	33	19	12	30	16	2	16	15	2	27	11	6	3	25	16	23	11	2	7	3	7		
TOTAL SUB APPEARANCES									(1)		(2)		(2)	(17)	(7)	(12)	(10)	(7)		(4)	(7)		(11)	(1)	(9)	(1)	(3)		(1)		(1)	(1)
TOTAL GOALS SCORED							1	1	1	2	3	3		6	4		1	8			2	1		1	2	6						

Small bold figures denote goalscorers. † denotes opponent's own goal.

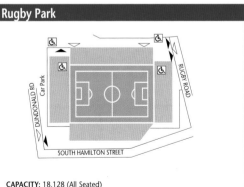

Rugby Park

DUNDONALD RD — Car Park
RUGBY ROAD
SOUTH HAMILTON STREET

CAPACITY: 18,128 (All Seated)

PITCH DIMENSIONS: 112 yds x 74 yds

FACILITIES FOR DISABLED SUPPORTERS:
Contact: Grace Jamieson, Secretary, Persons with a Disability Association
Tel: (01563) 555933

Team playing kits

FIRST CHOICE
Shirt: Royal Blue and White Broad Vertical Stripes.
Shorts: White with Royal Blue Trim.
Stockings: White.

SECOND CHOICE
Shirt: Yellow with Navy Blue Trim.
Shorts: Navy Blue with Yellow Trim.
Stockings: Yellow.

How to get there

Rugby Park can be reached by the following routes:
BUSES: The main bus station, which is served by buses from all over the country, is ten minutes walk from the ground, but there are three local services which run from here to within a two minute walk of the park. These are the Kilmarnock-Saltcoats, Kilmarnock-Ardrossan and Kilmarnock-Largs.
TRAINS: Kilmarnock Station is well served by trains from Glasgow and the West Coast, and the station is only 15 minutes walk from the ground.
CARS: Car parking is available in the club car park by permit only. Entry **ONLY** from Dundonald Road. Visiting supporters enter **ONLY** from Rugby Road Entrance.

Killie

Kilmarnock F.C. is a member of The Scottish Premier League

Livingston

West Lothian Courier Stadium,
Alderstone Road, Livingston,
West Lothian, EH54 7DN

CHAIRMAN
Dominic W. Keane

VICE-CHAIRMAN
John McGuiness

DIRECTORS
Anthony K. Kinder, James Leishman
& Derek J. Milne

HON PRESIDENT
John P. Blacklaw, C.Eng, M.I.E.E.

HON VICE–PRESIDENTS
William L. Mill &
John L. Bain, B.E.M.

SECRETARY
James R. S. Renton

PA TO CHAIRMAN
Diane Blair

GENERAL MANAGER
David Wakefield

CHIEF EXECUTIVE/TEAM MANAGER
James Leishman

HEAD COACH
David Hay

ASSISTANT COACH
John Robertson

YOUTH DEVELOPMENT MANAGER
John McLaughlan

YOUTH TEAM COACHES
Allan Preston (U21)
John McLaughlan (U18)
Alan Morgan (U15)
John McLaughlin (U14)
Alex Gordon (U13)

GOALKEEPING COACH
Roy Baines

FITNESS COACH
George McNeil

CLUB DOCTOR
Dr. Gerald Canning

FULL-TIME PHYSIOTHERAPIST
Michael P. McBride

PART-TIME PHYSIOTHERAPIST
Arthur Duncan

COMMERCIAL MANAGER
Charles Burnett (01506) 417000

CATERING MANAGER
Allison Ross

HEAD SCOUT
James McArthur

KIT MANAGER
Danny Cunning

**FOOTBALL SAFETY OFFICERS'
ASSOCIATION REPRESENTATIVE**
John O'Lone (01506) 432142

OPERATIONS DIRECTOR
Alistair Hood

MEDIA LIAISON OFFICER
Archie Reid (01506) 417000

**MATCHDAY PROGRAMME EDITOR/
ASSISTANT SECRETARY**
Duncan Bennett (01506) 417000

TELEPHONES
Ground (01506) 417000
Sec. Home (07802) 933263
Fax (01506) 418888

E-MAIL & INTERNET ADDRESS
livingstonfc@btinternet.com (General)
jrenton@pkc.gov.uk (Football)
www.livingstonfc.co.uk

CLUB SHOP
Contact Stadium (01506) 417000

OFFICIAL SUPPORTERS CLUB
Duncan Bennett, 63 Granby Avenue,
Howden, Livingston, EH54 6LD
(01506) 495113

TEAM CAPTAIN
Stuart Lovell

SHIRT SPONSOR
Motorola

KIT SUPPLIER
Jerzees

160

LIST OF PLAYERS 2001-2002

Squad No.	Name	Place & Date of Birth	Previous Club	Lge Career Apps	Gls
6	John Anderson	Greenock 2.10.72	Morton	30	3
5	Marvin Andrews	Trinidad & Tobago 22.12.75	Raith Rovers	13	–
26	Darren Brady	Glasgow 4.11.81	Dundee United	–	–
11	David Bingham	Dunfermline 3.9.70	Dunfermline Athletic	94	39
3	Gary Bollan	Dundee 24.3.73	St. Johnstone	–	–
2	Phillipe Brinquin	France 2.6.71	Le Havre	11	–
1	Javier Sanchez Broto	Barcelona, Spain 25.8.71	Airdrieonians	5 (1)	–
25	Massimiliano Caputo	Brescia, Italy 10.9.80	Brescia	–	–
23	Thomas Courts	Kirkcaldy 10.8.81	Cowdenbeath	–	–
24	Paul Deas	Perth 22.2.72	Stirling Albion	87 (5)	6
10	David Fernandez	Corvina, Spain 20.1.76	Airdrieonians	6 (2)	2
16	David Hagen	Edinburgh 5.5.73	Falkirk	8 (12)	1
21	Michael Hart	Bellshill 10.2.80	Aberdeen	19 (6)	–
14	Marino Keith	Peterhead 16.12.74	Falkirk	15 (5)	7
9	Nathan Lowndes	Salford 2.6.77	St. Johnstone	–	–
17	Stuart Lovell	Sydney, Australia 9.1.72	Hibernian	–	–
19	Mark McCulloch	Inverness 19.5.75	Inverness Caledonian Thistle	35	5
18	David McEwan	Lanark 26.2.82	Shotts Bon Accord	– (1)	–
27	David McGuire	Bellshill 27.9.80	Dundee United	–	–
29	Brian McPhee	Glasgow 23.10.70	Airdrieonians	36(48)	26
12	Quino*	Malaga, Spain, 5.3.71	Deportivo Badajoz	–	–
4	Oscar Rubio **	Portugal 17.5.76	Farense	–	–
32	Vincent Sullivan	Waterford 19.4.81	Celtic	–	–
8	Steven Tosh	Kirkcaldy 27.4.73	Raith Rovers	24	1
20	Stephen Whalen	Irvine 3.5.82	Morton	–	–
7	Barry Wilson	Kirkcaldy 16.2.72	Inverness Caledonian Thistle	34 (1)	13
13	Davide Xausa	Vancouver, Canada 10.3.76	Inverness Caledonian Thistle	6 (3)	4

* Abbreviated from Francisco Cabrera Guinovart

** Abbreviated from Oscar Montalban Ramos

Milestones

YEAR OF FORMATION: 1974 (From Seasons 1974/75 to 1994/95 known as Meadowbank Thistle F.C.)
MOST LEAGUE POINTS IN A SEASON: 55 (Second Division – Season 1986/87)(2 Points for a Win)
    77 (Third Division – Season 1998/99)(3 Points for a Win)
MOST LEAGUE GOALS SCORED BY A PLAYER IN A SEASON: John McGachie (Season 1986/87)
NO. OF GOALS SCORED: 21
RECORD ATTENDANCE: 2,818 (-v- Albion Rovers, 10.8.1974 at Meadowbank Stadium)
    10,024 (-v- Celtic, 18.8.2001 at West Lothian Courier Stadium)
RECORD VICTORY: 6-0 (-v- Raith Rovers – Second Division, 9.11.1985; -v- Alloa Athletic – First Division, 26.8.2000)
RECORD DEFEAT: 0-8 (-v- Hamilton Academical – Division 2, 14.12.1974)

Livi Lions' ten year league record

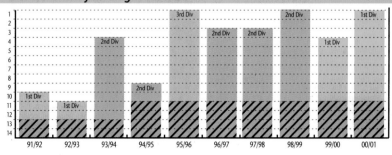

LIVI LIONS' CLUB FACTFILE 2000/2001
RESULTS... APPEARANCES... SCORERS... ATTENDANCES...

Date	Venue	Opponents	Att.	Res	Alexander N.	McManus A.	Deas P.	Dolan J.	Coughlan G.	Anderson J.	Wilson B.	Keith M.	Crabbe S.	McCulloch M.	Bingham D.	McPhee B.	Fleming D.	Hagen D.	Britton G.	McCormick M.	Sweeney S.	Smith Grant	Burns A.	Hart M.	Tosh S.	Andrews M.	McCaldon I.	Jackson D.	Madsen J.	Brinquin P.	Xausa D.	Fernandez D.	Broto J. S.	McEwan D.	Ormiston D.
Aug 5	A	Morton	1,729	2-0	1	2	3	4	5	6	7	8	9	10¹	11¹	16	14																		
12	H	Inverness Cal. Th.	3,838	3-1	1	2	3¹	4	5	6	7¹		9¹	8	10			11	17	12															
19	H	Clyde	1,781	1-1	1	2		4	5	6¹	7		9	8	10	15	3	11	16	14															
26	A	Alloa Athletic	983	6-0	1	2		4	5		9		8²	10¹	7	3¹	11¹	14	12¹	6	16														
Sep 9	H	Ayr United	5,271	2-0	1	2			5	6	7¹	16	4	10¹	8	3	11	9	15																
16	H	Raith Rovers	3,961	0-4	1	2			5	6	7	15	16	4	10	8	3	11	9	14															
23	A	Airdrieonians	1,826	2-1	1	2	12		5	6¹	7	8	9	4	10¹	14	3	11			16														
30	A	Falkirk	3,547	2-3	1	2		4	5¹	6	7	9	12	8	10	3	14	11¹		16															
Oct 7	A	Ross County	3,466	3-1	1		3	14		6	7	11²	15	8	10¹								9	2	4	5									
14	A	Morton	3,468	1-0	1		3			6	7	11	16	8	10¹	15							9	2	4	5									
21	H	Inverness Cal. Th.	2,147	2-2	1		3			6	9	11	16	8²	10		7							2	4	5	18								
28	H	Alloa Athletic	3,149	4-0	1			14		6	7	15	9	4	11²	3	16						10¹	2	8	5¹									
Nov 4	H	Ayr United	3,082	1-1	1					6	7	15	9	4	11	3¹	16						10	2	8	5									
11	H	Airdrieonians	3,915	2-2	1		12		5	6	7	9¹		4	11	3	16						10¹	2	8										
25	A	Ross County	2,723	2-0	1		4		5	6	14		9	8	11¹	15	3						10¹	2	7										
Dec 2	H	Falkirk	4,464	2-0	1		14		5¹	6	7¹		9	4	11¹	15	3						10¹	2	8										
5	A	Raith Rovers	1,626	2-1	1		12		5	6	7		9	4	11²	15	3						10	2	8										
9	H	Clyde	3,230	2-0	1				5	6	7		9¹	4	11	15	3	16					10	2	8¹										
16	A	Morton	888	2-1	1		3		5	6	7		9	4		14	11	15	16¹				10¹	2	8										
Jan 2	H	Raith Rovers	3,305	2-0	1				5		7		9	8	11¹		3	16					10¹	2	6	4									
6	A	Airdrieonians	2,382	1-1	1				5		7		9¹	8	11	15	3	14	16				10	2	6	4									
13	A	Falkirk	4,914	0-1	1		14			6	7		9	4	11	15	3	16					10	2		5		8							
30	A	Alloa Athletic	684	2-0	1	2	3			6¹	9¹			4	10	7	14	11	16				12			5		8							
Feb 3	A	Clyde	2,506	3-0	1	2	12	3		6	9²	15		4	10	7¹	11						2			5		8		14					
24	H	Alloa Athletic	3,014	1-0	1		4	3		6	9			5	11¹	15							10	12	8		7			2					
Mar 3	H	Ayr United	2,726	1-1	1			3		6	9¹	16		4	11	7							10	12	8	5				2					
20	H	Ayr United	2,731	0-1				3		6	9			7	4	11		15					10	12	8	5	1			2	16				
27	H	Ross County	1,736	1-1				3	5	6	9¹			7	4	11	14						16		8		1	10		2	15				
31	A	Raith Rovers	1,794	0-2				3	5	6	9			4	11	14	15						10		7		1			2	8	16			
Apr 3	H	Inverness Cal. Th.	2,136	4-1				6			7²			4	11	3	16						12	8			1	14		2	9²	10			
7	A	Ross County	2,549	1-0				6		5	7¹			4	11	3	15						16	8			1			2	9	10	18		
21	H	Morton	2,727	2-0				6	5		9	14	4		15	3¹	16						7					10		2	8¹	11	1		
24	H	Falkirk	3,659	3-0				6	5		9¹	15		4	11	14	3	16					7					10¹		2		8¹	1		
28	A	Inverness Cal. Th.	2,824	3-2				6	5		9¹	15		4	11	14	3						7					10		2	16	8²	1		
May 1	H	Airdrieonians	3,295	5-0				4		6	9¹				7¹		3	11³					10	2		5		8			15	1		18	16
5	H	Clyde	6,835	0-2				6	5		9	15		4	11	12	3	16					7					2			10	8	1		
TOTAL FULL APPEARANCES					26	11	19	6	21	30	34	7	17	35	33	7	24	8	3		1		20	16	24	13	5	8		11	6	6	5		
TOTAL SUB APPEARANCES						(1)	(5)	(2)		(1)	(4)	(11)			(16)	(4)	(12)	(9)	(5)		(2)		(4)	(6)			(1)	(1)	(1)	(3)	(2)	(1)	(1)	(1)
TOTAL GOALS SCORED							1		2	3	13	3	4	5	14	2	3	1	4	1			7	1	1		1			3	3		

Small bold figures denote goalscorers. † denotes opponent's own goal.

West Lothian Courier Stadium

EAST STAND
NORTH STAND
CAR PARK (AWAY SUPPORTERS)
SOUTH STAND
WEST STAND
ALMONDVALE BOULEVARD
ALMONDVALE SHOPPING CENTRE
POLICE STATION
BUS STATION
CAR PARK (HOME SUPPORTERS)
ALDERSTON ROAD
RAILWAY 2 MILES

CAPACITY: 10,004 (All Seated)

PITCH DIMENSIONS: 107yds x 75yds

FACILITIES FOR DISABLED SUPPORTERS:
By prior arrangement with Secretary.

Team playing kits

FIRST CHOICE
Shirt: Gold with Black Undersleeve and Two White Vertical Stripes down Arms. Broad Black Chest Band.
Shorts: Black.
Stockings: Gold with Two Black Hoops on Tops.

SECOND CHOICE
Shirt: White with Red Undersleeve and Side Panels.
Shorts: Red.
Stockings: White with Two Red Hoops on Tops.

How to get there

West Lothian Courier Stadium can be reached by the following routes:

BUSES: By bus to terminus at Almondvale Shopping Centre. Follow direction signs for St. John's Hospital or West Lothian Courier Stadium and it is a short 5 minute walk.

TRAINS: To either Livingston North or South Stations, and by taxi to stadium. Approximate cost is £2.00.

CARS: Leave M8 at Livingston Junction (East). Follow signs for St. John's Hospital or West Lothian Courier Stadium.

Livingston F.C. is a member of The Scottish Premier League

Motherwell

Chapman Building, Fir Park Stadium, Firpark Street, Motherwell, ML1 2QN

HON. LIFE PRESIDENT
James C. Chapman, O.B.E.

CHAIRMAN
John Boyle

DIRECTORS
William H. Dickie, R.I.B.A., A.R.I.A.S, Alisdair F. Barron, Fiona Boyle, Andrew Lapping, John Swinburne & James McMahon

DIRECTOR OF FOOTBALL
Patrick Nevin

SECRETARY
Alisdair F. Barron

MANAGER
William Davies

COACH
Miodrag Krivokapic

UNDER 21 COACH
John Phelliben

YOUTH COACH
Michael Weir

CLUB DOCTOR
Dr. Robert Liddle

PHYSIOTHERAPIST
John Porteous

S.F.A. COMMUNITY OFFICER
Colin McKinnon

YOUTH DEVELOPMENT OFFICER/ CHIEF SCOUT
Dave McParland

FOOTBALL SAFETY OFFICERS' ASSOCIATION REPRESENTATIVE
Kenneth Davies
(07711) 237800 (Mobile)

GROUNDSMAN
Grant Murdoch

COMMERCIAL MANAGER
Mrs Karen Paterson
(01698) 338011

HOSPITALITY CO-ORDINATOR
Amanda Gwynne

MATCHDAY PROGRAMME EDITOR
Graham Barnstaple

KIT CO-ORDINATOR
Alan MacDonald

TELEPHONES
Ground (01698) 333333
Ticket Information (01698) 333033
Fax (01698) 338001
Clubcall (09068) 121553
Hospitality Hotline (01698) 338008/9

E-MAIL & INTERNET ADDRESS
mfc@motherwellfc.co.uk
www.motherwellfc.co.uk

CLUB SHOP
Motherwell Football & Athletic Club, Firpark Street, Motherwell, ML1 2QN Tel (01698) 338025. Open Tues, Thurs & Fri from 10.00 a.m. to 3.00 p.m. Saturday (Home Match days), 10.00 a.m. to 3.00 p.m. and Saturday (Away Matches) 10.00 a.m. to 1.00 p.m.

OFFICIAL SUPPORTERS CLUB
c/o Fir Park, Firpark Street, Motherwell, ML1 2QN.

TEAM CAPTAIN
Scott Leitch

SHIRT SPONSOR
Motorola

KIT SUPPLIER
XARA

LIST OF PLAYERS 2001-2002

Squad No.	Name	Place & Date of Birth	Previous Club	Lge Career Apps	Gls
12	Derek Adams	Glasgow 25.6.75	Ross County	43 (26)	7
1	Mark Brown	Motherwell 28.2.81	Rangers	–	–
29	David Clarke	Glasgow 22.6.83	Motherwell Youth	–	–
13	Jon Connolly	Glasgow 3.4.81	Thorniewood United	2	–
2	Martyn Corrigan	Glasgow 14.8.77	Falkirk	50 (5)	1
18	Stephen Cosgrove	Glasgow 29.12.80	Manchester United	–	–
28	Brian Dempsie	Bellshill 4.2.83	Motherwell B.C.	–	–
3	Andy Dow	Dundee 7.2.73	Aberdeen	–	–
11	Stuart Elliott	Belfast 23.7.78	Glentoran	20 (14)	12
25	John Fallon	Bellshill 14.1.82	Calderbraes B.C.	–	–
4	Edward Forrest	Edinburgh 17.12.78	Airdrieonians	–	–
16	Steven Hammell	Rutherglen 18.2.82	'X' Form	35 (3)	–
21	Paul Harvey	Glasgow 28.8.68	Queen of the South	16 (8)	–
9	David Kelly	Birmingham 25.11.65	Sheffield United	–	–
22	Keith Lasley	Glasgow 21.9.79	Cathkin United B.C.	6 (6)	1
8	Scott Leitch	Motherwell 6.10.69	Swindon Town	23 (3)	–
31	Kevin McDonald	Glasgow 5.2.83	Gleniffer Thistle	–	–
27	James McFadden	Glasgow 14.4.83	Motherwell BC	1 (5)	–
10	Roberto Martinez	Balaguer, Spain 13.7.73	Wigan Athletic	–	–
19	Steven Nicholas	Stirling 8.7.81	Stirling Albion	8 (37)	3
23	Ange Oueifio	Bangui, Cen Africa Rep 29.3.76	Denderleeun	14 (3)	–
26	Stephen Pearson	Lanark 2.10.82	Motherwell B.C.	3 (3)	–
20	Douglas Ramsay	Irvine 26.4.79	Bearsden B.C.	3 (14)	1
5	Karl Ready	Neath 14.8.72	Queens Park Rangers	–	–
6	Greg Strong	Bolton 5.9.75	Bolton Wanderers	41 (1)	1
14	Neil Tarrant	Darlington 24.6.79	Aston Villa	–	–
7	Kevin Twaddle	Edinburgh 31.10.71	Morton	38 (12)	7
30	Scott Wilson	Bellshill 20.4.82	Netherdale B.C.	–	–
24	Martin Wood	Aberdeen 28.8.82	Rothes	3 (5)	–
17	Stephen Woods	Glasgow 23.2.70	Preston North End	109 (1)	–

Milestones

YEAR OF FORMATION: 1886
MOST CAPPED PLAYER: Tommy Coyne (Republic of Ireland)
NO. OF CAPS: 13
MOST LEAGUE POINTS IN A SEASON: 66 (Division 1 - Season 1931/32)
MOST LEAGUE GOALS SCORED BY A PLAYER IN A SEASON: William McFadyen (Season 1931/32)
NO. OF GOALS SCORED: 52
RECORD ATTENDANCE: 35,632 (-v- Rangers – Scottish Cup, 12.3.1952)
RECORD VICTORY: 12-1 (-v- Dundee United – Division 2, 23.1.1954)
RECORD DEFEAT: 0-8 (-v- Aberdeen - Premier Division, 26.3.1979)

The Well's ten year league record

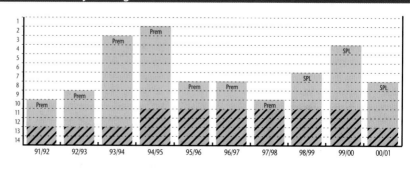

THE WELL'S CLUB FACTFILE 2000/2001
RESULTS... APPEARANCES... SCORERS... ATTENDANCES...

Date	Venue	Opponents	Att.	Res	Goram A.	Corrigan M.	McMillan S.	Kemble B.	Strong G.	Davies J.	Brannan G.	Townsley D.	Harvey P.	Twaddle K.	Nicholas S.	Wood M.	Elliott A.	Quelfio A.	Hammell S.	McCulloch L.	Spencer J.	Goodman D.	Leitch S.	Adams D.	Ramsay D.	Woods S.	McClen J.	Lasley K.	McFadden J.	Pearson S.	Okoli J.	Chiba S.	Connolly J.
July 29	H	Dundee	5,961	0-2	1	2	3	4	5	6	7	8	9	10	11	12	13	14															
Aug 5	A	Celtic	59,057	0-1	1	2	3	4	5	8	7	22	9		23	11	14		6	10													
12	A	Dundee United	6,201	1-1	1	2	3		5		7	8	9						6	4	10	11^1	12	13									
16	H	Dunfermline Athletic	5,257	0-1	1	2	3		5		12	9	8						6	4	10	11	24	7	23								
19	A	Kilmarnock	6,533	2-3	1	6	7	4	5		8				13			9^2	2	3	11	10	12										
27	H	Aberdeen	6,009	1-1	1	2	3		5		7		12					14	13	4	10^1	11	9	6	8								
Sep 9	A	St. Mirren	5,264	1-0	1	14	3	4			7	13	8				9		2	5	10^1	11	12	6									
16	A	Hibernian	9,868	0-2	1	14	3	4	12		7	6	8				9		2	5	10	11	13										
23	H	Rangers	11,275	0-1	1		3	4	6		7		8				12		2	5	10	14	13	9	11								
Oct 1	A	Heart of Midlothian	10,460	0-3		12	3		5		7	13	6				9		2	4	10	11	14	8		1							
14	H	St. Johnstone	4,483	†4-0		2	3		5		7^1		6				9^1	14		4	10^1	11	12	8		1	13						
21	A	Dundee	7,344	2-1		2	6		5		7		12				9^1	14	3	4	10^1	11	13	8		1							
29	H	Celtic	12,421	3-3		2	6		5		7^1		14				9			4	10^1	11	12	13	8^1	1							
Nov 4	H	Dundee United	6,864	2-1		2	6	3	5		7^1		12				9^1			4	10	11	14	13	8	1							
11	A	Dunfermline Athletic	4,146	2-1		2	3		5		7^1	12^1	13				9			4	10	11	6	8		1							
18	H	Kilmarnock	6,571	1-2		2	3		5		7^1	8	12	14			9			4	10	11	6	13		1							
25	A	Aberdeen	11,502	3-3	1	2	6	3	5		7	9^1	14				12			4	10^2	11	8	13									
29	H	St. Mirren	5,312	2-0		2	3		5		7	9	8^1	12^1			11			4	10		6	13		1							
Dec 3	H	Hibernian	5,715	1-3		2	6	3	5		7	9	11	13			12^1			4	10		8	14		1							
10	A	Rangers	46,058	0-2	1	2	3		5		7	8					11	12		4	10	14	9	13	6								
16	H	Heart of Midlothian	5,440	2-0	1	2	3		5		7	9^1	8				13			4	10	11	6	12^1									
23	A	St. Johnstone	3,489	3-2	1	2	3		5		6^1		8				13	14		4	10	11^1	7	9^1		12							
26	H	Dundee	6,183	0-3	1	2	6	3	5			9				10				4		11	7	8		12	13						
Jan 2	A	Dundee United	6,311	0-2	1	2	3		5		7	9	8				13			4	10	11	14	6		12							
31	H	Dunfermline Athletic	4,601	1-1	1	2	3	4	5		7	8	22								10^1	11	23	6	9								
Feb 3	A	Kilmarnock	6,018	2-1	1	2	3		5		7^1	8	13^1							4	12	10	11	6		9		14					
10	H	Aberdeen	6,680	0-1	1	2	3		5		7	8	12					14		4	13	10	11	6		9							
21	A	Celtic	58,736	0-1	1	2	6	3	5			8	13							4	10	11	7	9		14		12					
24	A	St. Mirren	3,704	1-0	1	2	6	3	5			8^1	9	14			12			4	10	11	13	7									
Mar 4	A	Hibernian	8,225	1-1	1	2			5^1			8	9			22				4	10	23	6	11	3			7		14			
17	H	Rangers	11,208	1-2	1	2			5				12	13	11	11					10^1	6	3			9		7		14		4	8
31	A	Heart of Midlothian	11,581	0-3		2			5		7		9	13	11					4	6	10	14			1					12	3	8
Apr 7	H	St. Johnstone	4,600	1-0		2			5			8	9	12	11^1					4	10		7			1				14	13	3	6
21	H	St. Johnstone	3,195	0-1		2			5			9	8	10	11					4			7	13		1					12	3	6
28	A	Dundee United	5,928	0-1		12			5			9	10		11	14			2	4			13			7				6	8	3	1
May 5	H	Aberdeen	3,905	0-2					5		7	9	8		10	11			2	4						12				14	13	3	6
12	A	Dunfermline Athletic	2,437	2-1		2		3	5		7	9	10	14	11^2					4			13			1					12	6	8
19	A	Dunfermline Athletic	4,158	3-3		2			5		7^1	9	10	12	11^1					4			3			1				6^1	13	8	
TOTAL FULL APPEARANCES					22	31	25	23	31	2	23	22	10	20	5	3	20	14	32	26	20	6	23	17	3	14	1	6	1	3	6	7	2
TOTAL SUB APPEARANCES						(4)		(1)			(8)	(1)	(5)	(13)	(5)	(13)	(3)	(2)		(2)	(12)	(3)	(9)	(8)		(2)		(6)			(5)	(3)	
TOTAL GOALS SCORED									1		6	6	2	1			10			8	2	1		3						1		

Small bold figures denote goalscorers. † denotes opponent's own goal.

Fir Park

DALZELL DRIVE

KNOWETOP AVENUE

Chapman Building

FIRPARK STREET

CAPACITY: 13,757 (All Seated)

PITCH DIMENSIONS: 110 yds x 75 yds

FACILITIES FOR DISABLED SUPPORTERS:
Area between Main Stand and South Stand. Prior arrangement must be made with the Secretary and a ticket obtained.

Team playing kits

FIRST CHOICE
Shirt: Amber with Claret Collar and Cuffs.
Shorts: Claret with Amber Piping and Bands.
Stockings: Amber.
SECOND CHOICE
Shirt: White and Purple Horizontal Bands with Black Collar and Sleeves.
Shorts: White with Black Band.
Stockings: White.

THIRD CHOICE
Shirt: Claret with Amber Piping.
Shorts: Claret with Amber Piping.
Stockings: Claret with Amber Trim.

How to get there

The following routes can be used to reach Fir Park:
BUSES: Fir Park is less than a quarter of a mile from the main thoroughfare through the town and numerous buses serving Lanarkshire and Glasgow all pass along this road. De-bus at the Civic Centre.
TRAINS: Motherwell Station is a main-line station on the Glasgow-London (Euston) route, and the station is particularly well served by trains running from numerous points throughout the Strathclyde Region. Motherwell Station is a twenty minute walk from Fir Park, while the station at Airbles Road is only ten minutes away. East Coast access is via Motherwell Central Station on the Glasgow-London East Coast line. Travel from West Coast and Glasgow areas is via the low level Glasgow Central line to Airbles and Motherwell Central. This is a regular service on a 30 minute basis (8 mins & 38 mins past).
CARS: Controlled supervised car parking is available in the immediate area of Fir Park. Car park season tickets are available for closest proximity car parks. Away fan car parking is extensive in the grounds of Motherwell College on a day rate basis of £5.00. Access to South Stand is within a maximum of 5 minutes walk.

The Well

Motherwell F.C. is a member of The Scottish Premier League

Rangers

Ibrox Stadium,150 Edmiston Drive, Glasgow, G51 2XD

CHAIRMAN
David E. Murray

DIRECTORS
R. Campbell Ogilvie, Ian B. Skelly,
Douglas Odam, Daniel P. Levy,
Donald Wilson, David C. King
& John McClelland

ASSOCIATE DIRECTORS
Ian Russell & Bill Thornton

SECRETARY
R. Campbell Ogilvie

MANAGER
Dick Advocaat

ASSISTANT MANAGER
Bert van Lingen

FIRST TEAM COACH
Jan Wouters

DIRECTOR OF FOOTBALL DEVELOPMENT
Tommy McLean

UNDER 21 TEAM COACH
John McGregor

UNDER 18 TEAM COACH
John Brown

GOALKEEPING COACH
Billy Thomson

YOUTH DEVELOPMENT OFFICER
Jan Derks

CHIEF SCOUT
Ewan Chester

CLUB DOCTOR
Dr. Gert Jan Goudswaard

PHYSIOTHERAPIST
Grant Downie

PUBLIC RELATIONS EXECUTIVE
John Greig, M.B.E.

FINANCIAL CONTROLLER
Douglas Odam

RANGERS HOSPITALITY MANAGER
Peter Kingstone

COMMERCIAL MANAGER
Martin Bain (0141) 580 8569

HEAD OF SALES
Suzie Lang

CUSTOMER SERVICES MANAGER
Michael Patterson

INFORMATION SYSTEMS MANAGER
James McGlynn

GENERAL MANAGER–RETAIL,
LICENCING & DIRECT MARKETING
Nick Peel

OPERATIONS EXECUTIVE/
FOOTBALL SAFETY OFFICERS'
ASSOCIATION REPRESENTATIVE
Laurence MacIntyre (0141) 580 8630

PITCH SUPERINTENDENT
David Roxburgh

STADIUM FACILITIES MANAGER
Ken Crawford

MATCHDAY PROGRAMME EDITOR
Lindsay Herron

TELEPHONES
Main Switchboard (0141) 580 8500
Football Administration (0141) 580 8609
Fax–Football Administration (0141) 580 8947
Ticket Centre
0870-600 1993 Fax (0141) 580 8504
Customer Services 0870-600 1972
Hospitality 0870-600 1964
Commercial 0870-600 1899
Retail/Mail Order 0870 600 599 1997
Fax Enquiries 0870-600 1978

E-MAIL & INTERNET ADDRESS
dorahowie@rangers.co.uk
www.rangers.co.uk

CLUB SHOPS
1873 Superstore, Ibrox Stadium,
Glasgow G51. Open until 10.00p.m.
on Matchdays and 9.30a.m.-5.30p.m.
Mon to Sat and 11.00a.m. to
5.00p.m. on Sun.
The Rangers Shop,
84-92 Sauchiehall Street, Glasgow, G2.
Open 9.00a.m.-5.30p.m. Mon to Sat
and Sun Noon-4.00p.m.
The Rangers Shop,
St. Enoch Centre, Glasgow. Open
9.00a.m.-6.00p.m. Mon, Tue, Wed, Fri
and Sat., 9.00a.m.-8.00p.m.
Thurs and Sun, 11.00a.m.-5.00p.m.

OFFICIAL SUPPORTERS CLUB
Rangers F.C. Supporters' Association,
250 Edmiston Drive, Glasgow, G51 1YU

TEAM CAPTAIN
Barry Ferguson

SHIRT SPONSOR
NTL

KIT SUPPLIER
Nike

LIST OF PLAYERS 2001-2002

Squad No.	Name	Place & Date of Birth	Previous Club	Lge Career Apps	Gls
–	Dariusz Adamczuk	Stettin, Poland 20.10.69	Dundee	6 (7)	–
4	Lorenzo Amoruso	Bari, Italy 28.6.71	Fiorentina	96	5
–	Michael Ball	Liverpool 2.10.79	Everton	–	–
7	Claudio Caniggia	Buenos Aires, Argentina 9.1.67	Dundee	–	–
22	Jesper Christiansen	Roskilde, Denmark 24.4.78	Odense BK	3	–
14	Ronald de Boer	Hoorn, Holland 15.5.70	Barcelona	17	6
16	William Dodds	New Cumnock 5.2.69	Dundee United	32 (16)	19
6	Barry Ferguson	Glasgow 2.2.78	Rangers SABC	90 (1)	7
9	Tore Andre Flo	Stryn, Norway 15.6.73	Chelsea	18 (1)	11
27	Stephen Hughes	Motherwell 14.11.82	'S' Form	– (2)	–
24	Allan Johnston	Glasgow 14.12.73	Sunderland	9 (4)	–
17	Andrei Kanchelskis	Kirovgraci, Ukraine 23.1.69	Fiorentina	58 (8)	12
–	Jani Kauppila	Finland 16.1.80	Tervarit	1 (3)	–
1	Stefan Klos	Dortmund, Germany 16.8.71	Borussia Dortmund	74	–
15	Bert Konterman	Rouveen, Holland 14.1.71	Feyenoord	36 (1)	3
20	Russell Latapy	Port of Spain, Trinidad 2.8.68	Hibernian	–	–
26	Peter Lovenkrands	Horsholm, Denmark 29.1.80	AB Copenhagen	1 (7)	–
11	Neil McCann	Greenock 11.8.74	Heart of Midlothian	43 (27)	11
–	Robert Malcolm	Glasgow 12.11.80	'S' Form	4 (5)	1
23	Kenny Miller	Edinburgh 23.12.79	Hibernian	12 (15)	8
10	Michael Mols	Amsterdam 17.12.70	FC Utrecht	19 (3)	14
3	Craig Moore	Canterbury, Australia 12.12.75	Crystal Palace	95 (6)	6
8	Christian Nerlinger	Dortmund, Germany 21.3.73	Borussia Dortmund	–	–
5	Arthur Numan	Heemskerk, Holland 14.12.69	PSV Eindhoven	59 (3)	1
29	Tero Penttila	Finland 9.3.75	FC Haka	3	–
12	Claudio Reyna	Livingston, USA 20.7.73	VFL Wolfsburg	47 (6)	7
2	Fernando Ricksen	Heerlen, Holland 27.7.76	AZ Alkmaar	26 (1)	1
21	Maurice Ross	Dundee 3.2.81	Rangers SABC	– (2)	–
46	Graham Smith	Edinburgh 8.6.83	Rangers B.C.	–	–
25	Tony Vidmar	Adelaide, Australia 4.7.70	NAC Breda	66 (16)	7
19	Scott Wilson	Edinburgh 19.3.77	Rangers B.C	36 (6)	1

Milestones

YEAR OF FORMATION: 1873
MOST CAPPED PLAYER: Alistair McCoist
NO. OF CAPS: 58
MOST LEAGUE POINTS IN A SEASON: 76 (Division 1 - Season 1920/21) (2 Points for a Win)
97 (Scottish Premier League - Season 1999/2000) (3 Points for a Win)
MOST LEAGUE GOALS SCORED BY A PLAYER IN A SEASON: Sam English (Season 1931/32)
NO. OF GOALS SCORED: 44
RECORD ATTENDANCE: 118,567 (-v- Celtic – 2.1.1939)
RECORD VICTORY: 14-2 (-v- Blairgowrie – Scottish Cup, 20.1.1934)
RECORD DEFEAT: 2-10 (-v- Airdrieonians – 1886)

The Gers' ten year league record

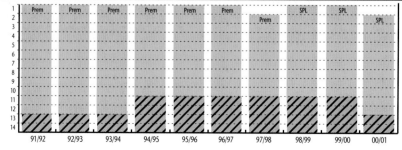

	91/92	92/93	93/94	94/95	95/96	96/97	97/98	98/99	99/00	00/01
	Prem	Prem	Prem	Prem	Prem	Prem	SPL	SPL	SPL	

THE GERS' CLUB FACTFILE 2000/2001
RESULTS... APPEARANCES... SCORERS... ATTENDANCES...

Date	Venue	Opponents	Att.	Res	Klos S.	Ricksen F.	Amoruso L.	Konterman B.	Vidmar T.	Kanchelskis A.	Ferguson B.	van Bronckhorst G.	Albertz J.	Dodds W.	Wallace R.	McCann N.	Reyna C.	Miller K.	Porrini S.	Kerimoglu T.	Lovenkrands P.	Wilson S.	Numan A.	de Boer R.	Mols M.	Johnston A.	Brown M.	Negri M.	Adamczuk D.	Christiansen J.	Flo T-A.	Carson S.	Ross M.	Malcolm R.	Hughes S.	Moore C.	Kauppila J.	Gayle M.	Fernandes F.
July 29	H	St. Johnstone	48,062	2-1	1	2	3	4	5	6	7	8	9	10²	11	12	13	14																					
Aug 5	A	Kilmarnock	14,680	4-2	1	2	3	4		12	7	8		10²	11	9	6	24¹	5	23¹																			
13	A	St. Mirren	9,251	3-1	1	2	3	4	12		7	5	9²	10¹	11	8					6																		
19	H	Dunfermline Athletic	47,452	4-1	1	2	3	4		22	7	5¹	8¹	10¹	11¹	9	23				6	14																	
27	A	Celtic	59,476	2-6	1	2	3	4	5	13	7	8		10¹	11	9	6¹				12	14																	
Sep 9	A	Dundee	10,439	1-1	1	14	3				8		10		9¹	2	13				7	12	4	5	6	11												
17	H	Heart of Midlothian	47,496	1-0	1	2	3	4	13		8	9	10		12		14				7		5	11¹		6													
23	A	Motherwell	11,275	1-0	1		3	4	14		9	8			2	13				7	12		5		10¹	6													
Oct 1	H	Dundee United	44,324	3-0		2	3	4	12	6¹		8¹	9¹	13		14				7		5	11			1	10												
14	A	Hibernian	14,524	0-1		3	4	5	22	8		9	10			23	2	7	11					6	1														
22	A	St. Johnstone	7,763	1-2		3	4		6			10	23	8		11¹	2	7	22		9				1	5													
28	H	Kilmarnock	49,659	0-3	6	3	4		9			12	11	8		13	2	7			5	10				14	1												
Nov 4	H	St. Mirren	48,795	7-1		2	3	14			8		9	12¹		13¹		11⁵			7		4	5	6	10			1										
12	A	Aberdeen	16,798	2-1		6	3	4	2		7		9	12		11¹					5		8	10¹					13	1									
18	A	Dunfermline Athletic	10,706	0-0			3	4	2		7		8		12		11				5	6	9	10															
26	H	Celtic	50,083	5-1	1		3¹	4		7¹		8		24	2	11		23			5	6	9¹	12¹						10¹									
Dec 3	A	Heart of Midlothian	16,710	1-0	1		3	4		7		8¹	13		2	11		12			5	6	9							10									
10	H	Motherwell	46,058	2-0	1	2		3¹	5	6¹		9	13		7					12	4		11	8						10	14								
13	H	Aberdeen	45,285	3-1	1	2		3			6	12¹	13¹		8	7	10				4	5	9	11¹															
17	A	Dundee United	10,750	1-1	1	2	3	4	5		6	14	10		8	7¹	12						9	11	13															
23	H	Hibernian	49,993	1-0	1	2	3	4		6		9	14		8	7	13	5	12				10¹	11															
26	H	St. Johnstone	46,180	3-0	1	2¹	3	4		6			8¹	7	12		9				5	10	11	14			13¹												
Jan 2	A	St. Mirren	8,142	3-1	1	2	3	4¹		6		12		8	7	11					5	9	13				10²		14										
31	A	Aberdeen	45,621	1-0	1	7		6	4			9		10	2	8¹		3	5				12				11		13										
Feb 3	H	Dunfermline Athletic	46,302	2-0	1	2		6	4			7	10		8¹		3	5	12¹		9						11			13									
11	A	Celtic	59,496	0-1	1	7		4		6	9		8		10		12	3	5				13				11		2										
24	A	Dundee	9,778	1-0	1		3	7¹		6		12		10	13	2	8	5			9						11		4										
Mar 3	H	Heart of Midlothian	49,003	2-0	1		3	7		6	8	10			13	2		5			9						11²			14		4	12						
14	H	Dundee	45,035	0-2	1		4	7		6		12			2			5			9						11	8		13		3	14	10					
17	A	Motherwell	11,208	2-1	1		4			6		13			10	2		5			9						11		3¹				7	8	12¹				
31	H	Dundee United	48,382	0-2			4	5		6	9	13	10		2			7	3								11							8	12				
Apr 8	A	Hibernian	9,704	0-0	1	7		4		6	12	11	10		8		2	3	5								9												
11	A	Kilmarnock	14,585	2-1	1	7		4		6		11	10		8	12	2	3	5								9²												
21	A	Dundee	10,687	3-0	1	2	3	7		6		8¹	11	10¹		14		13	4	5							9¹												12
29	H	Celtic	50,057	0-3	1	2	3	7		6		8	11	10			13	5									9							4					14
May 5	H	Heart of Midlothian	15,315	4-1	1	2	3	7		6		8²		10¹	9			5									11¹							4					
12	H	Kilmarnock	46,577	5-1	1	2	3¹	7			8	13	10²				6	12			5	9¹					11¹							4	14				
20	H	Hibernian	47,023	4-0	1	2	3	7	4¹		13	8¹	14	10			6	12			5	9²																	11
TOTAL FULL APPEARANCES					32	26	29	36	11	3	30	10	20	16	14	16	16	12	12	17	1	19	22	17	10	9	3	1	1	3	18	1		3		5	1	4
TOTAL SUB APPEARANCES						(1)		(1)	(4)	(4)		(1)	(4)(14)	(1)	(5)	(2)(15)		(9)(7)	(1)				(3)	(4)			(2)		(1)	(1)	(1)	(3)	(1)		(3)		(4)
TOTAL GOALS SCORED						1	2	3	1		1	2	2	10	9	5	3	2	8		3			6	5					11			1				1

Small bold figures denote goalscorers. † denotes opponent's own goal.

Ibrox Stadium

EDMISTON DRIVE

CAPACITY: 50,444 (All Seated)

PITCH DIMENSIONS: 115yds x 75yds

FACILITIES FOR DISABLED SUPPORTERS:
Special area within stadium and also special toilet facilities provided. The club also have a Rangers Disabled Supporters' Club. Contact: David Milne, Secretary, Disabled Supporters' Club, c/o Ibrox Stadium, Glasgow, G51 2XD. This is free of charge.

Team playing kits

FIRST CHOICE
Shirt: Royal Blue with White/Blue 'V' Neck with Red Insert, Red Mesh Panel with White Piping running along Sleeves and down Sides, White Cuffs.
Shorts: White.
Stockings: Red with Black Tops **OR** Black with Red Tops.

SECOND CHOICE
Shirt: White with Red Band on 'V' Neck with One Red and One Navy Blue Band on Sleeves.
Shorts: Navy Blue with Red Trim.
Stockings: White with Navy Blue Horizontal Bands at Top.

THIRD CHOICE
Shirt: Red with Black Trim Running from Neck to Sleeve. Black Trim on Sleeves.
Shorts: Red with Black Trim.
Stockings: Red with Black Horizontal Bands at Top.

How to get there

You can reach Ibrox Stadium by these routes:
BUSES: The following buses all pass within 300 yards of the Stadium and can be boarded from Glasgow city centre:- Nos. 4, 9A, 23, 23A, 52, 53, 53A, 54A, 54B, 65, 89 and 91.
UNDERGROUND: GGPTE Underground station is Ibrox, which is two minutes walk from the Stadium.
CARS: Motor Vehicles can head for the Stadium from the city centre by joining the M8 Motorway from Waterloo Street. Take the B768 turn-off for Govan. This will then take you to the ground. A limited number of parking spaces will be available in the Albion Car Park.

The Gers

Rangers F.C. is a member of The Scottish Premier League

St. Johnstone

McDiarmid Park, Crieff Road,
Perth, PH1 2SJ

CHAIRMAN
Geoffrey S. Brown

DIRECTORS
Douglas B. McIntyre, Robert Reid,
James Donnachie
& Dr. Alistair McCracken

**MANAGING DIRECTOR/
SECRETARY**
A. Stewart M. Duff

MANAGER
Alexander Clark

FIRST TEAM COACH
William Kirkwood

YOUTH COACHES
Alastair Stevenson & Henry Hall

CLUB DOCTOR
Dr. Alistair McCracken

PHYSIOTHERAPIST
Nick Summersgill

S.F.A. COMMUNITY OFFICER
Atholl Henderson

STADIUM MANAGER
Jimmy Hogg

**FOOTBALL SAFETY OFFICERS'
ASSOCIATION REPRESENTATIVE**
Alistair Drummond (01738) 459090

MARKETING EXECUTIVE
Paul Fraser (01738) 459090

SALES EXECUTIVE
Susan Weir

COMMERCIAL MANAGER
Diane Knight (01738) 459093

LOTTERY MANAGER
Keith Pitken

CATERING MANAGER
Stuart MacColl

MATCHDAY PROGRAMME EDITORS
Alistair Blair & Helen Green

TELEPHONES
Ground (01738) 459090
Ticket Office (01738) 455000
Fax (01738) 625771
Information Service (09068) 121559

E-MAIL & INTERNET ADDRESS
anyone@saints.sol.co.uk
www.stjohnstonefc.co.uk

CLUB SHOP
Mon-Fri at Main Reception
at Ground. A shop is also open on
matchdays and is situated at
Ormond (South) Stand

OFFICIAL SUPPORTERS CLUB
157 Dunkeld Road, Perth
Tel: (01738) 442022

TEAM CAPTAIN
Jim Weir

SHIRT SPONSOR
Scottish Hydro-Electric plc

KIT SUPPLIER
XARA

LIST OF PLAYERS 2001-2002

Squad No.	Name	Place & Date of Birth	Previous Club	Lge Career Apps	Gls
14	Paddy Connolly	Glasgow 25.6.70	Airdrieonians	32 (13)	6
31	Chris Conway	Glasgow 17.7.83	'S' Form	– (1)	–
23	Brendan Crozier	Glasgow 7.10.82	Busby B.C.	3 (1)	–
21	Kevin Cuthbert	Perth 8.9.82	St. Johnstone B.C.	–	–
4	Nick Dasovic	Vancouver, Canada 5.12.68	Trelleborg FC	111 (2)	1
24	Rachid Djebaili	France 26.4.75	Noisy le Sec	–	–
2	Darren Dods	Edinburgh 7.6.75	Hibernian	82 (4)	5
16	Willie Falconer	Aberdeen 5.4.66	Dundee	–	–
37	Mark Ferry	Glasgow 19.1.84	'S' Form	–	–
20	Ross Forsyth	Glasgow 20.11.82	Aberdeen B.C.	9 (2)	–
30	Martyn Fotheringham	Perth 23.3.83	Forfar B.C.	– (2)	–
17	Paul Hartley	Glasgow 19.10.76	Hibernian	16 (7)	2
25	Darren Jackson	Edinburgh 25.7.66	Livingston	–	–
9	Graeme Jones	Gateshead 13.3.70	Wigan Athletic	24 (4)	6
11	Paul Kane	Edinburgh 20.6.65	Viking Stavanger	117 (6)	6
6	Benito Kemble	Nieuw Nickerie, Holland 27.8.68	Motherwell	–	–
28	Martin Lauchlan	Rutherglen 1.10.80	Partick Thistle	– (6)	–
7	Tommy Lovenkrands	Copenhagen 30.5.74	AB Copenhagen	16 (7)	3
10	John Paul McBride	Hamilton 28.11.78	Celtic	40 (8)	4
22	David McClune	Glasgow 8.2.83	'S' Form	5	1
3	Stuart McCluskey	Bellshill 29.10.77	'S' Form	51 (12)	3
19	Marc McCulloch	Edinburgh 14.3.80	Musselburgh Athletic	13 (9)	3
27	Peter MacDonald	Glasgow 17.11.80	Rangers	–	–
1	Alan Main	Elgin 5.12.67	Dundee United	212	–
26	Stuart Malcolm	Edinburgh 20.8.79	Hutchison Vale B.C.	– (1)	–
12	Grant Murray	Edinburgh 29.8.75	Heart of Midlothian	–	–
36	Emmanuel Panther	Glasgow 11.5.84	'S' Form	–	–
18	Keigan Parker	Livingston 8.6.82	St. Johnstone B.C.	36 (13)	12
8	Craig Russell	Jarrow 4.2.74	Manchester City	7 (8)	2
5	Jim Weir	Motherwell 15.6.69	Heart of Midlothian	173 (1)	5

Milestones

YEAR OF FORMATION: 1884
MOST CAPPED PLAYER: Sandy McLaren
NO. OF CAPS: 5
MOST LEAGUE POINTS IN A SEASON: 59 (Second Division – Season 1987/88)(2 Points for a Win)
80 (First Division – Season 1996/97)(3 Points for a Win)
MOST LEAGUE GOALS SCORED BY A PLAYER IN A SEASON: Jimmy Benson (Season 1931/32)
NO. OF GOALS SCORED: 38
RECORD ATTENDANCE: 29,972 (-v- Dundee 10.2.1951 at Muirton Park)
10,545 (-v- Dundee – SPL, 23.05.1999 at McDiarmid Park)
RECORD VICTORY: 8-1 (-v- Partick Thistle – League Cup, 16.8.1969)
RECORD DEFEAT: 0-12 (-v- Cowdenbeath – Scottish Cup, 21.1.1928)

The Saints' ten year league record

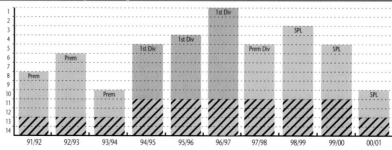

166

THE SAINTS' CLUB FACTFILE 2000/2001
RESULTS... APPEARANCES... SCORERS... ATTENDANCES...

Date	Venue	Opponents	Att.	Res	Main A.	Sylla M.	Bollan G.	Weir J.	Kernaghan A.	McBride J.P.	Dasovic N.	Kane P.	Parker K.	Lovenkrands T.	Jones G.	Russell C.	Connolly P.	Dods D.	O'Neill M.	Hartley P.	McCulloch M.	Forsyth R.	Evers S.	Lauchlan M.	Malcolm S.	McCluskey S.	Lowndes N.	Frail S.	Crozier B.	Ferry M.	McClune D.	Fotheringham M.
July 29	A	Rangers	48,062	1-2	1	2	3	4	5¹	6	7	8	9	10	11	12	13															
Aug 6	H	Heart of Midlothian	6,165	2-2	1	2	3	4¹	5	6	7	8	9	10	11¹		13	12														
12	A	Dunfermline Athletic	3,477	1-1	1	2	3	4		6	7	8	9	10	11¹	12	13	5														
19	A	Dundee United	6,636	2-1	1	2	3	4			7		9¹	10	11¹		13	5	6	8	12											
26	A	Kilmarnock	3,773	1-1	1	2	3	4		14	7	12	10¹	11	9			5	6	8	13											
Sep 9	A	Aberdeen	10,464	1-1	1	2¹	3	4	5		7	8	9		11	12			10	6												
16	H	Dundee	5,055	0-0	1	2	3		5	6	7	8	13	10	11	12		4		9												
23	A	St. Mirren	4,119	1-0	1	2	3	4	5		7	8	9¹	12	11		6			10												
30	H	Hibernian	5,464	0-3	1	2	3	4	5		7	8	9	13	11		6		12	10		14										
Oct 14	A	Motherwell	4,483	0-4	1	2	3		5	6	7	8	22	10			11		4	9			23	14								
17	H	Celtic	8,946	0-2	1	6	3	4	5		7	8	10		11	2			13	9		12										
22	H	Rangers	7,763	2-1	1	6¹	3	4	5	13	7	8	10¹	12	11	2				9												
28	A	Heart of Midlothian	10,883	3-0	1	6	3	4	5		7	8	10¹	12	11²	2				9												
Nov 4	H	Dunfermline Athletic	4,287	0-2	1	6	3		5	12	7	8	10		11	2		13		9			4									
12	A	Celtic	56,952	1-4	1	6	3		5	12	7	8	10		13¹	11	2		14	9			4									
18	H	Dundee United	4,295	1-0	1	6	3	4		9	7	8	10¹		11	13	2		12				5									
25	A	Kilmarnock	6,330	2-0	1	9	3	4			7	8	10²		11		2		12	6			5									
28	H	Aberdeen	4,897	0-0	1	9	3	4			7	8	10		11	12	2			6			5									
Dec 2	A	Dundee	7,014	1-1	1	6¹		4		12	7	8	10		11	2		9	3				5									
9	H	St. Mirren	4,434	2-0	1	9		4		6¹	7	8	10¹		11	2			3				5									
16	A	Hibernian	10,374	0-2	1			4	9		7	8	10		11	2	13	12	6				5									
23	H	Motherwell	3,489	2-3	1	9¹	3	4		6	7	8	10¹	12	13	11	2						5									
26	A	Rangers	46,180	0-3	1	9	3	4			7	12	8	10	11		2	6			13	14	5									
30	H	Heart of Midlothian	5,173	2-2	1	9¹	3	4			8	7	10		11¹	2	6		5								12					
Jan 2	A	Dunfermline Athletic	6,117	0-0	1	9	3	4			8	7	10		11	2	6		12								13	5				
Feb 3	A	Dundee United	6,482	1-1	1	9	3	4		6	7	8	10		11	2	13										12¹	5				
11	H	Kilmarnock	6,627	1-2	1	9	3	4		6	7	8	10		11¹	2	13										12	5				
Mar 3	H	Dundee	5,065	2-3	1	9	3¹	4	5	7		8¹	10		14	11		6	13	12							2					
14	H	Celtic	8,993	1-2	1	9		4	5	7		8	11	12				13		10							2¹		3	6		
17	A	St. Mirren	4,563	0-1	1			4	5	7			11	12			8	10	14	9							2		3	6	13	
27	A	Aberdeen	8,496	3-3	1			4	12	9²	7	8	11	6				10	13	5							2	14¹	3			
Apr 1	H	Hibernian	4,346	2-0	1	8		4	5	6	7		13	9²				10	12	3							11				2	
7	A	Motherwell	4,600	0-1	1	8		4	5		7	13	12	9				10	3	6							14	11			2	
21	A	Motherwell	3,195	1-0	1	9¹		4		8	11	7					12	10	3	6							5	13			2	
28	H	Aberdeen	3,611	0-3	1	8	3	4		14	7		11	9				5	10	6							2	12				14
May 5	H	St. Mirren	4,122	2-2	1	9		4		8	7	12	11				5¹	10¹	3	6							2	13				
12	H	Dundee United	6,497	2-3	1	9		4		8	7	12	11				5	10¹	3	6									13	2¹		
20	A	Dunfermline Athletic	4,084	0-0	1		3			10	7		11			12	4		5	8			2				9		6			13
TOTAL FULL APPEARANCES					38	34	28	33	17	20	35	27	30	16	9	6	15	26	7	16	13	9	5					18	2	6	3	5
TOTAL SUB APPEARANCES									(1)	(6)	(1)	(1)	(7)	(7)			(8)	(6)	(3)	(3)	(7)	(9)	(2)	(1)	(1)	(1)	(1)	(8)		(1)	(1)	(2)
TOTAL GOALS SCORED						6	1	1	1	3		1	9	3	3		1	4	1		2							1	2		1

Small bold figures denote goalscorers. † denotes opponent's own goal.

McDiarmid Park

◀ GLASGOW AND EDINBURGH - A9 - INVERNESS ▶

Car Park
WEST STAND
SOUTH STAND
NORTH STAND
EAST STAND
CRIEFF ROAD
CAR PARK

CAPACITY: 10,723 (All Seated)

PITCH DIMENSIONS: 115 yds x 75 yds

FACILITIES FOR DISABLED SUPPORTERS:
Entrance via south end of West Stand and south end of East Stand. Visiting disabled fans should contact the club in advance. Headphones available in West and North Stands for blind and partially sighted supporters.

Team playing kits

FIRST CHOICE
Shirt: Royal Blue with White Piping on Shoulders and Sides. Collar and Cuffs White.
Shorts: White with Royal Blue Piping down Sides and around Hem.
Stockings: Royal Blue with two White Hoops on Tops.

SECOND CHOICE
Shirt: Yellow with Blue Trim on Shoulders and Sides. Blue Trim across Chest.
Shorts: Blue with Two Yellow Stripes down Sides.
Stockings: Yellow with Two Blue Hoops.

THIRD CHOICE
Shirt: White with Royal Blue Sleeves with White Panel.
Shorts: White with Royal Blue Side Panels.
Stockings: White with Two Royal Blue Hoops.

How to get there

The following routes can be used to reach McDiarmid Park:
TRAINS: Perth Station is well served by trains from all parts of the country. The station is about 40 minutes walk from the park.
BUSES: Local services nos. 1 and 2 pass near the ground. Both leave from Mill Street in the town centre.
CARS: The car park at the park holds 1,500 cars and 100 coaches. Vehicles should follow signs A9 to Inverness on Perth City by-pass, then follow "Football Stadium" signs at Inveralmond Roundabout South onto slip road adjacent to McDiarmid Park. Vehicle charges are £2.00 for cars and no charge for coaches.

St. Johnstone F.C. is a member of The Scottish Premier League

Dates for your Diary Season 2001/02

TENNENTS SCOTTISH CUP 2001/01
First Round .... Saturday, 17th November, 2001
Second Round .... Saturday, 8th December, 2001
Third Round .... Saturday, 5th January, 2002
Fourth Round .... Saturday, 26th January, 2002
Fifth Round.. Saturday, 23rd February, 2002
Semi-Finals .... Saturday, 23rd March & Sunday, 24th March, 2002
Final .... Saturday, 4th May, 2002

FIFA WORLD CUP 2002 – QUALIFYING MATCHES
Scotland v. Croatia.................................. Saturday, 1st September, 2001
Belgium v. Scotland .... Wednesday, 5th September, 2001
Scotland v. Latvia .... Saturday, 6th October, 2001

EUROPEAN 'UNDER-21' CHAMPIONSHIP –
QUALIFYING MATCHES
Scotland v. Croatia...................................... Friday, 31st August, 2001
Belgium v. Scotland .... Tuesday, 4th September, 2001
Scotland v. Latvia.. Friday, 5th October, 2001

UEFA MEN'S "UNDER 19" CHAMPIONSHIP –
QUALIFYING MATCHES
Qualifying Group 12, Tournament in Slovenia
Faroe Islands v. Scotland ....Wednesday, 24th October, 2001
Greece v. Scotland ....Friday, 26th October, 2001
Slovenia v. Scotland ....Sunday, 28th October, 2001

UEFA MEN'S "UNDER 17" CHAMPIONSHIP –
QUALIFYING ROUND
Mini Tournament in England
England v. Scotland .... Wednesday, 6th March, 2002
Lithuania v. Scotland .... Friday, 8th March, 2002

2003 FIFA WOMEN'S WORLD CUP – QUALIFYING MATCHES
Austria v. Scotland................................... Saturday, 29th September, 2001
Scotland v. Wales .... Saturday, 27th October, 2001
Belgium v. Scotland .... Sunday, 25th November, 2001
Scotland v. Belgium .... Saturday, 20th April, 2002
Scotland v. Austria .... Sunday, 5th May, 2002
Wales v. Scotland... Sunday, 19th May, 2002

WOMEN'S 'A' INTERNATIONAL CHALLENGE MATCH
Scotland v. Sweden Under 21 .... Sunday, 9th September, 2001

UEFA WOMEN'S "UNDER 19" CHAMPIONSHIP –
QUALIFYING MATCHES
First Qualifying Tournament in Styria, Austria
Scotland v. Belarus ....Monday, 10th September, 2001
Scotland v. Austria ....Wednesday, 12th September, 2001
Scotland v. Greece ....Friday, 14th September, 2001

UEFA CHAMPIONS LEAGUE
Qualifying Round 1
First-Leg matches...Wednesday, 11th July, 2001
Second-Leg matches ....Wednesday, 18th July, 2001
Qualifying Round 2
First-Leg matches...Wednesday, 25th July, 2001
Second-Leg matches...Wednesday, 1st August, 2001
Qualifying Round 3
First-Leg matches ....Wednesday, 8th August, 2001
Second-Leg matches ....Wednesday, 22nd August, 2001

First Group Stage:
1st Match Days: ....Tuesday, 11th September and
....Wednesday, 12th September, 2001
2nd Match Days: ....Tuesday, 18th September and
....Wednesday, 19th September, 2001
3rd Match Days:..Tuesday, 25th September and
....Wednesday, 26th September, 2001
4th Match Days:..Tuesday, 16th October and
....Wednesday, 17th October, 2001
5th Match Days:..Tuesday, 23rd October and
....Wednesday, 24th October, 2001
6th Match Days:..Tuesday, 30th October and
....Wednesday, 31st October, 2001
Second Group Stage:
1st Match Days: ....Tuesday, 20th November and
....Wednesday, 21st November, 2001
2nd Match Days:...Tuesday, 4th December and
....Wednesday, 5th December, 2001
3rd Match Days: ....Tuesday, 19th February and
....Wednesday, 20th February, 2002
4th Match Days: ....Tuesday, 26th February and
....Wednesday, 27th February, 2002
5th Match Days: ....Tuesday, 12th March and
....Wednesday, 13th March, 2002
6th Match Days: ....Tuesday, 19th March and
....Wednesday, 20th March, 2002
Quarter Finals:
First Leg: ....Tuesday, 2nd April and
....Wednesday, 3rd April, 2002
Second Leg: ....Tuesday, 9th April and
....Wednesday, 10th April, 2002
Semi-Finals:
First Leg: ....Tuesday, 23rd April and
....Wednesday, 24th April, 2002
Second Leg: ....Tuesday, 30th April and
....Wednesday, 1st May, 2002
Final: ....Wednesday, 15th May, 2002

U.E.F.A. CUP
Qualifying Round:
First-Leg matches: ....Thursday, 9th August, 2001
Second-Leg matches:......................................Thursday, 23rd August, 2001
First Round:
First-Leg matches: ....Thursday, 13th September, 2001
Second-Leg matches:...............................Thursday, 27th September, 2001
Second Round:
First-Leg matches: ....Thursday, 18th October, 2001
Second-Leg matches: ....Thursday, 1st November, 2001
Third Round:
First-Leg matches: ....Thursday, 22nd November, 2001
Second-Leg matches: ....Thursday, 6th December, 2001
Fourth Round:
First-Leg matches: ....Thursday, 21st February, 2002
Second-Leg matches: ....Thursday, 28th February, 2002
Quarter Finals:
First-Leg matches:...Thursday, 14th March, 2002
Second-Leg matches: ....Thursday, 21st March, 2002
Semi-Finals:
First-Leg matches: ....Thursday, 4th April, 2002
Second-Leg matches: ....Thursday, 11th April, 2002
Final: ....Wednesday, 8th May, 2002

2002 WORLD CUP – KOREA/JAPAN
First Round – Group Matches ......Friday, 31st May to Friday, 14th June, 2002
Round of 16 ....Saturday, 15th June to Tuesday, 18th June, 2002
Quarter-Finals.................Friday, 21st June and Saturday, 22nd June, 2002
Semi-Finals ....Tuesday, 25th June and Wednesday, 26th June, 2002
3rd and 4th Place ....Saturday, 29th June, 2002
Final...Sunday, 30th June, 2002